In Pursuit of Lakshmi

In Pursuit of Lakshmi

The Political Economy of the Indian State

**Lloyd I. Rudolph and
Susanne Hoeber Rudolph**

The University of Chicago Press

Chicago and London

The University of Chicago Press, Chicago 60637
The University of Chicago Press, Ltd., London

96 95 94 93 92 91 90 89 88 87 54321

Library of Congress Cataloging-in-Publication Data

Rudolph, Lloyd I.
  In pursuit of Lakshmi.

  Bibliography: p.
  Includes index.
  1. India—Economic policy—1947–   .
  2. India—Economic conditions—1947–   . 3. India—
  Politics and government—1947–   . I. Rudolph,
  Susanne Hoeber. II. Title.
  HC435.R77 1987   338.954   86-24903
  ISBN 0-226-73138-3
  ISBN 0-226-73139-1 (pbk.)

LLOYD I. RUDOLPH and SUSANNE HOEBER RUDOLPH
are both professors of political science at the University
of Chicago. Susanne Hoeber Rudolph is president of
the Association for Asian Studies, and Lloyd I.
Rudolph is chair of the Committee on International
Relations at the University of Chicago. They are the
authors of numerous books on India, among them *The
Modernity of Tradition* (1967), also published by the
University of Chicago Press.

She has no temples, but being goddess of abundance and
fortune, she continues to be assiduously courted, and is not likely to
fall into neglect.

John Dowson, "Lakshmi," in *A Classical Dictionary of
Hindu Mythology*

From thy propitious gaze, oh mighty goddess, men obtain wives,
children, dwellings, friends, harvests, wealth. Health, strength,
power, victory, happiness are easy of attainment to those upon whom
thou smilest. . . . Oh thou who purifiest all things, forsake not our
treasures, our granaries, our dwellings, our dependents, our persons,
our wives.

Hymn to Lakshmi, *Vishnu Purana*

As the goddess of fortune, the epithet fickle is sometimes applied to
Lakshmi, in contradistinction to Parvati, or Sati, who is called the
constant, or faithful.

Edward Moor, *The Hindu Pantheon*

Even the Communists learnt that an Indian's vote was not wooed by
Marx alone. In Bengal, the Congress was making a heavy play of the
fact that its party symbol was a pair of bullocks on a yoke, which
represented the peasantry. The Communist Party of India countered
this by saying that its own election symbol, the ear of corn and
a sickle, was an image of the Goddess Lakshmi, the goddess of
prosperity.

M. J. Akbar, *India: The Siege Within*

Contents

Figures

Tables

Preface

This is a book about the pursuit of wealth and power by the people and state in India. Wealth and power are elusive, subject not only to the frailties of human design but also to ever-changing fortune—what some social scientists call conjunctures. We have titled this book on the political economy of the Indian state *In Pursuit of Lakshmi* because this fickle goddess's favor is sought by those who desire worldly prosperity. We conceive of today's Lakshmi in national and secular terms: if her favor was once sought by individual pious Hindus, it is now sought by persons of all communities, ranks, and conditions and by state actors concerned about national power, social justice, and collective goods. Five-year plans, even annual budgets, and the political economy doctrines that inspire them become the slokas and mantras of an age less confident that knowledge and power produce results without the blessings of good fortune.

Writing a book about the political economy of the Indian state over the past nine years has been an experience in discontinuity. Repeatedly, events have pulled the rug out from under our scholarly feet. We began the book in the midst of intense concern with governability and state "overload," not only in India but also in advanced industrial democracies. India was under emergency rule. Indira Gandhi had dealt with the Indian variant of a governability crisis by imposing an authoritarian regime. We had to take seriously the possibility that it might endure. The momentous sixth parliamentary election in 1977 overturned the authoritarian regime, restored constitutional democracy, and suggested that Mrs. Gandhi's solution to the overload problem was unacceptable. In the process, India seemed to have acquired an alternating-party system. This too proved illusory. With all the heedlessness of Pandavas casting dice,[1] the victorious Janata party destroyed a historic opportunity to establish a credible national party.

When Indira Gandhi's Congress party returned to power in 1980 in India's seventh national election, the one-party-dominant system of the first national elections appeared to have returned. Mrs. Gandhi had promised a government that works but led the country into its most severe crisis. In June 1984, the Indian army shot its way into the Sikh's

Golden Temple, and in October, Indira Gandhi was dead, shot by Sikh bodyguards. We had our last go at revisions in 1985, after Indira Gandhi's forty-year-old son, a dynastic heir and representative of the postindependence generation, restored national unity by winning an unprecedentedly large majority in the eighth parliamentary election and crafting a settlement for the Punjab crisis.

India's economy at that time was characterized by less dramatic changes. When we began writing, India seemed locked into a modest 3.5 percent annual increase in national income, what the late Raj Krishna, in his inimitable manner, characterized as the Hindu rate of growth. By 1985, Jagdish Bhagwati and others were asking "Is India's Economic Miracle at Hand?" and answering in the affirmative.[2]

One consequence of the kaleidoscopic nature of political and economic change was to force us to rise above the flotsam and jetsam on the surface of political and economic events and reach for the more durable elements beneath. But we are aware that we are still at the mercy of conjunctures.

We have many debts. We gratefully acknowledge the care with which Pradeep Mehendiratta, director of the American Institute of Indian Studies, has always attended to our multifarious problems. We thank the Smithsonian Institution, particularly Francine Berkowitz, for allowing us to think about the historical aspects of state formation, and the Committee on Southern Asian Studies and the Social Sciences Divisional Research Committee of the University of Chicago for facilitating our work on current problems. For thoughtful comment and criticism we thank Sanjib Baruah, James Warner Bjorkman, John Echeverri-Gent, Elfriede Fischer Hoeber, and George Rosen. For "pretesting" the manuscript in their undergraduate and graduate classes and giving us an impression of how we were doing and what was needed, we thank Tsou Tang of the University of Chicago, Brantly Womack of Northwestern Illinois University, Philip Oldenburg of Columbia University, James Warner Bjorkman, then at the University of Wisconsin, Franklin Pressler of Kalamazoo College, and Barnett Rubin of Yale University. Howard Erdman's eagle eye improved both style and content.

Laura Jackson and Frances Haman became more familiar with Indian electoral data than they might have wished as they worked to construct the results of the 1984 and 1985 elections. Laura Jackson struggled with the construction of results from the newspapers before unofficial summaries became available from the Election Commission. She also practiced her art on the graphs. The chief election commissioner of India, Mr. R. K. Trivedi, and the secretary to the Election Commission, Mr. R. Ganeshan, were unfailingly courteous and helpful in supplying official data. So were Messrs. Shankar Kumar, Ullal, and Maggu of DCM Data Products, New Delhi.

Katherine Sellers of the cartographic unit of the Geography Department at the University of Chicago prepared the final graphs. The manuscript has gone through many hands. In India, we were greatly aided by M. L. Sharma of Jaipur. In the United States, the first draft was created by means of the old technology, mere typewriters, by Kathy Anderson and June Mattick; the last version was a creature of the personal computer, as operated first by Mary Haynes and then by Betty and Earl Raaf.

Richard Ulmann, director of the New York Council on Foreign Relation's 1980s project, launched this book by asking us in 1976 for a contribution to the project. The effort not only got out of hand, it has come to coexist with the decade it was meant to anticipate.

Juliann Lipson's extraordinary subject and author indexes provide the reader with easy access to the book's ideas, evidence, and bibliography.

Introduction:
The Weak-Strong State and the
Rich-Poor Economy

India is a political and economic paradox: a rich-poor nation with a weak-strong state. We try to unravel this paradox by examining interactions between polity and economy. Our conclusions are contingent, but not because India is part of a mysterious East that resists formulation by the Western mind. They are contingent because India is a populous subcontinent whose variety and complexity generate contradictory forces. If our formulations are contingent, it is because India defies simple generalizations or easy projections.

When we speak of India's weak-strong state, we mean to convey the paradox of a state that has, over the four decades since independence, alternated between autonomous and reflexive relations with the society in which it is embedded. The strength of this state derives from the institutions and expectations created by 350 years of Mughal and British subcontinental rule. The result is a level of "stateness" and administrative capacity that exceeds those in other Third World and even some First World countries. It accounts for the vigor and effectiveness with which the state created a basic-industries sector in the 1960s. On the other hand, the capacity of the state to penetrate the countryside and to influence the unorganized economy, particularly its agricultural sector—which accounts for 67 percent of the work force and 39 percent of the gross national product (GNP)—remains attenuated. The rising levels of mobilization since the mid-1960s impinged on the relative autonomy that characterized the state in the Nehru era. Moreover, the deinstitutionalization of the past decade has diminished the state's capacity to make policy and manage conflict—that is, to govern wisely and well.

Among the Indian state's sources of strength has been a centrist pattern of partisan politics that minimizes the political salience of major cleavages. The country seems agreed ideologically on secularism, socialism, and democracy, on the merits of a mixed economy—part socialist, part capitalist—and on a nonaligned foreign policy. In society as in politics, social pluralism prevails over class solidarity. Although Bengal and Kerala are often governed by class-oriented Communist parties, India's many aspiring national parties as well as its one

1

actual one, the Indian National Congress, are centrist. Contrary to what one might expect in a country with great disparities of wealth, no national party, right or left, pursues the politics of class. And in a country where secularization has advanced slowly and religious cleavages remain significant, there are no strong national confessional parties, although there are important regional ones.

The two economic forces that might support class politics—organized workers and private financial and industrial capital—are politically marginal. Organized workers are marginal because they are divided by party, union competition, and government manipulation. Private capital is politically marginal because private capitalism lacks ideological legitimacy in face of the widely held belief that the profit motive and private gain are inherently antisocial; because the private sector is overshadowed by the public, which occupies the economy's "commanding heights"; and because state control has made private capital dependent. Capital and labor face a third actor, the state, whose dominance of capital and employment in the organized sector dwarfs their influence in the conduct of policy, politics, and market relationships. To varying degrees and in different times and arenas, the third actor has served public interest or socialist objectives, the interests of private capital, and its own partisan, patronage, and resource interests. In the early 1970s, the third actor came increasingly to serve itself.

Class polarization between wage workers and capitalist farmers in India's massive agricultural sector and rural society is constrained by the leading role played in production and politics by small-scale, self-employed "bullock capitalists," cultivators who benefited from land reform and the "green revolution" and who rely more on family labor and their own human capital than on wage workers and machines. The bullock capitalists oppose both industrial capital (state and private) and urban workers in the name of remunerative prices and better terms of trade between the countryside and the city. The Congress party, which has been the principal aggregative force for thirty-eight years, has played centrist politics with sufficient skill to win seven of eight parliamentary elections.

Another source of strength for the Indian state was the country's "permanent government"—its highly professional, technically expert, and well-institutionalized bureaucracy. Most Third World states have struggled at the time of independence to build qualified and effective career services, and most have failed. In India, the Indian Administrative Service (IAS)—successor to the Indian Civil Service (ICS), which was the British raj's "steel frame"—provided the Indian state with talent, expertise, and continuity. In recent years, politicization and deinstitutionalization have affected IAS performance. Civil service morale was badly damaged by the alternations of regimes and governments between 1975 and 1980. The 1975 Congress-imposed emergency, the 1977 backlash against it that brought the Janata party to power, and the backlash against the backlash in 1980, when Indira Gandhi's Congress government returned to power, put a premium on loyalty and put professional independence at risk. Senior officers were transferred to remote posts for devoted service to fallen political advisors. After 1980, Indira Gandhi relied increasingly on palace advisors, many of whom were senior civil servants. In Nehru's time, confidential advice and deliberation on policy and politics had been the province of cabinet colleagues, state chief ministers, the Planning Commission members, and senior party leaders. Unmediated exposure to power left many civil servants intimidated and cautious.

The international environment is far less salient for explaining Indian economic or political development than is the case for other Third World countries, unless it is salient in a negative sense, as an environment to exclude or keep at bay. India's economic and security dependency have been slight. Its participation in the international economy, which we discuss below, has been highly selective. Its goal has been self-reliance, a goal that has led it to participate in world markets less than other large Third World countries, in order to maintain control of the sources of economic power. Nonalignment, which was to a considerable extent founded and defined by India under Jawaharlal Nehru, has helped India moderate security dependency. It has been an increasingly successful alternative to the superpower's bipolar definition of international politics and security, giving India (and other countries) the means to remain relatively independent of superpower blandishments. By featuring diplomacy more than armed strength, nonalignment has limited opportunities for India's military services to appropriate state power. Moreover, because nonalignment has been supported by parties of all political tendencies, it has minimized foreign policy cleavages in domestic politics, reinforced the centrist political consensus, and strengthened the hands of Jawaharlal Nehru, Indira Gandhi, and Rajiv Gandhi in Indian domestic politics.

India's need for high-technology armaments has introduced some external constraints, such as its reliance on the Soviet Union as a major arms supplier. But this constraint has been balanced to an extent by arms acquisitions from Europe and, more recently, the United States. Nonalignment also enabled India to gain the advantages of international economic support for development while skirting the disadvantages of dependency. After a decade of bilateral foreign aid, in which the United States played a leading role, India was instrumental in constructing less political multilateral frameworks, such as the International Development Association (IDA), of which it became the prime beneficiary in absolute terms. When India's needs were greatest, at the time of the third plan (1961–66), aid constituted 28 percent of plan investment, but as it built up its economy, the percentage shrank, to 10.6 percent in the sixth plan (1978–83). In 1983, India decided not to take advantage of the last tranche ($1.2 billion) of the International Monetary Fund's (IMF's) largest loan.

The Indian state's relative independence of the international system at the global level is complemented and reinforced by its leading role in the South Asia region. Its present dominant position followed the formation of Bangladesh in 1971, a development made possible by an Indian military victory over Pakistan. The South Asia region differs significantly from Southeast Asia, Latin America, Africa, and the Middle East in two crucial respects: the predominance of one power, India, and the small degree of political fragmentation. All five Third World regions share economic backwardness and liberation from colonial rule or imperial domination. But South Asia was less afflicted than other regions by political division into sovereign states during the imperial and decolonization eras. Rather than being the aftermath of divisive competition among colonial powers, the South Asian states of India, Pakistan, and Sri Lanka were shaped by the Mughal and British subcontinental empires, and Bangladesh emerged as the late fruit of internal war in Pakistan. As a result, fewer nationalist movements sought recognition in South Asia as independent states, and fewer and more viable states were founded.

India's relative position among South Asian states is characterized by a degree of asymmetry not present in the other four Third World regions (see table 1). India leads its region decisively (by ratios of 2 : 1 or more) in GNP, population, armed forces, military expenditures, installed energy, and world trade; Brazil is the only other single country that leads its region in all six measures, and Brazil's proportions and ratios are substantially lower than India's.

Asymmetry increases the risks that lesser powers face if they engage in conflict and hence can constrain or eliminate intraregional state conflict. Although state asymmetry in South Asia—and its consequence, Indian predominance—has lessened the level and likelihood of conflict, it has not eliminated it. The Soviet military intervention in Afghanistan in December 1979 reintroduced superpower rivalry into the region. How India plays its dominant role determines whether or not

TABLE 1

Indicators of Regional Hegemony: Leading-Country Shares of Regional Aggregates (Percentages)

Aggregates	South Asia	Middle East		Latin America			Africa		Southeast Asia[a]		
	India	Iran	Egypt	Brazil	Mexico	Argentina	Nigeria	South Africa	Indonesia	Philippines	Thailand
GNP	79.4	34.7	7.6	35.7	19.4	12.0	16.4	23.0	30.3	21.0	18.4
Population	75.7	30.0	31.7	33.7	18.6	8.2	17.8	7.0	42.5	13.0	12.9
Armed forces	67.9	22.8	23.7	35.1	7.3	12.3	26.9	5.0	15.6	7.0	13.5
Military expenditures	81.2	40.5	7.0	38.6	17.3	13.5	22.9	32.5	28.4	11.0	10.7
Installed energy	86.7	42.4	27.5	35.0	19.8	16.6	3.4	56.0	10.8	29.7	24.6
World trade (exports and imports)	63.0	28.3	4.8	32.0	13.3	15.0	21.0	19.0	26.1	13.2	12.4

SOURCES: The 1975 figures for GNP, population, armed forces, and military expenditures are from United States Arms Control and Disarmament Agency, *World Military Expenditures and Arms Transfers, 1966–1975* (Washington, D.C.: United States Government Printing Office, 1976). The figures for installed energy and world trade are from United Nations, *Statistical Yearbook, 1976* (New York: United Nations, 1977). The two sources differ slightly in country composition of regions, but these differences should not affect the comparisons made in this table.

Note: Reprinted, by permission of the publisher, from our "The United States and South Asia," in John P. Lewis and Valeria Kallab, eds., *U.S. Foreign Policy and the Third World: Agenda 1983* (New York: Praeger, for the Overseas Development Council, 1983). The countries to which the Latin American installed energy and world trade figures refer are members of the Latin American Free Trade Association, including eleven "mainland" states, excluding Central American and Caribbean states, but including Mexico. For all other categories, Latin America includes Mexico, Central America, and South America. For all sets of figures, Egypt is included in the Middle East.

[a] Vietnam commands 38.5 percent of the armed forces in the area. In addition to Indonesia, the Philippines, and Thailand, this group includes Malaysia, Vietnam, Burma, Kampuchea, Laos, and Singapore.

lesser South Asian states will collaborate with or reject India's regional leadership. A regional bully that uses economic power and the threat of force to get its way, insisting on the privileges and prerogatives that accompany great power and "responsibility," invites lesser states to turn to outsiders for help. A permissive "big brother" willing to pay any price for family harmony and compliance invites exorbitant demands and blackmail. In fact, India's behavior has fluctuated between these extremes, never reaching either but occasionally leaning toward one or the other. Powerful voices in government and among attentive elites, by calling attention to impending untoward consequences and the benefits of the neglected posture, have always constrained successive governments from moving too far to one extreme or the other. India's role as the predominant power in the South Asia region, like its leadership of the nonaligned movement at the global level, has added more to state sovereignty than it has subtracted.

Sovereignty at home is more problematic. Although often severely challenged, the Indian state, in the form of successive Congress party governments, has shown considerable capacity to manage, manipulate, or repress a society that is eager but only partially able to speak for itself. Despite a competitive party system, high levels of social mobilization, and a plethora of voluntary organizations, India's associational life has proved too fragmented to agree or act on alternative national political doctrines that challenge Congress's version of the nationalist legacy and centrist consensus. Repression replaced politics during the 1975–77 emergency regime. After its return in 1980, Indira Gandhi's Congress government enacted preventive detention and antistrike laws, although it relied on them only intermittently. Its relationship to organized labor was paradigmatic of the state's relationship to organized interests and classes: tenuous control of the trade union sector resulted less from repression than from organized labor's competitive fragmentation into eleven weak national federations and many, often powerful, local unions.

The paradox of India's weak-strong state arises from the juxtaposition of the Congress party's durable command of a centrist ideological and foreign policy consensus, social pluralism, permanent government, and a dynastic charisma, on the one hand, with highly mobilized albeit fragmented social forces that threaten governability, political stability, and national purpose, on the other. Four developments have given concrete shape to state weakness: (1) governments led by Indira Gandhi deinstitutionalized the Congress party and state structures; (2) increasing levels of political mobilization, embodied in demand groups that press for immediate and hard-to-fulfill demands, have created an overload on the state; (3) unofficial civil wars among castes and classes have beset the countryside, particularly in North India; and (4) a new religious fundamentalism is exacerbating hitherto latent or low-level social cleavages, making it difficult for the state to accommodate them.

Deinstitutionalization accompanied Prime Minister Indira Gandhi's successful attempts, between 1969 and 1984, to centralize power in her own hands. Beginning in 1969, when she split the party by routing the "syndicate" (state party bosses who managed Congress party affairs and hoped to manage her), and continuing in 1972, when she used her personal triumph in state assembly elections to take the selection of chief ministers out of the hands of the Congress's state legislative parties, she systematically eliminated actual and potential party rivals. She thus undid the remarkable institutionalization of the party at the state and district levels that had been the distinguishing mark of the Congress since 1920, when Mohandas Gandhi built a political organization unparalleled in Third World countries. By cutting the national and state parties' links to local organizations (to free herself from demands on the one hand and to take personal change of resource allocations and patronage on the other), Mrs. Gandhi jeopardized the support and legitimacy that a state generates when it engages in mutual substantive exchanges with local elites, associations, and governments. Instead, she tended to reply on plebiscitary methods: direct, unmediated mass appeals enabled by ample funds (often of dubious provenance) and government's monopoly over the electronic media, the national name recognition and magic that the Nehru dynasty uniquely possesses, and the continuing but declining identification of Congress with both independence and *sarkar* (government in the generic sense). During the Indira Gandhi era, the Indian state—like the old regime before the French Revolution—gained formal authority but lost power, as the government loosened the state's connections with society by making them tenuous and arbitrary. In the mid-1980s, Rajiv Gandhi's efforts to revivify the party had not yet succeeded.

The deinstitutionalization of party was accompanied by the erosion of the autonomy and professionalism of state institutions. During the Indira Gandhi era, India's political capital was depleted as the independence, professional standards, and procedural norms of the Parliament, courts, police, civil service, and federal system gave way to centralization based on personal loyalty. Erosion was also the consequence of increased political mobilization, which invited authoritarian measures by threatening governability. The arrival and successes of new political classes untutored in the procedural decencies of a government of laws and parliamentary conventions also washed away the legacies of British rule and the nationalist and Nehru eras. Nationalist politicians were succeeded by professional politicians and they in turn by a generation of political condottieri. Mrs. Gandhi's effort to maintain governability by centralizing power in her own person and her secretariat and palace retainers led, paradoxically, to her son Rajiv's becoming prime minister of a state diminished in both legitimacy and effectiveness.

Increasing levels of political mobilization have expressed themselves through demand groups that have pressed the state since the mid-1960s. They have acted at least as much through extraparliamentary and extraconstitutional channels as through regular political institutions. Writers on the European welfare state have developed the concept of the "overloaded" state, in which the overload arises from the increased responsibilities of the welfare state on the one hand and the heightened expectations of mobilized constituencies on the other. Because it is the state that stands surety for India's economic progress, demand groups have targeted the state, more than fate, nature, or private capital, as the defaulting party in the process of economic transformation. The problems of ungovernability that arise as the state becomes the target of protest against unfulfilled agendas are a challenge the Indian socialist state shares with European welfare states.[1]

The unofficial civil wars that have erupted in rural India since the mid-1970s have exposed the state's limited or perverse penetration of the countryside. Sporadic and unorganized, if not entirely spontaneous, local civil wars have often taken the form of group atrocities perpetrated by higher castes and classes against local Harijans, ex-untouchables who generally are landless and work as agricultural laborers. Such warfare reflects several trends: the decreasing willingness of untouchable laborers to acquiesce to the molestation of their women, unjust wages, and debt dependency and their increasing willingness to defy local elites; the backlash by new and established elites against programs targeted toward poor constituencies and discriminated-against minorities; and the fact that, at the grass roots level, the state is too weakly articulated and dependent on powerful local elites to insure the security of persons and property or intervene effectively on behalf of citizens' civil rights and economic transformation.

Overall, the medium-term prospects for state performance and political stability are sufficiently positive to sustain steady if slow economic growth. The beginning of Rajiv Gandhi's term of office suggested that he wished to strengthen some of the institutions that deteriorated in his mother's time. But the deinstitutionalization, un-

official civil wars, and evidence of state violence and the "criminaliza-
tion" of politics that characterized the early eighties heavily encum-
bered Rajiv Gandhi and indicated that restoring the Indian state would
be a formidable task.

Recent conversions, religious revivalism among Sikhs, Hindus, and
Muslims, and related regional political movements accompanied by
political extremism and violence remind us not only that Iran is not
unique, but also that India's secular state, civil society, and federal system are increasingly at risk. The new politics of religion and region
express the aspirations and fears that accompany upward and downward mobility among reconstituted religious communities, castes,
classes, and peoples. The prospects of these groups in political struggles depend on the ability of their elites to revitalize or create identities
and organizations. Religious and regional ideologies often have proved
more accessible, meaningful, and effective in the defense of interests
than more abstract and less familiar secular ideologies of class, nationalism, or citizenship. Migration and the politics of region and religion feed on each other, as "locals" and "foreigners" (outsiders)
struggle for their fair share of whatever benefits and opportunities a
slowly expanding economy makes available. The circumstances of the
early and mid-eighties have led to a gradual redefinition of the state's
religious stance, from a secularism that recognized individual citizens
entitled to the free practice of religion to a secularism that is obliged
to recognize corporate religious groups clamoring for protection and
advantage.

The politics of revivalism and subnationalism has created a dilemma
for the state. A "strong" state response may generate more extremism
and resistance; a "weak" state response may invite further mobilizations that challenge a state whose legitimacy and capabilities have been
in decline since the mid-1970s. Finding the proper balance of responsiveness and firmness, as Rajiv Gandhi has attempted to do, will be
critical to the meaning of secularism in the late eighties and nineties.

If the paradox of the Indian policy is the weak-strong state, the paradox of India's economy is its rich-poor quality. India shares features of
the "Northern" (rich) industrial states in that it is an industrial country with a large GNP. Specifically, in a world of 154 states, it ranks fifteenth in industrial production and twelfth in GNP.[2] India produces
basic, heavy, and intermediate industrial goods (e.g., machine tools,
steel, and mature-technology engineering products) for domestic consumption as well as for export, and it exports technology overseas via
its own multinational firms. Other indicators of India's Northern

status include its technical and scientific personnel (ranked third in the world), its food self-sufficiency, and its falling fertility rate and rising life expectancy. These assets create dilemmas for India. Should it continue to be placed among needy African and Asian "Southern" (poor) states whose economies have almost no organized sector? Do its interests coincide with those of other Southern countries that form part of the "Group of 77," the organized voice of developing countries in economic issues? Is it not a "closet" Northern country within the South?

Yet the poor side of India's paradoxial condition clearly places it in the ranks of the South. As much as 50 percent of India's population lives under variously drawn poverty lines, a proportion that has not changed since the 1950s. In 1981, 67 percent of the country's work force was in agriculture, a proportion that has changed very little since the first decade of the century. These stark figures should not be taken to mean that very little has changed. Economic development may not have altered the basic parameters of poverty and the work force, but it has brought important and visible changes to the social, cultural, and technological conditions of rural society and village life. In India, as in other parts of the Third World, reduced mortality rates (and higher life expectancy) have countered declines in fertility; between 1971 and 1981 the population growth rate decreased almost imperceptibly—from 2.48 to 2.475 percent per year—instead of declining to an anticipated 1.9 percent.[3] If poverty proportions remain constant and population growth rates do not decline much below 2 percent per year, at least four hundred million people will be living below a putative poverty line by the year 2000. Having said this, we want to remind our readers that such poverty estimates are seriously compromised by the large proportion of production, services, and exchange that is either nonmonetized or unaccounted for, and also that the calorie counts and consumption baskets, far from being standard, tend to exaggerate the quantity and quality of poverty in India. Even so, the glacial pace of poverty reduction contrasts with India's rapid development as an industrial self-reliant power.

India's size itself is an asset and a liability—an element on both sides of the rich-poor equation. The subcontinent is large enough to provide a potential market for indigenous manufactures and to reduce the appeal of or need for export-based growth, to warrant large investments in industrial growth and infrastructure, to provide the basis for diversification that can support independent development, and to create a critical mass in technical personnel and investment resources. On the other hand, every asset has to be divided, as it were, by 710 million. The poor side of the Indian equation—that is, India viewed in per capita rather than in aggregate terms—reveals that India properly ranks as a Southern state and that its needs parallel those of other Southern states.

India has sought to control and regulate the impact of the international environment on its domestic economic and political choices. It has done so successfully enough to minimize the dependency constraints that afflict many Third World economies. Our analysis of the political economy of the Indian state, therefore, focuses more on internal determinants and dynamics than on external ones. India's development plans have been oriented toward one overriding and widely accepted national goal: *maximizing self-reliance*. Nehru's basic industries strategy, launched in the second five-year plan (1957–62), succeeded insofar as India, compared with other Third World (and many First and Second World) economies became relatively self-sufficient with respect to the production of capital and intermediate goods. The import substitution of the first three plan periods (1951–66) has created a situation in which India home-produces most consumer durables. Even if a discriminating buyer might prefer a lively Rabbit to the Birla's heavy-footed Ambassador, Indian consumers, until the mideighties, made do with the locally produced product. Import substitution and industrial diversification have, moreover, released India from heavy reliance on finished industrial imports—thereby freeing it from the dependence on particular trading partners that characterized its trade at the time of independence in 1947 and still characterizes the trade of many Southern countries. Unlike most Third World countries, India invested in agricultural technology. Agricultural production since the mid-1970s has made India self-sufficient with regard to food, an achievement that distinguishes it not only from most Third World countries but also from the Soviet Union and most of Eastern Europe.

Self-reliance has an external as well as an internal dimension, which is determined by aid, external debt, investment, and trade. Aid continues to be important for India's development progress but makes a smaller relative contribution today than it did in the 1950s, having declined from 28 percent of plan expenditures in the third five-year plan (1961–66) to 10.6 percent in the sixth plan (1978–83).[4] Despite large absolute external borrowings, India's debt service payments have remained low, at about 10.7 percent of exports in 1982–83, a figure well below those for comparable large Third World countries, such as Mexico and Brazil, whose debt service ratios in 1979 were 32.1 and 34.5 percent.[5] By limiting the proportion of equity that foreign capital may hold in Indian firms, and by steering its acquisitions of foreign technologies in the direction of agreements that allow coproduction, India has minimized investment dependency. Foreign inflows were expected to constitute about 4 percent of corporate private investment in the Seventh Plan, and all foreign inflows about 6 percent of total investment (i.e., both public and private). This level is in marked contrast to the 20–35 percent ratios common in Latin American economies, the homeland of dependency theory.[6] India has also diversified its exchanges with both market-developed and non–market-developed economies as well as with areas of the South (see table 2). No foreign buyer or seller can hold it to ransom. India is no longer dependent on primary products for its export earnings. By 1975–76, over half of India's exports were industrial goods.[7]

Oil has become a significant element in shaping the autonomy of states in the last ten years. The effect of the oil surplus on many Middle Eastern states has been to free them partly or wholly from the constraint of extracting revenues from their citizens. This has been a significant determinant of both state autonomy and state disregard for political pressure and demands. Revenue extraction enmeshes states in bargains with their citizens; collection entails exchanges, in which state responsiveness to citizen demands is traded for revenue compliance. While India has some chance of achieving oil self-sufficiency in the next ten years, it depends now and in the foreseeable future on

TABLE 2
India's Trade with the United States and Others (Percentages)

	1971–72		1979–80	
	Imports	Exports	Imports	Exports
United States	22.9	16.4	10.3	12.6
European Common Market	26.0	18.2	24.1	27.1
(United Kingdom)	(12.1)	(10.5)	(7.9)	(7.9)
East European countries	11.5	21.4	12.2	13.2
USSR	(4.8)	(13.0)	(9.2)	(10.0)
ESCAP countries[a]	20.0	26.4	27.2	25.4
(Japan)	(8.9)	(11.3)	(6.8)	(10.0)
Other countries[b]	19.7	17.6	31.0	21.7

SOURCES: Reserve Bank of India, *Report on Currency and Finance*, vol. 1 (Bombay, various years); and Government of India, Directorate General of Commercial Intelligence and Statistics. *Monthly Statistics of the Foreign Trade of India*, vols. 1 and 2 (Calcutta, 1980).

Note: Reprinted, by permission of the publisher, from our "The United States and South Asia," in John P. Lewis and Valeria Kallab, eds., *U.S. Foreign Policy and the Third World: Agenda 1983* (New York: Praeger, for the Overseas Development Council, 1983).

[a]Member states of the Economic and Social Commission for Asia and the Pacific.
[b]Primarily the oil-exporting countries.

revenues that require citizen compliance. It neither reaps the benefits—autonomy—nor suffers the costs—an unresponsive state—that
can accompany revenues based mainly or exclusively on oil.[8]

India's drives to achieve economic self-reliance have led to losses as
well as gains. Private and public firms have grown lax with respect to
costs of production and quality, behind the shields of import substitution, protection, administered prices, and subsidized credit. The increasing capital-output ratios that have eroded the yield from new investment in recent years are in part the result of insulating private and
public firms from domestic and international competition.[9] Without
competition, particularly international competition, there is little likelihood that these economic maladies will be remedied. While Rajiv
Gandhi appears to favor a more open economy, and the mid-eighties
witnessed an increase in foreign import agreements for consumer durables such as cars and for communications equipment and other high-
technology products, the vested interests in protection of both public
and private sectors are powerful.

Parts 1 and 2 of this volume are about the state in its sovereign
mode, about state formation, "stateness," and party politics. Parts 3
and 4 are about the state in its policy mode, about how policy choice
and implementation shape political actors, who in turn make demands
that shape policy and affect state autonomy. In part 1, we introduce the
notion of the state as a powerful "third actor" that diminishes the significance of capital and labor, the two classic protagonists of class politics. The state's dominance is related to its material condition, to its
overwhelming control of investment and employment in the organized
sector, and to its ideological advantage, as the presumed defender of
the collective interest and socialist purposes and as the enemy of private and partial gains. Because its dominance makes class politics marginal, the state is itself an element in the creation of the centrist-
oriented social pluralism that has characterized Indian politics since
independence.

Conceiving the relationship of the state to society as a continuum
from reflexive to constrained to autonomous to totalistic, we locate the
Indian state on a shifting continuum between constrained and autonomous. While autonomy has occupied a privileged position in state
theory oriented toward economic development, we treat it as more
problematic. Autonomy's positive face implies that it is free of en-
tanglements with social forces that would appropriate the state to partial and interested ends. The Nehruvian state of the 1950s provided a
credible if partial embodiment of that image. Autonomy, however, has

a negative face: the "state for itself"—as interested actor, reproducing itself—appropriates public powers and resources to partisan and private interest. The Indian state has sought over the last two decades to insulate itself from the exigent pressures of a mobilized society—by the Draconian suspension of rights and intimidation of opposition during the emergency of 1975–77 and by the more incremental de-institutionalization of parliamentary, federal, and party mechanisms since then. Even if one does not judge responsive and participatory government as a good in itself, these strategies for enhancing state autonomy would have to be judged in light of which "face" of state autonomy they serve.

In parts 3 and 4, we conceptualize the state in its policy mode in terms of two models—the command polity and the demand polity—and society in its political mode in terms of demand groups. In the real world, features of command and demand polities can be found in both the authoritarian and the democratic regimes that have characterized Indian governments since independence.

In the command polity model, the state is sovereign—differentiated, autonomous, and authoritative. Command politics can orient policy toward future societal benefits and public and collective goods or toward the appropriation by state political elites, officials, and employees of state-generated wealth, power, and status. In the demand polity, citizens are sovereign, that is, the state is linked to societal values and interests by processes of representation and accountability. Demand politics orients policy toward satisfying short-run consumption needs, services, and input requirements of mobilized constituencies. It can do so in ways that promote social justice, enhance human capital, and encourage investment and productivity or in ways that reward the powerful at the expense of the weak, allow consumption that limits savings and investment, and move the state toward entropy.

When we related periods of command and demand politics and of authoritarian and democratic regimes to investment taken as a summary indicator of economic performance, we found that economic performance was at best marginally and contingently affected by type of politics and type of regime. Exogenous factors—such as the quality of the monsoon, oil shocks, and the level or quality of foreign aid—and certain key policies—such as the creation and use of new agricultural technologies—appear to be regime neutral. Our analysis also reveals that a long-term trend toward higher levels of political mobilization, a trend driven in part by the student, worker, and agricultural producer demand groups that we examined, has been an important determinant of policy choice and economic performance by both types of regime and both types of politics. The trend has increased the pressure on all governments to allocate resources to current consumption rather than investment in the future. It has moved the state along the continuum from autonomous to constrained. At the same time, the dichotomy between consumption and investment expenditure that were built into our models of demand and command polities has given way in the face of new theory and practice. Policy applications of development theory that call for expenditures on basic needs and human capital in the short and medium term seem, after the creation of industrial infrastructure, as promising as continued longer-term investment in basic physical capital. Indeed, the alarming growth in the capital-output ratio and the associated decline of productivity in the organized economy strongly suggest the continuing need for improvements in human capital. In any case, the old theory that growth in GNP depended on a balance favoring investment over consumption expenditures no longer seems as compelling as it once did.

The vanguards of higher levels of political mobilization have been demand groups, India's version of pluralist representation. In part 4, we feature worker, student, and agricultural producer demand groups and the policies that both create and respond to them. Demand groups mobilize ready but inchoate interests and attentive publics. They are unlike organized interests, which rely on permanent organizations and specialized knowledge to pursue fixed interests and long-term goals and which work in camera in the corridors and salons of power. Demand groups rely on ad hoc organizational means to pursue historically contingent objectives and work "out of doors" on the *maidans* and public roads of India. They are more akin to social movements than to the organized interests and political parties that they sometimes build on or use. Their influence on policy comes more from successful agitation and large numbers than from expert knowledge, political donations, or patronage networks. Demand groups are more apparent in the unorganized than in the organized economy, particularly among agricultural producers, but they are also important, if less dominant, in the organized economy. If interests, more than classes, provide the main link between state and society in India, mobilized interests have proved as decisive as organized interests for policy determination and state formation. In the multifaceted political economy of the Indian state, the demand group stands out as both a distinctive and a powerful determinant of the state in its policy mode.

Part 1

STATE

I Centrist Politics, Class Politics, and the Indian State

The most striking feature of Indian politics is its persistent centrism. During the thirty years and five parliamentary elections that the Indian National Congress was the dominant party among India's several parties, it benefited from three interdependent characteristics: (1) an apex organization whose national goals and leadership provided democratic legitimacy and bargaining advantages for a subcontinental state encompassing diverse regional political formations; (2) a centrist (for India) ideology of secularism, socialism, and democracy and centrist policies epitomized in the "mixed economy"; and (3) a pluralist basis of support that encompassed a wide spectrum of interests, classes, status groups, regions, and communities. These characteristics were shared by the Janata party, victor in the sixth parliamentary election of 1977; the Congress-I (for Indira), victor in the seventh and eighth parliamentary election of 1980 and 1984; and the several parties that split from Congress and Janata between 1978 and 1980.

Why, in a country with significant objective class differences in its industrial and agricultural sector are India's national parties centrist and pluralist rather than left or right class parties? Why, in a country with a confessional majority (Hindu) and prominent religious minorities, have there been no enduring national cleavages and no national confessional parties based on religion as there are in the Middle East or Western Europe?[1]

The conditions that have maintained centrism in national politics are long term and enduring but not without challenge. They include (1) the marginality of class politics; (2) the fragmentation of the confessional majority; (3) the electoral strength of disadvantaged confessional and social minorities; (4) the increasing political consciousness and effectiveness of "bullock capitalists" and "backward classes"; (5) the imperatives of capturing power in Delhi; (6) the constraints imposed on India's federal system by cultural diversity and social pluralism; and (7) the advantages that accrue to a centrist national party or coalition when parliamentary seats are won by pluralities in single-member constituencies. What are the meanings and consequences of each of these conditions?

Class Politics

A leading condition for centrism is the marginality of national class politics. To many, class politics may seem likely or even inevitable in a country with as much inequality, poverty, and injustice as exist in India, and in a country that ranks fifteenth in industrial production among the world's economies.[2] But class politics has not been and is not likely to become the principal medium for representing India's "weaker sections," wage workers, and capitalists or for expressing conflicts among them. Consciousness and organization with respect to social and economic asymmetries have been provided more by status groups, cultural communities, sectors of the economy, and regions than by classes. Organizations representing language, caste, and territorial (sons of the soil)[3] interests and those speaking for disadvantaged minorities (backward classes, scheduled castes and tribes, Muslims) and sectoral interests such as agriculture have been more successful than class-oriented organizations in creating consciousness and identity and in influencing political action and policy agendas.

If class is to become a stronger determinant of political action and policy, suitable objective conditions are required. Conventionally, this has meant that as capital accumulation accelerates and capital becomes more concentrated, with larger proportions of the work force working for wages in industry, organized capital and labor become the principal actors in politics and policy. Despite some movement in this direction, class politics in India is likely to remain as marginal in the future as it has been in the past.

What do we mean by class politics? First "politics." By "politics" we refer to regulated conflict over the extraction of resources, the allocation of values, and the condition and terms of legitimate authority. Our use of the term does not refer to the elimination of conflict—the totalitarian extreme—or to unregulated, pervasive conflict—the extreme of civil war or revolution. When we argue that class politics in India is marginal, we mean that, in the context of regulated conflict, India's parties do not derive their electoral support or policy agendas from distinct class constituencies or from organized representatives of workers and capital.

By "class" in the phrase "class politics," we refer to the historic adversaries in industrial democracies, capital and labor. Our framework for judging the centrality or marginality of class politics in India is industrial democracies, generally the universe comprising the countries in the Organization for Economic Cooperation and Development (OECD). Although class-oriented left parties in industrial democracies have reached beyond their initial constituency of organized wage-workers to encompass middle-class professionals and salaried employees, the British Labour party, the German Social Democratic party, the Spanish Socialist party, and the French and Italian Communist parties also retain a wage-worker electoral base and policy orientation. Similarly, despite the ambiguities concerning the class interest and identity of salaried managerial, professional, and service employees, to whom they appeal, class-oriented right parties based on private property and capital—such as Margaret Thatcher's Conservative party in Britain, Giscard d'Estaing's Independent Republican party in France, and Helmut Kohl's Christian Democratic Union in Germany—remain spokesmen for the voters and interests of organized capital.

Class politics is not always dominant in industrial democracies. When Marx and Engels wrote about early industrialism in mid-nineteenth-century United States, they entertained the possibility of American exceptionalism. Nor are class politics evident in preindustrial peasant economies. Marx, who spoke of "the idiocy of rural life," thought peasants were incapable of class consciousness and organization and had to be represented by others if they were to be represented at all. Faced with peasant economies in Russia and China but committed by their Marxist ideology to revolution, Lenin and Mao used or transformed poor and middle peasants to help defeat tottering and degenerate autocratic states.[4] India is no longer a preindustrial society, but its industrial economy coexists with a very large and politically participant agricultural sector whose collective and particular interests severely constrain the scope and prospects for class politics.

We begin our explanation of the marginality of class politics in India with a sectoral analysis of the economy that depicts the relative objective position of actual or potential political actors (fig. 1). We do so to show the marginality in Indian politics and policy of the two historic adversaries of class politics, capital and labor, and the centrality of a "third actor," the state. Since independence, the industrial sector has grown enough to place India fifteenth in the World Bank ranking of economies by value added from manufacturing. In 1981, workers in the organized economy (large-scale enterprises subject to social and economic legislation) numbered twenty-three million, a figure comparable to that for work forces in OECD countries.[5] But, as figure 1 shows, the twenty-three million workers in the organized economy constituted only 10 percent of India's total work force; 90 percent is in the unorganized economy—23 percent in small-scale and cottage industry, petty trade, and services, and so forth, and 67 percent in the agricultural sector.[6] While the absolute number of workers in India's organized economy is comparable to the numbers in other industrial democracies, their proportion in the work force is much smaller. India's agricultural sector is enormous, employing 67 percent of the total work force, compared with 10 percent for the agricultural sector in Western European countries and 3 percent in the United States.[7]

Of the 10 percent (23 million) of the work force in the organized economy, only an estimated 30 to 40 percent (six to ten million) are members of trade unions,[8] a proportion that further diminishes the objective conditions supporting organized labor, one of the two classic adversaries in class politics. The 90 percent of the work force in the unorganized economy has remained beyond the ambition or capability of organized labor.

Is there a possibility for class politics based on an alliance of agricultural and industrial wage workers and poor and middle peasants? After all, poor agricultural producers in India are in a position to play a much more important political and policy role than peasants in Europe who, at comparable stages of industrialization, either lacked the franchise or could not adequately represent their interests in elections or policy choice. Such an agriculture-based class politics is unlikely. What we will refer to as the "new agrarianism" of the seventies and eighties is indeed an important part of national politics, but it is more

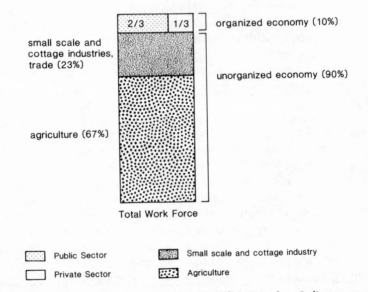

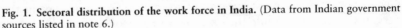

Fig. 1. **Sectoral distribution of the work force in India.** (Data from Indian government sources listed in note 6.)

sectoral than class based. In chapters 12 and 13, we show that the politics of the agrarian sector (the countryside) is mainly opposed to the politics of the organized economy (the city) and that mobilization of the rural poor has been both exceptional and independent of workers in the organized economy.

Perhaps the most important determinant of the marginality of class politics is the presence in the economy of a powerful third actor, the Indian state. Our sectoral analysis of the work force shows that of the small proportion (10 percent) of workers in the organized economy, two-thirds are employed by the state in public-sector enterprises and government services. Having occupied the "commanding heights" of the industrial economy (basic and heavy industry and infrastructure) and nationalized financial institutions (banks and insurance companies) and monopolized long-term lending institutions, the Indian state came to dominate the country's industrial and finance capital as well as employment in the organized economy. In consequence, organized private capital and organized labor face a third actor, the state, whose control of capital, market power, and standing as employer overshadow theirs in the conduct of policy, politics, and market relationships.

On three critical measures, the third actor is the dominant producer interest in the organized economy. From the third to the sixth plan, the ratio of planned investment in the organized economy between the private and public sectors was 40:60, 40:60, 34:66, and 48:52, respectively,[9] and the ratio of employment in 1981 was 32:68.[10] Among India's hundred largest firms, the larger the firm, the more likely it is to be in the public sector. As appendix A at the end of the book shows, India's eight largest firms (in terms of total capital employed) are in the public sector, as are eighteen of the top twenty and twenty-four of the top thirty. Conversely, among the bottom fifty firms in this group, thirty-five are in the private sector. The net sales in 1981–82 of the ten largest public-sector firms were more than six times those of the ten largest private-sector firms (table 3). Finally, the public sector overwhelmingly dominates the capital employed by the top hundred firms, with forty-six public-sector firms employing 76 percent and fifty-four private-sector firms employing only 24 percent.

The presence of the state as a third actor contributes to the marginality of class politics by making the state—rather than private capital—labor's principal counterplayer. In contrast with private capital, the Indian state as employer claims to represent workers' collective interest because of its commitment to socialism and pursuit of national economic goals. It features itself as a model employer to the fifteen

TABLE 3
Comparison of Public and Private Sectors among the Top One Hundred Firms,
1981–82

	Rs. Crores[a]
Sales	
Top ten public-sector firms	23,536.00
All public-sector firms (N=47)	31,870.55
Oil public-sector firms (N=7)	13,803.23
Non-oil public-sector firms (N=40)	18,068.00
All private-sector firms (N=53)	8,770.35
Top ten private-sector firms	3,706.54
Profit	
All public-sector firms	742.80
Oil public-sector firms	585.15
Non-oil public-sector firms	157.65
Private-sector firms	384.99
Capital employed (1981–82)	
All public-sector firms	26,253.00
Oil public-sector firms	4,512.00
Non-oil public-sector firms	21,741.00
All private-sector firms	8,356.00
Profit ratios[b]	
Public-sector firms	2.8%
Non-oil public-sector firms	0.7%
Private-sector firms	4.6%

SOURCES: See appendix A.
[a]Rs. 1 crore (10 million rupees) = $1 million in 1983.
[b]Ratio of after-tax profit to capital employed.

million workers on its payroll. Rather than being an adversary or
"class enemy" of organized labor and the working class, the Indian
state presents itself as their representative, friend, and protector. Defined in this way, the state and labor as counterplayers do not seem to
be in a conflictual relationship. In fact, however, the state does not
adequately represent labor's interests and, as we will show in chapter
10, weakens its capacity to represent itself.

Organized labor as a potential actor in class politics must contend
with formidable obstacles. Its marginality as a proportion of the total
work force and of the organized economy is compounded by debilitating internal weaknesses, some of which are state induced.

In India, unlike in countries that industrialized earlier, white-collar
unions constitute a large proportion of the organized work force. National unions, those with the greatest capacity to act on an all-India
basis, tend to be predominantly white collar: employees of the Life In-

surance Corporation of India, of the Post and Telegraph Department, and of nationalized banks. While they have often been militant, their working-class identities are compromised by their identification with middle-class interests and lifestyles.

Organized labor is fragmented at the top into eleven national federations whose ideological and partisan divisions inhibit organized labor's capacity to act as a body for political, policy, or bargaining purposes. There is no equivalent in India of the OECD countries' apex labor federations or even of America's AFL-CIO.[11] At the middle and bottom, the level of industries and firms, trade unions are weakened by degenerative development or what we call organizational involution, that is, enterpreneurial business unionism and state-imposed conditions and procedures encourage multiplication, fragmentation, and competition. Organizational involution undermines the possibility of collective bargaining by a few powerful, representative unions and of a major voice for labor in national policy.[12]

Organized capital, the second actor, also faces formidable ideological, sectoral, and structural constraints that inhibit its capacity and will to engage in class politics. Private capitalism in India is dependent capitalism. It relies on the patronage and protection of the third actor, the state, for its profits and security. Private capitalism is protected from the rigors of competition by government-licensed production and by protectionist trade policies that continue from the import substitution development strategy. In the absence of private finance capital, private producers must rely on the policies and discretion of government-owned banks and long-term lending institutions. Private-sector boards are heavily infiltrated by government representatives. Under what Raj Krishna called the *dharmshala* model (a shelter for the pious poor), government guarantees capital against failure by taking over "sick" industries.[13]

Private capital does not have a public political voice. Private capital is able to protect and advance business interests, but mainly through *in camera* political and policy channels, not in the public arena.[14] Between 1959 and 1974, the Swatantra party represented the interests of private capital in industry and commerce and landed property in agriculture.[15] Since its demise, the voice of capitalism (but not of agrarian producers) in party politics has been muffled and defensive. After Swatantra, the centrist limits set by the national ideological consensus on "secularism, socialism, and democracy" have gone unchallenged. The question whether the centrist limits—especially their socialist component—represent the consensus of the eighties was reopened in the wake of Rajiv Gandhi's entrepreneurial, managerial, and market-oriented proclivities.

Table 4 shows that the share of private firms in paid-up capital in the organized economy has declined from 29 to 24 percent between 1978 and 1982. As we noted above, the ratios of planned investment and employment in the organized economy favored the public sector, including public services, over the private sector (60:40 and 68:32). Only two of the top ten firms and nineteen of the top fifty firms were privately owned. Because some "big houses" in the private sector are conglomerates controlling numerous firms, these figures understate the economic power of private capital. If one were to aggregate all the companies controlled by the two largest conglomerates, then Tatas and Birlas, controlling thirty-eight and seventy-seven firms, respectively, would rank fourth and fifth in sales. However, the private sector's sales among the top hundred firms are still overshadowed four to one by public-sector sales.[16] The concentration of private capital qualifies but does not alter the fact of state dominance of the organized economy and private capitalism's dependent status. The private sector's decisions in all significant areas—investment, expansion, use of foreign exchange, and imports—are regulated by a system of licensing and controls that imposes social objectives and public priorities on the calculations, decisions, and costs of private firms.

Until the mid-seventies, modern capitalists in India had to contend with preindustrial cultural prejudices and postindustrial ideological doctrines that picture them, on the one hand, as heartless money-lenders or greedy merchants and, on the other, as antisocial profiteers or powerful exploiters. The celebration of entrepreneurship that fol-

TABLE 4

Increasing Dominance of Public-Sector Firms in the Organized Economy, 1978–82, as Measured by Total Paid-up Capital

	Paid-up Capital (Rs. Crores)[a]	
	1978	1982
Private sector	3,497 (29)	4,083 (24)
Public sector	8,527 (71)	12,879 (76)
All firms	12,024 (100)	16,962 (100)

SOURCE: Government of India, Ministry of Law, Justice and Company Affairs, Department of Company Affairs, *Annual Report on the Working and Administration of the Companies Act, 1956* (Delhi, 1982–83).

[a]Percentages in parentheses.

lowed Rajiv Gandhi's accession has not yet eclipsed this imagery.[17] "Profit," in the public as well as the private sector, is more often perceived as ill-gotten gain at the expense of workers, consumers, or society than as a sign of efficiency or a source of capital accumulation for productive investment and growth. It is said that the proposal to ban the profit motive failed in the Constituent Assembly,[18] which wrote the Indian constitution of 1950, but it survives in the public mind. Like profit, competition in India's mixed economy is also suspect. The Monopolies and Restrictive Trade Practices Act, unlike American antitrust legislation, attempts to limit the concentration of private power by regulating the size and market shares of large firms rather than by promoting competition among them. The increase permitted in 1985 in the size of firms governed by this act did not alter its basic philosophy but does reflect a more lenient government attitude toward private economic power. The visible hand of state regulation, administered prices and wages, and protective import substitution measures is said to safeguard planning and social objectives and to insure a self-reliant economy. It takes precedence over the invisible hand working through competitive markets whose prices and products respond to consumer preferences and promote the efficient allocation of scarce resources.

In addition to direct measures to limit and control private capitalism via licensing and the control of monopoly—what is referred to in India as the "permit-license raj"—the state under Congress and Janata governments has used indirect measures that have the effect of marginalizing private capitalism in class politics and making it dependent on the state. Government policies toward capital have promoted its involution, that is, the multiplication of more and smaller enterprises, the counterpart of the fragmentation and multiplication that characterize the trade union arena. The ideological justifications of these policies include Mohandas Gandhi's preference for human-scale, labor-intensive craft and commodity production by self-employed workers,[19] the belief that small-scale enterprises generate more employment per unit than large, the socialist goal of increasing industrial production without increasing private economic power, and populist dislike for size and asymmetry. The instruments of these policies are reservation of production for the small-scale sector and substantial financial and fiscal incentives. Promoting small-scale industry in order to enhance employment, economic development, and competition has accelerated the powerful entrepreneurial propensities of India's small business and commercial classes. It has also attracted the family conglomerates known as "big houses" and large firms. Because licensing and regulation significantly raise large firms' costs of production, many have invested in the much less regulated small-scale industry sector. The unintended consequence for capital has been similar to that for labor; involution, an increase in the number of firms and a decrease in their average size.

As table 5 shows, the number of private firms increased by 50 percent, between 1978 and 1982, from 47,210 to 70,795, and the paid-up capital per firm decreased by 22 percent, from 0.074 to 0.058 crores. At the same time, the number of public-sector firms increased only by 20 percent, from 745 to 894, but paid-up capital per firm *increased* by 26 percent, from 11.4 to 14.40 crores. Involution within the private sector varies widely between small family firms and large national and international corporations. The rate of involution is far more marked among the former. The difference among small and large firms is to some extent captured by the designations, "private limited" and "public limited." These terms have nothing to do with private or public control; they refer to forms of incorporation that entail different degrees of public accountability. The rate of involution in the private sector is most marked among the small, closely held, less publicly accountable private limited firms, which are five times more numerous and command much less capital per firm than public limited firms. The number of private limited firms in the private sector increased, by 55 percent between 1978 and 1982, even as capital per firm declined by 19 percent. Public limited firms in the private sector—which are larger, and more publicly accountable and include those owned by "big houses"—have been less subject to involution. While they increased in number by 23 percent over the same five years, capital per firm declined by only 8 percent.

Soviet economists, who usually take the view that scale and efficiency coincide, have been sensitive to the involuted nature of Indian capitalism. Thus G. K. Shirokov unmasked the Gandhian and populist sheep tricked out in socialist wolves' clothing. The policy encouraging the multiplication of small firms, he noted, was "aimed not so much against the monopolies as against big production units in general. The encouragement of comparatively small undertakings was often [wrongly] interpreted as a struggle against 'monopolistic tendencies.'" [20] Some Indian economists, such as Isher Ahluwalia, have begun to see the policies favoring small-scale industries as militating against "the choice of the optimum scale of production for a production unit." [21]

Another way by which private capital is constrained in the conduct of class politics and made dependent on the state is the progressive

TABLE 5
"Involution" in the Private Sector, 1978–82, as Measured by Paid-up Capital per Firm

	No. of Firms			Paid-up Capital per Firm (Rs. Crores)		
	1978	1982	% of Change	1978	1982	% of Change
Private sector						
Public limited[a]	7,725	9,530	23	0.343	0.317	−8
Private limited[a]	39,485	61,265	55	0.021	0.017	−19
Total	47,210	70,795	50	0.074	0.058	−22
Public sector						
Public limited	300	372	24	2.4	3.4	42
Private limited	445	522	17	17.5	21.03	20
Total	745	894	20	11.4	14.40	26

SOURCES: Association of Indian Engineering Industries, *Handbook of Statistics* (New Delhi, 1983), table 14-4; Ministry of Law, Justice and Company Affairs, *Annual Report on the Working and Administration of the Companies Act, 1956.*

Note: "Involution" refers to an increase in the number of firms together with a decrease in average size.

[a] The terms "private limited" and "public limited" refer not to sector but to different forms of incorporation: private limited firms are typically smaller and have to meet less exigent standards of public accountability; public limited firms are typically larger and more publicly accountable.

blurring of the line between private and state capital and private and state management of private firms. The line has never been very clear and became less so after nationalization of life insurance in 1956 and of general insurance in 1973, the formation of Unit Trust of India (a government-operated mutual fund) in 1964, and several other measures that cumulatively made state agencies plurality holders of equity capital in most large private firms.[22] This made it possible for the state to control and direct the management and personnel of private firms. But the conventions and rules surrounding investment by state agencies set objectives that left private firms free to conduct their own affairs. The basic principles were laid down by the terms created in 1958 for the Life Insurance Corporation of India, which took over the assets of the nationalized private insurance companies. The primary concern of this corporation, like any privately owned insurance company, was that "its funds should be invested so as to safeguard and promote the interests of the policy holders."[23] As the Industrial Licensing Policy Inquiry Committee of 1969 held, "investment policy is mainly guided by the consideration of obtaining maximum return on invested funds consistent with the security of capital."[24] Until the Escorts case arose in 1984, the prevailing convention was that government directors sitting on boards of private firms must observe self-restraint. As the licensing committee said of the Life Insurance Corporation, "it should not acquire control or participate in the management of any concern in which it has interest as an investor."[25]

In 1984, this standard was called into question when the Life Insurance Corporation called for a special meeting of the board of directors of Escorts, a highly profitable, well-managed firm producing a variety of high-quality products. The Life Insurance Corporation and other state commercial and financial agencies held over 50 percent of the equity in Escorts. The stated objective of the meeting was to replace nine of fifteen private directors with representatives of state commercial and lending institutions. The call for a meeting occurred subsequent to Escorts' blocking the effort by Swraj Paul, a British businessman and financier of Indian origin close to Prime Minister Indira Gandhi, to take over the company by purchasing approximately 5 percent of its shares. Many informed observers believed that the Life Insurance Corporation was aiding and abetting this takeover effort. Regardless of its motives and objectives, it appeared that the corporation, speaking for government investors generally, was reversing the convention not to "acquire control or participate in the management of any concern in which it has interest as an investor."[26] The import of the

BUT NOT INDUST
GOOD UNIONS IN
UK

Life Insurance Corporation effort was to move from a blurring toward an obliteration of the line between private and state capital.[27]

Finally, the blurring of the line between the private and public sectors is apparent from the functioning of "joint-sector" enterprises, that is, enterprises that are private but in whose financing and management state or national governments participate significantly.[28] Because Government of India–sponsored financial institutions are a major source of private-sector loans, and because such loans are converted into equity, even firms not formally "joint" tend to become so. Government lending institutions are strongly represented on the boards of the borrowing firms. Howard Erdman, whose studies of large-scale fertilizer firms in Gujarat and Bangalore explore both joint and private firms, generalizes his findings to conclude that "there are few, if any, purely private, large-scale enterprises in India today."[29] An aspect of the dependent nature of private capital is that public opinion is less exercised about maintaining a distinction between private and public power than in Western industrial democracies.

"Business" interests in India, while not publicly represented in competitive party politics, are better represented than those of organized labor in bureaucratic, parliamentary, and (informal) party processes. Because the state owns or directly controls the economy's industrial and financial heights, business is prevented from organizing or being organized along the neocorporatist lines for the representation of interests found in OECD industrial democracies. Business interests in India have adopted pluralist forms and methods to influence state policy and public opinion. Industry associations and apex bodies abound.[30] The most visible and vocal of the apex bodies are the Federation of Indian Chambers of Commerce and Industry and the Associated Chambers of Commerce and Industry. Their elected presidents, permanent secretariats, and sponsored or friendly research organizations and publications comment regularly on government's national economic objectives: management of the economy and sectoral and industry policies. Representatives of the several apex bodies and industry associations are "vested" in the sense that they are often consulted or sit on ad hoc or longer-term government commissions, councils, and committees, including the sporadically assembled bipartite or tripartite bodies convened to advise on industrial relations, wage policy, and productivity. Lobbyists for organized interests or firms regularly attempt to influence interpretation and implementation of policy by government departments, bureaus, and commissions. Unlike with the pluralist representation of organized interests in the United States—where

Congress matters—business interests in India focus their attention on executive agencies rather than Parliament, which plays a limited role in the formulation, choice, and implementation of policy.

Business contributions to political parties are an invisible but important channel of influence. Until 1967, when the second Indira Gandhi–led Congress government enacted legislation barring corporate giving, financial contributions by business houses and lesser firms to political parties could be monitored. Subsequently, such payment went underground until 1985, when Rajiv Gandhi's government, as part of its effort to make political influence visible and accountable, once more legitimized business campaign contributions.[31] A finding in 1982 by Justice B. Lentin of the Bombay high court that Maharashtra Congress-I chief minister A. R. Antulay had allotted government-controlled cement in return for very large donations to various "trusts" he headed partially and temporarily revealed that nether world of political funding that firms, sugar cooperatives, etc., used in Maharashtra to gain access, influence, and benefits.[32] Such political funding taps the unaccounted-for income, the black money of the dual economy whose scope has been estimated at 15 percent or more of the national income.[33] Before 1967, the Congress party, as the ruling party, was the principal beneficiary of legal partisan giving. It increased its advantage under the act barring corporate contributions, because the risks of surreptitious giving became higher for opposition parties when the Congress-controlled government, rather than an independent body, became responsible for enforcement.

Private-sector capitalists can also influence how the government applies and implements controls and regulations that affect every major area of decision: investment, expansion, new products, foreign exchange and collaboration, location, and pricing. Controls and regulations can be bent and manipulated to the advantage of influential capitalists. Indeed, some argue that private-sector capitalism has benefited more than it has suffered from the protected markets and monopoly profits of India's "permit-license raj." The significant private sector resistance after 1984 to Prime Minister Rajiv Gandhi's efforts to open up the economy to foreign and domestic competition supports this argument. As the Birla-owned *Hindustan Times* put it in an editorial commenting on the Antulay case, "Over the last thirty years of Indian socialism and mixed economy, the private sector has flourished and prospered many times over; much of the prosperity can be traced to the private sector's capacity and ability to influence governmental policies and laws."[34]

This interpretation of the relationship between private-sector capitalism and the state has led the neo-Marxist left to argue that the tail wags the dog, that despite the state's socialist claims and its command of the economy's industrial and financial heights, it serves capitalists and capitalism. Such a convergence of right and left views misses the dependent nature of private capitalism in India. Its lack of autonomy and bargaining disadvantages vis-à-vis state agencies prevent it from challenging the extensive regulatory framework that makes it a client of state patronage or, more broadly, the minority position of private capital in the organized economy. That it benefits objectively from state protection and tutelage and sometimes says so does not make it any less dependent or more able to engage in the kind of class politics (and policy influence) that characterizes organized capital in other industrial democracies.

The ability of business to influence implementation obscures its inability and unwillingness until 1984 to change the basic parameters of its dependent status in the mixed, patronized, and protected economy. Kochanek writes:

> Business has never succeeded in blocking or even in modifying a major distributive policy in India . . . [it] could not delay or modify the decisions to nationalize life insurance . . . [or] stop the nationalization of private sector banks . . . what business *can* do, however, is to try to convert a redistributive issue into a regulatory issue in which its interest seems self-evident rather than self-serving.[35]

It is questionable whether business will transcend these basic parameters in the late 1980s. Business could bend established policies but could not disestablish or replace them. It could circumvent obstacles by cultivating personal equations and networks, employing lobbyists and fixers, or expanding production of old or new products in the unregulated and subsidized small-scale industry sector. The general ability of firms and businesses to manipulate the state's system of control and regulations to their advantage showed the strength of overt and subterranean private economic power, not the existence of conservative class politics or a state controlled by private capitalist interests.

Fluctuations in the scope and severity of government controls reflect changing political forces as well as leaders' interests and personal preferences. Liberalizations are associated with the declining legitimacy and influence of the Planning Commission in bureaucratic politics after 1967; the death in May 1973 of Mohan Kumaramangalam, leader of the progressive faction in the Congress party that had pressed inter alia for bank nationalization; the rise in the mid-1970s of Sanjay Gandhi's anticommunist, procapitalist influence in the Congress party; the advent of Janata rule in 1977; and the Indira Gandhi government's negotiation and acceptance in 1981 of the IMF's $5.6 billion loan. But liberalizations are just that; they do not dismantle or replace the ideology and basic parameters that a nominally "socialist" state managing a mixed economy uses to direct, regulate and patronize private capitalism. Liberalizations have not created the objective or subjective conditions for class politics.

Even though the basic parameters of the public power—private power relationship are unlikely to change, the relative ideological standing of the two sectors is being altered. In recent years, the antipathy to private profit has come to be balanced by criticism of the antisocial effects of public-sector inefficiency. This modification in perceptions and attitudes has eroded commitment to the public sector, diminished the power and standing of the state as third actor, and increased the confidence of capital in the political arena.

Declining confidence in the public sector has been fueled by a growing perception that an overdirected and overregulated economy has become an obstacle to rather than an agent of growth; that the unfavorable capital-output ratio of the public as against the private sector reflects inefficiency, corruption, and poor management; and that socialist benefits of the public sector have become less apparent and convincing.

Public-sector firms controlled by the third actor, which constitute the largest producer interest in the organized economy, are markedly less efficient than private firms. While the public sector dominates the capital employed by the top hundred firms (76 percent), its profits in 1981—82 constituted under 3 percent of the total capital they employed (table 3). This proportion shrinks to less than 1 percent (0.7) when profits earned by public-sector oil firms—who monopolize a seller's market—are subtracted. Even though the profitability of the fifty-three private-sector firms in India's top hundred is not impressive by world standards, at 4.6 percent of total capital employed it is significantly higher than the profitability of non-oil public-sector firms and even of all forty-seven public-sector firms.

What accounts for the low profitability of the public sector and the rising capital-output ratio has been disputed in recent years. Some argue that persistent losses or low profitability can be attributed to forces internal to India's public-sector industries: poor management, absent or limited professional and expert knowledge among top managers, the lack of industry experience of the frequently transferred generalist administrators who direct much of the public sector, the disruptive effects of inappropriate political and patronage interference, and "rent seeking."[36] Others account for the unfavorable capital-output ratio of the public sector in terms that would exculpate it from the charge of gross inefficiencies. They cite factors external to the public sector, such as the relatively greater increase in the price of capital goods as compared with the prices of other products and services; the increased investment in public-sector industries—electricity, petroleum, coal, steel—in which capital-output ratios are characteristically high; and more generally, as capital intensity increases, a universal tendency— visible in other economies—toward a rising capital-output ratio.[37]

Yet another explanation for inefficiency in the public sector is the slowdown in public investment after the 1960s. The slowdown particularly affected coal, railways, and energy, leading to severe infrastructural constraints. Later in this volume (chapters 7 to 9) we offer a political explanation of the decline in investment. Increased pressures by mobilized demand groups led governments to allocate more to consumption than to investment expenditures. Rising levels of mobilization coincided with the declining capacity of political institutions to mediate demands. Pranab Bardhan and Prem Shanker Jha also link the economic ineffectualness of the public sector to political factors, in Bardhan's case to the heterogeneity of the dominant coalition, and in Jha's to the power of the "intermediate class" to penetrate politics.[38]

The slow economic growth that undermined confidence in the state's capacity to plan and direct the economy was accelerated in the 1975–84 decade by disillusion with the conduct of the politicians who led and managed the state. Their conduct identified the state with self-aggrandizing public officials who used their power to benefit themselves and their friends and clients. This image crowded out the image of dedicated nationalists and public servants and, over the decade, the state came to be seen less as the means to realize national goals and socialist objectives and more as a vehicle to advance the interests of elected officials and those the state employed and patronized. By 1984, the third actor was perceived by many as the problem rather than the solution. This shift in the public perception of the state diminished the legitimacy of its claims to direct the economy and opened the way for Rajiv Gandhi, whose generation and class shared the new perception of the state, to enhance private capital's public standing and policy.

Despite this altered ideological climate, the state as third actor continued to dwarf both of the historic adversaries of class politics, capital as well as labor. Neither was in a position to challenge the centrist future of Indian politics.

Confessional Politics

Centrist ideology in India includes secularism as much as it does socialism and democracy. If there are reasons why India does not have national class parties, why not confessional parties? Why not, in a country whose population is over 80 percent Hindu, a national Hindu party? From independence, secularism as an ideology and as a constitutional arrangement has been controversial and difficult to define. Nevertheless, the prospects for centrism have been buttressed by the national committment to secularism. National centrist parties, of which the Congress party has been the preeminent example, retained their commitment to secularism despite temptations to adopt a Hindu confessional identity and program. To create a broad national base, a confessional party would have to challenge India's centrist ideological consensus, a formidable task in the face of India's founding myth, secular state, and enormously diverse cultural and social pluralism.

By using the term "confessional politics" we mean to invoke European rather than American ideas and practice with respect to the role of religion in politics. The American constitutional doctrine of maintaining a wall of separation between religion and the state—of confining religious freedom to the private realm—is as alien to the Indian as it is to most Western European political systems.

To confess a religion is publicly to acknowledge and express commitment to a religious identity. In Western Europe the roots of confessional politics go back to the Reformation in the sixteenth century. It unleashed civil and international war. It also occasioned a secularizing process that, over several centuries, contributed to the separation of church and state and to religious tolerance. In post–World War II Europe, confessional politics took the form of support for political parties that acknowledge a commitment to Catholic or Protestant Christianity, or to Christianity generally, and pursue policy objectives that implement or at least are consistent with their religious commitment. Other parties, to a greater or lesser degree, advocate laicizing or secularizing politics, that is, freeing politics and the state from ecclesiastical control or religious influence. In this sense, an important political cleavage that can affect party competition is that between confessional parties or between them and nonconfessional or anticonfessional parties.[39] It is the European sense of confessional politics that we have in mind when we inquire whether in independent India confessional politics will again become, as it was prior to independence, not only an important but also a destructive cleavage in national politics.

The obvious candidate for national confessional politics is the "Hindu majority." But this majority, 83 percent according to the 1981 census, is an artifact of categorization. The Hinduism of the "Hindu majority" encompasses a diversity of gods, texts, and social practice and a variety of ontologies and epistomologies. Without an organized church, it is innocent of orthodoxy, heterodoxy, and heresy. Thus, until the transforming historical events and experiences that surfaced during the Janata government (1977–79) and crested in the early 1980s, the "Hindu majority" remained an illusory support base for a national confessional party. At the same time, minority religious communities—Muslims, Sikhs, and Christians—were able to play a role in state politics.

In addition to the 17 percent (115 million) of the population who are not Hindus, another 15 percent (105 million) are members of the scheduled castes or ex-untouchables. Their categorization as Hindus is as much a result of census enumeration as of their own choosing. Most are not susceptible to political appeals based on a Hindu identity or Hindu interests.[40] Similarly, it is questionable whether the forty-two million of fifty-two million tribals classified as Hindus in the 1981 census share a Hindu identity.[41] They too are not available for appeals to Hindu nationalism and interests. Indeed, many are actively engaged in asserting a variety of cultural or subnational identities and defending their interests against "Hindu" encroachment and appropriation.

Together, Muslims, other non-Hindus (Christians, Sikhs, Buddhists, Jains, and others) scheduled castes, and scheduled tribes counted as Hindus constitute 38 percent of India's population (11, 6, 15, and 6 percent, respectively). Of the 62 percent of the population that is left after we deduct 38 percent, only a fraction of uncertain magnitude shared, until about 1980, a Hindu identity that had political saliency. More important, the Hindu majority was more fragmented and competitive along sect, class, caste, and regional lines of cleavage than were India's minority religious communities.

Prior to the 1975 emergency regime, it was the Jan Sangh and its sister organization, the Rashtriya Swayamsevak Sangh (RSS), that articulated the ideology of Hindu Rashtra (nation) and symbolic, cultural, and social policies that addressed Hindu interests and values. Hindu confessional politics thrived on partition and was sustained by the perception that an Islamic Pakistan posed an ideological and military threat to India. Even though these external forces were sometimes the occasion for considerable sound and fury, Hindu confessional politics prior to 1980 did not attract much political support.

A rough measure of support for Hindu confessional politics prior to

Mrs. Gandhi's return to power in 1980 was the proportion of the vote captured by the Hindu nationalist Jan Sangh party before its merger with Janata in 1977. Its best showings were in 1967, when its vote share was 9 percent, and in 1971, when it was 7.4 percent. The fading away of the partition generations, particularly the Hindu refugees who migrated from Pakistan under violent conditions, and the fading away of the international threat after the breakup of Pakistan in 1971 as a result of India's military victory substantially reduced for a time the saliency of Hindu confessional politics.

India's founding myth is grounded in the traumatic circumstances of partition in 1947. Mohammed Ali Jinnah, the founder of Pakistan, insisted that Muslims in an undivided India would be oppressed by a Hindu majority. India was two nations, one Hindu, the other Muslim. A Muslim nation required an Islamic state.[42] Gandhi and Nehru, leaders of the Indian National Congress, spoke for a secular nationalism that tried but failed at partition to represent all Indians. Independence meant partition as well as freedom from British rule. Half a million died and ten million migrated. Pakistan became a Muslim state, India a secular state. Gandhi's assassin was a Hindu who believed that the Mahatma was betraying Hinduism in his efforts to be fair to Pakistan.

The lesson of partition that informed India's founding myth was that religious politics kills. What in India is called "communalism" destroys civil society and the state. As a result, India began its career as an independent state with a powerful commitment not only to a secular state but also to secularism as an ideology. The Indian constitution declares India to be a secular (as well as a socialist and democratic) state, that is, one that is neutral and impartial toward all religions; it prohibits the state from establishing a religion; and in article 25, it guarantees freedom of conscience and the right freely to profess, practice, and propagate religion. "Communalism," exclusive identification with and commitment to one's religious or social community, became a Congress party term of opprobrium, the antithesis of the inclusive nationalism and cosmopolitan secularism preached and practiced by Gandhi and Nehru.

The founding myth was constructed between 1885 and 1947 out of the experience of the nationalist era and the trauma of partition. It was sustained for thirty years after independence by Nehru's avoidance of the latent contradictions in the meaning of secularism as the nationalists had defined it. It was challenged after 1980 when mounting distrust and conflict among Sikhs, Hindus, and Muslims made the latent contradictions manifest.

The contradiction in India's concept of secularism was its simultaneous commitment to communities and to equal citizenship. The group component was rooted in the history of representation under British rule. Englishmen, who at home conceived of the political community in terms of equal citizens, in India saw it in terms of distinctive groups. This group vision of the political community, they thought, was an appropriate reflection of Indian society. Indian nationalists appreciated and sought to realize a political community composed of equal citizens but early on realized that they could not build a nationalist movement without recognizing cultural and territorial communities.

Political safeguards to minorities were a key element of British efforts to represent groups in Indian society. They were first elaborated in the Morley-Minto constitutional reforms of 1906, then in the Montagu-Chelmsford scheme of 1919, and finally in the constitutional framework that received the royal assent in 1935.[43] Safeguards gave statutory recognition to communal representation by providing for separate electorates and reserved seats for religious and other minorities. Nationalists saw these provisions as a policy designed to divide and rule Indians.

For different reasons and in different ways, Mohandas Gandhi, the dominant figure in the freedom movement, also recognized groups. He transformed Indian nationalism from a movement of the anglicized few to a mass movement by speaking the language of the people, including regional speech and religious idioms. Gandhi brought Muslims and Sikhs into the nationalist fold by leading movements on behalf of saving the caliph, then the religious head of all Muslims (1920–22), and on behalf of reform and self-government of gurdwaras (Sikh temples) (1920–25).[44] Gandhi made Hindus self-conscious as a national religious community in 1932 when he turned a "fast unto death" against separate electorates for untouchables into a fast against the Hindu community's practice of untouchability.[45] From jail and then in an extended nationwide tour he launched a massive campaign against untouchability that politicized Hindu India just as his caliphate agitation had politicized Muslims and his campaign for gurdwara reform had politicized Sikhs. Confessional politics for him was a vehicle for community reform that could bring communities together, not only as brothers who respected the truths of each other's religions but also as Indians whose unity could be found and maintained in diversity.

By contrast, Nehru, free India's first prime minister, could not take religion seriously or credit groups as valid components of the Indian nation. In his eyes, the Muslim League in the 1937 provincial election in Uttar Pradesh used religion as a cover to further the landed interests of its leading members. The political community of independent India was to be based on equal citizenship and committed to economic and social justice. But Nehru's commitment to scientific humanism and his confidence that the future lay with secularism, socialism, and democracy was tempered by a deep concern to insure that Muslims in secular India would feel not only safe but at home. They were to be not only citizens with equal rights but also a self-governing religious community in charge of its own personal law. The potential contradiction between Nehru's commitment to anticommunal secularism and to Muslim community autonomy, in other times and other hands, would be exposed in contradictory standards for action.

In the Constituent Assembly (1946–50), the nationalist leaders had to confront concretely how they would balance the claims of equal citizenship and of group identities and interests. After prolonged debate, members of the assembly eliminated reserved seats as well as separate electorates for Muslims, Sikhs, Christians, and other minorities provided for in the 1935 constitution, but not reserved seats for untouchables and tribal peoples. It was a decision that almost, but not quite, eliminated the group as a defining element of the political community.

Yet groups survived, not only in the provision of reserved seats for untouchables and tribals but also in the provisions of article 29, which explicitly recognized the rights of groups, including religious communities: "Any section of the citizens of India . . . having a distinct language, script [read Gurmukhi for Sikhs and Urdu for Muslims] or culture [a euphemism inter alia for religion] shall have the right to conserve the same." Article 30 established all religions on an equal footing by guaranteeing the right of religious minorities to establish and administer educational institutions and barring the state from discriminating against them when granting financial support to private educational institutions.

Paradoxically, the elimination of group safeguards was accomplished by a decision rule that gave groups the right to veto decisions affecting their interests. First adopted in the Congress party's constitution and later incorporated in the Lucknow Pact in 1916 that united the Indian National Congress and the Muslim League on nationalist objectives, it held that no bill or resolution affecting a minority community should be proceeded with if three-fourths of the representatives of that community were opposed.[46] The Muslim community was in fact deeply split on the issue of safeguards. Partition had diminished their numbers and influence. Did they not need safeguards—separate electorates and reserved seats—more under a majoritarian Congress than under the

British raj? But major Congress leaders in the convention "quietly and privately put a great deal of pressure on the minorities to relinquish special privileges." Also, partition had "altered the views of many Muslims, who now thought that they must drop this highly controversial point [reservation of seats] in order to ingratiate themselves with the Congress." [47] Perhaps foregoing reservations in legislatures in order to create an at least politically homogeneous society would help to insure fair treatment from a Hindu-majority society. When on May 11, 1949, H. C. Mookerjee, a Christian, moved the resolution that reservations be abolished, he assured the minorities that all they needed for their protection was the fundamental rights of citizens guaranteed by the constitution. His resolution carried "with almost complete support." [48]

The challenge to centrist politics after independence and until the late 1970s came from linguistic movements and class conflict in the countryside, not from confessional politics. Selig Harrison foresaw authoritarian rule or the balkanization of India as a result of linguistic cleavages. But states reorganization in 1956 dispelled them, and repression and prosperity in time tamed Naxalite violence. These challenges, while extraordinarily threatening in their time, did not ultimately disrupt the effective practice of centrist politics by national parties. As Paul Brass has said of this period, most Indians comfortably accommodated "to recognition of themselves as members of two nations: a Sikh, Bengali or Tamil nation at one level of identity and an Indian nation at another." [49] With regional and local exceptions, of which the movement for a Punjabi Suba (created in 1966) was one, these identities rarely came into conflict with each other.

In the 1980s, the Hinduism that had been an "artifact of categorization" began to become a condition of national consciousness. This development signaled the possibility of a national Hindu confessional politics. Religious performances, celebrations, and demonstrations began to transcend localities and to acquire national dimensions. As they did so, they became more strident and militant. The agitations and *yatras* (pilgrimages) of the Hindu solidarity and unity movements, such as the Vishwa Hindu Parishad,[50] were no longer the local phenomena they had been in the 1880s when Bal Gangadhar Tilak aroused Hindu political solidarity around the Ganesh festival at Poona.[51] Aided by the proliferation of religious symbolism in the print and electronic media, Hindu themes and organizations crossed state boundaries and helped diverse sects, castes, and classes to acquire the consciousness of a popular and more homogeneous Hinduism.

Popular Hinduism has expressed itself in fashionable symbolism. "Imagine," an alarmed Romesh Thapar wrote in 1986, sects of Hindu priests . . . moving from mandatory caste signs to other symbols of the faith—*dhoti* clad, bare to the waist, trident equipped, and with the *bodi* tuft of hair . . . soon the cult could take over in our offices as an exercise of the fundamental rights embodied in our constitution . . . the Muslims . . . could overnight don the red fez . . . to this could be added the trimmed bear of the mullahs and maulvies . . . we are on the edge of encouraging a multitude of what are called "psyches," one for each community, each caste, each tribe.[52]

Social mobility has contributed to the rise of popular Hinduism and Hindu nationalism. In the years prior to the Janata government of 1977–79 and Indira Gandhi's return to power in 1980, the support base for Hindu confessional politics had been the traditionally literate, spiritually initiated upper castes located for the most part in the relatively backward "Hindi Heartland" states of northern India and in Maharashtra.[53] But in the course of the 1970s, new generations of mobile middle castes born after independence and partition and located as often in the countryside as in the city were attracted to Hindu revitalization movements and political appeals. As social moorings gave way in a rapidly changing society and rapidly growing population, these groups found that patronizing Hinduism and practicing it in new ways not only earned respect but also provided a familiar and satisfying world view and social identity.[54]

Patronizing Hinduism in order to acquire status and power has an ancient pedigree in India. In the "old days," alien, newly victorious, or ambitious rajas seeking to legitimize their power patronized deities and temples, endowing them with land, offices, and income. Landlords, merchants, and state servants used religious patronage in a similar fashion.[55] Today, newly rich sugar barons and beneficiaries of the green revolution, as well as successful first-generation professionals and entrepreneurs, have channeled their new wealth into temples, Ramayana recitations,[56] and more elaborate and expensive ritual practices. What is a positive identity for socially mobile groups, however, often becomes a controversial identity in intercommunity relations.

Economic competition that upsets received status and power differentials has lead to resentment and envy. In some communities in northern India and Kerala, investments in religion by Muslims returning from lucrative employment in the Gulf countries have spurred similar Hindu investments. Educated, prosperous untouchables converted to Islam in and around Meenakshipuram (Tamil Nadu) in 1981 to win as Muslims the respect and equality Hinduism had denied them.[57] In Maharashtra and Gujarat, where there are large local concentrations of mostly poor Muslims, communal violence became endemic as a result of struggles between Hindus and Muslims over reservations, employment, property, and business opportunities.[58]

Hindu confessional politics also became a form of cultural nationalism for the Hindi Heartland states. Under certain conditions, such as those prevailing after 1980, Hindu nationalism was exported to regions where Hindus are a minority. In Punjab and Kashmir, Sikhs and Muslims, respectively, are the majority. In Kerala, Hindus confront large numbers of Christian, Muslim, and communist voters. In these states, minority Hindus resorted to defensive mobilization and sought outside support and protection. Hindu confessional politics was exported from the Hindi Heartland to all three states. By contrast, the social structure and consciousness needed to support Hindu confessional politics is marginal in the southern states of Tamil Nadu and Andhra Pradesh, where regional nationalisms are the dominant ideology. These examples suggest that because Hindu confessional politics is weak in most of the periphery, it is dangerous for a national centrist party to become overcommitted to Hindu confessional politics.

The Janata party's victory in the 1977 national elections put proponents of Hindu confessional politics in the seats of power in Delhi for the first time. This was evident in the party's abortive effort to block conversions to Christianity through national legislation limiting the right of Christians to propagate religion[59] and in its attempt to decertify textbooks that allegedly failed to depict Hinduism in a sufficiently favorable light and glossed over the flaws of Muslim rulers.[60]

After Mrs. Gandhi's return to power in 1980, Sikh extremism and terrorism in the Punjab entered national consciousness and politics at about the same time as the much publicised conversion of untouchables to Islam in Meenakshipuram. These Christian-, Sikh-, and Muslim-inspired events were used, by those who held that Hinduism was threatened by India's minority religions, to launch nationwide efforts to save Hinduism. The supporters of the Hindu backlash alleged that the minorities were privileged and pampered. Governments, particularly Congress governments, long accustomed to protecting and aiding the minorities in the expectation of electoral support, were charged with appeasing the minorities out of political expediency.[61]

The Indira Gandhi–led Congress-I government that was returned to power in the 1980 parliamentary election was the first Congress government openly to court Hindu support. This was evident in the Kashmir assembly and Delhi municipal corporation elections in 1983 when voters who had traditionally voted for the Hindu-oriented Jan Sangh supported Congress-I candidates.[62] It was evident in Mrs. Gandhi's personal attention to Hindu temples, priests, and gurus. Most important was the crisis involving Sikhs in the Punjab that began to unfold soon after the Congress-I government's return to power in 1980. Congress-I's attempt to recoup its position in the Punjab by patronizing Sikh extremists loosed a storm of communal politics. Mrs. Gandhi's subsequent attempts to crush the terrorism of secessionist Sikhs who were murdering moderate Sikhs and Hindus led to the army's invasion of the Golden Temple, the Sikh's holiest shrine,[63] an event that alienated even moderate Sikhs and triggered mini-mutinies by recent Sikh recruits. The spiral of distrust and fear wound its downward course from the October 31, 1984, assassination of Mrs. Gandhi by her Sikh bodyguards, through the retaliatory slaying by Hindus of at least two thousand Sikhs in the three days after Mrs. Gandhi's death, to the reciprocal violent "self-protection" among Sikhs and Hindus in Punjab, Haryana, and Delhi.

A parallel, if less dramatic, spiral of fear and distrust affected Muslims. The spiral included the national Hindu reaction in 1981 to the local conversion of a few untouchables to Islam; the killing at Nellie in Assam of more than a thousand Muslims during the 1983 state elections; the terms of Rajiv Gandhi's settlement in 1985 of the festering Assam regional agitation, which deprived some Muslim immigrants of their citizenship and others of their right to vote for ten years; a court ruling in 1985 that a disputed, historic building in Ayodhya was a temple, not a mosque;[64] and, finally and most important, the Shah Bano case of 1985, a supreme court ruling that Muslims perceived as depriving them of control over their personal law. These events in isolation might not have precipitated a crisis of distrust. But in conjunction with the Sikh-Hindu communal confrontations that had already agitated North India, they were construed as part of a larger pattern of Hindu revivalism and nationalism. Muslims became alarmed that in the name of secularism they would have to give up their religious identity. As Syed Shahabuddin, an aspirant for national leadership of the Muslim community and a Janata member of Parliament (MP) put it: "Ours is not a communal fight. It only amounts to resisting the inexorable process of assimilation. We want to keep our religious identity at all costs."[65]

The clearest indication of Muslim alienation was Shahabuddin's December 1985 by-election victory. By-elections in Assam, Gujarat, Orissa, and West Bengal told the same story: massive Muslim defection from the Congress.[66]

In 1986, the Rajiv Gandhi Congress-I government, in an effort to

break and reverse the spiral of fear and distrust, forced through a reluctant Congress-I party and national Parliament the Muslim Women
(Protection of Rights on Divorce) Bill.[67] The law preserved the independence and integrity of Muslim personal law that orthodox
Muslims alleged the supreme court's judgment in the Shah Bano case
(1985) had put at risk. The court had held that a divorced Muslim
woman was entitled to support from her former husband. According
to orthodox Muslim opinion, by contrast, the *shariat* held that when
the marriage contract is terminated by divorce, the husband's financial
responsibilities cease. It is the responsibility of blood relatives—fathers and sons—and perhaps Muslim religious bodies to see to the
maintenance of divorced Muslim women. The decision had a national
impact on Muslim consciousness because its challenge to Muslim personal law aroused a common concern in a community otherwise divided by region, historical experience, ethnicity, urban-rural differences, and language.[68]

The bill passed on May 5, 1986, only by dint of a stringent three-line
whip to enforce Congress party discipline. Prime Minister Rajiv
Gandhi's initial response to the supreme court's Shah Bano judgment
had been to accept it. He remarked in Parliament that he hoped in the
twenty-first century Indians would be recognized as Indians and not as
a collection of sects. But as orthodox Muslim objections mounted and
the election returns confirmed massive Muslim resistance to the decision, he reconsidered his position. Equal citizenship, it seemed, was
not a sufficient definition of secularism. Secularism had not only to
take account of "sects" but also to allow them some measure of self-
regulation. It was, he said, for the "Muslims themselves to look at
their laws"; "it is not for us to be arbiter between" the traditional and
westernized Muslims. Spokesmen for the government argued in Parliament that however regressive some might think the Muslim personal
law, government was bound to respect what it believed to be the majority opinion of the Muslim community.

The Punjab crisis and the Shah Bano case became an occasion for
confronting what secularism meant in an era of resurgent religious
politics among Hindus, Muslims, and Sikhs. The Rajiv Gandhi government had reverted to a version of secularism implied by the Congress party's informal "rule," observed in the Constituent Assembly,
that no act directly affecting a particular (religious) community should
be taken without support of an extraordinary majority in that community. Like article 29 of the constitution, which protects the right of any
group to preserve its culture, it is a rule that moves some way toward
conceiving of the political community as constituted of distinctive

groups as well as equal citizens. His concept of secularism, the prime minister said, was *sarv dharm sambhaav* (respect for all religions), a concept closer to Mohandas Gandhi's views than to those of Rajiv's grandfather, Jawaharlal Nehru.[69]

By the mid-eighties, the secularism of India's centrist consensus no longer commanded the understanding and commitment of the postindependence generations. With the rise of confessional politics, particularly its communal and violent version, these generations had to relearn the lesson of partition: in a diverse, plural society, communal politics can destroy civil society and the state. The Congress-I had moved dangerously close to becoming a Hindu confessional party. Denying Christians the right to propagate their religion in the name of freedom of conscience, making war on Sikhs and their religion, and threatening to deprive Muslims of their law and their mosques were signs that centrist national parties, such as Janata and Congress-I, had been tempted by the option of Hindu confessional politics. Rajiv Gandhi's 1984 election campaign was based in part on Hindu backlash support: sympathy for a bereaved son whose mother had died as martyr to a Hindu cause and a campaign appeal for national unity that spoke to Hindu nationalism.

But there was another face to the possibilities of the mid-eighties. All of India's national parties remained nominally committed to a secular state. Only regional parties, in Punjab, Kashmir, and Kerala, had explicit confessional identities, and they were not new. Congress drew back from the prospect of confessional politics in the face of its consequences for the party's principles and electoral success. Many of Rajiv Gandhi's words and actions after the 1984 elections made it clear that he thought reliance on Hindu confessional politics was not a viable alternative for Congress-I in the states or nationally. He made peace with the Sikhs in Punjab and with Muslims by reversing legislatively the supreme court's judgment in the Shah Bano case. Asked in May 1986 whether he had won the December 1984 election on the basis of a Hindu backlash vote, he offered a secular interpretation: "No, I don't. Not at all . . . more than just Hindus voted [for the Congress] and in the same sort of percentages."[70]

For Congress to become a confessional party would not only threaten its principles but would also jeopardize its standing as a national party. The principle support for Hindu confessional politics is in the Hindi Heartland, and even there Congress's comparative advantage over rivals who can compete effectively in the Hindu confessional mode lies with maintaining the support of the minorities. To embrace Hindu confessional politics would be to risk becoming a regional party.

Reliance on Hindu confessional politics is not compatible with Congress's legacy as the party of secularism. The meaning of that secularism historically has encompassed the celebration and constitutional protection of cultural diversity as well as the protection of equal rights of citizens in a secular state. The result has been an ambiguous and sometimes contradictory relationship between the confessional politics of the majority and the minority communities. The lessons of partition were there to remind the Congress, the opposition parties, and the country of their fate should they forget the consequences of allowing confessional politics to become a major cleavage in national politics.

Minority Politics

The scale and cohesiveness of India's minorities not only contributes to the illusory quality of the Hindu "majority" but also constitutes an obstacle to the practice of Hindu politics and the success of a Hindu confessional party. Secularism in the centrist ideology of secularism, socialism, and democracy speaks to the needs of India's poor and discriminated-against minorities by delegitimizing the claims of the old and the new Hindu politics.

India's minorities, like American blacks, seem to share a "group consciousness" that helps to explain higher levels of political participation than individual measures of their social and economic status would lead one to expect. Group consciousness (including prudence and fear) may also help to account for evidence that up through the third national election in 1962 scheduled castes and Muslims voted more cohesively (i.e., in higher proportions) for the secularist Congress than did other voters.[71] Subsequently, their self-protective tendency has led them, in state as well as national elections, to vote more for the party most likely to win than for parties representing class or community appeals particular to their condition. However, since the fourth national election in 1967, the scheduled tribes have voted together more than scheduled castes and Muslims.[72]

The minorities' community identity has been more pervasive and politically salient than the Hindu majority's, in part because the minorities share common economic and social conditions to a much greater degree. Like American blacks and Hispanics, they suffer simultaneously from poverty, discrimination, and powerlessness, objective circumstances that have been translated into subjective awareness of economic exploitation, status deprivation, and political repression.

The objective conditions and consciousness of India's minorities have been less subject than the Hindu majority's to the crosscutting or divisive effects of class, caste, and region.

Muslim and scheduled caste and tribe support is particularly vital for electoral success in the five Hindi Heartland states of northern India where vote swings have been widest since 1967.[73] Minorities are most significant numerically in just those states where elections since 1967 have been most volatile. In Uttar Pradesh, Bihar, Madhya Pradesh, Haryana, and Rajasthan, which include India's two most populous states and elect 39 percent of Parliament's 542 members, the three minorities together constitute 37 percent of the votes in the first three, 34 percent in Rajasthan, and 23 percent in Haryana (table 6). Congress victories in 1971, 1980, and 1984 were due in part to strong support among minorities. Defeat (1977) and low voter support (1980) were associated with defection by the minorities.

Because minority support is vital to electoral success, gaining or holding it has become a common feature of party strategy and ideology. Secularism is, among other things, an ideology for the minorities. Parties that rely primarily or exclusively on class appeals to reach the poor and disadvantaged have been less successful than centrist parties that seek to represent minority interests and identities. The electoral successes of the Congress party under Jawaharlal Nehru and Indira Gandhi were largely enabled by support from India's largest minorities, Muslims and the scheduled castes. In the early years after independence, these minorities regarded Congress as their friend and

TABLE 6

Parliamentary Seats and Minority Population Proportions in Hindi Heartland States, 1977

	No. of Seats	%			
		Muslims	Scheduled Castes	Scheduled Tribes	Total of Three Minorities
All India	542	11	15	7	33
Hindi Heartland					
Uttar Pradesh	85	16	21	<1	37
Bihar	54	14	14	9	37
Madhya Pradesh	40	4	13	20	37
Rajasthan	25	7	15	12	34
Haryana	10	4	19	<1	23

SOURCE: Government of India, Ministry of Information and Broadcasting, *India: A Reference Annual, 1979,* (New Delhi, 1979), p. 10.

protector, and prudence in any case dictated a continuing adherence to Congress as the party most likely to win. Janata's success in the March 1977 election reflected a new minority alienation from Congress, in reaction to the vasectomy and slum clearance programs that disproportionately affected minorities. Minority support also reflected a prudential calculation that Janata would win the election. All three national parties contesting in 1980—the Congress-I, led by Gandhi, the Janata, led by Jagjivan Ram, and the Lok Dal, led by Charan Singh—tried to occupy the center by avowing that they were secular and socialist, that is, that they recognized the minorities' fear of "Hindu" as well as economic oppression, their need for protection and help, and the state's obligation to provide economic opportunities to the poor and disadvantaged. Each made symbolic and policy appeals designed to gain the support of India's minorities: Janata had its scheduled caste leader, Jagjivan Ram; Lok Dal, its son-of-a-*kisan* (cultivator) leader, Charan Singh, and its commitment to promote secularism; and Congress-I, the Nehru legacy of friendship and protection for Muslims and the scheduled castes, as personified in Nehru's daughter, Indira. Since 1980, in both center and state elections, the minority constituencies have consistently voted for the winning party, which has also been a centrist party. They voted for Telugu Desam and Janata centrist winners in the state assembly elections in Andhra Pradesh and Karnataka in 1983, and for Congress-I in the parliamentary election of 1984.

The distribution of minority electoral support in the 1977, 1980, and 1984 parliamentary elections indicates that the minorities, rather than engaging in bloc voting for Congress, have responded to the centrist appeals of winning parties. Parties whose ideology, policies, and electoral strategy do not attend to representing minority interests and identities cannot compete for power at the national level. Centrist parties, in the coded language of Indian politics, espouse secularism and socialism to signal their regard and concern for the 38 percent of the electorate who are poor and oppressed minority voters.

Bullock Capitalists and Backward Classes

The centrist character of India's national politics and parties is also a consequence of the balance among productive, social, and political forces in the agricultural sector and rural society. Even though the Nehru-led industrial strategy placed India among the world's leading industrial powers, its economy remains predominantly agricultural. In

1981, 77 percent of India's population was classified as rural, 67 percent of its labor force was in agriculture, and 39 percent of its national income (15 percent more than industry and 2 percent more than services) originated in the agricultural (primary) sector.[74]

Polarization based on left and right class politics in the agricultural sector and rural society is as unlikely as it is in the industrial economy and society. India no longer has an agrarian class corresponding to England's landed aristocracy, Prussia's Junkers, or Latin America's latifundia masters. The interpenetration of a quasi-feudal landlord class with an emergent class of tractor capitalists might have provided in India, as it did in Pakistan, the basis for a viable conservative politics.[75] However, the first wave of land reform in the 1950s nominally, and to a considerable extent actually, abolished "intermediaries," the quasi-feudal landlord class known as zamindars and *jagirdars,* which stood between the state and the cultivator by acting as revenue agents and performing some local government functions. The Swatantra party in the 1960s created an alliance between rural feudal and capitalist agricultural interests on the one hand and urban industrial and finance capital interests on the other.[76] Since Swatantra's merger with the agrarian Bharatiya Kranti Dal (BKD) in 1974, no party has represented an alliance of urban and rural capitalist producers. Swatantra's demise ended India's only experiment with class politics on the right.

In the 1960s, two producer groups occupied the dominant position in the countryside left vacant by the quasi-feudal zamindars and *jagirdars.* One included landlords with variously sized holdings who, having successfully blocked or evaded land ceilings legislation, rented to sharecroppers or tenants or employed attached or casual labor. The other included bullock capitalists, small to medium-sized self-employed independent agricultural producers[77] who were the principal beneficiaries of intermediary abolition. Overlapping bullock capitalists, an economic category, were the "backward classes" (read castes), a status group that came of age politically in the 1970s. The balance of power between these groups lay with landlords in the sixties but in the seventies it shifted toward bullock capitalists and backward classes.

In the late 1970s and 1980s, agrarian movements, organized on the issue of remunerative prices, became a major force in state and national politics. They put sectoral rather than class politics on the national public agenda. The organization and representation of these agrarian interests differs from that of the classic actors in class politics. Agrarian interests rely more on spontaneous issue and movement politics than on permanent formal organizations to represent their interests. The presence of agrarian interests in national politics has strengthened centrist rather than class politics.

With some important local and regional exceptions, the level of consciousness and organization among agricultural workers is too limited for them to represent themselves effectively, much less become a rural proletariat. As we show in chapter 10, India's "proletariat" in the organized economy is in fact a labor aristocracy composed of white collar and skilled blue-collar workers. It is sufficiently separated from rural wage labor by economic interest, life-style, and political tactics to prevent urban and rural workers from becoming allies in the foreseeable future, much less comrades.

The appearance in the late 1970s and early 1980s of agrarian mobilizations in state and national politics undid the political settlement of the Nehru era. The Nehru settlement had been based on a coalition of urban and rural interests united behind an essentially urban-oriented industrial strategy. Its senior partners were India's proportionately small but politically powerful administrative, managerial, and professional English-educated middle classes [78] and private-sector industrialists. Private-sector industrialists welcomed the freedom from foreign competition and dependency that was enabled by the second and third five-year plans' import substitution and industrial self-reliance strategies. The English-educated middle classes manned the senior services, built and managed the public-sector industries, and staffed large firms in the modern private sector. The junior partners in the Nehru settlement were rural notabilities, mostly large landowners who survived intermediary abolition and blocked the passage or implementation of land ceilings legislation. They consented to the import substitution and industrial self-reliance strategies, middle-class control of the central government, and the advantages that accrued to urban elites and organized workers on condition that they themselves control state governments. That control enabled them to allocate resources and monitor policy implementation for the agricultural sector and rural society in ways that protected their interests.

The defeat in 1977 of Congress by the Janata party and the formation of a Janata government in 1977 marked the ascendance of a political coalition in which agrarian interests were the senior partner for the first time. Since then, no party, including those on the left, has been able to ignore the political importance of establishing a mass base among independent cultivators.

As an only partially intended consequence of the 1977 election, agricultural interests were powerfully represented at the center as well as in the states for the first time since independence. At the same time, bullock capitalists rivaled or displaced large landowners in the agrarian power constellation. As a result, the Nehru-era policies favoring cities, centralization, bigness, and capital-intensive industrialization were modified by policies that favored the agricultural sector and rural society, decentralization of government and the economy, and small producers using labor-intensive technologies that promote employment.[79] The Gandhi-led Congress-I government returned by the 1980 parliamentary election recognized the claims of the agricultural sector by continuing, in somewhat attenuated form, Janata policies designed to support remunerative prices and cheap inputs and to provide more employment and productive assets for the rural poor.[80]

Independent agricultural producers are one component of the ascendant agrarian political class that strengthens the prospects of centrism. This group encompasses two overlapping categories, a producer group, the middle peasants we call bullock capitalists, and a status group, the "backward classes," an administrative euphemism for backward castes. "Backward classes" constitute about 25 percent of the population and are located in the lower reaches of the caste order but above the untouchables. Backward classes began to mobilize politically in the South and West after World War I, but only recently have come to be a political force in the North.[81] The centerpieces of the Janata economic and social policies in 1977 and of the Janata and Lok Dal policies in 1980 articulated this political class's interests, an agriculture-led employment strategy, and a call for reservation of places for backward classes in government jobs and educational institutions.[82] The convergence of economic and status interests in the agrarian political class makes it particularly potent in Indian politics.

Bullock capitalists are advantageously placed by their objective circumstances to become the hegemonic agrarian class, speaking for a broad spectrum of agricultural producers (see chapter 13, table 40). As of 1971–72, they constituted a larger proportion of agricultural households and controlled more land (34 percent controlling 51 percent) than any of the other three agrarian classes—landless (27 percent controlling 0 percent), smallholders (33 percent controlling 10 percent), or large landholders (6 percent controlling 39 percent). Large landholders, whose average holding increased marginally, lost ground to bullock capitalists between 1954–55 and 1971–72 in terms of the proportion of households and area controlled, and, we infer, in terms of capacity to mobilize vertically those dependent on them for work, land, credit, and so forth.[83] Some of the decline in area controlled by large landholders may be illusory, because of the prevalence of unreported fraudulent (*benami*) transfers, but the direction of change shown by the above data seems correct, if not the precise degree.

Bullock capitalists resemble "yeoman" farmers in that they are independent agricultural producers. They are not "kulaks" if that word is used to designate wealthy producers relying on tenants or wage labor in "imperfect" labor markets and on control of credit and marketing to enforce dependency and support for their local power. Bullock capitalists are self-employed and self-funded. Their holdings are large enough to support the use of a pair of bullocks and the new inputs associated with the "green revolution." Typically, they operate between 2.5 and 15 acres, although, as we shall emphasize in chapter 13, size per se is an imperfect means of identifying bullock capitalists. At the same time, their assets are not large enough to enable them to engage in capital-intensive agricultural production based on extensive use of machinery or to require them to rely wholly or mainly on wage labor. We prefer the term "bullock capitalists" to "middle peasants" because of the mix of capitalist, preindustrial, and noncapitalist features that characterizes their economic circumstances. They operate family farms that rely on household labor: the family, broadly defined to include the household, is the primary if not the exclusive source of capital and management as well as of labor. Because they are self-employed, they benefit from their own high-quality, committed labor. While they use and pay for capital and participate in markets,[84] they are "noncapitalist" producers in the sense that, because they are self-employed, their relations of production remain relatively undifferentiated and nonantagonistic.

Most important for consciousness and centrist politics, the economic circumstances of bullock capitalists unite the interests of capital, management, and labor. Bullock capitalists own the means of production, manage the productive unit, and provide most if not all the labor themselves. If there is exploitation involved in their relations of production, it is self-exploitation; they benefit from the "surplus value" of their own labor.[85] Their ideological propensities are familial and communitarian rather than state collectivist or capitalist; profit is pursued more for the independence and well-being of the household than it is for capital accumulation per se. Their objective interests do not place them in a necessarily antagonistic relationship with other agrarian classes. At the same time, to the degree that they supplement family labor with wage labor or compete for scarce land with tenants or landless laborers, their mainly noncapitalist relations of production do not preclude severe conflict with other agrarian classes. Nonetheless, bullock capitalists are in a better position than any other agrarian producer class to become the fulcrum of political centrism and to seek hegemony within the agricultural sector by making downward or upward alliances and by appealing to the common interests of all agrarian producers.

All these features conspire to make bullock capitalists not only a centrist class but also the agent of a centrist politics equally opposed to collectivist agriculture and capitalist agriculture based on wage labor. As the bullock capitalists' most articulate ideologue put it:

> A system of agriculture based on small enterprises, where the worker himself is the owner of the land under his plough, will foster democracy. For it creates a population of independent outlook and action in the social and political fields. The peasant is an incorrigible individualist; his vocation, season in and season out, can be carried on with a pair of bullocks or a small machine in the solitude of nature without the necessity of having to give orders to or take orders from anybody. That is why the peasant class everywhere is the only class which is equally democratic without mental reservations. Further, the system of family-sized farms or peasant proprietorship ensures stability because the operator or the peasant has a stake in his farm and would lose by instability.[86]

The political coming of age of bullock capitalists runs parallel with and is strengthened by the first wave of the so-called backward classes movement in the northern Hindi Heartland states and Gujarat and the second wave in the southern and western states of Karnataka and Maharashtra. While the objective overlap is hardly perfect, the backward castes are the status aspect of bullock capitalism. Bullock capitalists are an economic category grounded in the means and relations of production; the backward classes are defined by the traditional ritual ranking of caste, modified by the British and Indian "official" sociological rankings of India's disadvantaged.[87]

Both the British and the Indian government's backward classes commissions designated as "backward classes" castes whose ritual rank and occuaptional status was above the untouchables but in the lower reaches of the caste order of traditional society. The political coming of age of backward castes occurred in the 1970s when chief ministers belonged to or spoke for Yadavas (Ahir), Kurmis, Koeris, Vokkaligas, and other prominent backward castes who have traditionally worked the land but now aspire to higher social status and improved occupational opportunities.[88] The demand by "backward classes" for reservation of posts in government service and seats in educational institutions partly reflects the efforts of upwardly mobile lower-caste cultivators to challenge the traditionally literate upper castes' hold on clerical positions. Such families hope to diversify, to place one or two family members in office jobs and thus improve the family's social standing, income, and security. In Bihar, Uttar Pradesh, and Karnataka in the 1970s and in Gujarat and Madhya Pradesh in the 1980s, the demands of backward classes became a divisive political issue by generating a backlash among upper-caste Hindus and untouchables. Just prior to the 1980 election, abortive efforts were made by the Charan Singh caretaker government to have the central government follow Bihar and Uttar Pradesh in reserving jobs (1980–85) in government service for backward class members.[89] The adamant resistance in the 1980s by established and predominantly urban upper castes, especially in the Ahmedabad reservations agitation of 1985, made it clear that the issue of reservations based on caste will continue to trouble Indian politics.[90]

The interests and ideology of the political class formed by bullock capitalists and backward castes strengthens centrist politics in India. As self-employed agrarian producers, bullock capitalists have less antagonistic relations with capitalist farmers and agricultural laborers than the latter two groups have with each other. These circumstances help to explain the wide appeal of their agrarian ideology and policies and the emergence in the 1980s of the "new agrarianism."[91] This composite political class encompasses more potential voters than any other agrarian producer group taken by itself (34 percent of households) or any other status group[92] taken by itself (about 25 percent of the total population). While imperfectly mobilized and far from homogeneous in political outlook and behavior, on both counts its political performance and prospects compare favorably with those of other agrarian classes and status groups who have entered the political arena.[93]

The Imperatives of National Power

The goal of capturing power in Delhi or wielding political influence nationally impels parties and factional leaders to occupy centrist ideological and policy positions. Power in Delhi requires a parliamentary majority or opposition standing in Parliament. As a result, the powerful tendency toward party fragmentation is met by a countervailing tendency toward party consolidation or coalition formation. Factions and personalities motivated by short-run calculations designed to exploit the main chance defect from and split parties, even while India's political elites seek homes in the Congress party and other national parties in order to exercise power and influence at the national level.

Governing in Delhi means having access to the advantages of incumbency. India's federal system gives the center initial or residual control over most of the resources and rules that affect state governments and leaves a substantial portion under the center's direct authority. The governing party or coalition in Delhi gains bargaining advantages with its own and rival state-level party units seeking to influence policy choice and implementation. Even though a national party may lose an election, belonging to it may be a more attractive possibility than going into the political wilderness at the head of a minor party.

In the eighties, the success of regional parties at the state level in West Bengal, Tamil Nadu, Andhra Pradesh, Karnataka, Punjab, and Assam created an alternative to the goal of capturing power in Delhi. This bifurcation of state and national political realms began a decade earlier in 1971 with the delinking of state assembly and national parliamentary elections (see chapter 6). The rise of regional parties, however, has not undermined the necessity for those seeking national power to adhere to centrist ideology and to pursue centrist politics.

The Constraints of Social Pluralism and Federalism

India's cultural diversity and social pluralism, reinforced and compounded by its federal system, further motivate parties seeking national power to adopt centrist ideologies and policies. Social pluralism in India, like social pluralism in America, may be the basis for the "exceptionalism" that distinguishes the country from other industrial democracies. Issues and symbols highly salient for one or a few states are irrelevant to others. Madhya Pradesh, one of India's more backward states because of its marginal agricultural economy, predominantly rural society, large and backward tribal population, and residual princely state loyalties, is very different from its neighbor Maharashtra, whose productive, market-oriented agricultural economy, numerous industrial complexes, large urban centers, and advanced and well-organized ex-untouchable castes make it one of India's most advanced states. National parties must adopt ideologies and advocate policies that articulate and represent the formidable range of economic, cultural, and social differences that exist among and within India's twenty-two states and eight union territories. They often adopt different strategies—and attract different supporters—to cope with variations among state political systems. The result has bedeviled scholars' efforts to establish significant correlations between socioeconomic variables and party voting.[94] Associations between socioeconomic status and party preference have been found at the district and, to an extent, the state levels, but they wash out at the national (all-India) level.

If Indian politics at the national level does not feature national confessional or caste parties, at the state level it does reveal religious and caste-based parties or voting. The Muslim League is an important component of Kerala politics just as the National Conference (Muslim) is important in Kashmir, the Akali Dal (Sikhs) in the Punjab, the Lok Dal (Jat) in western Uttar Pradesh and Haryana, and the various factions of the Republican party of India (scheduled castes) in western and northern India. Not only are none of these parties national, but voting by Muslims and ex-untouchables also tends, with a few exceptions, to parallel prevailing electoral trends and party distributions. Castes at the politically salient level of *jatis* (endogamous groups) number over three thousand. Politically powerful locally, their cohesion and reach diminishes with distance and scale. Caste associations and caste voting can affect electoral outcomes at the constituency level and even the state level, but their political reach stops at state boundaries, which, for the most part, coincide with language boundaries. The number and diversity of caste groupings and the diversity of their interests make it difficult to mount national ideologies or issues based on caste. The cutting edge of caste consciousness and concern is status and power, not class. The backward classes movement stands virtually alone as an instance of caste-based national politics. If this movement represents a version of Sudra power, there are no other national parties or movements based on status groups or *varna,* that is, Brahman, Kshatriya, or Vaishya.

Nor have linguistic groupings been able as such to compete for power at the center. The increasing importance of linguistically based regional parties (e.g., the All-India Anna Dravida Munnetra Kazhagam [AIADMK] and the Telugu Desam) lies in their ability to defeat class-oriented as well as national centrist parties at the state level and to control enough MPs to play a role in national coalition politics.

India's social pluralism and federal system reinforce centrist ideologies and policies. Electoral pluralities and parliamentary majorities depend on articulating policies that reconcile contradictions among diverse and often conflicting interests yet avoid consensual formulas which, by speaking to everybody, speak to nobody.

The Electoral System and Centrism

Finally, the formal rule governing electoral competition among parties has favored centrism. Regardless of the number of candidates and the division of the vote among them, the candidate first past the post (with a plurality) wins the seat. The first-past-the-post rule rewards the party with the highest plurality by inflating its seat percentage over its vote percentage by 20 to 25 percent. Conversely, the rule penalizes parties with losing pluralities by deflating their seat percentages below their vote percentages. The rule has helped broad-based parties that appeal to a wide spectrum of classes, communities, regions, and interests more than those that limit their appeal to a single class, community, or caste.[95] It has helped such parties win a majority of seats without the support of an electoral majority. Over forty years and eight parliamentary elections, no party has won a majority of the national vote. Yet, except from November 1969 to February 1971 and from July to December 1979, national parties with comfortable parliamentary (seat) majorities have governed the country since the first election in 1952. Without a majority party, India has regularly produced majority governments.

The high proportion of plurality victories (46 percent in 1980) and the predominance of multicandidate contests (518 of 525)[96] are two phenomena that reflect the attempts by some candidates to represent narrow confessional, caste, tribe, and other diversities. Without the plurality rule, aggregative parties would play a smaller role in the electoral outcomes.

The center may not hold. There is a limit to how many parties can aspire to be national and centrist. Multicandidate contests involving several centrist parties enable levels of vote fragmentation that can benefit parties with more focused appeals to class, community, or special interests. If three centrist parties (or electoral coalitions), having failed to agree on seat adjustments, face each other in 300 to 400 of Parliament's 542 constituencies, their average vote per candidate could decline sufficiently for the first-past-the-post rule to reward candidates of narrow- rather than broad-gauged parties.

Regional parties are located between class, community, and narrow special interest candidates on the one hand and national centrist parties and coalitions on the other. At the national level, regional parties have cooperated with or supported national centrist majority governments and are likely to continue to do so.[97] On the other hand, if regional parties detract sufficiently from centrist party pluralities by opposing rather than allying with them, the first-past-the-post rule may reward class, community, or special interest candidates so that no national centrist party or national centrist coalition is able to form a majority government.

India's centrist multiparty system may self-destruct by failing to produce a parliamentary majority. The possibility was implicit in the 1980 parliamentary election and, prior to Mrs. Gandhi's death, in that of

1984. In 1980, one hundred seats won by Congress-I pluralities would have gone to Janata or Lok Dal if these parties had made seat adjustments. For the first time, an Indian national election would have failed to produce a parliamentary majority. In the event, the Congress-I won 353 rather than the 253 seats that would have resulted from a Janata-Lok Dal electoral agreement. Without such an agreement, Congress-I won two-thirds of the seats with 43 percent of the vote, while Janata/Lok Dal/Congress-U (for Devraj Urs) gained only 15 percent of the seats with 34 percent of the votes. As the losing party in 1977, Congress-I in 1977 suffered a similar fate; with the same vote share as the opposition parties in 1980 (34 percent), it won 28 percent of the seats. The plurality victory multiplier reached its apogee in 1984, when Congress-I's 49 percent of the vote yielded 79 percent of the seats.

In 1980 for the seventh time and in 1984 for the eighth, a minority vote produced a majority government. Repeatedly since 1952, the first-past-the-post (plurality wins) rule has produced centrist parliamentary majorities.

Despite the de facto regime changes of the 1975–77 period, when the Indian state changed from democratic to authoritarian and back again, the character of political ideology, electoral politics and public policy has remained basically centrist. After 1977, the temporary transformation of the party system by the change in the party controlling the national government led to a perceptible decline in the level of procedural consensus. The result was to increase conflict over state issues, such as the nature of the federal system and the independence (or "commitment") with which judges and higher civil servants interpret the law and carry on the administration. These issues became less conflictual after Rajiv Gandhi's government was formed in 1984.

Significant as the changes since 1975 have been, they are not likely to alter the centrist character of Indian politics in the foreseeable future. In the absence of state fragmentation, revolution, or international cataclysm, the social and institutional determinants of centrism are likely to prove more powerful and durable than those supporting class or confessional politics.

2 State Formation in India: Building and Wasting Assets

If India's relatively stable democracy and slow but steady economic development in the 1950s and 1960s seemed exceptional, they were in part due to the legacies of stateness and state formation that distinguish India from most Third World countries. Their proximate determinant was the viceregal state of the British raj.[1] Their more distant determinants included the Mughal empire, from whose ideas and practice the British benefited and which the British assimilated, and the imperial states and regional kingdoms of ancient and medieval India. The troubled history of Third World countries since independence following World War II has revealed that state building must precede and parallel nation building and economic development. Contrary to prevailing assumptions of scholarship and policy in the generations since decolonization, states create nations and economies more than nations and economies create states.

Political economy encompasses two powerful paradigms, liberal and Marxist. Until recently, both depicted the state as reflexive of social forces. Liberal pluralists construed the state and its actions in terms of successive equilibrums that followed from the play of organized interests. At best, liberal states could umpire contests among competing interests and execute outcomes but could not independently determine policy or set goals. Marxists construed the state and its actions in terms of a struggle among classes formed and motivated by the mode and relations of production. The state was the agent of a ruling class or of a hegemonic class coalition. Both paradigms depicted a reflexive state whose nature and actions mirrored equilibrums of either organized interests or classes.

Both now hold that under certain historical conditions or in particular policy arenas, the state in developed as well as developing societies can be autonomous as well as reflexive. For liberals, the revisionist position arose from experiences with the post–World War II welfare states that until the mid-seventies successfully managed economies and provided rights and entitlements for citizens. For Marxists, revision arose from Marx's observation, in *The Eighteenth Brumaire of Louis Bonaparte,* that under the second Bonaparte the state made

60

itself completely independent, with the result that the executive power subordinated society to itself. This observation seemed more germane under a wide variety of historical circumstances than his reflexive view of the state as an "executive committee of the ruling class."

For us, the heuristic for the state-society relationship can be located on a continuum ranging from complete state domination of society to complete societal domination of the state. We identify four potential positions on the continuum: totalitarian, in which the state completely dominates society, creating and controlling social formations, maintaining a closed milieu, and using force and terror without restraint; autonomous, in which the state can be self-determining because it is relatively insulated from societal forces, the only limits on its freedom to act being legitimacy and consent; constrained, in which the state's freedom to act is limited not only by legitimacy and consent but also by the representation of organized social forces; and reflexive or heteronomous, in which the state lacks self-determination because it is dominated by society, whose organized interests or classes appropriate state authority and resources. A state's location on the continuum depends on historical circumstances, including ideology, leadership, conjunctural effects, and the balance of public and private power.

State formation and maintenance is a continuous process located in history; the nature of the state cannot be known a priori from theory. Because state-society relationships vary with historical circumstances, the continuous process of state formation and maintenance produces polymorphous entities; that is, states occur in a variety of forms, characters, and styles. Peter Nettl captured this polymorphous nature of the state when he introduced the term "stateness" and argued that high and low stateness varied with historical experience, institutional legacies, and political culture.[2]

The Indian state is the residual legatee of a long tradition of high stateness that reaches back to India's ancient subcontinental empires and medieval regional kingdoms.[3] It has been more directly shaped by the more recent Mughal and British empires of the sixteenth through the twentieth centuries, which, like European absolute states of the seventeenth and eighteenth centuries, established internal sovereignty. The Mughal and British states made terms of high stateness, such as *sarkar* (government) and *raj* (rule), an integral part of popular consciousness that, like the monsoon, were perceived as an aspect of nature. After independence, the Indian state has been located in the middle positions of the continuum, autonomous or constrained, rather than at its extremes, totalitarian or reflexive. In this chapter, we analyze the ideas and forces that shaped the postindependence state and provide some of the explanation for why the Indian state was relatively autonomous in the fifties and early sixties, when Jawaharlal Nehru was prime minister, but subsequently became more constrained.

In chapter 1 we introduced a reason for the Indian state's being autonomous or constrained rather than reflexive: its superordinate relationship as a "third actor" to the historic adversaries of class politics, private capital, and organized labor. The state as third actor began its autonomous career in independent India as a creature of Nehruvian socialism. India's ideological consensus and constitution featured socialism along with secularism and democracy. For Nehru, socialism meant using the planned development of an industrial society to eliminate poverty, provide social justice, create a self-reliant economy, and assure national independence and security in world politics. In a mixed economy, the state would occupy the commanding heights. The socialist state would serve society by providing collective and public goods from which everyone would benefit. Equally important, concentrations of private economic power were to be eliminated or controlled so that they could not appropriate state authority or resources or unduly influence the choice and implementation of state policy.

The successful practice of command politics and the rise of the state as third actor created conditions for a powerful state sector of the economy. The state sector brought into being a potentially privileged political class whose interests were defined by and associated with it. Public-sector employees and managers, petty and high-level officials, and professionals and elected politicians became a class defined by their ownership or control of state property, resources, and authority. Although the political class associated with the state sector shared common interests when it entered competitive relationships with political classes defined by other economic sectors, it was not necessarily or always unified. Both horizontal cleavages, between politicians and officials and among different levels of officials, and vertical cleavages, among ministries and other functionally defined units, from time to time created tensions and even violent conflict within the state sector's political class.

Another variant of the state as autonomous third actor was the "state for itself," self-justifying and self-serving as well as self-determining, which arose when the socialist state was appropriated by its own functionaries. Building a socialist state required means. Resources had to be extracted and capital accumulated for planned investment to occur. State services and production required employees. The state expanded as well as reproduced itself. The state sector that burgeoned and flourished on the way to socialism began to acquire and vest interests.

Means began to become ends. Those in the pay of state firms became the beneficiaries of monopoly profits and administered prices; petty bureaucrats and senior officials became the beneficiaries of rents, the petty and grand larceny made possible by administrative discretion in the application of rules. The third actor spawned interests that increasingly diverted it from its socialist objectives.

The Indian state also appeared in a constrained variant. In chapters 9 through 13, we show how, after 1964, rising levels of mobilization and the ascendancy of demand politics modified state autonomy. In doing so, we argue that the 1975–77 emergency regime's attempt to reestablish an autonomous state based on command politics met with only temporary success.

Which version of the state as autonomous third actor is at work at particular times and circumstances, the socialist servant of the public interest or the self-serving political class associated with the state sector, depends in part on how actions are interpreted. When the state raises the pay and benefits of some section of its fifteen million employees is it being a model employer, buying labor peace, investing in political support, or serving the interests of a state class? If public-sector managers insist that the state buy their industrial goods rather than an imported version, are they supporting self-reliance or sheltering the high-cost and/or low-quality production on which their jobs and incomes depend? In an economy that is still building its industrial base, should the goal of an industrial relations regime that severely restricts collective bargaining and the right to strike be to maintain production and protect the public or to hold down wages and coerce commitment? Do permits and licenses insure socially justifiable investments and production or provide rents to those who issue them?

Which of its faces the polymorphous Indian state reveals is determined by policy as well as by ideology, historical circumstance, and the balance of public and private power. In this chapter, we discuss the historical forces and policy choices that initially provided the institutional assets for state autonomy but subsequently put them at risk.

Historical Legacies: The Subcontinental Empire

The state in India was not a European import, an ideological and institutional transplant from foreign climes rooted in India's exotic and alien soil. British rule profoundly influenced state formation and the level and quality of stateness in India, but it in turn built on Mughal rule and incorporated many of its features. The historical legacies of imperial states on the Indian subcontinent in the pre-Christian era established state conceptions and institutions that provided models for the subcontinental multinational state of modern India.[4] Regional kingdoms were the principal state form that characterized the history of the Indian subcontinent until the sixteenth century. But the subcontinental state conception was already realized in preclassical times, in the Mauryan empire, particularly under Asoka (312–185 B.C.), and under the imperial rule of the Guptas (A.D. 319–540). At their apogee, India's ancient empires established hegemony over diverse regional kingdoms. Such kingdoms stood in tension with the subcontinental empire and forced recognition of their standing on the imperial forms that triumphed after the sixteenth century. The regional kingdom as a state form has remained in a dialectical relation with the subcontinental empire throughout Indian history. Today the dialectical relationship is expressed through Indian federal forms. The history of Indian state formation is more comparable to that of Russia and China, where empires became multinational states, than to that of Western Europe, where regional kingdoms were transformed into absolute monarchies and then nation-states. India is the state Europe would have become had the Holy Roman Empire embodied itself in a modern polity. On the subcontinent, the regional kingdom and the national state became the recessive, the multinational subcontinental empire the dominant form of the state. The Mughal, British, and Indian states of the modern era incorporate the dialectical tension between these two pervasive state forms.[5]

India's subcontinental empires created means of penetration and control comparable to those developed by European absolutism in the seventeenth and eighteenth centuries: centralized fiscal mechanisms in the hands of the ruler; patrimonial bureaucracies barred from control of the means of administration and from inheritance of office and estates; and military formations funded and controlled by the ruler rather than by feudal chiefs or independent military entrepreneurs. Such arrangements were already known in the subcontinental fourth-century B.C. Mauryan empire and articulated in books of statecraft (*Artha*) dating from that period and subsequently.[6] Their actualization, however, has varied over time. Revived in later subcontinental empires and in regional kingdoms, they fade with the fragmentation of dominion under weak emperors or regional kings, whose servants—under various guises and arrangements—appropriate estates, office, fisc, and army.[7]

The Mughals (sixteenth to eighteenth century) succeeded in constructing a centralized military-revenue arrangement, the *mansabdari* system, which extracted the resources and provided the military force to conquer and hold in stable fashion an extensive empire. Comparable in size to the domains of Charles V, the Mughal empire probably controlled its area more securely.[8] The emperor's dominion was exercised through a centrally appointed court nobility, the *mansabdars,* not through decentralized prebendiaries as in European feudalism. *Mansabdars* were dependent on the emperor; the lands allocated to support their foot and mounted troops and pay their expenses reverted to the emperor at his pleasure or at their death. Noble estates were not hereditary. The emperors exquisitely calibrated, depending on performance, the honors and income associated with state service.[9] Ottoman models probably influenced the administrative and revenue systems of the Mughals and their predecessors, but the Ottomans penetrated further and eliminated intermediary classes more ruthlessly than was the case in India. The local rulers and chiefs beneath the *mansabdari* system survived, creating intermediary layers of economic, political, and cultural autonomy that contrast with Russian absolutism and the model of "oriental despotism" expressed in the Ottoman empire.

The administrative system of the Mughals provided the network, units, and conceptions of revenue obligation on which the British system was modeled. The division of the country into *subahs, sarkars,* and *parganas* was reflected in British administrative divisions. The *zabt,* measurement of land for revenue purposes, migrated from the administrations of Sher Shah Sur and Akbar to Cornwallis and the British raj. In the latter part of Aurangzeb's rule and under the last Mughal rulers in the eighteenth century, state autonomy and capacity markedly declined, only to be restored under British rule, which fell heir to and reformulated the imperial state's ideas and practice.

Indian empires also created a symbolic and cultural order that emphasized the overarching significance of rulership, if not the state. Akbar restored and benefited from the ancient and pervasive Hindu idea of a universal emperor (*chakravartin*), who turned the cosmological wheel (*chakra*) and was the hub of its spokes.[10] The *chakravartin* or emperor was *raja dhiraja* (raja of rajas) or *shahanshah* (shah of shahs), conceptions which signified his primacy in a layered and aggregative as well as centralized state. Akbar succeeded in sanctifying the person and office of the emperor in the face of an Islamic tradition hostile to such sanctification. Iconography, rituals, and performances celebrated and elevated the emperor, who became an object of awe and wonder.[11] Because the loyalty and obeisance he commanded were at once intensely personal and abstract, they created a separate state domain that dissolved and displaced loyalties to place, kin, and community.[12] The void left by this dissolution "was unconsciously sought to be filled by the special position of the Mughal emperor as spiritual guide, and the self-conscious view of the Mughal empire as a great new polity, essentially just and humane."[13]

Performances and exchanges amplified the emperor's presence: for the public, the daily royal audience in the *diwan-i-am* (hall of public audience); for the court attended by princes and nobles, appearances in the *diwan-i-khas* (hall of private audience) and at frequent durbars; for the crown servants in the field, intimate personal exchanges—the gift of a *khilat* (robe said to have been worn by the emperor) to mark appointment as his agent, letters from the emperor's hand, and the reciprocation of gifts by subordinates.[14] Streams of exchanges kept "thick" the emperor's relations with service nobles at the far corners of the subcontinent.[15] Here too there was continuity between British and Mughal empires. The British used Mughal ceremonies and language to revitalize the universalism and mystique of the imperial state. Through ceremonial enactments that closely emulated Mughal patterns, they revived in Queen Victoria's time imperial grandeur and patrimonial ties in durbars, jubilees, and coronation ceremonies and rituals of loyalty between the Queen-Empress and her subjects.[16]

The actualization of the subcontinental state has waxed and waned over the centuries. The regional kingdom ceased to be the dominant state form with the rise of the Mughal empire in the sixteenth century, although it experienced a brief revival in the eighteenth. After the collapse of Mughal power at the death of Aurangzeb in 1707 and the failure of Maratha rulers to establish a successor state, British power, followed by British rule, revived and restored the subcontinental imperial state. The formation of India and Pakistan in 1947 and Bangladesh in 1971 left the subcontinent with two latter-day representatives of the regional kingdom and one of the subcontinental imperial state.

In contrast with European nation states, whose strength rested on the extinction of regional cultures and identities, subcontinental empires in India have made accommodations with regional kingdoms. The strategy propounded in the fourth-century *Arthasastra*—that subordinate rulers shall be preserved and respected in their customs and territorial jurisdiction if they acknowledge, via respect and tribute, the superior authority of a ruler of rulers—governed the statecraft of subcontinental empires in Mughal and British times.[17] After independence, India's federal system became its modern embodiment within the twentieth-century subcontinental empire.

Indigenous Hindu and imported liberal state theory have also made substantial contributions to state formation and to the level and quality of stateness. At first appearance, they seem to differ sharply on key issues. Liberal theory posits the individual as the basic unit of society; Hindu theory emphasizes family, caste, and tribe. The theories also differ with respect to the primacy of consent and force for obedience, with liberal theory stressing the voluntary and contractual basis of individual obedience and Hindu theory stressing *danda,* the rod of punishment, as the indispensible requisite of order.[18] The severe realpolitik of might making right in the *Arthasastra* contrasts sharply with the liberal conception that natural law and right reason are the source of morality and order.

Yet the two theoretical traditions converge with respect to the priority of societal values over state goals. Both see society as preceding and limiting the state (and for liberalism, unlike Hindu theory, the individual precedes and limits the society). The society displayed in the *Dharmasastras,* the classical texts of good conduct that constitute the fundamental prescriptive canons of Hindu culture, is a society whose reality and legitimacy co-originate with the king but are not his creation. Its units are self-regulating within a larger architectonic. The state in India did not constitute a community of feeling; the state-society relationship was primarily instrumental. The state upheld and protected society and its values rather than itself constituting the highest form of community and the means for realizing value. The Indian state was constrained by a society whose ordered heterogeneity was prescribed and legitimized in the *Dharmasastras.* This doctrine implied restraints on the state that stood in tension with the more absolutist doctrines of *dandaniti,* just as doctrines of state sovereignty and reason of state stood in tension with liberal doctrines of consent and natural rights.

The good Hindu king is meant to protect the laws of the self-regulating orders of society. The liberal state is meant to protect individual rights and interests. Insofar as a liberal state has goals and policies, they are to be determined by the outcomes of interest group and party competition that organizes and represents individual preferences. At the extreme, both liberal and Hindu state theory countenance anarchism, as the convergence of Thoreau and Gandhi on the legitimacy and importance of civil disobedience suggests, and discountenance reason of state to justify acts that violate procedural norms and societal values.

The founders of modern India's constitution benefited from the leg-

acy of stateness bequeathed by the Hindu, Mughal, and British subcontinental empires. They combined centralized rule with a parallel
state form, the regional kingdom. The ideas and practice of the subcontinental imperial state from Mauryan to British times and the
Hindu conception that social order requires the state's force, left a legacy of high stateness. On the other hand, the sovereignty-limiting ideas
and practice of the regional kingdom and of the Hindu and liberal conceptions that society is prior to and autonomous of the state created a
legacy of low stateness. These paradigms and parameters structured
the possibilities and choices of those who created independent India's
state.

Historical Legacies: Liberal and Authoritarian Options in the Founding Period

Models for the founding of states and for political change arise in both
domestic and international environments. When a liberal theory of the
state became the principal ideological determinant of the 1950 constitution, it drew on both domestic and international exemplars. It expressed the liberal obligation to recognize civil and political rights embodied in the Westminster model gradually introduced from 1909 by
the British raj.[19] It also included a more traditional Indian understanding that claims to state sovereignty and monopoly over public and national interest were constrained by the traditional obligation of the
ruler to recognize and uphold the jurisdiction of prior social groups.
At independence, democratic, parliamentary, and constitutional government had become a familiar form to Indians, who had fought as
nationalists for four decades to make it their own. A variant of Hindu
state theory advocated by Mohandas Gandhi in the Constituent Assembly was little attended to.[20] It held that that society's dharmically
ordered heterogeneity was prior to and to a considerable degree autonomous of state authority and that local communities were capable
of self-rule. Arguments were offered too in favor of the viceregal variant of the imperial administrative state. Like Gandhi's ideas, they were
not endorsed by the small group of Congress leaders who managed the
Constituent Assembly and its eight standing committees.[21]

That a liberal state should have triumphed was strongly determined,
but by no means preordained. Fortuitous conjunctures and long-range
secular trends collaborated in the outcome. The partition of India into
two successor states, India and Pakistan,[22] and the integration of the

autocratically constituted princely states[23] spared independent India from having to grapple with several divisive and recalcitrant state issues that had plagued British efforts at state building. The creation of an Islamic state in Pakistan removed the principal challenge to Congress's secular state ideology. The weak federalism that alone by 1946 could have kept the Muslim-majority areas from leaving India would have been a significant obstacle to planned development and social transformation. The incorporation of the princely states, whose territories covered about a third of the subcontinent and whose subjects encompassed about a quarter of its people, eliminated from serious contention the monarchical alternative that had for so long characterized regional kingdoms.[24]

The Gandhians in the Constituent Assembly were disarmed with minor concessions. The constitution's directive principles of state policy made commitments to *panchayati raj* (decentralized local government) and to certain cultural values dear to some upper-caste Hindus, such as the abolition of cow slaughter.

The liberal state created at independence was not merely the result of four years of deliberation in the Constituent Assembly, or the political legacy of four decades of gradual parliamentary growth. The historical circumstances and accidents that made Nehru the principal founder of the state and that enabled him to shape its conventions also played an important part in determining its character. The historical outcomes we know seem natural only because we repress the memory of possible alternatives. The deaths of Subhas Chandra Bose in August 1945 and Vallabhbhai Patel in December 1950[25] removed not only Nehru's principal competitors for national leadership but also powerful spokesmen for authoritarian state ideologies. On the eve of World War II, Bose successfully challenged Gandhi's hold on Congress by being elected its president in 1938 and again in 1939. Bose, like Nehru, had been shaped by a Cambridge education and exposure to European events in the 1930s. For a time they worked together in Congress's socialist left. By 1938, they diverged on the prospects and value of fascism and on political means. Bose thought that Hitler and Mussolini represented the wave of the future and would win the war they both anticipated. Nehru believed that the Soviet experiment provided economic lessons for independent India, fascism should be opposed and would be defeated, and Gandhi's and the liberal state's concern for right means was essential.

In April 1943, Bose arrived by German submarine in Singapore where, with Japanese support, he formed a government in exile (*Azad*

Hind or Free India) and took command of the Indian National Army (INA), composed of twenty-thousand of the eighty-thousand Indian officers and men captured by the Japanese when Singapore fell. Styling himself *Netaji* (leader on the Führer model), he declared his objective to be liberation of India by military means.[26] "I am convinced more than ever before," he wrote the German government in May 1942, when first proposing that it support his plan to shift his efforts to the Orient, "that the Tripartite Powers [Germany, Italy, and Japan] and India have a common destiny."[27] Writing in *Wille und Macht* in August 1942 on the subject of "Free India and Her Problems," he found one thing clear: "There will be a strong Central Government. . . . Behind this Government will stand a well organized, disciplined all-India party, which will be the chief instrument for maintaining national unity."[28] Earlier in his career, Bose had identified with and come to represent the realpolitik and extremist versions of Indian nationalism that flourished in Bengal and Maharashtra. He ended by being an apologist for national socialism. Nehru came to represent the liberal moderate version whose lineage ran from Mahadev Ranade to Gopal Krishna Gokhale to Gandhi with an essential detour via democratic socialism.[29]

The fate of state formation in independent India depended also on the outcome of a related historical event, the trial of arms between the (British) Indian Army and Bose's Japanese-supported INA. Had the Japanese and the INA succeeded in reaching Calcutta or beyond and had Bose's government been established on Indian soil even for a time, or had Bose lived to return to independent India, the determinants of state formation in India would have included elements like those in Indonesia where a *Netaji* and a political army gained independence by military means. The maintenance of a nonpolitical, professional army was a close thing in 1946. Even Nehru, in November 1945, put on his barrister's gown for the first time in twenty-five years to help defend the three INA officers being tried by the British raj at the Red Fort, symbol of Delhi's empires.[30] As independence became increasingly imminent, Nehru and others came to accept another view, articulated by Lord Mountbatten to Nehru in 1946: that "The I.N.A. were not politically conscious heroes fighting for their country but cowards and traitors who betrayed their loyal friends. The people who will serve you well in your national army of the future are those who are loyal to their oath [to the head of state, whether the king emperor or an Indian head of state]; otherwise if you become unpopular a disloyal army may turn against you."[31] In the event, India opted for a professional army loyal to its oath and to the honor of its traditions and calling.[32] The INA trials were curtailed, but INA officers and men were barred from joining the Indian Army. Unlike in many Third World countries where armies have become political and governing institutions, the Indian state and Indian politics have been notably free from military control or even influence. This reflects in part the success with which constitutional democracy has been pursued by Indian parties and leaders, but it is also a consequence of the events and decisions of 1944–46.

An authoritarian alternative to India's state formation had other voices and legacies in the critical period of gaining independence and writing a constitution for the new state. If he had not had to share power with Nehru at independence, Vallabhbhai Patel, the "iron sardar," might have oriented the Indian state in a Hindu revivalist, economically conservative, and authoritarian direction. The Bismarckian adjective "iron" was not inappropriate. Patel was not a charismatic ideologist or master of words and crowds like his rivals for national leadership, Bose and Nehru. He despised political rhetoric and pleasing the multitude. His forte was control of the many by the few through command of the party organization, intelligence, police, and mass media. He was a past master at manipulating party factions and political elites.

Patel was a man of action rather than words, and his state theory must be inferred from what he did and how he did it. He was committed to Hindu tradition and interests as much out of convenience as out of conviction; they were key elements of the political forces that supported his leadership. As a Hindu traditionalist he understood and appreciated the viceregal state's use of *danda,* the rod of chastisement, to ensure order and obedience. Patel's voice was essential for saving the ICS, the "steel frame" of the imperial administrative state, and, until yesterday, the masters and jailers of India's political classes. His greatest accomplishment was integrating the princely states, but his success in quelling the naval mutiny at Bombay in 1946 and in directing the "police action" against a recalcitrant nizam of Hyderabad also project a state that makes order and obedience a necessary if not a sufficient condition for legitimacy.

Patel was not a committed or convinced secularist. His call for Muslims to pledge their loyalty to India as a condition of citizenship after partition, his one-sided defense of Hindus during the communal rioting and carnage that accompanied partition, and his refusal to honor India's commitment to turn over to Pakistan the assets due it were the occasion of Gandhi's last fast in January 1948. The riots in Delhi abated; Patel, after being told by Gandhi on the verge of death, "you are not the *Sardar* I knew," turned over the assets and deferred to Gandhi's call for brotherhood and forgiveness. Subsequently he honored his pledge to Gandhi to cooperate with Nehru, inter alia supporting a secular state in the Constituent Assembly.[33]

Patel's death in December 1950 left Nehru as India's unchallenged national leader, free for a decade or more to shape the Indian state in a liberal direction. His doing so was not a foregone conclusion. In 1937, when his second term as Congress president was drawing to a close and there was a talk of drafting him for a third, Nehru wrote an anonymous article revealing that he had authoritarian fantasies very close to the kind his daughter, Indira Gandhi, acted out. It was the decade of dictators; fascism seemed to be ascendant. Bose, who followed Nehru as Congress president, had begun to turn from democratic to national socialism. "He calls himself a democrat and a socialist," Nehru wrote of himself, "but every psychologist knows that the mind is ultimately slave to the heart and that logic can always be made to fit in with the desires and irrepressible urges of man. A little twist and Jawaharlal might turn dictator, sweeping aside the paraphenalia of a slow moving democracy . . . we all know how fascism has fattened on this language and then cast it away as useless lumber. . . . Jawaharlal . . . has all the makings of a dictator in him."[34]

But it was the liberal state of the moderate nationalists and Gandhi's commitment to right means that became Nehru's historical option. He shaped the liberal state in ways that accommodated it to the 1950 constitution's new commitments to universal suffrage, a federal system, and socialist objectives. He and like-minded colleagues in the Congress had been weaned on the parliamentary version of the liberal state, including its concern for a government of laws and civil rights.

The Government of India Act of 1935 became the text of reference and emulation for India's constitution. About 250 of its 395 articles are taken from the 1935 act verbatim or substantially intact. Nehru and his colleagues preferred the liberal state to the untried and utopian Hindu or administrative state alternatives advocated by leaders of minority factions in the Constituent Assembly: a Gandhian state, later elaborated by Jayaprakash Narayan,[35] that favored radical decentralization and the inversion of the pyramid of power; a Hindu state that repudiated Congress's secular commitment and confirmed Muslim fears of becoming second-class citizens or worse; and a highly centralized, authoritarian state on the viceregal model. Nehru had the votes in the Constituent Assembly and subsequently the national support to establish a liberal state in India.

Had Bose or Patel lived into the independence period, highly divisive state issues would have created a very different history of state formation and building. As it was, Nehru had more or less a free hand, a historical circumstance that goes a long way in explaining the initial success of the liberal state and constitutional democracy in India.

The proximate causes of the struggles of the 1970s over democracy and authoritarianism were contests for power and political survival. But, to summarize, there were also more distant determinants, struggles over the kind and degree of what Peter Nettl called "stateness."[36] India was advantaged by the fact that the subcontinental empire had effectively established its hegemony over the regional kingdoms and that this hegemony was institutionalized in administrative practices. But India's historical legacies and leadership at independence pointed to a variety of possible outcomes. The authoritarian variants of the Hindu, Mughal, and British empires and the rise of fascism in the 1930s created one broad option. The liberal variants arising out of a means-oriented nationalism, the parliamentary features of the Westminster model, and Nehru's leadership of Congress created another.

High stateness in India is associated with its imperial legacies and the contemporary requirements of an interventionist, managerial state pursuing welfare and socialist objectives. But unlike the high stateness of continental Europe based on the era of monarchical absolutism, claims to state sovereignty and monopoly over public and national interest in India were constrained by the traditional obligation of the ruler to recognize and uphold the laws of prior social groups and the liberal obligation to recognized civil and political rights. The claim that the state has a special relationship to the public good, that the state's interest is uniquely identified with the public interest, and that the interests of social groups are narrow, partial, and selfish dates from the early 1970s and finds its analogues in theory.

State formation is never finished. It is a continuous process. Nehru's capacity to shape India's traditions in the first two decades of Indian independence greatly strengthened a liberal and constitutional state but did not foreclose other options. When Indira Gandhi introduced an authoritarian state in 1975, some observers thought such an outcome natural. A reviewer surveying Barrington Moore's magisterial *Social Origins of Dictatorship and Democracy* wrote, "India's move toward authoritarianism in 1975 confirms Moore's thesis that democracy can not survive without social revolution."[37] And yet it is possible that India's social revolution will take a form different from the European and Asian models Moore surveyed. Social revolution from below may work itself out in incremental fashion. Upheavals scattered rather than concentrated in time and space can reorder society even as they interrupt processes of economic development and state building.

The struggle between liberal and authoritarian versions of the state in India have featured opposing arguments. One asserts that institutions and processes representing organized interests in society are the best means to reach approximations of the public interest. Another asserts that the state knows best because it speaks for a disinterested, long-run view of the public good and national interests. Such issues played a central part in the politics of the 1970s. The stage was set by Indira Gandhi's authoritarian regime, when the arguments for India's version of high stateness were rehearsed by those who justified the regime. The climax of the drama was the victory of the Janata party in 1977, when the virtues of the liberal state were recalled and in considerable measure restored. But party alternation in control of the state after the 1977 and 1980 elections, when the principal contestants made state issues central themes of their campaigns, have kept these issues at the fore. In the eighties, Nehru's grandson sought to revitalize a Nehruvian constitutional settlement. The process of state formation continues.

The State and Its Permanent Government

A leading state issue during the founding period that reappeared in the 1970s and will affect the course of events in the 1980s is the kind of policy-level bureaucracy India requires. India became a republic, casting aside the autocratic monarchical doctrines and administrative state of king-emperor and viceroy; a democracy, where for the first time the political masters, those who would represent and govern, were chosen on the basis of universal suffrage; and a welfare and socialist state, committed not only to economic growth and self-reliance but also social justice and national power. The ICS, which had governed and administered the British raj, was available. Acting within the imperial and viceregal tradition, British civil servants under the raj had not only represented state interests but had governed directly; they constituted a colonial version of bureaucratic absolutism. A distant king-emperor and his secretary of state and a viceroy close at hand were political masters of a sort, but the British raj approximated bureaucratic more than monarchical absolutism. The steel frame and the guardians needed and took little political or policy direction. Was such a service suitable for the new state and nation? If it was, what changes in orientation were required of its successor service, the IAS, and could they be realized?[38]

At a time when many Third World states were struggling to build qualified and effective career services, the standing of India's senior bureaucracy was exceptional. It gave the state after independence an autonomy and continuity that has persisted in times of uncertainty and unsteady political control at the national and state levels. In the era of Patel and Nehru and, after 1950, in the Nehru era of Congress party dominance, the services were relatively sheltered from challenge and attack. The policy-level bureaucracy returned to the center of controversy and political debate with the onset of party alternation, a new development for the Indian political system. It began with the election of 1967 and its aftermath, when opposition coalitions governed half of India's sixteen large states, and it became more pronounced with the elections of 1977 and 1980, when the central government changed hands. States issues focusing on the senior civil service were brought to the top of India's political agenda by the temporary sharpening of socialist objectives after the Congress split of 1969 and the ensuing demands for commitment, the strain on the constitutional and legal obligations of civil servants created by the emergency, and the penetration of IAS state cadres by state politics and regional nationalism.

A variety of issues were debated but unresolved. The doctrine of "neutrality" was challenged by the doctrine of commitment; the meaning and operational consequences of commitment were disputed. The rise of personal loyalty as the test of commitment threatened the viability of career services and a government of law.

The doctrine of neutrality was the product of an era of partisan party competition. In England, such an era followed the coming of political stability in the early eighteenth century and of the concept of loyal opposition in the early nineteenth.[39] The doctrine was exported to India when, at the provincial level in the 1920s, Indian party politicians took charge of a limited range of ministerial portfolios, and it became a central doctrine of state theory at independence when India embarked on its experiments with parliamentary democracy. It was a convenient doctrine. Of the approximately 1,000 ICS officers serving at independence, 453 were Indian and became the policy bureaucracy of the successor states.[40] Neutrality served not only to explain and legitimize their role in the context of party government but also to provide a cover for their translation from political masters and jailers of Congress leaders to loyal servants of the new state.

Congress members of the Constituent Assembly were not easily convinced that the ICS should continue. As yesterday's nationalists, democrats, and reformers, they preferred to rid the state of an imperial legacy known for its elitism and conservatism. But more statist counsel prevailed. Patel, referring to the interim government that took office in November 1946 and the Government of India that came into being on August 15, 1947, warned the Constituent Assembly in 1949: "I have worked with them during this difficult period . . . Remove them and I see nothing but a picture of chaos all over the country."[41] Nehru, who had been unconvinced, changed his stance as he had done with respect to the INA and the Indian Army: "The old distinctions and differences are gone. . . . In the difficult days ahead our Service and experts have a vital role to play and we invite them to do so as comrades in the service of India."[42]

Nehru's remarks were premature. "Distinctions and differences" from the colonial era were not so easily forgotten. The most powerful metaphor for the services, the "steel frame," lingered on. The ICS was the vehicle of colonial administration, which featured law and order and the collection of revenue. For nationalists, law and order meant repression; for nationalists and socialists, revenue collection meant a failure to promote economic growth and social justice.[43] The steel frame was a negative metaphor until, in the face of the difficulties of governing the country, it lost its pejorative meaning. A new question emerged: was the steel frame strong enough and neutral enough? It became apparent in the late seventies, even as the position of the services was subject to buffeting from all sides, that a steel frame was useful for maintaining continuity and stability and sustaining national integration. In the face of their dramatic deterioration, maintaining law and order acquired new standing as an administrative virtue rather than a colonial vice.

"The guardians" was another image from the colonial era that lingered on after independence to provide a target for nationalists, democrats, and socialists. Philip Mason, a leading scholar of the ICS and himself a member of it, used the phrase to characterize it. He explicitly compared its self-image and outlook to those of the rulers in Plato's *Republic,* whose special knowledge of the good made them superior to ordinary men and justified their rule over them.[44] Translated into vulgar imperial relations, the guardians were the bearers of the white man's burden, the "heaven-born" superior beings whose duty it was to civilize the lesser breeds without the law and to enlighten the benighted. The guardian and heaven-born mentality lingered on, providing that special sense of calling that fortified IAS officers against the often philistine and populist onslaughts of democratic politicians, the elected representatives and ministers who were their newly installed masters. It lingered on too in the mistaken belief that amateur generalists were equipped to perform the technical and expert tasks involved in managing a vast and complex industrial and financial public sector, and in an ideology that state servants were uniquely equipped to speak for the public interest.

The guardian mentality also provided ample ammunition to those who demanded that the civil service shed its superior airs and become more socially representative, on the mistaken premise that those who were of the people would ipso facto be for the people. It is doubtful whether a more socially representative IAS composed of the children of middle and small cultivators or of urban petty traders would be more socialist, secular, or democratic than the children of the English-educated professionals who have been disproportionately represented in the senior and central services.[45] In much of the furor about representativeness, class style and more equal opportunities for social mobility were as often the issue as ideological orientation. In any case, as ministers and elected representatives became more rural and less professional, educated, and anglicized, they found their role as political masters threatened and compromised by state servants cut from the very different cloth of elite colleges and high-income urban and professional families.[46] Noting that 80 to 95 percent of India's higher civil service, as in most other countries, was drawn from the professional middle classes, they called for a more socially representative bureaucracy.[47]

At the national level, the disparity in educational levels and cultural styles was less marked and caused less difficulty than at the state level. During the Nehru era, the ICS and the IAS were Nehru's allies as well as state servants. The shared objective of national power through the creation of a modern society and economy overrode whatever differences there may have been with respect to socialist commitment.[48] As Nehru's coauthors and implementors, civil servants were the vanguard of the lobby for an industrial strategy, collaborating in the creation of basic and heavy industry under the second and third five-year plans. They brought into being the third actor in the Indian economy, the state sector, which rivaled and then surpassed private capital and organized labor. As the "new class" of a semisocialist state, they were among its principal beneficiaries. In Marxist tems, the policy bureaucracy of the permanent government was a leading element of the progressive national bourgeoisie, dominating state policy and being rewarded for it. Its members shared a common life-style; they talked the same languages, not only the king's English but also state capitalism, science and technology, and secularism. And they were "committed" to the government's policies and programs.

A distinguished member of the ICS entitled his administrative autobiography *Commitment My Style*. He found that the services were "infinitely more efficient" following the departure of the British at independence. The reason was the enormous challenge and "bursting promise" of administration at that time. "It is policy and direction, integrity and depth, that give [the civil servant] cohesion and knit him, in spite of heterogeneity, to the thrust of effective, massive organization, pursuing and achieving difficult and complex tasks . . . It is in the failure of policy, direction and integrity" that "our present [1973] malaise" is to be located.[49]

After Nehru's death (May 1964) and two successions (1964 and 1966), the alliance forged between a prime minister and a policy bureaucracy to build a powerful nation fell on evil days. It was shaken by the weak direction and confused initiatives of less able and confident national leadership and by the onset, even before Nehru's death, of Congress's decline, followed by the first signs of party alternation (1967).

Neutrality as a doctrine was a suitable rationalization for the transition from imperial rule to party government. It posed few problems so long as one-party dominance put no strain on the loyalty of civil servants.[50] But it began to be questioned when civil servants were asked to serve a variety of party masters in the states after 1967 and at the center after 1977. Mrs. Gandhi successfully challenged the old guard state bosses by backing radical policies such as bank nationalization, split the Congress in November 1969, and then twice led Congress to victory—first early in 1971 with the slogan "abolish poverty," then in the 1972 "khaki election" that followed the Bangladesh war. It was in this context—of a weak and divided Congress organization and the striking early success of the plebiscitary politics that were to become her hallmark—that Mrs. Gandhi called for a committed civil service. Speaking to the Congress parliamentary party, she referred to the administrative machinery as a stumbling block, adding "the country would be in a rut" if it followed the British system in which civil servants were not supposed to be concerned with which political party was in power. Her then colleagues but future political opponents, the Congress's left leaders Chandra Shekhar and Mohan Dharia, joined her call for the "creation of an administrative cadre committed to national objectives and responsive to our social needs." "The present bureaucracy, under the orthodox and conservative leadership of the ICS with its conservative upper-class prejudices can hardly be expected to meet the requirements of social and economic change along socialist lines."[51] In 1972, the Gandhi government, in the name of equality, abolished by amendment constitutionally protected perquisites of the ICS. The gesture was not only vindictive but also gratuitous, since only eighty ICS officers remained in service, but it had high symbolic payoffs for a leader professing socialism and egalitarianism.[52]

Mrs. Gandhi was not satisfied when civil servants and public figures argued that neutrality meant giving one's best to the government of the day, from policy advice to ministers to program implementation. For her, commitment went beyond active support for Congress programs to belief in the party leader's mandate from the people. She wanted a style of commitment more suited to a bureaucracy serving a single party and its leader than to one serving alternating-party governments.[53] In the face of party deinstitutionalization and the rise of plebiscitary politics, she attempted to substitute state bureaucracies for party-based organizational support.

Mrs. Gandhi also wanted commitment of the sort patrimonial rulers command: personal loyalty to herself and, from 1975, to her son Sanjay. This view of commitment fed and grew first on prudence, then on opportunism and, under the emergency, on fear. Better to show loyalty even to the extent of bending or breaking the law than to risk disfavor or punishment by too principled conduct.

When the Janata party swept the Congress emergency regime from office in 1977, it further muddied the doctrinal waters, complicating and compounding the issue of appropriate behavior for civil servants. It meant to restore the doctrine and practice of neutrality. In fact, it began to discipline or put on trial the civil service loyalists of the emergency era who had engaged in excesses. The Janata government favored not just upright professionals but also those committed to its own people and measures. Some of its ministers confused good ends with partisan advantage and correct procedure with victimization. When Mrs. Gandhi returned to power in 1980, her party government, often invoking Janata examples and precedents, restored to office and favor those whom Janata had found most culpable.[54] As India entered the 1980s and victims became heroes and heroes victims, all three doctrines—neutrality, commitment, and loyalty—had to be reargued in the light of a transformed historical context.

With the rise of alternating-party or coalition governments, the need for a politically "neutral" but *professionally* committed policy bureaucracy that can shift masters has become more pressing. India's interventionist, managerial state can no longer pretend that its policy bureaucracy is neutral in the sense of being anonymous and voiceless.[55]

At the cabinet level, effective policy coordination and guidance requires officials who are loyal to the responsible minister and committed to the minister's policies. But it also requires that ministers are themselves professional. In France, prime ministers and cabinet ministers have for some time drawn directors and chiefs of ministerial "cabinets" from senior civil servants who seemed loyal to them personally as well as committed to their policy objectives. It is assumed that if senior officials are to help a minister make and coordinate policy they must loyally share the minister's interests, a mix of policy and politics distinct from and often in conflict with both the interests of the permanent bureaus and the organized interests in relevant policy arenas.[56] In America, at least since the creation of the executive office of the president in 1939, loyal as well as committed president's men have been a legitimate feature of policy bureaucracies at the cabinet and subcabinet as well as the presidential level. Often drawn from outside the ranks of the senior civil service, policy intellectuals and professionals are chosen for personal loyalty as well as for their special knowledge and policy commitment. They become members of a responsible political official's team and are vital to that official's ability to make and control policy.[57] In Britain, the Fulton Commission recommended that civil servants publicly explain and defend government policy. India's Administrative Reforms Commission of 1966 failed to deal with the issue, recommending only that the present arrangements be properly adhered to.[58]

Policy innovation and coordination require an Indian version of French and American institutional arrangements that will mitigate if not eliminate the struggle over neutrality, commitment, and loyalty. However, in the early 1980s, commitment and loyalty were not being interpreted in policy and professional terms. Instead many ministers, behind a facade of policy concerns, were more interested in patronage that served partisan and personal interests. Loyalty and commitment became willingness on part of civil servants to accommodate themelves to ministerial manipulations of this kind. Rajiv Gandhi's managerial orientation toward government; his reluctance to use the services for political and personal ends to the extent his mother did, and the resuscitation in 1985 and 1986 of the Administrative Reforms Commission's recommendations favoring professionalization and specialization of the services; provided a more favorable climate for dealing with this issue.

The demand that the IAS shed its superior airs and become more "socially representative" has been fulfilled in ways not anticipated by its proponents. The real salaries of senior officials both in the public services (IAS, Indian Foreign Service, Indian Police Service) and in public-sector enterprises declined significantly in the 1970s. The highly differential levels of "dearness allowance"—the inflation equalizer in government salaries—had the effect of eroding the emoluments of lower level clerks by 2 percent while those of higher officers and public-sector executives eroded by as much as 37 percent. The ratio between the highest and lowest paid in government shrank from 15:1 in 1973 to 10:1 in 1978.[59] Only in 1986 was this erosion halted and reversed by the report of the pay commission.

The more socially representative political milieu of state governments also weakened the IAS's national orientation and professional ethos.[60] The ways in which civil servants are posted have enabled local politicians to appropriate administration to partisan and personal ends. Frequent transfers, which render the life of a civil servant more difficult by disrupting the schooling of his or her children and the routines of life, have long been used by influential politicians to bring to heel or oust inflexible officers that resist inappropriate requests for resource allocation.

The 1984 crisis in the Punjab made it clear that civil and police services were incapable of maintaining public order. One cause was the capture of the services by local factions and communities. The formula for allocating officers of the centrally recruited but state-assigned IAS required that persons from the state not make up more than 50 percent of the state cadre. The rationale for the formula was "to insure that officials were not subject to local pressures and took a more objective and national view."[61] When Prime Minister Gandhi addressed an extraordinary meeting of secretaries to the Government of India soon after the Indian army had battled its way into the Golden Temple in June 1984, she "voiced concern over the growing tendency on the part of state government to dilute the original formula by not only reducing the proportion of officers hailing from other states but also making a systematic effort to remove them from key administrative positions."[62] She revealed that the fifty-fifty rule had been breached to the extent that 70 rather than 50 percent of IAS officers were serving in their state of origin.

The public services have not always strengthened the state as entrepreneur. The inability of the IAS to manage undertakings in the enormous public sector efficiently and profitably has contributed to the erosion of the Indian state. But for a few exceptional years, India's public sector has been in the red. Over the thirty-year period between 1950 and 1980, the incremental capital-output ratio for India as a whole has deteriorated, but in the public sector the position is considerably worse. For the economy as a whole, the ratio has roughly doubled (from 2.79 to 6.22), while in the public sector it has more than tripled (from 3.12 to 10.58).[63] We have discussed in chapter 1 the disputes over the meaning of these figures. Many critics have attributed some portion of this failure to the role of generalist IAS officers in public-sector undertakings. This role is played at two levels, policy guidance and the management of firms. Public-sector firms, instead of being allowed to operate autonomously, have been brought de facto under the close supervision of government ministries, whose IAS officer secretaries to government not only guide long-term policy—which is appropriate—but also intervene in day-to-day decisions. As a former chairman of the Food Corporation of India, one of the largest public-sector undertakings has observed, "Generally the ministries adopt a superior fatherly attitude, trying to run the whole show. The autonomy of [public-sector undertakings] is reduced to a myth, since all decisions of importance and magnitude are taken by them."[64]

The management of public-sector firms needs career professionals who combine technical knowledge with long-term experience in particular technologies and industries, such as steel, oil, transportation, and mining. The IAS officers do not possess such knowledge and skills, and their career experience fails to develop it. The insulation of IAS generalists from an understanding of their relevant specialties is illustrated by the career patterns of the officers in the Ministry of Information and Broadcasting, charged with overseeing Doordarshan, India's state-run television. In 1983, all three of the ministry's senior officers left before completing two years of service in that post. One had come from the chairmanship of the State Electricity Board of Madhya Pradesh and gone on to become secretary in the Coal Department; one had come from being commissioner of a division in Maharashtra and returned to manage that state's State Finance Corporation; and one had come from district administration and left for a training course abroad. "It is hardly to be expected," wrote the Joshi Working Group on Doordarshan, "that the problems of Doordarshan . . . can be appreciated and resolved by such birds of passage."[65]

The generalist traditions of IAS officers and the frequency with which they are transferred militate against their performance as managers of the still-expanding public sector. At the level of the states, IAS officers occupy 75 percent of the posts of chief executive officers of public-sector firms and their average tenure in such posts is fifteen months.[66] Occasionally, a good IAS officer is exempted from the rapid turnover characteristic of the service and can develop expertise via extended incumbency, but such experiences are the exception.

In 1986, the Rajiv Gandhi government introduced measures to address the professional quality of the services and insulate them from inappropriate political pressures. Many of these measures were based on recommendations of the Administrative Reforms Commission of 1966. The government proposed to prevent frequent transfers of officers, to protect them against appropriation by local interests, to encourage specialization, and to break the monopoly of the IAS on the highest positions by opening alternative recruitment channels to high-quality candidates from technical services and the nongovernment sector. Only time can tell whether these measures will survive opposition and achieve their goal.[67]

India was endowed at independence with a permanent government that surpassed that of other Third World countries and rivaled those of many industrial democracies. The forces that have challenged the services since independence, such as the call for partisan and personal commitment and regional loyalty are powerful and long term. They have taken their toll, but they have not as yet prevailed.

Wasting Assets: The Erosion of State Institutions

The Indian state has experienced two contrasting political eras between independence in 1947 and the assassination of Prime Minister Indira Gandhi in 1984, one associated with Jawaharlal Nehru, the other with his daughter, Indira Gandhi. When Nehru died in 1964, he had been prime minister for seventeen years. The national press used the twentieth anniversary in May 1984 of his death—when Mrs. Gandhi had been prime minister for sixteen years—as an occasion to compare the ideas and practices of these two eras. It found profound differences in ideals and conduct. Regardless of whether this judgment was warranted or took adequate account of different conditions, it was widely held. More important, perceptions construct reality by shaping expectations and behavior. Public perceptions of the Indian state have changed dramatically since the mid-1960s.

Nehru's advocacy of scientific rationalism and of principled, purposeful, politics, and his respect for persons and means influenced the conduct of politics in his day. For him, the procedures of parliamentary democracy and a federal constitution were both civilizing and a means to express and realize values in politics and society. He became teacher and mentor to the political class of his day. As Raj Mohan Gandhi wrote, "As Prime Minister for seventeen years he strove hard to coach Chief Ministers, M.P.'s, M.L.A.'s [member, (state) legislative assembly] and the masses in the norms of democracy. The letters he wrote to the Chief Ministers almost every fortnight are for the most part lessons in democratic procedure." [68]

Indira Gandhi's political aspirations and practice made a striking contrast, a contrast which she recognized. Her father was, she once said, a "saint strayed into politics." Because he never had to struggle, "he lacked the necessary ruthlessness." [69] This she was able to supply. She even acted out the negative identity that Nehru had depicted in his anonymous article when he said that with the adulation of crowds ringing in his ears he could easily become a dictator. [70]

Unlike her father, Mrs. Gandhi depleted India's political capital by eroding the autonomy, professional standards, and procedural norms of political institutions and state agencies. She tried to make those responsible for Parliament, the courts, the civil services, and the federal system answerable to her. The effort succeeded, to varying degrees, in orienting their conduct to her personal will. A paradoxical consequence was to diminish the legitimacy and effectiveness of the state. Centralization based on personal loyalty and obedience to a monocratic executive lessened the state's capacity to amplify itself through multiple agencies extending beyond the limited control and attention of one person. Jawaharlal Nehru was the schoolmaster of parliamentary government, Indira Gandhi its truant.

The changing political environment between the nationalist era and the 1980s also contributed to the erosion of state institutions. Nationalist politicians were gradually supplanted by professional politicians, who in turn were joined and to an extent displaced by condottieri seeking personal profit. The men and women of the nationalist era who continued to lead the country in the 1950s and 1960s had been socialized at a time when dedication to ideal goals and public service shaped political expectations and careers. In practical terms, there was nothing to gain and much to lose by becoming a nationalist politician. Under the raj, joining the nationalist movement meant sacrificing conventional career opportunities and risking jail. It meant pursuing goals that transcended self-interest and personal benefit. A generation of professional politicians emerged in the 1960s. They included Lal Bahadur Shastri, prime minister after Nehru's death; Kamaraj Nadar, the Congress president who presided over the 1964 and 1966 successions; and other state chief ministers and party leaders, including the members of the so-called syndicate that Indira Gandhi bested and "purged" in November 1969. They pursued power, prestige, and sometimes wealth by serving and satisfying the status and economic demands of their diverse and expanding constituencies. By the eighties, the era of A. R. Antulay and Ramrao Adik,[71] the erstwhile chief and deputy chief ministers in Maharashtra who came to epitomize the venality and degraded personal conduct to which Congress party "loyalists" could descend, politics had become a lucrative career. On the one hand, MPs and MLAs, besides receiving substantial salaries and allowances, received extensive perquisites—housing, telephones, travel, medical care, and medicine—which they used not only for themselves and their supporters but also for their family and friends.[72] Public facilities—from elegant modern guest houses to plain *dak* bungalows—were increasingly appropriated to the private comforts and pleasures of the families of legislators. Ministerial positions in the states—as many as one-third of the governing party's state legislators—and directorships of state public undertakings were now being used extensively to provide even greater benefits and opportunities for patronage and income. On the other hand huge amounts of black (underground economy) money were collected for political and campaign expenses and private gain.

Sanjay Gandhi's choices of legislators and chief ministers in the 1980 elections crystallized earlier trends by providing the new class of political condottieri with an institutional base. Politics became attractive to those unscrupulous enough to subvert, by corruption and violence, the procedures and institutions designed to protect civility and a government of laws. The effect on the system of government of Rajiv Gandhi's succession in 1984 to the prime ministership has still to work itself out. His self-image as an advocate of technocratic and managerial solutions has led him to address the long agenda of administrative reform and institution building that his mother ignored in her struggles for political survival. He is not seen, as his brother was, as a leader of the condottieri, and he recognizes, as his mother did not, that India can only be governed by significant sharing of power. The question is whether he can convert his strong commitment to institutions and professionalization into policies and programs.

State institutions and procedures were unevenly affected by the corrosive process that set in after Nehru's death, and the forces and agents were multiple. Our account in this chapter will attend to the armed services, the Election Commission's role in the conduct of free and fair elections, the police, legislatures (Parliament and state assemblies), and the federal system. We have already discussed the civil service, especially the IAS, and the judiciary will be examined in chapter 3. One corrosive force has been the long-term trend toward higher levels of mobilization, which will be documented in chapter 8. An increasingly active electorate found agitational politics more accessible and often more effective than parliamentary politics for making demands and shaping policy. Professional politicians were able to ignore crucial distinctions between public authority and private power in pursuit of partisan goals. To establish his leadership in the sixties, Punjab chief minister Pratab Singh Kairon politicized the police and civil service in the name of rapid development. He succeeded on both fronts. By 1984, when Punjab was threatened by terrorism and civil war, it became apparent that the Punjab services, particularly the police, had lost the capacity to act as professionals. In Bihar, under the aegis of corrupt or ineffectual chief ministers, locally dominant caste and landed elites have de facto appropriated police power in their struggles with increasingly assertive and resistant dependent castes and classes. Bihar's jails have acquired a national and international reputation for political bias and official violence. High-minded politicians of left persuasion also contributed to the erosion of state institutions. Mohan Kumaramangalam and H. R. Gokhale, central ministers close to the prime minister, provided the ideology and techniques for politicizing the judiciary in the name of social justice. Anticipating Indira Gandhi's advocacy of the same doctrine, Mohan Dharia, then a Congress socialist, weakened the claims of civil service professionalism by attacking neutrality in the name of "commitment."

These initiatives were not necessarily undertaken with the thought of weakening the state or eroding constitutional democracy and parliamentary government, but their effect was to subordinate institutional autonomy, professionalism, and impartial procedures to the partisan and personal pursuit of power. For Kairon, insistence on correct means and recognition of professional standards was the failing of ineffective politicians; for Kumaramangalam and Gokhale, judicial autonomy the hypocritical self-protection of bourgeois interests. The Westminster version of the golden rule that Nehru practiced, to treat opponents as he would be treated by them, and Mohandas Gandhi's preoccupation with personal ethics were declared unsuited to the conditions of Third World countries or India's genius. "The dominant literati traditions of India" reasserted themselves, Ashis Nandy wrote, through a statecraft "sanctified by the amoral, dispassionate politics preached in the Arthasastra . . . the Brahmanic concept of politics has always been that of a zero sum game . . . the Gandhian tradition in this sense is an aberration." [73] The paradox is that politics pursued in the name of realpolitik and a hard state reduced state legitimacy and institutional capacity.

Institutional autonomy depends on the viability of professionalism, which has become increasingly at risk in the face of populist and personalistic politics. The quality of the military services, police, civil service, courts, and Parliament depend on professional commitment. Professionalism implies a body of knowledge to be mastered by apprenticeship or formal education, control over recruitment and training to assure mastery of that knowledge, criteria of adequate and inadequate performance, of which the professionals themselves are the main judges, and an informal ethos as well as formal rules to govern what professionals regard as technically and ethically correct conduct in relationship to their clients or superiors. Because the application of professional criteria can serve to control entry, exit, and professional standing and thus to allocate status, power, and income, professional autonomy can promote monopoly and privilege. Professions require regulation—societal control—if they are to serve rather than merely profit by society. Even so, professionalism requires a certain insulation of societal demands and political pressures. Democratic politicians distrust professionalism, which they find inimical to the responsiveness appropriate to democratic institutions and popular sovereignty. So do politicians for whom personal loyalty and compliance count higher than professional performance. From the late 1960s, both kinds of politicians contributed to the erosion of professional and institutional autonomy.

The Military

The military services have been least affected by politicization, the call for partisan or personal political commitments to supersede professionalism and the appropriation of state authority and resources on their behalf. However, even the military has, in the last decade, suffered dilution of professionalism as it has been called in "in aid of the civil." Two crucial decisions were made at independence. Professional commitment was rewarded and political commitment discouraged when the British Indian Army was transformed into the Army of Free India and when the officers of the INA, commanded by Subhas Chandra Bose, were excluded from appointment in it (see above section on liberal and authoritarian options).[74] Political commitment was again discredited in October 1962 when the allegedly politically motivated appointment of General B. N. Kaul to command the army corps on the border facing China became associated with failure of Indian arms in the 1962 war with China.[75] The negative example of military rule in Pakistan may have helped bring home the importance of keeping the generals out of politics and politics out of the army.[76] When Sanjay Gandhi—who occupied no official position but exercised power by virtue of dynastic politics—used his connection to Defense Minister

Bansi Lal to insinuate himself into national security decisions under the emergency of 1975–77, senior commanders resisted the attempt.

The military, by being radically enclaved, is more insulated from its political environment than the permanent government. Military personnel undergo long courses of training in separate educational institutions; they live in cantonments, isolated from surrounding towns; they mess together; they are encouraged to develop a distinctive subculture and regimental loyalties. They are sheltered from the pervasive populist demands for democratic responsiveness that affect other state services.

Even so, the armed services are not immune from politicization and threats to their professional standing. Some military promotions in the eighties have attracted criticism.[77] Because the military services are volunteer as well as professional bodies, they depend for their viability on the market for pay and prestige. In the *enrichez vous* environment of the new India, modest pay scales and the invitation to a career of service make it increasingly difficult to compete for talent with more lucrative and less rigorous career lines. In consequence, the class character of the Indian army has changed over the last decade. As middle-class students have stayed away from officer careers and headed for private business, they have left the officer corps to the sons of noncommissioned and junior commissioned officers who were themselves recruited from the peasantry. The army has always had opportunities for corruption, both in recruitment and in the negotiation of arms purchases. These have increased and been more exploited with the growth of personal and institutional corruption in Indian politics and, some say, in consequence of the changing educational and class composition of the army.[78]

Most hazardous for the professional nature of the army has been the steadily increasing interventions by the army "in aid of the civil power." Stephen Cohen has documented the increasing deployments of the army to aid the civilian government in communal unrest arising out of religious, cultural, linguistic, and caste confrontations. His account shows heavy use of the military in civilian disturbances between 1973 and 1975 (fourteen cases) and again between 1980 and 1984 (fourteen, excluding "continuing" cases such as Assam and Punjab). His account also documents that, over the last eight years, the army has often been called in to pacify or disarm the forces of law and order, as in the police strikes in Gujarat, Tamil Nadu, and Bombay, or strikes by para-military forces such as the Central Reserve Police. The army's seizure of the Golden Temple, the Sikh holy shrine, in 1984 and its continuous role in Assam from 1980 onward, placed something like forty million people under army rule.

These interventions bear witness to the increased levels of mobilization and irregular and extrainstitutional protest of the last decade, and to the declining legitimacy of the state. "It is tempting," writes Cohen, "to ask the military to serve political ends—increasingly as saviors of the law and order situation—but each such request further politicizes the military by bringing them into too close contact with civilian society and by placing more and more civilian tasks in their hands." Yet, while the military services face difficulties, their professional standing and autonomy have been less seriously compromised than have those of other services and institutions.

The Electoral Process

The electoral process has also resisted the trend toward erosion of state institutions. The record of free and fair elections in India stands comparison with any Third World and most First World countries. Counting the 1984 election, eight national elections have been held since independence in 1947, and incumbent governments have been turned out of office at the center and in the states. Complaints of intimidation, the buying of votes, and the unfair uses of incumbency are frequently heard and sometimes documented, but no one has suggested that electoral verdicts have not generally reflected voter preferences.

Free India started its electoral life with a constitutionally independent body, the Election Commission (article 324), to supervise the entire procedure and machinery for national and state elections. The statutory provisions for the removal of the election commissioner make him independent of the government of the day and help keep elections free from partisan political influence. The commissioner is supported by a small professional staff of career civil servants. The commission depends on thousands of local officials deputed by the several state governments for registering voters and conducting elections. In the mid-1980s, the commission began to search for ways to protect the conduct of elections from the increasingly partisan and factional encroachments condoned or encouraged by incumbent state governments.[79] The election commissioner proposed that president's rule be substituted for state government rule some months before scheduled elections to obviate such encroachments. So pervasive is the problem of partisan influence on state officials that critics immediately responded that the party in power at the center could use president's rule to assist its own state parties.[80] The criticism gained strength in 1984, when Indira Gandhi's Congress-I government toppled opposition governments in Sikkim, Kashmir, and Andhra Pradesh, in preparation, it was alleged, for the upcoming eighth parliamentary election in December.

The commission is concerned not only with the integrity of the electoral process but also with assuring that those elected act in ways that guarantee the meaningfulness of the choices made by voters. The most important issues here are floor crossing and defections based on questionable motives and problematic inducements. The 1983 uproar over the "Moily tapes," which recorded an effort by a Congress party leader in Karnataka to bring down the incumbent government by buying its supporters, publicly documented a widely practiced offense.[81] Defections have frequently jeopardized the integrity of the electoral process by substituting perquisites of office and material gain for electoral choice in determining a legislator's political commitment.

The powers of incumbency have been used not only to influence state officials in their conduct of elections but also to influence voters directly by the timely allocations of benefits. National commentators interpreted a series of moves by the Indira Gandhi government in 1984 as designed to influence the upcoming eighth parliamentary election: a sudden and controversial nationalization of thirteen closed and "sick" textile mills in and around Bombay that put their workers back to work, a 25 percent wage increase for five hundred thousand government-employed coal miners, and the dispersal of unsecured loans to tens of thousands of educated unemployed at "loan fairs" throughout the country.

The incumbent party at the center has taken advantage of government's monopoly over radio and television broadcasting to portray itself in a favorable light.[82] In the name of promoting development, the electronic media have featured incumbent leaders and governmental programs at the expense of opposition criticism and alternatives to them. Opposition and independent access has been both sparse and closely monitored. Central control of the electronic media makes it difficult for opposition governments in the states of India's federal system to use radio or television to portray their personalities. Only during the three weeks of national and state election campaigns can the time allocated by the Election Commission to opposition party spokesmen modestly offset the incumbent government's monopoly position.

In summary, the independent position of the Election Commission has enabled it to resist the general trend toward institutional erosion. However, its ability to maintain free and fair elections has become increasingly difficult. The Rajiv Gandhi government's early moves in 1985 to protect the electoral process by enacting several measures long demanded by the Election Commission suggested a reversal in trends. A bill was enacted that obliges legislators to forfeit their seats if they defect (with or without payoff) from the party for which they were elected. Another bill legalized corporate party donations, thus driving the process of party and electoral finances above ground, where it can be regulated. While both measures are likely to have only an incremental effect, they suggest a new attention to institutional autonomy.

The Police

The police are the principal agents of the state's internal sovereignty. Their capacity to insure the security of persons and property, to maintain law and order, and to play an active yet fair role in the administration of justice are leading indicators of both the legitimacy and viability of the state. Insofar as the police have lost the capacity to do these things, the state is in trouble.

The erosion of the police as a professional force has been a long and gradual process. It is not clear that the quality of the police at the middle and lower levels—among the almost 90 percent who are constables—is different or worse than it was eighty years ago.[83] The Police Commission of 1902–3 "found strong evidence of widespread corruption in the police particularly among Station House Officers throughout the country."[84] What is clear is that performance of the higher ranks has declined since independence and that organized public opinion as well as "weaker sections" in many villages now demand a higher standard of police performance at all levels.

Constitutional responsibility for public order and police is vested in the states of the federal system. They have primary responsibility for recruitment, training, posting, transfer, pay and conditions of service. The constitutionally drawn line separating state from central responsibility for public order and the police is blurred by the existence of central police services such as the Border Security Force and the Central Reserve Police and by the center's responsibility for the Indian Police Service, one of three all-India services. An elite cadre, members of the Indian Police Service occupy the senior police posts in the states and staff certain specialized police organizations at the center, such as those concerned with intelligence. However, they constitute a miniscule fraction of the total number of police and a small proportion of officers.[85] Much of the responsibility for the crisis in the police rests with the states.

Today's police must deal with a dissatisfied public, more than 70 percent of which believed in 1978 that the police are corrupt as well as partial toward rich and influential people.[86] The higher ranks must also deal with politicians who use their power to protect personal, partisan, and factional interests. In the words of the National Police Commission, politicians weaken "the normal chain of command. . . .

Interference at the operational level in police stations, police circles, etc. results in the total by-passing of the supervisory officers in the hierarchy. . . . The frequent by-passing of the normal chain of command results in the atrophy of the supervisory structure. It, therefore, fails to operate effectively even in matters which do not attract any such extraneous interference.[87]

According to a note circulated in June 1979 by the Ministry of Home Affairs at a conference of chief ministers convened in the wake of police insurrections in several states, "there is a feeling in all States that interference not only in the matter of postings and transfers but also in the matter of arrests, investigations and filing of charge sheets is widespread. The principal grievance of the policemen is that if there is any unwillingness to comply with unlawful or improper suggestions the persons concerned are harassed and humiliated." [88]

These remarks may attribute too much responsibility to the machinations of politicians in explaining the deterioration of police professionalism. There have been professional failures within the police force itself, failures that are in part due to state and national governments' failures to provide policy leadership and the resources and attention required to maintain the professional capabilities of the police. At the same time, the National Police Commission's remarks about ubiquitous political interference reflect widely felt perceptions within and outside the police force. These developments are associated with a significant absolute increase in the number of police, especially those controlled by the central government, such as the Border Security Force and Central Reserve Police. Between 1970–71 and 1975–76, central expenditure on the police doubled from 101.6 to 209.1 crores, and it doubled again, to 424 crores, by 1982–83.[89] Myron Weiner has estimated that in the mid-seventies the centrally controlled police numbered 600,000 and those under the control of state governments numbered 750,000.[90]

The increase in special police and paramilitary forces has threatened as well as promoted internal peace. Since the mid-seventies, police strikes or strikes by special constabularies have occurred almost on an annual basis, and often constabularies have been pitted against each other. In the 1978 strike by the Central Reserve Police Force in Tamil Nadu, police were unwilling to act against them, and two battalions of Border Security Force had to settle the matter. Police strikes occurred in Gujarat in 1979, in Tamil Nadu in 1979, and in Bombay in 1982; strikes by various special constabularies (Central Reserve Police Force, Central Industrial Security Force) occurred in 1979 and 1980.[91]

One of the purposes of building up central police forces was to release the military from civil responsibilities for maintaining the peace in difficult political circumstances that might compromise them professionally and politically. This purpose has been at best only partially realized; the army after almost a year of martial law rule in the Punjab, was still used to quell civil strife. In June 1984, it stormed the Sikh's premier shrine, the Golden Temple in Amritsar, an action that resulted not only in heavy casualties but also in revolts by Sikh recruits and, indirectly, in the assassination five months later of Prime Minister Indira Gandhi.

Ordinary politicization has made considerable inroads on the standing and professionalism of the police. Perhaps more important has been the "higher politicization" associated with exploiting atrocities against the poor and oppressed to gain political advantage in national and state politics. One might expect that national attention focused on crime against the poor and oppressed would benefit them by making local oppression visible and thereby strengthening the hand of the police in combating such crimes. Instead, national attention has encouraged manipulation of both victims and police.

Publicizing police failures at the center or state level has become a way of incriminating one's political opponents. Paul Brass, in a close examination of the infamous Narainpur incident, shows how the political strategy of publicizing alleged atrocities for political gain was perfected. In Narainpur, a Muslim village with a substantial scheduled caste population, villagers and police clashed after an old woman was hit and killed by a bus. Uttar Pradesh, where Narainpur is located, was controlled at the time by a Janata government, the Congress-I's electoral enemy. The events occurred shortly after the Congress-I comeback victory in the 1980 national parliamentary elections but before the June state assembly elections in nine states. According to Sanjay Gandhi's account after he and his mother inspected Narainpur in a widely publicized visit: "There was not a single girl or woman . . . who was not raped." [92] His remarks bore no relationship to the facts as ascertained by an investigative commission,[93] or to what Brass learned at Narainpur: it is doubtful that anyone was raped, and no one was killed. These events set a new national standard in the political manipulation of alleged local violence, by preparing the ground rhetorically for the dismissal of the Janata in Uttar Pradesh, an event that was followed by the dismissal of opposition governments in the remaining eight states and by Congress-I victories in the June elections.

After Congress-I's return to power at the center and in most states, it became apparent that atrocities occurred as much under Congress as under opposition governments. Opposition politicians were able to exploit for a time the law and order failures of the "government that works," but soon overuse so devalued the currency that public attention and concern faded. Politicization of atrocities further eroded police autonomy and professionalism and thereby lessened the prospect that crimes against "weaker sections" could be prevented or punished.

In the interstices of these pressures, the public has come to believe that "complaints at police stations will not be registered" and that investigations of those that are registered will be "apathetic, dilatory and protracted." In national politics, the police have acquired a reputation as the prime instrument of a lawless state and of state violence. They are charged with the torture and illegal detention of accused persons,[94] the rape of poor women who are suspects or witnesses, the widespread use of "encounter" killings to remove opponents to local political notabilities or inconvenient elements, the incapacity to control lawless gangs in several northern states and to deal with the increasingly frequent train and bus robberies, and, finally, failure to deal with terrorism in Punjab. These charges brought the Indian police into disrepute in the late seventies and early eighties to an extent unparalleled in their history.

Some of the problems are due to the recruitment, structure, and conditions of the services, which were addressed at length by the police commission. The ordinary constables who make up the force are undereducated, undertrained, and underpaid. The structure of the force is weak at its middle and lower-middle levels, where a higher standard of professional training is needed.

But the problems are also due to the fact that India is conducting its social revolution in incremental fashion, through decentralized and sporadic disorder rather than a concentrated revolutionary act. The Indian social structure is being challenged from both below and above. The challenge from below comes from social classes that are no longer willing to bear their poverty and oppression compliantly and who resist economic and social injustice. The challenge from above comes from legislation—agrarian reforms, provisions favoring untouchables and backward classes—that enables the demands of the underprivileged. The increase in riots between 1965 and 1977 from 33,000 to 80,000 per annum, the increase in incidents of student indiscipline from 271 in 1965 to 10,600 in 1980; and the increase in workdays lost by strikes from 6.5 million in 1965 to 29.2 million in 1981 are all indicative of the social turmoil the public must face. (See fig. 5, chapter 8.) A weakened professional force must mediate sporadic class and community conflicts in which its own cadres have divided loyalties.

With all that said, even critical accounts acknowledge that there are honest, responsible officers, capable of inspiring ordinary police cadres with a sense of mission and obligation. Such officers have to cope with a maze of local and higher-level loyalties, interests, and powerful persons and with poorly educated, poorly trained, and poorly equipped personnel. Elected politicians and their party governments have so far found it easier to misuse the police politically than to support them professionally. The Indian state is paying the price for these failures in declining legitimacy and effectiveness.

Parliament

Parliamentary life has deteriorated in Delhi and even more so in the state capitals. The Parliament in India at independence was an honored institution, rooted in the "moderate" stream of Indian nationalism. Its leading exponent and Mohandas Gandhi's political guru, G. K. Gokhale, was widely admired by his nationalist generation for his artful parliamentary practice and budgetary analysis. Nehru was as much committed to the ideas of the moderates as he was to socialist ideals. At independence, the Constituent Assembly overwhelmingly chose to reaffirm India's prior experience with parliamentary forms of representative government. To be sure, Parliament was not the only institution that determined leadership and policy. The Indian National Congress, against Mohandas Gandhi's advice to dissolve itself at independence, instead continued as a political party contesting for power in the new state. As had been the case in nineteenth-century Britain, when elections based on expanded suffrage rivaled and then displaced King-in-Parliament, party overshadowed Parliament in the making of governments, policy, and political careers. The states of India's federal system also created paths to power. From the beginning, careers in Parliament counted for less than those in party politics at the center and in the states.

In the Nehru era, Parliament was effective in performing its contemporary role; defending and criticizing government policy, overseeing bureaucratic performance, and, perhaps most important, holding government accountable by exposing its policies and actions to informed opinion and voter judgment. It was able to do so in part because many of the MPs who sat in early parliaments had, as leaders of the nationalist movement, acquired considerable political and legislative experience. Many were lawyers whose métier featured procedural sophistication, command of the fine print, and adversary exchange.

Legislatures in India have suffered some of the same setbacks as legislatures in advanced industrial democracies; that is, they have lost power and influence to the political executive and specialized bureaucracies in the formulation and control of policy. Like parties and legislators in many other industrial democracies, parliamentary parties and committees in India have not developed the specialized knowledge and staff needed to challenge the experts and bureaucracies of the political executive. Parliamentary opposition has often exposed malfeasance and corruption; it has found it much more difficult to challenge government's policy agenda and to mount credible alternatives. As Kuldip Nayar wrote: "The opposition can also make Parliament more purposeful, but its eyes are mainly stuck to the headlines in newspapers. It does not pursue any subject diligently or doggedly, much less study it in depth. Even when the government has been caught on the wrong foot it has been let off because of lack of preparation . . . what the opposition lacks is persistence."[95]

There is no equivalent in India of the Labour or Conservative party's research bureaus to prepare policy options for the opposition parties. Above all, the absence of a functional equivalent for Her Majesty's loyal opposition—that is, a politically viable alternative (whether as one party or a coalition) to the Congress party, with a recognized role not only in Parliament but also in the media and among the electorate—has seriously impaired the effectiveness of Parliament to dramatize national politics and shape public opinion.

To help halt the decline of Parliament under the complex conditions of an industrial, welfare, and national security state concerned to plan and manage the economy, there have been calls for providing Parliament with adequately staffed, independent specialized committees. Presently the standing committees are ex post facto and less and less attended to by government, Parliament itself, and by the public. An emergency era committee of the Congress parliamentary party, headed by the late C. M. Stephen, proposed to subordinate parliamentary deliberations to a Congress party—dominated committee structure. As the *Indian Express* commented, "The intention was clear: to dilute the authority of parliament and to close all forums at which the opposition could express its point of view."[96] In 1984, Lok Sabha (lower house) Speaker Balram Jakhar proposed to establish less-partisan, speaker-appointed subject area "budget committees" but qualified this move toward a more independent Parliament by arguing that the committee meetings should be held in camera and not be open to the press.

Unlike the decline of legislatures in other industrial democracies, which has been associated primarily with domination by more expert executive agencies, the decline of Indian legislatures has been accelerated by political forces. The front bench must collaborate with the members if parliamentary procedures are to retain their integrity and effectiveness. Since the mid-sixties and the death of Nehru, there has been a failure by both to honor each other's parliamentary role. The prime minister and cabinet colleagues have neglected Parliament: "The single most important factor that has contributed to this slump in the prestige and influence of Parliament," said opposition leader Atal Behari Vajpayee, himself a formidable parliamentarian, "is Prime Minister Indira Gandhi's unconcealed disdain for Parliament . . . Pandit Nehru stayed away from the house only when it was absolutely unavoidable. She attends Parliament only when she must."[97] Rajiv Gandhi's civility toward the opposition and respect for Parliament created a more favorable atmosphere after 1984.

The election to early postindependence legislatures of members without parliamentary experience and often with little education was compensated for by the parliamentary concern and skill of government and opposition leaders in many states as well as by Nehru and his colleagues of the nationalist generation at the center. The legislatures of the 1950's and 1960's constantly had to socialize newcomers into a parliamentary outlook and procedures. In the first parliament, half of those elected had never before served in a legislature.[98] In 1967, opposition gains brought a new influx of inexperienced members into the state and national legislature. In 1980, Sanjay Gandhi inducted young, ambitious, inexperienced rowdies whose contempt for procedure and penchant for violent means further diluted the standard of parliamentarianism at the center and in the states. But by that time there was no compensating influence of a tutelary nationalist generation.

The changing social background of legislators is of some significance but cannot by itself explain the decline of parliamentary life in India. The proportion of professionals—especially lawyers but also scientists, doctors, teachers, journalists, and civil servants—has declined. The only category that has increased—and it almost doubled from 22 to 38 percent between 1952 and 1984—was that of agriculturists.[99] By itself, this proportional increase does not explain why Parliament has become less effective. Many agriculturists are educated and experienced parliamentarians. Speaker Balram Jakhar, for example, lists himself as an "agriculturist" and represents parliamentary as well as agricultural interests.

Decline took a new turn after Indira Gandhi's declaration of an emergency in 1975. The Congress-I government arrested and sent to jail the principal opposition party leaders, and it encouraged its chief ministers and party leadership to address workshops and political science study groups that deplored the waste of time and unnecessary garrulousness of legislatures.[100] The Janata government, returned in 1977, restored constitutional democracy, but no one would accuse Charan Singh of parliamentary punctiliousness or Raj Narain of parliamentary civility. Both Janata leaders lavishly contributed to bringing ridicule upon parliamentary government.

Deterioration of legislatures has advanced further in the states than at the center. Madhu Limaye, an experienced opposition leader and political commentator, has noted that the deterioration began in 1967 with opposition victories in the northern states. The legislators who supported the opposition governments were "inexperienced and, being a rag tag coalition, could not enforce discipline. The legislators were an unruly lot, almost a rabble."[101] Governments were afraid to face such legislatures, and legislators had no conception of their role. In Bihar, which in this as in other matters tends toward the lowest political denominator, first the opposition and then the Congress government began to circumvent the legislative process. The result was a reduction of legislative days from 179 and 263 in 1960 and 1961 to 57 (1967), 37 (1968), 33 (1969), 55 (1970), and 63 (1973). Governments, rather than risk the introduction of legislation, began to rule by executive ordinance, a procedure used when legislatures are not in session or for extreme emergencies. Ordinances were repromulgated when they expired. Between 1967 and 1981, the Bihar government repromulgated 256 ordinances.[102] The breakdown of the legislature in Bihar, while not typical, is suggestive of the atrophy that has beset most state assemblies.[103]

The quality of legislative life depends on the quality of parliamentary leadership and legislators and, more importantly, on the legislators' capacity to master and use legislative procedures. Parliamentary leaders have fled from the crisis of the legislature in India rather than come to grips with it. Baffled by policy complexities and legislative procedures, legislators have resorted to shouting matches, ceremonial profanations, and occasional physical violence. Government's refusal to address pressing and embarrassing issues is answered by opposition walkouts and the politics of the streets. Legislators are increasingly unwilling to play the parliamentary game or to accept the possibilities this form of regulated conflict provides. Legislative debate is a highly stylized form of verbal combat. Legislators who cannot use their tongues fling shoes. Legislators who do not know how to use the rules to their advantage prefer chaos. It is apparent that training legislators is as important as training administrators if parliamentary government in the states is to remain viable.[104]

Federalism

There are reasons to believe that India's federal system is in jeopardy, not the least of which is the personal centralization of power during the Indira Gandhi era that we have discussed. On the other hand, there are powerful countercurrents to personal centralization, not the least of which is the growing strength of regional nationalisms and the success of regional parties. Both currents have put the federal system under severe strain.

Apart from academic disputation about the nature and even the "authenticity" of India's federal system as defined in the constitution [105] lies the reality of an enormous country whose cultural heterogeneity is expressed in the federal organization of power. The population of many of its twenty-three states ranks with those of the largest countries in Western Europe. India's largest state, Uttar Pradesh, has a population of over 100 million, which puts it just behind Indonesia, the world's seventh-largest sovereign state. America's federal system divides a population of 220 million into fifty units, whereas India's divides a population of 710 million into only twenty-two units, five of which are marginal.

Since state reorganization in 1953 and 1956, state boundaries have roughly coincided with historically rooted linguistic and cultural regions. These differences reinforce the effects of size and continue in the federal system the tensions between regional kingdoms and subcontinental empire that have characterized the history of the state in India. A spate of studies, conferences, and commissions—beginning in the early seventies with the Rajamannar Committee (1971) in Tamil Nadu [106] and continuing into the eighties—reflected the fact that center-state relations had become a major issue on the national agenda. The opposition and regional parties' deep concern for center-state relations forced Mrs. Gandhi to appoint the Sarkaria Commission to reconsider the functioning of the federal system.

The deinstitutionalization of the Congress party, to be discussed in chapter 4, contributed to the crisis of the federal system by dismantling the party's federal features. Most visible and devastating to party federalism was the surrender by victorious state parliamentary parties of the right to select their leaders. In the wake of the "Indira wave" of 1972, an electoral surge powered by Mrs. Gandhi's personal appeal that swept Congress to victory in all but one state, Congress state assembly parties asked the prime minister to name their chief ministers, a practice that has continued under Rajiv Gandhi. In the absence of the internal democracy that party elections represent, pradesh (state) Congress committees too were appointed by the party presidents, Indira and Rajiv Gandhi. [107] Those selected found it expedient to feature loyalty to the party's president at the center rather than to represent the interests and aspirations of their respective states. As a consequence, they lacked the support that chief ministers and committee presidents with autonomous networks of influence and mutual obligation could command. At worst, the nomination from Delhi of government and party leaders produced politically impotent loyalists held in contempt by their local constituents. Andhra Pradesh voters interpreted the nomination from Delhi of five chief ministers between 1978 and 1982 as contemptuous of Andhra Pradesh's standing, and they overwhelmingly voted (January 1983) to install a regional leader and party in preference to Congress.

Another development that weakened federalism was the failure of the center to respect the integrity of state assembly elections that determine which party and leader should form the government. The 1977 elections, in which the Janata party defeated the Gandhi-led Congress, were parliamentary elections only. They did not affect the standing of state assemblies, whose terms of office were not synchronized with Parliament's. However, the Janata government pressed the view that the Congress governments' legally dubious actions under the emergency and, more important, Janata's sweeping victories in nine northern states (in many of which it won all parliamentary seats) compromised the legitimacy of the Congress governments, that is, that the state assemblies had ceased to reflect the views of the electorate. After consulting the supreme court—which, in a procedurally and substantively controversial opinion,[108] endorsed its proposal—the Janata government advised the president to dismiss the nine governments. Subsequently, it held (and won) state assembly elections. In 1980, after Congress swept back into power at the center, it used the precedent of the Janata government's action to again breach the autonomy and integrity of state assembly elections by dismissing nine governments and holding elections in which it (like Janata) succeeded in replacing opposition with Congress governments. Taken together, the two actions dealt a severe blow to the integrity of India's federal system.

The integrity of the federal system was threatened too by the actions of state governors. A governor serves two masters, the president of India who appoints governors on the advice of the central cabinet (which, in Indira Gandhi's time, meant the prime minister), and the state's council of ministers, which acts in the governor's name but in fact advises him what to say and do. The two masters may be of different political parties. As envisioned in the Constituent Assembly, the governor would be an eminent public person detached from the world of partisan politics and not beholden to it. Governors would "naturally cooperate fully with the state government in carrying out the policy of the Government and yet represent before the public something above politics."[109] Over time, and at an accelerating rate in the 1970s, governors acted in a more and more partisan manner, as agents not of a detached and respected president, but of power-seeking party leaders at the center.

The ambiguity of the governor's role arises too from the constitutional provision (article 163 [1]) that, apart from an obligation to act on the advice of the state cabinet, a governor may "exercise his functions or any of them in his discretion." In using their discretion, governors have been less and less constrained by parliamentary and constitutional conventions, acting more at the behest of party governments at the center. Prior to the 1984 parliamentary election, governors in Sikkim, Kashmir, and Andhra Pradesh helped destabilize and then topple opposition governments. The possibility of gubernatorial independence was further weakened when the supreme court held that the constitutional provision that governors are to serve at the president's pleasure took precedence over another provision that they serve for a fixed term of five years. For some time, it was assumed that the president's authority to dismiss a governor should "be sparingly used to meet with cases of gross delinquency, such as bribery, corruption, treason, and the like or violation of the Constitution." [110] Such expectations were belied when the supreme court held that the governor of Rajasthan, Gurukul Tilak, who had been appointed on the advice of the Janata government, could be dismissed before the end of his term on the advice of the restored Congress government. [111]

Governors use their discretion when they ask legislative leaders to form governments and when they dismiss governments that have lost their majorities, and they have abused their discretionary powers on both counts. When Congress leaders with unproved and doubtful majorities were asked to form governments in Rajasthan in 1967 and Harayana in 1980, they were able to use the prospect of office and other benefits to gain the majorities they needed to govern. When Governor Gopala Reddy dismissed Uttar Pradesh's chief minister Charan Singh in 1967, and when Governor Ram Lal dismissed Andhra Pradesh's chief minister N. T. Rama Rao in 1984, neither waited for the verdict of the state assembly.

Governors have also abused their discretion with respect to the imposition of president's rule under article 356 of the constitution, which allows governors to advise the president that the "government of (a) State cannot be carried on in accordance with the provisions of the constitution." Such advice enables the governing party at the center to take over the government of a state. In the words of D. D. Basu, a leading constitutional authority, use of this "drastic coercive power" takes the substance away from the normal federal polity described by the Constitution." [112] B. R. Ambedkar, a principal architect of the constitution, told the Constituent Assembly that "the proper thing we ought to expect is that such articles (as 356) will never be called into operation, that they remain a dead letter."[113] However, instead of being a matter of last resort, article 356 had been used sixty-five times by March 1982.[114] According to Basu, "this extraordinary power has been too often [used] to serve the *political* purposes of the party in power at the Union,"[115] a result that occurs when governors (and presidents) fail to observe their constitutional responsibilities.

Ambedkar's expectations were not met. Article 356 was increasingly used in a partisan and arbitrary manner. Instead of becoming guardians of the federal system, governors became agents of its decline. But Indira Gandhi's partisan centralization at the expense of the federal system generated countercurrents. The cases of Assam and Punjab, so prominent in the politics of the early 1980s, lie outside the framework of our analysis of the erosion of the federal system. There, perceived threats to cultural identity and survival could no longer be accommodated by conventional political processes. Elsewhere, countercurrents took the form of regional nationalism and regional opposition parties that gained power because they better represented the aspirations and interests of India's diverse peoples. After its return to power in 1980, the Congress government had to operate a federal system in which regional and opposition parties governed five of the sixteen large states (West Bengal, Kashmir, Andhra Pradesh, Tamil Nadu, and Karnataka), while the civil administrations and political process had broken down in two (Assam and Punjab). Regional politics and parties became a persistent aspect of India's political equations.

Such politics can be accommodated only if the federal system remains a viable and important aspect of the larger political system. Rajiv Gandhi as prime minister recognized this fact in his accomodating approach to opposition-controlled state governments. He initiated his government's federal policy in 1985 by accepting with good grace opposition victories in Punjab and Assam, where his mother's fear of sharing power had led to stalemate. He also reinforced the governor's role as a nonpartisan figure obligated to respect the wishes of state legislatures rather than the partisan interests of the governing party at the center. Federal systems are mechanisms for sharing power. Rajiv Gandhi's willingness to do so is likely to counteract the centralizing tendencies of the previous administration.

3 The Struggle over Stateness: Judicial Review versus Parliamentary Sovereignty

India's legal system—the supreme court, and the state high courts subordinate to it—has not been immune from the erosion that has affected the autonomy and professionalism of the civil service and police and marginally touched the military services. The courts have struggled on two fronts against institutional erosion, the larger constitutional front of judicial review versus parliamentary sovereignty and the related but separate front of the independence of judges from executive manipulation and control.

The consensual framework for the Indian state created by the Constituent Assembly did not settle or foreclose future state issues. The struggle between parliamentary sovereignty and judicial review, a struggle at once institutional and substantive, became acute in the 1970s. Less prominent in the 1980s, the struggle is likely to recur whenever the executive stretches the limits of its powers.

The state created by the 1950 constitution was more liberal than viceregal. With Jawaharlal Nehru's support and blessing, it manifested more low than high "stateness."[1] The introduction of universal suffrage and parliamentary democracy was designed to make party governments accountable to the people through open and free electoral competition, legislative deliberation, and public discussion. Judicial review of a written constitution guaranteed that fundamental law, a federal system, and the liberties of citizens would be essential features of the liberal state.

At the same time, Nehru and like-minded colleagues believed that a viceregal-like strong center was a necessary condition for the realization of their substantive goals: national power based on a modern and independent economy and socialist transformation of India's society and economy. The sufficient condition for the realization of their goals, strong party government in a parliamentary and federal system, became a reality when the Congress party gained a dominant position among its competitors and held it through three general elections.

Even so, during India's first two decades as an independent state, successive Congress governments bent on carrying out social and economic reforms, particularly land reform, confronted successive su-

103

preme courts bent on upholding fundamental rights, particularly property rights. In the face of India's radical inequalities and powerful political support for some redistribution, the court might have exercised its judicial imagination by drawing distinctions between property rights and other fundamental rights. Instead, the court's reliance on legal solipsism and formal and technical interpretations of the constitution inhibited the efforts of Congress governments to effect social and economic change. The inflexibility of the courts encouraged the state to circumvent and weaken them. The conflicts intensified after Nehru's death in 1964 and Congress's near loss of the fourth general election in 1967. They intensified further in the 1970s, when Congress, under Mrs. Gandhi's leadership, won impressive legislative majorities in the 1971 parliamentary and 1972 state assembly elections;[2] and they reached their height during her emergency regime, when the government seriously considered abolishing a supreme court capable of judicial review. The conflict gradually changed its meaning as the Gandhi government, credited in the sixties with opposing the court because it blocked social change, was accused in the seventies of opposing the court because it restrained the irresponsible exercise of power by a self-serving state. As India entered the eighties, the state issue of parliamentary sovereignty versus judicial review (although no longer a likely occasion for state transformation or breakdown) remained a principal line of political cleavage.

The country was divided and uncertain about this question. Authoritarian rule and political repression under the emergency cast an ominous light on the meaning of parliamentary sovereignty, and the Janata effort to restore a liberal state, liberty, and the rule of law only partly succeeded. So long as the Indian state remains committed to both constitutional government and social transformation, the political cleavage over judicial review and parliamentary sovereignty will remain a source of political tension and institutional ambiguity. In the shorter run, dilemmas and threats abound. A court that has learned that its authority, if not its survival, depends on reading the election returns must also find ways to protect and maintain judicial review and the constitution's essential features. Can the court be counted on to do so when for two years under the emergency it countenanced political repression, including depriving citizens of liberty without known cause or legal resources? Can the law of the land as interpreted by the court accommodate the legislative actions of party governments bent on economic and social transformation? Can the court maintain a government of laws when law has become a conventional weapon in the partisan political struggle?

The pendulum of doctrinal and institutional controversy over constitutionally defined state issues swung wider in the eleven years between 1967 and 1977 than it had in the first twenty years of independence. Several dimensions of constitutional interpretation were at issue: the amending power, property rights (particularly the acquisition of property), and citizens' liberties.[3] The pendulum swing reached its furthest points in 1967 and 1976. At one extreme, the court in *Golak Nath* restricted Parliament's amending power.[4] It barred Parliament from using its constituent authority to amend fundamental rights protecting the liberties of citizens. At the other extreme, Parliament barred the supreme court's power to review. Under a provision of the omnibus forty-second amendment passed during the emergency (1976), it laid down that there was "no limitation whatever on the constituent power of parliament to amend" the constitution.[5] For good measure it added another provision, that no law declared by Parliament to be giving effect to the directive principles of state policy[6] could be called into question by the court as abridging fundamental rights.

Between these extremes, court decisions and parliamentary amendments kept the pendulum swinging, but within narrower limits. Most notable of the decisions was that in *Keshavananda Bharati* (1973).[7] It reversed *Golak Nath*'s bar to parliamentary amendments affecting fundamental rights but protected judicial review by limiting Parliament's amending power to matters that do not destroy the constitution's "basic structure" or "essential features." After Janata's 1977 electoral victory, doctrinal controversy and institutional rivalry abated somewhat as a result of legislative stalemate and the caution of a chastened court. But the pendulum continues to swing between extremes widely enough separated to insure that the state issue of parliamentary sovereignty versus judicial review will continue to divide parties, the court, and the country.

The Changing Meaning of Parliamentary Sovereignty

In Nehru's time, parliamentary sovereignty took on a meaning distinct from its meaning for India's founding political generation. The Westminster model that had furnished this generation's understanding tempered the unlimited power of Parliament and the absence of judicial review with a keen sense for the conventional restraints of the unwritten constitution and of court interpretations of the common law. For Nehru and his like-minded colleagues, parliamentary sovereignty opened the way to legislate social transformation and a planned economy. The primacy of parliamentary will over a judiciary bent on protecting citizens' rights, particularly property rights, was a necessary condition for realizing a socialist society. Nehru's strongest statement on parliamentary sovereignty came during the course of the Constituent Assembly's debate on compensation for property, particularly landed property. "No Supreme Court and no judiciary," he aid, "can stand in judgment over the sovereign will of Parliament representing the will of the entire community . . . ultimately the whole Constitution is a creature of Parliament."[8] Even so, he remained silent during the debate on the amending article a few weeks later (September 17, 1949). Known to favor amendment by simple majority, he did not offer a motion to that effect. Instead, he acquiesced in a statement by B. R. Ambedkar, law minister and chairman of the assembly's drafting committee, that "the Constitution is a fundamental document" and that "utter chaos" would follow if it could be amended by a simple majority.[9]

A careful student of the Constituent Assembly concluded that, despite the diversity and relative ease with which the constitution it created could be amended, "it must not be assumed [that] the Assembly favoured parliamentary sovereignty. The members believed that the [Constituent] Assembly had superior status and that its product should be the supreme law of the land."[10] The Constituent Assembly also rejected an effort by Sir Benegal Rau, its constitutional advisor and a Nehru intimate, to give the directive principles of state policy precedence over fundamental rights in case of conflict.[11] Nehru and the Congress left were deeply concerned that the judiciary would create obstacles to the realization of socialist objectives, while "hard state" advocates, led by Patel, were concerned that the courts would jeopardize the state's capacity to maintain law and order.[12] Nevertheless, Nehru himself was sufficiently committed to a liberal state to accept a constitution whose supreme court could interpret fundamental law and protect fundamental rights and the federal system.[13]

In Nehru's time and in the early years of his daughter's prime ministership, the struggle between parliamentary sovereignty and judical review was translated into a conflict between socialism and property rights, between the legislative authority required for progressive social policies, particularly land reform, and the court's power to protect the principle of meaningful compensation against efforts to render it nominal. As Mrs. Gandhi's support ebbed, as she was threatened by Jayaprakash Narayan's movement to remove her from office (the "JP movement"), and as the executive democracy of 1971–74 gave way to emergency rule in 1975, the struggle took on a new cast reminiscent of

Patel's efforts to create a strong state. Parliamentary sovereignty eventually became a means to protect those in power from accountability and competition and a doctrine to legitimate authoritarian rule and repressive government. In the end, it was used to strengthen the executive's power of preventive detention (through the Maintenance of Internal Security Act [MISA]) and then, under the emergency, to remove all restraints on the state's authority to deprive citizens of their fundamental rights.

The question for the courts and the prime minister became, who spoke for the people? Judges of state high courts and of the supreme court claimed to speak from the authority of the written constitution that expressed the people's will as well as the fundamental law of the land. Ruling Congress governments claimed to speak with the authority of constitutional majorities in Parliament based on electoral mandates that expressed the people's will. Nani A. Palkhivala, one of India's leading constitutional lawyers and an opponent of the emergency, while recognizing that Parliament's claim to possess unlimited powers of amendment rests on its representation of the people's will,[14] argued that judicial review of parliamentary acts has a higher claim because the constitution is a superior expression of the will of the people: "Where the will of Parliament, declared in an amendment, stands in opposition to that of the people, declared in the Constitution, the will of the people must prevail."[15] It may be argued, and was in 1975, that the latter view of the will of the people includes the prior existence in a "state of nature" or in human nature of individual rights not contracted away in the formation of civil society and/or the state.[16] But advocates of both parliamentary sovereignty and judicial review repaired ultimately to democratic rather than statist or natural law grounds to legitimize their positions.

Judicial Review: Protection of Property or Protection of Liberties?

"Progressive" opinion in India often accused the court of using judicial review to protect the interests of propertied classes from Congress government policies that threatened them. Mohan Kumaramangalam was the most effective advocate of this view from 1966, when he left the Communist party to join Madras Congress chief minister Kamaraj Nadar as advocate general, until his death in May 1973. He was an old friend of Indira Gandhi from their student days in London, leader of the Congress Forum for Socialist Action—the progressive faction of the Congress parliamentary party that played a key role in shaping

Mrs. Gandhi's strategy and policies between 1969 and 1973—and minister for mines and steel in her 1971 government.[17] His Marxist legal theory shaped the Gandhi government's counterattack against the supreme court after it gained a two-thirds parliamentary majority in 1971. Kumaramangalam conceived the twenty-fourth, twenty-fifth, and twenty-sixth amendments, which struck back at *Golak Nath* and other decisions, as "a single whole" that would, by establishing Parliament's supremacy, enable it to enact progressive measures endorsed by the people. And it was Kumaramangalam that formulated the doctrine of a "committed judiciary," the legal counterpart to the doctrine of a committed bureaucracy.[18] The progressive view of the law and the court's role had, until November 1980, at least one voice on the bench itself, Justice V. R. Krishna Iyer. "Even after 30 years of independence," he argued, "the Indian judicial system followed the path of the Anglo-Saxon legacy left behind by the British. The law, framed by the British to suit their class interests, has no relevance to the present Indian social conditions."[19] The courts also had at least one justice whose admiration for Mrs. Gandhi seemed to transcend the decent respect due a prime minister: "I am sure that, with your iron will and firm determination, uncanny insight and dynamic vision, great administrative capacity and vast experience, overwhelming love and affection of the people . . . you will be able to steer the ship of state safely to the cherished goal."[20]

According to the progressive view, the struggle between Parliament and court for supremacy in interpreting the constitution pitted proponents of the oppressed many without property against the privileged few with property. The court's rejections in February and December 1970, just prior to Mrs. Gandhi's upset victory in March 1971, of her minority government's measures to nationalize the fourteen largest commercial banks and deprive the princes of their privileges and privy purses were only the most recent examples of the court's effort to maintain the viability of property rights. Yet even in the era from *Golak Nath* (1967) through the amendments of 1971 and 1972, a preference for judicial review was not restricted to the propertied classes and a preference for parliamentary sovereignty was not restricted to the poor. What congruence there was between class and attitude toward judicial review began to lose its meaning when the consequences of an unrestrained Parliament and a committed judiciary for constitutional government and the rule of law became more apparent. Congress socialists, such as Chandra Shekhhar and Mohan Dharia, who had supported the progressive view of law, recognized that "progressive" was becoming a code word for Mrs. Gandhi's partisan interest. With the death of Mohan Kumaramangalam in 1973, his left doctrine increasingly gave way to Sanjay Gandhi's free enterprise and antileft convictions.

In May 1973, Jayaprakash Narayan, whose socialist credentials included Marxist, democratic, and Gandhian variants, wrote a personal letter to Mrs. Gandhi pointing out the need to provide constitutional safeguards to prevent Parliament from "abrogating the fundamental freedoms of the citizens" and to insure the independence of the judiciary. Without these limitations, the proclaimed aim of national leaders to establish socialism by peaceful means would be defeated, and "the very foundations of our democracy will be in danger of being destroyed."[21]

As the emergency era (1975–77) and its Janata aftermath (1977–79) demonstrated, the struggle was as much over the continued existence of the 1950 constitution, the meaning of constitutional government, and the standing and enforcement of citizens' rights against the state as it was over the capacity of the state to enact socialist measures. Though the struggle between parliamentary sovereignty and judicial review is often animated by conflicts among classes and interests, it is not reducible to them and, for that reason, not merely "superstructural." The 1977 election demonstrated that the poor, like other citizens, appreciated the connection between a government of laws and their welfare and material interests. Activists on both the left and the right valued the liberty both had lost under the emergency.

Arena of Struggle: The Power to Amend and the Power to Destroy

The actual struggle between the supreme court speaking for a liberal state and the executive speaking for a more authoritative if not authoritarian state had begun soon after the commencement of the constitution in 1950. As we have noted, one of the principal substantive grounds on which the battle was fought was the meaning of and limitations on the right to property.[22] The principal formal arena was the amending power of Parliament. Congress, as a nationalist movement and as a governing party in the provinces (1937–39), had given very high priority to agrarian reform. Immediately after independence, when state legislation abolishing "feudal" intermediaries (zamindars and *jagirdars*) was passed, it was blocked in the courts by cases brought under articles 14, 19, and 31[23] protecting fundamental rights. Parliament responded in 1951 by passing the first amendment, which protected legislation acquiring the "estates" of intermediaries against application of these articles and, for good measure, added a new (ninth) schedule to the constitution that immunized from judicial review any state or union legislation placed in it by Parliament.[24] But the struggle continued in a series of cases about the meaning of compensation. The courts held that it meant market value. The government responded with new constitutional amendments, notably the fourth and twenty-fifth,[25] that attempted to protect from judicial review the amount it paid for compulsorily acquired property.

The issues of the scope of Parliament's authority to amend the constitution and its relationship to judicial review and fundamental rights were most seriously joined in the momentous *Golak Nath* case decided in 1967. It held that the fundamental rights provided for in part 3 of the constitution could be amended only by a new constituent assembly, not by Parliament. Parliament responded with the twenty-fourth amendment, which overrode *Golak Nath* by making fundamental rights amendable by Parliament. In 1973, the battle was rejoined in the equally momentous *Keshavananda Bharati* case. It may prove to be India's *Marbury v. Madison* by establishing an acceptable ground for judicial review. The decision in *Keshavananda* legitimized constrained versions of both principles: parliamentary sovereignty in the service of state purposes and interests and judicial review in the service of fundamental law and a government of laws. It provided a framework for accommodating a hard and/or socialist state with a liberal one. The court embarked on a path that continued to characterize its strategy in the late 1970s and early 1980s, firmly protecting its own jurisdiction and prerogatives while yielding to the executive and Parliament on substantive issues. It conceded that legislation and amendments giving effect to state purposes and interests may take precedence over fundamental rights and a government of laws, provided the court has an opportunity to review their bona fides and compatibility with the constitution's essential features.

While upholding the twenty-fourth amendment and thus reversing *Golak Nath*, *Keshavananda* nevertheless limited Parliament's amending authority. According to *Keshavananda*, Parliament's authority to amend is not the authority to destroy the 1950 constitution or to make a new one. The amending authority[26] is limited by the constitution's "basic structure" or "essential features," which include judicial review, the sovereignty and territorial integrity of India, the federal system, free and fair elections, and other disputed or as yet unspecified features. Amendments attacking the constitution's essential features or basic structure would be held unconstitutional. Nor can judicial review be eliminated or compromised, as it was in the twenth-fifth and twenty-sixth amendments, by parliamentary professions that particular laws give effect to the directive principles of state policy generally (twenty-fifth amendment) or to those particular ones (twenty-sixth amendment) providing for state ownership, control, or redistribution of "the material resources of the community" (article 39 [6] and [c]). On the other hand, *Keshavananda* recognized what the court reaffirmed seven years later in *Minerva Mills,* that in certain specified areas of stipulated state purposes, those that provide for control or redistribution of "the material resources of the community," the directive principles might override fundamental rights (twenty-fifth amendment) *subject to the court's review.*[27] And it in effect upheld the "Kumaramangalam package" of the twenty-fourth, twenty-fifth, and twenty-sixth amendments, the twenty-fourth (reversing *Golak Nath*) and the twenty-sixth (abolishing the privy purses of princes) wholly and the twenty-fifth insofar as it could do so without yielding up judicial review.

While the court was willing to accommodate state purposes, it continued to resist property rights' being made nominal by reopening the question of meaningful compensation for property compulsorily acquired by the state. The twenty-fifth amendment's substitution of the word "amount" for "compensation," did not, according to *Keshavananda,* open the way for legislatures to fix "arbitrary or illusory" sums or lay down irrelevant criteria. Although *Keshavananda* represented a retreat from *Golak Nath* and some accommodation to Congress's amendments after the 1971 election, it clearly limited Parliament's amending and legislative authority by reestablishing firm grounds for judicial review.

Keshavananda (1973) was the law of the land when the emergency was declared on June 26, 1975. Neither the courts nor the executive seemed able to separate the legislative pursuit of social transformation, particularly compensation for property compulsorily acquired by the state, and restraints on the state through judicial review. Even though Sanjay Gandhi, who once described the Communist Party of India (CPI) leadership as rich and corrupt and who thought decontrol of the economy would produce growth and equity,[28] had replaced Mohan Kumaramangalam as Mrs. Gandhi's political advisor, Mrs. Gandhi continued to claim that those who accused her of using the doctrine of parliamentary sovereignty to undermine constitutional government were opposed to her progressive policies. By 1974, her political support in the country and the party had deteriorated markedly in the face of failed policies, party factionalism, and political repression. By June 1975, she was fighting for survival. The electoral defeat of Congress in Gujarat and her conviction by the Allahabad (Uttar Pradesh) high court of corrupt electoral practices rendered her situation precarious, even desperate. Pending her appeal to the supreme court, she was barred for six years from sitting in Parliament. In the meantime, the opposition parties, now led by the JP movement, and elements within her own party were clamoring for her resignation. A desperate situation called for desperate measures. On June 26, 1975, a presidential declaration put the country under emergency rule on the grounds that an "internal disturbance" threatened the security of India. With fundamental rights suspended for the duration, parliamentary leaders from the opposition and her own party as well as Jayaprakash Narayan and hundreds of others throughout the country were arrested, and press censorhip was imposed.

Having successfully imposed a constitutional dictatorship on the country, Mrs. Gandhi still could be barred from Parliament if her appeal to the supreme court failed. Further, as long as *Keshavananda* remained the law of the land, judicial review could be used to protect the constitution's essential features. Mrs. Gandhi moved quickly to protect her personal and constitutional position. In August a depleted and intimidated Parliament passed the thirty-eighth and thirty-ninth amendments. The first made the emergency proclamation nonjusticiable.[29] The second removed from the jurisdiction of the supreme court the authority to review on appeal election petitions involving the prime minister and speaker. It also retroactively amended the Representation of the People Act (1951) to remove the provisions under which Mrs. Gandhi had been convicted.

For a time, it seemed that Mrs. Gandhi's emergency government meant to rely on the supreme court itself to enhance the authority of the executive and legislative branches by helping to keep her in office and to establish the clear supremacy of Parliament in constitutional matters. In 1937, a similar crisis in America pitted the president's executive leadership and reform legislation against the use of judicial review by the United States Supreme Court to declare New Deal measures unconstitutional. Franklin Roosevelt, after his massive electoral victory in 1937, tried unsuccessfully to "pack" the court with justices sharing his views. The country was spared further struggle by the "switch in time that saved nine," the realignment of the court's majority favorable to New Deal measures. Mrs. Gandhi may have expected a similar "switch" as a result of the highly controversial and much-disputed "supersession of judges" engineered by Mohan Kumaramangalam, a month before his death and one day after the *Keshavananda* decision was handed down on April 25, 1973. In the face of the well-established seniority convention, her government had superseded the three seniormost judges to appoint A. N. Ray chief justice. Ray had established his qualifications according to Kumaramangalam's doctrine that judges should be committed to the philosophy of the government that appointed them, by voting Mrs. Gandhi's way in three significant decisions.[30] The government hoped that as chief justice he would give a lead to the court by his stand on cases, his selection and ordering of business and his appointment of judges to the smaller benches through which the court processes particular cases.

Indeed, on November 7, 1975, the court gave a preliminary indication that it too was prepared to switch by unanimously reversing Mrs. Gandhi's June conviction by the Allahabad high court of two electoral offenses and quashing its order barring her from elective office for six years. It made its decision by recognizing as valid the August election law amendment that retrospectively removed the offenses at issue. But the court was not prepared to be fully committed. At the same sitting, it upheld *Keshavananda* when it struck down the clause of the recently enacted thirty-ninth amendment (adding article 329A) that removed election petitions against the prime minister and speaker from the courts' jurisdiction. The immunity jeopardized free and fair elections, which, the majority suggested, were an essential feature of the constitution not susceptible to constitutional amendment.[31] As in *Keshavananda*, the decision saved judicial review while yielding substance. At least one leading scholar of the court thinks that this decision precipitated the move, evident by the end of November, to bring in a new constitution, in which inter alia the judiciary would be subordinate to the executive.[32]

Despite the court's ruling, informed opinion expected Chief Justice Ray to find a way to accommodate government's request that the supreme court review *Keshavananda*. With a proposal already in circulation to scrap the 1950 constitution, it seems reasonable to suppose that the government anticipated a ruling that would repudiate *Keshavananda*'s basic structure justification for judicial review of parliamentary legislation, including constitutional amendments. In December, Ray convened a division bench (all thirteen justices), selecting a case from Andhra Pradesh from over three hundred writ petitions pending before state high courts. The petitions challenged a wide range of acts on the ground that they violated the basic structure of the constitution. But when court proceedings began, none of the state attorneys general present were prepared to offer a case to test the meaning or validity of basic structure; other justices questioned Ray's purpose in convening the bench, indicating that a majority was unwilling

to reverse *Keshavananda;* the attorney general of India, who had orally
asked for the review, virtually yielded to objections raised by eminent
counsel; and the chief justice, after the third day of the hearing, suddenly dissolved the bench. Government's effort to use the court to rid
itself of *Keshavananda* ended in inaction, not to say confusion.[33] It was
a reversal for government but not an entirely surprising one, given a
court interested in survival and reluctant to self-destruct.

While the court was struggling with the legal and constitutional
dilemmas posed by the emergency, unofficial documents that contemplated scrapping India's British-style parliamentary system for a
French-style presidential one, began to circulate in government circles
in October and November. They soon leaked to the underground opposition as well. The 1975 proposals would have subordinated Parliament and a cabinet only partially chosen from it to a directly elected
president, whose time "should not be allowed to be frittered away in
fruitless debate and discussion."[34] Particularly vital, given the battles
raging over judicial review and parliamentary sovereignty, was the proposal to subordinate the hitherto-independent judiciary to a presi-
dentially and ministerially dominated judicial council. The council
was to be oriented more to state than to citizen interests and distinctly
corporatist in selection and membership. The document explicitly
cited an annexed article of the French constitution, which deals with
France's state-dominated superior council of the judiciary.[35]

The document also proposed to undo *Keshavananda* by withdrawing jurisdiction over fundamental rights from the courts,[36] introducing
language that makes Parliament's judgment "conclusive" in disputes
between the government and the courts, and barring the courts from
calling into question restrictions on any of the rights provided for in
article 19, which specifies the fundamental—or civil—rights.[37] In consequence of these proposals, "the Court was faced for the first time in
its history . . . with a credible threat to its survival as a major institution of the Government," a fact of political life that Upendra Baxi
urges its critics to take into account when they find that the court, like
"those who were at the helm of other major institutions of the society . . . yielded in substance to the regime's demand in the interests of
self-preservation."[38]

Indeed, if in November the court found ways to avoid jeopardizing
its institutional interest, in April it found ways to placate the emergency executive. On April 28, the court upheld the government's authority under the emergency to jail its political opponents without
court hearings or subsequent review. The court, with only Justice
Khanna dissenting,[39] agreed that under an emergency not just funda-

mental rights but all safeguards protecting individual liberty are suspended. A five-member constitution bench had been convened in November 1975 to hear the union attorney general challenge decisions by seven state high courts allowing habeas corpus petitions. The bench's subsequent decision in April held that the state high courts were wrong in believing that courts could look into the bona fides and accuracy of preventive detention orders or decide whether they conformed to principles of natural justice or the common law. No persons could move the courts for a writ petition challenging the legality of a detention order. Further, the June 29, 1975, ordinance amending MISA, an act reviving preventive detention in 1971, validly removed the requirement that a prisoner be informed of the reason for his detention. According to Chief Justice Ray, the emergency provisions themselves were the rule of law under an emergency. Khanna, dissenting, held that the constitution did not provide for any authority to suspend habeas corpus. If life and liberty were not proteced by law, the distinction between a lawless society and one governed by laws would cease to have any meaning.

When a reconstituted court, purged of three dissenting judges, led by a committed chief justice, and surrounded by emergency pressures, nevertheless failed in late 1975 to abrogate *Keshavananda*'s doctrine of judicial review, Mrs. Gandhi took a more direct path to disestablish judicial review. Instead of finding a way to create a constituent assembly to write a new "presidential constitution," the Congress's annual session meeting in Chandigarh at the end of December appointed a committee chaired by Swaran Singh, a veteran minister and party stalwart, to recommend constitutional amendments that would make the fundamental law more responsive "to the current needs of the people and the demands of the present."[40] Its recommendations formed the basis of the forty-second amendment, a sweeping fifty-nine-clause constitutional revision. Tantamount to a new constitution, the amendment was accepted by a compliant Parliament fettered by censorship and intimidated by arrests of leading members.[41] The amendment purported inter alia to undo *Keshavananda* by barring the court from reviewing parliamentary legislation, declaring "that there shall be no limitation whatever on the constituent power of parliament to amend" the constitution. The "amendment" limited the court's authority in a variety of ways and added provisions that vastly strengthened the executive. It completely subordinated the fundamental rights of part 3 to parliamentary legislation giving expression to any of the directive principles of state policy in part 4[42] and severely restricted the courts' capacity under article 226 to issue writs to public authorities for the enforcement of rights conferred by part 3 and "for any other purpose."[43]

The electorate's massive repudiation in March 1977 of Mrs. Gandhi's authoritarian regime and emergency excesses and its affirmation of Janata's commitment to a liberal state that respected judicial review, citizen rights, and the rule of law raised the question of how the new government would "restore" the constitution. In particular, how would it redeem its pledge to reestablish judicial review of parliamentary legislation and amendments and right the balance between the executive and the supreme court?

Prime Minister Morarji Desai began by taking a difficult and controversial decision in favor of an independent judiciary. On the retirement of Chief Justice A. N. Ray soon after Janata assumed office, eminent members of the supreme court bar and other opponents or victims of the emergency called on a sympathetic Janata government to make a one-time exception to end exceptions by superseding Y. V. Chandrachud, the senior justice who had voted with the majority in the notorious habeas corpus case. But Prime Minister Desai chose to protect the independence of the judiciary by reinstating the seniority rule rather than appointing a chief justice with the right legal philosophy.[44]

Conflict over state issues was at the center of the Janata government's policy concerns and its relationship with the Gandhi-led Congress-I opposition in Parliament. Choosing the level and quality of stateness and framing and passing amendments that institutionalized hard-fought cabinet decisions proved difficult and frustrating. Now that Janata faced the responsibility of ruling the country, it could not easily or automatically redeem the pledges of an opposition party struggling against a tyrannical government and authoritarian regime. Even if it had known its own mind about what it meant to restore to the constitution, doing so would have proved difficult and complex. As it was, the staggered terms of the upper house (one-third elected every two years) deprived the Janata government of a majority, much less of the constitutional majority (two-thirds of those present and voting) required for amendments. In the lower house it had to rely on friendly and/or opposition parties to muster a constitutional majority. The Janata government's Forty-fifth Amendment Bill (later the Forty-fourth Amendment Act), which cleared both houses in December 1978, twenty-two months after Janata assumed office, and received the president's assent in May 1979, just two months before its government fell, reflected the limitations of Janata's parliamentary situation and the compromises and bargains required by the diverse preferences of influential actors within and outside the Janata government.[45]

If the Forty-fifth Amendment Bill did not restore a liberal state, it did go to considerable lengths to prevent the recurrence of an authoritarian one. Mrs. Gandhi, on June 26, 1975, had invoked the language of article 352, authorizing the proclamation of an emergency by the president if the country's security is threatened by an "internal disturbance," to repulse and repress political and legal threats to her power and authority.[46] In doing so, she may have abused power in two ways, by wrongly identifying such threats as an "internal disturbance" that constituted a threat to the security of India and by asking the president ab initio to act on her advice rather than, as the constitution requires, the advice of the council of ministers.[47] The Forty-fifth Amendment Bill provided remedies for these potential abuses of power by substituting "armed rebellion" for "internal disturbance" and prohibiting the president from issuing a proclamation of emergency "unless the decision of the Union Cabinet . . . that such a Proclamation may be issued has been communicated to him in writing." The clause also required that parliamentary resolutions approving declarations of emergency be passed by a constitutional majority (two-thirds) rather than by an ordinary majority. Other remedies of the bill for abuses of power under an emergency were guarantees: that the media can report freely and without censorship the proceedings in Parliament and the state assemblies;[48] that citizens' access to the courts on matters that touch their rights to life and liberty cannot be suspended; that protection against self-incrimination, retroactive laws, and double jeopardy cannot be suspended and that writs will be available from the high courts to enforce these protections; that persons arrested under laws authorizing preventive detention (e.g., MISA and Defense of India Rules) cannot be held for more than two months without court-supervised review procedures;[49] and that one-tenth of the total number of members of the lower house can call for a special sitting to consider disapproving the continuance in force of an emergency.[50]

In a surprising, even daring, decision four months after Mrs. Gandhi was swept back into power, the supreme court in May 1980 restored via judicial review what the Janata government was unable to restore by parliamentary amendment. In the *Minerva Mills* case, the court invoked *Keshavananda* to declare invalid, because they attacked the basic structure of the constitution, the two clauses of the forty-second amendment meant to reverse *Keshavananda*. The first prohibited court review of laws that contravened fundamental rights if Parliament declared that they gave effect to directive principles of state policy; the second proscribed judicial review of constitutional amendments.[51] The court's decision was reminiscent of its actions in November and December 1975 when it struck down the thirth-ninth amendment's attempt to immunize the prime minister's election from review by a competent tribunal and refused to follow the chief justice in his attempt to reverse *Keshavananda*. Without returning the pendulum to the extreme of *Golak Nath*, the court returned it to a position between *Keshavananda* (1973) and the twenty-fifth amendment (1971) by recognizing in *Minerva Mills* the limited primacy of directive principles created by the twenty-fifth amendment (article 39[b] and [c] only) but challenged by *Keshavananda*.[52] Buffeted by the constitutional storms of the emergency period and the alternation of Janata and Congress governments, the court seems to have adopted a dual strategy to assure its survival as a coordinate branch of government. It protected judicial review by asserting its special responsibility for defining what was constitutional. It practiced self-restraint with respect not only to legislative but also to executive action.

Self-Restraint: Will Saving the Court Save a Government of Laws?

The political innocence that accompanied the court's era of legal solipsism produced *Golak Nath*. Since then, the court has learned to read the election returns in ways that attend to long-run political currents as well as short-run opportunities. Its conduct since 1977 suggests a politically responsive and self-restrained strategy that seeks to protect the principle of judicial review while recognizing that the executive, acting through or with the support of parliamentary majorities and in the name of state purposes and interests, can make claims that constrain citizens' rights, the federal system, or even the rule of law.

When the 1977 election ended Congress's emergency regime and installed a Janata government in Delhi, the court showed its responsiveness in an advisory opinion (article 143).[53] The Desai government proposed to dissolve the assemblies and hold midterm elections in nine states with Congress governments. Congress had captured no parliamentary seats in some and one or two in others, and its vote shares had declined precipitously in all. The Janata government in Delhi held that the parliamentary results made it clear that Congress governments in the nine states no longer represented the people. In any case, their involvement in emergency excesses made it difficult for these governments to maintain law and order, because of their loss of legitimacy and the people's hatred of them. The supreme court advised the president that dissolution was justified. It was an unprecedented act that significantly undermined the constitution's federal arrangements.[54]

While acquiescing in the wishes of the country's new political masters, the court failed to specify adequately the special electoral and legal circumstances that could distinguish Janata's dissolution from similar ones that might arise in the future. It failed to give sufficient consideration to the consequences of the precedent. In March 1980, Mrs. Gandhi's newly elected Congress government, despite patent differences in electoral outcomes and extant legal and political circumstances, justified dissolution of nine state assemblies with non-Congress majorities and governments by invoking the court-sanctioned Janata precedent.[55]

The court again acquiesced in the purposes of the Janata government by providing a second advisory opinion that upheld the legality of legislation that would create special courts to try Mrs. Gandhi, Sanjay, and others for their alleged abuse of power, excesses, and criminal acts under the emergency.[56] After Janata's defeat and Mrs. Gandhi's return to power, the two special courts set up by the Janata government followed the election returns by invoking "improper procedures" in their creation to dismiss summarily cases against Indira and Sanjay Gandhi pending before them.[57]

When Mrs. Gandhi returned to power in January 1980, the courts accommodated themselves to the interests and needs of the country's new political masters in other ways. Not only did they find ways of winding up the special courts trying emergency offenses but also they found ways, between January and June 1980, to dismiss all the cases pending against Mrs. Gandhi and her emergency associates. Mrs. Gandhi dismissed them in her own way by characterizing all prosecutions against her and her political associates as merely politically vindictive. The supreme court in June seemed to agree when it held in the Baroda dynamite and Bansi Lal cases that the state need not prosecute criminal cases when it finds that the motives involved were political.

Before the court's decision was handed down, the country was treated to a spectacle of cavalier dismissals that jeopardized the rule of law. Four cases against Bansi Lal, emergency defence minister, former chief minister of Haryana, and a close associate of Sanjay Gandhi, were dropped when the then Lok Dal chief minister of Bansi Lal's home state, Bhajan Lal, found he needed the political support of a codefendant close to Bansi Lal.[58] The Delhi high court dismissed on a minor procedural detail an important defamation case against Maneka Gandhi, Sanjay's politically active and ambitious wife who edited *Surya*, a political weekly.[59] The Central Bureau of Investigation found that it had "insufficient evidence" to proceed with its case against Jag Mohan, the Sanjay intimate who, as commissioner of the Delhi Development Authority had played a key role in the demolition of "slums," such as those near the Jama Masjid and around Turkman Gate.[60] On the same grounds of insufficient evidence, the bureau stopped work on a case against D. K. Dhawan, the private secretary to Mrs. Gandhi who handled many of the repressive acts under the emergency and who was being investigated for misuse of party funds.[61] The special courts, trying the procurement without payment of 139 jeeps and Mrs. Gandhi's harassment of officials charged with investigating why and how five state chief ministers purchased equipment from Sanjay's Maruti Ltd. firm without proper bidding,[62] found that they themselves had been improperly constituted.[63] A hit-and-run case lodged at Dehra Dun against Sanjay Gandhi in September 1979 was adjourned after the election when the injured victim discovered that he rather than Sanjay was at fault and witnesses changed their testimony.[64] These are only a few of the nearly twenty cases dropped after Congress-I's electoral victory in January 1980.[65]

The supreme court directly confronted the problem of the balance between a government of laws and executive discretion in two cases handed down in May 1980. It skillfully paired its review of the two cases: the withdrawal by the Janata government of the Baroda dynamite case brought against Janata sympathizers under the emergency by a Congress government and the withdrawal by the Congress government of the Bansi Lal case lodged by the Janata government against Congress's defense minister under the emergency. The court asserted the principle of the nonpolitical nature of state prosecutions even while erecting a commodious shelter for governments wishing to withdraw cases on purely political grounds. On the one hand, Justice Reddy asserted that "criminal justice is not a plaything and a court is not a playground of politicking." [66] The court's function is to assure that the public prosecutor "had applied his mind as a free agent" and did not allow himself to be the "stooge" of the executive. On the other hand, in sanctioning the withdrawal of cases by both the Congress and Janata governments, the court's opinion offers special protection to politically motivated offenses.

The Janata government, the court notes, withdrew the Baroda dynamite case because "the motivating force of the party [Janata] which was formed to fight the election in 1977 was the same as the motivating force of the criminal [the Baroda dynamite] conspiracy." The court then poses a question: "To say that an offence is of a political character is not to absolve the offender of the offence, but the question is, is it a valid ground for the government to advise the public prosecutor to withdraw from the prosecution?" Indian history suggests it is indeed a valid ground: "A political offence is one which is committed with the object of changing the government of a state or inducing it to change its policy," and these are "the kinds of offences with which Mahatma Gandhi and his spiritual son, the first prime minister of India" as well as the present prime minister and president were once charged. In consequence, "one cannot say that the public prosecutor was activated by any improper motive in withdrawing from prosecution."

Is it then all right, under this doctrine, to commit crimes, provided they are politically motivated? Apparently so. Three days after the supreme court handed down its judgment, the metropolitan magistrate of Delhi used it to dismiss the Jan Path riot case involving Sanjay Gandhi and his Youth Congress followers. They were charged with mayhem and window smashing in New Delhi's central shopping area. Because the acts occurred during a political demonstration protesting the Janata government's policies—special courts, unemployment, and corruption—they fell under the authoritative judgment of the supreme court protecting such offenses. The magistrate cites the court, "To persist with prosecution where emotive issues are involved, in the name of vindicating the law may be utter foolishness tending on insanity."

In the midst of the wholesale withdrawal of emergency cases, a prominent Indian journalist argued that "we have not reached the stage of maturity in our development as a democracy" to make it possible for the Indian government to inquire into the transactions of close aides to the executive. Judges who have collaborated in the evaporation of cases "should be recommended for their common sense and realism" in avoiding a "confrontation between the concepts of popular sovereignty and an independent judiciary, if only because they cannot hope to win it." [67] Many leaders of India's legal profession do not deserve this judgment, written, in any event, before the *Minerva Mills* decision was handed down. However, this statement does suggest how the positive norm of judicial self-restraint toward the politically responsible executive can be used to defend judicial abdication in the interest of judicial survival.

State Issues in the 1980s

The issues of institutional rivalry have taken a more ambiguous form in the late 1980s. The court shows the battle scars it incurred in the seventies. As Upendra Baxi noted, "During the Chief Justiceship of Ray and Beg, the Court progressively became an assembly of individuals and lost much of its corporate institutional character." [68] Yet the end of Mrs. Gandhi's rule has eased the propensity of friends of the court to view as suspect all executive proposals for court reform. It is easier than before to assess the weaknesses of the court system without rousing fears that the courts are under attack. Thus, when Mrs. Gandhi's government proposed transferring sitting judges of the state high courts to other states, this was viewed, with good reason, as a potential weapon against uncompliant judges. When Rajiv Gandhi's law minister proposed a system for drawing a third of each state court's justices from outside the state, at the beginning of their appointment to that court, it seemed more credible that the move was in line with the recommendations of the Law Commission for deprovincializing the courts. Even then, in reviewing appointments to the Uttar Pradesh high court, the supreme court accused the government of "picking and choosing" in ways that might produce "a sycophant judge at the helm of affairs," which was "a complete antithesis of an independent judiciary."[69]

The eighties brought new issues. Attention shifted among legal observers and actors, from the macrodrama at the national level of conflict between between the supreme court and Parliament to the myriad microdramas at the local level between the disadvantaged and the petty oppressive agents of the state: police rape, police blindings, social agency corruption, jail inhumanity.[70] Justices such as Kirshna Iyer and P. N. Bhagwati, who had taken a permissive view, in the name of social justice, of a strong and even authoritarian state, led the movement against the state's agents at the micro level.[71] Legal aid, public interest litigation, and voluntary agencies intervening on behalf of poor clients victimized by state agencies flourished in the postemergency climate.[72] The "epistolary jurisdiction"[73] by which Justices Iyer and Bhagwati recognized even postcards from jail inmates as writ petitions focused attention on state impropriety and lawlessness.

Some of the early euphoria has worn off the public interest law movement. Its limitations have become obvious. Overloaded courts cannot handle the epistolary jurisdiction; courts have great difficulty enforcing their decisions; without a serious institutional base, public interest law cannot survive; and "top-down" bureaucratic institutions for legal aid soon become routinized and unresponsive.[74] But public interest law continues as a powerful reminder that the state, written in lowercase letters, has its own distinctive style of oppression.

Finally, attention has shifted in the eighties from whether the courts can provide justice to whether the courts can function at all.[75] When the government of India sought to sue Union Carbide in a United States court to establish the company's liability for the industrial accident at Bhopal that killed two thousand and injured many more, it claimed that Indian courts were too slow and ineffectual to deliver timely and adequate justice to Indian citizens—a claim both humiliating and partly true.[76]

Nevertheless, the state issues of the 1970s persist. Several of the justices are criticized in their fraternity for not observing a proper distance between themselves and the executive. Both Justices Bhagwati and Desai have been so criticized.[77] Other justices doubt the legitimacy of the system that they serve. Justice D. A. Desai, like Justice Krishna Iyer before him, finds the judicial system "utterly alien to the genius of the country" and a "smuggled system."[78] Yet others, such as Justice O. Chinappa Reddy, think fundamental rights have been given undue importance as against directive principles.[79] The seniority issue, which was considered closed after the supersession wars of the 1970s, is also still alive. When Chief Justice Bhagwati faced retirement in 1986, the prospect that his successor by the seniority rule would be the more conservative Justice R. S. Pathak led Justice Bhagwati to press for another supersession by a chief justice with views more in keeping with his own.[80]

In the late 1980s, state issues remained at the center of the political struggle. Institutional rivalry between Parliament and court, constitutional controversies over the relative standing of judicial review and parliamentary sovereignty, and conflict between citizens' rights and state interests will continue to orient leaders and parties seeking power. Constitutional doctrine in India is not explicit about a government based on a balance of powers and does not feature the pursuit of institutional self-interest as a restraint on power. Yet India will test whether the prescription offered in *Federalist 51* for the successful working of a division and balance of powers among several branches of government is viable. "The great security against a gradual concentration of the several powers in the same department," according to *Federalist 51*, "consists in giving those who administer each department the necessary constitutional means and personal motives to resist encroachments of the others. . . . Ambition must be made to counteract ambition. The interests of the man must be connected with the constitutional rights of the place. . . . In framing a government which is to be administered by men over men, the great difficulty lies in this: you must first enable the government to control the governed; and in the next place oblige it to control itself."[81]

The Janata government (1977–79), via the provisions of the forty-fourth amendment, and the supreme court, in reaffirming in *Minerva Mills* the basic structure doctrine of *Keshavananda*, restored a balance between judicial review and parliamentary sovereignty that gave the court and the parliamentary executive "the necessary constitutional means and personal motives to resist encroachments by the other." It remains to be seen whether the court will continue to be filled by judges whose personal motives will connect with "the constitutional rights of the place."[82] Chastened by the shocks and pressures of the emergency and alternating party governments, the Chandrachud court, to accommodate the political interests of governments of the day, circumscribed the meaning of the federal principle and a government of laws. At the same time, it protected the doctrine of fundamental law and the practice of judicial review. Whether balances struck over the next decade will reflect judicial self-restraint that protects the constitution and fundamental rights or judicial abdication that sacrifices both awaits the course of historical events and the country's judgment of them.

Part 2

POLITICS

4 The Congress Party: Deinstitutionalization and the Rise of Plebiscitary Politics

The Indian National Congress, India's leading political party, was founded over a century ago, in 1885. It has dominated the country's public and political life ever since. Its success as the governing party of independent India distinguishes Congress from nationalist movements and governing parties in other Third World countries. When Congress successfully ousted and replaced the British raj, it inherited its standing as *sarkar*, governmental authority in the generic sense. It also benefited from the political capital that it had accumulated by leading the nationalist struggle for independence and victory over the country's colonial masters. For the first fifteen years after independence, the Congress party's nationalist reputation enhanced its legitimacy and that of the state it governed. When India held its first universal-suffrage postindependence election in 1952, the sixty-seven-year-old Congress was one of the world's oldest and best-institutionalized political parties.[1] At its centenary celebration in 1985, it had won seven of eight national elections and governed independent India for thirty-five of thirty-eight years.

The Congress Party and the Dominant-Party System

Congress began as an organization of anglicized regional elites whose common language, interests, and lifestyle distinguished them from most of the Indians they purported to represent. In the 1920s, Mohandas Gandhi transformed the Congress from an organization catering to anglicized elites to a cadre-led mass organization based on regional language areas. Gandhi not only rationalized and tightened Congress's organization and procedures but also combined individual and group organizational strategies. Congress became a popular organization based on personal primary membership on the one hand and an alliance of service and cultural societies and linguistic, ethnic, and religious groups on the other.[2] Gandhi's campaign against untouchability explicitly introduced caste to India's public agenda by repudiating caste hierarchy, a repudiation that burgeoning caste associations furthered by political efforts to improve their status.

127

The post-Gandhi Congress, differentiated and rationalized, encompassed national executive and legislative bodies—the Working Committee, the All India Congress Committee, and the pradesh (provincial, later state) and district Congress committees—that were a liaison with India's regions, social formations, and, to a lesser extent, producer groups. They reached traders, artisans, and cultivators in towns and villages.[3] After independence, this is the Congress organization that with considerable skill won the first five parliamentary elections, governed and developed the country, and managed two successions (the first after Jawaharlal Nehru's death in May 1964, the second after Lal Bahadur Shastri's in January 1966). The Congress party retained its organizational cohesiveness until November 1969, when a struggle between the "syndicate" (an alliance of senior state and organizational party leaders) and the leader of the parliamentary party (and prime minister), Indira Gandhi, split the party for the first time. Lesser splits occurred again in 1977 and 1978. Except at the time of the Shastri succession in 1964, the Nehru dynasty faction led by his daughter, Indira, and his grandson, Rajiv, not only has defeated dissident factions, driven them into the political wilderness, or reabsorbed them but also has subsequently led the party to electoral victories that consolidated the dynasty's hold over the party and the country.

The Indian National Congress in the preindependence period was both a revolutionary nationalist movement that aspired to be the successor regime to the British raj and an opposition party that aspired to be an alternative government. Congress's early experience as both a governing and an opposition party taught India's political class that party politics and political participation could be competitive as well as revolutionary. This lesson powerfully shaped postindependence politics. Unlike the revolutionary politics of violence and coups that have characterized many Third World countries, regulated conflict in electoral and legislative arenas enabled government and opposition to survive and change sides by competing for popular support.

In the nationalist era, India's political class and political community learned to participate in competitive parliamentary politics. The 1919 reforms introduced "dyarchy," governments in the provinces responsible to popularly elected legislatures, in which certain subjects were "transferred" to Indian ministers. The Government of India Act of 1935 provided for elections (1937) that led to the formation of fully responsible Congress governments in seven of eleven provinces. From 1922 through September 1939, when the Congress provincial ministers resigned, Indian politicians, drawn mostly from Congress ranks, were active participants in party and parliamentary government and politics at the provincial level, even while, at the national level, Congress leaders pursued the confrontational politics of the independence struggle. The dual objectives of governance and the revolutionary struggle for independence fostered dual forms of political participation: (1) regulated conflict in the form of parliamentary and electoral party politics and (2) agitational collective action (particularly via Gandhian civil disobedience) that entailed unregulated conflict with authorities.

These legacies shaped political participation and collective action after independence. Indian subjects as voters were organized and mobilized by political parties seeking mandates to govern. They were also mobilized as revolutionary, albeit nonviolent, nationalists and as producers, consumers, and victims of private and state power by leaders of movements and demand groups seeking to bring about regime or policy change through agitational and extralegal means. The latter legacy inspires demand groups, whose form of politics will be discussed later in this volume, in chapter 9.

After independence, the Congress party became the lead player in a one-party-dominant system. Other parties were free to compete for power in electoral arenas to which entry was easy and constitutionally guaranteed, but they did not displace Congress, except in a few states. Congress's dominance in the first three general elections was expressed by overwhelming majorities of seats in Parliament and by victories in most of the states. The Congress won between 70 and 75 percent of the central parliamentary seats in the first three elections and between 61 and 68 percent of the seats in state legislatures. That it did so with only 43 to 48 percent of the electoral vote is a mark of both the success and failure of the opposition: success in mobilizing more than 50 percent of the electorate; failure in dissipating its potential seat majority when opposition parties competed as much with each other as with Congress (see figs. 2 and 3).

Simultaneous control of the central and state governments by the Congress party mitigated differences within the federal system. Congress governments in Delhi used party mechanisms and channels to coordinate central and state governmental policies and to accommodate divergent interests. Such party contexts supplemented the financial and administrative means normally available to the central government.[4]

As the hegemon of the dominant-party system, Congress was subject to "pressure at the margin" by opposition parties.[5] Rather than trying to replace Congress governments of the day by forming coalitions or merging, opposition parties influenced Congress policies by working on like-minded factions within Congress. As much out of necessity as out of choice, opposition parties responded to what the late Asoka Mehta referred to as "the political compulsions of a backward country" by engaging in criticism but not in opposition for opposition's sake, because "the axiom of opposition's job to oppose would make economic development difficult."[6] The dominant-party system and the roles of Congress and the opposition parties within it provided

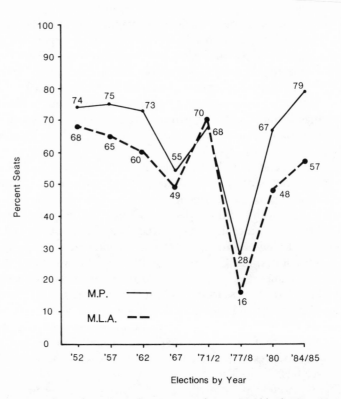

Elections by Year

Fig. 2. Congress's share of seats in parliamentary and state assembly elections. To calculate seats for the "1980" state assembly election, we have had to aggregate state elections for the period of 1979–83. The main election for nine large state assemblies was held in May 1980 (Bihar, Gujarat, Madhya Pradesh, Maharashtra, Orissa, Punjab, Rajasthan, Tamil Nadu, and Uttar Pradesh). Other elections were held as follows: 1979, Mizoram and Sikkim; 1980, Arunachal Pradesh, Goa, Pondicherry, Manipur, and Kerala; 1982, West Bengal, Haryana, Himachal Pradesh, and Nagaland; 1983, Assam, Delhi (Metropolitan Council), Meghalaya, Andhra Pradesh, Karnataka, Tripura, and Jammu and Kashmir (data from *Asian Recorder* [various issues]). For the "1985" state assembly election, we had the results from only nine states (data from *India Today,* March 31, 1985). For state and parliamentary elections through 1978 and for the 1980 parliamentary election, data were obtained from Election Commission reports; for 1984, from Government of India, Press Information Bureau, *Lok Sabha Elections, 1984* (New Delhi, 1985).

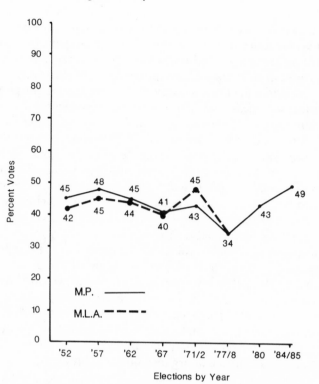

Fig. 3. **Congress's share of votes in parliamentary and state assembly elections.** Data through 1984 are from Election Commission reports. The vote figures for 1977–78 are based on a calculation for the seventeen major states minus Gujarat, which voted in 1975. The votes for the 1980 and 1985 state assembly elections were still not available when this volume went to press in 1986.

a fertile context for the rooting of India's democratic process during the first two decades after independence.

Until the 1970s, the Congress party concerted and led the mediated mobilization of voters and the representation of interests. It was in tension with rather than in control of or subordinate to public opinion and organized social groups, classes, interests, and local notabilities. In the context of policy choice and resource allocation, it led by creating political formulas that conciliated social groups and made bargains possible. But mediation meant more than skill in creating political formulas, consensual policy agendas, and aggregated interests. In its early postindependence years, Congress retained some of that strong normative dimension that inspired it as a nationalist movement, a dimension that was capable of enlisting not only the interests but also the ideals of its members and those who identified with it. Congress workers, candidates, and officeholders were meant to be bearers of Mohandas Gandhi's example and legacy, to live exemplary lives and selflessly render service to achieve *sarvodaya,* the uplift of all, particularly the most disadvantaged and oppressed. They were also to engage in the more mundane tasks associated with competing for power and representing the needs and interests of ordinary citizens.

For Gandhi, *sarvodaya* was essential if the Indian people were to be ready for and worthy of *swaraj* (self-rule). For him, Congress was both a movement with a cause—national independence—and a service organization that aimed to transform Indian society. The principled and disinterested conduct that Gandhi practiced and evoked contributed to popular trust in Congress, even among those, like Nehru, who were skeptical about Gandhi's ethical prescriptions for individual conduct, collective action, and social transformation.

At independence, Gandhi called for the dissolution of Congress as a political party engaged in the pursuit of political power and governmental office. The call was not heeded, even by those most closely associated with his political leadership. The nationalist generation and its immediate successors followed Nehru, Gandhi's chosen successor, some because of his call to make the Congress party a vehicle for social transformation and principled conduct, others because the Congress party he led was a powerful organization that promised influence and benefits.

Congress as the legatee and bearer of the nationalist era brought many valuable institutional assets to the early years of the independent nation. They reached well beyond the party itself and the party system that it dominated to the political community, government, and state that encompassed them. During the Nehru era, the political capital that Congress brought to independent India was replenished, perhaps enhanced. But in the 1970s and early 1980s, India's institutional assets began to dissipate as Indira Gandhi sought to maintain power in the face of an increasingly mobilized and demanding electorate and seemingly intractable problems of governability.[7]

The Deinstitutionalization of Congress

The nationalist era's committed political generations faded from view in the 1960s. Those for whom politics was an occupation, more a way to make a living and get ahead in the world than a cause worthy of sacrifice, filled Congress's offices and anterooms. In the nationalist era too, some Congressmen had lived off politics rather than for politics.

But in the 1960s they became the dominant element in the party's outlook and practice. The 1963 "Kamaraj plan," promulgated in the last year of a weary and chastened Nehru's life, attempted under the aegis of party president Kamaraj Nadar to revive party commitment and strengthen its professionalism. Party professionals, prominent cabinet ministers, and state chief ministers left the perquisites and privileges of government office to do party work. The idea was to upgrade the esteem and prestige associated with party service as well as to improve its organizational effectiveness. After Nehru's death in May 1964, party revitalization remained a prominent but elusive goal during Lal Bahadur Shastri's nineteen months as prime minister.

Kamaraj Nadar successfully managed the succession at Nehru's death but did not, as Nehru hoped he would, succeed in strengthening the party. "Unfortunately," writes Stanley A. Kochanek, a close student of the Congress party, "organizational reconstruction was ignored during the four years of Kamaraj's tenure as Congress President. . . . The inertia of the President affected the entire organization and particularly the central office. . . . Ironically, the man who came to the Congress Party leadership in the name of reconstruction failed most conspicuously to carry out his primary task."[8] Instead, in the absence of Nehru's vigorous central leadership, powerful state chief ministers began in Shastri's time to be more influential in national politics: the era of the "syndicate" had dawned. When Indira Gandhi attempted after three years in office to assert herself as Congress prime minister, she, the "Indicate," faced the syndicate as a rival force in the party's national affairs.

Under syndicate leadership, Congress ideology was more than ever perceived as empty rhetoric, mantras without meaning, repeated in manifestos and important party occasions. In Delhi, state capitals, and district towns, the politics of persons and factions crowded aside the politics of national purpose and high policy. The ground was being prepared for the electoral and organizational crises of 1967 and 1969, in the face of two consecutive bad monsoons (1965 and 1966), a draw in a major war with Pakistan (1965), and an unsuccessful devaluation (1966). In the fourth general election of 1967, Congress lost power in eight large states and almost did so nationally; two years later, it split for the first time.

In January 1966, after the sudden and unexpected death of Lal Bahadur Shastri, Indira Gandhi had become prime minister of India. Granddaughter and daughter of two of Congress's great national leaders, Motilal Nehru and Jawaharlal Nehru, she seemed to the state bosses of the syndicate who controlled the organizational wing of the party more likely to attract votes and to be compliant than Morarji Desai, her rival for party leadership after Shastri's death. By 1969, having shed her diffidence and uncertainty, she was ready to challenge those who in their view had been her patrons and benefactors and who continued to think of themselves as her mentors. In June, in an extraordinarily risky move designed to free herself from syndicate tutelage and constraints, she engineered the defeat of Sanjiva Reddy, a syndicate member whom the party had nominated for president of India, by unofficially backing V. V. Giri, an "independent" candidate who, conveniently, had entered the race. In November, after a series of defeats within the organizational wing of the party, Indira Gandhi successfully defied the syndicate first by endorsing leftist political positions the party had tabled but ignored and then by testing her strength in the parliamentary party. Congress MPs, however, were asked to choose not between the "Indicate" and the "syndicate" but once again between Indira Gandhi and Morarji Desai, whose imperious and self-righteous manner had alienated not only many MPs but also his senior Congress colleagues in the "syndicate." Mrs. Gandhi emerged victorious by a margin of two to one. After the split, she led a minority government that had to rely on opposition party support (primarily from the CPI and the Dravida Munnetra Kazhagam [DMK], but she had freed herself from the constraints and tutelage of Congress's organizational party.

Indira Gandhi's voice and actions in 1969 seemed to many at the time to be those of a savior. She was perceived, particularly by those at the center and left of the party, as breathing new life and purpose into a moribund body. She did so, but not in the way anticipated by those for whom Congress was the party of Mohandas Gandhi, Vallabhbhai Patel, or even Jawaharlal Nehru. Although not foreordained, Indira Gandhi's 1969 victory over the "syndicate" proved in retrospect to be the beginning of party deinstitutionalization. Over the next five years it became increasingly clear that Mrs. Gandhi's ideological and policy stances at the time were useful tactics in the struggle for power within the party, not revitalizing commitments intended to strengthen the party organizationally and electorally. Personal loyalty, not party commitment, became the touchstone for preferment and promotion. The simultaneous rise of plebiscitary and personal politics under Mrs. Gandhi's guiding hand obviated the need for an organization capable of articulating with society, serving and leading the political community, and fighting elections. The rise of plebiscitary and demise of mediated politics resulted as much from unintended consequences of ad hoc actions as from design or conspiracy. As Indira Gandhi became

Congress's most vital resource, the key to political power and personal advancement, the party and the person tended to become one until, in the rich prose of then party president D. K. Barooah, the phrase "Indira is India, India is Indira" could be spoken to a grateful but anxious party following. As the myth of Indira Gandhi began to inspire and diminish India, the party that she led lost its institutional coherence and élan.

The Congress under Mrs. Gandhi's leadership entered the 1971 parliamentary election at the head of a minority government dependent for its existence on opposition party support. Most informed observers believed that Congress was unlikely to win a majority of seats in the new Parliament, much less capture the two-thirds or better the party had won in the first three elections. They had not counted on Indira Gandhi's tactical and rhetorical skill nor on the revulsion many voters in Hindi Heartland states felt for the squabbling self-serving parties that had led coalition governments since 1967. By calling for an early (midterm) poll that "delinked" (separated) parliamentary from state assembly elections, Mrs. Gandhi was able to exploit her comparative advantage as India's only national political personality. Delinking also make it easier to turn the election in a plebiscitary direction by matching one known personality with one appealing slogan, "abolish poverty." The result surprised the experts and practitioners; the Gandhi-led Congress was returned with levels of support reminiscent of Nehru's, a two-thirds majority in Parliament based on 43 percent of the vote. The daughter seemed to have redeemed the ideological and electoral legacy of the father. Some observers held that the results heralded a new issue- and class-oriented politics.[9] Certainly delinking helped to "nationalize" parliamentary elections by liberating them to an extent from a reliance on "vote banks" and local notabilities.

Her impressive personal victory freed Mrs. Gandhi from the constraints of national and state party decision making. At one stroke she was able to discredit her erstwhile Congress opponents and to substitute plebiscitary national outcomes for intraparty deliberations. She began to circumvent or ignore Congress's widely ramified organizations and procedures. At the time, her well-wishers thought the newly found freedom from conservative party oligarchs would enable her to use her mandate in realizing the promise of progressive policies at home and independence abroad.

State assembly elections in early 1972 provided similar possibilities. As the heroine of India's sixteen-day victory over Pakistan in December 1971, Mrs. Gandhi benefited from the emotional surge of a khaki election. Large seat if not vote majorities in most states again enabled

Mrs. Gandhi, this time at the state level, to brush aside seemingly powerful regional leaders. Victory in the state assembly elections was attributed to her personal following among the voters. Electoral success once again validated authority within the party. The coattails once supplied by the Congress party's nationalist heritage, progressive image, and organizational muscle were now thought to be supplied by Mrs. Gandhi's sari.

Mrs. Gandhi used her commanding presence in the party to substitute patrimonial considerations for organizational standing and service. This was most apparent in the choice of state chief ministers. She overrode the established method of selecting them on the basis of support in state assembly parties and Congress committees. Instead, in the manner of the British raj, she "nominated" loyalists, leaders more dependent on her favor and pleasure than on the support of representative party bodies connected to state constituencies.

Party matters received low priority.[10] Party organs at the center, state, and district levels fell into disuse, and those who ran them became persons of lesser consequence unless they were thought to have Mrs. Gandhi's ear or enjoy her favor. Starting in 1971, elections to state Congress committees and of their officers, particularly the presidents, were superseded by appointments made by the Congress party president, who was either Mrs. Gandhi herself or one of her loyal dependents. The 1969 split removed most of the party's senior and experienced organizational leaders when men such as Kamaraj Nadar, a former president and architect of the 1964 and 1966 successions, the five most prominent "syndicate" members (Atulya Ghosh, S. K. Patil, and Sanjiva, Nijalingappa, and Brahmananda Reddy), and Morarji Desai, Mrs. Gandhi's Congress rival for the prime ministership in 1966 and 1967, formed a rival party, the Congress-O (for organization). Some constructed the meaning of the 1969 split and exit from what they took to be the lessons of similar intraparty struggle in 1950. Soon after the death of Jawaharlal Nehru's party rival, Vallabhbhai Patel, Prime Minister Nehru and Congress president Purushotamdas Tandon, thought to be a Patel surrogate, contested for ascendency. In the Congress canon, Nehru had saved the party from capture by conservative forces by forcing Tandon to resign and assuming the presidency himself.[11] The 1969 struggle was interpreted by Mrs. Gandhi's Nehruite and "progressive" supporters as a comparable struggle over ideology and policy.

With the benefit of hindsight, events beginning with the November 1969 split of the Congress party can be given a different reading. The 1971 and 1972 elections, for example, become the opening phase of a plebicitary politics that opened direct relation between Indira Gandhi's personalized leadership and individual voters rather than of an issue-oriented politics that mobilized classes and interests in support of Congress programs and candidates.[12] Both plebiscitary and issue-oriented politics radically reduce the explanatory significance of mediated politics based on vote banks, notabilities, and state-level factions. But unlike issue politics, plebiscitary politics reduces ideological commitments and policy preferences to one overriding question: whether or not to support the only person who is the dynastic heir to Congress's legacy and whose name and fame extend from the Himalayas to Cape Cormorin.

The trend away from politics mediated by party organization and social groups was reinforced by aspects of Mrs. Gandhi's character. She was a loner who did not feel comfortable with political peers and independent colleagues, neither trusting them nor inspiring their trust. She suspected rather than used autonomous political networks. Independent figures did not remain long in her cabinets or service. Out of these dispositions and their consequences arose her avoidance of the mediated politics of party networks, and of political collegiality. Her avoidance of mediated politics was balanced by a considerable talent for direct mass communication, for eliciting trust and confidence at a distance. Large crowds came to take her *darshan* (auspicious viewing of a sacred object) and felt rewarded by being in her presence.[13]

By 1974, Congress governments at the center and in the states had squandered their electoral mandates. The country was in crisis. Rather than implementing propoor redistributional policies and programs, the Gandhi government crushed the railway workers strike and faced Jayaprakash Narayan's movement for "total revolution."[14] The imposition of an authoritarian emergency regime in June 1975 signalled both the progressive deinstitutionalization of the Congress party and the radical erosion of Mrs. Gandhi's plebiscitary support. The twenty-month emergency regime accelerated state as well as party deinstitutionalization by substituting fiat for a government of laws, and fear for consent. The apparently voluntary dismantling of intraparty democracy and procedures in the name of loyalty and discipline that had accompanied reliance on "Indira waves" was compounded during the emergency by a miasma of fear. By "suspending" public liberties, particularly freedom of the press and representative and responsible government, emergency rule enveloped its perpetrators in an illusion of public support.

After extending the life of Parliament by one year, the Gandhi government eventually decided to face the electorate in March 1977. In-

dira Gandhi was concerned that her government's legitimacy was eroding in the eyes of the civil, police, and military services on whom
emergency rule depended. She had been shielded—by loyalists anxious
not to displease her and by the absence of public criticism—from
knowledge of the grievances, political alienation, and resistance that
emergency rule, particularly forced vasectomies, had created. She
might not have risked an election had she been aware of how much her
standing and the standing of her son and political heir, Sanjay Gandhi,
had deteriorated. Janata, the party of the united opposition, swept to
power on the crest of an antiemergency, prodemocracy wave.[15] In answering one fundamental question—democracy or dictatorship—the
1977 election result demonstrated the parallel and reinforcing effects
of plebscitary politics and Congress deinstitutionalization.[16]

Party deinstitutionalization was not only the result of centralized
personal leadership and of splits and purges that deprived the party of
seasoned national and state party professionals. It was also the result of
substituting loyalists and favorites at state and constituency levels for
party officials and candidates with local knowledge and support. Paul
Brass, for example, in his restudy of Uttar Pradesh politics after a
twenty-year interval, found that party officials from Delhi no longer
had access after deinstitutionalization to the kind of local information or networks needed to select viable candidates or ministers. In
Mrs. Gandhi's time, the party leadership in Delhi had bypassed state
and district party workers and notabilities to break the hold of factional leaders on the selection of candidates and ministers. Rather than
conciliate those bypassed by brokering differences and balancing
slates, party officials from Delhi had relied on those who professed loyalty to the Nehru family but lacked local knowledge or support.[17]
When "waves" could win elections, deinstitutionalization seemed not
to matter.

Congress deinstitutionalization also took the form of declining
party identification. Survey data analyzed by Eldersveld and Ahmed
for the second and fifth years (1967 and 1971) of Indira Gandhi's
party leadership show a precipitous decline, from 70 to 47 percent,
among all party identifiers. The decline was even more marked among
strong Congress identifiers, from 94 to 55 percent, a decline greater
than that for any other party.[18] The decline of party identification in
India should not be confused with a comparable phenomenon in the
United States, because the causes are different: in the United States, the
rise of media politics, independent voting, and personalized campaign
financing; in India, party deinstitutionalization in the context of plebiscitary politics.

Deinstitutionalization in the form of a radical decline in party iden- tification would not matter for elections if "waves," electoral surges re- sponsive to a particular personality or historical mood, were adequate substitutes. But waves are unreliable, the result of unpredictable or un- controllable circumstances, such as historical conjunctures, plebisci- tary decisions, and personal popularity. Waves may be too ephemeral and superficial a form of national decision making to respond to the electoral needs of a complex and variegated country.

A decline in the proportion of elected independent candidates, such as the one that has occurred in India, would seem to cast doubt on our analysis, as this decline has generally been read as a sign of the institu- tionalization of party voting.[19] However, despite the deinstitutionaliza- tion of the Congress party, voters continue to prefer and reward party candidates, including Congress-I candidates. As table 7 shows, the proportion of independents elected has declined steadily, from 8.4 per- cent in the first parliamentary election (1952) to 1.0 percent in the eighth (1984) (column 3). Paradoxically, voters' preference for party over independent candidates has been paralleled by a rising tide of in- dependent candidacies: in 1952, only 28 percent of the candidates were independents; by 1984, 69 percent were.

The 1971 parliamentary election was the first overtly plebiscitary campaign and the first to be delinked. Its results indicated three major changes in the relationship between party and independent candidates:

TABLE 7
Independents in the Party System over Eight Parliamentary Elections

Year	(1) Contested Seats	(2) No. (and %) of Independent Candidates	(3) % of Seats Won by Independents	(4) % of Votes Polled by Independents
1952	489	521 (28)	8.4	15.8
1957	494	475 (31)	7.9	19.4
1962	494	497 (25)	5.5	12.3
1967	520	865 (37)	6.7	13.8
1971	518	1,134 (41)	2.7	8.4
1977	542	1,224 (50)	1.7	5.5
1980	525	2,821 (61)	1.5	6.4
1984	508	3,679 (69)	1.0	8.4

SOURCES: Robert L. Hardgrave, Jr., *India: Government and Politics in a Developing Na- tion,* 3d ed. (New York: Harcourt Brace Jovanovich, 1980) (figures for 1952–77); Gov- ernment of India, Election Commission, *Report on the Seventh General Elections, 1980,* vol. 2 (New Delhi, 1981); and Government of India, Press Information Bureau, *Lok Sabha Elections, 1984: A Computerised Analysis* (New Delhi, 1984).

an *increase* in the proportion of independent candidates running (from 37 percent in 1967 to 41 percent in 1971), a sharp *decline* in the proportion of seats won by independents (from 6.7 percent in 1968 to 2.7 percent in 1971), and a sharp *decline* in the proportion votes polled by independents (from 13.8 percent in 1967 to 8.4 percent in 1971). The inverse relationship between the proportion of independents standing and winning and the proportion of votes cast for independents suggests a marked discrepancy between the perceptions of the political class and those of the citizen voter. Higher proportions of the political class saw Congress deinstitutionalization as an opportunity to gain office without party affiliation and support, while voters, whose identification with particular parties had declined, still strongly preferred candidates with party commitments and ties.

From 1971, when the notability politics of vote banks was put on the defensive by plebiscitary politics, independent candidates increasingly stood as spoilers. Typically, they had filed to get a party ticket but believed that, even if they did not win themselves, they could prevent the party candidate from winning. The voters took a different view by electing increasingly fewer of the increasingly more numerous independent candidates (compare column 2 with column 3). Voters made it clear that the deinstitutionalization of the Congress-I and other parties did not extend to their expectations about parties as the preferred vehicle for electoral choice. Particular parties may have experienced deinstitutionalization and a decline in voter identification, but parties as the framework of choice in the electoral process did not.

Sanjay Gandhi and Personalized Centralization

Congress deinstitutionalization was accelerated and deepened during the meteoric rise of Sanjay Gandhi, the younger of Indira Gandhi's two sons. During the emergency regime (1975–77), whose imposition Sanjay is said to have advised, Mrs. Gandhi collaborated in her son's efforts to establish a leadership position in the party and the nation. Many informed observers viewed such efforts as an attempt by Mrs. Gandhi to position him as her successor.

In an effort to supply Sanjay with a power base, and in the name of rejuvenating the party, Mrs. Gandhi not only endorsed his "Five-Point Program" but also supported him in supplanting the party's regular organization by the Youth Congress committees in each of six thousand blocs (development administration units intermediately between villages, of which there are three hundred and fifty thousand, and districts of which there are 352) and in promoting Youth Congress–sponsored associations for physical training, sports, and so forth. When Youth Congress president Ambika Soni told congressmen assembled for the party's 1976 annual session that the parent organization had lost its vitality and asked it, for the sake of the party's future, to subordinate itself to the more vigorous Youth Congress, Mrs. Gandhi supported the suggestion.[20]

Prior to the 1977 parliamentary election, Sanjay's star had risen enough among Congressmen loyal to the Nehru dynasty to risk allowing him to pick 150 to 200 of 542 Congress candidates from among his followers. They, like himself, were young, inexperienced, and unknown to the world of mediated politics in the constituencies for which they were given "tickets" (nominations). If the elections had turned out according to Sanjay's and his mother's expectations, Sanjay Gandhi would have become the leader of the Congress parliamentary party's largest faction.[21] The "new blood" that Sanjay tried to introduce were often young men on the make, of dubious provenance, some with criminal records, whose loyalty was to Sanjay and the Nehru dynastic idea rather than to Congress as the party of secularism, socialism, and democracy. The prospect of Sanjay's ascendency in the party triggered a second Congress split on the eve of the 1977 election and contributed to its defeat. Jagjivan Ram, the seniormost minister in Mrs. Gandhi's cabinet, and other party stalwarts resigned to contest the election with the newly formed Janata party.[22]

Ram was the leader of India's untouchables who, along with poor Muslims, were the principal victims of the Sanjay-inspired forced vasectomy program, an important cause of the vote swing against Congress in the election that followed. Three years later, in the January 1980 parliamentary election that climaxed her "comeback" by returning Congress-I to power, Mrs. Gandhi was more cautious than she had been in 1977 about Sanjay's role in the nomination process. Even so, it has been estimated that about 100 of the 351 party candidates who won parliamentary seats were or became Sanjay loyalists. In May 1980, when controversial midterm elections were held in nine opposition-governed states, Congress-I victories returned an even larger proportion of Sanjay loyalists.

The political novices who responded to Sanjay's call to oppose the Janata government often had done so by taking to the streets or physically disrupting Janata-sponsored public events and courtrooms where Sanjay had been called to answer criminal charges. Some were lumpen capitalists, entrepreneurs on the make who expected Sanjay to shift government licenses, quotas, and credit in their direction. Once elected, many proceeded to disrupt the legislatures in which they served, showing little knowledge of parliamentary conventions or respect for the civility required for deliberation or regulated conflict.

The selection of candidates for state assemblies and Parliament is an important determinant of party control and of its ideological, leadership, and programmatic orientation. Candidate selection, the giving of "tickets," determines the relative strength of factions, which, in turn, provide a route to ministerial posts and the perquisites of office. It also affects the prospects of those who aspire to be chief ministers. In what respect did Sanjay's selection differ from previous Congress practice? Rameshray Roy has provided an account of candidate selection at the end of the Nehru era:

> Selection of party candidates offers the first series of skirmishes between conflicting interests which grope for political articulation and control. If the party fails to adjust and reduce the intensity of conflicting claims, it will go to the final battle bruised . . . the selection process is a crucial test of the party's flexibility and adaptability in coping with the pressures and counterpressures that impinge upon it from both within and without.[23]

Roy's characterization depicts candidate selection as a party process that articulates with social forces, sometimes accommodating or yielding to them, sometimes shaping or leading them. But candidate selection as practiced by Sanjay Gandhi ceased to be such a process. Instead, it became a top-down affair in which favorites, loyalists, and their networks won the prize.

Sanjay's ways of giving Congress tickets contrasted sharply with those practiced in his grandfather's time. In the Nehru era and, indeed, through the 1967 (fourth) general election, candidate selection involved a complex balancing of personal qualifications, ideological orientation, and factional alignment. Prospective candidates' credentials were scrutinized for integrity, commitment to party goals, adherence to party rules of personal conduct (e.g., abstention from alcohol, wearing khaddar), and participation in approved forms of service, the latter two criteria particularly being residues of Mohandas Gandhi's influence. Tacitly considered were pragmatic factors, such as previous success in holding a constituency and current prospects of winning in one, standing in large or powerful social groups, and influence over political resources and networks. The principal organizational vehicles for the selection process were state-level Congress committees. In the sixties, district and even *mandal* committees (a smaller party unit) actively participated. The committees recommended MLA or MP candidates to the Central Parliamentary Board, whose members in principle made the final choice, a choice that often validated committee recommendations.[24] The board, which included the party's most influential national leaders, deputed "observers" to Congress committees in several states, where they mediated conflicts in the light of the board's ideas and preferences. Insofar as these procedures were perceived as fair and motivated by concern for the collective good of the party, they minimized defections and independent candidacies by disgruntled aspirants for party tickets, moderating factionalism and reducing its political costs.

In the 1950s, with independence still a recent event, persons who had served or suffered in the nationalist movement were particularly favored. In the 1960s, local notabilities and leaders of caste communities able and willing to convert their social power into political resources for party use became more prominent. In either case the selecton process rewarded apprenticeship and time in rank, overt signs of party discipline and loyalty to the party. In Indira Gandhi's time, those who proclaimed and were seen to practice loyalty to the Nehru dynasty were more likely to get a ticket. Political influence, including the likelihood of getting a ticket, was increasingly determined not by apprenticeship, party service, and local standing but rather by location in manifold networks of personal loyalty and patronage, at whose apex stood Indira and Sanjay Gandhi.

In the selection process for the 1980 parliamentary and state assembly elections, the party's apex bodies, which had umpired a bottom-up process, had been displaced by Indira and Sanjay Gandhi or their agents, who presided over a top-down process.[25] In the May 1980 candidate selections, Sanjay or his lieutenants overrode, often literally in the last minutes before official nominations closed, slates of candidates selected over a two-month period by district and state-level Congress committees, in order to allocate tickets to adherents of factional leaders loyal to Sanjay or to supporters of Sanjay's choices for state chief minister.[26]

The successful outcome of the May 1980 state assembly elections (Congress won majorities in eight of nine states, and Sanjay loyalists became chief ministers in six of them) was Sanjay's finest and last hour.[27] A month later, the triumphant heir apparent was dead. The world would have to imagine what the future course of Indian history would have been had he lived to reap the fruits of his ascendency. Unlike his elder brother Rajiv, the airline pilot, Sanjay was an inexperienced flyer. He crashed while violating the regulations against performing acrobatics at low levels over New Delhi's presidential palace. He died as he had lived: daring, impetuous, contemptuous of the rules, a danger to himself and others. His death removed a controversial and divisive figure from the inner life of the Congress party. His mother, grandfather, and great-grandfather had led the Congress and the nation. As a Nehru, he could use the family name to attract bigger crowds in most states than favorite sons or other aspiring national leaders. Those who wanted to get things done, to cut the red tape spun by bureaucrats and judges concerned about correct procedure and the rule of law, and those who saw in his meteoric career a way to make their political fortunes quickly, flocked to his side. The effect of Sanjay's leadership on the Congress was to deinstitutionalize it further by increasing its patrominial features. By the time of his death, the party had become his and his mother's bailiwick.

The Demise of Intraparty Democracy

The Congress party of the 1980s was the precipitate of Indira Gandhi's struggle as leader of the parliamentary party to free herself from the organizational wing and the state party bosses who had controlled the party since the mid-1960s.

After Nehru's death in 1964, the influence of the organizational party's apex bodies—the Working Committee, often loosely referred to collectively as the "high command"—had been diminished by the power state leaders or "bosses" came to wield in national politics and policy. Some described the result as party federalism, others as balkanization. State chief ministers and committee presidents demonstrated their role as national power brokers in 1964 and 1966 by presiding over the selection of Lal Bahadur Shastri and then Indira Gandhi as successors to Jawaharlal Nehru.

As the party became more federal, it also lost some of its organizational autonomy. Its electoral prospects became increasingly dependent on local elites and the resources and networks they could deliver. The interest of aspiring, newly mobilized social groups in gaining access to power complemented the needs of competing Congress factional leaders in widening the bases of their support. These leaders tended to attract such support because they were more likely than opposition factional leaders to influence the allocation of government benefits. Even so, by 1967, when the party almost lost the fourth general election, growing democratization and heterogeneity seem to have outpaced the party's proverbial capacity to absorb anything; the great boa constrictor was suffering from indigestion.

Although the party became more "federal" in the 1960s, it retained the forms and much of the substance of the intraparty democracy it had known in the immediate postindependence era. Periodic (usually biannual) organizational elections to offices and bodies at the district, state, and national levels were held through 1969, but they became increasingly problematic. Intraparty elections generated intense and disruptive factional conflict. Struggles for power within the party exacerbated the problem of "bogus" memberships as contestants sought to win by buying or coercing rank-and-file support and as factionalized Congress authorities lost the capacity to intervene. At the same time, intraparty elections provided a means, however imperfect, for aspiring party leaders to validate and thus legitimize their claims to support within the party.

Mrs. Gandhi, the author of the 1971 and 1980 Indira waves that swept the party into power, became the party's principal political resource. In 1972, she suspended organizational elections. None have been held since. Rajiv Gandhi's pledge at the Congress-I centenary session in 1985 to purge the party of "power brokers" and restore intraparty democracy by holding elections was stymied by revolt and resistance from "Indira loyalists."

Mrs. Gandhi used her plebiscitary endorsement by the people to legitimize her authority in the party. The result sealed the fate of intraparty democracy. It also ended the party's reliance on the organizational wing to conduct and win elections. Campaign resources could be paid for from the ample funds that flowed into the party coffers from interested and intimidated sources. As the government party, the Congress could use the powers of incumbency to target benefits in a timely manner and to take advantage of the help that committed bureaucrats were willing to render. The party in the 1980s could afford to ignore the power base that aspiring state leaders might attempt to build because it was free to bypass the local elites on which state factional leaders rely. Prior to Mrs. Gandhi's assassination in October 1984, the balance of power between the center and the states and between the parliamentary and organizational wings of the party had been reversed: members of the party's apex bodies as well as chief ministers and state Congress committee presidents were nominated from Delhi, not chosen by state party bosses, state legislature parties, or state committees.

With the benefit of hindsight, the problematic consequences of plebiscitary politics and personal leadership seem clear, but they were not in the 1960s. Many of Mrs. Gandhi's measures seemed to address problems of party management. In the mid-sixties, the rule of party bosses (the syndicate) and the effects of rampant factionalism in the states struck many observers and active politicians as vicious, destructive, and corrupt. Stanley Kochanek's postscript to *The Congress Party of India* (1968) and Rameshray Roy's account of the selection of Congress candidates" (1966–67) characterize the effects of active participation by lower levels of the organization in tones that are often skeptical. They are cautionary tales that warn us against romanticizing the intraparty democracy of that time. The national organs of the party appeared to have lost their capacity to moderate, broker, and channel the conflicts let loose by a party trying to make decisions and govern itself from the bottom up. The costs of contentiousness seemed to overshadow the virtues and benefits of intraparty democracy. The party's inability to conduct internal elections that commanded confidence (bogus membership in some states rose to 50 percent) generated cynicism too. These developments explain why suspension of organizational elections in 1972 could be regarded as a way to avoid destructive conflict as well as a way for state and national party leaders to evade the test of the vote.

Nor is the victory of the party's parliamentary wing over its organizational wing novel or problematic for parliamentary systems. Parliamentary parties in India, as in other parliamentary democracies, are often the seat of ideological tendencies or factional groupings that differ from those entrenched in the organizational wing. In the British Labour party, for example, the organizational wing and the parliamentary wing have often been at loggerheads, with the organizational wing typically taking the more radical stance. In India, by contrast, the parliamentary party has usually been the more progressive. In any case, leaders of parliamentary parties in Britain and India frequently acted independently of the policy decisions and discipline of their parties' organizational wings, and sometimes have become the dominant party influence. In a classic instance, Hugh Gaitskell retained the leadership of Labour's parliamentary party in November 1960, even though he defied Aneurin Bevan's efforts to make him adhere to the party conference's call for unilateral disarmament. Similar clashes have occurred in India with comparable results. We have already referred to Nehru's successful use in 1951 of the threat of resignation as prime minister to remove the conservative, Hindu nationalist Purushotamdas Tandon from the office of Congress president. The move secured his ascendency thereafter in the organizational wing of the party. These examples provide a context for judging Indira Gandhi's claims, after 1967, that it was only by asserting the prerogatives of the parliamentary leader of the party that she could save it from the conservatism and depradations of its organizational wing.

Was deinstitutionalization a necessary or inevitable response to decline in organizational autonomy or to increased centralization? Was Indira Gandhi merely the victim of historical forces? Did she act more out of necessity than choice? Another prime minister—for example, Lal Bahadur Shastri—placed in the historical circumstances of the decade from 1965 to 1975, might also have acted to correct organizational imbalances and to protect the party leader's prerogatives. But Indira Gandhi went further than correcting imbalances and protecting prerogatives. Autonomous centers of power became suspect; loyalty was rechanneled from the party to its leader. These consequences go beyond efforts to deal with the tensions that are bound to arise between the organizational and parliamentary wings of a party within a federal system. Brokering and bargaining skills and ideological creativity might have restored balance between the party's state and national levels and between its organizational and parliamentary wings. Mrs. Gandhi preferred other means. The outcome suggests that human agency mattered, that the values and acts of a leader were a vital component in the deinstitutionalization of the Congress party.

Party deinstitutionalization in India and elsewhere was overdetermined. The trend toward the erosion of party and unmediated national politics was not unique to India in the 1960s and 1970s. It bore a family resemblance to the fate of parties in American politics of the same period. National campaigns in India and America began to have less to do with local machines and their dedicated party workers and more to do with raising and spending large sums of money on opinion experts, instant organization, the mobilization of volunteers, and intense media efforts to start bandwagons rolling. The literature on party in America is replete with accounts of a decline in party identification and local organization, an increase in the proportion of voters who said they were independents, and a shift from organizational to media politics. The older-style ward committeemen who knew the voters were displaced by advertising firms, professional political consultants, and media specialists. Some observers read these trends as the demise of party.[28]

Indian elections since 1971 have shared some of these features. All-India and state party officials who provided policy guidance and arbitrated local disputes and committed party workers with their knowledge of local candidates and issues have been increasingly superseded. Heavy expenditure (often based on "black" money) on instant state and local organizations composed of temporary workers hoping to benefit from the spoils of victory have taken their place, as have a rural nation's equivalent of pervasive mass media—fast-moving jeeps equipped with loudspeakers, posters, leaflets. Most recently, sound and video cassettes have been added to the campaign repertoire. Rajiv Gandhi's 1984 and 1985 campaigns relied heavily on the newer forms and methods.

These changes are not necessarily the same as deinstitutionalization. In the United States, they were being interpreted as a new version of institutionalized parties. In India, in so far as such new forms and methods reflect professonalism and better management rather than personalism, they constitute a new form of institutionalized party rather than deinstitutionalization in the context of plebiscitary politics. India may be no more ready than the United States to dispense with party as an organization that links society to politics.

Rajiv Gandhi's Construction of Congress

Interpreting Rajiv Gandhi's ideas and actions in relationship to party deinstitutionalization is more difficult than interpreting those of Indira and Sanjay Gandhi, but his efforts in the early years after his succession gave signs that he wished to reverse deinstitutionalization. Rajiv's presence in the party and in public life began only after Sanjay's death, and even then, until October 31, 1984, he remained more in the shadow of his mother than had been the case when Sanjay was the heir apparent. After Sanjay's death in June 1980, it took some time for Rajiv to overcome what was believed to be a genuine reluctance on his and, even more, his wife Sonia's part about exposing themselves to the publicity and vicissitudes of political life. The life of an heir apparent was not one Rajiv seemed eager to begin. Whether calculated or not, Rajiv's earlier shunning of politics and his initial reluctance to join it after Sanjay's death spoke to the Indian belief that those who do not desire power or pursue it are more fit to rule than those who do.

When he gave up his career as an airline pilot some months after Sanjay's death and publicly began to help his mother, there seemed little doubt that she hoped and intended that he would succeed her. His intended course of action became apparent in 1981, when in a by-election he stood for and won his brother's vacant seat in the Uttar Pradesh constituency of Amethi. His initial years in politics left many in doubt about his ability to don the family mantle of national leader. Youthful, handsome and personable, he was dubbed "Mr. Clean" by the media, in part to contrast his conduct with his brother's unsavory reputation in his youth and as a politician. But he seemed to lack Sanjay's fire, guts, and, more important, political appeal and skill. His role in four state assembly campaigns in 1982 and two in 1983 did little to help his own or Congress-I's political standing. His much-touted managerial role in the extraordinarily expensive preparations for Asian Games held in Delhi in the fall of 1982, when new roads, flyovers, stadia, and hotels sprouted throughout the city, raised questions about whether Rajiv's politics would feature bread and circuses for the affluent. Some thought in February 1983 that the disappointments in the Andhra Pradesh and Karnataka state assembly elections in January were the reason for Rajiv's becoming one of the Congress-I's five general secretaries rather than, as some had expected, Congress party president.

Rajiv's activities as a general secretary were devoted mostly to a centralized effort at professionalizing the party by training cadres and to efforts at consolidating Congress's position in various states. In 1984, he played an active part in toppling state governments (in Sikkim, Andhra Pradesh, and Kashmir) in ways that raised questions about propriety and even constitutionality. His leadership of the 1984 parliamentary election campaign was perceived as communal. By attacking Sikh demands and conduct as separatist or fissiparous, he seemed to be exploiting the Hindu backlash to his mother's assassination. If the result could be heralded as a great victory for national unity and renewal, it could also be interpreted as exacerbating rather than reconciling communal animosity between Hindus and Sikhs. Rajiv Gandhi's record as a Congress general secretary and in the immediate succession period left open the question of whether his leadership would address Congress deinstitutionalization or continue the centralized personal politics of fear and loyalty associated with his mother and younger brother. Had Rajiv been biding his time, a victim of his mother's leadership and the historical circumstances that it provoked? Or was he the youthful, forthright, confident leader of a new India who would rejuvenate the party?

The answer to the question is complicated by the fact that the same evidence can be read in a number of ways: what looked to some like party rejuvenation and national renewal looked to others like a continuation of deinstitutionalization. The reading depends to an extent on perceptions of motives and goals. Indira and Sanjay Gandhi's rhetoric and action can be read in the light of their intolerance for opposition, their drive for centralized patrimonial control, and the public perceptions that personal loyalty mattered most. Rajiv's actions can be read in the light of a belief that he is a more secure person than his mother was and that he has a greater tolerance for opposition if not disloyalty and more confidence that deliberation and bargaining among relatively autonomous and responsible men and institutions can yield legitimacy and workable solutions. He is more capable of trusting and of being trusted, more tolerant of opposition and autonomy, more appreciative of the need and virtues of decentralization. In an interview that he gave to *Sunday* in March 1983, he observed that "over the last . . . ten maybe 15 years, the party has stopped functioning as a party. . . . We have to restore the responsibilities of the lower office bearers, the block presidents and district presidents and really restore a democratic functioning within the party." Decentralization was the "only way" the party could be made to work as a viable organization. The first step for party revitalization, he held, was party elections.[29]

Rajiv Gandhi's attitudes toward party building can be viewed from the perspective of the new space he has come to occupy in Indian politics. More than his mother and grandfather, whose political rhetoric featured socialist formulations of Congress politics and solidarity with the poor and dispossessed, Rajiv speaks for the "France in India," the 100 to 150 million who live like the middle classes in advanced industrial societies. But a winning political strategy cannot easily be constructed without addressing the interests of the much larger pre- and nonindustrial sectors in household-based craft and agricultural production and the bazaar economy. Can the "France in India" and the Indian version of "yuppies" who are its vanguard build a party whose appeal and support exends to India's new agrarians, independent producers who have benefited from the land reforms and the green revolution, not to mention its marginal cultivators and agricultural laborers?[30]

In an era in which media politics is displacing organizational politics, Rajiv Gandhi is even better equipped than his mother was to fight elections. Both were concerned to extend television coverage prior to the eighth parliamentary elections in December 1984, so as to better exploit their incumbent government's monopoly over the electronic media. Rajiv has a natural and attractive television presence. In an era in which the cassette recorder is replacing the local notability and vote banks, Rajiv's technological bent gives him an advantage.

Rajiv Gandhi's record in the four deinstitutionalization arenas previously discussed yields a mixed picture. Under Indira and Sanjay Gandhi, deinstitutionalization was particularly evident with respect to (1) intraparty democracy (i.e., the fate of party elections and of organizational decision making); (2) the sources of a leader's support and legitimacy (i.e., the extent to which they were located within the party or outside, in plebiscitary endorsements by the electorate); (3) the criteria used to select party candidates; and (4) the autonomy of state party leaders and organizations and the integrity of state governments.

Rajiv Gandhi's view of intraparty democracy, the first aspect of de-institutionalization, can be understood through his strategy as a party general secretary and later as party president, through his approach to party elections, and through his handling of intraparty opposition to his leadership. As a general secretary of the Congress party in 1983 and 1984, Rajiv Gandhi was less oriented to rebuilding the party at the state and local levels or reintegrating it with society than to creating a centralized national party bureaucracy whose local cadres could gather information for Delhi and communicate decisions made there. The emphasis was on top-down rather than bottom-up communications and authority. Rajiv's managerial ideology and professional style took the form of training camps, public relations campaigns, and information gathering and analysis by his "computer boys," all instruments of central control and coordination. Under Rajiv's party stewardship, one heard or saw little of "service" and "mass contact," Congress's organizational ideologies in the days of Mohandas Gandhi and Jawaharlal Nehru, when a socially connected party meant to change people and society.

Rajiv Gandhi's actions as general secretary did not ignore ties to society, but he pursued them through national organizations sponsored by or allied to Congress, whose youthful leaders he often chose and trained. Youth-oriented organizations, such as the Women's Wing, the National Students Union of India, the Seva Dal (Service Organization), and the Development Center of the Indian Youth Congress were resuscitated and refurbished. Like the Youth Congress in Sanjay's day, these organizations have proved to be the testing and recruiting ground for leading positions in the party and government. Rajiv purged many of Sanjay's followers, particularly those with questionable reputations, but recognized those who redeemed themselves by good conduct, ability, and personal loyalty. Two Youth Congress leaders became Rajiv Gandhi's parliamentary secretaries, and 438 "coordinators" appointed by the Youth Congress's Development Center provided data for the selection and rejection of Congress candidates for the March 1985 state assembly elections.[31]

Party elections were mandated by the revised party constitution of 1974, and Rajiv Gandhi pressed hard for such elections in 1982 and 1983. There is little evidence however, to suggest that he then confronted the hitherto-intractable administrative problems and governance issues associated with holding party elections.[32]

In August 1986, Rajiv Gandhi again called for reinstituting party elections. His hope was that by forcing state leaders to validate and thus legitimate their claims to support, elections would revitalize a corrupt and unresponsive party. At the same time, he hoped to use an election to strengthen his own following in the party. In a speech to the party's centenary celebrations in December 1985, in Bombay, he told his followers: "We [Congressmen] obey no discipline, no rule, follow no principle of public morality, display no sense of social awareness, show no concern for the public weal. Corruption is not only tolerated but even regarded as the hallmark of leadership." Intraparty elections, he told an interviewer, would address these evils. They would "expose all the paper tigers. We have not had elections for 13 years; so we have people who have lost their base, who don't have any standing. That will all get exposed."[33]

Whether elections can revitalize the party and retsore institutionalized leadership remains an open question. From the mid-sixties, when the party lost its capacity to insure fair procedures, elections have exacerbated destructive factional struggles for power in the state parties. Some fear elections might reestablish the local and state power brokers who, when elections were held in the days before 1972, had enrolled and mobilized bogus as well as valid primary members to insure the dominance of their faction's influence in party affairs, including the outcomes of party elections. Rajiv Gandhi expected elections in August 1986 to return effective and responsible party officials responsive to his leadership, but revolt and resistance by displaced "Indira loyalists" blocked his efforts to hold them.

The suppression of party leaders who showed signs of ambition and independent political bases was a mark of Indira Gandhi's deinstitutionalizing style. Rajiv Gandhi's response to intraparty opposition was complicated by the fact that he had to establish initial control over the party. Congress party leaders have had to strike a balance between coopting challengers and disciplining potential rivals. Like his grandfather in conflict with Purushotamdas Tandon in the early 1950s and his mother in conflict with Morarji Desai in the 1960s, Rajiv Gandhi in 1986 confronted and attempted to suppress a challenge by factional leaders. His challengers were leaders who had been close to Mrs. Gandhi. They resented their displacement in the party by Rajiv Gandhi's new men. Rajiv's expulsion from the party of former finance minister Pranab Mukherjee and suspension of several other senior members of the party in May 1986 can be read as paralleling the efforts of his grandfather and mother to establish their control of the party rather than as part of the pattern of deinstitutionalization.[34]

Rajiv Gandhi has not significantly altered the plebiscitary character of Indian politics and party leadership, the second aspect of deinstitutionalization. Catapulted into party and national leadership by his mother's assassination, he had little choice in the 1984 parliamentary election but to conduct the most plebiscitary of India's several plebiscitary election campaigns. The election featured a single overarching concern, the actual and potential consequences of violent conflict between the Sikh minority and an amorphous but overwhelming and aroused Hindu majority. The choice before the voters was said to be between national unity and national disintegration. Rajiv was perceived by the voters, particularly "Hindu" voters, as the spokesman and the vehicle of national unity. He benefited from being a Nehru and from being his martyred mother's only surviving son without having to pay, as she would have had to, for the incumbent Congress government's sins of commission and omission. These sins were forgiven or forgotten in the electorate's concern to restore order and hope.

In the third deinstitutionalization arena, candidate selection, Rajiv Gandhi's conduct is harder to interpret than in the arenas of intraparty democracy and leadership legitimation by party or plebiscitary support. On the one hand, his approach to candidate selection in the 1984 parliamentary and the 1985 state assembly elections was reminiscent of Sanjay Gandhi's in the 1980 elections; both operations were centralized, personal, and transformatory. On the other hand, Rajiv Gandhi showed greater concern for objective criteria and procedure.

The selection of MP candidates for the Congress parliamentary party is somewhat akin to the selection of delegates for presidential nominating conventions in the United States: elected delegates to presidential nominating conventions and Congress MPs choose the leader of the party and, potentially, of the government (the presidential candidate and the prime minister). Aspiring Congress prime ministers must command the support of a majority in their party before they can demonstrate to the president of India that they command the confidence of a majority in the lower house of Parliament.

Prior to the 1984 parliamentary election, Rajiv Gandhi, like Sanjay Gandhi prior to the 1980 parliamentary election, was believed to have considered using the nomination process to establish his supporters' ascendency in the parliamentary party. In the event, both acted more cautiously. Uncertain about the prospects of a "wave" that would sweep Congress candidates to victory, they feared the constituency effects of subversion, defection, and splits by factional leaders and local power brokers whose nominees were not accommodated. Instead of "replacing" an anticipated 50 percent of 339 sitting MPs, Rajiv Gandhi—like his brother in 1980—replaced about 25 percent, a proportion comparable to the "normal" level of attrition in prior elections. Similar caution was evident in the selection of candidates for seats held by opposition parties. Even though the financial aspects of the election were highly centralized—the central party office even-handedly funded each MP to the tune of Rs. 300,000 and provided campaign material—the selection process largely respected established local preferences.[35]

In 1980 and even more so in 1984, Congress won decisive parliamentary victories. In subsequent midterm state assembly elections designed to capitalize on the party's national victories, both Sanjay and Rajiv Gandhi carried out the purge and personal faction building exercise they had contemplated but not attempted prior to the parliamentary elections. Having won an unprecedented 79 percent of the seats and 49 percent of the vote in the December poll, Rajiv Gandhi, prior to the March 1985 assembly elections, replaced 40 percent of Congress-I's sitting MLAs, sixty-three of whom were ministers.

The severity with which Congress incumbents were eliminated created consternation among party stalwarts and factional leaders. The party cushioned backlash effects in those states most affected by giving "tickets" to sons or younger relatives of purged incumbents,[36] a practice reminiscent of Mughal times, when sons of dissident or obstreperous rajas replaced their fathers in Mughal service and at court. Rajiv Gandhi's greater commitment to objective criteria and known procedures was expressed in a ten-point guideline that addressed deficiencies and constructed a new image: preference was to be given to youth, professionals, and women.[37] The taint of public and private corruption that plagued the party, a taint that became particularly troublesome for the party in 1984, after the Antulay and Adik scandals, was to be removed by choosing candidates with unblemished records. As "Mr. Clean" and the yuppie leader of India's postindependence generations, Rajiv Gandhi meant to construct a party in his own image. Service in party or party-sponsored organizations, commitment to secularism and propoor policies, and prospects of success were also to be considered. (The MLAs from assembly segments of MP constituencies that Congress-I failed to carry in 1984 were barred).

Given the confidence engendered by the party's unprecedented victory in December 1984, the thrust of the guidelines exercise was more to build an image of the party that matched that of its new leader than to produce precise demographic, ideological, characterological, or even electoral results. The guideline exercise stands in contrast to Sanjay Gandhi's efforts in 1980 to rebuild the party as a personal following based on loyalty to him and his mother.

Rajiv Gandhi's effort to reconstruct the party, while successful nationally in image and institutional terms, proved costly in electoral terms. Compared with the highly successful parliamentary and state assembly performances in January and June 1980, Congress-I did poorly in March 1985.[38] In December 1984, Congress-I had won 79 percent of the MP seats, but in March 1985 it could win only 57 percent. The voters treated the state assembly elections as opportunities to reward good and punish bad governments in the respective states rather than as an opportunity to heed Rajiv Gandhi's call to reaffirm in the state assembly elections the national mandate he and the Congress-I had received in December. Insofar as the March state assembly elections carried a message for the conduct of national politics, it was to suggest that voters favored the restraints and balance provided by a multiparty federal system. Electing as well as nominating a new breed of candidate was more successful rhetorically than it was electorally. The voters returned incumbent Congressmen in higher proportions than they did new nominees.[39]

Rajiv Gandhi lost his gamble that in March 1985 he and the Congress-I could ride the wave that had carried them to victory in December 1984. The wave had been largely determined by conjuncture, the voters' response in a national election to Indira Gandhi's assassination and to fear generated by the violence and threat of disintegration that followed. But the gamble did pay off to an extent. Despite Congress-I's poor showing in seats and votes, the result produced a new generation of state leaders and legislators attuned to Rajiv Gandhi's professional style and managerial outlook.

Chief minister selection, like the nomination of MPs and MLAs, was another arena for party deinstitutionalization under Indira and Sanjay Gandhi. Rajiv Gandhi's doctrine and practice after he became prime minister, if not before, seems to have stemmed, and perhaps reversed, deinstitutionalization in this arena too. Indira Gandhi began the practice of "nominating" chief ministers in 1972, after she led the split and demoralized party to comeback parliamentary and state assembly victories in 1971 and 1972. "Nomination" had been practiced under the British raj; it was the process used by the viceregal state to choose loyal and usually qualified Indians to fill responsible or representative positions at the center and in the provinces. After Indira Gandhi's great plebiscitary and personal victories, state assemblies with Congress-I majorities asked her, the party leader and prime minister whose family name and personal fame some believed had swept them into office, to designate persons to lead them. Loyalty took precedence over party support; chief ministers served at Mrs. Gandhi's, not the legislature's, pleasure and often her pleasure proved short-lived and arbitrary. Chief ministers in some states were treated as if they were disposable, a practice that in Andhra Pradesh succeeded in alienating and angering a state that had been a Congress-I bastion and had supported Indira Gandhi in her darkest hour. In just four and a half years, between February 1978 and September 1982, Indira Gandhi had nominated five chief ministers to govern Andhra Pradesh,[40] treatment that led to Congress-I's defeat in January 1983. In a midterm state assembly election, the state's voters repudiated Congress-I and regained their honor and dignity by handling an overwhelming victory to the Telugu Desam, led by Andhra screen hero, N. T. Rama Rao, who campaigned against the government's trampling upon "the self respect of the Telugu people."[41]

The "nomination" of chief ministers, which began in 1972, reached its apogee after the Sanjay Gandhi–managed state assembly elections in June 1980, when five Sanjay loyalists with little else to recommend them were among the eight Congress chief ministers installed. Deinstitutionalization with respect to the selection of chief ministers took the form of courtierly politics, the politics of favorites managed from Delhi, which crowded out, if it did not wholly displace, factional and organizational politics at the state level.

Rajiv Gandhi's handling of the selection of chief ministers was more respectful of sentiment in the state parties than under Indira and Sanjay Gandhi. It is more difficult to say whether the differences are the product of prudence under difficult circumstances or of a conscious and deliberate effort to strengthen the party as an institution. Rajiv Gandhi's role when he was a party general secretary in toppling opposition governments in three states (Andhra Pradesh, Kashmir, and Sikkim) did not indicate an understanding of or commitment to the constitutional proprieties of federalism. On the other hand, he showed respect for these proprieties when, as prime minister, he rejected the opportunity to end opposition rule in Karnataka when Ramakrishna Hegde, Karnataka's Janata chief minister, offered his resignation to the governor after Congress-I had decisively carried the state in the December 1984 parliamentary election.[42] The circumstances of the March 1985 assembly elections in ten states were not, in any case, conducive to a Sanjay-like strategy for the selection of chief ministers; instead of replicating its success in the December 1984 parliamentary elections, the Congress-I had done poorly.

Rajiv Gandhi approached the chief minister selection process cautiously. His conduct was reminiscent of the Nehru era when the national leaders who staffed the "high command" acted as umpires, but umpires with opinions and preferences among contending state factions. Congress-I was in a position to form governments in eight states and one union territory. In five states and in the union territory, Rajiv Gandhi's high command left incumbent chief ministers in office.

It replaced only three chief ministers—in Bihar, Madhya Pradesh, and Rajasthan—and their replacement by veteran Congressmen with strong support from their respective state organizational and legislative parties was taken by most informed observers as tactical rather than strategic. Whether out of prudence or principle, Rajiv Gandhi did not attempt, as Sanjay Gandhi had, to impose loyal nonentities on intimidated and supine state legislative parties.[43]

On the other hand, the resignation of Vasantrao Patil—the incumbent chief minister and party boss in Maharashtra—tells a different story about Rajiv Gandhi's relationship to Congress-I state parties and chief ministers. The assembly result in Maharashtra had been very close but this was true of most states. After much soul searching and controversy in Delhi and Bombay about replacing Vasantrao Patil with an alternative leader, Vasantrao had become one of the five second-term chief ministers. But on the occasion of Rajiv Gandhi's uncontested election as party president soon after, when Vasantrao was perceived to challenge Gandhi by calling attention to the party's rule against holding more than one office, his resignation was quickly arranged. This action was read inside and outside the party as a warning not to interpret Rajiv Gandhi's commitment to decentralization and respect for state party leaders and organizations as "weakness."[44] Similarly his replacement of Madhav Singh Solanki as Gujarat chief minister, in response to the mishandling of communal rioting, reflected more the prime minister's judgment than the alignment of power in the Gujarat state party.

Rajiv Gandhi began his career as an elected prime minister by treating opposition chief ministers with respect and consideration. Indeed, this was so true that Congress-I chief ministers were heard to complain publicly about the advantages of being an opposition chief minister. Gandhi was even quoted as saying, in August 1985, that should there be elections in the troubled Sikh-majority state of Punjab, the people of the state might be best served if they returned an Akali Dal government, which indeed they did. It is hard to imagine such a thought occurring to Indira or Sanjay Gandhi. The new look in center-state relations was given formal recognition in the summer of 1985 at a governor's conference. After being "advised" by Prime Minister Rajiv Gandhi, the governors repudiated the practice of aiding and abetting "toppling" operations after party splits or defections by giving untested new chief ministers many weeks to muster support before facing the assembly. Henceforth, they agreed, new chief ministers would have to face the assembly to test their majority within two or three days. The result of the governors' conference was hailed as "a conscious effort" by the prime minister to strengthen party responsibility and the federal system.[45]

The prime minister's respect for his fellow politicians extended to leaders of the national opposition parties as well as to state chief ministers. As prime minister, he took them into confidence and sought to achieve consensual solutions on hitherto-intractable issues such as the Punjab, Assam, and reservations for "backward classes."[46] This cost him support within Congress among members who believed party interest was not sufficiently protected in these settlements.

Rajiv Gandhi's record as a politician is a mixed one. As a party general secretary working in his mother's shadow and even as prime minister in the period between his mother's assassination and Congress-I's unprecedented electoral victory, his conduct could not easily be distinguished from the deinstitutionalizing actions of Indira and Sanjay Gandhi. After leading his party to victory and becoming prime minister in his own right, Rajiv Gandhi's conduct took a different turn. The party remained centralized and subject to its leader's managerial ideology and professional style, but it was less subject than it had been under Indira Gandhi to arbitrary tests of personal loyalty that dissolve institutional commitment and procedural regularity. Talk of party elections indicated a preference for congressmen once again to seek local party support rather than rely exclusively on the favor of Delhi. Similarly, the selection of chief ministers, while it sometimes reflected the prime minister's more than the state party's preferences, showed a lighter hand from Delhi. The party under Rajiv Gandhi was not the institutionalized party of the Mohandas Gandhi or Nehru eras, nor was it the party of state bosses in the syndicate era. But collegiality, institutional autonomy, and decentralization seemed to have a better chance than they had had in a decade.

5 Janata's Historic Failure: A Competitive Party System Aborts

Since independence some forty years ago, India's polity had been dominated at the center and in most states by a single party, the Indian National Congress. Although, in the aggregate, the opposition parties captured more than half the vote in every national election, disunity among them prevented them from displacing Congress as the national governing party. Yet, in 1967 and even more so in 1977 (when they united in the Janata party), the opposition parties very nearly converted the elections of those years into critical elections that would have reconstituted India's political universe.

In 1967, an expedient "Grand Alliance" of national and regional parties for the first time came close to winning a parliamentary majority when Congress's share of votes and seats plummeted from 45 to 40 and from 73 to 54 percent, respectively. As Stanley Kochanek noted, "The 1967 General Election marked the beginning of a transformation of the Indian political system from a dominant one-party system to a multi-party system." For Eric da Costa, then India's leading interpreter of public opinion and electoral behavior, the election "was the beginning of a break with the past," because most demographic and social groups were "rewriting their basic loyalties."[1] Congress fared even worse in the 1967 state assembly elections, when its proportion of seats fell from 60 to 49 percent and opposition parties formed governments initially in six and later in eight of the then sixteen large states.

In 1977, Janata's victories in both parliamentary and state assembly elections[2] seemed to mark the end of the dominant-party system. Congress's thirty-year hegemony over India's national government and federal system was broken when Janata governments took office in Delhi and in nine of seventeen large states. Janata's successes and Congress's reduced but still substantial strength had put two fairly equal national parties at the center of the party system. Together, with about 77 percent of seats and votes, they appeared to constitute a competitive two-party system.

In the event, Janata failed to capitalize on its historic opportunity. Janata's political performance after 1977, like the ineffective policy and governmental performance of opposition coalition governments in northern states between 1967 and 1972, diminished public confidence

159

in the national opposition parties' capacity to govern. Between 1977 and 1979, Janata failed to establish that it could be a meaningful alternative to Congress as a governing party at the center. The extent and nature of Janata's failure has to be appreciated to understand why Indira Gandhi, shamed and discredited in 1977, was able in 1980 to lead Congress to a triumphant return to power and an apparent restoration of the dominant-party system. Janata's failure to remain united or to establish its credibility as an alternative governing party also helps to account for the extraordinarily poor showing of the national opposition parties in the 1984 parliamentary election and the progressive bifurcation of the party system into national and regional arenas, which is discussed in the next chapter.

Janata's unsuccessful challenge to Congress party hegemony in a dominant-party system had consequences for the Indian state. Party alternation can encourage nonpartisan use of state institutions and personnel. The long-term interests of alternating governing parties provide each with good reasons to observe the golden rule of "do unto others as you would have done unto you." Yet, the temptation to use the powers of incumbency to settle old scores and to win the next election pulls governing parties in the opposite direction. The Congress-I's abuse of power under the emergency regime gave the Janata government a historic opportunity to "restore democracy" and nonpartisanship in the use of public authority and resources. It restored the first, but its standards with respect to the second were hard to distinguish from those of the Congress-I.

Janata's pursuit of decentralization in politics, administration, public finance, and economic activity arrested and countered in some instances the effects of Congress-I's centralizing proclivities. The states of the federal system were accorded the recognition they once had had in policy formulation and implementation. Since Congress-I's return to power in 1980, the one issue that all opposition parties—national and regional, Communist and non-Communist—can agree on is to continue the restoration of a viable and vigorous federal system that Janata began. In retrospect, although Janata could have done more to retore the nonpartisan and federal character of the liberal state in India, its legacy is not inconsiderable: the restoration of democracy and the resuscitation of federalism.

The Opposition Challenge and the Promise of a Critical Election

To comprehend the political universe of the 1980s, we need to know why the election of 1977 was not ultimately a critical election.[3] The theory of critical elections has been used to explain transformatory changes in American and British politics. Because they are constitutive, critical elections preempt and, in a sense, substitute for revolution or a change in regime by enacting or establishing a new ordering of the political universe. Major shifts in voter preferences, party vote shares, and/or turnout express interrelated changes in political ideology, in the formation or reorientation of interest groups, communities, or classes, and in the composition and level of voter participation. Such changes in turn affect the party system by adding, subtracting, or reorienting specific parties and reshaping the pattern of party competition.

Four indicators suggested that 1977 might be a critical election: (1) the change in party vote shares, in comparison with previous vote swings of less than 4 percent, went well beyond any previous election; Congress's share of the parliamentary vote dropped by 9 percent, from 43 to 34 percent (see chapter 4, fig. 3), (2) a second national party was formed and had contested and won the sixth parliamentary election, so that for the first time a party other than Congress governed the country; (3) for the first time, national parties competed effectively in almost all (sixteen of seventeen) large states; and (4) the one-party-dominant system was displaced by a competitive two-party-plus system.

All of these developments except the third were prefigured in the 1967 general elections, the last in which the parliamentary and the state assembly elections were linked (conducted simultaneously). With the significant exception of the Jan Sangh, the parties that came together in 1977 to form the Janata party formed an alliance in 1967 that very nearly won the parliamentary election and overshadowed Congress in the state assembly elections. Between the 1962 and 1967 elections, Congress's share of parliamentary and state assembly votes declined from 45 to 40 percent and from 44 to 40 percent, respectively (see chapter 4, fig. 3); its share of parliamentary and state assembly seats decreased from 73 to 55 percent and from 60 to 49 percent (see chapter 4, fig. 2), and its control of the then sixteen large state governments was reduced from fourteen to eight.

Congress's loss of support and the marked (5 percent) increase in turnout in 1967 (see fig. 4) reflected voter dissatisfaction with poor economic and military performance in the preceding two years.[4] The depressing economic consequences of two consecutive bad monsoons, disappointment with the outcome of the 1965 war with Pakistan, and the unsuccessful devaluation of June 1966 were blamed on the Congress government. But Congress losses and opposition gains also reflected the electoral consequences of a more cohesive opposition. The "Grand Alliance" succeeded modestly in concentrating the major-

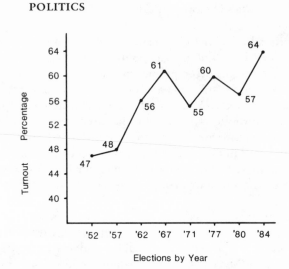

Fig. 4. **Voter turnout for parliamentary elections.** Data through 1980 are from Election Commission reports. The turnout figure for 1984 is from an analysis by the Press Trust of India and the Computer Maintenance Corporation, New Delhi (*India Abroad,* January 18, 1985).

ity non-Congress vote: except for the second and eighth parliamentary elections in 1957 and 1984, when it was 52 and 51 percent, respectively, the non-Congress vote has exceeded 55 percent in six of eight parliamentary elections. In the fourth election in 1967, the non-Congress electoral majority was for the first time sufficiently consolidated to threaten Congress's parliamentary majority.

In 1977, with the addition of the Jan Sangh, an expanded version of the 1967 "Grand Alliance" united to form a party, the Janata. The authoritarian emergency regime had generated widespread anti-Congress sentiment, particularly in the Hindi Heartland states. In the election, Janata won 43 percent of the vote and 55 percent of the seats; Congress-I, 34 and 28 percent. Again, as in 1967, voter turnout was high, at 60 percent, 5 percent above 1971 (fig. 4). For the first time, independent India was governed by a non-Congress government. In the state assembly elections that followed in June 1977 and February 1978, Janata gained control of nine of the seventeen large state governments.

These changes suggested that 1977 had been a critical election. But the course of events over the next three years, including the disintegration of Janata and dramatic reversal of Congress fortunes in the January 1980 midterm parliamentary poll, belied the possibility. So too did Congress-I's electoral victory in January 1984, when Rajiv Gandhi led the party to its most decisive parliamentary victory.

Why did the 1977 election fail to realize its promise of being a critical election? One reason is that the electoral outcome of 1977 was less a victory for the Janata party's leadership, ideology, or policies than it was a protest vote against Congress's emergency regime. The electorate had said no to the Indira and Sanjay Gandhi Congress, but at best it had said "perhaps" to that as-yet-unknown entity, the Janata party. To consolidate its incidental gains, it had to convert the antiemergency vote into positive commitments by varied sectors of the electorate. To meet this challenge, Janata had to resolve the numerous strains inherent in its heterogeneous origins.

Janata's Historic Opportunity: Alternating-Party Government

Our account of Janata's collapse is in part an exercise in counterfactual history, a study of what might have been and its consequences. Janata's victory in the March 1977 parliamentary election had the makings of a new departure. It created a historic alternative to India's Congress-dominated nationalist and postindependence history. The victory not only transformed the party system but also opened the way to new departures in ideology and policy.

The Janata government formulated and attempted to implement and institutionalize a neo-Gandhian alternative to the centralized state and industrially oriented growth strategy associated with Congress rule. It took seriously Mohandas Gandhi's concern to decentralize the state and the economy. It talked about and groped to find technologies that served rather than mastered their users and that enhanced workers' productivity rather than displaced them with machines. The federal system and local and village administrations were rejuvenated. State decentralization would make public authority more accessible to those it was meant to serve. Small-scale craft producers and independent cultivators were helped. Government invested in programs that created employment and generated income by relying on labor-intensive technology and the distribution of productive assets to those without them. For those without work or assets, it used food "surpluses" in "food for work" programs that improved the rural infrastructure. By putting labor output rather than capital output at the center of its development strategy, it believed itself more able to redistribute personal income as well as increase national income. The state and the economy were to be reshaped to a human scale capable of sustaining community and meeting basic needs.

The Janata government's neo-Gandhian ideology and programs were not "new" or even novel. It had taken a minor ideological and pro-grammatic theme from Congress's consensual score and made it a major one. Change under Janata rule, like change under Congress rule, proceeded at the margins of investment and programs. When Indira Gandhi's Congress-I government retuned to power in 1980, it con-tinued many of the Janata initiatives under different labels and some-what modified policy rhetoric, all the while protesting that whatever economic difficulties it faced were not of its own doing but had re-sulted instead from the Janata government's mismanagement of the economy. At the same time, 1980 marked something of a turning point in Congress thinking with respect to technology. The capital goods phase of economic development in the public sector had succeeded in making the industrial economy relatively self-reliant if not efficient and profitable; the problem was how to arrest and reverse deteriora-tion of the capital-output ratio in the public sector, not how to invest more in its "smokestack" industries.

In 1980, the new Congress-I government began to face questions with respect to the future course of political and economic develop-ment. Did the future lie with a viable federal system, in which the states and local government had the authority and resources to decide and to act independently, or with centralization, a Delhi-dominated political system in which the states and local units of government and administration were primarily agents of the center? Did the future course of economic development lie with agriculture-led, employment-oriented, labor-intensive, and decentralized "appropriate" technology or with industry-led, growth-oriented, capital-intensive, and central-ized advanced technology? The first course in each case would con-tinue Janata's neo-Gandhian policy orientation; the second would reassert Indira Gandhi's centralism and take India's economic develop-ment on a new course, different from that of both the Nehru and the Janata eras. From 1980, Indira and Sanjay Gandhi began vaguely to consider giving high technology a more central place in India's planned development, and Rajiv Gandhi considered the same thing in more in-formed and concrete ways after his entry to politics. Such an emphasis on high technology would run counter to Congress's Gandhian heri-tage and to Janata's neo-Gandhian revival.

The Janata era moved the question of "appropriate" technology and the related question of economic and governmental decentralization to a prominent place on the country's public agenda. Its ideas, policies, and performance had taken neo-Gandhianism from the drawing room to the drawing boards in ways that made it a viable option for the country.[5]

The Janata's ideological and policy alternatives provided a statement of national goals that challenged the tarnished and decaying image articulated with so much conviction and persuasiveness by Jawaharlal Nehru and P. C. Mahalanobis in the second and third five-year plans: heavy industry in the public sector was to occupy the commanding heights of the economy and lead the economy out of poverty into abundance and social justice. But it was not this statement that dominated the outcome. The Janata vision fell victim to the failure and inadequacies of its leaders, particularly the two men who succeeded in becoming prime ministers, Morarji Desai and Charan Singh. Their ambition and rivalry proved more powerful than the historic circumstances of Janata's founding and the cohesion of its neo-Gandhian commitment.

Why exactly was Janata unable to capitalize on its 1977 election victory? One reason was the conflicting historical legacies of the parties and fractions that constituted the fledgling party. The leaders of the erstwhile and subsequently reconstituted parties were old-time nationalists. Each had reason to believe that his claim to leadership of the new party was as good as or better than those of his rivals. The parties and fractions had become accustomed to functioning separately from each other and had adjusted their expectations to garnering the small rewards of permanent opposition. A second reason was that the party leadership avoided the mechanisms of party democracy—elections that would have required bargaining and compromise among components. They resorted instead to decision making by respected gerontocrats. Third, factional leaders resisted the integration of the functional organizations—such as youth and labor—that constituted the active base of the component parties. Finally, it is hard to understand the failures of the party without taking account of human nature. Ambition, pride, hypocrisy, and folly were spectacularly on display for three years. Ashis Nandy was probably right to conclude that with such a display of intraparty *matsyanyaya* (the state of nature in the Indian classical tradition, in which big fishes eat little ones and each other), it was not surprising that, in 1980, Indians were prepared to reelect the biggest shark of all to overawe the others.[6]

Jayaprakash Narayan (popularly known as "JP") stood at the center of Janata's short-lived effort to reconstruct a Gandhian alternative compatible with a modern economy and state. He had come to his neo-Gandhian socialism and anachist partyless democracy via his sojourn in the United States as a casual agricultural laborer, Communist, and sometime postgraduate student; the democratic socialism of the Nehru Congress's labor department; his 1947 personal commitment to Gandhi's leadership and world view; and his coleadership, with Vinoba Bhave, of the ultimately sterile Bhoodan (Land Gift) movement to create a more equal society by voluntaristic means.[7] By 1974, JP appeared to be a spent force in Indian public life. Nehru had hoped that someday he would become India's prime minister, but that hope had proved illusory.

His Gandhian values led JP to try to transform Indian society by moral rather than institutional means. He began his last and most effective effort to transform Indian society in 1974, following the Indira Gandhi government's ruthless suppression of a nationwide workers' strike and growing authoritarian measures and actions. He called for "total revolution." However hyperbolic its language, the JP movement aimed first to save and then to deepen democracy by transforming moral standards and practices. JP held no position in the Janata government, in part because he was sick and dying, in part because, like Mohandas Gandhi, he was reluctant to hold office. But he did help to "settle" who should lead the party by invoking the politically neutral doctrine of "seniority."

Two of the triumvirate who became Janata's leaders, Morarji Desai and Charan Singh, were professed Gandhians, the first a self-professed "ascetic" oriented to the urban business classes, the second India's most important agrarian and spokesman for independent cultivators. The third, Jagjivan Ram, had built his durable and extended career as a Congress minister on being of but not exclusively for the scheduled castes (as India's ex-untouchables are called in official parlance). His nonideological pragmatism, tactical skill, and identification with the disadvantaged poor enabled him to become a credible leader of Janata's Gandhian renaissance. The Jan Sangh fraction too declared itself to be deeply committed to JP's interpretation of Mohandas Gandhi's ideas and practice. The appreciable socialist component of the new party included many doctrinal orientations and organizational legacies. Not least among them was Gandhian socialism, an orientation that trade union socialists (e.g., George Fernandes) and "Sorelian" Lohia socialists (e.g., Raj Narain) if not Popular Front socialists (e.g., Madhu Limaye) could appreciate and support because of the redistributional thrust of its employment-oriented growth strategy and its concern for social justice.

Mohandas Gandhi's ideas, as mediated by JP's, Morarji Desai's, and Charan Singh's rendering of them, provided the ideological and policy framework of the new party, but its more proximate political orientations were shaped by the renewed opportunity to translate "anti-Congressism" into power and office. Unlike in their almost successful effort in 1967 and abortive effort in 1971, the "opposition" parties in 1977 united in one party rather than in a makeshift alliance. Their unity owed a great deal to Mrs. Gandhi's emergency regime. She revitalized anti-Congressism by putting her opponents in jail, tearing up the rule book for competitive politics, and terrorizing ordinary citizens. Party leaders of all stripes, RSS and Communist cadres, Muslim divines and Hindu pandits were arrested or went underground. Adversaries and strangers found they shared a common danger and common enemy. The immediate need to fight for survival and the possibility of at last being able to use the anti-Congress vote to gain power and office helped the five non-Communist parties to respond to JP's appeal to unite. So powerful was the magnet of anti-Congressism created by the Gandhi government's emergency excesses and destruction of freedom that the CPI broke its long-standing Congress alliance and the Communist party of India—Marxist (CPI-M) joined Janata in an anti-Congress electoral front.

The five parties that became fractions in Janata were a diverse lot, as often in conflict with each other as with Congress. The question for Indian history raised by the events of January through March 1977 was whether the parties joined in Janata could transcend their past rivalries to build a new future. To do so required a party that could use the circumstances of its origin to transcend deep-seated differences over ideology and interest and reconcile personal ambitions in order to govern effectively for five years. In the event, the outcome was tragicomic. The principal protagonists, Desai, Singh, and Ram—all of whom had lived beyond the biblical allotment of three score years and ten—proved incapable of distinguishing adherence to principle and the collective good from pursuit of the main chance. The party's electoral failure in 1980 resulted as much from self-destruction as from Mrs. Gandhi's remarkable comeback. In 1980 as in 1977, the voters rejected bad government.

Janata victories in the March and June 1977 parliamentary and state assembly elections transformed the party's objective circumstances. The common enemy was defeated and discredited. Janata was now a governing party responsible for the country's welfare and security. The election established the relative standing of the former parties that aspired to become a national party: Jan Sangh, led by A. B. Vajpayee, external affairs minister, had ninety seats (31 percent); Bharatiya Lok Dal (BLD) led by Charan Singh, home minister, had fifty-five (19 percent); the socialists, led by George Fernandes, industries minister, had fifty-one (17 percent); Congress for Democracy, led by Jagjivan Ram, defense minister, had twenty-eight (10 percent); and dissident Congressmen (who had broken with Mrs. Gandhi prior to or during the emergency), led by Chandra Shekhar, party president, and Mohan Dharia, commerce minister, had six (2 percent).

Contradictions abounded. Was the party to be confessional like its largest party fraction, the Jan Sangh, and promote the values and interests of the Hindu community? Or secular like its socialist fraction and pursue class politics? Was the new party to follow the socialists' redistributionist and conflictual strategy, support Congress-O's Gandhian commitment to consensual values and practice, or accept the Jan Sangh's Hindu justifications of cosmic inequality and dharmic social harmony? Was the party to rely on the paternalism and noblesse oblige of the upper (twice-born) castes who led the Congress-O and Jan Sangh fractions to mobilize mass support vertically, or should it rely on horizontal mobilization of cultivator castes, the scheduled castes (untouchables), and wage workers? Should the party speak for the agrarian interests of rural producers or the industrial and trading interests of urban capitalists and labor aristocrats, lines of cleavage that tended to divide the BLD and the Congress for Democracy from the Congress-O and Jan Sangh and to separate Lohia and Gandhian socialists from trade union socialists? Within India's massive agricultural sector, should the party help the poor but less productive tenants and laborers by land redistribution, tenancy reform, and higher wages? Or should it help relatively prosperous but more productive bullock capitalists and large landholders by high farm prices and low input costs?

The contradictions that these cleavages created for the Janata were not its exclusive concern; in some measure they affect all parties, and national centrist parties most of all. Congress used to be called a boa constrictor because of its capacity to swallow anything. The strain on the Janata was severe because it had become overnight not only a national centrist party but also India's majority and governing party. A necessary condition for remaining the majority national centrist party was the capacity to create political formulas and bargains that reconciled or papered over its cleavages. Congress's long tenure as the majority national centrist party was in part a measure of its capacity to handle such contradictions. Compared with Congress, with its nationalist heritage and organizational legacy, Janata was disadvantaged by the negative and fragmented circumstances of its origin.

The party began its effort to consolidate diverse factions with two main settlements, one in March 1977 on the question of national leadership and one in June on control of state governments. Both were resolved informally, behind the scenes, and "consensually," in the hope of avoiding conflicts among the party's diverse fractions and contending personalities and of strengthening the party's capacity to deal with difficult decisions.[8]

To avoid an immediate and potentially destructive test of strength among the three aspirants for prime minister—Morarji Desai, Charan Singh, and Jagjivan Ram—the party turned to two old Gandhians, Jayaprakash Narayan and Acharya Kripalani, for a decision. Their choice of Desai as prime minister (and of his younger and more leftist Congress dissident colleague Chandra Shekhar as party president) was legitimated by JP's charismatic laying on of hands and by Desai's seniority. Personal enmity and the conflicting status and economic interests of their support bases had kept Charan Singh and Ram from supporting each other's ambition to be prime minister. In the face of the Jan Sangh fraction's preference for Ram, Charan Singh wrote to JP in support of Desai, whom he regarded as the lesser evil. These considerations and developments sustained the plausibility of JP's choice. It was a gerontocratic decision in favor of a candidate twice rejected by the Congress parliamentary party. From the beginning, the choice of Desai contradicted the fresh possibilities inherent in Janata doctrine and its potential to be a new national alternative.[9]

The choice was not achieved by the usual democratic or formal processes within the Janata parliamentary party that tested the support of the contending candidates. While evading such procedures saved the party from starting its rule with a highly acrimonious controversy, it merely postponed the moment of reckoning.[10] This evasion came to haunt the party when, in response to Charan Singh's efforts to discredit and displace Desai, Charan Singh and Chandra Shekhar endeavored to establish and broaden their support in the parliamentary, state assembly, and organizational wings of the party.

The second settlement, after the June 1977 state assembly elections, resulted from a tacit bargain between the party's two largest fractions, the Jan Sangh and the BLD, who divided the seven state governments and Delhi (a union territory) in which the party had run.[11] As a result, Madhya Pradesh, Rajasthan, Himachal Pradesh, and Delhi were led by erstwhile Jan Sangh chief ministers or their equivalent and India's two largest states, Uttar Pradesh and Bihar, as well as Haryana and Orissa, were led by former BLD chief ministers.

The socialist (including the Congress-O's former socialist Asoka Mehta) and BLD fractions had the major voice in setting the party's policy agenda. It was expressed in the party's manifesto ("Both Bread and Liberty: A Gandhian Alternative") and in the economic and industrial policy statements issued after Janata had taken charge of the government. The settlement among Janata's components also included distribution of ministerial posts at the center and in the states. At the state and national levels, the initial settlements would have boded well if all the actors involved had made them in good faith and were prepared to abide by them.

At the level of party organization, however, they boded less well. While the constituent parties dissolved themselves, the youth and student organizations attached to component organizations did not.[12] The most developed cadre organization associated with any of the predecessor parties, the RSS,[13] remained independent, a source of contention and ultimately the ostensible cause of the three splits that disintegrated Janata. In the state assembly elections that followed soon after the March 1977 parliamentary election, partisan fractions and individuals raised their own funds in disregard of efforts to create a campaign chest.[14] Most fundamentally, the party was not able, by the time of the 1980 election, to conduct an organizational election that might have obliged candidates to bargain for cross-fractional support. Fear of Jan Sangh/RSS ascendancy inhibited other fractions from agreeing to a contest and led ultimately to the splits of July 1979 and February 1980 and the Jan Sangh "expulsion" in April 1980.[15]

Although the former Jan Sangh, with 30 percent of Janata's parliamentary seats, was the largest fraction in the new party, it had no aspirant for prime minister, held fewer major ministerial portfolios than Congress-O, the BLD, or the socialists, controlled fewer and smaller state governments than the BLD, was weakly represented at the top echelons of the party's organizational wing, and had less influence on party policy than any other fraction.[16] The gradual effort by the Jan Sangh, often in response to Charan Singh's provocations, to correct this underrepresentation by strengthening its position in Janata-governed states and supporting Morarji Desai more than Charan Singh was a significant element in upsetting the fragile settlements of 1977.

It is difficult to say whether the erstwhile Jan Sangh's initial self restraint was a matter of conviction, prudence, or tactics—that is, whether most of its leaders and activists, quite apart from its supporters, were a new breed transformed into committed supporters of Janata's leadership and policy by the suffering and fraternity of the emergency and the imperatives of governmental responsibility, whether they were trimmers prepared to adjust their ideological goals and political aspirations for the sake of party harmony, or whether behind their Janata masks lay the faces of RSS communalists who sought to impose at the propitious moment a Hindu nation and a Hindu state on a vulnerable and unsuspecting India. That each view is partially true helps explain the complex role the Jan Sangh fraction played in holding the Janata together during Charan Singh and Desai's struggle over the prime ministership and in occasioning its ultimate disintegration.

Beginning with a relatively peaceful settlement with the BLD, which brought out the Jan Sangh's capacity for secular alliances, the Jan Sangh fraction migrated gradually toward Desai, whose sympathy and support for "Hindu" cultural policies it found attractive.[17] It ended up, as it had begun in early 1977, in an alliance with Jagjivan Ram in his unsuccessful 1979 and 1980 parliamentary and electoral bids to become India's first untouchable prime minister.

Within a few months of the momentous March 1977 parliamentary election, political events began to undermine the conditions on which Janata's precarious equilibrium depended. Mrs. Gandhi surprised the Janata and political observers when Congress won an early by-election in Azamgarh, Uttar Pradesh, and she was able to make political capital out of atrocities committed against Harijans in Belchhi, Bihar. Uttar Pradesh and Bihar are India's most populous states. Their large scheduled caste and Muslim minorities had turned on Congress in March 1977, and with their help Janata had swept all 139 parliamentary seats in the two states with unprecedented and often overwhelming majorities. Mrs. Gandhi had launched an energetic offensive to recapture the minorities. Azamgarh and Belchhi signalled that Indira Gandhi's abuses of power had not, as Richard Nixon's had under comparable circumstances in the United States, so discredited her that she was no longer a force to be reckoned with.

In June, when voters in nine states went to the polls to elect state assemblies, Janata won reassuring majorities in seven. But turnout was radically reduced since March (down to 40 from 60 percent), as was Janata's proportion of the vote (down 10 to 20 percent in most states)[18] providing clear signals that the electorate in March had voted against the emergency more than it had for Janata and that Janata had to work hard to hold its gains.

In January 1978, the Congress split again over the question of Mrs. Gandhi's continued leadership, as the newly formed Congress-I (for Indira) made a strong showing in a second round of state assembly elections in February 1978. It won large absolute majorities of seats in Andhra Pradesh and Karnataka and finished a close third to Janata and Congress in Maharashtra. The results confirmed what had been feared by Janata leaders; that Mrs. Gandhi had managed to overcome the pariah status engendered by her authoritarian regime and was again a contender for national leadership. These fears were confirmed when on November 8, 1978, she turned back a massive Janata effort to prevent her return to Parliament in a by-election by winning the Chikmagalur (Karnataka) seat. Such storm warnings should have alerted Janata that a positive political performance had to accompany its restoration of democracy and imaginative policy initiatives if it meant to compete with the Gandhi-led Congress-I, but the warnings were ignored.

Policy Performance versus Political Performances: Politics Fails

Janata's historic failure had more to do with its political than with its policy performance. The paradox of the Janata years was that its commendable policy performance in terms of ideas, programs, and economic indicators was obscured and then negated by the demeaning political dramas enacted by its leaders. Like political leaders elsewhere, India's leaders are "on stage" before the voting public, not just for television screen and the front page but also for the local gossip networks. Their roles—as prime minister, as party or opposition leader—are defined institutionally and culturally, but their words and actions, their style and idiom, are of their own making. Within limits, political leaders define themselves through political drama. Roles are provided but scripts and plots are not. Unlike theater audiences, political audiences do not suspend disbelief; politics, not the play, is the thing. In democracies such as India, the resolutions and rewards of political drama are voters' judgments of political performances. As measured by economic indicators, the Janata government's policy performance, at least until Charan Singh's budget of March 1979, compared favorably with the best the country had known since independence. Janata's restoration of democracy and constitutional government was approved if not politically rewarded. It was its leaders' political performance that proved the party's undoing.

The demeaning political dramas began in March 1978, just a year after Janata assumed office, when Charan Singh launched his efforts to displace Prime Minister Morarji Desai. Soon they encompassed Jagjivan Ram and ended in early 1980 with all three leaders discredited and the party in shambles. The political drama's scenes, sometimes played separately, sometimes together, featured personal, political, and institutional themes. Family members, particularly sons, were used to discredit or embarrass rivals; the March and June political settlements about national leadership and control of state governments, were violated, first surreptitiously, then openly, to promote fractional interests; significant conventions that facilitate parliamentary government, such as collective cabinet responsibility, were also violated; and the search for a suitable institutional and legal response to the emergency regime was used as the occasion to gain personal and partisan advantage. In the end, Charan Singh, the advocate of strong measures to punish Mrs. Gandhi, sought her support to become prime minister, only to be outwitted and deposed by her.

There was a fatally predetermined quality about the heedlessness with which two stubborn old men, Charan Singh and Morarji Desai, sought to ruin each other even as their common enemy was gaining support. In the process of degrading each other, Janata's leaders degraded themselves; Charan Singh's not implausible attacks on Prime Minister Desai via the conduct of Desai's 55-year-old businessman son, Kanti, discredited Charan Singh because he launched them from inside the cabinet and with the obvious goal of capturing his rival's seat. Desai's moralistic strictures on Charan Singh's violations of cabinet responsibility and the inappropriate conduct of Charan Singh's relatives squared ill with his tolerance of Kanti Desai's behavior and Janata's condemnation of Sanjay Gandhi's improprieties.[19]

The political dramas were often full of pathos and sometimes absurd: Charan Singh displayed self-pity and tears during an interview soon after he was removed from the cabinet; Raj Narain—sometime minister, Charan Singh's stalking horse, buffoon, and inadvertent practitioner of guerrilla theater—invented a purity ritual for the party by pouring holy Ganges water on himself near Mohandas Gandhi's *samedhi* (death memorial) and rubbing rose attar on unwilling diplomats summoned to benefit from his views; Desai practiced "urine therapy" (the drinking of one's own urine) while preaching prohibition, to the delight of the cartoon industry; Charan Singh and Mrs. Gandhi exchanged bouquets and birthday greetings while contemplating each other's destruction.

Charan Singh's first open challenge to Desai's leadership took the form of a letter to him, soon leaked to the press, reviving charges that Kanti Desai, the prime minister's son and personal aid, had used his father's position improperly or illegally to further his own interests, a charge made more damaging by Janata's better-founded and more serious criticisms of Sanjay Gandhi's improprieties.[20] A new low in the art of attacking rival leaders via their sons and relatives was reached in August 1978, when an official of the Kisan Sammelan, a farmers' organization closely identified with Singh, was implicated in airing a sensational sex scandal involving Jagjivan Ram's son, Suresh. The son told the press that he and a woman companion had been kidnapped by supporters of Charan Singh and forced to pose for photographs in "compromising postures." The salacious pictures were circulated among eager members of Parliament by Raj Narain, then Charan Singh's close associate and cabinet colleague, and they later appeared in national magazines. The presumed object of this unsavory exercise was to make sure that if Charan Singh succeeded in ousting Desai, Ram would be a discredited alternative.

Soon after the second round of state assembly elections in February 1978, Raj Narain attacked Chandra Shekhar, the Janata party president, for his management of party affairs, particularly the selection of candidates in Andhra Pradesh and Karnataka, where Janata had fared badly.[21] On April 21, Chandra Shekhar offered to resign, but Desai refused the offer. Instead, he took a hard line toward Charan Singh, for whom Raj Narain spoke, warning that persons, "howsoever big and important," who criticized their colleagues in public would expose themselves to disciplinary action,[22] including expulsion from cabinet and party. Charan Singh, who suffered a heart attack three days after Desai's reprimand and warning, responded by resigning on April from the party's national executive and parliamentary board.

The conflict at the top, which challenged the March 1977 settlement about national government and party leadership, had a parallel state dimension. From his sickbed, Charan Singh alleged that "a section of the leadership" was encouraging efforts to replace the erstwhile BLD chief ministers of Haryana and Uttar Pradesh. These efforts reflected Desai's attempt to secure his uncontested selection as party leader by widening his support in the parliamentary and state assembly parties.[23]

Desai's efforts to undermine the BLD fraction's hold on state governments coincided with and complemented the efforts of the Jan Sangh to make its influence within the party as great as its share of seats. The Jan Sangh's offensive in turn jeopardized its national and state relationships with Charan Singh's BLD. Desai's Hindu cultural revivalism, noblesse oblige high-caste attitudes, and economic conservatism provided the political and ideological conditions for an evolving rapport between Desai and like-minded members of the Jan Sangh fraction.[24] Desai's cultural policies strongly appealed to the Jan Sangh fraction but alarmed the socialists, who, in response, created the secularism issue on which the power struggle in the party would be fought.

The incipient battle for control of state governments fueled the growing crisis at the top, but the proximate and principled cause of the first rupture between Desai and Charan Singh was the government's policy response to Mrs. Gandhi's abuse of power and illegal acts during the emergency and earlier. The country was confronted with a situation not unlike that in the United States in 1974, when the House of Representatives's impeachment proceedings against President Nixon led to his resignation. Was he to be prosecuted or pardoned? The Shah Commission had produced incriminating evidence comparable to that available against Richard Nixon;[25] were Mrs. Gandhi and her associates to be prosecuted? If so, when and how?[26]

Desai was forgiving, Charan Singh vindictive.[27] Charan Singh interpreted Desai's professed concern for correct procedure as a cover for inaction. Desai believed that a home minister (Charan Singh) who accuses the government of which he is a senior member with failure to act on matters under his own charge had ulterior motives.[28] On June 28, Charan Singh, circumventing the usual rule of cabinet unity and patently challenging the prime minister, called for Mrs. Gandhi's immediate arrest.[29] The next day the cabinet, responding to the challenge to its collective responsibility, endorsed Desai's call for Charan Singh—and Raj Narain—to resign immediately. On June 30, they were gone.

During the second half of 1978, the Desai government, under pressure from new circumstances, responded to the absent Singh's charge of impotence by supporting action against Mrs. Gandhi. In November, Mrs. Gandhi returned to Parliament by decisively winning the by-election at Chikmagalur (Karnataka). No sooner had she taken her seat (on November 20) and been elected chairman of the Congress-I parliamentary party than the privileges committee of the Lok Sabha tabled a report holding Mrs. Gandhi and several assistants guilty of breach of privilege and contempt of the House.[30] After a heated debate in which Mrs. Gandhi accused the Janata government of converting the house into a "medieval star chamber," Desai's motion calling for Mrs. Gandhi's expulsion and imprisonment until the prorogation of the session six days hence carried 279 to 138. The farce of imprisonment that followed confirmed Charan Singh's fear that the public perceived the Janata government as "impotent."[31]

Leading members of the Janata government quickly began to create suitable conditions for Charan Singh's return to the cabinet.[32] The conciliatory efforts bore fruit. On January 24, 1979, Charan Singh rejoined the Janata cabinet as home minister, but without his sometime alter ego, Raj Narain, and accepted equal status as deputy prime minister with his archrival, Jagjivan Ram. Though the Jan Sangh fraction had backed Desai's ouster of Charan Singh in July 1978, it now played the role of mediator in the reconciliation of the two antagonists. But this was the last time it was able to keep the party in equilibrium. Soon its increasing factional and ideological identification with Desai and the struggle at the state level, where the Jan Sangh engineered or sup-

ported the removal of three BLD chief ministers, broke its links to the
Charan Singh-led BLD.[33] By July 1979, when the Janata party and government finally broke up Singh belatedly noticed the Jan Sangh fraction's imputed communal stance. Communalism, in the form of "dual
membership" in the Janata and the RSS, was the issue he used to justify splitting the party.[34]

Reunification preceded the end by six months. The denouement was
expected by no one, even those in and outside the party who worked
for it. From January, when Charan Singh rejoined the government, to
July, when he finally split the party, he was isolated and in a weak bargaining position. The monsoon (July 1) session of Parliament began
peacefully. No one imagined that the debate on Congress-U leader
Y. B. Chavan's no-confidence motion would be anything but pro forma.
Only a lonely Raj Narain, abandoned even by Charan Singh after the
party national executive expelled him on June 12, 1979, for yet another irrepressible outburst against the party leaders, was still chip-
ping away at the unity of the party from the outside. He appealed to
a few old colleagues to keep him company in support of Chavan's
motion. How this small trickle suddenly became a stream and then a
flood, and how Parliament's mood suddenly shifted from resigned acceptance of Desai's Janata government to rebellion and rejection, is not
quite clear, but Charan Singh's conversations with Indira Gandhi via
Sanjay Gandhi and Raj Narain no doubt had some bearing on the fall
of the Desai government.[35] On July 15, 1979, Morarji Desai, having
lost his parliamentary majority, submitted his resignation.

The Janata party eventually split into three parts: the "original"
Janata, under president Chandra Shekhar; the Lok Dal (later the Dalit
Mazdoor Kisan party [DMKP]), under Charan Singh; and the Bhara-
tiya Janata party (BJP), encompassing the former Jan Sangh.[36] Jagjivan
Ram came to rest in the Congress-U, formed after the January 1978
Congress split.[37] The components roughly, though not precisely, ap-
proximated the elements that had joined to form the Janata in 1977.
But this outcome was by no means certain at the time Desai's govern-
ment fell. There was a real possibility that, under other leadership,
Janata could have survived as the largest party even without Singh. But
the same single-minded self-destructiveness that had dogged the party
since 1978 pursued it to the end.

The probability that Jagjivan Ram, less tarnished than the others,
could have formed a government and that an election could have been
avoided, was blocked by Morarji Desai, who doggedly refused to resign leadership of the parliamentary party even when it became apparent that he could not form a government. To Charan Singh it appeared

that at long last he would become the prime minister of India. But he was mistaken. Mrs. Gandhi snatched the prize from him. She raised his hopes initially by voting for Chavan's no-confidence motion and subsequently by offering support to the government he and Chavan were allowed to form on July 22, on the condition they could muster a vote of confidence within the month.[38] But the promise dissolved when she insisted that Charan Singh agree to protect her against present or past threats to her political career.[39] Without Congress-I's seventy-one votes on August 20, the appointed day for Charan Singh to prove his parliamentary majority, he failed.

Having failed, Charan Singh again played into Mrs. Gandhi's hands by precipitating the election. Desai had finally allowed Ram to be elected leader of the truncated Janata, still the largest parliamentary party. Ram was in a position to try to form a government, and many observers believe he might have succeeded. But rather than open the way for his old rival to form a government by telling the president that he himself could not do so, Charan Singh recommended dissolution and a midterm election. To Janata's consternation, the president acted in accord with the recommendation of a failed prime minister designate.

Mrs. Gandhi's strategy rested on the belief that an election was better for her than coalition politics in a Parliament where her party ranked fourth.[40] Her estimate was confirmed. The divided opposition parties lost to the Congress-I by one hundred seats, seats they would have won had their parties' votes been counted together rather than separately.

What had begun as a bold experiment in party building, political realignment, and national reconstruction along Gandhian lines ended in shambles. A potential critical election that promised to transform the party system was dissipated in a miasma of debilitating efforts at personal aggrandizement. Janata's term in office betrayed its founding and destroyed its promise as a great national party. Janata did not consolidate or expand its support because its leaders failed to inspire confidence in their integrity, ability, and vision. It performed well enough as government; its policies were imaginative and reasonably effective for over two years. But it failed to become a party organizationally or among the voters. It was not Janata's policy that failed. The voters rejected its political performance. Ironically, the party that took Mohandas Gandhi as an exemplary figure had not learned what he had tried to teach the Indian nation, that swaraj (self-rule) for India required swaraj for its leaders and citizens.

6 Decline of Congress Dominance and the Emergence of a Bifurcated Party System

The events of late 1984 confirm the importance of historical conjunctures in the determination of political events and behavior. Indira Gandhi was assassinated on October 31, 1984. She had been prime minister for fifteen years. Her father, Jawaharlal Nehru, Mohandas Gandhi's principal associate in India's independence struggle, had been prime minister for seventeen years. The day after Indira Gandhi's death, November 1, 1984, Rajiv Gandhi, Indira's eldest son, was sworn in as her successor. Two months later, at the end of December, he led the Congress-I party to its most decisive electoral victory since 1952.

In mid-1984, many political analysts had held that an Indira Gandhi–led Congress-I would lose ground in the upcoming eighth parliamentary election. A narrow majority comparable to the 1967 result was possible, but a plurality rather than a majority of seats, followed by a coalition government, seemed more likely to many observers. These predictions took account of Congress-I's responsibility for the violence, alienation, and threat to national unity of the Punjab and Assam crises; the shady manner in which opposition state governments were "toppled" in Andhra Pradesh, Kashmir, and Sikkim; the perception of pervasive corruption and abuses of power that the recent Antulay and Adik scandals in Maharashtra had highlighted; and the insecurity engendered by a rising tide of societal and state violence. In domestic if not in international politics, Indira Gandhi was increasingly perceived as taking actions that were motivated by personal and party advantage rather than by what was good for the country.

More important than these proximate causes of informed observers' expectations were long-term secular trends that indicated both erosion and volatility in Congress-I's regional and minority support base. In this chapter, we analyze these electoral trends and their consequences for Congress support and the party system, with respect to six regions (Hindi Heartland, West, South, East, North and Northeast and Islands) and three minorities (Muslims, untouchables, and tribals). As early as 1962, Congress began to lose its base in the Hindi Heartland, whose 42 percent of Parliament's seats makes it the largest of the five

178

regions.[1] This trend was paralleled by erosion of Congress's support among minorities. Though both trends were strikingly reversed by the postassassination election in 1984, they suggest a decay of the conditions that originally produced Congress dominance. The erosion of Congress's regional and minority support was paralleled by increasing volatility and unpredictability in regional party voting. Volatility affected Congress's regional support base and, from 1967, contributed to an emergent bifurcation between support for national and regional parties in parliamentary as well as state assembly elections.

The outcome of the 1984 election may indicate the beginnings of a new party system, in which Congress is dominant at the center but not in most states. But the conjuncturally determined "waves" that contributed to the volatility of national election outcomes since at least 1971, and that were very much in evidence in 1984, suggest that the system may be inherently less stable than the dominant-party system that characterized the Nehru era. In the Rajiv Gandhi era, regional parties operating within the federal system appear to be as important as centrist national parties in providing leadership and policy alternatives. Put another way, the majority of the electorate that supports "the opposition" to Congress will be represented by combinations of regional and national parties. At the same time, Congress rule at the center will rely on electoral alliances with regional parties and cooperation from the regional and national parties that govern many states.

The Breakdown of Congress's Hindi Heartland Base

Regional determinants, while leaving much to be explained about patterns and changes in party support, compare favorably with other determinants (such as socioeconomic status, urban-rural differences, and class) often used to explain such changes.[2] We have used marginal shifts in Congress's regional seat and vote shares to explain the transformation of the party system that began with the 1967 parliamentary election. Categorizing India's twenty-two states and eight union territories into five major and one minor region, we have analyzed regional voting patterns for eight parliamentary elections.

Although the parliamentary majorities needed to form national governments require multiregional party support, seat majorities in the Hindi Heartland have proved essential in determining which party has been able to obtain such support. Our analysis shows the breakdown between 1962 and 1980 of the Hindi Heartland support that sustained

Congress dominance of the party system in the first two parliamentary elections. It also shows the return of Hindi Heartland support as significant in the overwhelming parliamentary Congress victory of 1984.

Like Prussia in imperial Germany, the Hindi Heartland is by far India's largest region. Its six states, including the two largest, Uttar Pradesh and Bihar, and one union territory have provided five (all from Uttar Pradesh) of independent India's six prime ministers. With 42 percent of Parliament's seats, it occupies more political space than the two next largest regions combined (table 8). Its definition as a political region starts with a common language, Hindi, extends to its heartland characteristics of cultural parochialism and social and economic backwardness, as measured by most statistical indicators, and eventuates in voting patterns distinct from those of other regions. For example, low average turnout makes it the only region whose proportion of votes polled has been consistently below its proportion of seats (table 8).

The South, encompassing four states and one union territory, ranks second among the six regions, with 25 percent of total seats. Like the other two rimland regions (West and East), the South has a higher level of political participation than the Heartland (table 8). Its proportion of valid votes polled nationally has been consistently higher than its proportion of national seats, which reflects turnout disproportionate to its population and higher than the national turnout. The South's common features include Dravidian (as opposed to Sanskrit-based)

TABLE 8
Each Region's Seats and Votes as a Percentage of All-India Seats and Votes, 1967

	Seats (N=520)	Votes (N=146 million)
Hindi Heartland	42	38
South	25	29
West	14	14
East	14	14
North	4	4
Northeast and Islands	1	1

SOURCE: See table 9.

Note: These proportions have been relatively stable but were subject to some variations on 1967, which was a representative year: the Hindi Heartland had 44 percent of the seats in 1957 and 1984 and 41 percent of the votes in 1957 and 1977; the South, 26 percent of the seats in 1957 and 24 percent in 1977 and 1980, and 27 percent of the votes in 1957 and 28 percent in 1977; the West, 13 percent of the seats in 1957 and 13 percent of the votes in 1977; the East, 13 percent of the votes in 1977; the North, 2 percent of the seats in 1957; and the Northeast and Islands, 2 percent of the seats in 1980.

languages, higher levels of development by most socioeconomic indicators, and a more cosmopolitan history and outlook than in the Hindi Heartland. At the same time, it is more internally differentiated by language and political orientation than the Hindi Heartland. Its four languages are less mutually comprehensible than the wide range of dialects spoken in the Heartland. The upper South (Andhra Pradesh and Karnataka) became for a time the mainstay of the Indira Gandhi–led Congress when its Hindi Heartland support declined, while the lower South (Tamil Nadu and Kerala) favored regional parties, the cultural nationalist DMK and AIADMK in Tamil Nadu and the locally rooted CPI-M and other local parties in Kerala. Since 1983, Andhra Pradesh and Karnataka disavowed their Congress-I commitment by supporting a regional party (Telugu Desam) and national parties (Janata and BJP), respectively. The Telugu Desam held firm in both the 1984 parliamentary and 1985 state assembly elections. Congress-I carried Karnataka nationally, but Janata, just three months later, was given a clear mandate to continue governing the state.

Bombay and Calcutta, former capitals of presidencies under the British raj whose hinterlands encompassed the states of today's West and East regions, symbolize many of the characteristics that distinguish these two rimland regions. Equal at 14 percent with respect to proportion of seats, West and East are unequal with respect to economic growth. Both states of the Western region, Maharashtra and Gujarat, are leaders in industrial and agricultural production, while West Bengal, the largest of the East's three states, has lost ground in national rankings of state income and production as a result of Calcutta's commercial and industrial decline.

The North, composed of a twice-truncated Punjab, Kashmir, and the union territory of Chandigarh, includes the two states whose politics is heavily influenced by the presence of majority non-Hindu religious communities; Kashmir is about 70 percent Muslim, and the Punjab is just over 50 percent Sikh. Although Punjab is at the top and Kashmir near the bottom of states ranked by per capital income, their politics are similar, in that party strategy and electoral behavior are heavily influenced by confessional parties (the Akali Dal and the National Conference) that represent Sikhs in the Punjab and Muslims in Kashmir.

The smallest region, the Northeast and Islands, is made up of geographically and culturally peripheral states and union territories. Its thirteen seats constitute only 2 percent of the parliamentary total. The region's poverty, relative deprivation, cultural alienation, and resistance to immigrants from Bangladesh (formerly East Pakistan) and more advanced states of India have led to rebellions, civil strife, and incipient secessionism.

In the Nehru era of one-party dominance, Congress relied for its success on a tacit Hindi Heartland strategy. It won a disproportionate share of its votes and seats from the region's six states. This disproportionate electoral support was in turn based on strong support from India's principal disadvantaged minorities, Muslims and scheduled castes and tribes, who came to believe in the nationalist era and in Nehru's time that Congress was their friend and protector. One finding of our regional analysis is that the elections of 1962, 1967, and 1977 marked a deterioration of Congress support in the Hindi Heartland that the 1971 and 1980 elections only partially reversed. The great return swing of the 1984 parliamentary election, when Congress won 95 percent of the seats in the Heartland, was moderated but not cancelled when Congress won the state assembly election of 1985 with more modest majorities of 66 percent of the seats. Table 9 reviews seat and vote data for the eight elections from 1952 to 1984.

The first election, in 1952, was the best of the party's three Nehru-era parliamentary elections in the Hindi Heartland (50 percent of the vote and 85 percent of the seats). The outcome exemplifies a leading feature of the era of Congress dominance, the party's disproportionate support in the Heartland. In 1952, Congress won 12 percent more seats and 5 percent more votes in the Heartland than its national averages, and its performance there in seats and votes was better than in any other region except the West (see table 9). After 1957, with the exception of 1971, Congress did not attract more seat and vote support in the Hindi Heartland than in the country as a whole until the recovery under Rajiv Gandhi's leadership in 1984. In 1962, Congress's vote share in the Heartland dropped below its national average, and in 1962, 1977, and 1980, both seat and vote proportions were below its national average (table 10).

Comparisons between the 1952 election and elections held after 1967, when Congress dominance was challenged, demonstrate the changing nature of Congress support. Indeed, the challenge of 1967 was prefigured by Congress' weak showing in the Heartland in 1962. From 1962 onward, except in 1971 and 1984, Congress won higher percentages of votes and seats in the South and/or West than in the Hindi Heartland (see table 9).

Another way of measuring Congress support in the Hindi Heartland is to express it in terms of the proportions of total national Congress seats and votes located in the Hindi Heartland (see table 11). In 1952 and 1957, paradigmatic for the era of Congress dominance, 52 and 49 percent of all seats Congress won nationally and 44 and 42 percent of all votes were won in the Hindi Heartland. In 1962, both proportions declined dramatically, to 41 and 31 percent, respectively, recuperating somewhat in 1967. Even though Congress regained support in the Hindi Heartland in 1971, when Mrs. Gandhi engineered India's first midterm and first "delinked" election, the proportions of Heartland seats and votes were below the 1952 and 1957 levels. In the post-emergency election of 1977, Congress in the Heartland won only 2 percent of the national total of seats and 28 percent of the national votes. In 1980, while the proportions were considerably increased from 1977 (to 43 percent of seats and 36 percent of the vote), they were still below those of both 1971 and 1967. In 1980, a united opposition vote in Uttar Pradesh would have reduced the number of Congress seats from fifty-one to fourteen of eighty-five; in Bihar, from thirty to eleven of fifty-four.[3] As it was, Congress-I's vote in these two states was 17 and 9 percent below that of 1971, respectively. In the 1984 parliamentary election, Congress reversed its downward trajectory when it approximated its best Heartland seat and vote performance of 1952.

In the course of the 1970s, the South, particularly the upper South (Andhra Pradesh and Karnataka), and the West (Maharashtra and Gujarat) became the bastions of Congress support that the Hindi Heartland had been in the era of Congress dominance. Mrs. Gandhi's decision in 1978 to return to Parliament by standing in a by-election in Medak, Andhra Pradesh, rather than in her old constituency, Rae Bareli in Uttar Pradesh, made visible Congress-I's reliance on its Southern bastion. It was the upper South that rallied to Indira Gandhi in 1977, saving Congress from destruction when the Hindi Heartland massively defected. Congress nationally won only 28 and 34 percent of seats and votes but the South as a whole delivered 77 percent of its seats and 41 percent of its votes (table 9). Voting support levels in the South as a whole (but not in Andhra Pradesh) even increased in 1980 and 1984 (to 44 percent in 1980 and 47 percent in 1984 [table 9]), but these gains were crosscut by the state assembly elections of 1983 and 1985, when Congress lost convincingly in Andhra Pradesh and in Karnataka.

The West was the other major region that in 1977 supported Congress with proportions of seats and votes higher than the national averages. Except in the election of 1957, the West has consistently sup-

TABLE 9
Distribution of Congress Support in Parliament by Region, 1952–84

	1952	1957	1962	1967	1971	1977	1980	1984
				Seats (%)				
Total no.	100 (489)	100 (494)	100 (491)	100 (520)	100 (518)	100 (542)	100 (520)	100 (508)
Congress's support								
All-India	73 (357)	76 (371)	73 (358)	54 (282)	68 (352)	28 (154)	67 (352)	79 (401)
Hindi Heartland	85 (184)	85 (182)	71 (147)	58 (127)	75 (165)	1 (2)	66 (148)	95 (214)
South	51 (63)	76 (97)	75 (95)	46 (58)	56 (71)	77 (92)	72 (94)	53 (69)
West	87 (46)	58 (38)	86 (57)	68 (49)	76 (55)	42 (32)	84 (65)	90 (69)
East	68 (45)	57 (39)	66 (44)	39 (29)	55 (41)	22 (17)	32 (26)	57 (36)
North	75 (18)	100 (13)	64 (14)	70 (14)	80 (16)	15 (3)	70 (14)	43 (3)
Northeast and Islands	25 (1)	50 (2)	25 (1)	71 (5)	57 (4)	62 (8)	38 (5)	77 (10)
				Votes (%)				
Total no.	100 (106)	100 (121)	100 (115)	100 (146)	100 (146)	100 (189)	100 (197)	100 (232)
Congress's support								
All-India	45 (48)	47 (57)	45 (52)	40 (59)	43 (64)	34 (65)	43 (84)	49 (114)
Hindi Heartland	50 (21)	49 (24)	40 (16)	37 (20)	46 (26)	26 (20)	39 (30)	54 (50)
South	38 (12)	47 (15)	46 (17)	44 (19)	37 (16)	41 (22)	44 (24)	47 (28)
West	51 (6)	47 (8)	53 (9)	48 (9)	55 (11)	47 (12)	53 (15)	52 (17)
East	43 (6)	47 (8)	48 (7)	38 (8)	34 (7)	33 (8)	41 (11)	50 (17)
North	41 (3)	50 (2)	41 (3)	38 (2)	47 (3)	31 (2)	47 (3)	26 (1)
Northeast and Islands	25 (0.08)	47 (0.1)	37 (0.2)	47 (1)	30 (1)	35 (1)	23 (1)	— (1)

SOURCES: For 1952–80, Election Commission reports. For 1984, Government of India, Press Information Bureau, *Lok Sabha Elections, 1984: A Computerised Analysis* (New Delhi, 1984), and Government of India, Election Commission, "General Elections to the House of the People," provisional (New Delhi, 1985, mimeograph).

Notes: Figures in parentheses are numbers of seats, and numbers of valid votes in millions (rounded to the nearest million). The areas included in each region have shifted somewhat over time. We have not attempted exact totals, which would have required disaggregation of votes by district over time, but instead have used rough approximations. The Hindi Heartland includes Uttar Pradesh, Bihar, Himachal Pradesh, Rajasthan, Haryana, Madhya Pradesh, and Delhi. In 1952, it also included Madhya Bharat, Ajmer, Bhopal and Vindhya Pradesh, subsequently included in component states of the region. It included Haryana only after 1966; that state was previously part of Punjab and the North. The South includes Andhra Pradesh, Tamil Nadu, Karnataka, Kerala, and Pondicherry. Before 1956, it included Madras, Hyderabad, Mysore, Travancore-Cochin, and Coorg, some parts of which went to the West. The North includes Punjab, Kashmir, and Chandigarh, and before 1956 it included PEPSU and Bilaspur. Kashmir was not counted through 1962. The East includes Bengal and Orissa and some of Assam (some of Assam has been lost to the Northeast and Islands). The West includes Maharashtra, Gujarat, Dadra and Nagar-Haveli, and Goa. Before 1956, it included Bombay, Saurashtra, and Kutch, most of which have been included in component states of the West. The Northeast and Islands includes Sikkim, Tripura, Manipur, Mizoram, Arunachal Pradesh, Meghalaya, Nagaland, Lakshadweep, and the Andaman and Nicobar Islands; some of these were part of Assam, and some (Sikkim) have been added since independence. Because of disturbed conditions, Assam and Punjab did not participate in the 1984 parliamentary election. "Congress" refers to Congress (R) in 1971, Congress in 1977, and Congress-I in 1980 and 1984.

ported Congress at levels well above its all-India averages (table 10). Even though turnout has been inconsistent and many voters have deserted Congress in state assembly elections, over the eight parliamentary elections since independence, the West's high average level (51 percent) of support indicates that it has been Congress' strongest and most reliable regional support base.

The East has shown levels of support for Congress well below the national averages for seats and votes (table 10), except in 1962 and 1984. The North was more volatile, not only deserting Congress in 1977 but also recording strong support for regional parties in state assembly elections. Punjab and Kashmir remain highly problematic for Congress. In the Northeast, two regional parties grounded in class and tribal nationalism have competed with Congress on better than even terms.

In 1984, Hindi Heartland voters strongly supported the Congress-I. It received the disproportionate level of electoral support that in 1952 and 1957 made it the dominant party: 16 percent more seats and 5 percent more votes than the party's national averages (table 10). The outcome suggested the possibility that the dominant-party system of the Nehru era might have been restored. Why we believe this not to be so is explored in the next two sections.

TABLE 10
Divergence of Regional Support for Congress from National Support

	1952	1957	1962	1967	1971	1977	1980	1984
	Seats							
Hindi Heartland	+12	+9	−2	+4	+7	−27	−1	+16
South	−22	0	+2	−8	−12	+49	+5	−26
West	+14	−18	+13	+14	+8	+14	+17	+11
East	−5	−19	−7	−15	−13	−6	−35	−22
North	+2	+24	−9	+16	+12	−13	+3	−36
Northeast and Islands	−48	−26	−48	+17	−11	+34	−29	−2
	Votes							
Hindi Heartland	+5	+2	−5	−3	+3	−8	−4	+5
South	−7	0	+1	+4	−6	+7	+1	−2
West	+6	0	+8	+8	+12	+13	+10	+3
East	−2	0	+3	−2	−9	−1	−2	+1
North	−4	+3	−4	−2	+4	−3	+4	+1
Northeast and Islands	−20	0	−8	+7	−13	+1	−20	0

Note: Given as percentage differences between regional and national support, based on percentages in table 9, with positive and negative percentages indicating support higher and lower than the national average, respectively, and zero indicating no difference.

TABLE 11
Congress's Hindi Heartland Support as a Percentage of Its National Support

	1952	1957	1962	1967	1971	1977	1980	1984
Seats	52	49	41	45	47	2	43	54
Votes	44	42	31	39	40	28	36	44

SOURCE: See table 9.

Minority Support for Congress:
Special Relationship or Minority Prudence?

Conventional wisdom has held that the minorities vote disproportionately for Congress. The conventional explanation for this pattern
has been that the minorities regarded the Nehru-era Congress as their
special friend and welcomed its secular orientation. It was believed
that the disproportionate electoral support for Congress in the Nehru
era and for Indira Gandhi's Congress-I in 1971 was sustained in part
by a special relationship between India's principle disadvantaged minorities: Muslims, scheduled castes (untouchables), and scheduled
tribes. In 1977, after having fallen victim to the excesses of Mrs.
Gandhi's emergency, the minorities deserted the Congress en masse to
support the Janata party. But the 1980 and 1984 elections appeared to
have restored the close and consistent relationship believed to exist between the Congress party and the three large minorities discussed in
chapter 1 (see the section on minority politics and table 6). Our analysis reveals, however, that this relationship has been substantially altered and may never have had the electoral significance attributed to it.

Shifts in minority voting patterns since 1977 show that they have
paralleled regional and national outcomes, that is, that the minorities
have voted more like everybody else than with special favor for Congress. This pattern of minority voting raises the question of whether
the minorities' purported support for Congress results more from a
special relationship based on Congress's commitment to equal citizenship and secular values or from a perception of Congress as the
dominant party and as such the likely winner and prospective governing party.

The three universes of minority voters—scheduled caste, scheduled
tribe, Muslim—are similar in some important respects. All are based
on constituencies in which these voters are concentrated. They differ,
however, in their degree of concentration and in their relationships to
surrounding or adjacent local societies. Scheduled caste voters have
the benefit of constituencies reserved for scheduled caste candidates

(seventy-nine in 1980). However, in those constituencies, scheduled caste voters rarely make up 30 percent of total voters.[4] These circumstances reflect the dispersed but socially segregated and economically dependent conditions that affect their voting. Their relatively low levels of concentration make voting for exclusively scheduled caste parties more difficult and dangerous. It is prudent to show loyalty to multicaste parties. In contrast, scheduled tribe voters in the constituencies reserved for scheduled tribe candidates (thirty-eight in 1980) tend to be more concentrated and more isolated. Unlike members of scheduled castes, who are integrated into the Hindu social framework by virtue of their traditional positions as dependent service castes of higher social groups, tribals may or may not be integrated. Poor tribals involved as service castes in local economies—for example, agricultural laborers—may often be even more dependent economically than the modal scheduled caste voter. But other tribals, engaged in subsistence production and concentrated in socially and economically isolated areas, are sometimes politically conscious and organized enough to elect tribal rather than class or national party candidates.[5]

Although, for weighty historical reasons, Muslims have been denied reserved seats in specified constituencies in proportion to their population, our evidence on party voting in 1977, 1980, and 1984 is as good for "Muslim" constituencies as for scheduled castes and tribes.[6] Muslims fall somewhere between scheduled caste and scheduled tribe voters in their degree of concentration or scatter and in their degree of isolation or integration. Their party voting reflects not only this "middle" position but also differences associated with the range in the proportions of Muslim voters (from 10 to over 50 percent) in "Muslim" constituencies and the variety of their economic and social circumstances.[7]

How would one ascertain whether a "special relationship" exists between the Congress party and minority voters? We have done so by inquiring whether constituencies in which minority voters are particularly numerous elect a higher proportion of Congress candidates than the national average or give Congress a higher proportion of the vote.

We begin with scheduled caste voters. By our measure, scheduled castes did have a special relationship with Congress in the 1962, 1967, and 1971 parliamentary elections. In 1962, Congress won 82 percent of scheduled caste seats when its national average of all seats was 54 percent; in 1967, the contrast was 61 to 52 percent; in 1971, 66 to 64 percent (table 12). In all three elections, Congress' proportion of scheduled caste seats topped its proportion of all seats, but the intensity of the relationship steadily declined. (Comparisons with the earlier

TABLE 12
Distribution of Scheduled Caste (SC) Parliamentary Seats by Party, 1971–84

	1971			1977			1980			1984		
	No. of SC seats	% of SC Seats	% of All Seats	No. of SC seats	% of SC Seats	% of All Seats	No. of SC seats	% of SC Seats	% of All Seats	No. of SC Seats	% of SC Seats	% of All Seats
Congress	48	66	64	15	19	28	46	60	67	52	75	79
Janata	7	10	7	45	58	55	14	18	16	1	1	3
Communist parties	8	11	9	9	12	5	7	9	8	4	6	5
DMK, AIADMK, and Telugu Desam	6	8	4	4	5	4	4	5	3	9	13	8
Other	4	5	16	5	6	8	5	7	6	3	4	5

SOURCES: Election Commission reports for 1971–80 and provisional tables for 1984.

Notes: The figures are for the seventeen large states only; in 1980, there were seventy-nine scheduled caste constituencies in all; in 1984, because there were no elections in Assam and Punjab, the universe was reduced. "Congress" refers to Congress (R) in 1971, Congress in 1977, and Congress-I in 1980 and 1984. "Janata" refers to the component units that united in 1977; to the premerger components in 1971; to the Janata, Lok Dal, and Congress-U in 1980; and to the Janata and DMKP in 1984.

elections of 1952 and 1957 are not possible, because scheduled castes and tribes were mostly elected to double-member constituencies in which the other member was not scheduled caste or scheduled tribe.)

This special relationship was shattered by the 1977 election. At the most general level, scheduled caste voters have voted for the winning party, whether Congress or other: Janata in 1977 and Congress in 1980 and 1983 (table 12). Most important, regardless of the winning party, their support for Congress in seats and votes (where we have the data) has been below the national averages. Conversely, their support for the Janata (and its successors) and regional parties has been above the national or state seat and vote averages.

Congress's failure to reestablish its special relationship with scheduled caste voters in 1980 seems even more evident if the electoral outcome is disaggregated by region. In the five Hindi Heartland states where almost half (49 percent) of the seats reserved for scheduled castes are located, Janata closed out Congress-I in 1977 by winning, in all, thirty-eight scheduled caste seats (table 13). In 1980, Congress-I recaptured twenty-three of the thirty-eight seats, 23 percent below its share in 1971. Congress-I's recovery as measured in seats overstates its recovery in constituency vote shares. This difference is most apparent in Uttar Pradesh, which is not only India's most populous state but also the state with the highest proportion of scheduled caste voters (21 percent). Janata and Lok Dal candidates in Uttar Pradesh's scheduled caste constituencies in 1980 won 58 percent of the vote, a proportion 24 percent higher than Congress-I's share, and 6 percent higher than the average Janata/Lok Dal share in Uttar Pradesh (52 percent).[8] Congress-I, by contrast, polled only 34 percent in scheduled caste constituencies, 2 percent less than its average in the state as a whole.

In 1984, however, scheduled caste constituencies in Uttar Pradesh swung decisively behind the Rajiv Gandhi–led Congress-I. Their level of voting support (67 percent) was 16 percent greater than the enormous swing to Congress-I in all Uttar Pradesh constituencies (51 percent in 1984 as against 36 percent in 1980) and 33 percent higher than Congress-I's proportion (34 percent in scheduled caste constituencies) in 1980.[9] Some have interpreted this extraordinary swing to Congress-I in Uttar Pradesh's scheduled caste constituencies as a quasi-class variant of the "Hindu" and/or nationalist backlash to Sikh terrorism and secessionism in the Punjab. Scheduled caste voters, like other Congress-I voters, may have sympathized with the bereaved son of a mother martyred by her Sikh bodyguards and been concerned that national unity and personal security had been put at risk by Sikh "extremism." But scheduled caste voters differed from other Congress-I

TABLE 13

Distribution of Scheduled Caste Parliamentary Seats between Congress and Janata in Hindi Heartland and South, 1971–84

	1971		1977		1980		1984	
	Congress Seats	Janata Seats	Congress Seats	Janata Seats	Congress Seats	Janata Seats	Congress Seats	Non-Congress Seats
Hindi Heartland								
Bihar	5	1	0	8	6	2	8	0
Haryana	2	0	0	3	1	1	2	0
Madhya Pradesh	3	2	0	5	4	2	6	0
Uttar Pradesh	17	0	0	18	8	9	15	0
Rajasthan	2	2	0	4	4	0	4	0
Total[a]	29 (85)	5 (15)	0 (0)	38 (100)	23 (62)	14 (38)	35 (100)	0 (0)
South								
Andhra Pradesh	3	3	6	0	6	1	0	6
Karnataka	4	0	4	0	4	0	2	1
Kerala	0	0	1	0	0	0	2	0
Tamil Nadu	1	0	2	0	3	0	2	3
Total[a]	8 (73)	3 (27)	13 (100)	0 (0)	13 (93)	1 (7)	6 (38)	10 (63)

SOURCES: See table 12.

Note: The number of scheduled caste seats has increased over time.

[a]Percentages in parentheses.

voters in the degree to which class anger against Sikh merchants and employers may have affected their vote.[10]

We conclude that although scheduled caste support for Congress-I in Uttar Pradesh may have restored the special relationship in 1984, the outcome seems to reflect historical conjuncture and economic relationships more than a "special" (read ideological and/or patrimonial) relationship between Congress-I and the scheduled castes. Neither the scheduled castes nor the Muslims, to be discussed below, act as if they believe that Congress holds a monopoly over protecting, helping, or representing disadvantaged minorities.

The disaffection of scheduled caste voters in the South came later than in the Hindi Heartland, but, again, it paralleled but was more pronounced than the disaffection of Southern voters generally (table 13). In 1977 and 1980, when Congress-I support in the Hindi Heartland collapsed and then only partially recovered, the party was able to replace its waning support in the Heartland by strong showings in the South (table 9). In 1977, for example, when the Congress-I won 77 percent of the seats and 41 percent of the votes in the South, it did much better there than it did nationally (28 and 34 percent, respectively). In scheduled caste constituencies Congress-I did even better, winning 100 percent of the seats in 1977 and 93 percent in 1980. Scheduled caste support was an important aspect of Congress-I's "southern strategy" in the two elections.

Congress-I's support in the South dramatically collapsed in 1983 when in state assembly elections the Telugu Desam won overwhelmingly in Andhra Pradesh and a Janata/BJP coalition took power in Karnataka. The party's proportionate loss of seats between the 1978 and 1983 state assembly elections was more pronounced in scheduled caste than in all constituencies. In Andhra Pradesh, Congress-I's proportion of seats declined 40 percent overall but 48 percent in scheduled caste seats; in Karnataka the respective declines were 30 and 40 percent (table 14). As a result, the converse held: Congress-I's principal party rivals in the two states, Telugu Desam in Andhra Pradesh and Janata in Karnataka, won higher proportions of seats in scheduled caste constituencies than they did in all constituencies (table 14). Scheduled caste support in the South, as in the Hindi Heartland, had not been the product of the community's special relationship with the Congress-I. In both regions, the scheduled castes simply voted with the winning party.

The results of the 1984 parliamentary election in the South modified but did not reverse the relationship evident in the 1983 Andhra Pradesh and Karnataka state assembly elections (table 13). In the four

TABLE 14

Decline of Scheduled Caste Support for Congress in State Assembly Elections in Andhra Pradesh and Karnataka, 1978 and 1983

	% in 1978		% in 1983	
	All Seats	SC Seats	All Seats	SC Seats
Andhra Pradesh				
Congress-I	60	71	20	23
Janata	20	21	0.13	0
Telugu Desam	0	0	69	72
Other	20	8	10	5
Karnataka				
Congress-I	67	66	37	26
Janata	26	27	42	58
BJP	0	0	8	3
Other	7	6	13	13

SOURCES: Election Commission, *The General Elections to the Legislative Assemblies of Andhra Pradesh, Assam, Karnataka, Maharashtra, Meghalaya, Arunachal Pradesh and Mizoram, 1978* (Delhi, 1979) and "General Elections to the Legislative Assembly, 1983" (1983, mimeograph).

southern states, opposition parties won 63 percent and Congress-I 38 percent of the scheduled caste seats.

Together, the evidence from the Hindi Heartland and the South strongly suggests that after 1971, the scheduled castes have not had a special relationship with the Congress-I. Instead, scheduled caste voters' preferences resemble those of all voters, with the added caveat that they probably vote for the winning party in higher proportions than all voters. We take this as a sign both that, being dependent, scheduled caste voters use their vote to seek protection and benefits from governing parties and that all parties can and do court scheduled caste support. Because our analysis of Muslim voting since 1971 comes to similar conclusions, we conclude that Congress-I can no longer count on the support of India's two largest disadvantaged minorities.

The 1977 parliamentary election dramatically demonstrated that Muslims also might defect from the Congress-I. Our evidence from this and the 1980 and 1984 parliamentary elections suggests that Congress did not benefit from a special relationship with Muslims and may never have.

Conventional wisdom holds that Muslims in Jawaharlal Nehru's time also had a special relationship with Congress. This relationship was thought to have held through the fifth parliamentary election in 1971.[11] Already in 1961, survey evidence cast doubt on this view: 58

percent of the Hindus polled supported Congress, compared with 55.7 percent of Muslims, 71 percent of Christians, and 28 percent of Sikhs.[12] More telling, however, is our evidence with respect to seats and party vote shares from 207 parliamentary constituencies with Muslim populations of 10 percent or more. In the 1977, 1980, and 1984 parliamentary elections, Congress-I received a lower percentage of votes in Muslim than in all constituencies, and in 1977 and 1980 it won a lower proportion of seats in Muslim constituencies than it did overall. (In 1984, Congress-I's share of seats was the same in Muslim and in all seats, 79 percent [table 15]. In 1977, Janata won 61 percent of seats in Muslim constituencies, 6 percent above its national average. In 1980 and even in the disasterous 1984 election, it won higher percentages of seats and votes in Muslim than in all constituencies, while Congress did less well in Muslim constituencies in both respects (table 15).

Muslim voters' electoral behavior differs markedly depending on their degree of concentration, that is, the proportion of Muslims in a constituency. We have divided the 207 "Muslim" constituencies into three universes that range from low to high proportions of the Muslim population: Muslim-I (10–20 percent), Muslim-II (20–50 percent Muslim) and Muslim-III (over 50 percent). We infer that Muslims vote more for the two national centrist parties, Congress and Janata, when they are a vulnerable minority (Muslim-I) than they do when they are or approximate a plurality (Muslim-II) or are a majority (Muslim-III).

TABLE 15
Congress and Janata Support in Muslim Constituencies Compared with National Support

	Support in Muslim Constituencies (%)		Divergence from Party's National Support (%)	
	Seats[a]	Vote	Seats	Vote
Congress				
1977	25 (52)	27	−3	−7
1980	56 (116)	39	−11	−4
1984	79 (150)	48	0	−1
Janata				
1977	61 (126)	39	+6	−4
1980	20 (42)	36	+3	+3
1984[b]	5 (8)	—	+2	—

SOURCE: Calculations are based on data on party voting in Muslim constituencies identified from census information and provided by DMC Data Products, New Delhi.
    Note: There were 207 Muslim constituencies, in 1977 and 1980, and 190 in 1984.
    [a]Numbers are given in parentheses.
    [b]Janata vote data were unavailable for 1984.

Thus, in 1980, Congress gained 2 percent more seats in Muslim-I constituencies than it did in all constituencies (table 16), but it gained 28 percent fewer in Muslim-II constituencies and 57 percent fewer in Muslim-III constituencies. (In 1977, there was a deviation from this pattern for Muslim-III constituencies.) In 1984, Congress again gained more seats in constituencies with fewer Muslims. The same pattern characterizes Janata's votes for 1977 and 1980. Put another way, there is an inverse relationship between the proportion of Muslims in the population and Muslim voting support for national centrist parties; the lower the proportion of Muslims, the more likely it is that Muslim voters will vote for national centrist parties.

The same trends are apparent if we analyze Muslim support by vote shares (table 17). It appears that where Muslims feel themselves a distinct and vulnerable minority, they avoid antagonizing or seek the protection of mainsteam parties by voting as the general electorate does; they support the likely winner and governing party to be. In constituencies with high proportions of Muslims, however, Muslims tend to vote for class and Muslim confessional parties and candidates (other parties and independents). Support for the CPI-M (India's principal class party) and for Muslim parties and candidates (among "Other parties and independents" in tables 16 and 17) is very pronounced in Muslim-III constituencies and evident in Muslim-II constituencies.[13]

Our analysis and interpretation of the electoral data for Muslim constituencies shows that, in 1977, 1980 and 1984, Congress did not have a special electoral relationship with Muslim voters. According to the measure we used—the extent to which a party's vote and seat shares in minority constituencies exceed its national shares—Janata in 1977 and 1980 fared better than Congress in India's 207 Muslim constituencies taken as a whole and in Muslim-I and Muslim-II constituencies taken separately (tables 15–17). It is class and confessional parties and candidates, not centrist parties like Janata or Congress, that have support in constituencies where Muslims are a majority (Muslim-III) or approximate a plurality (Muslim-II). Indeed, it could be argued that it is they rather than Congress or other national centrist parties that have a special relationship to the Muslim minority.

Among the minorities, scheduled tribe voters alone seem to have a stable specific relationship with Congress. The diversity of tribal cultures, levels and kinds of development, and locations in state political systems has precluded even the limited level of national consciousness and organization characteristic of scheduled caste and Muslim voters. The constituency circumstances of scheduled caste and Muslim voters

TABLE 16

Variations in Muslim Support for Parties by Proportion of Muslim Population: Parliamentary Seats, 1977–84

	National % of Seats	Muslim-I (10%–20% Muslim) (126 Constituencies)		Muslim-II (20%–50% Muslim) (71 Constituencies)		Muslim-III (Over 50% Muslim) (10 Constituencies)	
		% of Seats	Divergence from National %	% of Seats	Divergence from National %	% of Seats	Divergence from National %
Congress							
1977	28	24	−4	23	−5	40	+12
1980	67	69	+2	39	−28	10	−57
1984	79	85	+6	75	−4	40	−39
Janata							
1977	55	67	+12	54	−1	10	−45
1980	17	21	+4	21	+4	10	−7
1984	3	5	+2	4	+1	0	−3
CPI-M							
1977	4	2	−2	14	+10	10	+6
1980	7	4	−3	23	+16	30	+23
1984	4	3	−1	11	+7	20	+16
Other parties and independents							
1977	8	5	−3	8	0	40	+32
1980	5	2	−3	6	+1	50	+45
1984	13	6	−7	11	−2	30	+17

SOURCE: See table 15.

TABLE 17

Variations in Muslim Support for Parties by Proportion of Muslim Population: Parliamentary Vote Shares, 1977–84

	National % of Votes	Muslim-I (10%–20% Muslim)		Muslim-II (20%–50% Muslim)		Muslim-III (Over 50% Muslim)	
		% of Vote	Divergence from National %	% of Vote	Divergence from National %	% of Vote	Divergence from National %
Congress							
1977	34	33	−1	30	−4	28	−6
1980	43	43	0	36	−7	30	−13
1984	49	49	0	47	−2	34	−15
Janata							
1977	43	53	+10	41	−2	4	−39
1980	33	41	+8	32	−2	7	−27
CPI-M							
1977	4	3	−1	12	+8	17	+13
1980	6	4	−2	19	+13	28	+22
Other parties and independents							
1977	11	9	−2	12	+1	50	+39
1980	10	9	−1	11	+1	35	+25

SOURCE: See table 15.
Note: Only Congress figures were available for 1984.

are quite different from those of tribal voters. Proportions of scheduled caste and Muslim voters rarely exceed 30 percent in a constituency, while tribal voters often account for a majority. As a consequence of their minority and often scattered circumstance, scheduled caste and Muslim voters more often reflect—by choice or because of intimidation—the pattern of local party preferences. Where they are concentrated, tribals, like Muslims in those constituencies where they are the majority, are free of the majority choices of other voters.

Tribals are the poorest and most disadvantaged of India's three largest minorities, and their economic and social circumstances are more bimodal: they tend to live either in social isolation under conditions of primitive subsistence production or as a segregated and exploited underclass within the organized economy. Their politics, too, tend toward bimodality, being either rebellious or loyalist. The tribal belt extending from the Darjeeling district in the northeast of West Bengal (site of Siliguri Tehsil and Naxalbari) down the eastern ghats of Orissa and Andhra Pradesh and up the western ghats of Kerala has been the homeland of Naxalism, the violent, antiparliamentary ideology of the Communist party Marxist-Leninist. Radicalism has been one mode of tribal politics, taking the form of Naxalite revolutionary violence or the sometimes violent efforts by tribal peoples in India's troubled northeastern states and union territories to gain greater political autonomy or drive out "foreigners." The other mode has been voting for the party ruling or likely to rule in Delhi, a mode particularly characteristic of the inland tribal peoples of Madhya Pradesh, Bihar, and western Indian states.

There is no conventional wisdom holding that tribals have a long and special relationship with Congress. The nationalist movement did not reach into tribal society as it did into the untouchable commu-

TABLE 18
Distribution of Scheduled Tribe Parliamentary Seats by Party, 1971–84

| | No. of Scheduled Tribe Seats[a] | | | |
	1971	1977	1980	1984
Congress	21 (68)	9 (29)	27 (82)	31 (86)
Janata	5 (16)	19 (61)	2 (6)	0 (0)
Communist parties	0 (0)	0 (0)	1 (3)	3 (8)
Other	5 (16)	3 (10)	3 (9)	2 (6)
Total	31	31	33	36

SOURCES: See table 12.
[a]Percentages in parentheses.

TABLE 19

Stability of Scheduled Tribe (ST) Support for Congress in Recent State Assembly Elections, Andhra Pradesh and Karnataka, 1978 and 1983

	% in 1978		% in 1983	
	All Seats	ST Seats	All Seats	ST Seats
Andhra Pradesh (N=15)				
Congress-I	60	40	20	47
Janata	20	20	0.3	0
Telugu Desam	0	0	69	40
Other	20	20	10	13
Karnataka (N=2)				
Congress-I	67	100	37	50
Janata	26	0	42	50

SOURCE: Election Commission, "General Elections to the Legislative Assembly, 1983."

nities. Weiner and Field have shown that there was, up to 1972, no systematic difference between the voting support Congress received from tribals and nontribals. However, since 1967, Congress and tribals have had a special relationship by our measure: a larger percentage of seats in tribal constituencies than the national average (see table 18 and compare table 11). In 1971, Congress-I won 68 percent of the seats reserved for scheduled tribe candidates. In 1977, Janata won 61 percent, but in 1980 and 1984, Congress-I more than recouped its commanding 1971 support by gaining 82 and 86 percent of those seats (table 18). In 1980 in Madhya Pradesh, the state with the largest scheduled tribe population and the most scheduled tribe seats (nine), Congress-I won comfortable voting majorities or high pluralities in all but one. Its average vote in Madhya Pradesh's tribal reserved seats was 55 percent, 8 percent higher than its average in the state (47 percent) and 12 percent above its national average.

Tribal loyalties held up in 1983 in the face of a swing against Congress in two major southern state assembly elections (table 19). The results in Karnataka, which has only two tribal seats, are inconclusive. But Andhra Pradesh has considerable tribal area and fifteen tribal seats in the state legislature. There, despite Telugu Desam's sweep and Congress-I's decline between the assembly elections of 1978 and 1983 (from 60 to 20 percent of all seats), Congress-I increased its proportion of tribal seats from 40 to 47 percent.

To summarize, Congress-I's alleged special relationship with India's disadvantaged minorities was shattered in the 1977 parliamentary election and was not restored in 1980 or 1984. Our analysis suggests that prudential calculations concerning which party is likely to win and be in a position to offer help and protection has generally governed the electoral behavior of the scheduled caste and Muslim communities. Tribal voters seem not to have been guided by such prudential calculations. Their more isolated, concentrated, and oppressed social and economic circumstances have led some of them to rebellion or nationalism but most to a special relationship with Congress, whom they continue to regard as a special friend and protector.

Congress in the 1980s: Bifurcation and Volatility of Political Universes

The 1980 and 1984 parliamentary elections restored aspects of the political universe characteristic of the 1950s and early 1960s, what we have referred to as the Nehru era. Congress's resurgence should not, however, be interpreted as a return of Congress dominance as it was understood in that era. The political universe in which the 1980 and 1984 parliamentary elections occurred, like the state assembly elections that followed soon after, was shaped by radically altered national and regional conditions.[14]

The post-Nehru era was marked not only by the rise of plebiscitary and personalistic politics and the delinking of parliamentary and state assembly elections but also by the decline of party organization as a determinant of voting, a growing bifurcation and volatility of national and regional voting behavior, and an increasing differentiation among regional voting patterns.[15] In the first three general elections of the Nehru era (1952, 1957, and 1962), the Congress party won convincing national and state legislative majorities on the basis of relatively uniform regional support. (See figs. 2 and 3 in chapter 4, and see table 9 in this chapter.) In the general election of 1967 and the parliamentary and state elections of 1977, Congress's proportion of the vote declined markedly. These political outcomes reflected important substantive changes in the political universe in which they occurred. Beginning in 1971, the structural conditions for voter choice radically altered when Indira Gandhi delinked parliamentary from state assembly elections.

The one-party-dominant system of the Nehru era was the product of relatively stable voter preferences at the broad center of the political spectrum and of parallel preferences at the parliamentary and state assembly levels. In 1967, the national and state political universes began to diverge. State and regional determinants of national voting contributed to a sharp decline (of 5 percent) in Congress's national vote and to the Grand Alliance of national opposition parties winning almost half the seats in Parliament. Congress's proportion of the state assembly vote declined too, dropping well below its 1952–62 average. As a result, national opposition parties and newly emergent or powerful regional parties captured control of half (eight) of the large states. Following what was to be the last concurrent parliamentary and state assembly election in 1967, Congress party leaders confronted a more complex and less manageable political world than that of the Nehru era and the Shastri interregnum, when policy issues and factional struggles at the center and in the states could be settled within the Congress fold.

A significant aspect of the post-1967 political universe has been its unpredictability; volatility rather than stability became the hallmark of India's electoral politics. Wide vote swings and party alternation at the center and the states in the 1970s and 1980s contrasted with the relatively stable electoral outcomes of the first three general elections. The largest swing in Congress's national vote in the first three elections was 2 percent. Since 1967, the swings have exceeded 2 percent in five parliamentary elections and have been much higher in four: 5 percent in 1967, 6 percent in 1984, and 9 percent in both 1977 and 1980 (table 20).[16]

Volatility since 1967 is related to the way politics changed after the 1962 general election. First, it reflects the decay of party organization as a determinant of electoral politics, including candidate selection. However faction ridden they were in the Nehru era, party organizations at the state and district levels were able to make decisions about candidates, leadership, and issues and to sustain some sense of party loyalty and commitment to organizational goals. Since then, plebiscitary politics has emphasized not only loyalty to particular personalities

TABLE 20
Electoral Swings in Congress's National Vote over Eight Parliamentary Elections

Year	% of Swing	Index No.[a]
1952	—	100
1957	+2	102
1962	−2	100
1967	−5	*95*
1971	+3	*98*
1977	−9	*89*
1980	+9	*98*
1984	+6	*104*

[a]Set at 100 for 1952, when Congress received 45 percent of the vote. Values set in italic type indicate volatility.

(Indira, Sanjay, Rajiv), but also issues concerning society or the regime: *gharibi hatao* ("abolish poverty") in 1971, "restoration of democracy" in 1977, "the government that works" in 1980, and "national unity" in 1984.

Great conjuncturally determined questions about the nature of the regime and its leadership have dominated electoral outcomes since 1971 more than the policy preference determinants associated with pluralist politics. Voters can answer such large, overarching questions without reference to particular interests of producer or consumer groups, castes, religious, linguistic or ethnic communities, regional subnationalities, or classes based on property or production relations. Such questions transcend party identifications and loyalties. By loosening politics from its roots in interests, party loyalties or social identifications, conjuncturally determined questions and the appeal of personalities in plebiscitary campaigns produced the "waves" to which we have referred in earlier chapters (as in "Indira wave"). The waves generated by the politics of personality, plebiscitary campaigns, and shaping historical events go a long way in explaining the volatility of Indian elections since the Nehru era. Volatility has been an important characteristic of electoral outcomes perhaps since 1967, when the inertial advantage of the nationalist and Nehru era was partially reversed by the incumbent Congress government's identification with dramatic economic failures, and certainly since the 1971 "abolish poverty" and the 1972 khaki elections.[17] Volatility may well be further exacerbated with the increasing role of the electronic media in elections.

Volatility is also associated with the progressive bifurcation of national and state political arenas. The 1967 election marked the beginning of the end of Congress dominance at the state level. From the 1971 parliamentary and 1972 state assembly elections, the determinants of national and state electoral outcomes became more distinctive. A key structural factor contributed to this change when Mrs. Gandhi—for short-term tactical reasons—delinked the 1971 parliamentary election from state assembly elections. She hoped to separate the effects of state issues and personalities and local "vote banks," which had operated to Congress's disadvantage nationally in the 1967 general election, from the question of who and which party should govern the country. In 1971, delinking operated to Congress's advantage, but at the next parliamentary election in 1977 it contributed to the Janata party's victory. Delinking, which has persisted, established two domains for the conduct of politics. Since 1971, Indian voters have cast their ballots for national and state representatives and for the governments they make on the basis of separate candidate and platform selection procedures and separate campaigns.[18]

We have measured the bifurcation of national and regional political universes in a variety of ways: the percentage differences between Congress's parliamentary and state assembly seats and votes over eight elections (see chapter 4, fig. 3); regionally weighted standard deviations that show for each of eight parliamentary elections the degree to which Congress's vote varied across five regions (table 21);[19] and a "volatility" index that measures the degree to which Congress's level of support in the five regions fluctuated from its average vote over the eight elections (table 22).

That the bifurcation of political universes is not wholly a recent phenomenon is apparent in figures 2 and 3 in chapter 4, which show state support for Congress uniformly below national support in all elections except those of 1971 and 1972. Congress in seven elections won from 5 to 22 percent fewer seats and from 1 to 3 percent fewer votes in state than national elections. The most recent three elections have exhibited the highest differential in seat percentages: −12, −19, and −22 percent. The 1972 state election that was an exception had the earmarks of a national election; it reflected the victory over Pakistan in the Bangladesh war that followed the 1971 parliamentary elections.

Table 21 shows the degree to which national voting patterns were unified and congruent. The Congress vote was more uniform across regions prior to 1971 (except in 1952) and more dispersed thereafter. A high standard deviation (a measure of dispersal) signifies strong regional divergence from Congress's national vote; a low standard devia-

TABLE 21
Regional Dispersion of National Vote over Eight Parliamentary Elections

Year	Weighted Standard Deviation	Rank Order[a]
1952	2.26	3
1957	0.61	8
1962	1.50	6
1967	1.84	7
1971	2.61	2
1977	3.06	1
1980	2.06	4
1984	2.04	5

Notes: Dispersion was measured in five regions; for description of the regions, see table 9. The Northeast and Island region, whose proportion of valid vote is less than 1 percent, was excluded from this exercise. The squares of the difference between Congress's national proportion and its proportion in each region were multiplied by the proportion of the national vote cast in each region.
[a]1 = most dispersed.

TABLE 22
Volatility Index for Eight Parliamentary Elections in Five Regions

	Average Vote for Congress (%)	Volatility Index	Rank Order
Hindi Heartland	43	55	1
South	43	26	4
West	51	20	5
East	42	42	3
North	41	49	2

Note: The volatility index is the sum of percentage differences from the average.
[a]1 = most volatile.

tion signifies more uniformity with the national average. Except for the first "experimental" and thus somewhat unformed parliamentary election in 1952, when Congress did exceptionally well in the Hindi Heartland (50 percent) and exceptionally poorly in the South (38 percent), the elections before 1971 had considerably lower standard deviations than the elections after 1971. Before the 1971 watershed election, Congress's more regionally uniform vote was due to its standing as the party of nationalism and independence, its advantage with respect to organizational resources and capabilities, and its perception as *Sarkar* (established authority), the successor to the British raj. These "advantages" faded with time. New generations, for whom the nationalist struggle was an increasingly distant memory, became voters, Congress's organizational resources became dysfunctional or atrophied, and the idea that Congress had a special claim to be the government lost credibility. Delinking in 1971 may have liberated Congress's national electoral fortunes from the play of local forces, but it also liberated local forces from some of the effects of national personalities and plebiscitary and conjunctural politics. We interpret delinking more as a watershed than as an incremental linear change, because both the qualitative evidence and the large standard deviation increase in 1971, from 1.84 to 2.61, with subsequent levels above 2 (table 21), strongly support such an interpretation. Delinking seems to have added a structural determinant to longer-term processes differentiating national and regional politics.[20]

In 1977, 1980, and 1985, the Janata or Congress parties, after being swept into power by large national waves in delinked elections, tried with some success to benefit from them in state assembly elections by restoring a modified version of linkage. Janata led the way in 1977. Indira Gandhi in 1980 and Rajiv Gandhi in 1985 followed suit when they called special state assembly elections within a few months of winning national elections. Despite the evidence that national waves can and have affected state assembly voting, the maneuvers involved reflected a deep appreciation that, except under very special circumstances, regional and national politics march to different drummers.

The effects of regional on national politics vary considerably by region; some regions are clearly more volatile than others. As table 22 shows, not only has the West supported Congress over eight parliamentary elections at a much higher average level (51 percent) than have the four other regions (41–43 percent) but it also, along with the South, has done so with marked consistency.[21] The volatility index in table 22 shows the volatility of the level of support in each region. The West's volatility index is the lowest at 20 and the South's the next lowest at 26. By contrast, support for Congress in the Hindi Heartland, North, and East has been subject to wide swings (index scores of 55, 49, and 42, respectively). Because the Hindi Heartland is the largest region, its marked volatility has been a principal cause of the waves that have characterized Indian politics in the post-Nehru era.

We are inclined to explain the differences in volatility qualitatively: the Hindi Heartland and North are closest to Delhi, the epicenter of Indian politics and policy, the South and West furthest removed. Voters in the Hindi Heartland and the North are more aware and more sensitive to events and personalities in Delhi than are voters in the more remote South and West. Conjunctural effects, policy change and implementation, response to leaders, and regime issues affect India's regions differentially. Viewing Delhi as an epicenter, the Heartland and the North lie closest to its concerns, personalities, and intrigues; the South and West furthest away; and the East in between. All five regions have political profiles and dynamics that distinguish them from each other and from the forces that determine national electoral outcomes.

The bifurcation of state and national universes is well institutionalized in seven of the seventeen large states. In four of these, regional parties have established themselves as durable parts of the political scene: Punjab (Akali Dal), Tamil Nadu (DMK and AIADMK), Andhra Pradesh (Telugu Desam), and Kashmir (National Conference). In the other three, national parties have carved out so persisting a regional niche that they function rather like regional parties: Bengal (CPI-M), Karnataka (Janata), and Kerala (CPI and CPI-M). In a number of these states, the regional party operates in a local two-party system with national parties. Some of these regional and quasi-regional parties have long histories in their respective states. But the appearances of Telugu Desam in Andhra Pradesh and Janata in Karnataka in the 1983 state assembly elections and their persistence in the 1985 assembly elections made the state political arena more distinctive and visible. Mrs. Gandhi's propensity to destabilize the state governments stimulated the state parties to collaborate with each other in self-defense. They articulated common programs emphasizing federal autonomy and rights[22] and moved to give more vigorous constitutional form to the bifurcation of the state and national party systems. Rajiv Gandhi's respect for duly constituted state-level opposition governments drew the teeth of the state opposition parties after 1984 and blunted the campaign for more generous federal rights. However, the distinctiveness of regional arenas for the party system seems here to stay.

The results of the 1985 state assembly elections that followed just three months after Rajiv Gandhi's unprecedented parliamentary victory dramatically demonstrated the persistence of bifurcated regional and national political universes. One way of showing the change is to compare the number of assembly constituencies within an MP constituency in which Congress won majorities in the 1984 parliamentary election with the number of assembly seats it won in the 1985 state assembly elections. Between the December 1984 parliamentary and the March 1985 state assembly elections, the Congress-I lost 26 percent of the state assembly segments it had carried ten weeks earlier. This was a more severe reversal than the party experienced between the January parliamentary and June state assembly elections in 1980, when it lost only 20 percent of the assembly segments it had carried five months earlier.[23]

In December, the party had won 79 percent of the MP seats, but in March it could win only 57 percent of the state assembly seats. Its proportion of the vote declined substantially too, from an unprecedented 49 percent in December to what, in the absence of official figures, we estimate to be a more "normal" 43 percent in March. It lost in three states (Karnataka, Andhra Pradesh, and Sikkim) and narrowly escaped defeat in Maharashtra and Rajasthan. In Uttar Pradesh, India's most populous state, it won only 266 of 425 seats, a poor showing compared with the 309 it had held in the old assembly and the 383 assembly segments it won in December 1984. Its vote in here, which had increased slightly (from 36 to 37 percent) between the January parliamentary and June state assembly elections in 1980, plummeted from 53 to 42 percent between December 1984 and March 1985.[24]

The bifurcation of state and national political systems, confirmed by the 1985 electoral outcomes, suggests the emergence of dual political arenas. These do not necessarily entail confrontation and standoff between the national and state governments. But the Congress "system" that held together state and national units has passed away and will now have to be replaced by new forms of cross-party bargaining and accommodation. Stable Congress dominance of the state and national elections has been supplanted by volatile electoral patterns. These accompany the plebiscitary politics from the top that has replaced the older politics from below rooted in local and regional social solidarities. Coordinating the outcomes of plebiscitary politics in national and parliamentary elections with the outcomes of regionally based politics at the state level will require new political conventions that have yet to be crafted and practiced.

Part 3

ECONOMY

7 Demand Polity and Command Polity

We address the relationship between polity and economy in independent India by using contrasting models: demand polity and command polity. These models allow us to raise questions about the tension between conflicting requirements of state sovereignty and popular sovereignty, which determines the degree of state autonomy on the one hand and state responsiveness on the other. We use this tension to illuminate the relationships between governability and mobilization, between saving and consumption, and between investment in future benefits and expenditures on welfare now.

The play of contesting sovereignties, the state versus the people, in the tension between command and demand polities helps us to explain India's political economy by tracing the interaction since independence between rising levels of political mobilization and the changing capabilities of the "state." The use of competing sovereignties in the form of command and demand polities avoids conventional but increasingly unproductive arguments about whether "capitalism" or "socialism" is better for prosperity, freedom, or equality. For example, both models allow, inter alia, for planned or corporatist capitalism or market socialism under conditions of more or less equality and freedom.

Demand and Command Polities

In our model of a demand polity, voter citizens are sovereign. Extractive and allocative decisions reflect citizens' preferences as they are expressed through party competition in elections and through representation by interests, classes, communities, and movements. In the theory of voter sovereignty, voters are said to be analogous to sovereign consumers in a competitive market economy, insofar as consumers' preferences and choices in markets, like those of voters' in elections, are not "distorted" by widely asymmetrical distributions of wealth, power, and information.[1]

211

In our model of a command polity, "autonomous" states are sovereign. Extractive and allocative decisions reflect the preferences of the elected and appointed officials who choose and implement policies. They favor, repress, license, or co-opt classes, interests, communities, and elites. Using the economic analogy again, the role of the state is like that of monopolistic or oligopolistic producers who can determine what and how much is produced because they control investment and product choice and shape consumer preferences accordingly.

The demand polity is oriented toward short-term goals; toward competitive processes for determining policies and the public interest (e.g., voting, deliberation, and bargaining); and toward the provision of private goods. It is constrained and directed by the imperatives of electoral victory and by pluralist and class influence on public choice. It is also oriented toward the "rationality" of incremental policy choice,[2] because the next step from a known position is better than a leap in the dark. The command polity is oriented toward state-determined long-term goals and formulations of the public interest and the provision of collective goods. Rationality in command polities derives from comprehensive and detailed calculations that relate social objectives to available resources.[3] A necessary condition for the command polity's ability to formulate goals, strategies, and policies is the state's ability to free itself from the constraints of societal demands through leadership, persuasion, or coercion.

Legitimacy, support, and producer commitment in both command and demand polities require equity in the allocation of benefits and sacrifice. Demand polities tend to maximize legitimacy, support, and producer commitment by stressing equity with respect to benefits; command polities, by stressing equity with respect to sacrifice.

Because demand and command polities are heuristic constructs and appear in the real world in mixed forms to varying degrees, we use the terms command and demand *politics* to signal their empirical referents. Democratic or authoritarian regimes sometimes express elements of demand and command polities, respectively, but there is no necessary congruence between regime and polity. For example, strong and skillful institutional or personal leadership in democratic regimes can practice command politics that favor long-run objectives and collective goods by appealing to national pride and social justice and by manipulating incentives and sanctions to achieve the desired goals. Democratic regimes, in arguing the trade-offs between investment in future benefits and expenditure on present consumption and welfare, can and do advance the former. Jawaharlal Nehru's Congress governments exemplified the possibility of combining command politics with a democratic regime. On the other hand, leaders of authoritarian regimes can distort or subvert the command polity commitment to future benefits and collective goods. Beset by the exigencies of the political struggle and the immediate needs of political survival, they may attempt to maintain themselves in power by claiming that their self-interested repression of current demands serves long-term goals and the public good.

Legitimacy in demand politics depends on the state's capacity to provide short-run equitable treatment of citizens' demands. Legitimacy in command politics depends on the credibility of the state's call for equitable sacrifice to achieve future benefits and avoid social costs. Short-term demands articulated by interest groups, elites, or classes need not be perceived as partial or unjust by large portions of society. For example, Polish workers' demands in 1980 for cheaper food and the right to independent representation were widely supported. But short-term demands can be perceived as partial and unjust. Such was the case in India when highly advantaged Life Insurance Corporation employees and Air India pilots in the early seventies struck for higher wages and other benefits. The efforts of Indira Gandhi's emergency regime to stop hoarding and black marketeering by punishing violators won wide support because they seemed to promote equity of sacrifice. On the other hand, the regime's vasectomy program was perceived by poor Muslims and untouchables as illegitimate, not only because it involved coercion and the violation of personal liberty but also because its implementation discriminated against them. An authoritarian regime can, up to a point, manufacture positive perceptions of its goals and performance, but it too is subject to tests of legitimacy. Ultimately, an authoritarian regime's legitimacy may hinge as much on its recognition of the demand for independent representation as on its performance with respect to its professed goals.

Economic and Political Correlates of Demand and Command Politics

Our models of demand and command polity include both political and economic characteristics. The demand polity is characterized politically by voter sovereignty and the societal direction of the state; the command polity, by state sovereignty and state hegemony (domination or control) over policy and politics. The economic characteristics of the demand model feature shorter-term market or state consumption and welfare expenditure; those of the command model, longer-term investment expenditure in public goods and future benefits.[4]

The Nehru years, 1950–64, represent a command politics under democratic auspices. Over the course of those years, the central government was able to increase the proportion of its annual budget allocated to investment (capital formation) from 30 to 50 percent (see chapter 8, fig. 6). With the onset in 1966 of the first period of demand politics (1966–75), the proportion declined rapidly. By 1969, it had returned to nearly where it began in 1951, about 32 percent. Central government investment continued at a low level until 1974, when many of the economic policies later pursued under the emergency regime were initiated. During the authoritarian regime (1975–77), the share of the central government's budget allocated to investment increased further. But when the Janata government restored a democratic regime in 1977, investment allocations did not decline. Instead, they remained at or above the levels reached under the authoritarian regime. Nevertheless, the investment levels reached in the mid-1970s and maintained through the mid-1980s remained below the level of the peak year, 1965–66. More seriously, central government investment expenditure during this period was increasingly negated by a rising capital-output ratio, an increase driven primarily by poor performance in the public sector.

The high levels of government investment attained under the Nehru and Shastri governments cannot be attributed exclusively to successful democratic leadership. International and domestic determinants beyond the reach of government policy made important contributions too. Cheap oil, for example, contributed to low levels of inflation and positive foreign exchange balances. High commodity prices during the Korean War boom helped. So too did the low defense expenditures that prevailed prior to the China and Pakistan wars in 1962 and 1965. Equally important, during the Nehru era the relatively low levels of political mobilization (measured and analyzed in chapter 8) paralleled and reinforced the helpful effects of international determinants.

India's dominant elites and policy intellectuals since independence have tended to favor command politics as a faster and surer means of creating a self-reliant economy and a powerful state. However, the practice of political economy in the postindependence era has strongly indicated not only that demand politics is compatible with economic growth and governability but also that it may promote them. The consumption and welfare expenditures that demand politics generates can improve the productivity of human capital and enhance legitimacy; the voter sovereignty that demand politics expresses can promote governability by enhancing the legitimacy and efficiency enabled by citizen and producer commitment.

The command polity's investment orientation has also raised questions about the extent to which, after a self-reliant industrial economy has been established, continuing to invest in basic and heavy industry will promote growth and employment or help alleviate poverty.

The links between command and demand politics and economic policy and performance have to be understood in the context of changing conceptions and the goals for development and the ways to achieve them. The future-oriented promise of command politics implied the postponement of immediate gratification in the interest of accumulating and investing capital to obtain future benefits. This was a social version of the this-worldly asceticism that Weber associated with the Protestant ethic and the rise of capitalism in the West. The scientific asceticism of socialist regimes collectivized the Protestant ethic when it called for postponement of current consumption in order to extract the surplus for state investment. For almost three decades, this psychology and morality of postponed gratification animated Indian planners and their economic policies. The short-run orientation of demand politics is associated more with the quality of life as it is lived now and less with the uncertain promise of future growth and its benefits. For supporters of future-oriented development theory, the current consumption they associated with demand politics ate up the income and assets needed to insure future benefits. Expenditure on current consumption reflected the spendthrift propensity of irresponsible politicians seeking quick fixes to obtain political support and cope with economic crisis.

More recently, postponement theories that call for sacrificing the present for the future have lost ground to development theories that identify goals other than growth in GNP and different means to reach them. Postponement theories have been impugned because of the high cost to current generations of a future orientation. In India, postponement development theory was translated into import substitution and basic industry strategies that bore fruit in a relatively self-reliant economy. Once self-reliance and growth in GNP had been achieved, it became clear that these goals did not address the distribution and character of benefits. Nor was it clear where to go next—what investment goals to address or how to address them.

New goals emerged from the realization that the poor were neither benefiting from nor contributing to development. Indeed, it became clear that they were the primary victims of postponement theories of development. Forty to fifty percent remained below the poverty line, under- and unemployment rates grew, and the poor lacked the skills, assets, and health to contribute to economic growth. Development that addressed "basic human needs" and unemployment became the established view of most multilateral agencies after the World Bank gave it its imprimatur.[5] The physical quality of life index (PQLI), a measure of development that combines literacy, life expectancy, and infant mortality, was devised as an alternative to measures based on growth in per capita GNP.[6] The PQLI gave a different meaning to the goals of development. Measures of per capita GNP do not address the distribution or character of benefits but the PQLI does.

Recently, Amartya Sen has attempted to estimate the cost to present generations of postponement-oriented development efforts. For example, in China and Sri Lanka, where short-term policies directly benefiting the poor were more in evidence than they were in India, the average life span in the late 1960s was 69 years, compared with 52 in India. Sen, in asking how long it would have taken the Sri Lankan economy to reach an income level likely to support an average life span of 69 years if it had invested more in capital formation and less in social expenditure, concludes that it would have taken somewhere between 58 and 152 years.[7] This kind of estimate has given a certain concreteness to the costs implicit in postponement theories.

Other economists have challenged the primacy of the long run in postponement theories by stressing that human as well as physical capital is an essential component of development. In its classic formulation, capital accumulation was seen as a process of maximizing nonperishable capital goods (physical capital). Physical capital would not be consumed but would instead be used to generate future production and long-term growth processes. John Toye, who has some faith in the conventional distinction between investment and consumption,[8] offers a Keynesian definition of investment as the goods produced in one year that are not consumed or extinguished but are still available at the end of that year to satisfy future consumption needs—that is, *not* current consumption.

On the other hand, the emphasis by Theodore Schultz and Gunnar Myrdal on human capital[9] has highlighted the fact that people as much as things are a requisite for future production and long-term growth. Gunnar Myrdal assumes that investment is any expenditure that raises production. In a context where the productivity of human beings is low and capable of vast augmentation by human investment, for example, by feeding people adequately or maintaining their health, this definition would include current consumption expenditure. And, indeed, Myrdal has argued that in less-developed countries "the basic distinction between investment and consumption does not hold [since] higher consumption forms 'investment'—that is, raises production—and at the same time remains consumption."[10]

This assertion is an extreme version of the idea that human capital contributes to development by adding to productivity. Its excess lies in its failure to distinguish between social services that have a large incremental effect on productivity and those that do not contribute to production or productivity or—except in the Malthusian or Marxist sense of reproducing labor—merely maintain or marginally increase them. At the extreme, consumption expenditures may be used by partisan controllers of the "state for itself" to attempt to purchase support. For example, Congress-I under Indira Gandhi repudiated the Charan Singh government's policy of linking wage increases in the public sector to productivity gains when, in anticipation of the 1984 election, it granted at the national level a 25 percent wage increase to five hundred thousand low-productivity public-sector coal miners. It also engaged in the notorious "loan melas" of 1984, where loans were distributed at public gatherings to young educated unemployed, without adequate investigation of the repayment capacities of the recipients or the soundness of the proposals. At the state level, in Tamil Nadu and Karnataka in the early 1980s, the AIADMK and Congress-I governments wrote off agricultural loans in profligate efforts to please powerful agricultural producer interests.

Human capital played a significant role in the economic recovery of Germany and Japan after World War II and in their subsequent ascendance in the world economy.[11] Conversely, the poverty of human capital in oil-rich Middle East economies made them dependent, because they had to import human capital in order to use the physical capital that their oil wealth could buy. Because of the interdependence of physical and human capital, current expenditure on people and on their health and education, becomes an element in capital accumulation and development.[12]

The political characteristics of demand and command politics raise questions other than those raised by their economic characteristics. Demand politics threatens governability when mobilizations overrun established channels. It jeopardizes regulated conflict and the representational infrastructure, and it undermines a government of laws. Even so, mobilization that articulates perceived needs and inequities can contribute to governability by making the state respond in ways that foster support and legitimacy. Command politics holds out the potential for governability and discipline but can be a rationalization for authoritarian suppression of demands that jeopardizes legitimacy, support, and labor commitment.

These ambiguous potentialities are exacerbated by the conditions of modern Indian politics. In the second half of the twentieth century, the political context for capital accumulation is dramatically different from that in the eighteenth century, during the first industrial revolution, or from the political context that affected the Soviet Union's industrialization in the 1920s and 1930s. Radical asymmetries in economic and political power enabled England to build an industrial economy on considerable mass suffering. A repressive regime that sacrificed millions enabled the Soviet Union to extract, from the countryside and elsewhere, the surplus required for industrialization.

Capital accumulation in England and the Soviet Union occurred under political conditions very different from those in independent India, which, ab initio, adopted universal suffrage and responsible government. India's attempt to create a political context for rapid industrialization comparable to that in England and the Soviet Union, the emergency regime of 1975–77, revealed that the "discipline" that accompanied the initial stage of authoritarian rule was ephemeral, more a question of bottling up political opposition and economic demands than of transforming consciousness, institutions, and commitments.

If demand politics features voter sovereignty and societal direction of the state, what have been the consequences in practice? An implication of the centrality of voter sovereignty in demand politics is that the many who are poor will benefit more than the few who are rich. However, in India as elsewhere, political participation in the context of interest group and social pluralism has favored the better organized and more affluent, who not only have been more influential in shaping the policy agenda than the unorganized or underorganized poor but also have often appropriated the benefits of state-inspired propoor policies. Bank employees, doctors, airline pilots, office workers, professionals, and the labor aristocracy—all located for the most part in the public sector of the organized economy—have benefited more from demand politics than have landless laborers, marginal cultivators, and workers in craft and small-scale industries in the private sector and unorganized economy. Our chapters on industrial workers (chapter 10) and agricultural producers (chapter 13) show that those with more organization and assets gain more from demand politics than those with less, an outcome not inconsistent with what critics of interest group pluralism have found in other industrial democracies.

One reading of demand politics holds that the poor are unable to represent themselves. Such a reading led some Indian political leaders and intellectuals to hold the view that an authoritarian version of command politics was preferable to demand politics because it could enable the state to act as the friend, benefactor, and protector of the poor.

The disenchantment with authoritarian rule in 1975–77 revived the belief that voter sovereignty in the form of demand politics can contribute to both social justice and development, that is, that it does not necessarily serve only the well organized and prosperous. Without being able to mobilize on their own behalf, the poor are voiceless and defenseless. Demand politics gives the many poor an opportunity to represent themselves, to assert and protect their rights and interests, to protest and, sometimes, to limit the diversion by vested interest of the benefits of propoor policies.

Amartya Sen has drawn attention to the contrast between the People's Republic of China, where famine did occur, and independent India, where it did not. Sen attributes this difference to the presence in India of channels of political communication and representation that draw attention to dramatic deprivations and to the absence of such channels in China. He adds, however, that these channels "easily allow the quiet continuation of an astonishing set of persistent injustices [such as] endemic malnutrition and hunger that is not acute, so long as they happen quietly." [13]

Mobilization of the poor via demand politics depends on their being organized and connected to political processes, including policy choice and implementation. The deinstitutionalization of the Congress party and the rise of plebiscitary politics associated with Indira Gandhi's national leadership substituted a leader–mass following relationship for the organizational infrastructure of the institutionalized party that connected the poor, among others, to political and policy processes. In plebiscitary politics, the leader gains and holds support by appealing directly to voters. Such appeals short-circuit the mediating role of a representational infrastructure summed and integrated by the competition among parties. Party competition encouraged the Congress party to extend its support base to previously unrepresented constituencies as well as to hold old constituencies and attract those of rivals. As demonstrated by the parties of chief ministers Devraj Urs in Karnataka, Karpoori Thakur in Bihar, and Sharad Pawar in Maharashtra and the CPI-M in Kerala and Bengal, parties often were mechanisms for disestablishing old political elites, widening participation, and representing new constituencies. The absence of agreed procedures for making demands and for bargaining and deliberating about them tends to radicalize demands. Deinstitutionalization not only reduced the likelihood that the poor and other constituencies would be represented but also weakened the capacity of the state to contain and redirect demands that could not or should not be accommodated. Without an open and effective representational infrastructure that mediates between demand politics and the state, the bargaining and deliberation that compromise interests and articulate common purposes will atrophy.

8 Types of Politics and Economic Performance

The relationship between politics and economics is one that continues to perplex politicians, policy intellectuals, and social theorists. Does poverty in developing countries lead to revolution or fatalistic apathy? Does economic growth yield frustrated rising expectations or contented cooperation?[1] Too often, the answers to such questions have been ad hoc and a prioristic deductions or inferences from theory, occasionally buttressed by examples. In this chapter, we examine the association in India since independence between types of politics and types of regimes and economic performance.

The Relationship between Politics and Economics

We recognize that economic performance has many determinants, that is, that types of politics and types of regimes are only one set among a variety of factors determining economic growth. Variables thought to account for growth are not independent of each other. They are affected by prior and intervening factors, some short term or conjunctural. In 1975, for example, Donald Zagoria attempted to counter the then-prevalent euphoria about all things Chinese, including the authoritarian path to development, that followed the reopening of relationships between the United States and the Peoples Republic of China. He observed that economic development in the twentieth century "has taken place in many different places and in many different ways [in] countries with different political and economic systems, some with conservative military dictators, some more or less authoritarian, some with free market systems. . . . Quite obviously economic development can and does take place under extraordinarily diverse cultural, economic and political circumstances."[2]

Barnett Rubin has examined the constraints on and causes of economic growth in India between 1951–52 and 1978–79 through a statistical analysis of the relative positive and negative effects over time of five economic variables (defense expenditure, tax revenues, public consumption, price level, and foreign resources) on public-sector gross capital formation—the principal measure of investment in India and a

220

principal "cause" of economic growth.[3] In two concluding chapters, he considers "how political pressures from various groups rendered it impossible for the development lobby to finance continued growth in public sector investment"—that is, how political determinants of economic growth dominate and drive the five economic variables.[4]

In this chapter, we, like Rubin in his concluding chapters and Dennis Mueller and his colleagues in *The Political Economy of Growth*, emphasize "the importance of considering both economic and political factors simultaneously when trying to understand the growth and development process."[5] Mueller argues that economic factors alone—including capital, labor, and "technological change or similar factors that might improve the efficiency of the utilization of both factors simultaneously"—are not sufficient to explain rates and differences among them. Political factors broadly conceived, he argues, must be considered if, for example, one attempts to explain why Japan grew at a rate three times that of the United Kingdom between 1951 and 1973.

Of the five economic variables that Rubin uses to explain variations in public-sector gross capital formation, price level or inflation accounts for more of the variation than any of the others. Inflation too has its causes. Primary among them for India have been two exogenous factors, the price effects of monsoon failures and the two oil shocks of 1973 and 1979, the first caused by "nature," the second by India's participation in the world economy. Both, to be sure, are relative—that is, subject to constraining policy measures—the first via modernization of agricultural technology, the second by adjustment measures with respect to trade, conservation, and fiscal and monetary policy. Nevertheless, both monsoon "failures" and oil "shocks" remain largely exogenous; they and some of their effects remain beyond the reach of domestic politics and policy.

In this chapter, we treat price level or inflation as an independent, not a dependent, variable. Inflation explains a lot of the variance in economic performance, primarily because of the political and policy response to it. When politicians in charge of fiscal policy have framed their annual budgets, they have cut investment expenditure more severely than consumption expenditure. (These terms are carefully defined in accounting terms in Rubin's *Public Power and Public Investment in India*.) The lobby for the future and for public and collective goods has less votes and is less well mobilized than the lobbies for consumption expenditure. Politically, it is easier to cut hoped-for but uncertain future benefits of unknown (even unborn) and unmobilized constituents than it is to cut incomes and benefits that have become part of the expectations or aspirations of mobilized or mobilizable constituents, or to raise taxes. In other words, politics matters for the most important of the five economic variables that Rubin used to explain variations in investment, the principal determinant of growth.

In this chapter, "politics" becomes two qualitative variables—type of regime and type of politics—and four quantitative mobilization variables—voter turnout, riots, workdays lost, and student indiscipline—that operationalize important aspects of demand politics. The intervening variables are politically determined levels of investment and consumption expenditure. The question we adddress is, how have variations over time in our qualitative and quantitative political variables affected economic performance, defined primarily as growth but operationalized in the four variables of public investment, agricultural and industrial production, and inflation?

Prime Minister Indira Gandhi and many of those in India who supported the 1975–77 emergency shared the view that in developing countries there is a positive relationship between authoritarian regimes and economic performance. So too did significant segments of world press and financial opinion that looked favorably on India's emergency regime. India seemed to be adopting the then-fashionable authoritarianism-cum-growth model, a model that seemed to be entailed if not necessarily intended in IMF conditionality. According to the model, authoritarian regimes are better able to keep wages down, cut or eliminate subsidies and transfer payments, foster savings as opposed to consumption, and, by virtue of their putative political stability and alignment, attract foreign aid, loans, and investment. Consent, representation, and human rights might have to wait; they were a luxury for poor peoples not accustomed to freedom.

Prime Minister Indira Gandhi justified the emergency by arguing that selfish, antisocial, and politically destabilizing activity had to be checked and replaced by state-imposed "discipline." Authoritarian, repressive rule won tacit approval abroad, particularly in banking and financial circles. Robert McNamara, president of the World Bank, and H. J. Witteveen, director of the IMF, praised the economic performance of the emergency regime. Their assessment supported Gunnar Myrdal's earlier diagnosis; India's inability to develop rapidly was attributable to its "soft state." [6]

The belief that an excess of democracy constrains economic growth and jeopardizes governability had a certain currency in developed countries too. By the mid-1970s, when Mrs. Gandhi was promoting authoritarian rule in India, the democratic "excesses" of the late 1960s had begun to influence social theory and policy prescription in the West. [7] Excessive and unruly demand led not only to "ungovernability" but also to expansive welfare states that diverted increasing proportions of GNP from investment in growth to "unproductive" expenditures on entitlements and social rights.[8] Stagflation accompanied by costly new demands and escalating established benefits put welfare states, themselves products of democratic politics, at risk and revealed cultural as well as political and economic contradictions.[9] Theories of the "overloaded state" and proposals for how to insulate government from democratic politics multiplied.[10]

In the developing world, the rise in the 1970s of newly industrialized countries (such as South Korea, Taiwan, Hong Kong, Singapore, and Brazil) suggested that the future lay with authoritarian regimes and export-led growth in an expanding world economy based on free trade and easy access to commercial bank credit.

However, in the 1980s, the authoritarian-cum-growth model began to unravel paralled with a rash of restorations of democracy. World recession, debt, worsening terms of trade for primary products (including the collapse of oil prices), and creeping protectionism seemed to show that it was the buoyant world economy of the 1970s, not authoritarian regimes, that accounted for economic growth.

Our analysis in this chapter suggests that in India there are discernible but indeterminant relationships between political variables and measures of economic performance. Under an authoritarian British raj, per capita income had remained stagnant between 1901 and 1946, the last forty-five years of colonial rule. Raj authoritarianism did make the trains run on time but did not make the economy grow.[11] Independent India under Jawaharlal Nehru's leadership proposed to do better. Over four decades of mostly democratic rule, per capita income increased by at least 1.3 percent per year.[12] India's economy has not grown as fast as those of postwar pacesetters among industrialized societies, such as Japan and Germany, or leaders among developing societies, such as South Korea and Taiwan. Until the 1980s, it seemed to be locked into what the late Raj Krishna identified as the "Hindu rate of growth," 3.5 percent of GNP. In the 1980s, when other Third World economies were faltering, the Indian economy seemed to have broken with the Hindu rate of growth by reaching a long-term annual rate of 5 percent.

Our findings in this chapter suggest that authoritarianism was not an important determinant of India's modest but significant economic growth and that it is not likely to become one. The notion that authoritarian rule in India has been positively associated with economic growth and that democracy has not is more contradicted than supported by the available evidence. Both good and bad economic performance occurred under both authoritarian and democratic regimes.

Authoritarianism in India lacks legitimacy. It is likely to have a short half-life without a Stalinist-type regime, which India seems reluctant to mount. Authoritarianism in India faces not only a legitimacy constraint but also a productivity constraint; that is, authoritarian rule can coerce workers in the short run, but in the long run the productivity of human capital depends on willing commitment. It also faces an investment constraint. As the decline in public investment during the emergency suggests, the regime used consumption expenditure to gain or hold support, in a sense substituting consumption expenditure for coercion. Finally, authoritarianism in India faces an efficiency constraint. As practiced in India (and the Philippines under Marcos), it exaggerated the already patrimonial and personalistic features that characterized democratic rule under Mrs. Gandhi's leadership. The quality of investment, commercial and professional activity, and public authority and the productivity of physical capital deteriorated as favorites and courtiers enlarged their ability to influence decisions and to extract rents and profits.

Over the four decades since independence, state capacity and autonomy declined. The decline encompassed both authoritarian and democratic regimes. The long-run deterioration in state capacity and autonomy was associated with the deinstitutionalization of both political parties and state institutions. As we showed in parts 1 and 2, there has been a secular decline in the authority and capacity of state agencies and political parties to articulate a public philosophy and to respond to and broker political demands within the framework of that philosophy.

In examining the association between politics (operationalized as type of politics and regime type) and growth, we focus on the rising levels of participation and mobilization that characterized the years after 1965. While authoritarianism was instituted in order to counter the pressure of such mobilization and while it did temporarily limit it, rising and persistent demand pressures have affected Indian politics and policy regardless of type of regime or type of politics.

We approach the relationship between politics and growth by distinguishing four periods since Indian independence. Each manifests a different combination of regime type (democratic or authoritarian) and type of politics (demand or command). Next we relate the four periods to various measures of economic performance and to indicators of demand politics. We conclude that demand and command politics are more associated with economic performance than are regime types per se but that neither association is very compelling. Politics seems not to matter as much for economic performance as politicians and political scientists would like to think. We also note that the higher mobilization of the post-Nehru era both narrowed and lowered the range within which economic performance varies.

In addressing the question of the association between demand and command politics and economic performance, we use a different mix of evidence for economic performance than we do for type of politics. The evidence for economic performance is mostly quantitative, while that for type of politics is more qualitative. Where available, we have also used quantitative evidence to make the case for the existence of demand and command politics. At the same time, we have resisted the temptation to pursue an attractive but spurious symmetry of quantitative measures for economic performance and type of politics and to attempt the statistical manipulations that then become possible. Not only is accurate medium- to long-term quantitative evidence for type of politics scarce, but also—and more important—the available qualitative evidence is more valid and reliable. Our explanatory project encounters the phenomenon of circular causation. While we are primarily interested in analyzing the effect of type of politics and regime on economic performance, we recognize that economic performance also affects the type of politics and regime. Problems about causal direction are inherent in analysis. The relationship is mutually determined.

The era of 1952–86 included four distinct periods for types of regime and types of politics. Our periodization starts with the period covering the first three five-year plans, when India embarked on a strategy of limited autarky based on investment in heavy and basic industry and import substitution: (1) 1952–53 to 1963–64: democratic regime/command politics I (mainly Nehru); (2) 1964–65 to 1974–75: democratic regime/demand politics I (mainly Indira Gandhi); (3) 1975–76 to 1976–77: authoritarian regime/command politics II (emergency); and (4) 1977–78 to 1985–86: democratic regime/demand politics II (Janata/Congress).[13]

1952–53 to 1963–64: Democratic Regime/Command Politics I

The Nehru era was characterized by a democratic regime and non-authoritarian command politics. Nehru-led Congress governments were able to invest in the future because they could rely on Nehru's persuasive leadership, the effectiveness of the Congress party's organizational wing at the center and in the states, and autonomous and authoritative state institutions. They benefited from the residual consensus of the nationalist era and a less mobilized, more dependent society and electorate. Quantitative indicators of demand politics—such as voter turnouts, workdays lost due to strikes, incidents of student "indiscipline," and number of riots—remained low (fig. 5 and table 23). The Congress party exercised firm control, winning two-thirds or

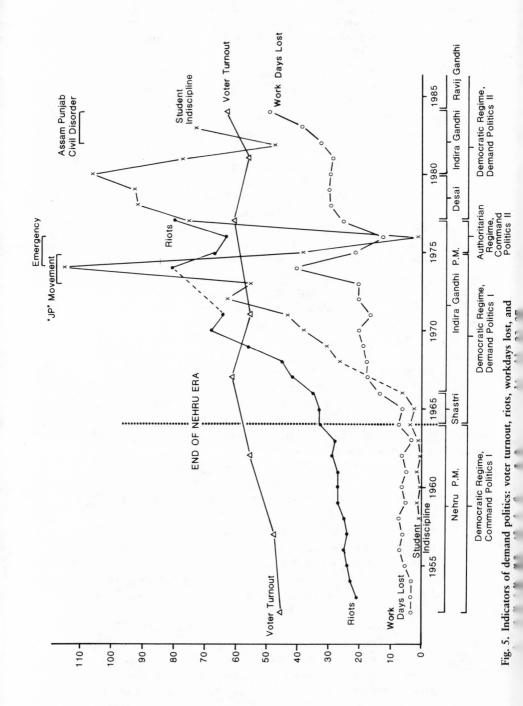

Fig. 5. Indicators of demand politics: voter turnout, riots, workdays lost, and

TABLE 23
Indicators of Demand Politics

Year	Riots (Thousands)	Student "Indiscipline": Reported Incidents	Workdays Lost (Millions)	Voter Turnout (%)
		Democratic Regime/Command Politics I (Nehru)		
1952	—	—	3.3	45.7
1953	21	—	3.4	—
1954	23	—	3.4	—
1955	24	—	5.7	—
1956	25	—	7.0	—
1957	24	—	6.4	47.8
1958	25	93	7.8	—
1959	27	120	5.6	—
1960	27	80	6.5	—
1961	27	172	5.0	—
1962	29	97	6.1	55.4
1963	28	109	3.3	—
		Democratic Regime/Demand Politics I		
1964 ⎫ Shastri	33	395	7.7	—
1965 ⎭	33	271	6.5	—
1966 ⎱	35	607	13.8	—
1967	42	—	17.1	61.3
1968	45	2,665	17.2	—
1969	56	3,064	19.0	—
1970 ⎰ I. Gandhi	68	3,861	20.6	—
1971	64	4,380	16.5	55.3
1972	—	6,365	20.5	—
1973	—	5,551	20.6	—
1974 ⎭	81	11,540	40.3	—
		Authoritarian Regime/Command Politics II (I. Gandhi)		
1975	67	3,847	21.9	—
1976	63	1,190	12.8	—
		Democratic Regime/Demand Politics II		
1977 ⎫	80	7,520	25.3	60.4
1978 ⎬ Desai	—	9,174	29.7	—
1979 ⎭	—	9,203	29.8	—
1980 ⎱	—	10,600	29.6	—
1981	—	7,740	29.2	56.9
1982 ⎰ I. Gandhi	—	5,200	33.2	—
1983	—	7,188	38.3[a]	—
1984 ⎭	—	—	49.4[a]	64.0
1985 ⎭ R. Gandhi	—	—	—	—

SOURCES: Riots: Baldev Raj Nayar, *Violence and Crime in India* (Delhi: Macmillan, 1975); Government of India, Ministry of Home Affairs, Bureau of Police Research and

more of parliamentary seats and three-fifths or more of assembly seats in the 1952, 1957, and 1962 general elections.[14] Economic performance was good to outstanding.

The era encompassed the second and third five-year plans, which, in retrospect, appear as a kind of political and economic golden age. Government's investment effort, as reflected in the central government's capital formation, grew vigorously from about 25 percent of total expenditure just prior to the first five-year plan (1950–51) to an average of just below 50 percent (fig. 6 and table 24) during the second and third five-year plans. Industrial production spurted forward during the last two years of the second plan and the first four years of the third (1959–60 through 1964–65, [fig. 7 and table 25]). Subsequent industrial production has not equalled the twelve-point average annual gain of these remarkable six years. Food grain production stayed abreast of population growth by increasing 20 percent between the last year of the first plan (1955–56) and 1964–65, the year before the great monsoon failure of 1965–66 (fig. 8 and table 26). In only two years of the 1956–66 period did the price index rise more than ten points (fig. 9 and table 27).

1964–65 to 1974–75: Democratic Regime/Demand Politics I

Demand politics surfaced in 1964–65 and continued through 1974–75, with a brief remission in 1971–72. Exogenous factors contributed to this change; these included shocks caused by security, political, and economic events: military failure in wars with China (1962) and Pakistan (1965); the deaths of two prime ministers (Nehru in May 1964 and Shastri in January 1966); and the "worst weather on record"

Development, *Crime in India* (annual); student indiscipline: Government of India, Ministry of Home Affairs, "Student Indiscipline" (1967, mimeograph), *Report* (annual), and *Third Report of the National Police Commission, 1980* (Delhi, 1980); and *Data India,* September 18–24, 1978, p. 594; workdays lost: Government of India, Ministry of Labour, Labour Bureau, *Indian Labour Statistics* (Chandigarh and Simla, annual), and *Indian Labour Yearbook* (Chandigarh and Simla, annual); and Government of India, Ministry of Finance, *Economic Survey* (Delhi, annual) (the figures in *Economic Survey* are for fiscal years; e.g., 1978–79 corresponds to 1978 in the table).

Notes: Data on riots and "student indiscipline" were not available after 1977 and 1982, respectively. As a result, our figures do not account for what may have been extraordinary increases in both. In the 1980s, riots and student indiscipline may have merged when highly mobilized student-led regional movements in Assam and Punjab engaged in (Punjab) or triggered (Assam) violence.

[a]Provisional, and excludes Bombay textile strike.

in 1965–66 when food production plummeted and prices soared.[15] Together, these events created the necessary but not the sufficient conditions for the rise of demand politics.

United States president Lyndon Johnson practiced a disruptive and politically counterproductive "short tether" food aid policy. World Bank, United States, and consortium foreign aid commitments remained unfulfilled. One of the first acts of the inexperienced new prime minister, Indira Gandhi, was to devalue the rupee (June 1966). Perceived as being imposed on India, devaluation politically embarrassed the Gandhi government and weakened its standing and authority.[16] Poor economic performance both reflected and compounded the effects of exogenous shocks on the rise of demand politics. Economic indicators for the fifth year of the third plan (1965–66) turned sharply downward. Industrial as well as agricultural production declined; plan investment, already adversely affected by the doubling of defense spending after the China war (October 1962) (see fig. 6), slumped further; and prices shot up.

The fourth general election (February–March 1967) illustrates the mutually determinative relationship between type of regime and of politics on the one hand and economic performance on the other. Voters turned out in unprecedented numbers (fig. 5 and table 23) to protest poor economic performance and to vote against government's domestic and foreign economic policy failures. The result was virtual repudiation of Congress, the party of nationalism and independence. Between the third general election in 1962 and the fourth in 1967, Congress's share of parliamentary votes and seats dropped from 46 to 40 percent and from 73 to 54 percent, respectively; its share of state assembly votes and seats, from 44 to 40 percent and from 60 to 49 percent,[17] and its control of sixteen state governments from fourteen to eight as regional parties or opposition party coalitions formed governments in half. In circular fashion, the electoral outcome fostered demand politics, as narrow and uncertain Congress majorities at the center and unstable and warring opposition coalitions in the states rendered governmental authority more suspect and vulnerable.

The election results weakened public authority. At the center, Congress government was inhibited by a razor-thin majority. After Congress split in November 1969, its minority government remained in power until the 1971 parliamentary election, with the support of the CPI and DMK. With eight opposition-governed states, it lost some of its capacity to initiate and coordinate policy between the center and the state governments. At the state level, party parochialism and rivalry

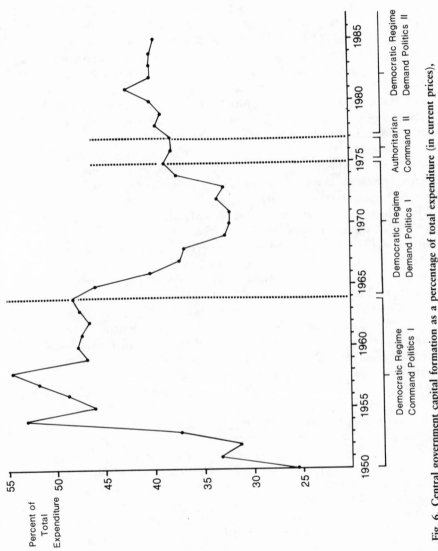

Fig. 6. Central government capital formation as a percentage of total expenditure (in current prices), according to regime type and politics type.

TABLE 24
Central Government's Capital Expenditure as a Percentage of Total Expenditure (in Current Prices)

Year	%		Year	%	
1950–51	25.56		1975–76	38.74	I. Gandhi — Authoritarian regime/command politics II (negligible point-to-point change in capital expenditure, 1975–76 to 1976–77; 38% average annual proportion)
1951–52	33.39		1976–77	37.95	
1952–53	31.45				
1953–54	37.23	Democratic regime/command politics I (86% point-to-point increase in capital expenditure, 1950–51 to 1963–64; 44.4% average annual proportion)	1977–78	37.98	Desai — Democratic regime/demand politics II (negligible point-to-point change in capital expenditure, 1977–78 to 1985–86; 40% average annual proportion)
1954–55	52.98		1978–79	39.49	
1955–56	46.62				
1956–57	48.77	Nehru	1979–80	39.06	
1957–58	51.77		1980–81	40.06	
1958–59	54.64		1981–82	42.5	
1959–60	46.75		1982–83	40.7	I. Gandhi
1960–61	47.73		1983–84	40.9	
1961–62	47.18		1984–85	40.1	
1962–63	46.46		1985–86	39.6[a]	R. Gandhi
1963–64	47.54				
1964–65	48.23	Shastri			
1965–66	45.83				
1966–67	40.22	Democratic regime/demand politics I (22% point-to-point decline in capital expenditure, 1964–65 to 1974–75; 37% average annual proportion)			
1967–68	37.24				
1968–69	36.74				
1969–70	32.74				
1970–71	32.37	I. Gandhi			
1971–72	32.20				
1972–73	33.48				
1973–74	32.77				
1974–75	37.58				

SOURCES: Barnett Rubin, "Private Power and Public Investment in India: A Study in the Political Economy of Development" (PhD. diss., University of Chicago, 1982), table 9. Rubin's sources include, Government of India, Ministry of Finance, *An Economic and Functional Classification of the Central Government Budget* (Delhi, annual) and *Economic Survey*.
^aBudget estimate

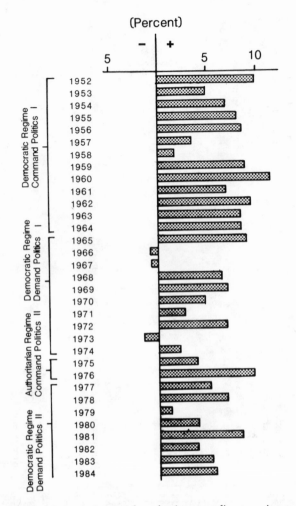

Fig. 7. Annual variation in industrial production according to regime type and politics type.

TABLE 25
Annual Variation in Industrial Production

Year		% Variation		Year		% Variation	
1952	⎫	10.0	⎫	1975	⎫ I. Gandhi	3.9	⎫ Authoritarian
1953	⎪	4.9	⎪	1976	⎭	9.8	⎭ regime/com-
1954	⎪	7.0	⎪				mand politics
1955	⎪	8.1	⎪				II (6.85% av-
1956	⎪	8.6	⎪ Democratic				erage annual
1957	⎬ Nehru	3.5	⎬ regime/com-				increase)
1958	⎪	1.7	⎪ mand politics I				
1959	⎪	8.9	⎪ (7.5% average	1977	⎫	5.3	⎫
1960	⎪	11.6	⎪ annual	1978	⎬ Desai	6.9	⎪
1961	⎪	7.0	⎪ increase)	1979	⎭	1.2	⎪ Democratic
1962	⎪	9.6	⎪	1980	⎫	4.0	⎬ regime/de-
1963	⎭	8.4	⎭	1981	⎪	8.6	⎪ mand politics
				1982	⎬ I. Gandhi	3.9	⎪ II (5.5% aver-
				1983	⎪	5.4	⎪ age annual
				1984	⎭	5.8	⎭ increase)
1964	⎫ Shastri	8.6	⎫				
1965	⎭	9.1	⎪				
1966	⎫	−0.8	⎪				
1967	⎪	−0.7	⎪				
1968	⎪	6.4	⎪ Democratic				
1969	⎪	7.1	⎬ regime/de-				
1970	⎬ I. Gandhi	4.8	⎪ mand politics I				
1971	⎪	2.9	⎪ (3.7% average				
1972	⎪	7.1	⎪ annual				
1973	⎪	−1.4	⎪ increase)				
1974	⎭	2.2	⎭				

SOURCE: Reserve Bank of India, *Report on Currency and Finance* (Bombay, annual).
Note: The index was set at 100 in 1951 and again in 1960 and 1970.

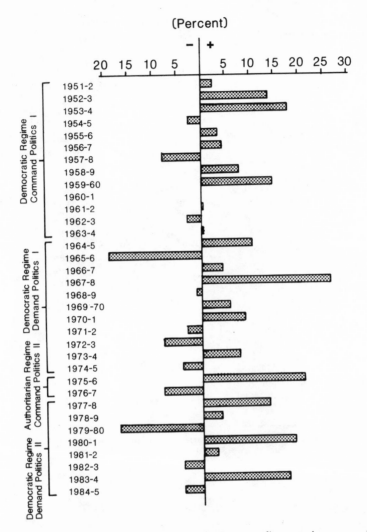

Fig. 8. Annual variation in food grain production according to regime type and politics type.

TABLE 26
Annual Variation in Food Grain Production

Year	Million Tonnes	% Change	Leader	Regime/politics
1950–51	50.0	—		
1951–52	51.2	2.4		
1952–53	58.3	13.8		
1953–54	68.7	17.8		
1954–55	66.9	−2.6		Democratic regime/ command politics I (4.3% average annual increase)
1955–56	69.3	3.6		
1956–57	72.3	4.3	Nehru	
1957–58	66.5	−8.0		
1958–59	71.7	7.8		
1959–60	82.3	14.8		
1960–61	82.0	−0.4		
1961–62	82.7	0.9		
1962–63	80.2	−3.0		
1963–64	80.6	0.5		
1964–65	89.0	10.4	Shastri	
1965–66	72.0	−19.1		
1966–67	75.1	4.3		Democratic regime/ demand politics I (2.6% average annual increase)
1967–68	95.1	26.6		
1968–69	94.0	−1.2		
1969–70	99.5	5.8		
1970–71	108.4	8.9	I. Gandhi	
1971–72	105.2	−3.0		
1972–73	97.0	−7.8		
1973–74	104.2	7.4		
1974–75	99.8	−4.2		
1975–76	121.0	21.2	I. Gandhi	Authoritarian regime/ command politics II (6.5% average annual increase)
1976–77	111.1	−8.2		
1977–78	126.4	13.8	Desai	
1978–79	131.4	4.0		
1979–80	108.9	−17.1		Democratic regime/ demand politics II (4.4% average annual increase)
1980–81	129.6	19.0	I. Gandhi	
1981–82	133.3	2.9		
1982–83	128.4	−3.7		
1983–84	152.4	18.7		
1984–85	146.2	−4.1		
1985–86			R. Gandhi	

Source: Ministry of Finance, *Economic Survey*.

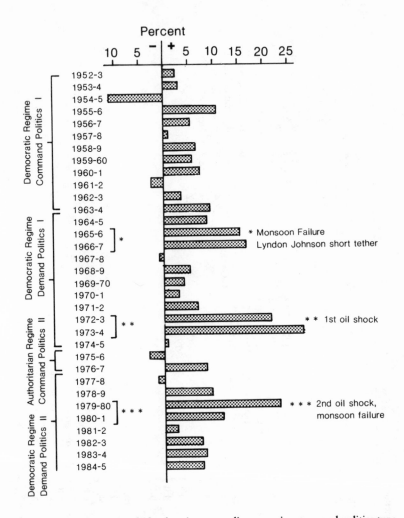

Fig. 9. Annual variation in wholesale prices according to regime type and politics type.

TABLE 27
Annual Variation in Wholesale Prices, All Commodities (Point to Point)

Year	% Variation	Leader	Regime
1952–53	2.0		
1953–54	2.3		
1954–55	-10.2		
1955–56	11.6		
1956–57	5.9		
1957–58	1.0	Nehru	Democratic regime/command politics I (3.5% average annual increase)
1958–59	6.6		
1959–60	5.8		
1960–61	7.2		
1961–62	-2.6		
1962–63	3.6		
1963–64	9.3		
1964–65	8.7	Shastri	
1965–66	15.2		
1966–67	16.5		
1967–68	-0.9	I. Gandhi	Democratic regime/demand politics I (10% average annual increase)
1968–69	5.2		
1969–70	4.0		
1970–71	3.1		
1971–72	6.8		
1972–73	21.7		
1973–74	27.9		
1974–75	0.6		

Year	% Variation	Leader	Regime
1975–76	-3.0	I. Gandhi	Authoritarian regime/command politics II (2.8% average annual increase)
1976–77	8.6		
1977–78	-1.3	Desai	Democratic regime/demand politics II (8.6% average annual increase)
1978–79	9.5		
1979–80	23.2		
1980–81	11.7		
1981–82	2.5	I. Gandhi	
1982–83	7.5		
1983–84	8.2		
1984–85			
1985–86	7.6	R. Gandhi	

SOURCE: Reserve Bank of India, *Report on Currency and Finance.*

in coalition governments fragmented and discredited authority. With the writ of government enfeebled, it became much more difficult to combine a democratic regime with command politics.

Quantitative and historical evidence for the rise of demand politics after 1965 include increases in electoral participation (turnout), riots, strikes, student "indiscipline" (see fig. 5), and agrarian unrest. Baldev Raj Nayar has shown that the ratio of riots to population was relatively stable for the decade from 1954–55 to 1963–64, slowly accelerated between 1964–65 and 1966–67, and then rose dramatically from 1967.[18] Between April and August 1966, when food shortages were acute, there were widespread *bandhs* (suspension of business) and demonstrations demanding food rationing and protesting price rises, tax increases, hoarding, and profiteering.[19] Industrial unrest, as indicated by workdays lost, more than doubled between 1965 and 1966, rose about 25 percent the following year, and continued to rise through 1970 (see fig. 5 and table 23). Incidents of student "indiscipline," an administrative euphemism for goals as various as postponing examinations and "total revolution," increased dramatically from 271 to 607 between 1965 and 1966, increased more dramatically to 2,665 by 1968, and continued steadily upward through the early seventies (fig. 5 and table 23).[20] Participation in the 1967 election increased 11.7 percent over the 49.6 percent average of the first three general elections (fig. 5 and table 23).

An agrarian version of demand politics began with alarming intensity after the defeated Congress government of West Bengal was replaced in February 1967 by a United Front government that included the CPI-M. Taking their name from Naxalbari, a village in the narrow neck of Darjeeling district that precariously connects Bengal to Assam, the Naxalite rebellions by tribal landless laborers spread west to Bihar and south along the tribal belt of the Eastern Ghats to Andhra Pradesh and Kerala.[21] By 1970, the state's use of force had crushed them. Naxalite rebellion was followed by a new version of agrarian protest, the land grab movement. Led by leftist parties (CPI, Samyukta Socialist party, and Praja Socialist party)[22] landless laborers engaged in symbolic occupation or harvesting of land large landowners should have given up under the land ceilings legislation. A Home Ministry study reflected the national alarm. In language uncharacteristic of Indian bureaucratic speech, it observed that "an explosive situation" existed and attributed it to the state governments' failure to carry out necessary land reforms. The patience of the cultivating classes was "on the verge of boiling over," and the resulting explosion "could rock India."[23]

The events of 1969 through 1972 suggested that under Mrs. Gandhi's leadership Congress could restore the party's credibility and government's authority and perhaps return to the democratic regime/ command politics of her father's time. In 1969, she split the party, purged the old guard state bosses, and began to advocate progressive and populist measures, such as the nationalization of the fourteen largest commercial banks, and, in 1971, the eradication of poverty (*gharibi hatao*). Her leadership for a time restored Congress's élan and support. In 1967, the electorate had voted against bad government by repudiating Congress. In 1971, the electorate voted against bad government again by using the "delinked" parliamentary election to signal its repudiation of coalition governments in the large North Indian states and in West Bengal. In a 1972 khaki election for state assemblies held soon after India's military victory over Pakistan in December 1971, the electorate not only confirmed its 1971 judgment but also rewarded Mrs. Gandhi's conduct of the war by returning Congress majorities in most states. Formal indicators of demand politics receded: the number of workdays lost declined in 1971, and the Home Ministry reported a respite in challenges to law and order.[24]

However, the party credibility and governmental authority gained in these elections were soon dissipated. Instead of using her mandate and the enhanced legitimacy and effectiveness of party and government to implement progressive measures at the center and in the states, Mrs. Gandhi began the process of deinstitutionalization that substituted centralized personal rule for party and state governance.[25] By 1974, it was abundantly apparent that the opportunity offered by the 1971 and 1972 elections to combine, as in the Nehru era, a democratic regime with command politics had been lost.

The intense pressure on government that had characterized the 1965–70 period quickly resumed (fig. 5). It was exacerbated by new exogenous shocks that lowered production and raised prices: the first oil price rise (1973) and a series of poor monsoons. The deterioration of party credibility and governmental authority quickened. All indications of unrest and discontent accelerated exponentially. The number of workdays lost jumped from sixteen to twenty million between 1971 and 1972 and reached an unprecedented forty million in 1974, the year of a national railway strike that challenged Mrs. Gandhi's government (fig. 5 and table 23). Incidents of student indiscipline grew phenomenally after 1965, increasing from 271 in 1965 to 11,500 in 1974;[26] the number of riots more than doubled, from 33,000 in 1965 to 80,000 in 1974. These indicators represent economic and political discontent, including a response to the extraordinary thirty-five-point price rise in 1974–75 following the oil shock, and student participation in the mobilization of protest by Jayaprakash Narayan that eventuated in the emergency proclamation. The JP movement for "total revolution" (i.e., fundamental transformation of Indian society) was most active in Bihar and Gujarat, where students were an essential component.[27] On June 26, 1975, Mrs. Gandhi imposed an emergency regime on the country.

1975–76 to 1976–77: Authoritarian Regime/Command Politics II

Mrs. Gandhi's authoritarian and corporatist version of command politics ended the 1965–75 period of demand politics by banning strikes and demonstrations, arresting opposition leaders, censoring the press, and depriving citizens of their civil and political rights. The declared purpose of the emergency regime was to restore civil order and economic discipline. Reported incidents of student indiscipline declined dramatically in 1976 (from 11,540 in 1974 to 1,190 in 1976) as did the number of workdays lost due to strikes (from forty to thirteen million) (fig. 5).

While the period of authoritarian rule may be too brief to support reliable findings, economic indicators suggested some positive performance. Food production increased, with help from a favorable monsoon. So too did industrial production (fig. 7 and table 25). Stimulated in part by gains in the industrial sector, the increase was associated with a lower level of workdays lost through industrial disputes, a result that, at least in the short run, supports one of the claims of the authoritarian growth model. However, as table 24 shows, the authoritarian regime, despite a price decline, was not able over two budgets to increase the proportion of total expenditure devoted to capital formation; proportionately, public saving declined and consumption expenditure increased.

1977–78 to 1984–85: Democratic Regime/Demand Politics II

The Janata party's unexpected election victory in March 1977 abruptly ended authoritarian rule. When its government restored constitutional government, a liberal state, and democratic political processes, quantitative and qualitative evidence indicated a resurgence of demand politics, which persisted after a Gandhi Congress government returned to power in 1980. Rates of student indiscipline in 1980 and workdays lost from 1979 to 1984 surpassed those of the 1960s. Student indiscipline rates approached figures for the most extreme prior year, 1974, and workdays lost by strikes exceeded them. The Home Ministry reported serious law and order problems for 1978–79, 1979–80, and again after 1982. It especially noted the appearance in 1980–81 of farmers' agitations for remunerative prices, a development that signaled the emergence of a new constituency for demand politics.[28] In 1984, labor unrest reached unprecedented levels.

The restoration in 1977 of a democratic regime and the consequent release of pent-up demands was not accompanied, as some had expected, with declines in economic performance. To the contrary, economic performance under democratic rule was equal to or markedly better than it had been under authoritarian rule. Both the Janata government and the Congress governments that preceded and followed it presided over substantial increases in agricultural production as well as the declines that accompanied poor monsoons in 1979 and 1982 (table 26). Industrial production accelerated slowly in the late 1970s but rapidly in the 1980s, apparently breaking through the "slow industrialization" of the 1960s and 1970s.[29] Contrary to what might be expected, gains in the rate of industrial growth were paralleled by marked increases in workdays lost. The proportion of central government expenditure on capital formation increased slightly over emergency levels, a gain that many regarded as futile given an apparent marked increase in the capital-output ratio.

In the accompanying figures, we plot regime types and then types of politics against measures of economic performance in order to judge whether they are correlated. Our project is limited and contingent, well short of causal statements but designed to examine the proposition that regime types and/or types of politics may be associated with variations in economic performance. To anticipate our findings, the emergency regime that institutionalized the authoritarian growth model did make some difference for economic performance, but not as much as Mrs. Gandhi's rhetoric claimed or as was anticipated in the IMF–World Bank conditionality era. Industrial production increased, and strikes, student indiscipline, and prices declined, but on the crucial performance variable of public savings for investment, the authoritarian regime faltered; that is, the level was below those that immediately preceded and followed the emergency years. By contrast, under the democratic politics of the Nehru era, when inflation was kept low, proportions of central government capital expenditures reached levels never attained subsequently. At the same time, type of regime does not seem to have made much difference for annual differences in the growth of industrial and agricultural production, which reached points as high after as during the emergency.

After 1965–66, there is a striking association between declining levels of economic performance, as measured by our four indicators, and increases in our four measures of demand politics (riots, student indiscipline, strikes, and voter participation). Higher plateaus in measures of demand politics indicate a qualitative change in the conditions under which politics influences economic performance. Regardless of regime type or type of politics, state actors after 1965–66 faced a differently constituted political universe that seemed to make outstanding economic performance more difficult. Yet the 1980s seemed to belie the inverse relationship between demand politics and improved levels of economic performance. As industrial production spurted upward, so too did mobilization indicators. The limited time frame calls for caution, but such figures seriously compromise the proposition that higher levels of mobilization necessarily impede economic growth.

In tables 23–27 and figures 6–9, we have plotted democratic and authoritarian regimes against four economic indicators: government capital formation, industrial production, food grain production, and wholesale prices. Wide variation in all four measures were apparent during the democratic regime of 1952–75 (Nehru-Gandhi). During the authoritarian regime, performance varied narrowly within plateaus reached just prior to its imposition. Under the democratic regimes of Janata and Congress (1977–86) investment showed slight and industrial production marked gains, while food grain production and prices, except during the "second oil shock," performed well. Overall, there is no consistent time-bound association between type of regime and economic performance, and the view that economies perform better under authoritarian than under democratic regimes is thus disconfirmed.

We have also plotted types of politics against the same four measures of economic performance. The most striking contrast is that between command politics I (1952–53 through 1963–64 [Nehru]) and demand politics I (1964–65 through 1974–75 [Gandhi]). Economic performance was better during the earlier period on all indicators except food grain production. However, there was little difference between economic performance under command politics II (1975–76 through 1976–77 [emergency]) and under demand politics II (1977–

78 through 1985–86). Capital formation did slightly better and growth in industrial production about the same under demand politics II, while prices did slightly better under command politics II (the emergency). Overall, the relationship between type of politics and economic performance is slightly more discernible than that between regime type and economic performance.

We conclude that there is an indeterminate relationship between type of regime and politics on the one hand and economic performance on the other. The indeterminant relationship holds in both the pre- and post-Nehru political universes. The success of authoritarian rule under the emergency in achieving state objectives—control of hoarding, recouping of black money, better attendance in government offices, compulsory deposits, more stringent tax collection, decline in prices, a wage freeze—lent some credence to the view that command features of an authoritarian regime provide short-term gains by repressing mobilization and participation. Yet during the Nehru era and under Janata, I. Gandhi, and R. Gandhi governments, democratic regimes were associated with good economic performance.

The view that there is a positive relationship between authoritarian regimes and economic performance and the view that state sovereignty is necessarily better for economic growth in developing economies than popular sovereignty is not supported by our analysis of the Indian evidence. A second finding concerns the association between economic performance and indicators of demand politics: riots, student indiscipline, workdays lost, and voter participation. There was a striking association after 1965–66 between declining levels of economic performance and increases in demand politics indicators (fig. 5). These quantitative changes suggest a qualitative transformation of mobilization and participation that affected subsequent economic performance and growth regardless of regime or polity type. In the post-Nehru era, state actors faced a differently constituted political universe that seemed to jeopardize growth. Yet events in the 1980s suggest otherwise. As industrial production spurted upward, so did the indicators of mobilization.

Mrs. Gandhi's effort from 1970 to free herself from the pressures of demand politics had a profound effect on Indian political institutions and conduct. Her strategy was to deinstitutionalize party, Parliament, public services, and the federal system. It was a strategy for narrowing or eliminating the channels through which demands might be articulated. Instead of engaging discontented or disgruntled constituencies and responding to or brokering their demands, Mrs. Gandhi sought to escape them. This strategy ultimately failed when demand groups, deprived of regular channels for expression, voiced their claims in the streets, that is, outside legal and conventional channels. The agitational politics of opinion "out of doors" developed highly elaborated political art forms to persuade or coerce public opinion and elected and appointed state officials. This is the subject of the following chapter.

Part 4

DEMAND
GROUPS

9   Demand Groups and Pluralist Representation

Interest group representation in India is marked by pluralist rather than corporatist forms and processes; its pluralism differs from that in other industrial democracies. Our conceptual vocabulary for the discussion of representation introduces three terms—"demand group," "state-dominated pluralism," and "involuted pluralism"—to designate distinctive aspects of the organization and representation of interests in India. Unlike organized interests, the demand group relies on ad hoc rather than bureaucratic organization. It uses mass mobilization more than expert knowledge and technical bargaining but combines issues and movement politics with the politics of organized interests. Other characteristics of the Indian variant of pluralism are its domination by the state and its tendency to excessive multiplication and fragmentation, a process we call involution. Finally, the pervasive and powerful state not only constrains and manipulates interest group activity, it is also itself a major interest, competing with and usually winning out over societal interests. On the one hand, the state sets policy agendas. It controls legal and economic incentives and both fosters and manipulates involuted pluralism. On the other hand, in its various industrial, financial, and commercial manifestations, it commands more resources than the societal interests with which it competes. State producer interests and policy bodies occupy much of the representational "space" that is occupied in other industrial democracies by pluralist and corporatist structures and processes. They also speak and act on their own behalf as institutional interests in the context of governmental pluralism.

Two parameters or initial conditions affect the organization of producer interests in India: (1) location in the organized or in the unorganized economies and (2) the dominance of the public sector within the organized economy. That only 10 percent of all workers are in the organized economy (see chapter 1, fig. 1) affects the base on which the formal representation of interest draws, and it also shapes the type of interest group organization specific to India. The demand group, a particular variant of interest representation that we discuss below, is in part a consequence of the scale of India's unorganized economy. As we

247

noted in chapter 1, about two-thirds of the salaried and wage workers within the organized economy are employed by public-sector firms or government, and public-sector firms control 76 percent of the paid-up capital employed by the hundred largest firms (table 4). Such state domination of the organized economy is a precondition for state domination of pluralist representation. Formally organized interests are more common and more important for policy choice and implementation in the organized economy than in the unorganized, where ad hoc issue and movement politics using agitational and symbolic means play a larger role.

In chapter 7 we advanced the theory of demand and command polities, and in chapter 8 we put the theory in motion by relating various measures of command and demand politics to measures of economic performance. In the next four chapters, we shall analyze the dynamics of command and demand politics. Here we attend to how interactions between command and demand politics are mediated by the organization and representation of interests. The framework of representation has an independent effect on the prevailing balance between command and demand politics.

Pluralism and Neocorporatism: Some Conceptual Distinctions

In treating representation in terms of pluralist and corporatist modes, we posit interest rather than class as the basic motivating and organizing principle of political economy. Unlike most Marxist treatments, which take it as axiomatic and predetermined that only the mode and relations of production define social formations and that class so defined is the ultimate determinant of consciousness and action, we treat interest phenomenologically and contingently. Interests can be expressed through a variety of social formations—class, caste, tribe, or status group; religious, linguistic, or territorial community; and profession or occupation defined in terms of skill, knowledge, and ethos as well as in terms of property relations. The existence, goals, and ascendance of such social formations are as much a matter of context and choice as of objective determination.

The most common conceptualization of pluralist representation is interest group pluralism.[1] American in its origin and development and closely related to liberalism, it became in the 1950s and 1960s a conceptual export that followed in the wake of a rising curve of American world power and influence. It posits an equilibrium model of competing but ultimately harmonious organized interests. Anybody who feels the need to represent his or her interest can participate by joining with like-minded persons in a formal organization. Tocqueville held that America's associational life helped to combine liberty and democracy. Unless equal but isolated and powerless individuals were to combine in associations, democracies would be prone to tyranny and citizens unable to limit and influence state action. Associations in democracies served to constrain and direct popular sovereignty.

Like classic theories of market economics, interest group pluralism relies on an equilibrium model for reconciling the pursuit of individual interest with realization of the public good. An invisible hand is said to guide market transactions and interest group bargains in ways that translate private into public interest. Just as buyers and sellers in markets get the goods they prefer for the prices they want to pay, so competing interest groups in policy arenas produce a policy outcome that is in the public interest. Persuasion, bargaining, and deliberation among interdependent but competing interests eventuate in harmonious equilibriums that approximate what is best for all and for each.

In America for some time, the frontier, abundance, and a rapidly expanding economy obscured, if not eliminated, the zero-sum possibilities of interest group competition. In time, sympathetic as well as hostile critics showed how the practice of interest groups pluralism led to consequences that were not anticipated by the model. Private power became the master of public power as vested interests appropriated public authority and resources by capturing state agencies. Just as inequalities of income, wealth, and power made for market imperfections that contradicted the assumption that consumers and workers could engage in mutually beneficial exchange with producers and employers, so the absence or inequality of organizational and political resources enabled vested interests to dominate policy choice and implementation. Many of those most in need of representation did not or could not benefit from interest groups. Members lost control or were alienated, as interest group bureaucrats became organizational masters. Those who managed interest group organizations found it difficult to distinguish their personal goals and interests from those of the members they were meant to serve.

Contradictions became increasingly manifest between party government and executive leadership on the one hand, and the representational infrastructure through which interest group pluralism operated, on the other. Instead of equilibrium and harmony that yielded the public interest, stalemate among group interests and among separated and balanced institutions became common. The multiplication and competition of interests often blocked legislative action.

Despite these and other criticisms, interest group pluralism as theory and practice persists in America, India, and other industrial democracies because it is more than an explanation of state-society relations. In part, it persists because associational life, like class, is a common feature of industrial democracies. It also persists because the right of citizen voters to associate independently is perceived as an essential aspect of liberty. If organized interests often represent the rich and powerful more than the poor and oppressed and if "overmighty subjects" in industrial democracies sometimes dominate policy and the state, at other times associations limit state power in ways that protect their members' values and interests. The workers in Poland who in 1982 rallied behind Solidarity to challenge an oppressive regime and the disadvantaged minority communities (Muslims, Harijans) who in 1977 helped turn Indira Gandhi's authoritarian regime out of office suggest that liberty to associate can serve unvested as well as vested interests. As long as sovereignty-seeking states and the elites that staff them serve themselves, the right to association and to independent representation that interest group pluralism makes possible will remain a collective good.

Pluralism and neocorporatism can be viewed as contrasting models of state-society relations. They posit contrasting patterns for the organization and representation of interests and for the formulation and choice of public policy. The pluralist model arose from a normative theory that values liberty for individuals and the voluntary associations they should be free to form. Voluntary associations are meant to pursue the interests of their members independent of state sovereignty or the compulsions of corporate and bureaucratic governance. Pluralist forms and processes of political participation and representation are held to determine public choices of policies and leaders in ways that both limit and direct state action. For these reasons, the pluralist organization and representation of interests has an elective affinity to demand rather than command politics.

Neocorporatism as a model for the organization and representation of interests echoes medieval and mercantilist forms for the compulsory and monopolistic representation of interests. Status orders (e.g., estates, *Stände*), craft producers (e.g., guilds) and state-licensed preindustrial commercial and manufacturing companies structurally prefigured neocorporatist forms and processes of representation. At the same time, neocorporatism is a response to the concentration, bureaucratization, and interdependence of producer interests in industrial economies.

The neocorporatist model posits vested, hierarchical, monopolistic, and compulsory apex bodies for producer interests organized in firms, unions, and professional associations.[2] Led by bureaucratic professionals, apex bodies negotiate with each other and with state agencies to gain benefits, avoid losses, and concert policy in well-established policy arenas. State civil servants and apex body professional bureaucrats shape policy agendas and bargain over the formulation of policy for whole industries, sectors, or the national economy. Whether by de facto appropriation or de jure command, apex bodies acquire not only collective but also para-statal (public) authority that enables them to govern and compel "members"—the individuals involved in firms, unions, and professional associations as well as the lesser intermediate organizations joined together in peak associations. The neocorporatist organization and representation of interests has an elective affinity to command rather than demand politics because it favors state over voter sovereignty and public over private power in policymaking.

Viewed historically, pluralism in contemporary industrial democracies has been associated with older patterns of policy determination by legislatures, neocorporatism with the functional representation of organized producer and professional interests. As cabinet or presidential governments have come to limit the influence of voters and interests acting through legislative representatives, the influence of the permanent government and of functionally organized producer groups has increased. The growth of oligopoly and monopoly in industry, labor, and professional markets was paralleled by the growth of hierarchical representative bodies that tended to impose policy choices rather than reflect members' preferences and to govern by compulsion rather than by consent. Under these emergent historical conditions, the pluralist vision of open, voluntary, and competitive but ultimately harmonious organized interests became harder to sustain. Concerting the functional interests of organized producers with professional counterplayers in the permanent government was said to be a better way to reconcile private and public power and private and public interests than pluralism's invisible hand guiding many competitive and conflicting interests to outcomes that were in the public interest. As neocorporatist representation, bargaining, and concertation in state-sanctioned policy arenas became more institutionalized, they tended to rival or displace not only legislative determination of policy but also pluralist representation.

In contrast to the Anglo-American world that is the home of pluralism,[3] Western Europe, Japan, and Latin America have proved more hospitable to neocorporatism. State-society relations in India are closer to Anglo-American relations than to those of the continental European world. India's associational life has not moved in the direction of a few monopolistic and compulsory apex bodies, capable of hierarchical domination of members' choices, but rather sustains a large variety of competitive associations, especially in the fields of labor and industry. In 1975, the Indira Gandhi authoritarian regime attempted to displace pluralist by neocorporatist forms in the organization and representation of interests. This effort proved abortive when the electorate in 1977 repudiated authoritarian rule and with it the initial attempts at state corporatism. What distinguishes Indian from Anglo-American pluralism is the emergence of the demand group as a representational form especially responsive to the unorganized sector, the extraordinary multiplication and fragmentation of pluralist associations that we call involution, and the role of the state sector, which crowds organized interests to the margin of the political and policy arenas and fragments their potential countervailing power.

The Demand Group as Pluralist Actor in Politics and Policy

In examining Indian pluralism, we conceive of interest groups as encompassing two forms: organized interests and demand groups. We use the term "demand groups" to signal that this unit of Indian pluralism is different from organized interests in other industrial democracies. Formally organized interests exist in India and affect state-society relations and the policy process but they have not been as important as demand groups, a more spontaneous and less formed type of collective action. The demand group is a form that interest representation can take in competitive, open democracies when political mobilization of mass publics outstrips or overflows the formal institutions of the political process.[4] Demand groups are an expression of movement and issue politics. They do not replace organized interests so much as they incorporate and transcend them. Unlike movement politics in other industrial democracies, which is usually an alternative to and competitive with organized interests, movement politics in India tends to complement formally organized interest groups. By raising new issues and mobilizing support for them, demand groups transform state and national policy agendas and gain bargaining advantages.

Formally organized interests work in institutionally defined policy arenas. They attempt to influence legislatures, bureaucratic agencies, and sometimes party policy. They develop elaborate organizational infrastructure, including a headquarters bureaucracy, means of internal communication to members and external communication to relevant publics, and research staffs. Their means of influence include technical and professional expertise and legal and legislative skills. The idea of an organized interest group implies a certain professionalization of the representative process. The force of its case rests at least as much on technical persuasiveness as on the pressure of numbers.

Demand groups, by contrast, do not work primarily in institutionally defined policy arenas. They rely less on expertise and lobbying skill than on symbolic and agitational politics. The tactics and style of demand groups have become a highly elaborated political art form that speaks to India's indigenous political culture, mobilizes support, influences public opinion, and gains bargaining advantages. Its ad hoc and spontaneous tactics include public dramas such as *padyatras* (political pilgrimages), *hartals* (shutdowns), *rasta rokos* (road blocks), and *gheraos* (lock-ins). The grandfather of such public dramas was Mohandas Gandhi's salt march to the sea in 1930. One of the more striking postindependence manifestations was agrarian leader Charan Singh's eightieth "birthday party" in 1979, when one hundred thousand North Indian cultivators arrived at Delhi's Boat Club grounds by tractor and bullock cart to attend the extravaganza.

Interest groups work more in camera, demand groups out of doors. Demand groups tend to agitate first and bargain later. The force of their case rests on its dramatic visibility and demonstration of massive support and sometimes on the disruption of public services. The transactions of organized interest groups take place between their knowledgeable professions and bureaucratic counterplayers, while the transactions of organized interest groups take place between their knowledgeable professionals and bureaucratic counterplayers, while the transactions of demand groups take place between supporters mobilized in favor of an issue on the one hand and governmental elites and public opinion on the other. While the organized interests represent functionally specific producer interests—dockworkers, steelworkers, tobacco growers—demand groups represent whole sectors—agricul-specific interests.

The demand group escapes some of the oligarchical aspects of formally organized interests: dominance by the organization's bureaucrats and professionals ("the iron law of oligarchy") and a propensity to underrepresent or ignore the less well placed members and the disadvantaged among potential constituencies. Demand groups arise when organized interests and political parties fail to represent or reach them. Because demand groups attempt to mobilize large numbers, they must appeal to and involve the poor and powerless even if they do not deliver equal benefits to them.

The natural habitat of the demand group is India's unorganized economy, which outnumbers the organized economy nine to one. While there is far from an absolute correlation between the presence of formal interest organizations and location in the organized sector of the economy, organized interests are more common and effective in the organized sector. At the same time, the scale of the unorganized economy (agriculture, small-scale industry, and commerce) affects the balance between organized interests and demand groups in Indian politics and policy. Demand groups share the less bureaucratized and less professional character of producers in the unorganized economy. The difference between organized interests and demand groups is also shaped by different levels of consciousness and articulation. As producers and as voters, potential supporters of demand groups have had little or no experience with organized representation and participatory politics. Organized interests assume that there is a "group" with an interest that it knows and wishes to advance.[5] The problem is to represent a manifest interest. The demand group has yet to recognize itself; it is still "becoming." The problem of demand groups is to create the group consciousness of an interest as well as to represent it.

Demand groups are lineal descendants of the "opinion out of doors" and "self-appointed" and "self-serving associations" that, according to Edmund Burke and George Washington, threatened republican government and representative democracy. Today, as in the late eighteenth century, the "opinion out of doors" that demand groups mobilize is perceived by authorities and vested interests as threatening governability. But "world time" casts a different light on demand groups in contemporary India. Universal suffrage, associational life, organized opinion, and political parties have become, as they were not in the late eighteenth century, legitimate aspects of representative democracy. The "opinion out of doors" that helped to establish civil, political, and, later, social rights was thought to be an unfortunate and dangerous aberration that could be eliminated once its goals were achieved. But this was not to be the case. Persisting discrepancies between formal equality and actual inequality of political and economic power justified the persistence of issue and movement politics. Demand groups persist but create dilemmas. They perfect democracy and promote more equal bargaining by mobilizing voters and lower constituencies slighted or ignored by organized interests. But they create problems of governability when they jeopardize public order and a government of laws.

Indian Variants of Pluralism

The validity of interest group pluralism as an explanatory social science concept has been vitiated by the anomalies and contradictions that have accompanied its application in industrial democracies. Nevertheless, it remains, with class-based theories, one of the reigning paradigms for explaining state-society relations in governance and policy. Efforts to keep the theory viable have produced variants that recognize the paradigm but make significant amendments or innovations. Two variants we find helpful for explaining state-society relations and the policy process in India are state-dominated pluralism and involuted pluralism.

Under state-dominated pluralism, the political arena is populated by relatively autonomous interest groups, but they are overshadowed by an omnipresent state. Much of the organizational and representational "space" occupied by pluralist actors and processes in the Anglo-American world and by societal corporatism in Western Europe is occupied in India by state agencies. This is not surprising in a state that opted, in the industrial policy resolutions of 1948 and 1956, for a mixed economy in which the public sector would dominate the "commanding heights"; that nationalized finance capitalism—banks and insurance—in the 1960s; and that had at its command a proliferating series of state long-term lending institutions. By occupying the co-manding heights of industrial and finance capital, the state also came to occupy the commanding heights of the representational infrastructure. At the same time, the line between the public and private sectors has become increasingly obscure, as state-controlled lending institutions and equity holders—(e.g., the Life Insurance Corporation of India, the Unit Trust of India)—have acquired sufficient equity in private-sector firms to give them, potentially, the power to control management.

The pervasiveness of the state in India also affects professional and occupational associations that occupy autonomous space in most other industrial democracies. While the "free professions" constitute a significant part of the autonomous associations in which middle-class society organizes itself in Europe, this is less true in India. The vast majority of doctors, scientists, engineers, teachers, and professors are employees of government organizations. Because government is the principal employer of managers, technicians, and clerics—generally speaking, the white-collar class—the interests of India's noncapitalist, non-property-owning middle classes are closely related to those of the state.

The state's prominence does not mean that there are no arenas of group autonomy. The political sociologist tells a different story than the political economist does. Religious communities, caste associations, cultural, ethnic and linguistic groups—a large range of nonproducer social forces generally—cannot be closely regulated or manipulated by the state. Although in the economic arena the state occupies much of the "space" occupied in America and Europe by pluralist and corporatist forces, in the social arena it occupies less. As a consequence, it faces powerful political and policy challenges from cultural, ethnic, and linguistic groups.

The state dominates pluralist representation through its direction of the policy process as well as through its control of public-sector industrial and finance capital and its employment of professionals. The state controls the policy agenda, (e.g., policy initiatives and choice); it directs, through the use of incentives and sanctions, the organizational and market behavior of organized interests, firms, and industries; and it powerfully influences particular policy arenas by establishing favored relationships with one among a plurality of organized interests in that arena.

The state controls the policy agenda to a remarkable degree. As Stanley Kochanek put it in his *Business and Politics in India:*

> Policy initiatives usually come from government . . . not from the larger society . . . so most groups are forced to take a negative or defensive rather than a positive stance . . . the pattern of public policy . . . has concentrated vast powers in the hands of government officials. This power enables them to control and regulate the internal affairs and external conduct of business, trade unions, and other organizations. . . . Far from being . . . an outcome of interest group activity, as group theory would have it, public policy in India exerts a significant impact on group mobilization and on behavior.[6]

State control of the policy agenda is most clearly expressed in the Planning Commission's perspective, five-year, and annual plans. Inter alia, targets for most of the investment in the organized economy and for infrastructure (power, irrigation, transport, etc.) are set by Planning Commission allocations. State incentives and sanctions—what critics at home and abroad call "permit-license raj"—are exercised through governmental licensing of production and production levels, control of foreign exchange and imports, and determination of agricultural prices and input costs. The state's monopoly of credit, together with its taxing powers, provides it with extraordinarily powerful means to encourage or deter market and organizational behavior.

The state's establishment of a special relationship with one of many organized interests in particular policy arenas is best illustrated by the arena of industrial relations, where the state, under Congress governments, has maintained a special relationship with the Indian National Trade Union Conference (INTUC). Congress party governments have been in power at the center almost continuously since independence, and INTUC has generally followed the party's—and thus the government's and the state's—policy line. INTUC does not have a licensed monopoly to represent organized labor as would be the case under neocorporatist arrangements. Its relationship with state agencies and the Congress-I party sometimes becomes strained when it tries to maintain both its competitive position in a pluralist universe and its special relationship with Congress governments. But without government support and patronage, INTUC could not have remained India's largest trade union federation, and without INTUC collaboration, Congress governments could not have been as successful as they have in manipulating and controlling organized labor and industrial relations policy.

The second distinctive pluralist variant found in India is involuted pluralism, one of the ways the state has dominated interest group pluralism. "Involution" refers to a continuing process and resultant structural condition, the excessive multiplication of less effectual units. A leading example is the agricultural involution that Geertz observed.[7] Pluralist involution contrasts with the oligopolistic and monopolistic tendencies of interest group pluralism that can eventuate in neocorporatism. We use involution as a metaphor for the decline or loss of vigor that results when a viable intensively elaborated pattern of development is extensively elaborated by continuous replication of units. Such replication not only weakens each successive unit but also weakens all units collectively and thus the activity as a whole. In this sense, more becomes less. Involution is thus a regressive, debilitating process that results in decreasing effectiveness or entropy, the reverse of evolution.

We showed in chapter 1 how change in industrial capitalism includes a mild form of involution, as smaller private-sector firms are encouraged to multiply by government incentives and deterrents (chapter 1, table 5). In chapter 10, on organized workers as a demand group, we show a more pronounced process of involution as an increasing number of trade unions compete for a limited constituency of easily organized workers. In both instances, the effect of involution is to enable the state to manipulate an increasing number of weaker units. Involuted pluralism as a form of representational mediation strengthens command politics and weakens demand politics.

In summary, pluralist representation in India is distinguished by two novel actors—the demand group and the state as the largest producer interest—and two novel structural variants—state-dominated pluralism and involuted pluralism. These elements of the representational infrastructure have an independent effect on the prevailing balance of command and demand politics. Demand groups favor the ascendancy of demand politics, while the state's role as producer, state-dominated pluralism, and involuted pluralism favors the ascendancy of command politics.

IO Involuted Pluralism and State Domination of the Industrial Relations Regime

The first demand group to which we turn is organized labor, a major participant in the demand politics that escalated in the 1960s. Labor's demands became more prominent as the public sector expanded and organized labor's role within it grew. While private employment in the organized sector grew slowly after 1966—9 percent between 1966 and 1981—public employment increased by 69 percent, almost 5 percent per year compared with 2 percent for population and about 3.5 percent for GNP. This rapid expansion of state instrumentalities, from nationalized banks through steel plants, fueled an increase of government consumption expenditures and contributed to the decline in public investment over the 1965–75 period. The 69 percent growth in public employment was due in part to the nationalization of key industries, notably insurance and banking, in part to ad hoc responses to the problem of unemployment among the educated, and in part to diffuse patronage pressures to create and allocate jobs.[1] High inflation rates from 1966 to 1968, and again from 1973 to 1975, indexed to cost-of-living ("dearness") allowances for public employees, exacerbated the problems of paying for so substantial an addition to the work force.

As the numbers and proportions of the organized-sector work force increased, the rate of strikes, lockouts, and labor unrest also increased dramatically (chapter 8, table 23). These developments paralleled the ballooning of student enrollment in higher education and the student unrest that accompanied it. Paradoxically, even while organized labor was extremely active, its influence on politics and policy did not increase.

Organized labor has not been able to challenge India's centrist ideology and politics, that is, to mount or support a left class party. We suggested in chapter 1 that the two traditional adversaries in class politics—labor and capital—are marginal forces in the Indian political arena. Neither finds expression in political parties. We attributed the political marginality of organized labor to several factors: workers in the organized economy, the pool for organized labor, constitute only 10 percent of the total work force; the state, which employs two-thirds of the workers in the organized economy, constitutes an ambiguous

259

adversary because of its claims to be a model employer and the vehicle for socialist objectives; and the multiplication and rivalry of national federations and of industry and enterprise unions lead to the progressive involution of the trade union movement.

In exploring the state-dominated industrial relations in India, we have stressed the nexus between labor and the state. Our analysis diverges from the emphasis common in writing on industrial relations in Europe and America, which stresses the labor-capital relationship as it is revealed in the work place, bargaining power, work place hierarchy, and worker control.[2] India invites a focus on the state's rather than capital's relations to labor, because the state is labor's most important counterplayer. Even where relations are primarily between labor and capital, the state controls many of the interactions that elsewhere fall in the realm of collective bargaining.

We begin this chapter by characterizing the conditions that separate labor in the organized and unorganized sectors and that distinguish the labor force in the organized sector into a hierarchy of more and less privileged strata. We then examine structural and ideological forces that have shaped the industrial relations regime and confined organized labor to a marginal role in national politics.

Trade Union Militancy and Its Failures

The expectations of public employees in the 1967–74 period, when the left Kumaramangalam faction was ascendant in the Congress, were shaped by the "socialist" orientation of Mrs. Gandhi's Congress governments. Freed from the profit and capital accumulation motives of private-sector capitalism, government firms could choose to share with their employees rather than appropriate the financial benefits of monopoly, administered prices, and tax-financed subsidies. Government, after all, held itself to be a model employer. But government servants, while nominally dependent on the ideals and good will of their model employer, could also attempt to coerce the state in order to correct grievances or gain benefits and advantages. In particular, the more skilled and privileged, who were also the best organized and most militant, used their organizational resources and capacity for mobilization to hinder, cripple, or stop the provision of services and production of goods by state agencies and public-sector firms. During this period, a number of groups struck for higher wages and better working conditions: employees of the Life Insurance Corporation of India and the

nationalized banks; secretariat employees of the central and state governments; the Central Reserve Police of Uttar Pradesh; airline pilots;
doctors and engineers in the service of the central and state governments; employees of public-sector steel plants, particularly those at
Durgapur; and railway employees (with two million employees, the
Railway Board is India's largest employer). These strikes, inter alia, dis-
rupted production and services and caused severe law and order problems. Table 23 in chapter 8 indicated the rapid increase in the number
of workdays lost from strikes or lockouts and the number of workers
involved in the period of 1961–75. Between 1965 and 1975, the number of workdays lost increased by almost 500 percent, a level of growth
over ten times greater than that for organized-sector employment.

Much of the most successful and conspicuous trade union activity
benefited middle-class and lower-middle-class employees whose condition was already good in comparison with that of the vast majority of
the nation's wage earners. Just as Congress's INTUC did, left unions,
such as the CPI- and CPI-M–affiliated All-India Trade Union Congress
(AITUC) and Centre of Indian Trade Unions (CITU) took the relatively
easy path of organizing and pressing demands on behalf of those who
are easily organized and whose employer—government—responds
readily. As a critic, Rakhahari Chatterji, has noted:

> The trade union leadership, especially of the leftist variety, was not a
> little responsible in facilitating the government's high-handedness.
> Generally, this leadership showed political adventurism and social
> irresponsibility through its direct or indirect encouragement to
> strikes by highly skilled and well-paid employees like the doctors,
> engineers, technocrats, life insurance employees or airlines staff.
> When an enormous portion of the working population . . . re-
> mained unorganized and severely low paid, the leftist leadership,
> rather than directing itself seriously towards them, opted for en-
> couraging those struggles which were for *luchi* and *mithai* [sweets]
> on top of bread and butter. Consequently, the general public was
> neither interested in nor sympathetic to those struggles even though
> they had to bear the harassment. And the unions' loss of pub-
> lic sympathy helped the government to put down even genuine
> struggles.[3]

The victories were pyrrhic from the long-run perspective of trade
unionism in India: militancy and disruption on behalf of the privileged
lowered trade unions' public standing and weakened their appeal to
unorganized workers. Prime Minister Gandhi could denounce unions

for economically harmful indiscipline and antisocial behavior. The agrarian party leader, Charan Singh, could castigate them as a privileged labor aristocracy and a principal beneficiary of urban parasitism.

The self-defeating nature of trade union activity was nowhere more apparent than in Bengal prior to 1977. Calcutta's economic decline was hastened by violent internecine warfare among party-dominated unions, the Naxalite strategy of urban guerrilla warfare, wildcat strikes and labor indiscipline, the CPI-M's doctrine that during strikes and civil disturbances "people's" rights were more important than property rights, and sabotage in public-sector undertakings. Over the years, West Bengal usually has accounted for half or more of the workdays lost nationally: thirteen of the twenty-two million lost in 1975, nine of twelve million in 1976, and eighteen of forty million in 1979.[4] Industrial unrest led many firms to close or flee elsewhere and contributed to the recession of 1967. Between 1961 and 1971, private-sector employment declined by 13 percent as West Bengal fell from first to fourth in per capita income. When the CPI-M formed a coalition government in 1977, a chastened, more prudent Jyoti Basu, a national leader of the CPI-M and the new chief minister, tried with only limited success to reverse the deindustrialization of what was once India's most industrial state.[5]

The Conditions of Labor: The Privileged and the Unprivileged

When public employees raised demands for higher wages and improved benefits, their demands reflected two concerns: the vicissitudes of real wages over time, and wage differentials within the organized sector. Government for its part was concerned with the relationship of emoluments in the organized sector to those in the unorganized sector. The available data on real wages does not distinguish public employees from other wage earners in the organized sector. However, we do have approximations that help to justify both public employees' claim that they were losing ground and charges that they were "privileged." These conflicting claims arise from the internal diversity among public employees, who include both civil servants, ranging from the lowest peon to the highest secretary to government, and employees of government enterprises, for example, steelworkers, airline pilots, bankers, and bank clerks. These categories gain and suffer differentially, and have to be distinguished. Moreover, the private sector with which one might compare government employees is also internally diverse due to differences in the amount and quality of capital. In the Bombay area, for example, knowledgeable persons speak of the industrial *chaturvar-nas,* the four castes, or status orders. In the mid-1970s, big multinationals, the first *varna,* paid workers Rs. 1,000–24,000 per month plus benefits; big Indian firms, Rs. 650–1,500; medium-sized firms, Rs. 350–1,100; and small firms, Rs. 200–700.[6]

We will start with manufacturing employees, even though the data are uneven and scattered. The real income of all manufacturing employees, a category that includes industrial workers in both public enterprises and private firms, remained static between the mid-sixties and the mid-seventies. The high demand-politics years of 1966–68 and 1973 were among those in which real wages declined (table 28). In 1967, wages reached an all-time low. At the same time, reports of per capita annual earnings within the manufacturing sector showed great variation, from approximately Rs. 2,000 to Rs. 4,000.[7] We surmise that the earnings of employees in public enterprises, especially central government public enterprises, were at or near the top of this range.[8] There are significant wage differentials by manufacturing product, differentials that attach to levels of technology. Public enterprises do not enter the low-technology, low-paying manufacturing areas. Thus, the Annual Survey of Industries for 1975–76[9] showed that low-technology industries (e.g., the processing of food, beverages, and tobacco) paid average daily wages of under Rs. 10; industries using middle-range technologies (e.g., textile and paper manufacturing, machine spinning, the production of clothing), Rs. 10–20; and those using mature tech-

TABLE 28
Index of Real Earnings for Employees in Manufacturing Industries, 1962–73

Year	Index	Year	Index
1962	103	1969	101
1963	103	1970	101
1964	94	1971	101
1965	97	1972	103
1966	95	1973	95[a]
1967	91	1976	100[b]
1968	94	1977	112
		1978	118

SOURCES: Government of India, Ministry of Labour, Labour Bureau, *The Indian Labour Yearbook* (annual) and *Pocket Book of Labour Statistics, 1983* (Chandigarh and Simla, 1983).
Note: For employees earning less than Rs. 400 per month.
[a]Provisional.
[b]New base.

nologies (e.g., the manufacture of plastics, petroleum, chemicals, alloys, iron and steel, and machine tools) (mainly in the public sector), Rs. 20–30.[10] When real wages declined, as they did in 1966–68 and 1973, the decline probably affected low-paid employees in private manufacturing, especially medium- and low-technology private-sector firms, more than well-paid workers in high-technology public-sector firms.

Workers in public enterprises are relatively more protected against inflation by indexed dearness allowance programs than many workers in the private sector. (This contrast does not hold for large, high-technology private firms, which provide inflation protection similar to that provided by the government.) Inflation had a limited effect on most public employees (i.e., those receiving less than Rs. 1,000 per month)[11] because of the dearness allowance. Furthermore, government's dearness allowance and wage and salary increases have had a leveling effect on the civil service component of public employment, because they are applied progressively, that is, in ways that protect the real incomes of lower- more than higher-paid employees.[12] Emoluments of lower-level clerks eroded only 2 percent, while emoluments of higher-level officers eroded as much as 37 percent. A similar conception of equity was leveling wages at the executive levels of public-sector industry.[13]

Income differentials among the more powerful and privileged public employees affect industrial relations. The central government wage and income structure is beset by odd and apparently irrational disparities between civil servants and those working for public-sector firms and also among the employees of public-sector industries and firms. The economic condition of employees in public enterprises sometimes reflects the nationalization of private firms that paid high wages. The Life Insurance Corporation of India, the nationalized commercial banks, and the shipping and air corporations were viewed by the Commission on Wages and Prices (1978) as "islands of privilege." Each of these enterprises is characterized by strong, unified, even militant labor organizations. The commission showed that the Life Insurance Corporation and nationalized commercial banks paid their employees, especially those at the lower ranks, 50 to 100 percent more than did government departments.[14] The commission was torn between its preference for standardizing pay across units and the need to recognize the autonomy of public corporations and of the collective bargaining process. Public corporations wanted the freedom to strengthen commitment and improve productivity by manipulating incentives. They feared that the gray uniformity of standard wages would defeat such efforts. There were low-order disparities as well. Low-level class III employees at the Life Insurance Corporation received higher pay than class I employees, an instance of the egalitarian thrust of wage policy within government.[15] Anomalies within and among firms and industries often fuel discontent as well as weaken incentives.

While old and new islands of privilege create disparities, the vast bulk of government employees, those earning less than Rs. 1,000 but benefiting from progressive dearness allowances, could comfort themselves with the growing equality of incomes created by substantial erosion in the emoluments of all-India and senior administrative services. For example, the real income of the most senior "privileged" IAS, which had declined appreciably betweenn 1960 and 1973, declined another 41 percent between 1973 and 1978.[16] The range from top to bottom of the central government's pay scale, expressed as a ratio, shrank between 1973 and 1978 from 15 : 1 to 10 : 1.[17] Government did not attempt to compete with the salaries of private firms. Along with the pressures on senior officials described in chapter 2, the declines in salary range and real income probably affected their morale and standing and may have contributed to the spread of corruption among them.

If some workers in the organized sector seem more privileged than others, the issue of whether workers in the organized economy as a whole were more privileged than those in the unorganized economy had become by 1980 a central issue in national politics. Wage and salaried workers in the organized economy (industrial and service sectors) are probably better off than agricultural laborers, most self-employed cultivators, and small household manufacturers in the unorganized economy. Given the present state of the data on income, expenditure, consumption, price levels, and benefits from public goods, it is difficult to obtain clear information about income inequality generally and about differences between the agricultural sector and unorganized economy on the one hand and the industrial sector and organized economy on the other. Nevertheless, Dharma Kumar, after reviewing disagreements and findings in the literature on income distribution, concluded (with respect to macrosectoral differences) that the decline from 51 to 44 percent in agriculture's share of total product between 1960–61 and 1969–70 "can be taken as a very rough sign that the ratio of average rural to urban *per capita* income has fallen." [18]

The available evidence gives some additional indication of the income differences between employment in the organized and unorganized economies. According to the 1971 census, 26.3 percent of workers were agricultural laborers,[19] 43.3 percent were cultivators, 9.4

percent were employed in manufacturing, and 8.8 percent were in "other services" of the tertiary sector.[20] It is generally assumed that the wages of agricultural laborers are low and approach subsistence. All states and union territories have statutory minimum wages, ranging in 1976 from Rs. 3 in Andhra Pradesh to Rs. 8 in West Bengal,[21] but in the absence of official means or unions to enforce them, they are more observed in the breach than in practice. Whatever the daily wage, payments in kind, or perquisites may be, for most workers they are paid only when work is available, which for casual adult male workers in 1974–75 was said to average 185 days of the year.[22] Dharma Kumar, following Herdt and Baker, concluded that all-India real wages in agriculture were lower in 1968–69 than in 1954–55.[23] On the other hand, Ahluwalia, who estimated the proportion of the rural poor under the poverty line, shows that the proportion declined between 1968 and 1974.[24]

Even if, as seems to be the case, real wages in industry, as in agriculture, have remained more or less constant since independence, per capita income levels in the organized economy are much higher than those in the unorganized economy (primarily agriculture and household or small-scale production of goods and services). According to the Labour Bureau, the average per capita annual earnings of approximately 5.5 million workers[25] in manufacturing industries in 1973–74 was Rs. 3,131.[26] To compare the approximate magnitude of difference between the annual per capita incomes of the organized and unorganized economies, we make the assumption that agricultural laborers worked 185 days in the same year and were paid—in cash, payments in kind, or perquisites—the equivalent of Rs. 3.27 per day.[27] The result would be an average annual income of Rs. 604. Differences in consumption baskets, price levels, or direct consumption of self-produced wage goods could not substantially affect the more than 5 : 1 income differential between industrial and agricultural workers. Again, to reach approximate magnitudes, we think it unlikely that the forty-one million or so dwarf cultivator households—that is, those who operated holdings of between 0.01 and 2.5 acres in 1970–71[28]—could have generated incomes (in cash or kind) approaching the Rs. 3,131 annual per capita income of wage workers in manufacturing in 1973–74.

Similar magnitude differences hold for the household industry sector. In 1971–72, the average per capita daily earning of 1.4 million workers in the household industry sector of the unorganized economy was Rs. 5.84, compared with Rs. 11.36 for those in the same industries within the organized economy, meaning that those in the unorganized economy earned about half as much as those in the organized economy producing the same product.[29] On the basis of these approximations, we conclude that the average income (if not the consumption) of workers in the urban organized economy is at least twice that of workers in the rural unorganized economy.

Rural-urban differences did not emerge as a live national issue until the second half of the seventies, when the politics of the new agrarianism began to take shape. Farmers' agitations in Mahaharashtra, Tamil Nadu, Karnataka, Gujarat, and Punjab and national *kisan* rallies in the early eighties made it plain that the issue of the organized sector's privileged position had come of age and would be central to the domestic politics of that decade.

The Indian wage and income structure raises difficult problems of justice and equity in its own and in comparative contexts. Capital accumulation for Soviet industrialization was in part based on a 2 : 1 differential between industrial and agricultural wages and an even more pronounced difference for investment in the two sectors.[30] In consequence, output grew enormously in industry but stagnated in agriculture. In India, spontaneous processes more than policy interventions have produced a comparable result for wages if not for capital accumulation or investment, yet output in agriculture has grown enough to give India a self-sufficiency in food grains not achieved in the Soviet Union. Redressing the balance in favor of agriculture by improving the terms of trade and investment ratios would presumably reduce government investment in the industrial more than in the agricultural sector, with hard to estimate consequences for economic growth and productivity of capital and labor.

It is difficult to judge the extent to which the growth of public employment is itself problematic. Does it, on balance, increase and improve public services or promote development? National accounts statistics make their own implicit judgment when they count public employment as a "nondevelopmental" expenditure. To what extent should it be counted as alleviating unemployment among the educated? To what extent as appropriation by an autonomous, expanding, and self-interested third actor, the Indian state?

In the organized sector, "islands of privilege" have emerged, especially among public employees but also in the private sector. As the privileged layers among the Bombay *chaturvarnas* and among public enterprises suggest, such islands reflect differentials in capitalization, technology, and management that are associated with market and political power. Leveling within the public sector—for example, between civil service employees and employees of public enterprises—threatens to deprive public enterprises of what little autonomy and capacity to employ incentives their anomalous position allows. Islands of privilege also reflect the capacity of workers to mobilize and organize, and the bargaining advantages their economic and political circumstances create. Disproportionate organization and mobilization of white-collar professional and skilled labor reveals that organized labor has elected to follow the path of least resistance, to work with the conscious and accessible rather than with vulnerable and dependent unskilled laborers in industry and agriculture. The doubtful assertion that in the rural sector the rich are getting richer and the poor poorer may in fact be more applicable to wage and income differentials within the organized economy.

On the other hand, not all public employees are privileged. Nor is an industrial work force whose average real wages have stagnated since at least 1951 and probably since the turn of the century likely to feel privileged. Marked vertical as well as less marked but nevertheless strongly felt horizontal disparities among industrial workers have compounded workers' sense of injustice. In the eighties, policymakers and spokesmen for the new agrarianism have increasingly drawn attention to the disparity between the incomes of industrial and agricultural workers. Government's capacity to define and implement "acceptable inequalities" through its wages and incomes, industrial relations, and sectoral policies has been severely strained by these perceived disparities.

The Nature of the Industrial Relations Regime

India's trade unions share the competitive pluralism of Anglo-American interest groups.[31] Such pluralism features union-employer relations based on private and voluntary agreements among a large number of individual actors, firms, and unions and restricts state action to the regulation of entry, bargaining, and conflict. In Europe, unions often convert this competitive situation into an oligopolistic one, aspiring to the power and standing of apex organizations.[32] Their relatively cohesive labor federations are in a position to bargain at the national level with industry associations and the state. This has not happened in India. The industrial relations regime within which Indian unions and national federations and firms operate inhibits both competitive pluralism and oligopolistic competition among organized producer interests. Instead, state strategies have created an involuted pluralism in which the state, by dominating the arena of industrial conflict, controls many weak and divided organizations rather than a few co-hesive ones.

The competitive pluralist model dominates the Indian trade unions' image of themselves and the world in which they live. Indian apex unions are multiple; entry is relatively easy. Their internal structure is characterized less by democratic and participatory arrangements and more by structural autonomy at regional, municipal, and shop floor levels that makes it difficult for national leadership to speak for followers. Indian unions do not concert with the state. The possible exception is INTUC, the Congress party's trade union that allows itself to be co-opted, reliably complies with government's directives, and derives many gains from its semiofficial standing. (It did not, for example, participate in the 1982 strike against preventive detention and antistrike legislation.)

The prospect that the Indian model can assume the oligopolistic form and consequent influence of European pluralism is made less likely by the radically different balance of forces that characterizes producer groups in India. When oligopolistic pluralism is successful in Western Europe, labor federations, management, and the state approach each other as relatively equal adversaries. In India, both labor and employer organizations are weaker relative to the state. The growth of the public sector through the fifties and sixties, by locating 60 percent of investment and 65 percent of organized-sector employment in the public sector, has weakened the standing of private producer groups. Labor's situation is compromised by the fact that the socialist state claims to be, and often is, the model employer. Agreements are far more determined by state goals and interests than by bargains struck between employers and employees.[33]

Trade unions conceive of themselves as acting within a self-determining pluralist world, while in fact the industrial relations regime is characterized by involuted pluralism and state domination. We use the term "involution" as a metaphor for a decline or loss of vigor that results from replication of units whose increase in number is accompanied by a decline in effectiveness. In Geertz's original metaphor, involution is used with respect to wet rice regimes to designate the intensive cultivation and overelaboration of tiny productive units in ways that proved self-defeating.[34] It is a regressive, debilitating process that tends toward entropy, the reverse of evolution or vigor. It serves the interests of the state to keep labor fragmented and prevent it from concentrating its force along oligopolistic lines, hence weakening its voice in policymaking and minimizing its political role. On the other hand, thousands of short-run micro-interest calculations by the manifold components of the trade union sector insure that labor collaborates in the fragmentation that damages its collective macro-interest. The state's strategy parallels its management of private industrial capital, which is also fragmented and kept subservient by the state's occupation of the commanding heights, by licensing, regulation, and control of investment and production.

State domination of the industrial arena has been shaped both by the paternalistic doctrines and practices of the administrative state under the British raj and by public choices that reflect Congress party ideology and state interests. State domination of the industrial relations regime features state-controlled compulsory procedures rather than open-ended bargaining among interested parties; the superior standing of government as an allegedly disinterested and fair third party; and its role as a spokesman for the public's interest in order, the provision of services, and the maintenance of production and development. The state believes itself responsible for imposing solutions from above. In the manner more of the civil than the common law tradition, the emoluments and working conditions that wage boards and industrial tribunals hand down for particular cases are meant to follow the disembodied principles found in legislation and in the reports of pay and other expert commissions. They are not meant to be the product of contested public policies or of open-ended collective bargaining, based on trials of strength among employers and employees. At the rhetorical level, the collective good is held to be served by harmony rather than conflict. Because the demands of organized labor, like those of other interest groups, are considered partial and self-interested, they are seen to be in conflict with the public interest and national goods.

State domination stands in tension with lively and tenacious pluralist doctrine and practice. The doctrine has been shaped by Indian and international versions of the doctrine of regulated conflict and democratic trade unionism[35] and has been represented by significant spokesmen of Indian labor at each of the abortive attempts to alter the Industrial Relations Act of 1926. It holds that tentative approximations of harmony and the public interest can result from regulated conflict and bargaining. The state should provide and apply agreed procedures and assume a facilitative role in order to support industrial democracy and regulated conflict. It should supervise elections to determine legitimate and representative bargaining agents, determine and validate unfair labor practices, and accept conflict in the form of open-ended collective bargaining. Regulated conflict among interested parties can be desirable and legitimate not only because it can produce approximations of the public interest but also because the use of state authority and the power it makes available to rulers is suspect. The partisans of a pluralist approach note that the state, as management and the larger employer, is an interested party even while it retains special responsibilities for maintaining order, providing essential services, realizing development objectives, and representing organized interests.

Whether involuted pluralism and state domination or regulated conflict will characterize Indian trade unionism in the future depends in part on economic as well as on political conditions. Indian trade unionism is favored by what Theda Skocpol calls "world time," recognizing that apparently similar chronological sequences have different causes and meanings because they occur in contexts transformed by prior sequences elsewhere.[36] The efflux of world time helps workers in industrializing countries such as India to benefit from the successful struggles of workers in countries that were industrialized earlier. The historical situation of trade unions in Great Britain, the first country to be industrialized, was significantly different from that in Germany, for example, which was industrialized somewhat later, and from that in India, industrialized later still.[37] Britain denied organizing rights to trade unions because laissez-faire doctrine held that "combinations" restrained equally free workers and employers from entering into work contracts. Manufacturing workers were employed without benefit of factory, much less social and welfare, legislation.[38] Today, the rights of workers to combine in organizations and bargain collectively, to be protected by factory legislation, and to benefit from the social rights of a welfare state are internationally recognized, if not always honored. Workers benefit too from the fact that factory acts and social rights have become conventional attributes of welfare states.

Yet later industrializing states share the suspicion their predecessors entertained for all interest groups. Those who ruled eighteenth-century Britain suspected the mobilization of "opinion out of doors" by organized associations, because they did not regard popular participation as legitimate. The rulers of late industrializing states such as India, while they may accept democratic participation, continue to fear associations because they threaten the autonomy and interests of weakly formed or vulnerable states.

Trends in the nature and composition of the Indian work force differ greatly from recent developments in the postindustrial democracies. Although India has already become the world's fifteenth-largest industrial economy,[39] its work force and labor movement are experiencing very different changes than those in the advanced or postindustrial economies of America and Western Europe. In America and Western

Europe, a decreasing proportion of workers are employed in industrial (blue-collar) jobs, and the rate of increase in office (white-collar) jobs is declining. Workers in low-skilled, low-paid, and unorganized personal service employment (e.g., fast food restaurants) and in high-skilled, high-paid, but unorganized knowledge and communications industry jobs are becoming a larger proportion of the work force. Partly as a result of such changes in the composition of the work force and partly as a result of related changes in ideological and political conditions, organized labor in "advanced" economies is in decline as a bargaining force in the economy and in electoral and policy domains. Even parties on the left have found that, because they have to rely increasingly on middle-class support to win elections and govern, they have to represent middle-class interests as much as—or more than—working-class interests.

In India, by contrast, trends and developments in the composition and organization of the work force and in the labor movement remain favorable to the economic, political, and policy prospects of organized labor. Not only is industrial and office employment still on the rise absolutely and proportionately but India's middle-class professionals (e.g., doctors, engineers, and airline pilots) are also disproportionately unionized and militant compared with those in America and Western Europe. While unorganized agricultural workers in India, like the low-skilled or unskilled workers in personal service jobs in the West, inhibit the economic bargaining and political and policy influence of organized labor, it seems likely in the 1980s that they will become increasingly organized and militant, as they have already done in Kerala and parts of Tamil Nadu.[40]

In the face of Indian unions' better prospects and the fluctuating but often high levels of labor unrest, analysts and leaders continue to differ over whether labor's and the country's interests are better served by the present pattern of state-dominated pluralism or by a commitment to regulated conflict. Some argue, for example, that the Congress-I government's July 1981 ordinance,[41] which formalized already extant discretionary authority to declare strikes illegal, was necessary if not desirable, because it strengthened government's hand in guiding and controlling industrial relations in ways required for order and development.[42] Others find that pervasive state guidance and control is the problem, not the solution. It shortcircuited the development of responsible representation and bargaining by denying or obfuscating real conflicts of interests behind a facade of economic and administrative rationality. The failure of collective bargaining and regulated conflict to strengthen industrial democracy and the further narrowing of the right to strike will continue to drive conflicts of interests among employees, employers, and the state into the streets, where agitations and violence breed repression and counterviolence. State management in the face of an expanding, better-organized, and better-coordinated labor movement is likely to exacerbate the vicious circle of extremism by workers and the state.

Seven conditions have contributed to the present balance of forces between labor and the state, to the weakness of trade unions, and to the strength of state initiatives:

1. The emergency regime of 1975–77 strengthened corporatist management of industrial relations.

2. State policy has created a legal and procedural environment that encourages unions to depend for recognition and benefits on government and management more than on their membership and their capacity to represent its interests. Many unions have collaborated to perpetuate this procedural environment where it favors their interests as particular actors even while it disfavors the position of labor in general.

3. The relative abundance of cheap labor and a labor market dominated by unskilled labor, a condition general to developing economies, weakens the capacity of trade unions to bargain effectively. This condition is being increasingly modified in the Indian case by the exceptionally rapid development of technical and professional classes that are not averse to unionization.

4. The ideological, partisan, and territorial fragmentation of unions and the much more rapid proliferation of unions than of unionized workers weaken the capacity of organized labor to affect economic bargaining, political competition, and policy formulation. Proliferating unions have tended to struggle among themselves over the control of a relatively fixed sum of organized workers rather than expand the sum of organized workers.

5. The world view of dominant elites, for a mixture of bureaucratic and neotraditionalist reasons, values efficiency and harmony. It distrusts and opposes the concept of regulated conflict on normative grounds, as irregular, chaotic, and disharmonious.

6. Wage and income policy has evolved as an extension of the Indian bureaucracy's technocratic efforts to regulate its own pay and benefits structure, treating employees in the public sector on the "pay commission" model, as if they were an extension of the state services, rather than attempting to develop a distinct political and social policy for the economic consequences of an emerging working class.

7. The state has won wide acceptance for its claim that it has a special responsibility for nation building and economic development.

This claim impinges on industrial relations, creating the need for labor commitment and discipline, uninterrupted production and productivity growth, and low wages to boost saving and capital formation.

These determinants are all central to the present balance of forces in the Indian industrial relations regime. We will examine each in light of the evolving political and economic situation in India and trends in the nature of the work force. Two qualifications should be noted. First, trade union activity varies by place and time. It is subject to phases or moods induced by events and developments in salient political environments. Ahmedabad with its legacy of Gandhian consensualism and Calcutta with its competitive radicalism create different contexts for trade union activity. The legalism and consultationism that characterized Bombay from the mid-fifties to the mid-sixties was succeeded by militancy.[43] Second, the determinants we analyze are neither immutable nor wholly determining of involution and weakness. When we examine the prospects for industrial relations in the late eighties at the end of this account, we will discuss alternative possibilities based on organized labor's changing relationship to management and the state.

The Emergency Regime as an Experiment in Corporatist Management of Labor

The emergency regime of 1975–77 contributed to the involution and political weakness of trade unions. Trade union demands and labor "unrest" were conspicuous among the factors leading to the emergency. As Rakhahari Chatterji has noted, "In an important sense, the Emergency was about the working class."[44] The emergency was preceded by a railway workers' strike that shook the country in May 1974. It was the first political challenge by a trade union to the central government at the national level. The strike, by a multimillion-member union in the state sector, revealed the weakness of established industrial relations doctrine and practice and the state's vulnerability to a unified national challenge.[45] It also demonstrated that opportunistic trade union rivalry easily destroys unity and that state repression could be sufficiently ruthless and systematic to break India's largest combination of industrial workers. The strike was never wholly effective.[46] Within three weeks, Mrs. Gandhi's government had broken it. Its repression greatly demoralized the trade union movement and led its leaders to shift their strategy from primary attention to the working class to one that stressed middle-class professionals and white-collar employees.

After the emergency was declared, the Congress government extended long-established mechanisms designed to promote "harmonious" relations between workers and employers, in ways that sought to strengthen corporatist linkages in industrial relations. Within weeks of the emergency proclamation, government established a National Apex Body (NAB), composed of twelve trade union and eleven employer representatives, to deal with industrial relations in the private sector.[47] Three of the four principal party-related trade unions (INTUC [Congress], AITUC [CPI], and Hind Mazdoor Sabha [socialist]) joined, but CITU, the CPI-M affiliate, did not participate. At least ten states set up parallel bodies. Bipartite national committees were brought into being by the central government in major private industries. In the name of worker participation in management, state governments also established or revived bipartite committees at the shop floor and enterprise levels for all public and private firms employing more than five hundred persons. The two-tiered committees were composed of nominated representatives of labor and management. Apex-level national consultative committees were formed for two major public-sector industries: steel and coal. The terms of reference of such industry-level committees included production targets, wage levels, and welfare measures. In announcing the steel industry committee, ministry sources pointed out that "labour participation and cooperation had been the main factors responsible for the record steel production from April to October in 1975."[48]

The NAB approach abandoned the tripartism of the Indian Labour Conference and the Standing Labour Committee, moribund since 1971. It built on the rival bipartite approach to industrial relations found in the works committees and joint management councils established by the Industrial Disputes Act of 1947 and the additional legislation of 1958.[49]

The earlier tripartite organizations were strongly state corporatist. The state rejected any trade union voice in setting agendas for the Indian Labour Conference and the Standing Labour Committee meetings and restricted labor management to a strictly consultative role in these bodies. By comparison, the structure of NAB seemed more responsive to trade union preferences for bipartite industrial relations organizations and for the voluntary, open-ended collective bargaining they implied. Such appearances were deceptive. The substitution of bipartism for tripartism under the emergency regime was spurious because of the tacit but powerful leading strings implicit in government's intimidation and repression and the explicit policy of more production for less cost that government's threatening rhetoric and actions supported.

The emergency regime preempted bargaining on key issues when it froze wages, phased out the wage-based 8.33 percent annual bonus,[50] transferred increments in the dearness allowance to a compulsory savings scheme, and de facto banned strikes. Government's objective in creating the NAB was to put industrial relations—which had been "bedevilled by strife, indiscipline and neglect of production and productivity"—on an "even keel," a euphemism for higher production with lower labor costs.[51] For about a year, this objective was achieved. The NAB responded to the prime minister's appeal for "harmony and higher production" by unanimously approving a proposal to achieve industrial peace.[52] The government also asked the NAB to concern itself with wider policy questions, such as the proposal for a seven-day workweek and the question of what to do about layoffs in a recession.[53] However, a rash of wildcat strikes and an upturn in the price level early in 1977 revealed the short-term viability of corporatist compulsion.

The corporatist approach to management of producer interests in the organized economy generally, and in industrial relations in particular, was not merely a formulation of the emergency. As will become apparent, emergency methods were an exaggerated and repressive version of the more general Indian approach to industrial relations common to national centrist parties.

The Procedural Environment and Trade Union Dependency

A second condition of trade union involution is the state's industrial relations policy as expressed under normal competitive politics. The state has created a legal and procedural environment that induces unions to depend on government and management more than on their membership for recognition as bargaining agents and for dispute settlement.[54] Three procedural issues are at stake: the absence of a secret ballot, the absence of a single bargaining agent, and the strong restraints on strikes. Under present legislation, trade union support in India is determined by counting the names on membership rolls, which are easily manipulated records, rather than by what opponents call the "populist" method of secret ballot elections. Present legislation also facilitates the multiplication of bargaining agents in the same enterprise, a situation in which management or government can easily manipulate the rivals.

Because check-off authorizations rather than secret ballot elections determine the extent of a union's support and because only rarely can one union qualify as the sole negotiating agent, workers in an enterprise or industry are often represented by rival unions more interested in scoring against each other than against management. These procedures assume that powerful friends and patrons in management politics are more helpful in securing members and benefits than is collective bargaining backed by the threat of strike. Strikes are legal under very limited circumstances. Unions must, in any case, go through drawn-out procedures prior to striking. As a result, strikes are often acts of desperation as well as illegal.[55] Unions usually shy away from them, preferring instead to rely on compulsory adjudication and failing that, arbitration procedures that government in any case often requires.

Trade union demands for more competitive and open-ended procedures have been lukewarm at best. Because INTUC, for long the largest national labor federation, has been affiliated since its creation in 1947 with the ruling Congress party, it has had good reason for collaborating with the present state-dominated arrangements. Using the advantages gained from Congress's incumbency, it became more influential than AITUC, the labor federation Congress despaired of controlling and whose leadership eventually passed into CPI hands. Given INTUC's strong vested interest in procedures that minimize competition, it has favored verification of extant registers as a basis of certification and opposed election based on secret ballot.[56] Its opposition to the secret ballot has been a significant element in the failure of Congress governments to commit themselves to competitive procedures.[57]

On the other hand, several smaller apex unions affiliated with opposition parties also have a vested interest in procedures that reward weak unions. Opposed to a single bargaining agent, they support the present proportionate representation and bargaining arrangements that enable minority unions to participate in negotiations with management.[58] They also support corporatist bipartite or tripartite bodies that enable the smaller federations to participate in national policy formulation.

The unions on the left have also given only ambivalent support to noncorporatist procedures. Because two of the three largest national federations, AITUC and CITU (founded in 1970, six years after the CPI split) are connected with the two principal Communist parties, the CPI and the CPI-M, they espouse the ideological view that industrial relations must reflect the interests of the working class and that organized labor is at the forefront of progressive forces.[59] AITUC's ideological line has been beset with contradictions and ambiguities. The S. A. Dange faction, ascendant until the emergency and active until Dange was expelled from the party in 1981, supported a strategy of alliance with what it perceived as the progressive Congress party of Jawaharlal Nehru and his daughter, Indira Gandhi. CITU, whose party patron, the CPI-M, has governed in Bengal and Kerala, has tried to take a line more independent of the state. Yet it too has found it prudent to adapt to the legal and economic conditions that make trade unions dependent on the state.

Because the state, INTUC, and most national federations have a vested interest in the system of corporatist dependency, they pay only lip service to the widely accepted goal of open-ended collective bargaining based on a single bargaining agent and the right to strike. The ambivalence of both unions and the state with respect to procedures that would institutionalize regulated conflict—such as the secret ballot, the single bargaining agent, and a wide scope for the right to strike—has stalemated efforts to reform industrial relations. The Janata and Congress legislative initiatives of 1978 and 1980 both foundered on the rock of this ambivalence.[60]

The pervasiveness of compulsory adjudication and arbitration and the increasingly limited circumstances under which strikes are legal perpetuates government's tutelary relationship to unions. Government dominance of dispute settlement procedures begins with the requirements for conciliation of the Industrial Disputes Act of 1947, the main legislative instrument of government intervention in labor affairs. Together with similar state acts, it mandated compulsory conciliation in disputes affecting essential services and optional conciliation for other cases. The National Commission on Labour noted as early as 1969 that "the optional provisions appear to be acquiring compulsory status in non-public utilities also."[61] As government, via legislative and discretionary measures, narrowed the conditions and terms under which legal strikes could occur, the use of compulsory adjudication and arbitration expanded.

One of the most frequent causes of industrial disputes and certainly the most vital issue for labor's economic interest is wage determination.[62] It is an area in which government's role is also dominant. As the Labour Bureau's 1974 report on wage fixation in industry and agriculture noted, "wage determination in India is mostly done by state action and compulsory arbitration, while collective agreements play an important part on matters of wage fixation in foreign countries."[63] Recommendations over time by ad hoc administrative bodies and pay commissions appointed by government are the source of policy for wage regulation. When such recommendations are endorsed by government, they are implemented by quasi-expert, quasi-judicial boards and tribunals. Meant to be autonomous bodies, these institutions determine wages on the basis of case law procedures. One might instance the Rau Court of Inquiry of 1940, which set a dearness allowance (D.A.) for railroad employees, thus launching the general practice of paying D.A.'s, or the Central Pay Commission of 1947, which established norms for considering how much price rises should be neutralized via D.A.'s for different income levels. These seminal recommendations in turn influenced the determinations of wage boards, whose heyday was in the fifties but which almost vanished from the scene until revived by the Congress-I government in April 1981.[64] Established for different industries, these boards were composed of management, labor, and independent experts appointed by government. Government described them as an alternative to collective bargaining, but the National Commission on Labour saw them as an obstacle to collective bargaining. The recommendations of such ad hoc administrative bodies and of wage boards are applied to specific disputes, in cases that constitute a body of precedent (e.g., *Madras Press Labour Union, Madras v. Artisan Press, Ltd., Madras*) by a network of labor courts—the industrial tribunals of various states, the Labour Appellate Tribunal, and the All India Industrial Tribunal.[65]

The Easy Path: Organizing Skilled Labor

The macroeconomic circumstances of labor in an industrializing economy seriously constrain the organizing and bargaining capacities of trade unions. Abundant and cheap labor has limited the economic leverage of trade unions in most industrializing countries, and so has the undifferentiated, unskilled nature of the labor required in low-technology industries. The exception to the prevalence of abundant and cheap labor was America, where until well into the nineteenth century, abundant land limited the availability of labor for industry and farm earnings put a floor under industrial wages.[66] The first of these constraints on trade unions, abundant and cheap labor, is more significant for India than the second, the unskilled nature of the labor force. In the framework of "world time," Indian economic development since independence has involved a high proportion of skilled workers employed in industries based on mature or advanced technology or in a rapidly growing tertiary (service) sector. It is much more difficult for trade unions to organize or bargain on behalf of unskilled and semiskilled workers who are easily replaced than on behalf of skilled workers whose skill constitutes a monopoly of sorts. The de facto organizing and bargaining strategies of Indian trade unions have featured skilled industrial, white-collar, and professional workers, while their often Marxist-inspired rhetoric has featured the struggle for working-class rights and power. Trade unions have taken advantage of the scarcity value of skilled labor while avoiding the challenge of organizing the unskilled. Despite affiliation with parties that purport to speak for the working class, their approach has been more like the skilled-labor strategy of Samuel Gompers' American Federation of Labor than the working-class strategies initially pursued by the German Social Democrats or the British Labour party. The result has been to focus trade union attention on a relatively small fixed sum of easily organized and strategically positioned workers rather than on expanding the sum of organized workers by reaching less accessible, more vulnerable ones.

The Conditions for Involution: Enervating Replication

The most significant measure of the labor movement's involution is its progressive fragmentation. The labor movement is fragmented at the apex as well as at the level of local industries and firms. At the apex, trade union federations are fragmented along ideological and party lines. In the period of 1920–28 and again in 1938–40, there was only one national federation (AITUC) but by 1970–74 there were eleven.[67] At the local level, such fragmentation is compounded by the mushrooming growth of unions that results from competition among trade union entrepreneurs, many of them pawns of party or management. They establish themselves on the industrial scene under cover of legislation that allows certification on the basis of as few as seven members.[68] Fragmentation at both the national and local level is exacerbated by government and management manipulation of the diverse and divided unions to assure acceptable representation and favorable policy and dispute outcomes.

Trade union membership statistics, incomplete and inadequate though they are, support the notion of progressive fragmentation. For statistical purposes, there are three types of unions: those that do not bother to register themselves and are therefore statistically invisible, those that register themselves but do not respond to the reporting requirement for information about their membership size, and those that register and "submit returns," including information on membership. The Trade Unions Act of 1926 does not require registration. The number of unregistered unions is probably quite significant; it may be as large as one-third to one-half the number of officially recognized unions (table 29) with one-fourth as many members.[69] "Registered" unions do no more than minimally establish their legal identity by registering their existence with government. They are unable or find it inconvenient to provide information about themselves to government. They lack the administrative resources or stable membership of the third category of trade unions, "unions submitting returns." Unions submitting returns have the apparatus to collect basic information concerning their membership and submit it annually to government. Registered unions are sometimes dummy organizations formed by trade unions, politicians, or management to influence or disrupt recognition or bargaining procedures. Unions submitting returns have higher levels of administrative capacity and stability, are more willing to accept public scrutiny, and are less likely to be dummy organizations. As is apparent in table 29, proliferation has occurred much more among registered unions than among those submitting returns, that is, it has occurred among the less stable and less organized. We may assume this is even more true of unregistered unions. Some states have been more prone to proliferation than others, depending on local circumstances and on which national federation has been dominant. In states such as Rajasthan and Karnataka, where CITU, the CPI-M affiliate, is the leading national federation, the trade union environment is more stable and the work force more committed and better represented than in West Bengal, the oldest industrial area, where political

TABLE 29
Registered Unions, Unions Submitting Returns, and Average Membership in Unions Submitting Returns, 1927–76

| | No. of Registered Unions | Unions Submitting Returns | |
Year		No.	Average Membership
1927–28	29	28	3,594
1937–38	420	343	1,137
1946–47	1,725	998	1,335
1955–56	8,095	4,006	567
1960–61	11,312	6,813	589
1966	14,686	7,244	606
1971	22,484	9,029	606
1976	26,193	6,698	707

SOURCES: Labour Bureau, *Indian Labour Yearbook* for 1947–48 (Simla, 1948) (p. 106), 1967 (Simla, 1968) (p. 82), and 1975–76 (Simla, 1976); and Government of India, Ministry of Information and Broadcasting, *India, 1980: A Reference Annual* (Delhi, 1981), p. 389.

struggles among national federations enhance fragmentation and conflict at the enterprise and industry level.[70]

Because of the incomplete nature of membership statistics for unregistered unions and for registered unions submitting no returns, the data to confirm fragmentation can come only from unions submitting returns. As these unions are better organized than the other two categories, the figures probably understate the overall degree of fragmentation. Our index of fragmentation is average membership per union, which shows a long-term decline (see table 29). It was 3,594 per union in 1927–28, 1,137 in 1937–38, 567 in 1955–56, and 710 in 1976 (a slight increase).

The cutting edge of fragmentation and involution is found in the private industrial sector, where a work force whose numbers have stagnated intersects with the phenomenal growth of registered unions. Fragmentation generates conflict. Private-sector industrial disputes are about ten times as frequent as those in the public sector.[71] By contrast, in the public sector, unions have not been subject to such fragmentation. Public employees are likely to belong to larger national trade unions organized to parallel large departmental and public-sector undertakings or industries such as the nationalized banks, the Post and Telegraph Department, and the railways. They are more likely to belong to unions "submitting returns," whose number has remained relatively stable (table 29) even while government and public-sector employment grew by 44 percent between 1966 and 1975. These figures suggest that even while the sum of organized workers is expanding, the real struggle by effective unions is over a fixed sum of easily organized workers. Adding hard-to-organize, low-paid workers—who do not work for government, for privileged multinationals, or large domestic business, but who work for the underprivileged industrial sector—is a less rewarding enterprise.

Doctrinal Alternatives: Social Harmony versus Regulated Conflict

State-dominated pluralism in industrial relations reflects a more pervasive Indian tradition that features social harmony and has been embodied over time in ideologically diverse and even opposed political forces. State-dominated pluralism continues the bureaucratic world view of the viceregal administrative state. The metaphors of the guardian and of the steel frame used to characterize the British raj captured a Platonic relationship between ruler and ruled that included hierarchy, administrative rationality, and discipline. Such a vision was not uncongenial to the rationalist calculus and social engineering that inspired the planned development of Congress's socialist intellectuals. Their socialist understanding of class conflict quickly yielded to the thought that such conflict was destructive in a state dominated by socialist policy. The viceregal tradition and planned socialism acquired strange bedfellows in this commitment to harmony, which parallels a similar commitment in Mohandas Gandhi's doctrine of trusteeship. Dimissing the notion of class conflict, Gandhians hold that, because wealth was socially created, the rich would use their wealth for the benefit of the poor and that all would observe their duties as defined by a commonly shared social norm.[72]

By contrast, the doctrine of regulated conflict that provides the framework for pluralist bargaining in Anglo-American and, to a lesser extent, Western European industrial relations has not made much headway in India. Regulated conflict requires (1) a public philosophy that welcomes adversary relations and political competition because they promote truth and the public interest, (2) economic and social differences that are more crosscutting than reinforcing, (3) agreement on the institutional and procedural means for competition and bargaining, and (4) enough symmetry among adversaries' competitive and bargaining resources to insure a rough approximation of countervailing power. None of these conditions holds in India.

It is difficult to find a voice—official, journalistic, or scholarly—that legitimates the role of conflict in unmasking the often spurious consensualism and disinterest of state corporatist claims. Workdays lost are interpreted as an index of the breakdown of law and order and of a loss of production rather than as a legitimate cost of industrial democracy.[73] The view that conflict has a positive role was represented in moderate form by the National Commission in Labour in 1969. Its thoughtful and substantial report failed to command government support, while the opinions of the dissenting INTUC commission members reflected the prevailing world view and carried the day.

The suspicion of group conflict based on group selfishness appeared in the remarks of the late Jagjivan Ram, then minister of labor, when he inaugurated the national commission. Despite his profession of support for the principle of collective bargaining, the core of his speech suggested that he did not credit the pluralist premise that interest group conflict could approximate the public interest. Collective bargaining would damage the interests of society as a whole:

> After all, historically and sociologically, the basis of the trade union group bond was the need to protect the group from opposing differ-

ent groups and to promote its interest against the interests of the group in opposition. The basis of the group bond was thus not creative association as in a cooperative, but negation and hostility and self-preservation. The consequences that the acquisitive action of one group might have on society as a whole did not figure into the calculation of the contending groups.[74]

Ram was not alone. L. K. Jha, the epitome of the talented expert bureaucrat, in his testimony before the commission as governor of the Reserve Bank of India, reminded the commissioners of the colonial and laissez-faire origins of collective bargaining but failed to recall for them its social democratic provenance:

> The British had a great genius for coining phrases, to make their self-interest appear to be virtuous. If we look to what is known as collective bargaining, which is a well enshrined and highly respected principle, its roots lay in the British *Laissez Faire*. Collective bargaining was the magic answer to avoid exploitation of labour. That answer did not originate in countries which had planning; much less in the countries which were socialist. The basic concept of what is a proper wage is not something to be decided by trial and error.[75]

The INTUC dissenters from the commission's report agreed with Jha. After opposing collective bargaining, they went on to decry the freedom to strike. They noted that the word "bargaining" was invariably used when "there is a commodity involved" and that "progressive thinkers all over the world [believe] that labour is not to be treated as a commodity," and they concluded that they would, "therefore, like to avoid the word 'bargaining' notwithstanding that it is very much in vogue." [76] The dissenters' profound distaste for bargaining and conflict was matched by their serene confidence in the state's capacity to know and protect the good of the community:

> The third party, the community, should be the real and ultimate master, and therefore, its interests should be paramount. The state, as the representative of the community must, therefore, have the right at all times and in all stages of an industrial dispute to step in and direct the parties to call off the strike or the lockout. . . . We therefore do not agree with our colleagues who want to reduce the appropriate government to the status of a mere petitioner before the Industrial Relations Commission, which Commission in its wisdom may disagree with the Government and may refuse to adjudicate a dispute which the Government as Government might feel it to be its duty to refer for adjudication.[77]

Raj Krishna, one of India's leading economists and an influential member of the Janata government's Planning Commission, lacked Jha's confidence in the Indian bureaucracy. "The greatest single constraint on industrial growth in India," he argued, "is bureaucratic overcontrol." Yet he too supported the bipartisan consensus that wages and industrial disputes are matters for expert and official determination and resolution:

> To promote industrial peace, national guidelines for wage contracts must be established. They should link increases in wages to increases in objective indexes of performance in every industry and to increases in cost of living indexes as determined by expert bodies. Whenever collective bargaining fails, arbitration must then be compulsory. The arbitration judgments should conform to the national guidelines.[78]

There are a few contrary voices. The "Giri approach" although defeated in its time, continues to serve as a rallying cry for moderate dissenters searching for a respectable way to challenge the state dominated system of industrial relations. V. V. Giri, already at independence a veteran union leader, served as labor minister between 1952 and 1954 and later as president of India. As labor minister, he held that compulsory adjudication discouraged genuine collective bargaining, which he tried to make statutory. His efforts to move in this direction aroused the opposition of INTUC, the newly formed Congress party affiliate, and government ministries. Giri was forced to withdraw his proposals, resigned soon thereafter and was replaced by Khandubai Desai, a former president of INTUC. As the Ramaswamys wrote: "When Giri resigned as Labour Minister, collective bargaining . . . suffered a setback from which it has yet to recover."[79]

The inability of the Janata government in 1978 and the Congress-I government in 1980 to pass much-needed new industrial relations legislation reflects the ambivalence of both governments and the uneasy standoff between interests and world views that has paralyzed action. Those elites who value social harmony, while more numerous and vociferous, are not sufficiently confident of their ground or powerful enough to crush those who value regulated conflict. Despite their 1975–77 differences over democracy and dictatorship, both the Janata and the Congress shared a common view that independent collective bargaining and conflict, especially strikes, expressed antisocial goals and attitudes more often than they promoted the industrial democracy and working-class interest they professed to value.[80]

The Pay Commission Model in Industrial Relations

State policy for the trade union sector has been fashioned not in response to the conditions of an industrial work force but by analogy to the regulation of the state bureaucracy. The in-house traditions of the Anglo-Indian bureaucracy for assessing and rationalizing its own pay and benefits structure have gradually been extended to the public sector and the organized economy more generally, introducing yet another element of policymaking from expertise and principle rather than bargaining. The Home Ministry appoints pay commissions to study the personnel policies and emoluments schedule of the government establishment and to make recommendations for their improvement.[81] The pay commission outlook has influenced subsequent committees and commissions concerned with wage and income policy. In Western Europe, state efforts to determine such policy are constrained by competition and bargaining among political parties, labor and industry federations, and expert knowledge. Indian policy, by contrast, has remained largely a bureaucratic matter, relatively insulated from trade union and political pressures and relatively out of touch with the world of social research.

Pay commissions provided a reliable vehicle for rationalizing anomalies and inequities within a hierarchical civil service. When, in the fifties, public employment expanded dramatically to become the largest component in the organized economy, the pay commission spawned a number of descendants. These included the aborted Chakravarti Committee of 1973, the Labour Bureau's report on wage fixation, and the Bhootalingam Study Group on Wages, Incomes and Prices, under the Janata government in 1978.[82] All shared the in-house, apolitical, technocratic orientation of their pay commission progenitor. The terms of reference and membership of the Bhootalingam group were such as to elicit no response from the trade unions. Among the reasons for the failure of its report as a policy document were its lack of trade union support and its thin research and analysis. Created in 1969 to coordinate public-sector industries and located in the Finance Ministry, the Bureau of Public Enterprise extended the pay commission's establishment mentality to the burgeoning public sector and added to it the Finance Ministry's concern for fiscal responsibility and expert opinion. Governing public-sector wages by a pay commission–like model was seriously proposed by the Bureau of Public Enterprise, leading to fears that collective bargaining would be banished from public-sector units. Rather than concerning itself with the wider, more amorphous, and disputed political and economic considerations that affect labor commitment and productivity, the bureau pursued administrative ratio-nalization and financial probity. It is strongly suspect in trade union circles, which see it as a tool of government and management with little concern for labor.[83] In confronting the problem of increasing pro-duction and profits in the public sector, it has turned more to the op-tion of disciplining labor and curbing wages and less to the harder task of upgrading management and technology.

Development Imperatives and the Desire for Low Wages

A final factor detrimental to labor's interest is the state's self-proclaimed responsibility for development.[84] This takes two potentially contradic-tory forms, maximizing industrialization based on capital-intensive in-vestment and maximizing employment based on labor-intensive meth-ods. Both development strategies entail cheap labor. If labor remains a low-cost factor of production under capital-intensive methods, savings for capital formation can be increased. Labor-intensive development methods that spread employment while attempting to meet market competition from manufactured products also entail low wages. The state's development goals accord with a wide range of economic theory that concludes, "unpalatable as it may be, the economy in India needs a policy of low wages."[85]

The state's commitments to represent the whole community, to be a model employer, and to be a friend of labor ultimately have proved less important than these development imperatives. Labor's political weak-ness and trade union involution serve government's development goals.

In 1955, Oscar Ornati summed up the immediate postindependence industrial relations scene in India by remarking that "within the cur-rent Indian socio-political climate, recurrent pious expressions glorify-ing the virtues of unhampered bargaining are no more than lip service to an ideal and a goal agreed upon as desirable."[86] Much of what we have said suggests that Ornati's remarks remain relevant at the ideologi-cal level because they help to explain the persistence of state-dominated pluralism in India's industrial relations. Since the mid-fifties, however, macroeconomic changes have affected the composition of workers in the organized economy and the structure of organized labor. By the early eighties, India had become the fifteenth-largest industrial econ-omy. The number of its technical and professional personnel ranked third in the world. These changes facilitated the process of trade union proliferation and involution that have been the dominant themes of this chapter. On the other hand, they have also facilitated contrary developments that could open the way to more symmetrical and independent bargaining relationships with management and political relationships with the state. Industrial relations have been affected by the emergence of national-scale labor organizations that parallel newly created, state-managed, industrial, financial, and commercial enterprises. They have been affected too by the emergence of independent national federations, particularly CITU. INTUC, the Congress party's chosen instrument, and AITUC, affiliated with Congress's sometime political ally, the CPI, have adopted pro-Congress ideological orientations and political commitments that make it difficult for them to challenge the state management of industrial relations favored by Congress.[87] CITU is better placed ideologically and politically to challenge Congress's state corporatist doctrine and practice because its patron, the CPI-M, has been a resolute Congress opponent. As a result, its claim to represent the interests of the working class and to oppose those of a Congress-dominated state is more credible and effective than those of its two principal rivals. To an extent, it has become the spokesman for a view of industrial relations that recognizes regulated conflict as desirable and legitimate.

Finally, industrial relations have been affected by the successful formation of local, regional, and national labor fronts. They have united workers hitherto divided by rivalries among local unions and national federations. They have created conditions of countervailing power capable of challenging industry associations and the state. At the local level, the Delhi textile labor alliance challenged Delhi's textile industry firms by maintaining a long, even though ultimately disappointing, strike. In Maharashtra's industrial areas, the charismatic Datta Samant successfully capitalized on postemergency (1977–80) worker militancy to raise the wage floor of India's largest industrial state. Samant's short-run success may entail longer-run difficulties. It was based on the personal leadership and loyalty characteristic of the entrepreneurial trade unionism that has fostered proliferation and fragmentation. Unlike the Delhi textile alliance, which united unions affiliated with a spectrum of national federations, Samant's front was achieved in opposition to them. His utilitarian mobilizations have gained wage benefits at the expense of working-class consciousness and trade union solidarity. Yet it is the demonstration effect of Samant's efforts and those of the Delhi textile workers alliance that could signal a change in industrial relations.

At the national level, the Congress-I government's July 27, 1981, antistrike ordinance and the parallel legislation passed by Parliament in September united eight opposition trade union federations in a national front, the National Coordination Committee. The front was reminiscent of the broad spectrum of political forces brought together during and after the emergency, when political parties on both left and right worked together to save democracy by opposing authoritarianism. In 1981, it was the threat to organized labor, particularly the right to strike, that united CITU (CPI-M), AITUC (CPI), Hind Mazdoor Sabha (socialist), and the Bharatiya Mazdoor Sangh (BJP). What had not been possible at the party level since the struggle against authoritarianism collapsed under Janata rule did become possible in the face of the threat of summary trials followed by imprisonment and fines for those inciting or participating in an illegal strike. Left and right joined forces to oppose the Indira Gandhi-led Congress-I. Opposition trade union federations agreed that the state in the form of the Congress-I act was an unequivocal threat to organized labor.

However, unlike Solidarity in Poland, whose opposition to authoritarianism, corruption, and economic mismanagement electrified the country and soon mobilized farmers and middle-class professionals in support of united industrial workers' demands, India's broad labor front was isolated from cultivators and middle-class professionals, and it did not include INTUC. While India's 1981 labor front did not succeed in blocking or in mobilizing broad national support, it was, like the repressive antistrike bill and the appearance of national unions and local and regional labor fronts, the possible harbinger of new possibilities in industrial relations.

National level trade unions and labor fronts are creating conditions that may be incompatible with state-dominated pluralism. History does not allow us to argue that greater industrialization and larger work forces necessarily favor the more oligopolistic patterns of interest aggregation that characterize the strong trade union presence in many European states. Such trends are not universal; the United States, for example, is characterized by pluralist trade union organization. Even so, the European experience is strongly suggestive. Despite the embattled political circumstances of Indian trade unions and their increasingly limited freedom to engage in legal strikes, the emergence of aggregation would indicate the possible reversal of processes that produce political weakness and involution. Industrial relations in India in the 1980s will continue to combine state corporatist and pluralist features, but it may take much more repression to prevent pluralist features from becoming pronounced and from assuming a more oligopolistic and influential form.

II Students as a Demand Group: Educational Policy and Student Mobilization

Students, including educated unemployed youth, have become an important demand group in Indian politics. They caught the country's attention in the mid- and late 1960s, when student "unrest" and student "indiscipline" began to affect state and national politics and entered Home Ministry calculations of trends affecting law and order. It was an era of worldwide student politics, not only in the Third World, where students were sometimes the vanguard of regime change, but also in advanced industrial societies, such as France, Germany, and the United States, where they challenged the authority and policies of governments and universities. While students in India share some of the characteristics of students elsewhere, their history and circumstances are sufficiently distinct to justify treating them in the framework of our demand group analysis rather than in the framework of Third or First World political systems.

Student political participation and mobilization in India is referred to officially and in the media as student "unrest" or student "indiscipline." These are cultural constructions implying that students, like "the natives" under colonial regimes, can become "restless" and, like badly socialized children, unmannerly and disrespectful. The cultural construction of students as, potentially, a lesser breed without law and as less than adult (i.e., mature and responsible), as wards rather than citizens of the state, helps to explain why students have rarely been counted as an interest group or a political actor. Being neither producers nor consumers and neither workers nor capitalists and lacking an unidentifiable social function, they do not fit interest group, class, or functional theories of social action. If, however, a demand group lens is used, students become visible as an important actor in Indian politics not only since independence but also in the nationalist era.

Recently industrializing countries reverse sequences experienced by those that industrialized early: state-enforced and -funded schooling and universal suffrage preceded or paralleled rather than followed industrialization. It is only since World War II that higher education in Europe's advanced industrial economies expanded beyond elite boundaries. By contrast, in India the expansion of education began soon after independence and the onset of universal suffrage, more or less paralleling the effort to industrialize. These contrasting sequences affected the relative numbers of potential recruits for demand groups in the political process: thirty years after independence, the number of students had grown to almost half that of organized labor. In 1979, there were about 22 million workers in the organized economy, between 7 and 12 million trade union members, 4.6 million students enrolled at the intermediate level and above, and 3 million unemployed educated persons (again at the intermediate level and above) in the live registers of government employment exchanges, the latter a conservative measure at best. The stage had been set for students to be a political class and a demand group in Indian politics.

The character of student groups stands somewhere between the continuity and professionalism generated by capital and organized workers on the one hand and the ad hoc quality of agriculturalists' demand groups on the other. Student organizations, like those of workers, develop out of the large-scale organizations in which both groups are concentrated. Like labor organizations, student organizations are aggregated in national, party-affiliated federations, but the control of such federations over local activities is minimal, as in the case of labor. The short generational cycles that define the role of students, along with their dependent status as consumers, rather than producers, works against the institutionalization of student interests in ideology and organizations, lending them an ephemeral quality. The organizational expressions of students lack the bureaucratic professionalism and continuity of firms and unions. Like cultivators, students do not run a high risk of job loss when they participate in strikes and protest movements and their activity as a demand group consists of ad hoc movements far more than of regular, institutionalized pressure and influence on the bureaucratic and legislative process.

Students played a major role in the nationalist movement, and at independence they were already a significant political class. But in 1947, higher education was an elite phenomenon. Twenty years later, higher education had been significantly democratized by increasing the numbers and proportions of students in ways that multiplied the links between college students and society. While we cannot say precisely what critical mass is needed for a group to become a political class, during the expansion of the sixties students did achieve such a critical mass.

Students as a demand group have not generally offered a challenge to the centrist ideological and policy consensus, although they have threatened centrist regimes. Their agitational politics and mobilizations gave them the appearance of revolutionary potential. Yet student politics has been mainly about issues internal to universities, issues arising out of students' interest in certification and the oppressive conditions of their "work"—examinations, grades, fees, hostels, admissions. Their style has been of the business unionism rather than the class politics variety. Students have provided the cadres of mainstream parties more than of left and right organizations. When they have espoused explicitly political causes, those have often reflected regional demands—in Tamil Nadu, Assam, and Punjab, for example.

In this chapter, we will explore the objective conditions that accompanied the phenomenal expansion of higher education and created an even larger, more discontent body of educated youth. The favoring of higher over lower levels of education laid the groundwork for the growth in student mobilization, marked by the exponential increase of student "indiscipline" and student participation in extraparliamentary politics in 1966–67, 1973–75, and sporadically since. We will also explore the attempt, after 1977, to put the genie back in the bottle through policies that restricted expansion and reallocated priorities between levels of education. Finally, we will review the effect of unemployment on student alienation.

Students and Industrial Workers as Political Classes

Students are more than able industrial workers and public employees to be a political class. Like workers, students are concentrated in large institutions that provide the community essential to a common consciousness. Unlike workers, they are not economically dependent on their institutions. While their immediate interest in credentials, fees, examinations, hostels, and jobs dominates their consciousness, their relatively unfettered condition leads them to search for personal identity and social meaning in ideologies and issues. The often undemanding conditions of their work free them for the work of partisan and movement politics. Unlike workers, they can begin practicing politics as a profession while carrying on their other "work."

The different historical contexts in which Indian workers and students entered the political arena account for their differences in commitment and political consciousness. Rural recruits to factory employment in eighteenth-century England were often thrown into inhuman conditions, faced with unfamiliar rationalized work routines, and subjected to degrading and unhealthy living conditions that were radically different from (if not necessarily "worse" than) those they had known on the farms and in the rural communities from which they came. If they had known toil and exploitation before, it had been mitigated by tacit social controls, local institutions, and the obligations of masters and servants. They resisted the new urban conditions of work, often violently. While no one would argue that the process of industrialization in India has taken place without suffering by its participants, it has been less violent than that of the first industrializers. The Luddite response to factory employment of some British workers in the eighteenth century has not characterized Indian factory workers in the twentieth. Instead, compared with their European counterparts, Indian workers in the early stages of industrialization appear remarkedly committed.[1] This difference is in part a consequence of the factory and social legislation, associational rights, and public philosophies that later industrializing nations have adopted from early industrializers after the latter became welfare states. It also reflects different patterns of urban migration. Often workers are brought to the Indian city for factory work as segments of kin and/or village communities by known foremen-cum-recruiters and settled together in localities already populated by people of their kind. While there are tremendous variations in their work and living conditions, such workers have adapted to industrial discipline more readily than rural students enrolled in urban colleges have adapted to academic discipline and its uncertain rewards.

It is the students, not the workers, who are not committed. Like rural recruits to urban factory work at the dawn of industrialization, they are uprooted and alienated. To the first-generation literates from rural areas or backgrounds, who formed the bulk of the millions involved in the rapid expansion of higher education in independent India, the "work" and the institutional discipline of urban university education seemed more uncongenial than jobs in urban factories seemed to workers recruited from rural areas. Students were uprooted from a world they only thought they were willing to lose.[2] They were brought together under one roof for reasons they dimly perceived and little understood or accepted. Alienated, for the most part, from the education they endured, students came to share the conditions of work and the consciousness that fed discontent and rebellion. Many found that what they were asked to do and learn was incomprehensible or meaningless. Many rural students in urban colleges are first-generation literates who lack the work habits, life goals, and cultural background that academic administrators and college teachers assume or require. Perhaps most important is the specter of unemployment among the educated that hovers over college students and recent graduates.[3]

Students adapted to their alienated circumstances by developing consciousness and organization, often with the help of political interests within and outside the university context.[4] Discontented with their education and with their employment prospects, and more concerned with certification and employment than with learning,[5] they struck, demonstrated, and agitated as much against academic rules, tests, and fees as against government policies.

If the shaping conditions for student politics in India have made students more of a political class than workers, they have still not played as decisive a role in national politics as students in other Third World countries. In Thailand, South Korea, and Iran, for example, students have been in the vanguard of national movements that changed regimes. Only from time to time, under crisis circumstances, have Indian students provided the cadres and become the vanguard of issue or movement politics that threatened to change governments and exceptionally even regimes. In Tamil Nadu in 1965 and in Gujarat in 1974, students launched and led massive anti-Hindi and anti–price rise agitations that challenged policies and toppled governments. In the 1980s, students led or collaborated with regional movements in Assam and Punjab. Nationally, students provided the cadres for the Jayaprakash Narayan–led movement in 1974–75 that threatened to displace Indira Gandhi's Congress-I government and induced it to save itself by imposing an emergency regime.

Even when they have threatened regimes, students have not threatened the centrist consensus. If the JP movement spoke of "total revolution," its main tenets were decentralization, honest government, and a more just society, hardly revolutionary goals in the Indian context. Ordinarily, Indian students have provided the personnel and political resources for partisan and factional politics. The easy access to political careers and the benefits of power have led students to participate in rather than challenge the established political system. Success in student government elections opens the way to political careers in partisan politics. Sanjay Gandhi's mobilization of educated and ambitious but frustrated youth in the Youth Congress was paradigmatic of this process. During the emergency (1975–77) and again after Congress-I's 1980 parliamentary and state assembly electoral victories, the Youth Congress was resuscitated and transformed. As Sanjay Gandhi's personal vehicle, it became the means for him to displace the "adult" Congress organization and those who held office in its name. Sanjay's success in building a support base of educated youth and young entrepreneurs indicates the propensity of student politics to respond to mainline political opportunities. After Sanjay's death, his brother Rajiv also used the Youth Congress to build his strength.

The Objective Conditions Shaping Students as a Demand Group

The number of students in higher education, at 4.6 million in 1975–76, approached the number of workers in organized labor, at 7 to 12 million. Their concentration in formal organizations made students readily susceptible to mobilization. The number of students in higher education grew even more rapidly than that of government and public-sector employees, increasing by over a million in each of the three five-year periods between 1960–61 and 1975–76. Enrollment increased by 220 percent between 1960–61 and 1970–71 (table 30), compared with 42.5 percent for government and public-sector employees.[6] The unprecedented increase in enrollment between 1960 and 1970 overwhelmed extant institutions and created the objective conditions for the student role in demand politics.

The largest spurt in enrollments began in the five-year period im-

TABLE 30
Growth in Number of College Students, 1950–79

Year	No.	Increase in No.	% Increase
1950–51	423,326	—	—
1955–56	736,124	312,798	74
1960–61	1,094,991	358,867	49
1965–66	2,095,217	1,000,226	91
1970–71	3,502,357	1,407,140	67
1975–76	4,615,992	1,113,635	32
1976–77	4,616,609	617	0
	(4,875,558)	(259,566)	(6)
1978–79	4,192,934	−423,675	−9
	(5,049,957)	(+174,399)	(+4)

SOURCE: This table is based on the Education Ministry's annual (but three to five years late) publication, *Education in India.* The table we have used is entitled "Number of Pupils in Recognized Institutions by Stages of Instruction," which, in recent years, changed its title to "Number of Pupils by Stages of Institutions," and then returned to the previous title. For higher education, we have aggregated figures for intermediate, B.A./B.Sc., M.A./M.Sc., research, professional, technical, and special education, undergraduate diploma, and "other education" (collegiate).

Notes: The stabilization and then decline of 1976–79 partly reflect the application of the so-called ten-plus-two pattern, in which students previously educated in eleventh- and twelfth-year intermediate or preuniversity courses, whom we counted for higher education, were shifted to the eleventh and twelfth years of higher secondary education. The shift has implications not only for education but also for political mobilization, which has been less active, though not negligible, at the secondary level. Numbers in parentheses include students shifted to the secondary level under the ten-plus-two program and indicate that there would have been a decline in growth rate even without the shift. Data were not available for 1977–78.

mediately preceding 1966–69, years characterized by demand politics. Higher-education enrollment increased by 91 percent between 1960–61 and 1965–66 and by 67 percent in the next five years (1965–66 and 1970–71), with the growth rate tapering off somewhat to 32 percent in the five years preceding the emergency (1971–77). At the end of the emergency regime and under the Janata government (1976–79), for the first time in two decades, the rate dropped to a negative figure or one only slightly exceeding the rate of population growth, depending on how one defines higher and secondary education (see notes to table 30).

The unprecedented growth of higher education was a response to powerful political demands pressing for a pace of expansion that quickly outran adequate funding. State governments, constitutionally responsible for education,[7] ignored the advice of planners and education officials in Delhi, who counseled that adequate staffing and facilities of new institutions and appropriations were beyond the means of the states. Instead, state governments responded to the insistent demands of influential urban middle-class and rural notable constituents for more college seats by creating intellectually and physically jerry-built institutions or underfunding expanding enrollments in existing ones. State legislators responded by demanding that government sanction both neighborhood colleges in their districts and regional state universities. Educational entrepreneurs and sect and caste benefactors took advantage of the degree boom by founding private colleges that entailed government subventions. Motives of profit, influence, and political power conspired to accelerate foundings as local politicians created colleges to secure the reliable political machine a loyal staff and students could provide.[8] Parents, who wanted their children to have the higher, more secure incomes and social status that degrees were thought to provide, fueled the demand for seats in increasingly malleable institutions. The number of universities multiplied from 27 in 1950 to 119 in 1975 (table 31).

Until the early 1970s, enrollment in higher education grew faster than national income and population, which grew at an annual average of 3.5 percent since independence and 2 percent in recent years, respectively. Spending on education in real terms lagged well behind growth rates. The result was deteriorating conditions as per capita expenditures dramatically declined.

Higher education also grew at a faster pace than secondary and primary education, a fact that had the only partly intended consequence of expanding the sector of education that was most likely to act politi-

TABLE 31

Growth in Number of Colleges and Universities, 1950–81

Year	Colleges		Universities	
	No.	% Increase	No.	% Increase
1950–51	816	—	27	—
1955–56	1,204	47	32	19
1960–61	2,140	78	45	40
1965–66	5,632	163	79	76
1970–71	6,886	22	100	27
1975–76	8,395	21	119	19
1980–81	—	—	128	8

SOURCES: Government of India, Ministry of Planning, *Statistical Abstracts: India, 1977* (Delhi, 1978); Ministry of Education, *Education in India, 1975–76;* Ministry of Information and Broadcasting, *India, 1980.*

Note: We have defined "colleges" broadly, because we are interested in the political rather than educational implications of the numbers of institutions and their enrollments. Our figures include universities, "institutions deemed universities," "institutions of national importance," boards of intermediate and secondary education, research institutions, institutions for higher education (degree standard and above), postmatriculation diploma/certificate (below degree level), and intermediate predegree or junior colleges. This provides a higher figure than that given in Government of India, University Grants Commission, *Report for the Year 1979–80* (New Delhi, 1980), appendix 8, p. 120, which excludes junior colleges and colleges having only diploma or certificate courses. Our definition of "universities" includes "institutions of national importance" and "institutions deemed to be universities." The latest figure available for colleges is 8,529 for 1976–77.

cally (table 32). Of the funds allocated to education under the fourth plan (1969–70 to 1973–74) only 30 percent went to the elementary level,[9] which accounted for 68 million enrolled students, while 18 percent and 25 percent went to secondary and higher levels, respectively, with enrollments of only 22 and 3.5 million. (The balance was allocated to vocational and special education.)[10] Fifth-plan allocations showed a comparable pattern.

The much lower per capita expenditure for elementary education cannot be accounted for in terms of the lower costs associated with elementary education. Higher education received a disproportionate share of the available funds in part because of the political influence of the urban middle classes and rural notabilities on public policy and the absence of countervailing pressure for allocations to elementary education. Even when poor nonliterates had the political resources to press for elementary education, most of them valued the short-run returns from their children's labor more than the longer-run and uncertain benefits of literacy and more advanced education.

TABLE 32
Enrollment Growth Rates for Primary, Secondary, and Higher Education

Year	Primary		Secondary		Higher	
	Enrollment	% In-crease	Enrollment	% In-crease	Enrollment	% In-crease
1950–51	18,677,641	—	4,817,011	—	423,326	—
1955–56	24,511,331	31	6,826,605	42	736,124	74
1960–61	33,631,391	37	10,942,293	60	1,094,991	49
1965–66	48,912,678	45	17,132,945	57	2,095,217	91
1970–71	55,167,533	12	21,773,019	46	3,502,357	67
1975–76	63,108,492	14	25,999,227	19	4,615,992	32
1978–79	72,390,000	14	27,090,000	4	4,192,934	−9
					(5,049,957)	(+4)

SOURCES: See table 30. Figures for 1978–79 are from Ministry of Information and Broadcasting, *India, 1980,* p. 47.
   Notes: Primary education includes, in most states, grades 1–5, although in 1950–51 there was greater variation. Secondary includes the middle, senior basic, and higher stages, that is, grades 6 through 11 or 12. We have not included in either category school-level (precollege) technical and professional courses or "other" and special education. All three are relatively small categories. See table 30 for explanation of parenthetical numbers. For disparities between the text and this table, see note 9.

Skewed allocations favoring higher education, besides accelerating the mobilization of students, generated other advantages and disadvantages for India's economy. The failure to invest adequately in human capital at the elementary level limited productivity growth in the agricultural and industrial sectors of the economy and limited the quality of opportunity in the society as a whole. Skewed funding also helped to perpetuate the disproportionate influence of the educated few in the political system and produced a large cadre of educated unemployed. On the other hand, investment in human capital in higher education created the world's third-largest professional class, an asset that distinguishes India from most other Third World developing countries, providing inter alia what plentiful oil revenues cannot buy. The class has proved to be a critical component in India's economic growth, a significant element in India's economic independence and technological capacity, and a source of the substantial remittances of foreign exchange that have mitigated India's balance of payments and foreign debt problems.

   The conventional wisdom that bemoans the decline of higher education in India does not ordinarily take into account the creation of national, high-level engineering and managerial institutions (such as the Indian Institutes of Technology and Management), postgraduate degree programs, and advanced research institutions in the natural and social sciences or the agricultural universities.[11] The humanistic, liberal arts conception of higher education that prevailed under British rule was designed to turn out clerks and administrators to serve the imperial mission,[12] not to create technical and scientific talent for economic development. The new institutions, by contrast, have not only transformed the pattern and capabilities of higher education in India but have also played a vital development role.

India's investment in higher education and research stands in marked contrast to Chinese doctrine and practice. In China, particularly during the Cultural Revolution (1966–76), radical egalitarianism, ideological and political distrust of the expert, fear that meritocratic formal education might lead to the capitalist road, and the practice of sending students to the country to work in the agricultural sector generated consequences inimical to schooling generally and to higher education and research in particular. The costs to China's development performance and potential became apparent only after Mao Tse-tung's death, when the new regime began to reveal his policy errors and began energetic efforts to undo and reverse them. Thus, in considering the disproportionate expansion of higher education in India, developmental gains must be considered along with the negative effects on education and the increases in political mobilization.

The Incidence of Student Protest and Its Goals

The pattern of educational expenditures from elementary through higher education also laid the groundwork for the disillusionment and alienation that fueled demand politics. Too often, elementary and secondary education did not adequately prepare students for higher education, and all three levels often failed to prepare students for jobs or careers. The too-rapid expansion of higher education led to collegiate slums, custodial institutions, and high levels of wastage. Perhaps most important, many degree holders failed to find jobs, remained unemployed for long periods, or could only find jobs for which they were "overqualified," jobs that blighted their aspirations and often their potential. The incidence of student agitations and violence rose steadily throughout the 1960s, accelerated exponentially after the fourth general election in 1967 to a crescendo in 1974, the year before the emergency, receded with the emergency, rose to new heights in the late 1970s, and remained high into the early 1980s (table 33).

The magnitude of the increase is striking. In the mid- and late 1960s,

TABLE 33
Student "Indiscipline" (Reported Incidents)

Year	Incidents	Year	Incidents
1958	93	1971	4,380
1959	120	1972	6,365
1960	80	1973	5,551
1961	172	1974	11,540
1962	97	1975	3,847
1963	109	1976	1,190
1964	395	1977	7,520
1965	271	1978	9,174
1966	607	1979	9,203
1967	—	1980	10,600
1968	2,665	1981	7,740
1969	3,064	1982	5,200
1970	3,861	1983	7,188

SOURCES: Government of India, Ministry of Home Affairs, "Student Indiscipline" (1967, mimeograph), *Report, 1979–80* (Delhi, n.d.), *Report, 1980–81* (Delhi, n.d.), and *Third Report of the National Police Commission* (Delhi, 1980); and *Data India,* September 18–24, 1978, p. 594.

observers considered extraordinary the great increase in student indiscipline (from 109 incidents per year in 1963 to 607 in 1966) that characterized the period of political unrest beginning with Jawaharlal Nehru's death in 1964 and continued with the food shortages of 1965–66, the Indo-Pakistan war of 1965, and the challenge to Congress in the 1967 election. Yet these rates were dwarfed by those of the late seventies, which rose to 9,000 and 10,000 incidents per year. The early seventies was the time of the student-led Nav Nirman agitation in Gujarat and Jayaprakash Narayan's student-supported drive for "total revolution" in North India, especially in Bihar and eastern Uttar Pradesh. The year 1974 was characterized by the highest rates of student indiscipline ever, far above those for the emergency years of 1975–76, when strong measures repressed campus turmoil.

The goals of student mobilizations in the 1960s to 1980s included both bread-and-butter interest issues and wider political objectives. An inquiry that we conducted in the late sixties into factors associated with student indiscipline supported the proposition that expansion proceeding without regard to resources, and the low prospects associated with such overexpansion, were indeed probable causes of indiscipline. The inquiry compared 112 high-performance colleges (with at least 60 percent of students passing exams) and 154 colleges with high rates of indiscipline to the all-India averages on a number of indicators.[13]

Colleges on our indiscipline list were more likely to be low-prospect arts and science rather than high-prospect professional schools, to have low proportions of faculty to students and books to students, to spend Rs. 1,000 or less per student, to have high proportions (30–60 percent) of students in the less well endowed preuniversity or intermediate courses. These factors help suggest why we have described student movements as largely a response to bread-and-butter issues.

The inquiry, however, also suggested the significance of the more diffuse and psychological "alienation" thesis. Urban colleges with many rural students, who found themselves in an unfamiliar environment and away from the usual social definitions and restraints, made up a disproportionately high share of the indiscipline-prone colleges. These were colleges with 20–70 percent rural students. Colleges whose student bodies were almost entirely rural, that is, made up of rural students in rural settings, were not especially conspicuous in the indiscipline group.[14]

These distant and proximate causes of student unrest spawned action that varied over time and place but increasingly involved state and national politics.[15] As enrollments increased throughout the 1960s, students increasingly joined protest and movement politics, often acting as the vanguard. The groundwork for such action had been laid in the nationalist period, when Mohandas Gandhi had called on students to leave colleges and join the movement. During the 1960s, students played an increasingly visible and influential role in party politics. They found that leadership in student organizations was the career path to "tickets" (nominations), elected office, and even ministerial posts.[16] In the early 1970s, students again began to play an increasingly important role in movement politics, as they had during the nationalist era. As movement politics shifted its objectives from blocking or demanding policies to bringing down governments and changing regimes, students became a critical component of national politics and of the problem of governability. This led to the widespread agitation in 1974 against the ineffective and discredited Congress government in Gujarat and to its defeat in June 1975 in a state midterm election.[17] The election results were announced the day after Prime Minister Indira Gandhi was held guilty of corrupt electoral practices and threatened with disqualification from Parliament for six years, and they are assumed to have influenced her June 25th decision to declare an emergency. So too did Narayan's movement for "total revolution." Students provided much of its leadership and support, first in Bihar, then in Gujarat, and then throughout northern India.[18] Mrs. Gandhi had every reason to fear that the parties and political forces brought together by the JP movement might carry the day in the general election scheduled for February 1976.

Nav Nirman and the JP movement, as regime-threatening student movements, were exceptions rather than the norm in Indian student politics.[19] However, they suggest that ordinary interest and party politics does not exhaust student potential. When the emergency was imposed in June 1975, most student, faculty, and staff associations were suspended. An uncommon peace descended on the college and university world. Students attended classes and took examinations. Unrest virtually vanished. The threat of repression and intimidation worked wonders—for the moment. Faculty who deplored the emergency praised the unaccustomed peace. In northern India particularly, committed vice-chancellors with their handpicked aides and advisors took charge. They not only dispensed with the teacher, student, and staff organizations recognized in university statutes but also, in several notable instances, excluded the faculty from admissions and faculty recruitment and selection procedures. Coupled with the state corporatist strategy of patronizing, licensing, or creating like-minded professional and intellectual organizations,[20] Mrs. Gandhi's emergency regime appeared for a time to lay the groundwork for political and ideological control of higher education.

The completeness with which the emergency was able to subdue the universities and students was startling. While students had played a major role in precipitating the emergency by their protest movements, they played no special role in the defeat of the emergency, which was accomplished through the ordinary political procedures of the electoral process.

Policy Intervention in Student Conditions

Student "indiscipline" and "unrest," like workers' strikes, cannot be dealt with merely as a law-and-order problem to be solved by repression and patriotic exhortation. Both policy intervention and more or less spontaneous changes in the general economic conditions of graduates can affect the civic incorporation or alienation of students. The Janata (1978–83) and Congress-I (1980–85) versions of the sixth five-year plan constituted important policy interventions. Both governments significantly reduced welfare allocations generally and educational allocations in particular. Allocations fell from a high of 6.9 percent in the third plan, when the demand for education was at its height, to a low of 2.2 percent of the sixth (see table 34), with a slight

TABLE 34
Expenditure on Education as a Percentage of Plan Expenditure (Center and States)

	Education Expenditure
Third plan (1961–65), actual	6.9
Annual plans (1966–69), actual	4.6
Fourth plan (1969–74), actual	4.9
Fifth plan (1974–78), actual (three years) and anticipated (one year)	3.7
Draft sixth plan (Janata) (1978–83), outlay	2.8
Sixth plan, (Congress-I) (1980–85), outlay	2.2
Seventh plan (1985–90), outlay	3.5

SOURCES: Ministry of Information and Broadcasting, *India, 1980;* table 5.2, Ministry of Finance, *Economic Survey, 1979–80* (New Delhi, 1980), table 2.5, p. 106; Planning Commission, *Sixth Five Year Plan, 1980–85,* (Delhi, 1981), table 21.2, p. 361, and *Seventh Five Year Plan, 1985–90,* 2 vols. (Delhi, 1985), tables 3.4(a), 3.4(b), pp. 27, 28.

recuperation to 3.5 percent in the seventh. The notion that spending on education and health programs and facilities represents investment in human capital is accepted only to a limited extent by Indian planners and administrators.[21]

Within these overall reductions in proportion, there was a relative reallocation of funds among educational levels. Janata's concern for increasing the assets, opportunities, and income of the poor produced plan ratios more favorable to elementary (and adult) education and less favorable to secondary and higher education (table 35). Elementary education received 45 percent and social (adult) education 10 percent (increases of 12 and 9 percent), as against 14 percent for secondary and 13 percent for higher education (a reduction of 14 percent).[22] When a Congress-I government returned to power in January 1980 and redrafted the sixth plan, it revised the Janata pattern, restoring some funding to secondary and higher at the expense of elementary education.

One consequence of treating education primarily as a low-priority welfare cost rather than a high-priority human capital investment was to reinforce spontaneous trends toward a decline in the growth rate of enrollments. As tables 30 and 32 show, of the three levels of education, higher education, the level that generated most student mobilization, has experienced the most pronounced shrinkage in enrollment growth. Higher education's average annual rate of enrollment growth in the three decades between 1950 and 1980 has been 12, 15, and 4 percent respectively. In 1978–79, it was only −9 or + 4 percent, depending on how one counted the "ten-plus-two" level (see table 30).[23]

TABLE 35
Changes in Plan Allocations to Levels of Education (Percentages)

	Four Five-Year Plans and Annual Plans (1950–69)	Fifth Plan (1974–78)	Sixth Plan	
			Janata (1978–83)	Congress-I (1980–85)
Elementary	33	33	45	36
Secondary	17	18	14	17
University	20	23	13	19
Social (adult education)	3	1	10	5
Cultural programs	1	3	3	3
Other	8	10	6	9
Technical	18	12	9	11

SOURCES: Ministry of Information and Broadcasting, *India, 1980*, table 5.2; Planning Commission, *Sixth Five Year Plan, 1980–85*, table 21.2, p. 361.

Spontaneous Changes in Enrollment Trends

Policy interventions were not the only factor affecting enrollments. We can infer that the spontaneous forces of the job market also marginally affected choices among degree programs as well as reduced enrollments in higher education generally. Tables 36 and 37 summarize the enrollment and employment situations, respectively. The most striking response to the job market was occasioned by the high unemployment rates affecting the graduates of arts and B.A. programs, by far the most numerous of all degree progress (table 36). Enrollments in these programs, whose graduates registered usual-status (chronic) unemployment rates of 22 percent in 1980, higher than for graduates of any other program, declined significantly, from 45 percent in 1975–76 to 39 percent in 1983–84 (table 36). On the other hand, enrollments in postgraduate second-degree programs (M.A., M.Sc., and Ph.D.), whose graduates have very low unemployment rates (table 37), increased, from 9.8 percent in 1975–76 to 11.1 in 1979–80, at the expense of first-degree courses.[24] In these fields and levels, enrollments were responsive to changing job markets trends.

However, enrollments in the next two most numerous first-degree programs, (science and commerce) (table 36), with unemployment rates of 21 percent and 18 percent, respectively (table 37), did not decline in the face of weak employment prospects. Commerce enrollments went up, as a fashion for business management swept the country, while science enrollments remained steady. Enrollments in engineering and technology (B.E.), a high-opportunity field where enrollment has a propensity to remain steady because of high costs per student and government's de facto monopoly on foundings, nevertheless increased from 4.0 to 4.7 percent in 1983–84. Medical enrollments (M.B., B.S.) have declined to 3.6 percent, again because of high per-student costs and government's tight control of foundings. However, state governments have recently begun yielding to considerable political pressure for additional foundings generated by the earning prospects of medicine. The government of Karnataka has been in the lead in allowing private entrepreneurs, relying for their funding on very high capitation fees paid by applicants, to open new medical colleges. If allowed to expand in Karnataka or spread to other states, the practice may affect the recent steady state of medical enrollments.[25] The number of doctors per capita in India is among the world's lowest, but in prosperous urban areas approaches the numbers for comparable areas in industrial societies. The demand for places in medical schools is enormous and unrestrained by the fact that ten thousand doctors were unemployed in 1980. The demand was unrestrained not only because of the high incomes available in urban areas but also because of the prospects of migration to North America and the United Kingdom. Despite protests from national professional bodies, other states, in the absence of federal intervention, may follow Karnataka's lead.[26]

These spontaneous trends, together with policy intervention, have mitigated but not eliminated the most obvious objective conditions contributing to student unrest. They have sharply reduced the rate of

TABLE 36
Student Enrollment in First-Degree Courses of Study, 1975–76 to 1983–84

| | Enrollment (%) | | |
	1975–76	1979–80	1983–84
Arts	44.5	40.6	39.1
Science	19.1	19.2	19.8
Commerce	17.1	19.5	22.4
Education	3.2	2.8	2.2
Engineering/technology	4.0	4.5	4.7
Medicine	4.3	4.2	3.6
Agriculture	1.2	1.5	1.3
Veterinary science	0.3	0.3	0.3
Law	5.8	6.7	5.4
Other	0.5	0.7	0.7

SOURCES: University Grants Commission, *Report for the Year 1979–80*, appendix 6, p. 118, and *Report, 1983–84*, appendix 6, p. xiii. The figures exclude preuniversity and intermediate enrollments.

TABLE 37
Usual-Status Unemployment Rate among First- and Second-Degree Holders, 1980

Type of Degree	% Unemployed
Engineering (B.E.)	7.09
Medical Graduate (M.B., B.S.)	6.50
Agricultural	11.41
Veterinary medicine	3.60
Education (B.Ed.)	15.67
Arts (B.A.)	22.43
Arts (M.A.)	4.00
Science (B.Sc.)	20.57
Science (M.Sc.)	4.87
Commerce (B.Com.)	17.63
Commerce (M.Com.)	6.52
All degrees	15.76

SOURCE: Planning Commission, *Sixth Five Year Plan, 1980–85*, annexure 13.9, p. 220.
   Note: rate is calculated as the percentage of unemployed among "economically active" degree holders.

enrollment increase in higher education so that this rate now approximates the population growth rate. If disproportionate spending on higher education developed human capital for the tertiary (service) sector of the economy, it may be that spending proportionately more on elementary and secondary education may help develop human capital in the primary (agricultural) and secondary (industrial) sectors of the economy. Market forces and policy intervention also seem to have marginally shifted degree preferences toward degrees offering better job prospects. Nevertheless, absolute levels are such that unemployment among the educated continues to be an important conditioning factor for the existence and sometimes the direction of student politics.

Unemployment among the Educated and Student Mobilization

Whether the politics of students in particular and youth in general tends toward alienation and rebellion or toward incorporation in established forms of regulated conflict and political competition depends in considerable measure on yet another objective condition, the level and meaning of unemployment among the educated. The objective conditions of such unemployment are not sufficient to explain student politics and its role in demand politics. How the educated perceive their opportunities, rights, and political influence is shaped but not wholly determined by their levels and kinds of employment. Uncertain and unsatisfactory unemployment along with irrelevant or inadequate education prepares the ground for student politics. But it is how students construe the ambiguous career probabilities before them that finally determines the intensity and direction of student and youth politics, whether they will respond to what they perceive by angry protest or by prudent lowering of their expectations.

Tracing the links between the prospect of unemployment, student consciousness, and student mobilization is made more difficult by the considerable variation in unemployment estimates and the ambiguous nature of the conditions lying behind the estimates. If data professionals disagree by magnitudes of more than 100 percent about the extent of unemployment, how should the observer who is interested in the consequences of unemployment on student perceptions interpret its impact? If unemployment is a life-stage phenomenon that is less common in older age groups and if many of those listed on unemployment registers are actually employed how do these contingencies affect the perception of students anticipating their future?

Different statements of the seriousness of the problem have different political implications and consequences. Hypothetical unemployment calculations based on the estimated growth of the labor force in relation to the estimated growth in unemployment produce the most horrifying magnitudes. Recent official estimates of hypothetical or so-called backlog unemployment include 32.6 million in 1977, 52.6 million in 1978, and 122 million in 1988 (anticipated).[27] These figures suggest unemployment rates in the range of 20–25 percent of the labor force. Such estimates were used in connection with the fourth five-year plan but now elicit some skepticism among planners.

These very high estimates must be distinguished from the actual rates of employment compiled by the National Sample Survey (NSS), which are relatively modest, in the range of 4 or 5 percent.[28] In 1977–78, the thirty-second round of the NSS found that nationally (all-India) 3.04 percent of those between 15 and 59 years of age were unemployed (weekly status).[29]

Even if one defines unemployment more broadly, using the "daily-status" unemployment rate (which includes daily unemployment among persons who have some employment each week, the unemployment rate does not reach very high levels. Janata and Congress-I's sixth plan calculations agreed that daily-status unemployment, which always has higher rates than weekly-status or usual-status unemployment, affected about twenty-one million persons, or 8 percent of the labor force.[30]

The hypothetical unemployment estimated by the time the fourth plan was being formulated had grown so astronomically as to strain its claim on credulity even more than its claim on the exchequer. The figure produced by empirical methods, on the other hand, seems modest by comparison with unemployment rates in industrial economies. Its small size, which conflicts with the intuitive expectations raised by India's poverty, is no doubt related to the conceptual and empirical problems involved when employment is largely in the unorganized sector, among self-employed farmers and small operators or wage workers enmeshed in patron-client relations. Are agricultural workers unemployed when, due to the season, their landlords don't need them for agricultural work but, also due to the season, they cannot work their own plots either? Are self-employed weavers unemployed when, due to low demand, they work their looms only eight months of the year?

At any rate, hypothetical unemployment and the variations in employment for the urban and rural labor force do not pinpoint the range and changing magnitude of educated unemployment. The thirty-second round NSS figures do suggest that unemployment increases with level of education. They show that the usual-status ("chronic") unemployment rate was 2.28 percent among illiterates, 3.61 percent among those who had finished primary school, 15.5 percent among those who had finished secondary school, and 15.76 percent among college graduates and above. The live register statistics of the employment exchanges also suggest that more than 50 percent of the job-seekers are educated.[31] The educated, by this calculation, experience far more unemployment than do other people, the average usual-status unemployment for all persons being only 4.33 percent.[32] Even if we take these figures with a pinch of salt, noting, for example, that the educated unemployed will register more in employment exchanges than the uneducated, they remain striking.

The absolute number of the unemployed among those who have passed through higher education is between 4 and 7 million, depending on the definition of higher education and the source of data. If we add together the 1.3 million (1979) first-degree holders in the live registers and the very large number of students who have only a partial higher education, the "intermediate" students and those who have taken the same intermediate years as part of their high school education, the figure on the live registers rises to 3 million for 1979.[33] From our point of view, which focuses on college-level students as the social group that has become a political class, this figure is the most important.[34]

The disparities between modes of estimation are at least partly related to the nature of the live registers. The total unemployment reported by them has risen tenfold over twenty-eight years, a change that partly reflects changes in coverage, that is, the increase in the number of employment exchanges from 126 in 1951 to 563 in 1980.[35] In addition, a 1968 survey of registrants by the director general of employment and training in the Ministry of Labour revealed that 42.3 percent of the job seekers on live registers were already employed, and an additional 7 percent were students.[36] On the other hand, many unemployed persons do not register themselves, as many as 50 percent according to some estimates. Changes in the live registers as a social institution and their dependence on "consumer" initiative make them a more variable source of data than the NSS with its dependence on samples and on the routinized initiative of professional staff.

The existence of some three million college-educated unemployed youth not only influences the consciousness, expectations, and plans of college students, but creates a population prepared to join movement politics when conditions are ripe. Unemployment among the educated, however defined, will increase. It increased by as much as 36 percent between 1980 and 1985, from 3.4 million to 4.6 million (including matriculates). One would expect this growth to increase the chances for political mobilization. Yet students, like all other social groups, are difficult to meld into a national class because of their regional and ethnic fragmentation. Furthermore, the condition of "educated unemployment" appears to be an age-related phenomenon that persons "grow out of," quite possibly by taking jobs for which they are at least formally overqualified. It is in the 15-to-29-year age range that the unemployment rate is highest, 17.63 percent (usual status) for urban males, and it declines precipitously thereafter, to 3.03 percent (table 38). Do students regard unemployment as a permanent threat? Or are they aware that it will be, for most of them, a passing condition?

As we have seen, unemployment is a statistical concept or artifact,

TABLE 38
Usual-Status Unemployment Rates by Residence and Age Group, 1977–78

	% Unemployed	
Age Group (yr)	Urban	Rural
5–14	8.46	3.05
15–29	17.63	6.02
30–44	3.03	1.74
45–59	1.71	1.14
60+	1.66	.64
All ages	8.77	3.26

SOURCE: Thirty-second round NSS data, in *Sixth Five Year Plan, 1980–85*, annexure 13.2, p. 214.

subject to the perils of conceptualization and measurement. We have also seen that unemployment can be a state of mind; that is, many urban unemployed do not list themselves on live registers and many of those who do are already employed or students. How many college educated have to be unemployed to make their successors desperate? Four million, as at present? Six million? Similar state-of-mind-problems afflict discussions of rural unemployment. Do agricultural workers believe they are unemployed when they cannot find work 50, 100, or 150 days a year?

Throughout this account we have assumed, in line with the commonsense wisdom of Indian policy intellectuals and politicians, that unemployment among the educated is a significant element in student discontent and influences students to mobilize. Our investigation suggests that overall unemployment rates are not high by comparison with rates in industrialized countries, but that the rate for the age group that overlaps with students—15–29 years—is, at 17.63 percent, well above the national rate of 4.23 percent, producing a minimum figure of four million unemployed holders of intermediate and first degrees. Judging the effect of this figure on the political mobilization of students, however, is by no means easy. We do not know whether most students regard early unemployment as an inevitable life stage, a warning to adjust their expectations to lower levels, or a battle cry to challenge an unjust system. We do not know what increments in the extent of unemployment among the educated under what historical or sociological conditions will create a critical mass for revived mobilization. We know that unemployment among the educated matters, but we have not yet learned to specify just when and how it matters.

The rate of "student indiscipline," which we take as an indicator of the mobilization of this class, was still rising at the beginning of the eighties. However, in the late seventies, the historical phenomena that had fueled the creation of this class and exacerbated its discontent— the expansion of higher education and overexpansion in relation to resources—had been slowed down by acts of policy and spontaneous adjustments. Unemployment among the educated was expected to increase, but its meaning to students and its significance for mobilization remained ambiguous.

In the mobilizations of the sixties and seventies, students for a time appeared as a more visible political class than organized workers, perhaps because rapid educational expansion, combined with the inadequacy of facilities and the considerable migration of rural students to urban institutions, created higher levels of alienation than existed among industrial workers absorbed into organized employment.

Throughout their postindependence career as a demand group, students have rarely challenged the centrist consensus, even when they have challenged particular centrist regimes. They have concentrated mainly on interest, not class, issues, especially those affecting their environment—examinations, hostels, admissions—and their prospects, especially employment. However, by virtue of their relative freedom from the dependency and from the control associated with embeddedness in work relations, students are also able to become an effective political class in partisan and movement politics. They have shown their potential, in 1974–75 in Gujarat, in the JP movement in North India, and more recently in Assam and Punjab.

Although the student wave that crested between 1965 and 1975 in world and Indian politics has for the moment receded, students remain one of the principal components in India's demand politics.

I2 Policies and Politics of the Agricultural Sector

Large proportions of India's population, work force, and national income are accounted for by the agricultural sector, yet its voice in national politics and policy during the years of the Nehru settlement (1950–64) was little heard or attended to. Seventy-two percent of the labor force was employed in agriculture, which produced almost half of the net domestic product. Eighty percent of the population lived in rural areas, and rural voters participated in politics as much as urban voters.[1] But until Nehru's death in May 1964, agricultural interests and values were poorly represented in New Delhi. Low levels of planned investment in agriculture reflected its limited influence.

There were structural reasons for the limited effectiveness of agrarian demand groups during the years of the Nehru settlement. By the nature of their work, agricultural producers are scattered. Unlike urban workers and students who are concentrated in large industrial or commercial enterprises and in universities, they work under dispersed conditions that inhibit their capacity to communicate, organize, and mobilize. At the ideological level, conditions have not been favorable either. Mohandas Gandhi's concern for rural employment and development went into eclipse with his assassination on January 30, 1948. Nehru recognized Gandhi's concerns and constituency when he launched the Community Development Program in 1952 (on Gandhi's birthday, October 2) and *panchayati raj* in 1959, but his mind and heart lay with industry. It and only it could make India powerful and independent.

Starting with Lal Bahadur Shastri's government (1964–66) and accelerating in the 1970s, agricultural producers have become increasingly visible and audible in national policy and politics. Their assertiveness is partly the result of long-term changes that are not specific to the rural sector, such as the spread of education and political organization and consciousness. It is also the result of increased agricultural commercialization and prosperity creating powerful economic interests. Most important, it is the result of the migration of agricultural policy from state capitals (e.g., land reform policy) to New Delhi (e.g., the cost of new inputs and commodity prices).

312

The form of agrarian demand politics has changed too, from notability politics to party and demand group politics. In the fifties and sixties, local notabilities used vertical mobilization of dependents and direct representation in state legislatures and cabinets to influence state governments. Myron Weiner was right about the 1950s and early 1960s when he observed that "thus far, the Indian countryside has not produced effective peasant movements capable of exerting a major influence on government policy."[2] In 1959, Nehru's plan to move toward Chinese-inspired production cooperatives was defeated at the Nagpur annual session of the Congress party, and this defeat was a harbinger of things to come. In the mid- and late sixties, North Indian cultivators rallied to the hero of Nagpur, Charan Singh, who had split from Congress to form an explicitly agrarian party, the BKD, later BLD.[3] With Janata's victory in 1977 and the farmers' movements in the early 1980s, agrarian politics came of age. Agricultural producers joined in making demands, as workers and students had, using direct action techniques such as roadblocks and "long marches."

The issues have changed and with them the arenas for action. In the fifties and sixties, the key issues were land reform, compulsory procurement of food grains, and taxation of agricultural production and income. All fell within the constitutional jurisdiction of the states. As technological upgrading (the green revolution) transformed Indian agriculture from the late 1960s on, policies that fell within the purview of the central government, such as commodity and input prices, became more important. The states continue to command attention as sources of agricultural credit and agricultural services. But countryside versus the city, Bharat versus India, to use Sharad Joshi's phrase, has become an important cleavage in national politics, if not the principal one.

The central government can control demand politics in the organized sector better than in the unorganized. Its reach and penetration become attenuated in the unorganized economy, particularly its massive agricultural sector. New Delhi's contrasting capacity to manage demand politics in the organized and unorganized sectors was highlighted under the emergency (1975–77). The central government was able to control wages and extract compulsory savings from organized workers and to repress student strikes and violence. It was not able to impose wholesale trading in food or an agricultural income tax. The increased organizational resources and mobilization capability of agricultural producers and the increased role of the central government in agricultural policy have strengthened Delhi's hand in the agricultural sector even as it grows more capable of articulating its demands.

Four policy strategies for agriculture have paralleled and sometimes shaped the evolution of demand politics in the agricultural sector and rural society. The first, the agricultural strategy of the Nehru era (1947–64), featured land reform. Nehru's advisers pictured land reform (intermediary abolition) as enhancing equity and productivity, larger proportions of second-plan investment were allocated to industry than agriculture. The second strategy began soon after Nehru's death and extended into 1971. It featured new agricultural technology. It was production oriented and aimed at self-reliance in food. The third strategy began with Mrs. Gandhi's *gharibi hatao* (abolish poverty) appeal in the 1971 parliamentary and 1972 state assembly elections. It emphasized basic needs and income redistribution. The fourth was launched in 1977 by Janata's agrarian-oriented government. It emphasized rural employment and asset creation, continued to stress income redistribution, and sought to relate increased investment in agriculture to a demand-investment cycle based on enhanced and redistributed rural and agricultural incomes. It continued with new names on established programs under the Gandhi-led Congress-I government that took office in February 1980.

All four strategies developed within a common constraint: that for the foreseeable future, the problems of rural poverty have to be solved on the land. Industrialization has not reduced the rural labor force, which has remained static at about 72 percent of the national labor force for the last sixty years.[4]

The First Strategy: Land Reform and "Releasing the Forces of Production"

The agricultural strategy of the Nehru era was shaped by two purposes: to advance justice and equity among agricultural producers and to increase agricultural production without diverting resources from the priority goal, creation of basic and heavy industry. Intermediary abolition sought to alter the balance of agrarian economic and political power by vesting operational control of land in tillers of the soil. Intermediary abolition expropriated with compensation the feudal landlord classes of zamindars and *jagirdars*. Nehru's effort in 1959 to collectivize agriculture failed. So too did a second wave of land reform based on ceilings and designed to reduce the size of holdings not affected by or benefiting from intermediary abolition. If the strategy's dominant orientation was toward equity, its secondary orientation was growth. It was believed that the redistribution of land acquired after the imposition of ceilings could significantly enhance production by "releasing the forces of production." Because basic and heavy industry absorbed the lion's share of planned investment, little was left for agriculture. In the event, the growth in agricultural production in the fifties came not from structural reorganization or from new inputs and technologies (which were, in any case, not yet available) but from bringing additional land under cultivation.

The intermediary abolition in the mid-fifties succeeded because the ideology and policy of the Nehruvian Congress suited an interested and mobilized producer class. It has been estimated that the abolition of intermediary holdings reduced tenancy from 60 to 25 percent and increased the proportion of owner cultivators from 40 to 75 percent.[5] Abolition had a profound effect on Indian politics. A class that might have played historical roles comparable to those played by Britain's landed gentry and aristocracy, Prussia's Junkers, Japan's daimyos and samurai, or Latin America's latifundia masters was removed from the historical stage. As a result of intermediary abolition, about twenty million tenants became owners and about 14 million acres were acquired and distributed. The state also acquired large amounts of privately owned forestland, grazing land, and wasteland.[6] Abolition also had unanticipated consequences, including the expulsion of uncounted numbers of tenants from land that landlords claimed for "self-cultivation."[7]

The abolition of intermediaries transformed agrarian relations by shifting the locus of rural power from feudal landlords to market-oriented independent cultivators, whom we categorized earlier as bullock capitalists. Marginal tenants, dwarf holders, and agricultural laborers did not benefit from intermediary abolition. Change occurred at the top and near the top of the agrarian pyramid. The landlord politics that persisted in Pakistan were eliminated. Political control of the agrarian sector at the state and local levels shifted to independent cultivators and large landowners, who were more diverse socially than economically, ranging from high-caste Rajputs to the lower-caste Hindus lumped together in the administrative and policy term, "backward classes." Large landowners were sufficiently influential in state politics to veto or block New Delhi–inspired agricultural policies, that threatened their interests such as ceilings legislation.

The agrarian strategy of the 1950s included an attempt in 1959 to institute cooperative farming. The attempt failed. It suffered from the inadequate or erroneous information about the Chinese model that

Nehru and his advisors and collaborators used to frame their proposal. The initiative also revealed astonishing economic and political miscalculations. Accepting erroneous economic information was not surprising; until Mao's death in 1976, the data supporting the Dhazhai model were accepted by Western observers less ideologically sympathetic than the two Indian delegations dispatched to China in 1956; reports from China crediting productivity gains to local initiative and self-help based on cooperative management of capital and labor were widely credited in the United States. Influential members of India's Planning Commission also believed the productivity claims made on behalf of Chinese agrarian reorganization. The two delegations brought back seemingly credible accounts of high levels of labor mobilization in cooperative farming areas, intensive utilization of underemployed labor in the construction of physical assets, reclamation of wasteland, and water management.[8] They concluded that the reports of 15 to 30 percent increases in agricultural production over a three-year period were not only valid for the intensive projects—as they may have been—but general to China. These methods, they believed, could be transplanted to India.[9] After Mao's death in 1976, increased availability of long-term aggregate statistics and revelations discrediting the Dhazhai approach destroyed the myth that China's agriculture had been transformed by collectivization and ideology. In fact, long-term food grain growth rates for China lagged behind those for India. Between 1954–57 and 1971–74, China's annual growth averaged 2 percent while India's averaged 2.5 percent. After 1976, and particularly after 1980, when China's agriculture became more like India's with the implementation of the "responsibility system," China's and India's average annual growth rates in food grain production were similar.[10]

Some Indian planners shared Mao's belief that ideological commitment, land redistribution, and agrarian reorganization could accomplish as much as or more than investment in agriculture. In 1956, during the second five-year plan, the Planning Commission's deputy chairman, V. T. Krishnamachari, circulated a note in which he reiterated the view that more efficient use of labor-intensive techniques could assure an increase of 40 percent in agricultural production during the second plan without any increase in investment outlay.[11] The figure was not wholly fanciful in view of the great productivity differences, especially on rice land, between India and East Asia. In fact, the norm for increases in agricultural production for five-year plan periods in both China and India has been about 15 percent.

The political miscalculation was to underestimate the high levels of ideological, institutional, and political control that lay behind the Chinese effort. Nehru's appreciation of and talent for party organization were never strong. Indian planning officials were better at formulating than at implementing policy. The fact that implementation is the focus of resistance to unwanted legislation in India became more evident in the 1970s. Together, Nehru and the planning officials persuaded themselves that purported Chinese gains could be achieved without the costs of creating a massive cadre organization imbued with suitable ideological fervor and dismantling open competitive politics. The party delegations that returned from China emphasized the voluntarism of Chinese reforms. Nehru and the planners seem to have thought that introduction of an additional layer of administration, the new block-level administration of the Community Development Program initiated in 1952, supplemented by "non-official leadership," [12] would be able to inspire, organize, and manage the collective transformation of Indian agriculture.

To achieve productivity via collective farming, the Nagpur session of the Indian National Congress in 1959 approved a resolution in favor of what was called cooperative joint farming. Its revolutionary possibilities seem to have dawned on Congress members only after it had been introduced. It said that

> the future agrarian pattern should be that of cooperative joint farming, in which the land will be pooled for joint cultivation, the farmers continuing to retain their property rights, and getting a *share from the net produce in proportion to their land.* Further, those who actually work the land, whether they own the land or not, will get a *share in proportion to the work put in* by them on the joint farm [our italics].[13]

Depending on which of the italicized passages would count, non-cultivating landowners or cultivating tenants and laborers could be expected to benefit most. Many Congress delegates thought the last passage was the one that would count, and envisioned de facto expropriation. It is hard to imagine why the Congress leadership supposed the resolution would be placidly accepted. And it is hard to understand why Nehru thought it could be enforced without massive coercion and ideological mobilization. He was not prepared to apply coercion even if others were. The resolution did not encounter opposition in its passage through the Congress state and national party committees prior to Nagpur, because few thought Nehru and his Congress allies and supporters meant it.

In the event, the resolution was swiftly followed by a crescendo of criticism, the prospect of a split in the Congress party, and the formation of India's only conservative party, the Swatantra, to defend property rights in land.[14] Led by rural notabilities, it counted on support from the much-expanded class of independent cultivators who, after landlord abolition, also had a stake in landownership. Their leader-to-be in North India, Charan Singh, led the forces in the Congress party that defeated the Nagpur resolution. Mao's prediction, that abolition of landlords without other measures, such as collectivization, will deter later land reform was amply borne out. Landlord abolition simultaneously deprived agrarian reform politics of its most conspicuous target and resulted in the embourgoisement of the beneficiaries.

The retreat of Nehru and the Planning Commission from the cooperative joint farming resolution was accelerated by signs that China might not be the friendly Asian power that Nehru supposed. In March and April 1959, a major rebellion in Tibet was followed by the flight of the Dalai Lama to India. A few months later, evidence surfaced of Chinese encroachments on the Indian border in Ladakh. Both cast an unfavorable, if irrelevant, light on Chinese models.

The defeat of the Nagpur resolution marked the end of efforts at the national level to bring about large-scale structural change in Indian agriculture and triggered early manifestations of agrarian politics. Congress's efforts to lower ceilings on landholding became suspect beause they were now read as threatening property rights in agriculture. Meant to redistribute land to tenants and landless laborers at the expense of large landowners, efforts to lower ceilings survived the Nagpur debacle but encountered stiff resistance at the state level, where landed property interests were entrenched and powerful. The result was flawed, easily evaded legislation and ineffective implementation after protracted delays. Agriculture is a state subject under the constitution, and ceilings legislation and its implementation are state responsibilities. Congress party leaders in New Delhi could bring state Congress committees and Congress governments to water but had difficulty making them drink. Their leadership and electoral support were based on cultivators and large landowners who were reluctant to pass and even more reluctant to implement the second wave of land reform. Neither the ceilings legislation of the early 1960s nor that of the early 1970s has borne much fruit.

The CPI-M—led governments in West Bengal and Kerala have passed and implemented second-wave land reform legislation. In Kerala, "land to the tiller" legislation implemented in the seventies affected 40 percent of all operational holdings by transferring control from "large" landowners to their tenants.[15] West Bengal tenancy and administrative reforms, although yet to be fully documented by nongovernment sources,[16] have made tenants more secure and enabled them to be active participants in the enforcement of legislation and allocation of resources by local government and administrative bodies.

During the Nehru era, India was able to pursue an industrial strategy by relying on P.L. 480 grain shipments from America. These shipments made adequate amounts of food available at relatively low prices to India's urban and industrial population. Some criticized reliance on P.L. 480 food as a form of dependence. Others argued that it was bad for India's agriculture because it depressed farm prices, thereby depriving the Indian farmer of the incentive needed to increase production. Nehru used the food aid to pursue investments in industry that he believed would make India economically independent. The P.L. 480 food aid made it possible for India to avoid the political costs of extracting food from the countryside. India would industrialize like the Soviet Union but would avoid sacrificing lives and freedom to do so. It was a bargain that benefited both participants. Nehru got what he wanted while American farmers, who were producing enormous surpluses during these years, got the prices and income they wanted. The publicly funded purchases of the Commodity Credit Corporation helped maintain a floor under American agricultural prices. Once the "structural" solution of collective farming was defeated, Nehru no longer relied on Indian farmers to feed the country. In any case the technological means—new seeds, chemical fertilizers, increased major and minor irrigation—that could justify large-scale investment in agriculture were not yet available. Gains in agricultural production were achieved in the 1950s but they were the result of increases in the amount of land under cultivation.

The Second Strategy: Agricultural Technology and Self-Reliance

The second agricultural strategy focused on new technologies and inputs, increased investment in agriculture, and food production for self-reliance. It grew out of a series of independently caused but conjuncturally related events: the death, in May 1964 of Prime Minister Jawaharlal Nehru, the primary advocate of the industrial strategy, and his replacement by Lal Bahadur Shastri, more a country than a city man; the 1965 Indo-Pakistan and Vietnam wars that led United States president Lyndon Johnson to put Indian food supplies on a short and arbitrary tether and, as a result, led Indian officials and policy intellectuals to give top priority to food self-sufficiency; World Bank and

United States bargaining with the Government of India that linked increased investment in agricultural programs (along with devaluation, economic liberalization, and an export drive) to the availability of increased foreign aid for planned investment and for meeting balance of payment problems; disappointment with the capacity of the industrial strategy to address the problem of rural poverty by generating large increases in employment; and the timing of scientific and technological breakthroughs, particularly the adaptation to Indian conditions of new high-yielding varieties of seed, such as the dwarf wheat initially bred in Mexico.

By the early 1960s, modest levels of investment in agriculture began to be blamed for low levels of food output. The agricultural product, which had grown by thirty-three index points (or about 3 percent per year) between 1950 and 1960, remained stagnant throughout the first half of the 1960s, except for one good year (1964–65). Population increased between 1961 and 1971 at a rate of 2.2 percent per year. Table 39 suggests the considerable disparity between increases in agricultural and manufacturing income that characterized the 1960s. The effects of low agricultural growth greatly diminished the positive effect on national income of the increases in mining and manufacturing. By 1964, when Shastri succeeded Nehru, agriculture had become a critical political issue for central and state cabinets. It sharply divided proponents of Nehru's industrial strategy in the Planning Commission from proponents of an agricultural strategy, who included some cabinet ministers and many state chief ministers. The Planning Commission sought to retain second- and third-plan investment proportions for industry in the fourth-plan draft and to fend off proportional increases in spending on physical inputs, such as chemical fertilizers or irrigation. It argued that if there was a food shortage, it was due to hoarding, not to production shortages, and could be solved by market intervention, such as government control of wholesale trade in food, not by diverting investment to agriculture.

The minister of agriculture, C. Subramaniam, Prime Minister Shastri, and most state chief ministers thought that agriculture had been slighted in the Nehru era. Stagnation called for greater investment in agriculture and a more generous incentive price policy to increase production.[17] These considerations were strengthened by reports in 1964 that the combined efforts of scientists supported by the Rockefeller Foundation and the Indian Council of Agricultural Research had developed new varieties of maize and that plant geneticists funded by the Rockefeller Foundation had achieved a breakthrough by creating a hybrid of Mexican wheat and Japanese dwarf strains that could achieve twice the output of Indian varieties.[18]

TABLE 39
Growth in National Income, 1960–69

National Income	1960–61	1961–62	1962–63	1963–64	1964–65	1965–66	1966–67	1967–68	1968–69
Total	13,274	103.9	106.0	112.1	120.1	113.3	114.6	124.7	128.4
Agriculture and allied sectors	6,785	101.6	98.9	101.7	110.9	94.5	94.3	111.3	112.6
Mining and large-scale manufacturing	1,213	109.2	120.1	132.0	141.3	146.0	147.7	146.6	155.4

SOURCE: Government of India, Planning Commission, *Fourth Five Year Plan, Draft, 1969–74* (Delhi, 1969), p. 5, constant prices.
Note: The 1960–61 income is given in crores (at 1960–61 prices). Growth in subsequent years is shown by an index on which the 1960–61 levels equal 100.

The food crisis of the early 1960s precipitated a debate on patterns of allocation between Nehru-style planners and post-Nehru leaders. Another debate on the social consequences of the industrial strategy was underway inside the Planning Commission. A 1962 paper of the Planning Commission's Perspective Planning Division noted that undifferentiated GNP growth had not affected the problem of absolute poverty.[19] The effect of plan investments on rural poverty inspired a third agricultural strategy. By 1962 it was already being argued that the industrial emphasis ignored and even exacerbated rural poverty and unemployment.

The war with Pakistan in 1965 and World Bank and United States government pressures strengthened those arguing for increasing agricultural production and achieving food self-sufficiency. "The events following the outbreak of hostilities with Pakistan have been from one point of view a blessing in disguise," noted K. N. Raj. "They have brought home to most people the essential correctness of the attention given to the development of heavy industry in Indian planning . . . [but] it leaves open other possibilities of arm-twisting, such as the thinly disguised pressure now being applied by the United States on India by planning the supplies of foodgrain under P.L. 480 on a month-to-month basis." V. K. R. V. Rao, agriculture member of the Planning Commission and a leading proponent of the capital-intensive strategy, now held that the fourth plan's highest priority should be maximization of food production, with a goal of self-reliance in food.[20] Such advice was fortified by the 17 percent drop in food production that followed two successive monsoon failures in 1965–66 and 1966–67. In the meanwhile, the World Bank commissioned Bernard Bell to undertake a critical examination of India's economic policies. Four of the twelve volumes of Bell's report were prepared by Sir John Crawford and devoted to agriculture. They criticized the secondary emphasis placed on agriculture in India's development plans and stressed the importance of India's producing more to meet its large and increasing food requirements.[21] In case India was not convinced by its own policy processes and by parallel international policy advice, President Lyndon Johnson made it his personal business to manipulate food shipments during the 1966–67 shortage in an effort to "make" India adopt a new agricultural policy and support American foreign policy.[22]

The question of whether India adopted a production-oriented agricultural strategy in 1964–65 because of United States and/or World Bank pressure or whether the World Bank and the United States were "leaning against open doors," probably requires a "both/and" answer. Prime Minister Shastri, C. Subramaniam, L. K. Jha, Asoka Mehta,

V. K. R. V. Rao, and most chief ministers speaking on behalf of agricultural interests in the states had concluded that India needed to be self-reliant with respect to food and that Indian farmers needed better inputs and price incentives. Professional opinion among Indian economists and policy intellectuals coincided with professional opinion at the World Bank, the United States Agency for International Development, and the American Embassy, and with the policy preferences and imperatives of state leaders.[23]

This combination of forces produced the second agricultural strategy that eventuated in the green revolution. Bringing additional land under cultivation accounted for an almost fifty-point growth in the agricultural index from 1950 to 1965 but was no longer feasible. Nevertheless, the agricultural index grew by approximately another fifty points, from 147 to 198, in the next fourteen years (1964–65 to 1978–79) largely as a result of technological innovation and increased investment. Wheat cultivation in a limited area of northwestern India—Punjab, Haryana, and western Uttar Pradesh—accounted for much of the increase. For three years, between 1972 and 1975, there was widespread apprehension that the green revolution had exhausted its impetus. This apprehension proved premature. So too did the fear that the effects of the green revolution would be confined to a handful of districts in a few states. Increases have been less marked outside the major growth areas in northwestern India. In what had been the rice-growing areas of West Bengal, Orissa, and Assam, wheat production expanded rapidly, and in Punjab, the star performer in wheat, rice production and productivity did too. Production growth based on higher-yielding varieties of rice, the main crop in much of the East and South, was slower. Yet rice production also increased steadily. By 1977–78, 35 percent of rice- and 70 percent of wheat-growing areas were under high-yielding varieties (HYV).[24]

The three-year period of apparent stagnation in production growth after the onset of the green revolution coincided with an increasing perception that the revolution's economic benefits were accruing mainly to the better-off farmers. The early optimism of the Nehru era, based on the production consequences of land reform, the attitude and democratic transformations of the Community Development Program, and *panchayati raj,* and the post-Nehru optimism, based on putative productivity gains of the HYV program and the greater availability of other green revolution inputs, was displaced by pessimism and discouragement as production growth flattened out. The belief spread that, in any case, the green revolution made the rich richer and the poor poorer. This happened, it was argued, because the gains of the green revolution benefited mainly the better-off farmers. Households operating 5 acres or more constitute only 24 percent of rural holdings but include 75 percent of the land (see chapter 13, table 40, 1972). Their holdings are large enough to generate the capital or secure the credit to pay for the inputs of the new technology. The 49 percent of rural households that operate less than 5 acres, on the other hand, often cannot generate the capital or obtain the credit to invest in the new technology. This argument exaggerates by dichotomizing the distribution of benefits for operational holdings above and below 5 acres. We suggest below in our discussion of smallholders that households with less than 5 acres did profit from green revolution technology, although they sometimes profited less than those with larger holdings.

Also leading to the perception that the rich were becoming richer and the poor poorer were the findings in the late 1960s and early 1970s that one of the consequences of green revolution technology was to reduce the demand for labor and, as a result, to lower the income of agricultural workers by depressing real wages.[25] As we suggest below, more recent findings suggest that the demand for labor and real wages increased in green revolution areas. Regardless of whether agricultural workers' incomes were rising or falling, some observers in the mid-1970s believed that the disparity in gains from the green revolution would in any case bring on class conflict by substituting horizontal for vertical mobilization. Disparities, they held, would lead to "the breakdown of vertical patterns of peasant mobilization. Over the long run, large numbers of the landless [would] become available for participation in new political commitments and groups based on egalitarian values and class-struggle doctrine."[26]

Anticipations of agrarian revolt spread among scholars and policy intellectuals as increasing research described polarization based on immiseration or relative deprivation. Political revolts of a sort did occur, but their proximate determinants were political, not economic. The JP movement in Gujarat, Bihar, and elsewhere in northern India helped trigger the authoritarian, repressive emergency regime of 1975–77. It in turn brought on Janata's electoral victory (January 1977). In 1975–76, the economy, including the agrarian sector, resumed growth rates comparable to those of the good years before 1965. These rates held through at least the first two and a half years of the Janata government (until July 1979). The positive effects of the green revolution after 1975 were less dramatic than some of its earliest advocates hoped, but there was more economic benefit and less political polarization than reported or anticipated by the analyses of the late 1960s and early 1970s. Depending on region, crop, and local agrarian structure, the consequences of improved agricultural productivity proved to be differentiated and variable, advantageous to many smallholders and agricultural workers, irrelevant to others, and disadvantageous to still others. The policy result of the debate about the uneven gains and losses from green revolution technology was the emergence of a propoor third agricultural strategy that addressed income distribution and basic needs.

The Third Strategy: Basic Needs and Income Redistribution

The determinants of the propoor third agricultural strategy were political and economic. They include Mrs. Gandhi's political problems from 1966, when she was installed as prime minister by the Congress party's old guard (the "syndicate"), until November 1969, when she split the Congress party to free herself from its control. Again in 1971 and 1972, she needed to confirm in the national and state elections that she had indeed triumphed over the syndicate, now her rival in the shape of the Congress-O. Another determinant of the propoor strategy, beginning in the mid-sixties, was a growing awareness among Indian and World Bank policy intellectuals of poverty as a social fact and a development problematic.[27] The growth in GNP had not enabled the poor to benefit from development. How to make the poor better off and more productive became the new problematic.

In November 1969 and subsequently, Mrs. Gandhi fought the factional battle within Congress and then between the Congress-I and the Congress-O and other opposition parties by occupying a leftist ideological and policy position. She said that she spoke for the poor and the people and that her opponents spoke for privilege and property. Her principal policy challenge in 1969 to the syndicate and to her rival for party leadership, Morarji Desai, was one of several "stray thoughts" addressed to the Congress Working Committee, a presidential ordinance nationalizing the fourteen largest commercial banks. The move helped to precipitate Desai's resignation as deputy prime minister when Mrs. Gandhi relieved him of the finance portfolio and drove him and the syndicate of state party leaders together, in common opposition within the party to Mrs. Gandhi's leadership. When in July Mrs. Gandhi's candidate for president, V. V. Giri, defeated the syndicate's candidate, Sanjiva Reddy, the stage was set for the denouement in November, when Mrs. Gandhi decisively turned back, by a vote of 226 to 65, a syndicate-Desai challenge to her leadership of the Congress parliamentary party.

Mrs. Gandhi held that the banks, as bastions of some of India's largest business houses (conglomerates), were not sufficiently responsive to the investment priorities of government's development policies. Especially neglected were the credit needs of poor cultivators. Bank nationalization was justified in part as a means to provide credit to those not considered worthy by private banking standards. Such credit would help to extend the benefits of the green revolution to all.

After fourteen months of minority government, during which she was dependent on CPI and DMK support, Mrs. Gandhi gambled on winning an absolute majority by calling an early parliamentary election for March 1971 and delinking it from the state assembly elections that hitherto had been held at the same time as parliamentary elections. She made her slogan "*gharibi hatao*" (abolish poverty), and the four-party alliance, led by the syndicate's Congress-O, answered with "Indira *hatao*" (abolish Indira). With the organizational wing of the Congress largely in the hands of her Congress-O opponents[28] and with both sides agreed that her leadership and slogan were the principal issue, the election became a plebiscite: Mrs. Gandhi, yes or no. The answer was yes in terms of seats won (352 of 518) and maybe in terms of votes (44 percent). The third agricultural strategy had come of age.

Mrs. Gandhi's propoor strategy had world as well as domestic determinants. B. S. Minhas, a member of the Planning Commission from 1971 through 1973, captured Indian perceptions of the time:

> Although the poor do not have strong political organization of their own, nevertheless, the elitist regimes, so long as they find it necessary to face their electorates to seek their mandate to rule, cannot ignore the poor who are in the majority. . . . The Third World governments' concern with the poor and the eradication of absolute poverty as an objective of development would, therefore, seem to be in the nature of a sociopolitical compulsion.[29]

Indian social scientists had come to recognize that the basic industries strategy of the second and third five-year plans (1956–66) had strengthened the country but hardly touched the poor. Most of the poor lived in rural areas and sought employment in the unorganized sector. Industrialization had not drawn them into the cities by providing employment there. A propoor and a rural strategy were almost by definition allied. Beginning with B. S. Minhas's estimates, first published in 1969, a spate of studies over the next four years estimated the number of people living below a hypothetical poverty line. Dantwala,

Dandekar and Rath, Bardhan, Vyas and others provided measures that placed from 40 to 60 percent of the population beneath various hypothetical poverty lines.[30]

The studies generated heated debates as to whether poverty was advancing or declining. All could agree that the absolutely poor remained sufficiently numerous to justify policies specifically targeting their particular needs. Both versions of the fifth five-year plan (1974–79), a Gandhi government version drafted in 1973 and a revised Janata version of 1978, focused attention on the poor. After her second electoral success in the March 1972 state assembly elections, Mrs. Gandhi's handpicked state chief ministers met as members of the National Development Council to consider the new science of poverty deciles. Planning Minister D. P. Dhar's inspirational view of planning led them to endorse a fifth-plan target of a 60 percent increase in real terms in the per capita consumption of the poorest three deciles. This promise, needless to say, was not fulfilled[31] but it epitomized the third strategy's propoor populist rhetoric.

The international community of development specialists in such organizations as the International Labor Organization, the World Bank, and the Dag Hammerskjöld Foundation joined the chorus of skepticism about undifferentiated GNP growth in its capitalist or socialist incarnations.[32] Hollis Chenery, et al., in a joint study by the World Bank and the University of Sussex's Institute of Development Studies noted, "It is now clear that more than a decade of rapid growth in underdeveloped countries has been of little or no benefit to perhaps a third of their population."[33]

The World Bank's growing cadre of Third World economists contributed to the two-way infiltration of international and Third World economic thinking. Mahbub al Huq spoke for the Economic Department of the World Bank when he damned the single-minded pursuit of GNP growth because it contributed to local poverty.[34] Bilateral providers of development assistance, from Sweden and Holland to the Agency for International Development and Britain (e.g., the 1975 white paper, "The Changing Emphasis in British Aid Policies: More Help for the Poorest") began to finance programs that could be shown to benefit the poor. Employment-generating projects and programs specifically targeted to minimum or basic needs—rural health and water supply, house sites for the landless, nutritional programs, primary education—received increased attention. Quality-of-life indexes challenged per capita income growth measures of development by showing that properly designed and implemented programs within low-income countries could significantly reduce infant mortality and increase life expectancy and literacy by reducing the incidence of malnutrition, disease, and death.[35]

India's third agricultural strategy generated two policy streams. The first took the form of increased ad hoc transfer payments by the central to the state governments for famine and drought relief. The transfer payments began with the extreme food shortages of 1965 to 1967 but continued at increasing levels through 1973–74. Anticipating the fourth strategy introduced by the Janata government in 1977, the second stream took the form of programs specifically targeted to employment and asset creation for poor constituencies. They included the Small Farmer Development Agency (SFDA), the Marginal Farmers and Agricultural Laborers Scheme (MFAL), the Drought Prone Areas Program (DPA), Rajasthan's Antyodhya Program (credit for productive assets to the five poorest families in particular villages), the Crash Rural Employment Scheme, Maharashtra's Employment Guarantee Scheme, and the Food for Work Program.[36] Their objectives ran a gamut from short term (e.g., the politically tinged emergency relief measures) to long term (e.g., the creation of productive assets and skills). The famine relief programs generated by the food emergencies of 1965–67 and 1972–74 became entrenched in the national budget until the mid-1970s. Following severe criticism by the Sixth Finance Commission, the emergency regime (1975–77) cut them back sharply.[37]

The Small Farmer Development Agency and the Marginal Farmers and Agricultural Laborers Scheme, consolidated in the fifth plan period (1974–79), were specific responses to the critique that agricultural development policies and programs discriminated systematically against small producers who lacked the capital or access to credit to invest in the new inputs. Small farmers were defined as those holding less than 5 acres of dry land and marginal farmers as those holding less than 7.5 acres. Macroaggregative indications of program impact were visible but modest. The six and a half million households—about one-eighth of those eligible—reached in the period of 1969–77 received on the average about Rs. 200 of credit per beneficiary. Microstudies suggest that the programs had a significant impact on those whom they reached: the Program Evaluation Organization study of thirty-four projects showed an additional annual income of Rs. 1,017 per beneficiary family. Other microstudies indicated even higher gains—especially in animal husbandry and dairying.[38] A positive indicator was the finding that of the credit granted, 86 percent was allocated for asset creation and only 14 percent for short-term crop credit. The rationale for such programs was that credit for productive assets or inputs increased not only employment and income but also demand and production. The goal was to lift increasing numbers above the poverty line and to enhance rather than waste the productive capacities of the poor.

Poverty in India has a marked areal dimension. The Drought Prone Areas Program and other areal programs addressed regional and local poverty. A state such as Maharashtra, home of India's largest industrial complex (Bombay) and of one of its most productive cash crop economies, also includes some of India's poorest and most barren land. Only 9 percent of Maharashtra's land is under irrigation. The Drought Prone Areas Program concentrated resources on backward areas in need of irrigation, in seventy-four districts of thirteen states.[39] In conjunction with the Integrated Rural Development Program agricultural service and credit programs could be coordinated in ways that enhanced their impact because directors of such programs were given the authority of state chief secretaries, that is, direct charge of all line agencies in their command areas.

The Fourth Strategy: Rural Employment and Increased Investment in Agriculture

The fourth agricultural strategy, inaugurated by the Janata government in 1977, continued the third's propoor orientation but dropped its populist rhetoric and tendency to throw money at problems and potential voters in the guise of relief and welfare. Instead, the third strategy's secondary concern of creating jobs and new income streams by providing productive assets and work for the poor became the fourth strategy's principal concern. It also broke with earlier strategies by elevating investment in the agricultural sector above investment in industry. Agriculture was to be a source of growth and development in its own right, not a handmaiden to industry. The two sectors, agriculture and industry, were to complement and supplement each other.

The fourth strategy was the child of the first "opposition" party to control the union government. It is not surprising that the Janata government highlighted discontinuities more than continuities by stressing the innovative nature of its strategy and programs. It made explicit the implied critique of Nehru's industrial strategy represented by the Congress-I government's rural employment and asset creation programs. The center of Janata's development strategy was said to be investment in the agricultural sector and the employment, income, and demand such investment would generate.

Janata's critique of Nehruvian industrial strategy found a conspicuous place in the party's policy statements. Prime Minister Morarji Desai put it: "We are not only producing steel, aluminum or all the materials of the railway or sugar machinery, or electrical machinery, we can even produce a steel mill now. But with all this advance in heavy industries, dissatisfaction today is much greater than when we became free."[40] Desai's solution for this apparent paradox lay in attention to agriculture and small-scale industry, which, he declared, had been neglected, and in the decentralization of political and economic power. "The big city, the big machine, and big science have their place," he said, "but they can not claim a prescriptive right to preference and dominance."[41]

Janata turned to Mohandas Gandhi for policy guidance. Gandhi had stressed employment, the principal objective of his Khadi program; decentralization of political power and economic activity; viable human-scale communities; and meaningful work, including technologies that liberated and enhanced rather than enslaved and diminished those who used them. Janata's policy intellectuals tried to identify appropriate and efficient technologies to justify protection of enlarged markets for small-scale industry products. The econometrically oriented neo-Gandhians in the Planning Commission upgraded and modernized Gandhi's appreciation of the employment and income that labor-intensive "cottage" industry could provide. Some of the impetus for neo-Gandhian doctrine and policies grew out of the remigration to India from advanced industrial countries of a self-critical concern for appropriate technologies that featured labor-intensive rather than capital-intensive development strategies.[42]

The fourth strategy counted on enhanced agricultural investment to generate additional employment from the labor required for increased double and triple cropping and for constructing rural public goods— for example, irrigation systems and roads, which were given high priority because of their contributions to productivity and marketing. The improved income streams from agricultural production, public goods creation, and small-scale industry were in turn expected to generate increased demands for locally produced goods and services, to accelerate the already buoyant growth in household savings and investment and, in circular fashion, to increase employment, income, savings, investment, and production of goods and services. The strategy was also expected to have intersectoral consequences. Greater demand in the agricultural sector would stimulate the private industrial sector by increasing the demand for simple and necessary consumer goods, from crockery and utensils to radio sets and bicycles, and the private industrial sector would increase its demand for the producer goods of public-sector firms. The increased demand of the agricultural sector would justify investment in private- and public-sector industries producing needed agricultural inputs.[43]

The Janata party's economic policy and industrial policy statements, both issued in 1977, represented a rhetorical reversal of Congress's industrial strategy. They congratulated the country for the infrastructural gains and manufacturing capacity built in the previous twenty-five years. They then proposed a 4 percent increase in plan investment in the agricultural sector, from 22 to 26 percent, a 4 percent decrease in investment in mining and manufacturing, and a doubling of the previous five-year plan's allocations to power and irrigation.[44]

The Janata statements and acts reflected an effort to meld into one program a number of political and policy imperatives. Its emphasis on investment in agriculture was pleasing to the bullock capitalist element that Charan Singh had led into the party. The emphasis on rural employment redefined the beneficiaries of agricultural investment. Investment in agriculture had been perceived as mainly benefiting large landowners and bullock capitalists. Now it was to create employment and new income streams for poor people. Agricultural investment was pictured as harmonizing rather than polarizing the interests of agrarian classes and interests.

Under Janata, India began to experiment with programs that directly addressed rural unemployment or underemployment. Maharashtra's Employment Guarantee Scheme guarantees up to thirty days of continuous employment to rural unemployed. In the most recent reported year, it provided 163 million workdays at approximately the minimum wage.[45] This program distinguishes itself from earlier relief programs by featuring the creation of durable assets, roads, minor irrigation works, *panchayat* (local government) houses, land conditioning, etc. The Food for Work Program, launched at the national level by Janata in April 1977, also attempted to combine propoor and asset creation features. It aimed to use the country's surplus food stocks for insulating the economically handicapped section of the rural community from hunger. At the same time, it aimed to strengthen the rural infrastructure, in order to speed up the conversion of natural endowments into durable assets meaningful to the people.[46]

The Food for Work Program was in part a response to a crisis of success. In 1976–77, with twenty million tons of food in storage, critics observed that the unequal distribution of income made food self-sufficiency meaningless to the poorest, who could not afford to buy their requirements. After Congress-I returned to office in 1980, the

Food for Work Program was absorbed into the National Rural Employment Program. It is something less than a national guaranteed employment program, but does move in that direction. Because its success and expansion depend on ample food supplies, which were not satisfactory during the first two years of the post-1980 Congress-I government, the National Rural Employment Program initially accomplished less than Janata's Food for Work Program.

When Mrs. Gandhi and Charan Singh campaigned against each other in 1980, one might have supposed that they were deeply divided over the scale of investment in agriculture and industry. Each made the other out to be the enemy of his or her brand-name policy. As we have seen with respect to Janata's Food for Work Program and Congress-I's National Rural Employment Program, the Congress-I government, after returning to power changed some of the labels on Janata's agricultural programs even while moving very much in the same direction. The second, third, and fourth agricultural strategies have all become part of a 1980s policy consensus. They are a response to the perception that the problem of the Indian poor cannot be solved by industrialization and urbanization. Nor will it be solved by a dramatic breakthrough on the population front; the coercive methods used during the emergency are not likely to be repeated. And it is not likely to be solved by "structural change"—collectivization of agriculture, for example, or massive land redistribution. It has to be confronted mainly on the land and in the context of extant political, economic, and demographic circumstances.

Investment in the agricultural sector and in programs targeted to the rural poor can do more than prevent further immiseration, provide relief from destitution, or prevent civil disorder by regulating the poor. An agriculture-cum-industry strategy can provide the growth with employment and equity that the industrial strategy of the second and third plans did not provide. Whether it will depends in part on how the emerging cleavage between city and countryside translates politics into policy.

13 Agrarian Producers as a Demand Group

We began this book by arguing the case for the centrist future of Indian politics. One argument was based on the fact that the organized sector of the Indian economy is considerably smaller, by various measures, than the unorganized sector, whose principal component is agriculture. The fact that India, unlike Western democracies and most Third World countries, adopted universal suffrage and competitive party politics at the beginning of its industrialization considerably enhanced the potential significance of agricultural producers for electoral politics and policy choice. In chapter 12, we showed how, since independence, the agricultural economy has become productive and, for many of its producers, profitable. In this chapter, we examine its political role. Do the politics of the agricultural economy strengthen centrist or class politics? Our answer features the politics of independent cultivators, whom we designate "bullock capitalists," and the politics of the rural poor. The emergent new agrarianism of the 1970s attempted to speak not only for bullock capitalists but for the agricultural sector as a whole. Even though the objective conditions of the rural poor appear to favor class more than sectoral mobilization, the potential for the former has not been realized. Insofar as sectoral rather than class politics characterizes the political orientation of the agricultural economy, centrist rather than class politics is likely to remain ascendent in the unorganized as well as the organized economy.

The literature on "peasant" studies depicts agrarian producers, particularly "middle peasants" (small owners) as either passive or revolutionary. These contradictory polarities ignore the vast middle ground between acquiescence and revolt that peasant mobilizations have occupied under varying historical and objective circumstances. Incremental change redistributing resources and power has been the characteristic form of social change in India and is more typical than passive support of the status quo or revolt eventuating in revolutionary transformation.

Our analysis of bullock capitalists after zamindari abolition and the green revolution parallels in one respect the literature on peasant or "subaltern" revolt in the nineteenth or early twentieth centuries. Their

333

relative independence and capacity to take risks equipped middle peasants with the motive and means to revolt against feudal and imperial domination, just as these same qualities equip bullock capitalists to mobilize in support of remunerative prices. But insofar as it neglects changing historical circumstances, the parallel between middle peasants and bullock capitalists is only partial.

The nineteenth and early twentieth centuries were a time when commercial agriculture was in its infancy and "feudal" domination and imperial rule more important than property and market relations for defining agrarian classes and their interaction. Times change. Scholars of agrarian revolt after independence were more concerned with the capitalist features of commercial agriculture than they were with feudal domination, a concern that led them to identify wage laborers as the class that could bring about revolutionary transformation in the countryside and even the state. By contrast, yesterday's middle peasants, having rid themselves of imperial rule and benefited from zamindari abolition and the green revolution, have become today's bullock capitalists. They remain the most mobilizable agrarian class, but their objectives have changed from ridding themselves of imperial rulers and their feudal allies to achieving remunerative prices and sectoral prosperity. If India has not experienced a revolutionary transformation, it has experienced regime and structural change within broad parameters that blur the distinction between incremental and systemic change.

Unlike public employees, industrial workers, and students, agricultural producers, as we showed in chapter 12, were latecomers to demand politics at the national level. In approaching the question of whether the politics of the agricultural economy support class or centrist politics at the national levels, we begin by differentiating agrarian classes by size of operational holding. Our purpose is to distinguish agricultural producers in terms of their objective economic interests. We turn next to the polarization thesis and its alternatives, to assess objectively the current and future prospects of class politics in the agricultural economy. The polarization thesis holds that agrarian producers are experiencing class formation. Commercial agriculture enhanced by green revolution technology is in the process of creating two antagonistic classes: capitalist farmers and wage laborers. We raise questions about the empirical and ideological evidence for this view. When agrarian politics became national in the 1970s and early 1980s, it was not the agrarian radicalism of the rural poor but the demand of independent cultivators and capitalist farmers for remunerative prices that rallied agricultural producers generally in support of the new agrarianism.

We next address the emergence and prospects of the new agrarianism. It introduced a new cleavage in Indian politics, the countryside versus the city, and featured the interests of its principal component, independent (self-employed) cultivators. Can the politics of agrarian producers be both prosectoral and propoor? To answer this question, we first identify the determinants of rural poverty and estimate its incidence. In the aggregate, the condition of the rural poor has neither improved nor deteriorated, but at the regional and micro levels their number and condition vary enormously and have been subject to considerable change. Our findings provide the background for assessing why and how the rural poor do or do not mobilize. We find that mobilization by the poor is less an expected phenomenon than one whose occasional occurrence requires explanation. This enables us to return again to the questions of whether the politics of agrarian producers can be both prosectoral and propoor and whether Indian politics will remain centrist or become class oriented. Despite the occasional successes of agrarian radicalism and pervasive undeclared civil wars at the local level, we conclude that the politics of the agricultural economy will remain more sectoral than class oriented and that its sectoral orientation will sustain the centrism of national politics.

Differentiating Agrarian Classes

Agricultural producers in the organized economy, like workers in the organized economy, exhibit considerable variation in social circumstances, incomes, and political influence. They control and use a total area of about 365 million acres (1976–77)[1] with about 122 million agricultural producers (1971 total)[2] divided into about 80 million households.[3] We begin our analysis of agrarian demand groups with a taxonomy of agricultural producers that differentiates them by operational holding size and then considers their interests and political influence.

We distinguish four agrarian classes—agricultural laborers, smallholders, bullock capitalists, and large landowners—and focus on their characteristics and interests. The categories are both empirical (i.e, based on the size distribution of operational holdings [see table 40] and ideal-typical (i.e., based on global qualitative or nonquantified characteristics). We follow Weber's heuristic injunction to select the dominant (stereotypical) qualities that, for the purposes of the investigator, yield knowledge about actors' orientation for social action.[4] We recognize that those within particular categories do not wholly

TABLE 40
Changes in Holdings of Agricultural Households, 1954–72

Size of Operational Household Holding (Acres)	1954–55		1971–72	
	Households (%) (N=61 Million)	Area Controlled (%) (N=335.7 Million Acres)	Households (%) (N=80 Million)	Area Controlled (%) (N=365.7 Million Acres)
1. Landless[a]				
0	28	—	27	—
2. Smallholders				
0.01–0.99	14	1	15	2
1.00–2.49	14	4	18	8
Total	28	5	33	10
3. Bullock capitalists				
2.50–4.99	15	10	16	15
5.00–7.49	9	10	9	13
7.50–9.99	5	9	4	9
10.00–14.99	6	13	5	14
Total	35	42	34	51
4. Large landowners				
15.00 and above	9	53	6	39

SOURCE: S. K. Sanyal, in Pravin Visaria and S. K. Sanyal, "Trends in Rural Unemployment in India: Two Comments," *Economic and Political Weekly*, January 29, 1977, pt. 2, table 3, pp. 245–48.

Note: All percentages are rounded.

[a]These figures should not be read as giving the households of "agricultural workers," who have increased in number and can be found in both categories 1 and 2.

or uniformly share the ideal-typical or nonquantified characteristics attributed to each. We rely on tendencies and prevalences, not isomorphic uniformities. For example, relations of production in the four quantitative categories are affected by variable mixes of labor- and capital-intensive production techniques and of family and hired labor. The degree to which each is present is uncertain or unknown at macrostatistical levels. Yet we know from microstudies, proxymeasures, and inferences from other aggregate data that cultivators in the bullock capitalist category, for example, are more likely than large landowners to rely on family rather than on hired labor and are more likely than smallholders to possess the quality of human capital needed to complement the improved physical capital and inputs of green revolution agricultural technology.

The figures in table 40 suggest the magnitudes of each class. Note that the categories are based on operational holdings, which are holdings *controlled* by a household as cultivators, regardless of ownership. Thus, "smallholders" may include both tenants and owners. The categories in the table and our four agrarian classes do not overlap perfectly; for example, agricultural laborers may be found in category 1 (landless), category 2 (smallholders), and even category 3 (bullock capitalist), because many smallholders and some bullock capitalists supplement their incomes by agricultural labor. We draw the boundaries for the bullock capitalist class, which we determined in chapter 1, at 2.5 and 14.9 acres, because within this range independent, self-employed agricultural producers can be productive and prosperous. Holdings within this range are large enough for agricultural producers to take advantage of new technology and credit institutions, to use their own human, physical, and financial capital, and to benefit from the quality and "surplus" of their own labor. Again, the category is not homogenous. Caste conventions often inhibit 10-acre Rajputs, Bhumiars, and Brahmans in the East Gangetic plains from cultivating, while 20-acre Jats in western Uttar Pradesh often put their hands to the plow. We have designated producers at 15 acres and above as "large landowners," because at that scale they are, figuratively, more often "tractor" than "bullock" capitalists. Large landowners are more prone than bullock capitalists to use capital- rather than labor-intensive production techniques, to rely on less-committed and less-skilled wage and/or attached labor or on insecure tenants, and, as a consequence, to be more involved in capitalist and/or feudal (master-servant, patron-client) relations of production.

Our agricultural labor category designates households with little or no land (owned or leased-in) who rely for their income on wages and/

or payment in kind. This category too is not without complexities that can affect the formation of subjective interests and political orientation. Agricultural labor can take a variety of forms: attached or casual, organized contract or unorganized, protected or unprotected by enforceable minimum wage legislation. Agricultural laborers can have variable access to nonagricultural labor markets and productive or service activities, and thus to alternative sources of additional income.

Compared with bullock capitalists and large landowners, smallholders (0.01–2.49 acres) are less likely to benefit from new technology and its enhancement of the value of labor.[5] Many operate holdings below the level required to support a pair of bullocks, cannot easily afford to rent them or a tractor, and often find it difficult to finance easily divisible inputs (seeds, fertilizer), much less lumpy ones (e.g., tube wells). It is common for them to rely on wage labor as a source of income, either as a supplement to earnings from cultivation or, particularly for those who lease out their land, as a primary source of income. At the same time, macro and micro evidence (see below) strongly suggests that a substantial proportion of smallholders produce as much or more per unit of land and use proportionally more improved inputs than bullock capitalists or large landowners. Because of the ambiguities of their objective circumstances, the subjective interests of smallholders are more prone to variation and instability than the subjective interests of the other three agricultural classes.

The proportion of smallholder households (category 2) and of agricultural laborers (categories 1 and 2) increased between 1954–55 and 1970–71, while proportions of households in categories 3 and 4 decreased. Table 40 does not reflect the change in the proportion of agricultural laborers, because landless households (category 1), whose number *decreased* slightly, are not congruent with agricultural laborers, whose number increased. (This problem will be dealt with at greater length below.) Agricultural laborers and smallholders, the two poorest and most disadvantaged classes of the agricultural sector, together constitute a majority of rural households and share certain characteristics. The political significance of this numerical majority will depend on the plausibility of the objective grounds used to distinguish them and on whether these grounds coincide with subjective determinants that orient behavior. For example, can smallholders whose incomes derive from both agricultural labor and cultivation be distinguished in objective or subjective terms from landless agricultural laborers? Are the classes depicted in table 40 becoming more homogeneous or more heterogeneous? In either case, are the subjective interests that orient their respective political action becoming more conflictual or more cooperative?[6]

Some studies have shown that large landholders benefit from developments in agricultural technology more than smallholders do.[7] These studies, however, do not speak fully to the matter of the economic interests of smallholders. Smallholders do participate significantly in the new technology. Raj Krishna showed at the macroaggregative level that "though the share of the small farm sector in cultivated area is only 21 percent, its share in all important inputs, namely, irrigated area, fertilizer consumption, institutional credit, and total inputs per unit of land is more than that of large farmers, though per household it is less."[8] Harrison showed that small operators (with less than 3.8 acres) used new technology and inputs as much (per unit operated) as medium and large operators.[9] Mutiah found that holders with less than 5 acres accounted for 39 percent of the cultivated area but 42 percent of the high-yielding variety seed area.[10] In many growth regions, smallholders are apt to develop interests in common with larger landowners; that is production costs and commodity prices will form part of their calculations.

The increases shown in table 40 in the proportion of smallholder households and in the proportion of land under their control are less disputed than the increase in the proportion of agricultural laborers. The 1961 and 1971 censuses showed a 10 percent increase in the proportion of agricultural laborers, from 15 percent in 1961 to 25 percent in 1971.[11] Scholars who accept these figures tend to support K. N. Raj's (1976) polarization thesis: India's agrarian economy is being reduced to two antagonistic classes, a decreasing number of rich capitalist farmers and an increasing number of landless wage workers (see the following section). Other scholars, working with NSS rather than census data, question both 1961 and 1971 census figures on the ground that changed census definitions accounted for most of the shift in proportions. Those responsible for the 1971 census operations attempted to distinguish cultivators from workers by counting as workers those whose principal source of income was wages and counting as cultivators those whose principal sources of income was cultivation. Enumerators' instructions were revised accordingly. Apparently, many cultivator-workers who in 1961 described themselves as cultivators, and were so counted, were counted as workers under the 1971 procedure. Critics therefore argue that the 1961 and 1971 figures for agricultural workers are not comparable.

Visaria, working with NSS data, came to different conclusions. He reported that the proportion of agricultural laborers in 1961 was between 19 and 20 percent rather than the 15 percent given in the 1961 census, that the proportion in 1971 was 22 rather than 25 percent, making the increase over the decade approximately 3 percent rather than 10 percent. The 1981 census, which retained the 1971 census definitions, supports the skeptics by showing a small decline (1.72 percent) from 1971 in the proportion of agricultural workers.[12]

The dispute over the increase in the proportion of agricultural workers arises out of the ambiguous and changing nature of those we have included in the bottom two classes. Our categories, like most used in the social sciences, are not isomorphic. Those included in a particular category (e.g., "smallholder") may overlap with or in some ways resemble those included in other categories.[13] As a result, investigators will inevitably disagree over the properties and sizes of particular categories.

We use the term "bullock capitalists" heuristically, to suggest a congery of qualities that other linguistic usages do not evoke.[14] Bullock capitalists are self-employed and self-funded producers. Their holdings are large enough to support a pair of bullocks and use of the new inputs associated with the green revolution. Their costs of production tend to be more efficient than those of large landowners.[15] At the same time, their assets are not large enough to enable them to engage in capital-intensive agricultural production based on extensive use of machinery or to require them to rely wholly or mainly on wage or tenant labor. Their costs and gains are powerfully but not wholly determined by market forces. We use the term "bullock" more figuratively than literally. Bullock capitalists may use tractors or other lumpy forms of physical capital on their modest-sized holdings typically by renting such items in or out.

The important point is that they are cultivators of moderate means who own or control the physical capital involved in farm production, and they and members of their household provide the complementary and differentiated human capital to operate and manage it. The late Daniel Thorner used actors' language to distinguish three agrarian classes: *maliks* (bosses), *kisans* (cultivators), and *mazdurs* (workers). Insofar as bullock capitalists are managers and entrepreneurs as well as cultivators and workers, they combine the interests of all three.

At the time of zamindari abolition, the objective and perceived interests of an emergent bullock capitalist class clashed with those of feudal landlords. Bullock capitalists as well as large landowners fell heir to the land surrendered by zamindars. In the absence of serious administrative, legislative, party, or movement efforts to enforce or further lower ceilings on landholdings, bullock capitalists' interests with respect to landholding are not likely to place them in antagonistic relationships with other agrarian classes. Under such circumstances, they are in a position to make appeals and alliances up or down in defense of agrarian-sector interests.

Bullock capitalists are not kulaks. The term "kulak" carries with it the specific historical baggage of nineteenth- and twentieth-century Russian usage. Before the revolution, it referred to an agrarian class of prosperous, noncultivating landowners and middlemen. This usage is not appropriate for India's independent farmers. The term acquired a more contemporary meaning from Stalin's use of it to refer to an enemy class that required elimination.[16] It can be used today for certain normative or polemical purposes, as Walter Neale showed when he observed that "*kulak* is the product of a conjugation: 'you *talk* to farmers, you *shout* at peasants, you *shoot kulaks,* and in each case the appelation justifies the action."[17] The Indian backlash against rural demands often finds it convenient to use "kulak" in this pejorative manner. For social scientific purposes, there are problems about employing the term to designate heterogeneous groups, especially to elide the distinction between self-employed owner-cultivators and noncultivating owners and middlemen, for example, between a self-employed wheat farmer and a sugar magnate.

Our definition of bullock capitalists as an agrarian class distinguishes them from kulaklike Indian farmers (large landowners) on the one hand and marginal farmers or landless agricultural workers on the other. Because they are neither capitalists nor workers, neither exploiters nor exploited, they pose a conceptual problem for liberals as well as Marxists concerned to identify suitable interests or classes with which to conflict or ally. If bullock capitalists are workers with property interests—self-exploiters—what is the justification for making them a class enemy or class ally? Their "categorical invisibility" in agrarian class theory is due precisely to their anomalous standing.[18]

As of 1971–72, bullock capitalists were probably more numerous and controlled more land than any one of the other three agrarian classes. Between 1954–55 and 1971–72, large landowners as a statistical category lost ground to bullock capitalists in terms of households and area controlled, a change that was punctuated by the 1977 election when Congress's rout by the Janata party made bullock capitalists rather than large landowners the senior partners in many state governments and for the first time placed them in an advantageous position at the center. Table 40 shows bullock capitalists as representing 34 percent of agricultural households in 1971–72 and operating about half the cultivated land. These proportions suggest a higher level of concreteness than is warranted. We use them because the heuristic category of bullock capitalists has its nearest empirical referent in the size class from 2.5 to 15 acres. Anomalies arise because similar size does not invariably capture similar properties. We have already mentioned that East Gangetic high-caste landholders are not likely to self-cultivate.

Some of the 2.5-to-15-acre holdings are spurious, parts of larger land-holdings disguised by legal fictions as smaller in order to evade, at least for a time, land ceilings legislation. On the other hand, some small-holders [19] and some large landowners no doubt qualify as bullock capitalists in their uses of physical capital and family labor. Ronald Herring, Utsa Patnaik, and Biplab Dasgupta have, in different contexts, seriously challenged the congruence of size categories with qualitative production relations. In the absence of relevant macrodata about qualitative aspects of size holdings, we have used the 34 percent of households between 2.5 and 15 acres to approximate the magnitude of the bullock capitalist agrarian class.[20]

Bullock capitalists are advantageously placed by their objective circumstances to become the hegemonic agrarian class. Smallholders (table 40) may collaborate politically with bullock capitalists if they can be led to believe in the Indian equivalent of America's Horatio Alger myth about mobility in industrial society. The myth held that, with pluck and luck, poor boys can become if not millionaires like Andrew Carnegie at least successful members of America's vast middle class, a myth that mixed enough fact with its fiction to inhibit the growth of class consciousness among America's poor and antagonistic class relations. The bullock capitalist myth holds that smallholders and even some of the landless can cross the subsistence or poverty lines to become independent farmers. Insofar as many smallholders and some landless accept India's mobility myth, bullock capitalists can lead a coalition that encompasses much of India's agricultural sector. From this position of political strength, bullock capitalists can bargain effectively with the components of the predominantly urban organized economy and society: organized white- and blue-collar workers, private and state industrial and financial capitalists, state bureaucrats, professionals, small business classes, and the "parasitical intelligentsia."[21]

Our analysis of bullock capitalists so far has considered the all-India level, but we recognize that what is true for all of India may not be true for South, West, East, and North India, much less for particular states, districts, or villages. All-India generalizations may miss differences that can prove decisive for national historical outcomes. As a result, bullock capitalists may remain more dominant in northern, western, and upper southern states than in the eastern and lower southern states or than at the center. Bullock capitalists are more significant in the economic and political life of the wheat-growing areas of the North and West than in the rice-growing areas of the East and South. In the North, independent cultivators and household farm helpers greatly outnumber agricultural wage laborers, but the two groups are evenly balanced in the lower South and Bengal. According to the Farm Management Survey, the ratios of independent cultivators using family labor to those using hired agricultural laborers in the wheat-growing areas of Punjab, Uttar Pradesh, and Haryana are 2:1, 3:1, and 4:1, whereas in the rice-growing areas of Tamil Nadu, West Bengal, and Kerala, they are 1:1, 1:1, and 1:2.[22] These figures support the proposition that in wheat-growing areas family labor predominates and in rice-growing areas wage labor is more important. Important rice-growing areas such as the Thanjavur district in Tamil Nadu, Hooghly and 24 Parganas in West Bengal, and Alleppey and Quilon in Kerala, for example, show a far lower proportion of family labor engaged in farm work than do important wheat-growing districts such as Muzzafarnagar, Meerut, Amritsar, Ferozepur, and Nasik.[23]

Our table 41, based on data from the NSS twenty-seventh round (October 1972–September 1973) also shows marked regional variations in the relative proportions of family to wage labor. In the southern rice-growing states of Tamil Nadu and Andhra Pradesh, for example, the proportions of household labor to hired labor in the total work force are even (25 vs. 25 percent and 26 vs. 27 percent, respectively), while in the northern wheat-growing states of Rajasthan, Punjab, and Uttar Pradesh, household labor significantly overbalances hired workers (55 vs. 4 percent, 27 vs. 10 percent, and 33 vs. 8 percent). These proportions are consistent with those noted by the Farm Management Survey as well as the 1981 census "provisional population totals," which showed that agricultural workers outnumbered independent cultivators as a percentage of the work force in Andhra Pradesh, Tamil Nadu, and Kerala (37 vs. 32 percent, 31 vs. 29 percent, and 28 vs. 13 percent).[24] Nevertheless, the fact of bullock capitalist cultivation and the appeal of its ideology remain powerful in the South too, where many cultivators operate holdings that fully and remuneratively employ family labor.[25]

Bullock capitalists' political significance depends in part on their ability to maintain their economic base, that is, the proportion of land under their operational control and the technology that makes their operational holdings at least as productive and profitable as large holdings that use capital-intensive technology and hired labor. While the proportion of large landowners and the amount of land under their control declined between 1954–55 and 1970–71, the proportion of bullock capitalists remained stable and the amount of land under their control increased. In agricultural production, the commitment and quality of labor matters more than its specialized division or, within limits, the size of the productive unit. Improved technology

TABLE 41
Variation by State in Proportion of Family Labor to Wage Labor

	(1) Household Employment: Owners and Helpers (%)	(2) Wage Labor (%)	(3) Ratio (2):(1)	(4) Non-Farm Employment (%)	(5) Not Working (%)	(6) Domestic Labor (%)
Rajasthan	54.58	3.91	0.07	7.47	28.13	5.61
Uttar Pradesh	32.53	7.92	0.24	7.43	33.65	18.46
Madhya Pradesh	42.10	13.86	0.33	4.23	32.32	7.49
Punjab	27.20	10.21	0.38	10.58	32.88	19.13
Gujarat	30.04	16.39	0.55	6.26	35.78	11.53
Karnataka	31.70	21.96	0.69	5.55	30.54	11.20
Orissa	23.81	17.34	0.73	7.36	31.72	19.77
Bihar	20.21	15.56	0.77	6.49	36.41	21.53
Maharashtra	26.30	21.53	0.82	6.33	29.96	15.88
West Bengal	15.20	14.50	0.95	8.61	38.32	23.37
Tamil Nadu	24.52	24.68	1.00	10.89	28.49	11.42
Andhra Pradesh	25.93	26.58	1.03	9.09	27.35	11.05

SOURCE: The categories used in this table are compiled from Government of India, Ministry of Planning, Department of Statistics, National Sample Survey, Twenty-seventh Round, (October 1972–September 1973), "Selected Tables on the Survey on Employment and Unemployment," no. 222 (New Delhi, 1975).

Notes: The categories are composed of the following subcategories: household employment (column 1): usual activity codes 11 ("working in own farm") and 16 (working in household farm as helper"); wage labor (column 2): codes 13 ("working as regular salaried employee/wage labourer in farm") and 15 ("working as casual wage labourer"); non-farm employment (column 4): codes 12 ("working in household non-farm enterprise/ farm") and 14 ("working as regular salaried employee/wage labourer in non-farm enterprise"), and 17 ("working in non-farm household enterprise as helper"); not working (column 5): codes 21 ("not working but seeking or available for employment"), 31 ("attending educational institution"), and 33–35 ("too young," "old and disabled," and "others" [including "pensioners, remittance recipients, beggars, prostitutes, etc."]); and domestic labor (column 6): code 32 ("domestic work"). Figures for Kerala, Haryana, and Jammu and Kashmir, among large states, were not available in this series.

combined with improved human capital and entrepreneurship can cancel or reverse economies of scale. The family labor bullock capitalists use is on the average markedly better than the wage or dependent labor on which large landowners rely. As among smallholders, bullock capitalists, and large landowners, we anticipate that, over the medium term (the next ten years or so), bullock capitalists will gain the advantage.

In world-historical perspective, the "large landowners" who benefited from or survived intermediary abolition are a less formidable agrarian or national class than owners of latifundia in Latin America, Prussian Junkers, Japanese daimyos, or English landed gentry. In table 40, large landowners are defined as those with operational holdings of 15 acres and above. Their average and median holdings in 1970–71 were about 23 and 25 acres.[26] We follow Rudra and Herring in not distinguishing capitalist and feudal large landowners, because noncultivating owners or operators have become increasingly alike with respect to the mix of economic and social power they command and their use of private power as "entrepreneurs."[27]

"Large" is a relative as well as a functional term. Functionally, it refers to holdings too large for self-cultivation and to the status that still attaches to those who do not toil by putting hand to plow. Many upper-caste and some upwardly mobile Indians have their land cultivated for them by tenants or workers in order to maintain or enhance their self-esteem and social status. "Large" in a relative context refers to those with more rather than less private power, that is, the material and ideological resources that yield economic control and social domination. Holdings that average 23 acres seem "small" compared with those of preabolition feudal estate holders in India, the "landed upper classes" analyzed by Moore,[28] or contemporary capital-intensive farmers in Pakistan or the United States but seem large compared with traditional peasant holdings in Asia. The "large landowners" we identify in table 40 are local notabilities. They control others by hiring them for wages or engaging them as tenants and by being an important source of credit, inputs, and influence. It is not so much greater land control as greater private power that makes owners of 15 acres or more "large." Their private power constrains local markets, bargaining, electoral choice, and administrative access.

Table 40 shows that between 1954–55 and 1971–72 the proportion of large landowner households and the amount of land they controlled declined from 9 to 6 percent and from 53 to 39 percent. Some of this shrinkage in the amount of land controlled may be illusory. Typically, landowners have protected themselves against the threat of ceilings legislation by so-called *benami* transfers: registering land in the name of relatives or dependents who could be counted on not to make good on their legal claim, at least in the immediate future. As a result, some land in the bullock capitalist category may be the *benami* holdings of large landowners. Nevertheless, intermediary abolition, ceilings legislation, and market transfers have caused a real decline in the aggregate in the proportion of large landowners and the amount of land they control. In a political system where numbers as well as wealth and status affect electoral and policy outcomes, it is not surprising that, from the late 1970s, large landowners lost ground to bullock capitalists.[29]

The Polarization Thesis and Its Alternatives

Since the "green revolution," scholars of India's political economy have tried to relate economic change to political action and political action to policy and historical change. What, they have asked, are the likely effects of technological change and policy on the character, outlook, and mutual relations of agrarian classes? Our analysis of agrarian classes depicts their variety and ambiguous nature. Is there a common structure or historical necessity that determines the properties and behavior of agrarian classes? We think not, but a substantial literature in the 1970s held otherwise. It alleged that immiseration of the poor and the enrichment of large landowners was polarizing agrarian class relations and would continue to do so. The spread of commercial agriculture was creating two classes, capitalist farmers and wage laborers. Polarization was being accelerated by the differential gains associated with the green revolution. Smallholders and dwarf holders would be pushed into the ranks of a rural proletariat as control of land fell increasingly into the hands of capitalist farmers employing growing proportions of wage laborers. This process was said to be driven by the dynamism of capitalist forces in the agricultural sector of the economy. These forces simultaneously increased the productivity and profit of capitalist farmers and decreased the land and income available to the growing numbers of agricultural wage workers. This interpretation of the quality and direction of economic change was used by scholars of pluralist as well as Marxist persuasion.[30]

In our view, the evidence suggests a more complex and ambiguous future for agrarian relations in India. Capitalist farmers and wage workers have not been nor are they likely to be the only or even the principal actors in the agricultural sector of the economy. As we suggested above, independent cultivators using their own and household labor (bullock capitalists) are likely to remain a larger and politically more influential economic class than wage workers or capitalist farmers (large landowners). Contrary to the polarization thesis, the proportion of land under the control of large landholders has been declining, and that held by smallholders and middle-sized holders has been increasing. Other trends too have not confirmed the polarization thesis. The purported increase in the proportion of agricultural workers between 1961 and 1971 was probably substantially less than reported by the census of 1971. According to the census of 1981, the proportion decreased slightly. The immiseration aspect of the polarization thesis holds that the incomes of agricultural wage workers will decline. The ambiguous evidence on agricultural incomes and on the proportions living below the poverty line over time does not support this view. Real wages, the number of days worked, the terms of trade between countryside and city, and opportunities for off-farm collateral employment vary by areas and their national aggregate seems to have neither deteriorated nor improved.

In judging the polarization thesis and an alternative view that finds small- and middle-sized holders have more than held their own, the kind and quality of evidence matters as much as the way the evidence is interpreted. The two main sources of aggregate data are the decennial censuses and the various rounds of the Indian Statistical Institute's National Sample Surveys.[31] The debate is affected by the validity of statisticians' and economists' concepts and by the reliability of census and NSS data as well as by the interpretative and explanatory modes applied to them. Further complications arise from the fact that the knowledge gained over thirty years of data gathering dictates revisions in concepts and their applications. Such changes, in turn, raise problems about comparability of the data over time.

Another factor affecting judgments about the future of agrarian relations is the problematic nature of statements about and interpretations of national characteristics and trends over time. Can "India" be used diachronically or synchronically as a unit of analysis for explanatory purposes? The Indian economic and social landscape is not only incredibly varied but also more segmented than in more-advanced industrial societies. Even when parallel conditions exist in different regions and states, they often are the result of different causes and remain innocent of each other. National data are sometimes spurious because what appear to be common properties or consequences are the result of different variables (objective or subjective) or different combinations of them. National aggregates wash out or obliterate variables that powerfully determine regional or local circumstances and behavior. These are some of the reasons for holding that macroaggregative data, while increasingly important for identifying objective determinants of social action, remain a less valid source of such determinants than regional and local data. Indeed, as E. P. Thompson has argued with respect to Britain, national aggregate historical summaries often obscure particular regional configurations that are relevant for political action.[32]

An equally compelling reason for remaining agnostic about national data is the difficulty for explanatory purposes of translating objective into subjective determinants. Causes or objective determinants are not self-executing. They must be translated into subjective determinants or reasons before social action can occur. Pursuing purpose or power or both is not an automatic or natural act. Translating objective into subjective determinants requires leadership that makes ideology and interest meaningful and compelling to vulnerable, uncertain, and risk-averse actors more prone to recognize private advantage than collective goods and bads. Even if a statement such as "the rich are getting richer at a faster rate than the poor" proved valid, it remains a statistical summary, not a statement about social action or political probabilities.

With these considerations in mind, we turn to 1970s studies that dealt with the future of agrarian relations. One of the more influential and characteristic studies was conducted by K. N. Raj.[33] Its central theme was rural immiseration and polarization. Raj's version of the polarization thesis was set in the Indian context, where the single largest category of agricultural producers is that of cultivators who use their own and household labor. He argued that there had been a secular increase in the number of agricultural employers and employees and a corresponding decrease of family farms (i.e., cultivators using their own and family labor)[34] (see appendix B, table B-1). Family farms were losing ground to capitalist agriculture based on wage labor.[35]

Raj's article was followed by "comments" that questioned his use and interpretation of macroaggregative data and challenged his conclusions.[36] One response, by Visaria,[37] was based on his reading of the NSS data and suggested a rather different pattern of change than the one suggested by Raj of capitalist farmers employing increasing numbers and proportions of wage laborers. According to Visaria's revisions, a relatively stable proportion of "employers" and an increasing proportion (+ 3.2 percent from 1960–61 to 1972–73) of "own account workers" (smallholders) were paying wages to a slightly increased proportion (+ 2.1 percent) of "employees" as well as relying on about the same proportion (+ 1.3 percent) of "unpaid family labor" (appendix B, table B-1). Several microstudies indicated that many "employers," rather than being "capitalist farmers," were small farmers ("own account workers") engaged in more intensive use of the land (such as double or triple cropping) that required more family and some wage labor[38] and mixed market with subsistence agriculture. To further complicate the picture and render it more ambiguous, there is reason to believe that an appreciable number of those classified as "employers" augmented their incomes by agricultural wage labor.[39] According to Visaria's reading of NSS data, the pattern of change was dominated by family farms ("own account workers" and "unpaid family labor") using some wage labor rather than capitalist agriculture based on wage labor. Visaria saw bullock capitalists where Raj saw capitalist agriculture.

Raj's formulation of the immiseration thesis held that between 1953–54 and 1970–71 large landowners had evicted tenants, with a resultant decline of 12.4 percent (from 45.3 to 32.9 percent) in the proportion of smallholders and a substantial increase in the number and proportion of households not operating any land, from 6.6 to 21.91 million and from 11 to 27 percent[40] (appendix B, table B-2). Sanyal's comment on Raj's article, published together with Visaria's, challenged Raj's reading of the data and interpretation of trends. According to Sanyal's reading of NSS data, the proportion of smallholders increased rather than decreased between 1953–54 and 1970–71, from 28 to 33 percent[41] (appendix B, table B-2).

Raj conveyed the impression of precipitous changes in the size of agrarian classes that suggested increased polarization. Sanyal's and Visaria's modifications suggest the initial importance and increasing significance of independent cultivators operating family farms. In Sanyal's version of agrarian change between 1953–54 and 1970–71, the proportion of households not operating land (most of whose members are agricultural wage workers) decreased slightly rather than increasing precipitously and the proportion of smallholders increased by 4.9 percent rather than decreasing by 12.4 percent. Both Sanyal and Raj show that the proportion of medium-sized holders remained constant and that the proportion of large holdings declined by about 4 percent.

In judging the immiseration thesis, it is also important to consider the direction and scale of change with respect to area held, that is, the proportions and the average sizes of the three categories of holding— small, medium, and large. While Raj and Sanyal disagree on other figures, their data are more or less the same for 1953–54, 1960–61, and 1970–71. This means they agree that the proportion of land held (i.e., operated) and the average holding of small and medium-sized operators *increased* between 1953–54 and 1970–71, the proportions from about 5.5 to 9.2 percent and about 29 to 37.5 percent, respectively, and the sizes from about 1 to 1.3 acres and about 5.4 to 5.8 acres, respectively (appendix B, table B-3). They also agree that the proportion of land held and the average holding of large operators *declined* over the same period, from about 65 to 53 percent and from 25 to about 23.6 acres. On the basis of area held, it seems unlikely that operators of small and medium-sized family farms were *objectively* more miserable in 1970–71 than they were in 1953–54.[42]

We have argued that macroaggregative national data sometimes obscure more than they reveal. For that reason, we turn to contrasting microanalyses set in two regional contexts, Gujarat and Punjab, the first by V. S. Vyas, the second by Ashok Rudra and colleagues. Vyas's Gujarat study supports Visaria's and Sanyal's interpretations of NSS data but disconfirms Raj's polarization thesis. Vyas shows some of the dynamics behind the growth of small holdings operated as family farms.[43] Vyas found that the proportion of smallholders (up to 4.99 acres) was increasing (from 33.9 percent in 1960–61 to 47.89 percent in 1970–71)—that is, that some agricultural producers were leaving rather than being driven into the ranks of tenants and agricultural wage workers. Further, the increase seems not to have been the result of fragmentation: the average size of holdings increased marginally (from 2.48 to 2.54 acres). Vyas attributes the increase in the proportion of smallholders to the land reforms of the mid-1950s and early 1960s, which "enabled a large number of landless and tenants to obtain ownership rights in land . . . a sizeable redistribution of land did take place following the land reform legislation. Also a greater convergence of ownership and management took place and tenancy as a category of relationship to land declined."[44] Other evidence also supported the view that the proportion of tenants and landless wage workers was declining and that of smallholders growing: The number of market transactions in land since the mid-1950s was low,[45] evidence that Vyas interpreted as indicating that, for the most part, smallholders were not selling out to larger ones. The increase in the proportion of smallholders, Vyas found, was accounted for by "arrivals from below (116 from below as against 14 from above); landless persons acquired small holdings much more than medium size holders caused fragmentation by sub-dividing and selling land."[46]

The microanalytic study in the Punjab by Rudra and his colleagues suggested patterns more akin to Raj's polarization thesis.[47] They estimated that between 1955–56 and 1967–68, the proportion of land controlled by big farmers (above 20 acres) increased by 9.5 percent. This aggregate result, they suggest, may have masked an even more severe concentration: the proportion of land controlled by the smallest of the big farmers (i.e., those operating 20–25 acres) increased by only 4 percent, while land controlled by the biggest (controlling 100–150 acres) increased by 40 percent. Concentration implies polarization; small and medium-sized family farms were being driven out by capitalist farmers employing wage labor.

A number of qualifications must be considered before accepting that in Punjab, India's most advanced agricultural state, polarization best characterizes the pattern of change or that Punjab may be showing India its future. First, it is difficult to judge the extreme concentration thesis—that is, that the proportion of land controlled by farmers with 100–150 acres increased by 40 percent between 1955–56 and 1967–68—because we are not given the actual numbers. If this category was very small to begin with, the increase would be less telling than if it constituted a significant proportion of all big farmers. Nor are we told how many cultivators there were in the class with more than 20 but less than 100 acres. As a consequence of these two lacunae in the data, we do not know how much of the overall increase of 9 percent in land controlled by big farmers can be attributed to those with 100–150 acres and how much to those with 20–99 acres. Without this information, the degree of concentration occurring between 1955–56 and 1967–68 remains moot. At the same time, the 9 percent overall increase in land controlled by big farmers is significant because it stands in marked contrast to Raj's and to Sanyal's findings about national trends. As appendix table B-3 shows, both Raj's and Sanyal's analysis of NSS data revealed that the proportion of land controlled by largeholders (defined as those with 10 acres and above) *declined* between 1953–54 and 1970–71 by 11 to 13 percent.

The study by Rudra and colleagues has to be further qualified by the findings of other regional studies or microstudies that have a bearing on the concentration-cum-polarization thesis in Punjab. Here we cite two, by Montek Ahluwalia and by G. S. Bhalla and G. K. Chadha.[48] Ahluwalia attends to trends at both the all-India and individual state levels with respect to the incidence of poverty and inequality. His data base includes the various NSS consumption surveys, which report the distribution of the population across per capita expenditure classes. Here we are interested in poverty and inequality as they relate to trends in Punjab. In six states, including Punjab, per capita agricultural output had increased. But Ahluwalia was particularly "disquieted" by evidence from Punjab "which does not support the hypothesis that improved agricultural performance will help reduce the incidence of poverty."[49] Punjab "has experienced a dramatic growth in agricultural output per rural person but there is no evidence of a downward trend in the incidence of poverty," nor was there evidence that factors operating independently of changes in the level of per capita output had affected the incidence of poverty.[50]

At this stage of the argument, Ahluwalia's analysis complements that of Rudra et al., insofar as it suggests that, in the Punjab at least, increased per capita output had not reduced the incidence of poverty. Ahluwalia explains this unexpected outcome by the "heavy migration into rural Punjab in response to the growth of labour demand." The poorest quarter of the rural population contains an increasing proportion of *purbeas* (migrant labor from the East). Their "consumption is higher than it would have been if they had not migrated . . . 'trickle down' benefits have taken the form of increased employment benefiting migrants from other states, rather than increased wages benefiting the pre-existing poor."[51] We find it difficult to know whether this picture of objective determinants should or should not be counted as favoring polarization, but we are fairly confident that migrant *purbeas* with improved incomes are even less likely to engage in polarizing social action or political participation than erstwhile Punjabi wage workers engaged, for the most part, in more desirable employment. Also "particularly worth noting," according to Ahluwalia, is the fact that "the Gini coefficient for Punjab . . . shows a statistically significant decline in inequality over the period as a whole."[52] Even if, as Rudra and colleagues hold, Punjab experienced a trend toward concentration of landownership between 1955–56 and 1967–68, its potential for polarization is likely to have been seriously compromised by the displacement of Punjabi by *purbea* wage labor and by declining inequality in consumption expenditure in the state as a whole.

Bhalla and Chadha's findings with respect to the input use, production, and income streams of marginal and small cultivators (0.10–4.99 acres) in the Punjab complement Ahluwalia's analysis of NSS aggregate data.[53] Such cultivators spend somewhat less on fertilizer and other inputs (except draft cattle) than do larger cultivators (12.5 acres and above), but their more intense, assured, and higher-quality labor results in higher output per acre.[54] Except in the most advanced areas (i.e., the central Punjab plain), Bhalla and Chadha, unlike Krishna Bharadwaj,[55] found very little difference in cropping patterns between small and large cultivators. They described the small cultivators as participating actively in the green revolution in terms of inputs, yield rates, cropping patterns, and so forth, and as deriving significant incomes from dairying, poultry, and wage income (often off farm). These observations help to explain Ahluwalia's finding of declining inequality in consumption expenditure and cast further doubt on the polarization-immiseration thesis.

The Gujarat and Punjab evidence under review suggest that in Gujarat family farms have gained ground as landless workers have become owner-cultivators, while in the Punjab an appreciable number of large landowners have become capitalist farmers by employing increasingly larger proportions of migrant laborers rather than by driving small and medium-sized cultivators into the ranks of wage laborers. West Bengal presents yet another regional pattern to fit into a composite picture of the possibilities and influences that can shape the future of agrarian relations in India. Its pattern of landholding has been confined to so narrow a range that polarization no longer seems possible. The 87 percent of West Bengal's cultivators who hold less than 2 hectares (about 5 acres) control 87 percent of the cultivated land. It would be hard to cast the 10 percent who control between 2 and 4 hectares in the role of large landowners or capitalist farmers, while the remaining 3 percent who control more than 4 hectares, far from being an expanding, powerful class, are politically in decline.[56]

In Kerala too, agrarian reform has exhausted the possibility of polarization. In a miasma of minor differences among roughly equal holders who employ increasingly secure and well-paid workers, alienation and indifference has resulted in lowered efficiency and production.[57]

What are the political implications of these ambiguous findings concerning objective determinants for the future of agrarian relations in India? Historically, the polarization thesis has been associated with the expectation of agrarian radicalism in national politics. The alternative we have offered, emphasizing the growth of small and medium-sized family farms, suggests a counterforce to polarization, and is less compatible with the likelihood of agrarian radicalism. However one judges the trend—toward polarization, concentration, and immiseration or toward family farms operated by independent cultivators—no reading of objective determinants can anticipate the future of agrarian relations. Objective determinants do not translate automatically into social formations possessed of political consciousness and capable of social action. Objective determinants (causes) are necessary but not sufficient conditions of social action. Macroaggregative categories found in regional and local data are abstracted from political contexts and policy. They are not informed by nor do they take account of the subjective determinants that precipitate and guide political participation or social action. For some time, they are likely to remain more regional and local than national.

Our reading of the future of agrarian relations suggests not only that mobilizations that result from the translation of objective into subjective determinants will occur more at the regional and local than at the national level but also that they will feature a variety of voices and loyalties: capitalist and family farmers who have benefited from state policies and economic growth but who, in the name of equity between countryside and city and of economic growth, demand higher commodity prices and lower input costs; dissatisfied marginal cultivators and agricultural workers who must balance the costs of challenging or allying with socially dominant and economically powerful local elites and classes against the benefits likely to be gained; and landless laborers (often untouchables) whose resistance to oppression and exploitation sometimes results in atrocities against them and unofficial civil wars.

Self-Employed Cultivators and the New Agrarianism

Proponents of the polarization thesis anticipated that the growth of capitalist farming based on wage labor would increase the likelihood of agrarian radicalism in national as well as state politics. Instead, in the 1980s, regional and national mobilizations of farmers demanded remunerative prices and lower input costs. Farmers agitated in many states and staged giant rallies in Delhi. This new agrarianism opened a fresh cleavage in national politics, between the countryside and the city.

The new agrarianism articulates the politics of the countryside's agrarian classes (see table 40). Among them, cultivators using their own and family labor probably constitute half of the households working in the agricultural sector, and of such households those we identify as bullock capitalists constitute the single largest proportion (34 percent).[58] Unlike large landowners ("feudal"-style landlords, capitalist farmers, or the emerging blend of the two) whose origins and resources are located in the history of the British raj, self-employed cultivators are largely the product of postindependence agrarian policies. They were the principal beneficiaries of the first wave of land reform in the middle 1950s that nominally, and to a considerable extent actually, abolished "intermediaries," the legal euphemism for noncultivating rentiers and/or revenue collecting landlords such as zamindars and *jagirdars*. The primary goal of the first wave of land reforms, to make ownership rights available to erstwhile tenants, was to a considerable extent realized in spite of large-scale evictions of tenants by intermediaries claiming the *khudkhast* (land for personal cultivation) allowed them under the terms of state laws.

The second wave of land reform, which began in the 1960s and extended into the 1970s, was less successful than the first. It attempted to impose ceilings on landholdings, with the aim of redistributing over-ceiling land to dwarf holders, insecure tenants, and landless workers. During the second wave, self-employed cultivators, who were, for the most part, only marginally affected, held their own or improved their position. Large landowners, who were the principal target but who were influential in state-level politics and government blocked, stalled, amended, and evaded ceiling laws and their implementation. And, as we indicated in the previous section, self-employed cultivators (as well as large landowners) benefited from the green revolution by using as much and sometimes more of the divisible new inputs as capitalist farmers with wage labor.

The political influence of self-employed cultivators first became visible in North India when, in Uttar Pradesh, Charan Singh brought down the C. B. Gupta Congress government in April 1967, formed the agrarian-minded BKD, and in alliance with the Jan Sangh party, formed the state's first non-Congress government. In 1974, the BKD merged with an increasingly moribund Swatantra party and five smaller parties to become the BLD. It in turn became a principal component of the hastily assembled Janata party. Formed in the wake of the emergency regime to contest the 1977 parliamentary election, with Charan Singh a reluctant deputy to Morarji Desai, it swept the northern states, gaining almost all the seats.

With the formation and victory of the Janata party, agrarian politics were for the first time transposed from the state to the national level. From being junior partners in Congress governments, agrarian interests and classes became senior partners in Janata's ruling coalition. The new configuration put agrarian ideology and policy at the forefront of national attention and concern and was reflected in policies and reoriented investment patterns. The new agrarianism challenged the political settlement of the Nehru era favoring industry, professional (particularly official) classes, and cities. Under it, rural notabilities, drawn primarily from the ranks of large landowners, had supported Nehru's (and Mrs. Gandhi's) urban-oriented industrialization strategy in return for a tacit understanding that agrarian interests (as they defined them) would retain control of state politics and policy. It was this understanding that enabled rural notabilities to stymie the second wave of land reform and to hinder or blunt other agrarian policies meant to help the poor and threatening what they perceived to be their interests.

The emergence of agrarian classes in national politics paralleled the progressive exhaustion of obvious basic- and heavy-industry investment targets. As a result, spokesmen for the new agrarianism could challenge the Nehru era's obsolescent investment strategy favoring industry and urban workers with demands that investment be reoriented toward the agricultural sector and rural areas, where most of the voters, national product, and poor were located.

Agrarian producers include a large spectrum of landholders and workers. In addition to a substantial proportion without land (27 percent), there exists a broad range of landholders: the few thousand-acre farmers (allegedly most prevalent in Bihar) who have induced or intimidated local and state officials to ignore their (often well-hidden) evasion of land ceiling legislation; a small but significant proportion of hundred-acre holders who, through tacit leases and *benami* transfers (land nominally transferred to relatives or dependents) also have evaded land ceilings; a larger proportion of 15- to 20-acre holders who are recognizable locally as village notabilities and leaders of dominant castes; the largest proportion of holders, those operating 2.5 to 15 acres, who constitute the solid core of self-employed bullock capitalists; and holders of less than 2.5 acres, who make up the second largest proportion of self-employed cultivators and contribute substantially to the pool of agricultural workers (table 40).

The challenge to the new agrarianism is to what extent and under what conditions actors in this spectrum of agrarian producers believe they share economic interests and political outlooks. The response to this challenge depends as much on the identification and perception of collective goods and bads as it does on the aggregation of individual interests and preferences. Whatever the differential benefits of remunerative prices for agricultural commodities and low costs for inputs, are remunerative prices and low input costs perceived as a collective good for the countryside? Are the adverse terms of trade between the agricultural and industrial sectors widely understood as a collective bad for agricultural producers? Collective goods and bads are, of course, constrained by objective calculations, but, for the new agrarianism's spokesmen, objective calculations are sufficiently contradictory or ambiguous that ideological interpretations can color the past and portray the future. The extent to which landless workers, dwarf holders and smallholders, bullock capitalists, and large landowners believe they share collective goods and bads has only recently begun to be visible in political action and remains subject to the influence of differing ideologies and interpretations of interest.

Some observers interpret the agrarian politics and movements of the last decade or so as essentially vehicles for the promotion of the interests of large landowners, whether feudal, capitalist, or a blend of the two. Large landowners have appropriated and will continue to appropriate a disproportionate share of the gains from public investments and programs in the agricultural sector, higher commodity prices, and input subsidies. They also point out that the incomes of large landowners, unlike comparable incomes in the urban organized economy, are not taxed. Such observers explain the participation of small and marginal farmers and of agricultural workers by invoking false consciousness or distorted interest perception. Some discount the success of the new agrarianism because, by their reading of objective interests, workers in the countryside and in the city have more in common with each other than they do with their employers in the agricultural, industrial, and service sectors. Given the right circumstances and leadership, workers can be expected to act together in transsectoral class politics.

Whatever the assessment made of objective class or producer interests, the subjective response to the new agrarianism in the last decade has led all parties, national and regional, left and right, to adopt multiclass agrarian strategies that feature agrarian themes and issues. Even parties whose ideologies would lead them to appeal primarily to marginal cultivators and workers have been sufficiently constrained by electoral considerations to seek the support of self-employed cultivators.

What is the "new" agrarianism? It is new in contrast to the "old" agrarianism that Mohandas Gandhi's leadership instilled in the nationalist movement and to the erstwhile Swatantra party's antistatist defense of the agrarian status quo in the 1960s.[59] Gandhi's leadership of the nationalist movement established a mass base by revitalizing the values and interests of India's agrarian and craft producers. His ideology was village and employment oriented. Influenced by Ruskin's and Tolstoy's utopian responses to industrialism, Gandhi argued that, given a commitment to simple wants, India's villages could be economically self-sufficient and politically autonomous. In *Hind Swaraj* (*Indian Self-Rule*), the text par excellence of the old agrarianism, Gandhi called on Indians to achieve the moral understanding and self-discipline required for national, economic, and cultural independence. He warned the country about the consequences of becoming an urban, industrial civilization: machines and wants that degrade and enslave, the destruction of community and meaningful work by impersonal, specialized, large-scale organizations and cities. The endless consumption that industrial production entailed was more likely to dehumanize than to liberate consumers, and its specialization and economies of scale more likely to eliminate craft than to create new factory jobs. Finally, Indians would become dependent on indigenous and foreign masters as the owners of industrial and finance capital at home and abroad destroyed the local bases of production and exchange.

The new agrarianism often invokes Gandhi's ideology and concerns but speaks in a more pragmatic, even technical language. It recognizes the interdependence of the industrial, agricultural, and service sectors of the economy that thirty-five years of planned investment have brought into being. It has come to accept the state and its policy interventions. Spokesmen for the new agrarianism do not so much oppose interdependence and the state's role in the economy as object to what they allege is the privileged and exploitive relationship between the unorganized agrarian and the organized industrial and service sectors of the economy. At the same time, because many independent producers have not yet become part of the market for discretionary consumer goods, they still respond to Gandhian messages deploring the growth of centralized economic and state power and the frivolous activity and consumption they associate with urban life, and celebrating individual discipline and local self-reliance.

The language employed by the ideologues of the new agrarianism invokes tacit or explicit socioeconomic theories. The terms in use differentially join or divide agrarian classes and urban and rural interests. Cultivators described as "peasants" (*kisans*) and "farmers" (*shetkari*) share a family resemblance despite the very different ideological provenances of the two terms. Those who talk about "farmers" usually include all agricultural producers involved in market relations, while those who talk about "peasants" are likely to exclude capitalist farmers and feudal landowners. The two languages converge, however, by explicitly placing agrarian and rural in opposition to industrial and urban interests. The nonpartisan new agrarian of the early eighties, Sharad Joshi, a former United Nations civil servant, and the partisan left's new agrarian, Harekrishna Singh Surjeet, long a leader of the CPI and CPI-M Kisan Sabha (Peasant Association), both hold that producers in the agricultural sector share a common interest in opposing and reversing development strategies and policies that have slighted agrarian interests. "Every section of the peasantry," Surjeet holds, "from the rich peasant to the marginal and small one, is affected" by the

Congress-I's antipeasant price policy.[60] Joshi's efforts to mobilize the countryside against the city is less constrained than Surjeet's. Unlike Surjeet, Joshi does not have to accommodate an ideology that attempts to bridge the division between city and countryside by featuring class as the principal political cleavage and strategic commitment to a worker-peasant alliance.

Joshi provides reasons for farmers to mobilize: for him, the principal cleavage in Indian politics is Bharat versus India, the countryside versus the city. All rural families, he believes, from agricultural laborers to rich farmers, "have a basic unity of interest on the issue of higher prices for agricultural products."[61] More broadly, all producers engaged in farming and related occupations share a "class interest." Farmer prosperity will "free blocked and warped productive forces of the country for new industrial and agricultural development."[62] Transposing the doctrine of unequal exchange from the world economy to the national economy, he argues that comparative costs and relative prices are rigged against agrarian producers. The view has attracted wide political and some ideological and scholarly support.[63]

An agrarian strategy has well-placed defenders on the left even if not all leftists support it. Although Surjeet opposes Joshi's effort to lead the new agrarianism in ways that accentuate the urban-rural cleavage, he argues along remarkably similar lines. Surjeet perceives the new agrarianism as a peasant uprising "unparalleled in the history of free India." "The peasants are fighting for common demands—the most important being the demand of remunerative prices for their produce." He denies that remunerative prices for agricultural commodities benefit only landlords and rich peasants: "Every section of the peasantry, including the poorest of them, is forced to sell a part of his produce . . . to purchase food grains for his family's consumption . . . and is therefore interested in such a level of prices as would meet the cost of production."[64]

The wide partisan and interest group support for the new agrarian policy demands masks important differences over substance as well as language. Those who espouse the cause of the peasant would like to exclude rich farmers and to mitigate or transcend the primacy of the cleavage between Bharat and India. Surjeet dismisses Joshi as a spokesman for rich farmers who grow commercial crops. At the same time he contributes to Joshi's successful mobilizations of a broad spectrum of producer interests and agrarian classes by swelling their ranks with leftist supporters.[65] Surjeet's version of the urban-rural cleavage is qualified by his call for an alliance—yet to be consummated—between peasants and workers who are meant to find common ground in their opposition to the Congress-I government's antipeasant and antiworker laws[66] and policies and to its repressive measures against both groups. Both the left and the new agrarians would like to have it both ways: by defining peasant broadly and loosely, the left can pursue vote-winning multiclass agrarian policies that divide countryside and city, and by ignoring sectoral cleavages, it can pursue Marxist class politics that unite workers against owners; conversely, the new agrarians would have self-employed cultivators, capitalist farmers, and agricultural wage workers ignore their differences in the conviction that the rising tide of agricultural prosperity will lift boats, not only of agrarian producers but also of those in the industrial and service sectors.

The new agrarianism first captured national attention in December 1978 when hundreds of thousands of *kisans* thronged to Delhi to celebrate the birthday of India's leading agrarian ideologue, Charan Singh.[67] The significance of the event did not escape Mrs. Gandhi's attention. In 1980, soon after the electoral victory that brought Congress-I and Mrs. Gandhi back to power, she too mounted a mammoth *kisan* rally, only to be challenged by an equally large rally staged on March 26 by the "democratic" opposition's Central Kisan Coordinating Committee.

In the winter of 1980–81, the new agrarianism moved from urban spectaculars to rural agitational politics organized by various interest groups, supported by a wide spectrum of political parties hoping to capitalize on or to control the new force.[68] Farmers in several states were mobilized to demand remunerative prices for agricultural commodities,[69] a demand that raised the broader issue of the terms of trade between the agricultural and industrial sectors. According to the Agricultural Prices Commission, the price index for agricultural products as a percentage of the price for manufactured goods declined from 100.7 in 1974–75 to 83.5 in March 1980.[70] The issue of remunerative prices had moved out of party headquarters, secretariat corridors, and legislative chambers to the unmediated politics of *rasta rokos* (roadblocks), *gheraos* (sit-ins), and "long marches." In western India, Sharad Joshi's Shetkari Sangathana adopted the Poujadist tactics of French petty merchants and farmers[71] by blocking roads to enforce their demands.[72] G. Narayanaswami Naidu's Tamil Nadu Agriculturists Association used similar tactics to press for cancellation of debts[73] as well as remunerative prices. In early 1983, Congress-I bastions in the upper South collapsed as organized farm interests played a major role in the defeat of Karnataka's Congress government by a Janata-led coalition, and the rural poor along with rich farmers helped N. T. Rama Rao's Telugu Desam rout a Congress government in Andhra Pradesh.[74] Organized farmers joined all-India industrial and commercial interest groups such as the Federation of Indian Chambers of Commerce and Industry in the pantheon of influential and controversial organizations that shape national policy agendas and policies.

The appeal of the new agrarianism posed a national and historical threat to the ruling Congress party, because Congress was identified with the Nehru-inspired industrial development strategy and the urban outlook and interests that informed and guided it. Congress's Nehru legacy opened the way for parties, interests, and movements opposed to Congress rule to articulate agrarian ideologies and advocate agrarian policies that promised substantial popular support and electoral dividends. As we mentioned in chapter 12, as early as 1959, at the Nagpur annual session of the Congress, Charan Singh (then a Uttar Pradesh Congress leader) attracted national attention when he successfully opposed the Nehru-sponsored resolution on joint cooperative farming, a move that most self-employed cultivators viewed as the first step toward a collectivized and industrialized agricultural sector. The failed Nagpur resolution triggered the formation of the Swatantra party. Subsequently, parties led by Charan Singh helped to shape agrarian consciousness and the politics and policies associated with it. By the 1970s, culturally nationalist regional parties (e.g., the DMK and AIADMK in Tamil Nadu and the Akali Dal in Punjab) and left regional parties (e.g., the CPI-M in West Bengal and Kerala) as well as national centrist parties were advocating agrarian ideologies and policies and pursuing multiclass agrarian strategies. By the 1980s, when farmers' interest groups and movements in various states began to demand remunerative prices, subsidized fertilizers, cheaper inputs, and rectification of the terms of trade between the agricultural and industrial sectors, all political parties, including by now the Congress-I, had entered the contest to lead or at least to capture a share of new agrarian political support.

If all the parties responded to the electoral and mobilization imperative of a voting population composed largely (about 70 percent) of agricultural producers, there was considerable variation at the state level. In eastern Uttar Pradesh, Bihar, and Andhra Pradesh, for example, local elites drawn from large landowners and rich farmers from dominant upper castes allied against smallholders, marginal holders, and agricultural laborers. In Bihar and Uttar Pradesh, party coalitions and governments led by Charan Singh and Karpoori Thakur countered with broad-spectrum coalitions of agrarian classes and disadvantaged minorities that were similar to those organized by the late Devraj Urs and Ramakrishna Hegde in Karnataka, Sharad Pawar in Maharashtra,

Bhairon Singh Shekawat in Rajasthan, and Madhav Singh Solanki in Gujarat. By contrast, coalition building among agrarian classes and minorities by the Congress-I was for the most part subsumed by loyalty to Indira Gandhi, dependence on her voter appeal, and the Gandhi family's factional politics of favorites and patronage.

The most significant shift from a single to a multiclass agrarian strategy was by the Communist party (the CPI, which, in 1964, split into the CPI and the CPI-M). In West Bengal, the CPI-M, in conquering the countryside, was transformed from an urban party supported primarily by organized industrial workers to a rural party supported by cultivating classes and agricultural workers. After independence, the CPI in West Bengal, whose support at that time was primarily among industrial workers in and around Calcutta, tried to penetrate and lead the countryside by demanding that sharecroppers' rights be recorded. The possibility of implementation led to large-scale evictions by superior tenants and landowners who, in turn, came to fear and oppose the CPI. After the second general election in 1957, the CPI moderated its stand by advocating policies that benefited cultivators generally, such as insuring the availability of cheaper inputs and higher prices for agricultural commodities. In 1967, at the fourth general election, the CPI-M–led United Front put its post-1957 multiclass agrarian strategy at risk by identifying itself with the land grab and forcible harvesting movements against *jotedars* and smaller landowners. The United Front won the 1967 election, but its government immediately faced contradictions. Its police had to keep law and order and protect property on pain of furthering the disorder and insecurity that was contributing to West Bengal's economic decline and, at the same time, protect its supporters' right to agitate, protest, and strike.[75] The United Front's tenuous multiclass rural base required nurturing, even as CPI-M cadres in and around Naxalbari were trying to transform the agrarian structure (and, for some, trigger a political revolution) by leading a violent rebellion by poor, mostly tribal sharecroppers against local *jotedars*. Defeated by the Congress-I in the 1972 khaki election, the CPI-M swept into power in the post-emergency 1977 election and won again in 1982 with the aid of a refurbished agricultural strategy better suited to the politics of a multiclass but increasingly homogeneous rural economy. By the 1980s, what had been an urban-led party, principally supported by organized industrial workers in and around Calcutta, had become master of the West Bengal countryside.

The transformation of the CPI-M's support base arose as much from the effects on agrarian class structure of land reform implemented through multiclass local committees as it did from the imperatives of party competition in a multiclass rural electorate.[76] By the 1970s, 87 percent of all Bengali cultivators controlled less than 5 acres.[77] In this context, the CPI-M government also tried vigorously to pursue Operation Barga, registering the entitlement to cultivation of local sharecroppers and thereafter attempting to enforce the legislatively mandated crop division of 25 and 75 percent between landowner and sharecropper. After reaching about half the two million sharecroppers, Operation Barga encountered an impasse. Why? When sharecroppers' "landlords" are themselves cultivators whose holdings are only marginally greater than those of the sharecroppers, and sharecroppers are in any case entitled to three times as much of the harvest as "landlords," local cadres found it hard to proceed further. A sense of fairness among sharecroppers, cadres, and owners and anticipation of the net political effect of pursuing Operation Barga slowed its momentum. The class enemy had dissolved into a sea of small holdings. It became apparent that when most agricultural producers share similar economic conditions, enlarging an electoral base, much less promoting class conflict, through redistributional means can become both unjust and politically counterproductive.

The CPI-M in West Bengal and other left parties have also been led by the pervasive complexity and ambiguity of class identity and interests to abandon class-conflict agrarian strategies for multiclass ones more compatible with the new agrarianism. Economic classes are rarely isomorphic; usually they overlap. Tenants are also owners; owners are agricultural workers and rentiers as well as cultivators; cultivators earn incomes from off-farm employment. Here is a CPI-M activist's newspaper account of the difficulty:

> I remember a peasant who cultivates two *bighas* of his own land, three or four *bighas* of leased-in land and has a betel leaf orchard of about 1.2 *bigha*. Apart from it, he has about a *bigha* of land in another village, which he does not cultivate himself, but leases out to a sharecropper. Once in a while, he works as an agricultural worker for wages and once for some reason he even had to employ workers on his land. What is this peasant's class character?[78]

In Kerala too, the CPI-M has adjusted its agrarian strategy to accommodate the imperatives of party competition in a rural economy composed of a variety of classes. It has appealed to "peasant masses" rather than exclusively to poor laborers and tenants. Its objectives have been redistributionist rather than collectivist. It has pressed for land reform and its effective implementation, rights and security for tenants and sharecroppers, and improved wages, working conditions, and job security, not for the elimination of property rights through the establishment of cooperative or collective production units. Pressure from the CPI-M brought about most land and tenancy reform and the establishment of agricultural workers' rights and benefits, but it had to share the political credit and rewards with its rivals, the CPI and local bourgeois parties (including the Congress-I), because it was their coalition governments that adopted, enacted, and implemented the CPI-M's programs.[79]

To summarize, agrarianism introduced a new cleavage in Indian politics and policy, the countryside versus the city. Unlike Western democracies and most Third World countries, India adopted universal suffrage and free and competitive party politics early in its industrialization. The result has been the increasing influence of agrarian interests and classes in politics and policy. Agrarianism introduced the new cleavage by influencing or capturing the ideologies and political strategies of all parties, national and regional, left and culturally nationalist. The result has been to give the agricultural sector of the economy and rural society a voice in national and state affairs more commensurate with their share of the electorate. The agrarian politics of local large landowners and dominant castes that characterized state politics through the 1960s has been superseded by the politics of "farmers" and self-employed cultivators. Some argue that because rich farmers benefit disproportionately from the policy benefits of the new agrarianism, lesser agricultural producers are being deceived and exploited. Others argue that the prosperity of the agricultural sector has benefited and will continue to benefit most agricultural producers sufficiently to warrant their supporting new agrarian movements, policies, and candidates. In our view, the ideology and class character of the new agrarianism have varied and are difficult to determine. They are likely to remain subject to the vagaries of leadership and historical conjunctures. In any case, it seems clear that unlike Indian politics in the first quarter-century after independence, Indian politics in the 1980s and beyond will reflect the electorate's predominantly agricultural and rural character.

Objective Conditions of the Rural Poor

Countryside versus city, sectoral rather than class conflict, became in the 1980s the leading manifestation of agrarian politics at the national and state levels. At the same time, the claim of the new agrarianism to speak for a collective sectoral interest was challenged by the question of whether agricultural politics can be both prosectoral and propoor.

We address this question by examining, in this section and the next, the objective conditions and the politics of the rural poor.

Despite the several decades during which national and international politics have been concerned with the issue of poverty—abolish poverty, growth with equity, meeting basic human needs, a new international economic order—at the all-India level poverty's basic parameters have not changed much since independence. The proportion of those living below the poverty line has remained more or less stable although there are some signs of improvement in the mid-eighties; the physical quality of life index (PQLI) has risen considerably since 1950, but not fast enough to improve substantially India's standing in world rankings; rural income inequality, as measured by Gini coefficients, has diminished slightly between 1957–58 and 1973–74, as the top quartile's proportion declined by 2 percent and the bottom's increased by a like amount; and marked state and local disparities have persisted, despite marginal shifts in some leading and lagging regions.

Among Indian officials and policy intellectuals, the most commonly used definition of the poverty line has been the expenditure required to buy a conventionally defined minimum caloric intake. In 1962, the Planning Commission adopted as its measure Rs. 20 per person per month at 1960–61 all-India prices, an amount that corresponds with the Dandekar and Rath "norm" of 2,250 calories per day.[80] Applying this consumption expenditure criterion, government and most policy intellectuals at the time and since have placed about half of India's population below the poverty line.

In recent years, the Dandekar and Rath caloric intake–based criterion has been subjected to several telling critiques. In 1982, McAlpin and Morris questioned the validity of 2,250 calories per day as a "universal" norm by pointing out that it was originated and tested in middle-class meat-eating populations of Western industrial societies.[81] P. V. Sukhatme had already pointed out in 1980 that "when correct meaning is put on requirement and allowance is made for intra-individual variation, it will be found that 15 to 20 percent of the population can be considered as malnourished for want of adequate income," a finding also supported by T. N. Srinivasan.[82] Not only was the conventional caloric minimum of 2,250 seen as a doubtful criterion, but the use of standardized per capita income data in relation to minimum expenditure levels for food was also subject to serious challenge. For example, Morris argued in 1979 that if the World Bank per capita income data for India were corrected to take account of purchasing-power parity, at least 50 percent of those placed under the poverty line would move above it.[83]

But even if only 25 rather than about 50 percent of Indians were living below the poverty line, the poverty issue would remain an important one for agrarian policy and politics. Parties that now compete for support from the poor would continue to do so, leaders of the new agrarianism would still face the problem of making the prosperity of the agricultural sector relevant to the poor, and adherents of the polarization thesis and class politics would still have to look for signs that the proportion of those living in poverty remained constant or was increasing.

Poverty as a policy or class issue is one thing; the politics of the poverty line is another. Mrs. Gandhi's Congress government might have welcomed the opportunity to mitigate India's negative image abroad as the land of the poor and enhance the Congress party's image at home as the friend and protector of the poor by engaging in one grand statistical act of state that reduced poverty by half. But doing so might also have entailed risks and costs. Those who claim that India has "graduated" from the ranks of Southern poor states (e.g., the Reagan administration) and should fund its planned investments and foreign exchange needs from market-rate commercial bank loans rather than from multilateral concessional assistance would welcome such an act. The credibility of the Gandhi government's rhetoric as the friend and protector of the poor would be put at risk too. Whatever the merits of reducing the proportion of the poor on statistical, expenditure, or caloric intake grounds, the reality of mass poverty would render its claims hollow and strengthen its opponents' arguments that the Congress-I leadership talks left but acts right. Left parties and many policy intellectuals would greet with deep suspicion an act of technical legerdemain that, to them, understated the extent of poverty in India.

Differences over identifying the poor and the poverty line have not yet spilled over into the literature on the incidence of poverty. Modified versions of the standards adopted by the Planning Commission in 1962 continue to inform most analyses. One of the most widely used studies of the incidence of rural poverty in India was done by Montek Ahluwalia while he was at the World Bank.[84] According to Ahluwalia, there is not statistically "significant evidence for asserting a trend increase or decrease in rural poverty over the period [1956–57 to 1973–74] as a whole." Within that period, he found a decline in the incidence of rural poverty up to the early 1960s, then an increase that peaked in 1967–68, and a decline thereafter.[85] When the series began in 1956–57, the proportion below the poverty line was 54.1 percent and, at its end it was 46.1 percent, with a low in 1960–61 of 38.9 percent and a high in 1966–67 of 56.6.[86] Only two states (Assam and West Bengal) showed a significant trend increase in poverty and only two (Andhra Pradesh and Tamil Nadu) a trend decline.

It is likely that the poverty measure has shown improvement since this study. The seventh five-year plan, published in 1985, showed a decline, based on NSS data, from 48.3 percent below the poverty line in 1977–78 to 37.4 percent in 1983–84. The caveat that this may prove a short-term change, as did some earlier declines, should deter premature optimism.[87]

Ahluwalia also found upon analyzing Gini coefficients applied to NSS data on consumption expenditure that there was "a significant *decrease* (author's emphasis) in relative inequality for India as a whole and for seven of fourteen states."[88]

Identifying the poor and establishing a poverty line on the basis of consumption expenditures (particularly on food) without taking into account consumption based on access to public goods and services (e.g., education, health care) as they are affected by subsidies and transfer payments may give a misleading picture of the meaning and incidence of poverty. Morris David Morris developed the PQLI to measure the extent to which minimum human needs are being met.[89] The PQLI eschews ethnocentric measures (e.g., telephones or steel per capita) that imply only one method of meeting human needs; it measures outputs (e.g., welfare) not inputs (e.g., income); it is sensitive to the distribution of benefits; and it is subject to synchronic and diachronic comparisons within and among states. Of many intercorrelated indicators considered, three relatively independent and widely available ones were chosen: infant mortality per thousand live births, life expectancy at age one, and literacy of those aged 15 and over.[90] These three indexes were averaged to produce the PQLI.

When applied to the incidence of poverty in India, the PQLI tells a different story than consumption expenditure on food. Whereas Ahluwalia found that the incidence of poverty based on caloric intake at the all-India level remained more or less steady between 1957–58 and 1973–74 and the proportion of the national product spent on private final consumption for food increased by only 10 percent between 1970–71 and 1979–80 (from Rs. 190 to 210 crores),[91] India's PQLI almost tripled (+ 285 percent) between 1950 and 1970, from 14 to 40.[92]

The discrepancy between income-based consumption measures and the PQLI is even more marked at the state level, where poverty as an objective determinant of politics and policy is more readily translated into subjective determinants of social action. Kerala, a state with a history of progressive social policy, presents the most striking example of this discrepancy. By one reckoning, Kerala, distinguished by high literacy rates and social welfare (including Communist) governments, in 1970–71 ranked eleventh in net per capital state domestic product but first in PQLI (1971 measures).[93] At 100, Kerala's PQLI was 38.4 points higher than that of the second ranked state, Punjab (61.6), whose per capita net state domestic product at Rs. 1,030 in 1970–71 ranked first, and was almost twice as much as Kerala's (Rs. 564). Again, although Kerala's per capita state domestic product was only 16 percent higher than fifteenth-ranked Uttar Pradesh's (Rs. 564 vs. Rs. 486), its PQLI was almost twenty times greater than bottom-ranked Uttar Pradesh's (100 vs. 5.3).

If per capita–based measures of income do not necessarily reveal the nature and levels of poverty because they fail to penetrate the quality of life, they also do not tell us much about how the presence or absence of income streams affects the incidence of poverty. Money income has a host of determinants, including the availability and duration of employment, wage levels, the range of income sources, access to new technologies and inputs, and regional variations in economic development. Although we have dealt with these income-determining factors elsewhere, we highlight findings about them here as they relate to the incidence of poverty. Our purpose in this section is to provide the background for our analysis, in the concluding section of this chapter, of the prospects for political mobilization by the poor.

The 1981 census figures show that, in the face of an increase of 80 million in India's rural population, a slightly higher proportion "worked for a major part of the year preceding enumeration" than in 1971 (33.09 vs. 33.44 percent) and that the "work participation rate" ("main workers" plus "marginal workers") was 4.13 percent higher in 1981 than in 1971 (39.46 vs. 35.33). Both increases reflect marked increases in the proportion of rural women working, 3.05 percent (27.6 to 40.4 million) for main workers and 7.97 for marginal workers.[94] Earlier, using different concepts and data, Raj Krishna had estimated that rural unemployment and underemployment declined between 1958 and 1972–73.[95] These data on work and employment indicate that rural poverty has not increased in recent years. Indeed, the increased proportions of work participation by women may add to the family incomes of the poor.

Wage rates of agricultural workers are another determinant of rural income and the incidence of rural poverty. The discussion of wage rates in the early 1970s occurred in the context of the green revolution and the assumption by many political economists that it would accelerate the polarization they associated with the spread of commercial agriculture. The new technology, particularly mechanization, was expected to displace labor and lower wage rates as more workers competed for fewer jobs. Since the early 1970s, the discussion of wage rates has become more complex as regional analyses of advanced and backward agricultural contexts revealed the effects of social policy and long-term consequences of higher productivity. For example, Pranab Bardhan reported in 1970 that in Kerala, one of the states least affected by the green revolution but most affected by progressive social policies (including a concern for minimum wages for agricultural and plantation workers), real wage rates had risen between 1960–61 and 1967–68. On the other hand, in Punjab and Haryana, states most affected by the initial phases of the green revolution, real wages in the same period had not increased. Subsequent studies, however, including another by Pranab Bardhan in 1973, revealed that the longer-term effects of increased agricultural productivity included a rise in real wages.[96] Deepak Lal, writing in 1976, reported that between 1956–57 and 1964–65, a period just preceding the onset of the green revolution, rural real wages rose in seven states and fell in eight but that between 1963–64 and 1970–71, a period that included inter alia the beginning phases of the green revolution, rural real wages rose in all states except Orissa.[97] Kalpana Bardhan showed a strong positive correlation of irrigation and multiple cropping with wage rates and income.[98] The effect of these and other studies was to cast doubt on the proposition that improved agricultural productivity would have a negative effect on agricultural wages. Indeed, Ahluwalia's previously reported findings for 1956–57 through 1973–74—that "improved agricultural performance is definitely associated with reductions in the incidence of poverty" and that "there has been a significant *decrease* in relative inequality for India as a whole"—suggest the reverse.[99]

Agricultural wage rates by themselves do not tell us much about annual income. Annual income depends on the amount of employment (e.g., the number of days worked per year; and the number of jobs held at a time) and the availability of alternative income streams. Indeed, as the Kerala instance makes clear, high wage rates can be a mixed blessing. Kerala agricultural workers tend to be unionized and to enjoy high, state-enforced wage rates.[100] Under the Kerala Agricultural Workers Act of 1974, their employment is guaranteed by a provision of the law that requires employers to employ workers confirmed under the act. Job security, improved working conditions, and high wages have not, however, resulted in high-quality, committed labor. Quite the reverse; they have led to a decline in labor quality and productivity. The high cost and low quality and productivity of labor has led employers to switch from labor-intensive rice cultivation to less labor-intensive commercial crops, to mechanize, and to evade the consequences of "socialism in one state" by hiring cheaper, more compliant labor from across Kerala's borders.

In the face of state-enforced higher wages and progressive social policies in Kerala, the average number of days worked per year by agricultural laborers in the late 1970s was 99, nowhere near enough (in the absence of other income sources) to maintain workers above the poverty line, and far below the all-India norm of 200 days per year.[101] In Punjab, by contrast, growth of agricultural productivity has been associated with increased employment. In the years preceding the green revolution, the average number of days that male laborers worked per year increased from 185 in 1950–51 to 282 in 1964–65.[102] Since the green revolution, we infer that the number of days worked per year has been at least 282. Our inference is drawn from the heavy migration of agricultural laborers into Punjab in response to the growth of labor demand,[103] and from Punjab's 38 percent increase between 1971 and 1981 in the number of employed agricultural laborers.[104] This growth in employment occurred in the face of tractorization, which has advanced faster in Punjab than elsewhere in India. Because tractors facilitate double and triple cropping and other forms of crop intensification, their use tends to generate rather than reduce employment. More labor is needed for cultivation and agricultural tasks, maintaining and repairing equipment, transportation, and other services.[105]

Rural poverty is in part the result of a radical decline in the private welfare benefits and subsistence security that many laborers once enjoyed as attached members of rural households. The employment and welfare insecurity of the rural poor constitutes a hidden asymmetry between the organized industrial and service sectors and the unorganized agricultural sector of the postindependence Indian economy. Insecurity is hard to measure because it involves qualitative dimensions of employer-employee relations. As impersonal market and profit calculations replace dominance, they dissolve the sentimental bonds and mutual obligations linking master and servant or patron and client. Agricultural laborers become "free" but insecure as they leave the fold of household economies to enter labor and wage good markets. The private welfare benefits and subsistence security that masters and patrons extend to servants and dependents for loyal service are replaced by uncertain wage employment. As labor becomes a commodity that figures prominently in the cost and quality of production, the private welfare aspect of traditional interdependence disappears. In the absence of public welfare programs for the aged, sick, hurt, disabled, and unemployed, the dissolution of traditional obligations leaves employees and their families at the mercy of what their wage incomes can buy in consumer and services markets.

Ironically, as Herring has shown for Kerala, state surrogates for household and patrimonial welfare and security have not improved the lot of the poor or the productivity of paddy agriculture. Under state-imposed work rules and public welfare programs, agricultural laborers cannot be fired, but neither can they quit. Minimum wages are high, but annual incomes have declined with the number of days worked per year. Without traditional, market, or collective incentives, labor produces less and costs more. In the face of all-India increases in agricultural employment and production, Kerala's paddy economy is in decline.[106]

The proposition that the spread of commercial agriculture, particularly after the green revolution, increases insecurity by dissolving patrimonial relations between landowning employers and attached workers has been pursued by several scholars, including Epstein in Karnataka, Breman in South Gujarat, and Herring in the Palghat district of Kerala.[107] They confirm that commercial agriculture does indeed dissolve traditional bonds and mutual obligations, but they question whether insecurity is necessarily the universal consequence. In one form or another, each found that in some cases a process of "repatronization" was apparent. Sometimes, its consequences served the interests of both employers and employees and, in doing so, the collective interest of the agricultural sector. For example, profit-oriented cash crop farmers in search of reliable, committed labor have established neopatrimonial relations with their employees through "gifts," accessible credit, job security, and other private welfare arrangements. Sheila Bhalla, who regards repatronization as primarily a device for making workers dependent, discusses a new type of long-term labor contract in Haryana designed to provide reliable, high-quality labor.[108] Marshall Bouton's work in the Thanjavur district of Tamil Nadu revealed that a significant number of workers preferred attached to casual labor status because of the employment and welfare security that attached status was thought to provide.[109]

Some would argue that repatronization is a mask for extractive neofeudal relations between dominant landowners and dependent workers. No doubt many workers find themselves in relationships that are too asymmetrical to allow for bargaining based on countervailing power, much less for sharing the benefits of productivity increases. However, neopatrimonial ideology and arrangements do not, as aspects of industrial relations in Japan show, foreclose conflicts of interest between employers and employees. The bargaining power of wage laborers is strongest where productivity and profit depend on reliable, high-quality labor and where mobilized agricultural producers can affect politics and policy outcomes. "Repatronization," by making wage workers household surrogates who share in the collective good of a production unit, can serve the interests of both employers and employees in commercial, profit-oriented agriculture and promote agrarian prosperity. On the other hand, by multiplying the bonds of mutual dependence between employers and employees, the new security can also diminish the capacity of employees to press for their share of the gains of productivity.

Above we have cited studies by Raj Krishna, Chadha and Bhalla, and others that suggest that small farmers, while not as advantaged as large, have come to participate in the new technology to a significant extent.[110] Here we address one critical factor affecting the use of new technology and improved inputs by small and marginal cultivators: the availability of institutional credit. Between 1950–51 and 1970–71, the proportion of rural credit given by moneylenders declined from 77 to 50 percent, while that made available by instructional lenders (primarily the twenty nationalized commercial banks and cooperatives) increased from 7 to 30 percent.[111] Since then, institutional credit's proportion of rural credit has continued to grow. Because the goal of reaching "weaker sections" who have few assets to pledge has animated public policy since bank nationalization in 1969, institutional lenders have had to entertain unconventional, riskier banking practices. Nationalized commercial banks are mandated to provide specific proportions of credit to priority sectors, of which the agricultural sector constitutes a significant component (42 percent).[112] The Small Farmers' Development Agency and the more recent Integrated Rural Development Program specifically targeted small and marginal farmers. But they have not received credit in proportion to their share of agricultural households because extant physical assets rather than anticipated production (e.g., crop loans) continue to be the most important criterion for advancing loans. Because the sixth five-year plan found that small and marginal farmers' share of agricultural credit was "short of needs," the plan document called for raising the proportion available to "weaker sections" to 50 percent.[113]

Table 42 suggests, as might be expected, that poor cultivators are faring proportionately less well than those with more assets. Nevertheless, the data suggest that the effort to supply credit to the weaker sections has gained ground. Table 42 gives a breakdown by holding size of credit advanced by commercial banks and cooperatives for short- and long-term loans. (The holding size breakdowns are less finegrained for cooperatives than for commercial banks.) The proportion of short-term loans (crop loans and production inputs) channeled to smallholders (2.5 acres and below) in 1979–80 was 34 percent,[114] a proportion equivalent to their share (33 percent) of agricultural-sector house-

TABLE 42
Credit Shares of Poor Cultivators

Size of Holding (Acres)[a]	% of All Households (1971–72)	% of Short-Term Loans (1979–80)	% of (Medium/Long-) Term Loans (1979–80)	% of All Loans[b] (1979–80)
Scheduled Commercial Banks				
Up to 2.5	33	34	12	—
2.5+–5	16	23	13	—
5+–10	13	21	19	—
Above 10	11	22	56	—
Landless households (0)	27	—	—	—
Cooperative Banks (PACs)				
Tenant cultivators agricultural labor, etc. (0)	—[c]	—	—	4
Up to 5	49	—	—	34
Above 5	32	—	—	62

SOURCE: The figures for scheduled commercial banks are from Reserve Bank of India, *Report on Currency and Finance, 1981–82,* (Bombay, 1983), vol. 2, statements 41 and 42, pp. 58–61; the figures for cooperative banks, from statement 43, p. 62; and the figures for primary agricultural credit societies (PACs), from table 43, pp. 81–82.

Notes: The percentage of all households is taken from our table 40. Short-term loans (including crop loans) are given for purchase of production inputs, such as seeds, fertilizers, and pesticides, and to meet the costs of cultivation, which include labor charges for carrying out agricultural operations, irrigation charges, etc. These loans normally are repayable within a period of twelve months and in certain cases within fifteen and eighteen months, the repayment schedule being related to the harvesting and marketing of the particular crop. Term (medium- or long-term) loans are granted for development purposes, such as development of irrigation potential, purchase of tractors and other agricultural implements and machinery, improvement of land, development of plantations, constructions of godowns and cold-storage facilities, and purchase of pump set/oil engines, plow animals (bullocks), etc. The period of payment of these loans generally extends from three to ten years. Table 43 in *Report on Currency and Finance* presents figures in hectares. We count 2 hectares as 5 acres (1 hectare = 2.47 acres).

[a]It is not clear whether the size holdings given in statements 41 and 42 of the *Report on Currency and Finance* are legal or operational holdings.

[b]Sixty-eight percent of loans from cooperatives in 1980–81 were short-term loans (*Report on Currency and Finance,* vol. 1, p. 175).

[c]Our table 40 does not give figures for tenant cultivators, only for landless households (27 percent).

holds. On the other hand, smallholders' share of long-term loans was only 12 percent, about a third their proportion of households. Cooperatives, more subject to the influence of local elites than commercial banks staffed by career professionals, did less well in reaching small and marginal cultivators: although 49 percent of all households, those 5 acres or under obtained only 34 percent of cooperative bank loans,[115] households above 5 acres (only 32 percent of households) received 62 percent of loans. Larger holders also did better than medium-sized holders in obtaining commercial bank credit. While those in the 2.5 + −5 and the 5 + −10 acre categories received credit in rough proportion to their shares of agricultural households, those with more than 10 acres received short- and long-term loans at proportions twice and five times their proportion of households, respectively. These findings suggest parallels between small and marginal cultivators' access to credit and to new technology and improved inputs: they are disadvantaged in relation to more prosperous farmers, but they are still significant beneficiaries of both the new technology and the credit required to use it.

The future of government-subsidized agricultural credit targeted to the poor remains obscure as the problem of nonrecovery mounts. Overdue loans in cooperatives and public-sector commercial banks were 42 and 50.20 percent of demand at the end of June, 1978, a situation that does not augur well for the future.[116] Like the cost of inputs, including water and electricity, the cost of credit to public exchequers, particularly those at the state level, is subject to powerful and mounting political pressure by organized agricultural producers to limit and even reduce costs of production.

Regional disparities are another important determinant of rural poverty. Unlike regional poverty in advanced industrial societies, which results from structural unemployment in industries with obsolescent technologies (e.g., shipbuilding and the manufacture of textiles, shoes, and more recently, automobiles and steel), regional poverty in India is associated with primary backwardness and the deterioration of the traditional household sector. India's advanced regions have benefited from the cumulative effects of colonial and/or postindependence investment in agriculture, industry, human capital, and infrastructure, while its poor regions, hindered by endowment, social structure, or politics, have not. Whether in irrigation, power, education, communications, or industry, the skewed regional distribution of public and private investment has been a principal cause of differences in regional prosperity.

In 1970–71 and in 1977–78, the same five states (Punjab, Maharashtra, Haryana, Gujarat, and West Bengal) ranked at the top among India's seventeen "large" states in per capita net state domestic product, the same four (Bihar, Orissa, Uttar Pradesh, and Madhya Pradesh) ranked at the bottom, and seven (Karnataka, Himachal Pradesh, Tamil Nadu, Andhra Pradesh, Kerala, Rajasthan, and Jammu and Kashmir) remained in roughly the same positions in the middle. Stability in regional disparities is also evident in the persistent ratios between the top and bottom per capita state domestic product in 1970–71 and 1977–78 (2.6 vs. 2.7).[117] Given a 3.8 percent average annual growth rate over thirty years, it may be commendable that regional disparities in India, unlike those in many developing countries, have not become more pronounced. But it remains worth noting that, like the incidence of poverty, the regional distribution of prosperity and poverty has not varied much over these years.

Krishna Bharadwaj attributes the relative backwardness of regions such as eastern Uttar Pradesh, some parts of Tamil Nadu, and Madhya Pradesh, where a relatively active household sector exists, to the absence of industrial (nonhousehold) employment. Bharadwaj relates the absolute backwardness of large parts of Bihar, Orissa, and the eastern region of West Bengal, where there is some industrial employment, to a decline in household employment.[118] Overall she finds that productively invested agricultural surpluses are a precondition for industrial development. A general level of well-being "creates effective demand" for industry and agriculture to grow. Punjab, Haryana, and Gujarat are leading examples of these positive effects while Bihar, Orissa, eastern Uttar Pradesh, and parts of Rajasthan and Madhya Pradesh exemplify how poverty fosters moneylending and trading at the expense of productive investment.

The practical effects of these differences are visible in the incidence of rural poverty: in the agriculturally prosperous states of Punjab, Haryana and Gujarat, only 23 and 35 percent of the population was under the poverty line in 1973–74, compared with 58 and 66 percent in the agriculturally stagnant states of Orissa and West Bengal.[119]

Within states such as Karnataka and Maharashtra, which combine advanced industrial and agricultural production with poor unirrigated cultivation, disparities can be very sharp. For example, eleven districts of Karnataka grew at an annual compounded rate of 4.5 percent between 1962–65 and 1970–73, while six experienced no growth.[120] Because agricultural production differs from industrial in that it varies markedly by microregion, there is often a powerful relationship between local conditions and rural poverty.

Conventional modernization theories often posit that the "solution" for rural poverty is the urbanization associated with the migration of agricultural workers from the countryside to the city to work in factories and offices. In England, in the face of resistance by rural producers to factory employment, enclosures helped to push the rural poor off the land and into industrial employment.[121] In Germany, early industrialization in the Rhineland helped captive land workers on Prussian estates to become "free" wage workers. The less attended to "solutions" to rural poverty found in Switzerland, Sweden, and Norway involved less urbanization because new forms of primary and processing production kept workers employed in the countryside.[122]

Despite the expectations of India's second and third five-year plans, urban industrial and service employment has not become a solution for rural poverty. Since the first decade of this century, the proportion of the agricultural to the total work force has remained stubbornly stuck at about 70 percent. Even the small decline to 67 percent in the proportion of the agricultural work force reported in the 1981 census has been disputed.[123] Small declines between 1971 and 1981 of 27–25 and 43–42 percent in the proportions of agricultural laborers and cultivators in the agricultural work force do not suggest a significant shift by agricultural producers to other types of employment.[124] Population increases that are not likely to abate soon have greatly increased the absolute number of agricultural workers, both laborers and cultivators.[125] In the medium term at least, the solution to rural poverty lies on the land and in the countryside, not in urban industrial and service-sector employment.

Mobilization of the Rural Poor

In the previous section, we addressed the question of who are the rural poor. Here we ask, what are the determinants and varieties of their mobilization? Mobilization of the rural poor is often portrayed by observers as historically inevitable or morally desirable. Often they conflate the two; what is inevitable is desirable and what is desirable is inevitable. The historical record and contemporary circumstances of the rural poor suggest that the causes of mobilization are too indeterminate to be readily predicted by scientific theory and its consequences for the rural poor too uncertain to be unequivocally recommended on moral grounds. As actors confronted with risks and uncertainty, the poor often find compliant adaptation more rational than collective action on their own behalf. Sometimes their response is anomic apathy. We take mobilization to be an exceptional response to rural poverty, a possibility to be explained, not a probability to be anticipated.[126]

Further complicating the explanation of mobilization by the rural poor is the reified nature of the unit of analysis. Global characteristics, such as low income and low consumption, mask diverse social and economic conditions and world views. Of the rural poor who find employment, many work for wages as casual laborers; others do so as attached laborers or on contract. Still others possess a small holding. Landless households, most of whose members are laborers, constitute about 27 percent of agricultural households; small cultivators, who work for wages as well as cultivate, constitute about 33 percent. But many small cultivators' perception of their interest and world view lead them to identify with self-employed independent cultivators (about 34 percent).[127]

Divided from each other by economic interest and world view and facing larger, more powerful groups of self-employed independent cultivators and large landowners, the rural poor are not in a position to become a dominant, hegemonic, or revolutionary class in the agricultural sector of the economy. Wage workers in agriculture and those in the organized sector of the economy have not responded to ideological constructions that describe them as a homogeneous class. Nor do poor and middle peasants perceive themselves as natural allies of urban workers in struggles against capitalism, imperialism, or feudalism. Indeed, the emergent cleavage of the 1980s between countryside and city pits urban producers and consumers against rural.

Mobilization of the rural poor has not been the reflexive result of nationally aggregated global characteristics or putative historically determined class formations. Nor has it occurred automatically as the result of favorable local objective determinants or historical conjunctures. Such determinants can be necessary but not sufficient conditions for collective action by the poor. When mobilization has occurred, it has been mediated by leaders' social and ideological constructions of varied local conditions, historical circumstances, and ideological currents. In the face of adverse local power and palpable risks, objective determinants are not self-actuating or self-executing. Mobilization of the rural poor has occurred when known and trusted leaders have been able to translate favorable conditions into ideological and policy terms that capture people's sense of who and what they are and what they are prepared to risk. The rural poor have not readily or often responded to the idiom or goals of class ideology.[128] But they will remain an important component in Indian politics because they can be mobilized in particular contexts and historical moments, and because national, sectoral, regional, and class organizations will continue to vie for their support.

How leaders relate objective determinants and historical conjunctures to actors' perceptions is best observed in local contexts. Here, we look at two sets of studies: one in Thanjavur district, Tamil Nadu, where mobilizations have occurred; the other in diverse locations in the North, where adaptive compliance or anomic apathy has prevailed.[129]

Thanjavur district in Tamil Nadu has attracted mobilization research because of its history of agrarian radicalism. Studies by Bouton, Mencher, Alexander, and Beteille attempted to account for the presence, goals, and intensity of mobilization.[130] They attended to variables such as the effect of technology, particularly as it is interwoven with and modified by ecological conditions (e.g., irrigation, type of soil);[131] the distribution and nature of rights in land (e.g., self-employed cultivators, tenants, landless wage laborers employed by landowners); historical conjunctures (e.g., war, monsoon failures that result in price rises, new technology); and the presence of active, credible leaders and organizations. The district's considerable ecological and socioeconomic variations make it possible to assess the significance and interactions of a broad range of variables in a limited area with common political institutions and processes. Objective ecological and socioeconomic conditions tend to covary systematically between *talukas* (administrative subunits) that coincide roughly with the Old Delta area in the north and east and the New Delta in the south and west of the district.

In the wet (irrigated) double-cropped paddy lands of the Old Delta, large concentrations of agricultural laborers work for a few large landowners who do not personally cultivate. This area overlaps with *talukas* whose percentage of agricultural laborers in the work force reaches 50 to 70 percent. Among the laborers, the proportion of Harijans (ex-untouchables) reaches 60 to 80 percent.[132] The result is a rare degree of congruence of class and caste under conditions in which the concentration of agricultural workers approximates those found in industrial production.

The Old Delta's radicalism contrasts with the New Delta's moderation. Unlike irrigated coastal and central areas of the Old Delta, the upland and dry cultivation of the New Delta features family-operated tenant or owner holdings that rely on their own and household labor more than on wage labor. Among wage laborers, the proportion of Harijans in the New Delta is lower than in the Old Delta. Bipolarity and inequality are less pronounced in the New than in the Old Delta because caste and class asymmetries are less severe and congruent. The New Delta lacks the upper-caste (mostly Brahman) noncultivating owners and the many Harijan landless wage workers characteristic of the Old Delta. In the New Delta, middle- and lower-caste independent cultivators using their own and household labor employ proportionately fewer wage laborers than in the Old Delta. Mencher's findings in nearby Chingleput district,[133] where small holdings operated by tenants or owners on the basis of their own and household labor are the norm, confirm that conditions like those found in the New Delta are less polarized and radical than those found in Thanjavur's Old Delta.[134]

Why has agrarian radicalism been less evident in the New Delta and Chingleput district than in the Old Delta?[135] Initially, objective determinants seem to have been decisive. Bouton's survey findings show that in the Old Delta, the objectively least secure and most exploited workers, casual landless laborers who hire out for wages on a daily basis, support the Communist parties in much higher proportions than the objectively somewhat better-off landless laborers who work on a contractual (seasonal or annual) basis, the laborers who cultivate some rented land (labor tenants), and the laborers who own and cultivate some land (labor owners).[136] Bouton's analysis also shows that the political consciousness and solidarity of landless laborers can counter the tendency of dwarf holders to think of themselves as tenant or owner cultivators rather than as wage workers. In the Old Delta, 90 percent of the Communist parties' supporters and members are landless wage workers. Their political consciousness and solidarity affect labor tenants and labor owners, whose participation in a large concentrated labor force, common caste status, and marginal involvement in cultivation outweigh "any conservative pull that their attachment to the land might exert."[137]

Both caste and labor status are important correlates of support for and membership in the Communist parties. In the coastal and central areas of the Old Delta, all Communist party members were Harijans, i.e., no backward- or forward-caste members sampled were Communist party members. Indeed, the association between Harijan status and Communist party membership is stronger than the association between being a casual laborer and Communist party membership. At the same time, not all Harijans among those sampled in Thanjavur were Communist party members. But where economic conflict between workers and noncultivating (mostly Brahman) owners was endemic, Harijans overwhelmingly supported the Communists. Under these conditions, caste identity became "the major factor underlying Communist mobilization in Thanjavur" by providing the "idiom and cement for radical mobilization."[138]

When and how did these predisposing conditions in Thanjavur's Old Delta result in mobilization? How were necessary objective determinants transformed into sufficient subjective ones, i.e., how did causes become reasons for vulnerable and risk-averse poor Harijan laborers and marginal cultivators to act politically? Agrarian radicalism began with the politically organized conflicts of the 1940s and re-emerged in the late 1960s and early 1970s. But the Old Delta's objective conditions that favored radicalism also obtained in the 1950s, 1970s and 1980s when electoral politics and bargaining pluralism rather than agrarian radicalism prevailed. What circumstances, beyond objective conditions, precipitated radical mobilization at some times and not at others? The answer is historical conjunctures and leadership.

We start with the historical conjunctures that transformed Thanjavur district's socioeconomic and ecological circumstances in the late 1960s and early 1970s and then turn to how Communist party leadership during World War II established a base in the Old Delta that enabled it to articulate the reasons and organizational means for radical and electoral mobilization. The introduction in the mid- and late 1960s of the new technology associated with the green revolution, by advancing the fortunes of commercial agriculture, destabilized an already shaky social equilibrium. The effects of new technology were refracted in many ways by the prism of varying land, production, and caste relations. For example, the effect of the new technology on tenant- and owner-operated small holdings in the New Delta or Chingleput was not easily translatable into reasons for radical mobilization. Because small operators used new inputs as much per unit as medium and large operators,[139] the uneven gains to large and small operators encountered in other contexts were not marked. On the other hand, when the introduction of new inputs in Thanjavur district's highly polarized Old Delta enhanced commercialization and crop intensity, it exacerbated conflict. Workers demanded higher wages and more workdays, and land owners resisted these demands by importing labor and introducing tractors.

Wage disputes in the Old Delta proved more intractable than elsewhere. Unlike in other areas of the district where several forms of employment and sources of income were available, wage labor in paddy production was the only work available in the Old Delta and then for only a few months of the year during the harvest. Workers' economic survival depended on the level of wages paid during these few months. Economic conflict in the Old Delta was also affected by the low average but high peak demand for labor; there was no or little work most of the year but a shortage of labor at harvesttime when it was most needed. Labor scarcity during harvesting accentuated differences of interest between laborers and owners and raised the level of disputes and conflict. Owners faced laborers when laborers' bargaining advantages were greatest; by 1972, prevalent wage rates in the Old Delta were the highest in Tamil Nadu.[140] Unlike in other areas of Thanjavur where wage bargaining took place in the context of productivity increases that allowed differences over wages to be compromised, owners in the Old Delta faced severe limits on total productivity that made paying a larger share of production costs to labor a matter of owners' economic survival.

Another historical conjuncture, the poor monsoons of 1965 and 1966, preceded and paralleled the introduction of new technology and enhanced commercialization. Their effects on the prices of essential commodities were both immediate and delayed. The monsoon failures led to price rises followed by demands for higher wages by agricultural workers. The combined effects of commercialization and price rises reached a climax of sorts in December 1968 at Kilvenmani, a Harijan village, when forty-two landless laborers and family members burned to death after they were confined to a hut that was set on fire. The laborers were members of the CPI-M's union, the Tamil Nadu Tillers Association; the farmers who attacked Kilvenmani were followers of the Thanjavur Paddy Producers Association. The tillers' association had called a strike in support of higher wages, and the paddy producers had responded by importing "volunteers" to break the strike. In the conflict that followed, one of the volunteers was killed, and the paddy producers retaliated with the night raid on Kilvenmani.[141]

The Kilvenmani atrocity had an electric effect on national consciousness. The first atrocity to be interpreted by policy intellectuals and politicians in terms of class and caste conflict, it established a framework of meaning and language that has shaped political rhetoric, policy analysis, and scholarly interpretation since then. The national response to Kilvenmani anticipated the accelerating pace of anti-Harijan atrocities that was highlighted nine years later when Indira Gandhi launched a political comeback by rushing to Belchhi, a Harijan village in Bihar, where seventeen landless laborers were murdered in September 1977.[142]

Historical conjunctures help to explain radical mobilization. Like favorable objective determinants, they are necessary but not sufficient conditions. The agrarian radical tradition and politics of Thanjavur's Old Delta, like radicalism in Kerala and West Bengal, cannot be explained without taking leadership into account. In this respect, the Communist parties of Thanjavur have been essential. It was the Communists who translated objective into subjective determinants by raising the agroeconomic issues that lay at the heart of the conflict between Harijan workers and high-caste landowners. But the extent and effectiveness of their translation varied over time. In the 1940s and 1960s, Communist leadership produced agrarian radicalism; in the 1950s, 1970s, and 1980s, it produced cross-class politics and policies. Why?

Variations in Communist party strategy and variations in the state's support or opposition to it help account for the fluctuating fortunes in radicalism in Thanjavur.[143] The party's line, in turn, responded to shifting international, national, and Tamil Nadu political environments. As the party's strategies changed over the decades, they affected its construction and use of objective determinants in Thanjavur.

A historical conjuncture, World War II, helped the CPI to establish its hold in the Old Delta. In 1939–40, Communist-led strikes by Harijan workers and tenants for higher wages and shares of produce succeeded when the British raj's provincial government, eager to maintain production in wartime, not only lent its support to their demands but accorded unprecedented equal treatment to Harijan labor leaders in its arbitration proceedings.[144] These early state-aided successes amplified the party's credibility and appeals. After Hitler's forces attacked the Soviet Union in June 1941, the CPI broke with the Indian National Congress for not supporting the British raj's war against Nazi Germany. While Congress leaders were in jail and its organizational activities at a standstill, the CPI received sympathetic treatment from government. Continued state-aided bargaining successes after Germany attacked the Soviet Union further enhanced the CPI's standing among the Old Delta's workers and tenants.[145]

In 1948, soon after the war's end and at the inception of independence, the CPI concluded that "a revolutionary upsurge was in motion in India" and called for armed conflict and the seizure of power.[146] Thanjavur's Old Delta, where the party was well established, was one of several areas from which it launched armed insurrections. Like the party's larger, more successful armed struggle in the Telengana area of princely Hyderabad, the Thanjavur rebellion was crushed by the armed forces of the newly independent Indian state. Nevertheless, by the late 1940s, party leaders and cadres in the Old Delta had come to be seen as heroic defenders of workers' and tenants' class and caste interests.

The 1950s were a decade of adjustment. The party's 1951 decision to try "constitutional communism" and parliamentary politics was rewarded in the 1952 and 1957 elections by successes in Thanjavur, Kerala, and elsewhere. It also encountered competition in its role as the party of the rural masses when Congress party governments in Tamil

Nadu undercut its appeal by enacting progressively more favorable protenant legislation in 1952, 1955, and 1956.[147]

In the 1960s, the party's strategy continued to be shaped by Tamil Nadu's changing political environment. With the rise of the DMK (Dravidian Progressive Federation),[148] the regional politics of cultural and linguistic nationalism crowded class ideology and issues to one side. The hold of DMK and—after its split in 1973—AIADMK cultural and film celebrities on mass imagination and opinion[149] and the repudiation of "northern" Congress rule after the central government's heavy-handed effort in 1965 to "impose" Hindi were signs of the ascendance of regional cultural nationalism.[150]

Agrarian radicalism revived in the late 1960s as a consequence of national and international divisions within the Communist party. In 1964, the CPI split. As a result, the two successor parties, the CPI and the CPI-M, began to compete in Thanjavur for local bases of support. This competitive period coincided with the onset of the green revolution and its intensification of commercial agriculture. Both parties took the lead in organizing strikes, leading agitations, and provoking conflicts designed to win higher wages and better working conditions for agricultural laborers. In 1969 and again in 1972, laborers credited the parties and their unions for gaining favorable wage settlements.

These successes contributed to the receding radicalism of agricultural laborers in the 1970s. As in Kerala, where the CPI-M–induced agrarian reforms converted tenants into owners and gave workers higher wages, job security, and welfare benefits, policy success engendered political failure. In Thanjavur, "satisfied" workers, like the satisfied tenants of the 1950s, were less responsive to class appeals. Instead, they were increasingly attracted to movements and organizations that advocated policies favoring agricultural prosperity.

Both Communist parties adapted their appeals to the transformed political environment of the 1970s that G. Narayanaswami Naidu's Tamil Nadu Agriculturalists Association brought into being. The association's mass-based and sometimes violent agitations on behalf of cultivators' interests established it by 1980 as the arbiter of politics and policy in Tamil Nadu. Its thousands of units and three million members made it a much more influential force in rural society and the agricultural economy than the Communist parties, whose largest organization, the CPI-M's Tamil Nadu Kisan Sabha, claimed eighty thousand members, most of whom were concentrated in Thanjavur district. The parties stopped identifying wage laborers as the pivotal class for agrarian radicalism and turned instead to multi- and cross-class appeals that spoke to the needs and interests of a wide range of agricultural producers and to the collective interests of the agricultural sector.

If the politics of the 1950s featured agrarian reform and that of the 1960s regional nationalism, the politics of the 1970s featured demands by agricultural producers for policies benefiting the agricultural sector of the economy. Agricultural producers proved their mastery of Tamil Nadu politics and policy at the end of the decade when Naidu's association punished a recalcitrant AIDMK government, led by M. G. Ramachandran, by assuring the defeat of its candidates in the January 1980 parliamentary election and their victory six months later in the June 1980 state assembly election after Ramachandran had conceded most of the association's demands.[151]

We have seen that successful mobilization of the rural poor in the favorable objective conditions of Thanjavur district's Old Delta depended on the presence of leadership. Communist party cadres in turn provided the sufficient determinants for the agrarian radicalism of the 1940s and late 1960s. Without leaders to give meaning to the Old Delta's polarized agrarian and social structure and to provide political resources and guidance, it is unlikely that the labor bargaining and armed insurrection of the 1940s and the agitations and strikes of the late 1960s and early 1970s would have occurred. However, Communist local cadres were not free agents. Continuous changes in the international, national, and regional political environments and subsequent historical conjunctures shaped their ideological formulations, political strategy, and policy preferences. Objective determinants prepared the ground for mobilization. But objective determinants are not self-executing. It is their construction by leadership into frameworks of meaning and reasons for action that lead to mobilization and its policy consequences.

Microstudies in Tamil Nadu's Thanjavur district have the satisfactory quality of having something to explain. Objective determinants were translated by leaders into subjective determinants that on occasion led risk-averse laborers and tenants to act collectively. Studies elsewhere remind us to eschew the assumption that objective determinants are self-actualizing or self-executing, that causes automatically become reasons. Accounts by Breman in Gujarat, Echeverri-Gent in Uttar Pradesh, and Juergensmeyer in Punjab depict poor status groups—tribal Halpatis in Gujarat, Harijans in Uttar Pradesh and Punjab—unwilling to act cooperatively or collectively.[152] Why should this be so?

These and other studies indicate that the rural poor perceive insecurity as more pervasive and impersonal under capitalist-tending market conditions than under traditional forms of domination. Although state agencies associated with a market economy nominally represent a government of laws, their administration of justice and welfare in local contexts is biased against the poor. Under forms of traditional domination, the legitimizing ideologies and power asymmetries of local hierarchies sustained interdependence within relatively stable local social equilibriums. Legitimizing ideologies sanctioned rights and obligations as well as duties and dependencies by linking putatively nonantagonistic strata in harmonious social orders.[153] Under the structural and normative conditions of declining traditional domination, master-servant, patron-client, and ritually ranked caste relations are subject to decay and displacement by an impersonal labor market and discriminatory state administration of order, justice, and development programs.

In the studies analyzed below, traditional social equilibria have been badly eroded. However, the poor—whether Halpatis in Gujarat or Harijan laborers in Uttar Pradesh or the Punjab—lack credible leaders who can help them interpret and respond to market and state induced inequalities. Nor have they experienced the triggering effects that new agricultural technology can have on commercial agriculture. Finally, the socioeconomic configuration of poverty in Gujarat, Uttar Pradesh, and Punjab, unlike that in the Old Delta, inhibits mobilization of the rural poor.

In the Old Delta hired agricultural labor was preponderant over family and household labor. Agricultural workers constituted 50 to 70 percent of the agricultural work force. Such proportions are often found in the rice-growing areas of Tamil Nadu, West Bengal, and Kerala, where, as we noted above, the ratio of family to hired labor is approximately even or favors wage workers. The ratios in the wheat-growing areas of Punjab, Uttar Pradesh, and Haryana, by contrast, favor family labor over hired workers.[154]

In North India, where the microstudies being examined were conducted, hired workers usually do not outnumber self-employed cultivators. In "Gaon," a Maharashtra village studied by Orenstein, some 600 persons belonged to the cultivating castes. Most of them were self-cultivators of small plots. They employed 117 Mahars and 112 Mangs, ex-untouchable castes available for field labor.[155] In the Gujarat villages of Chikhligam and Gandevigam studied by Breman, the concentration of workers was greater: 125 landowning Anavil Brahmans could employ 200 Dubla laborers in the first and 225 Anavil Brahmans could employ 429 Dublas in the second.[156] In practice, however, concentrations of hired labor were less pronounced than these figures suggest; for example, one Anavil Brahman might employ only one or two

Dublas, and that only on a seasonal basis. The Madhya Pradesh village that Mayer analyzed encompassed about 300 substantial cultivators (with 14–20 acres) in a village of 900, but numerous service castes with small holdings limited the use of hired workers.[157] Only 24 persons regularly served as agricultural labor. In Shoron, the Uttar Pradesh village studied by Pradhan, Jat cultivators outnumbered ex-untouchable Chamar field-workers in the three *pattis* (administrative divisions) of the village, by ratios of 170:97, 110:72, and 96:56.[158]

These ratios suggest that the decisive numerical advantage of agricultural workers in the Old Delta is exceptional. Most villages have few large landholders, if any, and self-cultivation on small plots is preponderant. Indeed, the all-India proportion for agricultural workers— about 27 percent,[159] many of whom are simultaneously smallholders— confirms the statistical unlikelihood in most localities of a numerical parity between workers and cultivators, much less a ratio that favors workers.

These figures take on additional significance for constraints on mobilization of the rural poor when one considers the pattern of employment. Agricultural workers in most villages of North India are not concentrated by work place; they are scattered across the social landscape. One or two or three laborers are attached by dyadic ties to a cultivator, although the word "attached" conveys a durability of relations that is less and less characteristic. Most farmland in a given village is self-cultivated by its holders. Even more prosperous cultivators controlling what in India passes for a "large" holding—20–30 acres— often employ only a few laborers and only at the time of high-intensity cultivation and harvesting. Where such patron-client relations persist, their vertical pull counters the potential for horizontal solidarities based on class, caste, regional nationalism, or religion.

More often, however, such relationships decay. T. Scarlett Epstein in 1962,[160] Orenstein in 1965, and Breman in 1974, reported the decay of patron-client relations in their respective areas in Mysore, Maharashtra, and Gujarat. Decay of the "moral economy"[161] (incipient social disequilibrium) is often taken as a precondition for the emergence of horizontal solidarities. Moore's argument that the rise of commercial agriculture encouraged class politics and Frankel's argument that the green revolution encouraged issue politics turn on this assumption: that the consequences of enhanced market relations and improved technology will dissolve dependent but affective patron-client ties and thus prepare the ground for class and issue politics.[162] However, Epstein found that commercial agriculture and improved technology intensified rather than dissolved traditional ritual and agrarian relations.

If Orenstein found that the horizontal ties of regional caste associations or egalitarian religious movements (Ambedkar-inspired neo-Buddhism) were beginning to affect village consciousness and action,[163] Epstein and Breman paint a picture of insecurity whose correlates were apathy or anomie. "The process of 'depatronization' has left the agricultural laborers in a condition of isolation," Breman writes.[164] We infer that isolation accompanied by normlessness and apathy has replaced decaying vertical ties in many other local contexts, rather than class or issue politics.

Apathy or anomie among the poor in local settings can be reinforced by the growth of alternate forms of employment outside the village, district or state that further fragment the labor force. Typical are the Dublas who left Gujarat villages to work as brick makers in Bombay part of the year and the contract laborers who left a Mysore village part of the year to work on earthworks in the region. They remained part of village society, but an increasingly ephemeral part. Of the ninety-five Dubla workingmen in Chikhligam, thirty-eight remained agricultural workers in Chikhligam, while fifty-two went to the Bombay brickyards much of the year. Formerly, they shared parallel interests as clients of adjoining patrons. Now, "as sharecroppers, servants, casual laborers, and gang laborers, they have no parallel interests."[165]

Given such inhospitable objective conditions, it is not surprising that in Breman's and Echeverri-Gent's studies, and in one by Juergensmeyer, leaders were shown as unable to transform apparent objective parallel interests into subjective interests that create group consciousness and reasons for collective action. Breman describes Halpati passivity, amoral individualism, and fatalism. Echeverri-Gent and Juergensmeyer provide similar accounts of Harijans.

Is passivity a "chosen" or "determined" response? When the "culture of poverty" literature argued that destitution and discrimination cause anomie, social disorganization, and selfishness,[166] critics noted that the analysis failed to take into account the extent to which such responses were rational adaptations. Failure to act collectively may be a rational response in contexts where the margin to take political and economic risk is absent or minimal, the costs of failure seem high, and the likelihood and benefits of success seem uncertain. Without the employment security and private welfare benefits associated with traditional dependent relations, some economic margin—that is, control of productive assets or labor market bargaining power—seems to be required. Laborers who lack assets, income, and bargaining advantages also often lack that sense of self-worth and efficacy that they need in order to believe that they can influence their fate through collective action. Unless they reach a certain economic and psychological threshold, mobilization based on group consciousness is unlikely. Juergensmeyer's comparison of the levels of ideological or religious commitment and the organizational affiliations of three different Harijan communities differentiates two that have reached this threshhold from one that has not.[167]

What did leadership make of the conditions found in the Breman, Echeverri-Gent, and Juergensmeyer studies? When objective determinants are less favorable and congruent with each other than in the Thanjavur Old Delta context, leadership has less to work with. In the three studies at issue, leadership was either absent or unable to translate the conditions of impoverishment and insecurity into reasons for collective or cooperative action.

Breman found that the class collaborative ideology of the Gandhian *sarvodaya* (service) workers engaged in organizing the Halpatis and the co-optive effects of government subsidies to Halpati schools preempted the possibility of conflictual mobilization. Echeverri-Gent reports that his one-year effort (over three crops) to build a self-sustaining production cooperative collapsed with his departure. In "Bimla," one of the three Harijan communities Juergensmeyer studied, there were no signs of leadership. Yet leadership of the "right kind," leadership that is in a position to translate adverse objective conditions into meaningful ideological and policy formulations, remains a critical mediating determinant for mobilization.

Gandhian *sarvodaya* workers and left party leaders of poor untouchables and tribals were outsiders whose high-caste backgrounds, considerable education, vested career interests, or ideological orientations were alien to those they professed to serve and benefit. *Sarvodaya* leaders in Gujarat were known as "service workers," volunteers in the well-established Gandhian style. They sought to "uplift" the lower orders by exposing them to a Sanskritic equivalent of the "Protestant ethic" or Methodist virtue, urging their benighted and depraved members to be self-disciplined, to abjure drink, to join in communal singing (*bajan mandlis*), and to become educated. As E. P. Thompson and earlier students of the history of the working class in England have pointed out, in saving the souls of England's lower orders, Methodism also helped to create a compliant and disciplined work force. Breman sees the less successful efforts of *sarvodaya* service workers among the Halpatis in a similar light.

When Halpati Seva Sangh leaders began to be recruited from among the Halpatis themselves, another dimension of finding the right kind of leaders arose. Halpati Seva Sangh leaders were co-opted. They joined the ranks of masters. They donned terylene shirts, accepted the rules and style of government officials, and observed conventions designed to keep poor Halpatis in their place. Some used their new positions for personal gain.

Indigenous leadership is often subject to co-optation and self-aggrandizement. Those raised up adopt the ideology and interests of their former masters and answer the call of individual rather than collective interests. Personal desire for mobility and respectability overcomes earlier commitments to the collective needs of their community.

Nonindigenous leadership can be problematic too. Its social provenance and ideas can be alien, and it can patronize those it seeks to serve out of a spirit of noblesse oblige. Upper-caste or upper-class leadership of the poor and oppressed can symbolize their inferiority. It was recognition of this meaning and its rejection that led to the expulsion in 1963 of white leaders of the civil rights movement in America's South. In Juergensmeyer's account of "Bimla" in Punjab, the Harijan fourth of the population may have not responded to the class ideology of upper-caste or upper-class leadership because they believed it would mean replacing the appropriation of their identity and interests by upper-caste landlords with another appropriation by upper-caste political leaders. Those below the economic and psychological threshhold for collective action needed to recognize themselves in symbolically separate terms that give meaning and dignity to what they knew of their culture and history before they could acquire the self- and social esteem required for collective social action. Juergensmeyer's work on the Ad Dharm and Dalit movements shows the importance of symbolic separatism and indigenous leadership for such esteem.

Our discussion of agrarian conditions and leadership in Thanjavur's Old Delta suggested the kind of circumstances favorable to mobilization of the rural poor. The contrasting circumstances of the North Indian microstudies show that the objective conditions, historical conjunctures, and leadership of the Old Delta are more the exception than the rule.

Our account of mobilization of the rural poor has shown not only that it occurs rarely, but also that the prospects are dim for it to be a vehicle of revolutionary transformation. Yet for over a decade there has been pervasive evidence of violent rural conflict in local arenas, what we refer to as undeclared civil wars. They are in part a consequence of the state's limited penetration of the countryside. But their causes lie deeper in the dissolution of traditional interdependence and the absence of a reconstituted moral order. Sporadic and unorganized, if not entirely spontaneous, local civil wars typically have taken the form of atrocities against Harijans, ex-untouchables who generally are land-less and work as agricultural laborers. Such warfare reflects several trends: the decreasing willingness of Harijan laborers to acquiesce in the destruction of their property, sexual molestation of their women, physical abuse, and unacceptable terms of employment and their in-creasing willingness to defy their erstwhile masters when provoked; the backlash by upwardly mobile backward castes and established elites against programs and reservation of places for "weaker sec-tions"; and the fact that the state is too weakly articulated and too much influenced by local elites and factions to protect citizens' rights or effectively implement redistributional policies.[168]

The December 1968 death of forty-two untouchables at Kilvenmani marked the beginning of an era when such atrocities became an impor-tant part of India's symbolic politics and their manipulation an impor-tant political tactic.[169] As mentioned earlier, in September 1977 Indira Gandhi launched her political comeback at Belchhi, a Harijan village in Bihar where eleven landless laborers had been killed, by com-miserating with survivors and victims of an atrocity for which she held Janata rule responsible. She and her son and political heir, Sanjay Gandhi, used the same tactic with respect to Narainpur, a Uttar Pra-desh village, immediately after Congress-I's January 1980 electoral vic-tory, to justify the dismissal of that state's Janata government.[170] Con-gress-I's claim that it was a government that works and that helps the "weaker sections" did not end the reality or rhetoric of atrocities. In-stead, spurious charges and empty rhetoric by all parties devalued the use of atrocities in symbolic politics.

The opportunistic use of atrocities by politicians has not undone the reality of undeclared civil wars. They constitute another form of mobi-lization of the rural poor. We distinguish undeclared civil war from mobilization by legally recognized political parties, trade unions, and service organizations pursuing policy and collective bargaining objec-tives, by placing the former in the "unorganized" and the latter in the "organized" sectors of Indian politics.[171] The leading characteristic of the unorganized political sector is spontaneous, leaderless violence against property and persons; of the organized, legally or conven-tionally recognized organizations, procedures, and leadership. In the twilight area between the organized and unorganized political sectors lie extralegal and illegal political movements whose objectives often entail violent means. Preeminent in this twilight zone are the Naxalite rebellions that crested between 1967 and 1969 (associated with the Communist party Marxist-Leninist) and the "land grab" movement of the early 1970s.[172] The embers of what the Naxalite movement's leaders had hoped would be a revolutionary conflagration yielding state power occasionally flares into local violence that is hard to distinguish from the spontaneous violence of undeclared civil wars. Indeed, it often suits government's convenience to label local social banditry as Naxalite, because doing so legitimates the use of state violence against declared "outlaws." The land grab movement, like the Naxalite rebellions, was the child of the crisis years between 1965 and 1969 when India's economy, political leadership, and military prowess faltered badly. Indira Gandhi's policy responses and political leadership in the 1971 parliamentary and 1972 state assembly elections and India's victory in the 1971 war with Pakistan restored for a time government's credibility and state legitimacy. Nevertheless, the experience of the mid- and late 1960s stand as a constant reminder that in times of policy failure and institutional decay the rural poor can be mobilized by movements whose objectives and means threaten not only law and order and property relations but also state power.

Agrarian revolts and local civil wars, like mobilizations of the rural poor, keep pressure on parties and governments to support policies and implement programs that address the interests and aspirations of "weaker sections." These forms of mobilization constitute a constant and sometimes ominous presence whose influence on party strategy, electoral competition, and policy choice is palpable if not precise. Despite the appropriation of benefits by better-placed cultivators and landowners, targeted propoor programs designed to enhance the assets, incomes, or employment of the rural poor have become and are likely to remain an imperative for party support and state legitimacy.

We began this volume with an explanation of why the politics of an emergent industrial democracy such as India has been more centrist than class oriented. We attributed the residual character of class politics at the national level to two factors: the relative weakness of the classic protagonists of class politics, organized labor, and private capitalism in relation to a "third actor," the Indian state, whose assets, employees and capital accumulation dominate the organized economy; and the fact that the organized economy accounts for considerably smaller proportions of national income and employment than the unorganized economy generally and its agricultural sector in particular. In this chapter, we showed that the politics of the agricultural sector's producers tended to strengthen centrist more than class politics.

In demonstrating the contribution of the agrarian sector to centrist politics, we featured the role of bullock capitalists in the new agrarianism. The new agrarianism opened a new cleavage in national politics. This sectoral cleavage occupies a middle ground between what peasant studies describe as the contradictory orientations of "middle peasants"—acquiescence and revolt—and the consequences of these orientations—system maintenance and system transformation. By contrast, the sectoral politics of the new agrarianism accepts the system but calls for changes within it; that is, it is incremental rather than either status quo or revolutionary. It aims to speak both for the collective good of the agricultural economy and for the particular interest of its principal actors: bullock capitalists, capitalist farmers, and the rural poor. It does so by making policy demands that can be brokered within the system via intersectoral and pluralist bargaining and cross-class alliances.

Our account of the mobilization of the rural poor depicted great differences by condition, time, and place in the propensity of the poor to act collectively in their own interest. The record of agrarian radicalism in Thanjavur's Old Delta and elsewhere, the Naxalite and land grab movements, and pervasive and unremitting undeclared local civil wars have influenced national and state policy and the ideology and demands of the new agrarianism. At the same time, we do not foresee the rural poor's becoming the basis for class politics in the agricultural economy or, by joining or allying with workers in the organized economy, for class politics at the national level. Our anticipation that Indian politics will remain centrist for some time is qualified by our recognition that history, while determined in some respects, is open-ended in others. Historical conjunctures, leadership, and—above all—actors' goals and choices are the stuff of open-ended history. Much will depend on the perceptions, choices, and performance of those guiding the economy and sectoral politics. If those who lead the new agrarianism credibly and effectively represent the interests of the rural poor and if the economy expands in ways that foster agricultural prosperity, the rural poor are likely to support rather than challenge the centrist orientation of Indian politics.

Conclusion

We conclude this book by considering what it means for social science and for India. We want here to interpret our interpretation. We also want to highlight our findings about the course of events in India and to relate our analysis of the political economy of the Indian state to concepts used to explain the dynamics and direction of change.

Our title—*In Pursuit of Lakshmi: The Political Economy of the Indian State*—contains key terms for our mode of inquiry, analysis, and explanation. We use "Lakshmi" as a metaphor that establishes a language of discourse. The name invokes an Indian world view, one that orients and organizes how many Indians, although not necessarily intellectuals, think about political economy. Lakshmi, the goddess of wealth, is a figure out of the popular pantheon, not a term from the economists' lexicon. It is precisely the exotic nature of Lakshmi's name, as it intrudes into the homogenized, decultured language of political economy, that forces the reader to recognize political economy has to accommodate the unique or particular as well as the universal. The name serves as a bridge, a way of translating our concerns as Western social scientists into a salient indigenous category. Invoking Lakshmi is an effort in translation, an effort to relate terms from otherwise alien systems of meaning (e.g., West and East, United States and India, social science and humanities) in ways that may make them mutually intelligible and add value to both sides.[1] Put another way, it is an effort to create through the metaphor of Lakshmi a commensurable yet liminal language, a term that in context lies "in between" alien language communities but that speaks to both.

Lakshmi's jurisdiction is wealth, power, and good fortune. Note that in this formula good fortune, not individual or collective rational choice or internal or external structural determinants, is associated with wealth and power. This is not because we do not credit such modes of explanation; we have explicitly or implicitly used them throughout. We invoke good fortune because social scientific explanations of large, complex, and variable social phenomena such as wealth and power are partial and indeterminant. At the margin, good or bad fortune—the

393

breaks, conjunctions, leadership—makes the difference not only for relative success or failure in human endeavors but also for the historical turns and conditions that constrain and orient them.

The name Lakshmi in the title establishes a link between the meaning in the popular pantheon of wealth, power, and good fortune and their meaning in the world of the social sciences that engages in political economy modes of inquiry, analysis, and explanation. Some of the actors in the social science world are more at home with the language of our subtitle—*the Political Economy of the Indian State*—than they are with Lakshmi. British rule, important aspects of the nationalist movement, and India's involvement in the world of scholarship and commerce have yielded intellectuals, politicians, and businessmen who command and use the language of political economy.

Both Mohandas Gandhi and Nehru, in very different ways, produced "translations" that made political economy modes of thought accessible to wide publics and many generations. They did not agree about questions of political economy, but they launched a public debate about them that educated Indian thought and opinion and that endures to this day.

Gandhi's *Hind Swaraj* (*Indian Self-rule*) was published in 1908. The multivalent term of his title linked individual self-rule or self-mastery to national independence. It soon became central to Indian thought about political economy questions. It reverberates to this day in the country's concern to be self-reliant, nonaligned, decentralized, democratic, and self-critical. Gandhi argued that there were mutually determining relationships among production, consumption, and power. Their quality and forms shape the civilization by which a society lives. Industrialization for Gandhi ran the risk of relying on machines that mastered rather than liberated workers, stimulating an unending cycle of more and more wants and more and more production and creating centralized, bureaucratic, and impersonal power that destroyed community and spread alienation and anomie. Such industrialization seemed to Gandhi an unlikely way to become or remain civilized. For Gandhi, industrialization lacked limits or purpose, threatened "self-rule" at the individual, community, and national levels, and put the quality of life and the environment at risk. The limits of growth for Gandhi were moral as well as social.[2]

Jawaharlal Nehru's *Discovery of India* introduced another understanding of political economy. More in keeping with the language of the modernist West, its language supplanted Gandhi's in the public discourse of independent India. It was the language of self-reliance and power through industrialization directed by a benign and wise state acting for the common good and social justice. Together, Gandhi and Nehru made languages of political economy an important aspect of India's public discourse,

We chose our title to remind our readers that this book is about the political economy *of* India, and also to remind them that it is a book about political economy *in* India. Political economy aspires to generality, even universality, but it must deal with particular cases, with political economy on the ground, as it is known and practiced in history under discrete and changing circumstances. Insofar as we are standing on the shoulders of those who have gone before, what we have written is in part a theoretically informed case study.[3] But we have attempted to go further by introducing a theory of political economy, the command and demand polity,[4] to guide many of the questions we ask and to determine how we answer them and what counts as evidence. Our theory informs the concepts we use to analyze and explain the political economy of the Indian state (e.g., command and demand politics, the state as third actor, state and involuted pluralism, demand groups).

Because we have attempted to go beyond a theoretically informed case study in political economy by deploying a theory and related concepts of political economy, the questions we ask and the ways in which we ask them, the terms and evidence we use, and the consequences and outcomes we seek to explain do not always accord with those used in extant political economy literatures. For example, the dependency theories that scholars of South America in the 1970s found so helpful in explaining bureaucratic authoritarian regimes and "the development of underdevelopment," and that they often generalized to the political economies of all peripheral economies and states, have not proved helpful. Foreign investment in India has been marginal and controlled, commercial debt has been low, and trade diverse. Like China, India can feed itself and has developed basic and heavy industries, mainly with its own capital. Moreover, India is not heavily dependent for its security on one or more foreign powers. As a founder and leader of the nonaligned movement, it shapes its international environment as much as it is shaped by it.

The 1980s has become the decade of methodological individualism and rational choice.[5] They provide another possible framework of analysis. Self-determined, egotistic individuals are said to ask, what's in it for me? Will I be better or worse off if I buy this rather than that, vote for *x* rather than *y*, join or support this or that group? Ahistorical, asocial, and amoral individuals choose or act collectively according to what are purported to be self-evident or at least transparent "rational" reasons, because they are said to have easy access to knowledge about their own personal preferences and utilities and can make simple, straightforward calculations about substantive, transaction, information, and other costs. Society, culture, the state, ideologies, and world views are epiphenomenal, mere aggregations of the choices of rational individuals.

In the rational choice canon, what determines preferences and how individuals order them remains relatively unproblematic. What Amartya Sen refers to as second-order preferences (e.g., commitments to rules, the values and interests of intermediate groups, and responses to leadership) are underattended or ignored. So are strategic considerations (e.g., exit, voice or loyalty),[6] and learning (sometimes referred to in game theory as "iteration"). At best, learning is believed to result in a simple rule, tit for tat.[7] Methodological individualism and rational choice seem to have leapt from the frying pan of social overdeterminism (e.g., the structural functionalism of Durkheim or Parsons and the historical and/or functional determinism of Marx) into the fire of an exaggerated atomistic rationality by ignoring the social, deliberative, and historical determination of private as well as public choice and action.

Having skirted dependency theory and given marginal attention to rational choice, we have adapted class and state concepts for use in our explanations of centrism and of the state as third actor. Translations of class and state concepts for use in India required mutual adjustments, reformulations that gave them meaning across the divides of historical experience, social circumstances, and cultural frameworks.

The marginality of class politics that helps to explain centrism in India has several causes, including the variety of social formations and identities that organize and represent society in India, the sectoral characteristics of the Indian economy, and the timing of industrialization and democracy. Of the many cleavages that animate Indian politics, class usually matters less than other social formations, such as caste, religious and language communities, and regional nationalisms. Other cleavages rival or surpass class in political saliency because the consciousness and commitment focused on them are usually more transparent and accessible than those focused on class. How interests are defined and pursued, how causes (objective determinants) become reasons (subjective determinants) is more powerfully determined—for most Indian people most of the time—by social formations other than class.[8]

Our use of class as a concept to explain the marginality of class politics in relation to Indian centrism and the role of the state as third actor arises from the Marxist claim that modes and relations of production ultimately determine the course of history and the collective action that animates it. Several difficulties arise with respect to such a claim. One is that arguments based on the ultimate determination of social change and history can not be disproved, because the moment of ultimate determination can always be placed just beyond the historical horizon. Another is that some readings of Marx deny that humans in all their variety can, within limits, construct their own history. A third is that other kinds of social formations rival or surpass class in the determination of collective action, historical change, and state orientation.[9]

The marginality of class politics in India has been affected too by the historical timing of democracy and industrialization and the sectoral composition of the Indian economy at the beginning of universal franchise. The sequential relationship of democracy and industrialization helped to revitalize and reorient traditional social groups and to enfranchise the agricultural sector before the objective conditions for postfeudal class formation were well established. In independent India, voting based on universal suffrage paralleled and to an extent preceded industrialization. Earlier, Gandhian nationalism gave primacy to village over city India and to social harmony over social conflict. The agricultural sector of the unorganized economy in the 1980s includes about two-thirds of the voters and produces somewhat less than half the national income. It is better positioned by numbers and ideology to make itself heard in national and state-level politics than are private capital and trade unions in the proportionately much smaller organized economy, and this is more true than in European industrializing nations. After primary industrialization (second and third five-year plans, 1957–67), two-thirds of the workers and the industrial capital in the organized economy and all of the finance capital are in the state sector, conditions that help make private capital and organized labor dependent on the state.

The marginality of class politics and the predominance of centrist politics is also related to another of our principal conceptualizations, the state as "third actor." The state is the third actor in relation to the two actors—private capital and organized labor—identified by analyses of advanced industrial democracies in Western Europe and by Marxist thought as the principal actors in class politics. In India, the state not only benefited from historically determined high stateness, legal sovereignty, and cultural orientations (the state as father and mother and as chief patron) but also benefited from its sectoral resources, what in India terms is referred to as the economy's "commanding heights."

The state could be a third actor in the organized economy partly because its sectoral resources (the state sector) made it in considerable measure self-determining. The possibility of a self-determining state opened up another possibility, the "state for itself" and raised yet another question: under what conditions and for what reasons would the state, in claiming to be the means for solving problems and achieving goals, itself become the problem?

The state's third actor role in India's organized economy was aided and abetted not only by the marginality of class politics and the state's self-determining resource position but also by the state's bargaining advantages with respect to organized interests, particularly those of private-sector industrial capitalism and trade unions. State-dominated pluralism and involuted pluralism, concepts that have been subject to translation from the Western social science language of pluralism, help us to analyze and explain how the state in India limits and controls the influence of organized interests in politics.

At the most general level, our analyses and explanations of the political economy of the Indian state start with a theory, the models we have drawn of the command polity and the demand polity. We postulate two tendencies that, in their extremes, result in state sovereignty and popular sovereignty. Both sovereignties take various forms: popular sovereignty can be expressed through voter domination of policy choice and implementation or through consumer domination of the production of goods and services, and thus of investment; state sovereignty can be expressed through public authority, coercion, or ideology. As Andrew Shonfield put it, there is a differentially weighted and unstable balance between public and private power. Either state or society, in their multifarious forms and processes, knows best and has the last word.

In India, popular sovereignty expresses itself more through the voter than consumer sovereignty. We have said very little about consumer sovereignty per se, except in our discussions of the orientations and operations of India's mixed economy. Consumer sovereignty in India is limited, because markets are believed to be the source of unacceptable inequalities and dangerous concentrations of private power that threaten state-determined social objectives. It is true that markets are valued and some attempts are made to perfect them because they promote allocative efficiency through prices. Nevertheless, the economy remains mixed because it is believed that markets in practice are imperfect—they allow and even promote inequality and accumulations

of private power that jeopardize the realization of state-determined social objectives—and because, ultimately, consumer sovereignty is regarded as a less desirable source of investment and distributive decisions than a putatively benign and wise sovereign state.

In the 1980s, states ruled by conservative governments in leading
and influential industrial democracies, such as the United States and
Great Britain, adopted antistate, promarket ideologies that took up
the cause of consumer sovereignty by dismantling or contracting state
services and regulation. The cause of consumer sovereignty in the market sense has not had similar champions in India. Prime Minister Rajiv
Gandhi's call in early 1985 for "liberalization" of the economy, that is,
for reducing some of the burdens of "permit-license raj," should not be
interpreted as a call for abandoning the mixed economy in favor of a
market economy dominated by consumer sovereignty and the private
power of large corporations. The Indian state will remain the economy's guide, tutor and patron, particularly with respect to investment.
Nor is it likely to surrender the industrial, financial, and infrastructural resources it controls, that is, abandon the economy's commanding height. Those resources and the state's strategic and bargaining advantages make it possible for the state in India to be not only relatively
autonomous and self-determined but also self-interested. It is for these
reasons that, in its struggle with state sovereignty, popular sovereignty
will be based more on voter than on consumer sovereignty.

In chapter 7, "Demand Polity and Command Polity," we spelled out
the characteristics and orientations of the two models. They are offered as heuristic devices to guide the lines of inquiry and explanation
followed in our analyses of the political economy of demand and command politics. Demand and command politics, in turn, are played out
in sectors and sectoral cleavages, in party politics and elections, in
state-dominated and involuted pluralism in private-sector capitalism
and the industrial relations regime, and in the formation, orientation
and effectiveness of student, worker, and agricultural producer demand groups.

Our conceptualization of demand groups draws on Weber's understanding that social action is powerfully determined by ideal and material interests and on Tocqueville's that liberty in democracies depends
on a viable and vigorous associational life. Demand groups are a form
of collective action that subordinates organized interests and classes to
issue and movement politics. Demand groups require leadership, ideology, and articulations of collective goods. Their scope and effectiveness depend on the ability of key actors with hegemonic advantages to
make hegemonic bargains. Demand groups and political parties (inso-

far as they can effectively articulate and represent societal interests) have been the principal vehicles of demand politics in India.

Our treatment of the state in the context of command politics goes beyond treatments of the state as potentially autonomous in advanced industrial democracies, by introducing the concept of the state as third actor. In this reading, the state not only provides order, justice, and security, enhances social goods and benefits, and reduces or eliminates social costs, but it also directly commands enough resources to be self-determining in a variety of policy arenas and historical contexts.

State sovereignty is usually understood to refer to the claim that the state in principle has a territorial monopoly and a monopoly over certain activities—for example, the use of force, national security, currency, communication, education, and welfare. Even if state sovereignty is not exercised through monopoly, it can be expressed in public authority that legitimizes, permits, and regulates the activities of lesser entities and settles conflicts among them. States can share sovereignty in federal and other arrangements and by creating or recognizing parastatal bodies such as banks, industry associations, and labor and professional organizations. Not least among the activities subject to state authority are those of producers and consumers in markets. If markets are to be created or are to operate more rather than less "perfectly," state intervention and supervision are required. The array of possible states ranges from the juridical or liberal state to the totalitarian state that attempts to monopolize not only force and security but also ideas, property, investment, and employment.

Our concept of the state as a self-determining third actor adds to this array of state possibilities. Its direct command of economic resources as well as of public authority and force makes it possible for the state not only to resist determination by societal forces but also to act in its own interest. Instead of having to extract resources from society, the self-determining state directly controls a significant proportion of physical and financial capital and employs a majority of workers in the organized economy.[10] Even while retaining conventional state attributes and powers, the state as third actor has become a major component of the economy and of society. It may or may not be subject to direction by command or demand politics or become the agent of dominant class, elite, or interest group coalitions. The self-determining state is in a position to serve itself and, like other self-interested actors, to be a source of exploitation or injustice.[11]

Like Hindu conceptions of the divine, the state in India is polymorphous, a creature of manifold forms and orientations. One is the third actor whose scale and power contribute to the marginality of class politics. Another is a liberal or citizens' state, a juridical body whose legislative reach is limited by a written constitution, judicial review, and fundamental rights. Still another is a capitalist state that guards the boundaries of the mixed economy by protecting the rights and promoting the interests of property in agriculture, commerce, and industry. Finally, a socialist state is concerned to use public power to eradicate poverty and privilege and tame private power. Which combination prevails in a particular historical setting is a matter for inquiry.

APPENDIX A
India's Hundred Largest Firms

Rank[a]	Name of Company	Total Capital Employed[b] (Rs. Crores)	Net Sales[c] (Rs. Crores)	Profits after Tax (Rs. Crores)
1	Steel Authority of India (SAIL)	5,127.07	2,948.59 (3)	39.11
2	Food Corporation of India (FIC)	2,512.92	3,723.99 (2)	0.40
3	Coal India	2,491.29	10.27	−0.49
4	Oil and Natural Gas Commission (OnGC) (O)	2,394.08	1,330.31 (8)	376.97
5	Indian Oil Corporation (IOC) (O)	1,313.39	7,943.99	106.53
6	Bharat Heavy Electricals (BHEL)	865.12	946.39 (9)	29.98
7	Shipping Corporation of India	801.87	545.47	4.63
8	Central Coalfields	790.05	461.02	117.63
9	TATA IRON AND STEEL (Tisco)	650.07	592.65 [2]	36.03
10	TATA ENGINEERING	605.18	693.09 [1]	43.60
11	National Fertiliser	562.28	319.70	59.75
12	Fertiliser Corporation of India (FCI)	558.79	176.80	−130.09
13	National Textile Corporation (Holding Company)	485.68	24.21	−1.77
14	Rashtriya Chemicals and Fertilisers	482.28	246.32	21.26
15	Hindustan Fertiliser Corporation	467.99	120.30	−48.13
16	Neyveli Lignite	450.88	137.69	37.92
17	Air India	436.57	608.35	10.36
18	Western Coalfields	434.31	374.79	41.28
19	Indian Airlines	429.43	348.51	11.34
20	Bharat Coking Coal	421.16	357.06	−23.76
21	Indian Petro-Chem Corporation	418.60	406.22	55.53
22	Hindustan Aeronautics	408.39	226.64	22.64
23	Eastern Coalfields	333.33	345.95	−92.15
24	Bharat Aluminum	299.74	85.74	−39.63
25	CALCUTTA ELECTRIC SUPPLY	273.55	155.27	3.98
26	RELIANCE TEXTILE	262.03	293.38 [5]	19.72
27	Hindustan Copper	260.46	99.48	−42.55

403

Rank[a]	Name of Company	Total Capital Employed[b] (Rs. Crores)	Net Sales[c] (Rs. Crores)	Profits after Tax (Rs. Crores)
28	Hindustan Petroleum Corporation (HPC) (O)	254.97	1,884.53 (4)	14.40
29	ASSOCIATED CEMENT	241.17	202.81	1.36
30	HINDUSTAN LEVER	240.20	474.11 [3]	22.54
31	ASHOK LEYLAND	236.33	261.70 [7]	14.98
32	Hindustan Zinc	227.37	90.60	0.25
33	SCINDIA STEAM	225.91	108.42	2.51
34	Hindustan Machine Tools	221.10	260.46	24.58
35	GWALIOR RAYON	216.66	290.91 [6]	5.37
36	J. K. SYNTHETICS	210.38	140.93	11.63
37	INDIAN TOBACCO COMPANY (ITC)	210.19	177.82	7.76
38	Cement Corporation of India	203.75	73.26	8.82
39	HINDUSTAN ALUMINIUM	201.97	116.65	3.61
40	AMBALAL SARABHAI	199.95	170.10	2.68
41	DELHI CLOTH MILLS	185.03	357.65 [4]	6.86
42	GUJARAT STATE FERTILISERS	178.96	149.73	8.20
43	Indian Telephone Industry	178.66	157.26	10.43
44	Oil India (O)	172.02	314.23	65.50
45	SOUTHERN PETRO CHEMICAL	168.74	209.80	8.75
46	Cotton Corporation	168.59	362.22	1.06
47	INDIAN EXPLOSIVES	164.09	125.18	7.36
48	DUNLOP	163.83	210.15	3.68
49	State Trading Corporation (STC)	161.26	1,866.85 (5)	25.69
50	GREAT EASTERN SHIPPING	155.93	56.75	12.23
51	INDIAN ALUMINIUM	155.62	136.46	2.84
52	TATA POWER	154.51	137.35	5.85
53	Fertilisers and Chemicals, Travancore	152.61	168.86	−10.99
54	CENTURY SPG	150.59	180.94	13.27
55	Indian Drugs and Pharmaceuticals	148.70	104.48	−27.44
56	HIND MOTORS B	147.06	248.66 [9]	14.22
57	Minerals and Metals Trading Corporation (MMTC)	146.64	1,736.57 (6)	25.03
58	Bharat Petroleum (BPL) (O)	144.15	1,515.42 (7)	14.07
59	LARSEN AND TOUBRO	142.21	82.36	6.88

Rank[a]	Name of Company	Total Capital Employed[b] (Rs. Crores)	Net Sales[c] (Rs. Crores)	Profits after Tax (Rs. Crores)
60	ENGINEERING CON-STRUCTION	140.64	16.54	1.32
61	Bongaigaon Refineries (O)	134.76	81.95	5.00
62	MAHINDRA AND MA-HINDRA	129.50	234.35 [10]	9.56
63	Bharat Earth Movers	129.41	221.93	12.13
64	VOLTAS	128.18	260.04 [8]	3.87
65	RENUSAGAR POWER	126.42	18.31	−3.72
66	Mazgaon Dock	124.88	103.67	5.63
67	ACC BABCOCK	120.54	72.92	3.96
68	Cochin Shipyard	120.43	32.72	0.02
69	National Mineral Development Corporation	120.37	106.63	3.80
70	GUEST, KEEN, WILLIAMS	120.15	152.15	0.36
71	Heavy Engineering	117.20	108.90	−22.82
72	AHMEDABAD ELEC-TRICITY	112.97	91.50	7.20
73	AHMEDABAD MANU-FACTURING AND CALICO	111.34	129.43	1.03
74	UNION CARBIDE	110.11	159.61	9.45
75	INDIA STEAMSHIP	109.38	54.99	−6.64
76	International Airport Authority	108.07	52.63	10.66
77	BALLARPUR IND.	105.35	148.10	7.66
78	ESCORTS	104.51	217.90	8.33
79	STRAW PRODUCTS	104.08	51.06	3.86
80	METAL BOX	101.86	109.47	−1.32
81	NATIONAL ORGANIC	101.21	140.73	4.11
82	BOMBAY SUBURBAN	100.65	107.15	4.44
83	Madras Refineries (O)	99.08	732.80 (10)	2.68
84	EAST INDIA HOTELS	98.57	35.99	5.41
85	PEICO ELECTRONICS	96.49	133.48	6.54
86	Central Warehousing Corporation	95.51	25.49	7.56
87	Bharat Electronics	94.67	128.44	9.37
88	Indian Road Construction	94.19	24.22	1.24
89	MODI RUBBER	93.78	127.89	6.91
90	BIRLA JUTE	92.93	91.52	1.04
91	SIEMENS	92.35	104.98	5.44
92	CROMPTON GREAVES	90.45	132.18	5.88
93	ANDHRA VALLEY	89.55	83.13	3.18
94	Mogul Lines	89.02	37.51	0.37

Rank[a]	Name of Company	Total Capital Employed[b] (Rs. Crores)	Net Sales[c] (Rs. Crores)	Profits after Tax (Rs. Crores)
95	TATA CHEMICALS	88.15	67.12	9.37
96	NIRLON SYNTHETICS	88.08	76.15	6.53
97	TATA OIL MILLS	86.81	140.13	1.57
98	BOMBAY DYEING	86.48	110.96	4.93
99	MAHINDRA UGINE	86.41	66.88	7.10
100	RAYMOND WOOLLENS	84.34	62.82	1.88
	All Public-sector firms (N=47)	26,253.00	31,870.55	742.80
	All Private-sector firms (N=53)	8,356.00	8,770.35	384.99
	All Oil public-sector firms (N=7)	4,512.00	13,803.23	585.15

SOURCE: Hannan Ezekiel, ed. *Corporate Sector in India* (New Delhi: Vikas, 1984), tables 1.2, 7.2.

Notes: Private-sector firms are given in uppercase letters. (O) = oil company. Rs. 1 crore = Rs. 10 million, or, in 1983, $1 million.

[a]Based on total capital employed 1981–82.

[b]For private-sector firms "total capital employed" (assets) involves net investments, sundry debtors, loans, advances (excluding advance payment of taxes), cash and bank balances. Because the Bureau of Public Enterprises does not provide data on inventories separately for public-sector companies, total capital employed for them involves the total of assets as shown by the bureau minus accumulated depreciation and accumulated deficits, i.e., the aggregate of net fixed assets, investments, cash and bank balances, and working capital (Ezekiel, *Corporate Sector,* p. 142).

[c]Parenthetical numbers indicate public-sector rankings for net sales (top ten); bracketed numbers, private-sector rankings.

APPENDIX B

Agricultural Labor and Landholdings

TABLE B-1
Statistical Conflicts in the "Capitalist Agriculture" Debate: Raj and Visaria's Reports of NSS Estimates for the Percentage Distribution of the Rural Males by Activity Status

(1) Activity Status	(2) September 1958–August 1959 (14th Round)	(3) July 1960–June 1961 (16th Round)	(4) September 1961–July 1962 (17th Round)	(5) July 1964–June 1965 (19th Round)	(6) July 1966–June 1967 (21st Round)	(7) October 1972–March 1973 (27th Round)	(8) October 1972–March 1973 (Adjusted)[a]
Own account workers							
1. Raj	27.47	22.72	21.74	18.11	—	30.66[b]	—
2. Visaria	27.47	22.72	21.74	20.81 (Schedule 16)[c] / 18.11 (Schedule 17)	21.30	30.66	25.93
Unpaid family labor							
3. Raj	11.24	8.82	7.96	5.95	—	11.83	—
4. Visaria	11.24	8.82	7.96	8.36 (Schedule 16) / 5.95 (Schedule 17)	8.85	11.83	10.11
Employers							
5. Raj	0.80	5.79	4.52	13.83	—	—	—
6. Visaria	0.80	5.79	4.52	7.81 (Schedule 16) / 13.89 (Schedule 17)	5.32	—	—
Employees							
7. Raj	15.30	16.60	15.83	13.69	—	21.92	—
8. Visaria	15.30	16.60	15.83	14.27 (Schedule 16) / 13.69 (Schedule 17)	17.32	21.92	18.73

SOURCES: K. N. Raj, "Trends in Rural Unemployment in India," *Economic and Political Weekly*, August 1976 (special no.); Pravin Visaria and S. K. Sanyal, "Trends in Rural Unemployment in India: Two Comments," *Economic and Political Weekly*, January 29, 1977.

[a] The adjustment is designed to make the twenty-seventh round figures comparable to those of previous rounds, on Visaria's ground that the twenty-seventh round excluded children five years old and younger, while the previous rounds had included them.

[b] Discounted by Raj as pertaining to the "busy season" only. Visaria counts it because enumerations inquire for "usual activity," not current activity.

[c] Visaria argues that there was a significant difference between schedule 17 (abridged, published) and schedule 16 (unabridged, unpublished) of the nineteenth round and that the criteria of consistency suggests that there must have been serious nonsampling errors in schedule 17. He uses schedule

TABLE B-2

Distribution of the Number of Households by Size of Household
Operational Holding: Estimates by Sanyal and Raj

Household Operational Holding	1953–54		1960–61		1970–71	
	No. (Millions)	%	No. (Millions)	%	No. (Millions)	%
0	17.2	28.2	18.5	26.6	21.9	27.4
	(6.6)	(10.9)	(18.6)	(27.0)	(21.9)	(27.4)
0.01–2.49 (small)	17.1	28.0	21.2	30.5	26.3	32.9
	(27.6)	(45.3)	(21.0)	(30.6)	(26.3)	(32.9)
2.50–9.99 (medium)	17.8	29.2	21.2	30.5	23.5	29.3
	(18.2)	(29.9)	(20.6)	(30.0)	(23.6)	(29.5)
10 and above (large)	8.9	14.6	8.6	12.4	8.3	10.4
	(8.6)	(14.0)	(8.5)	(12.4)	(8.2)	(10.3)
	61.0	100.0	69.5	100.0	80.0	100.0
			(68.7)			

SOURCES: See table B-1.
Notes: Figures without parentheses are taken from Sanyal, figures in parentheses from Raj. The years cited indicate the reference periods of the eighth, seventeenth, and twenty-sixth NSS rounds.

TABLE B-3
Distribution of Area Operated by Size of Household
Operational Holding: Estimates by Sanyal and Raj

Household Operational Holding	1953–54			1960–61			1970–71		
	Total Operated Area (Million Acres)	%	Average Size (Acres)	Total Operated Area (Million Acres)	%	Average Size (Acres)	Total Operated Area (Million Acres)	%	Average Size (Acres)
0.01–2.49 (small)	18.2	5.4	1.1	25.0	7.1	1.2	33.8	9.2	1.3
	(19.9)	(5.9)	(0.8)	(31.8)	(9.0)	(1.5)	(33.8)	(9.2)	(1.3)
2.50–9.99 (medium)	96.1	28.6	5.4	119.2	33.8	5.8	137.2	37.5	5.8
	(100.0)	(29.8)	(5.5)	(112.2)	(31.8)	(5.5)	(137.3)	(37.5)	(5.8)
10 and above (large)	221.4	66.0	25.0	208.8	59.1	24.4	194.7	53.2	23.5
	(215.8)	(64.3)	(25.1)	(208.6)	(59.2)	(24.5)	(194.8)	(53.2)	(23.8)
Total	335.7	—	—	353.0	—	—	365.7	—	—
				(352.6)			(365.9)		

SOURCES: See table B-1.

Notes: Figures without parentheses are taken from Sanyal, figures in parentheses from Raj. The years cited indicate the reference periods of the eighth, seventeenth and twenty-sixth NSS rounds.

Notes

Preface

1. In the epic *Mahabharata*, Yudhishtira, senior brother of the Pandavas, gambles away his kingdom, his wife, and the freedom of his lineage.
2. Jagdish Bhagwati, "Is India's Economic Miracle at Hand?" *New York Times*, June 9, 1985. Lawrence Veit's and Catherine Gwinn's editors used a similar title—"The Indian Miracle"—for an upbeat assessment in *Foreign Policy* 58 (Spring 1985).

Introduction

1. See, for example, Claus Offe, *Contradictions of the Welfare State* (Cambridge: MIT Press, 1984), chap. 9. See also Colin Crouch's summary of the literature of the "overloaded state" in "The State, Capital and Liberal Democracy," in *State and Economy in Contemporary Capitalism* (New York: St. Martin's, 1979).
2. India's industrialization rank in 1979 is based on the value added in manufacturing as given in International Bank for Reconstruction and Development (World Bank), *World Development Report, 1982* (New York: Oxford University Press, 1982), table 6, pp. 120–21. India's GNP rank in 1981 is taken from *World Bank Atlas, 1982* (Washington, D.C., 1982) (preliminary data subject to revision). The World Bank data on industrialization do not include data for the People's Republic of China or the USSR (or other centrally planned economies), which no doubt rank above India in value added in manufacturing. If they were included, India would rank seventeenth in level of industrialization. On the other hand, India's aggregate economy ranks higher on a world scale than does its industrial sector.
3. Government of India, Census Commission, Census of India, 1981, *Provisional Population Totals*, ser. 1, paper 1 of 1981 (Delhi, [1981]), p. 4. India's population grew from 548,159,652 in 1971 to 683,810,051 or 15.63 percent of the world population in 1981. The World Bank estimates India's population in the year 2000 at 973,580,000 (*Economic Situation and Prospects of India*, report 3401–IN [April 15, 1981], table 1.1, p. 205).
4. Reserve Bank of India, *Report on Currency and Finance, 1979–80* (Bombay, 1981), vol. 2, *Statistical Statements*, statement 76, pp. 100–1.
5. Government of India, Ministry of Finance, *Economic Survey, 1983–84* (Delhi, 1984), p. 72.

411

6. See table 4.4, "Financing of Investment," in Government of India, Planning Commission, *Seventh Five Year Plan, 1985–90* (Delhi, 1985), 1:48. Foreign private investment accounted for approximately 14–18 percent of investment in the private corporate sector under the second and third five-year plans. See K. K. Subramanian, *Import of Capital and Technology: A Study of Foreign Collaborations in Indian Industry* (New Delhi Peoples Publishing House, 1972), table 3, p. 34. For Latin American estimates, see United Nations, *Multinational Corporations in World Development*, UN pub. sales no. E.73.11.A.11 (New York: United Nations, 1973), p. 20.

7. Government of India, Ministry of Finance, *Economic Survey, 1976–77* (Delhi, 1977), table 7.3, p. 41.

8. For a discussion of oil-based autonomy in the Middle East, see Lisa Anderson, "The State in the Middle East and North Africa" (Paper presented at the annual meeting of the American Political Science Association, August 1985).

9. Raj Krishna, "The Economic Development of India," *Scientific American*, September 1980, p. 139. For a more extended analysis of the self-reliance strategy and liberalization, see our "The United States, India and South Asia," in John P. Lewis and Valeriana Kallab, eds., *U.S. Foreign Policy and the Third World: Agenda 1983* (New York: Praeger, for the Overseas Development Council, 1983). This chapter has drawn on ideas that were first developed in that essay.

Chapter 1

1. For the varying nature of class and confessional voting in Europe, see for example, Arend Lijphart, "Class Voting and Religious Voting in the European Democracies," occasional paper no. 8 (Glasgow: University of Strathclyde, Survey Research Center, 1971). More generally for Western Europe, see Richard Rose, ed., *Electoral Behavior: A Comparative Handbook* (New York Free Press, 1974).

2. Calculated from table 6, "Industrialization: Value Added in Manufacturing," in World Bank, *World Development Report, 1982*, pp. 120–21.

3. See Myron Weiner, *Sons of the Soil: Migration and Ethnic Conflict in India* (Princeton: Princeton University Press, 1978); Mary Katzenstein, *Ethnicity and Equality: The Shiv Sena Party and Preferential Policies in Bombay* (Ithaca, N.Y.: Cornell University Press, 1979); R. A. Schermerhorn, *Ethnic Plurality in India* (Tucson: University of Arizona Press, 1978); and Lloyd I. Rudolph and Susanne Hoeber Rudolph, *The Modernity of Tradition: Political Development in India* (Chicago: University of Chicago Press, 1967; Midway Reprint, 1984).

4. Theda Skocpol, *States and Social Revolutions: A Comparative Analysis of France, Russia and China* (Cambridge: Cambridge University Press, 1979).

5. The total labor forces in 1981 for France, Italy, the United Kingdom, and Germany, respectively, were 23,230,000, 23,100,000, 26,548,000, and 27,395,000 (OECD, Department of Economics and Statistics, *Labour Force Statistics 1970–81* [Paris, 1983], p. 477).

6. The "organized sector" is commonly used in public policy and economic

discourse in India to refer to the industrial or secondary sector of the economy. It stands in contrast to the agricultural or primary sector and to the service sector that, rather than being a tertiary sector controlled by corporations or firms as in advanced industrial economies, remains heavily the domain of family economic activity. More precisely, employees in firms with enough workers to be subject to the terms, conditions, and reporting and statistical requirements established by factories, labor, and companies acts count as workers in the organized sector. The unorganized sector includes cultivators, tenants, agricultural laborers, workers in cottage and village industry, contract laborers, and most construction workers. Standard sources include Government of India, Ministry of Planning, Central Statistical Organization, Department of Statistics, *Statistical Abstracts: New Series* (various numbers); Government of India, Ministry of Finance, *Economic Survey* (Delhi, annual). The latest figures are 7 million factory workers in 1980 (Government of India, Ministry of Labour, Labour Bureau, *Pocket Book of Labour Statistics, 1983* [Chandigarh and Simla, 1983], table 2.4(a), p. 45); 220 million in the total work force (Government of India, Census Commission, Census of India, 1981, *Provisional Population Totals: Workers and Nonworkers,* paper 3 of 1981 (Delhi, 1981), p. 3); and 23 million organized-sector employees, with 16 million in the public and 7.5 million in the private sector (Ministry of Finance, *Economic Survey 1983–84,* tables 3.1, 3.2, pp. 121–22).

7. World Bank, *World Development Report, 1982,* table 19, pp. 146–47.

8. The statistics of trade union membership are unreliable. The Government of India's Labour Bureau is able to report the membership only of unions submitting returns, not of all registered trade unions. In 1978, when the bureau reported six million union members, only 8,351 unions submitted returns out of 32,207 unions registered (Labour Bureau, *Pocket Book of Labour Statistics, 1983,* table 6.1, pp. 129–31). But, for reasons discussed in chapter 10, the unions that submit returns are probably larger and better organized than those that do not. Hence, we attribute two to four million more members to unions.

9. Alak Ghosh, *Indian Economy: Its Nature and Problems,* 22d rev. ed. (Calcutta: World Press, 1979–80), p. 312. The planned investment ratio for the seventh plan was significantly more modest, 52:48. The sixth plan figures were projections (Government of India, Planning Commission, *Sixth Five Year Plan, 1980–85* (Delhi, [1981?]), p. 63. The seventh plan projections represent a significant downward shift in the public sector's share. It is important to keep in mind that of the private sector's 52 percent, the corporate private sector accounts for only 17 percent, and the unincorporated and household, which includes farms, cottage industry, and the bazaar sector, accounts for 35 percent (Government of India, Planning Commission, *Seventh Five Year Plan, 1985–90,* 2 vols. (Delhi, 1985), 1:26.

10. Government of India, Ministry of Labour, Labour Bureau, *Pocket Book of Labour Statistics, 1984* (Chandigarh and Simla, 1984), p. 2. This figure includes the public services as well as industrial and commercial employment in the public sector.

11. Since the passage in 1980–81 of the National Security and Essential Services Act, there has been some national coordination and action by trade union apex organizations.

12. *India Today,* May 16–31, 1979, p. 83.

13. For an argument that the economic policy of the Rajiv Gandhi government is designed to reverse this dependency, see Barnett Rubin, "Economic Liberalization and the Indian State" (May 3, 1985, mimeograph).

14. For a careful account of capital's effort to influence its environment, see Stanley A. Kochanek, *Business and Politics in India* (Berkeley and Los Angeles: University of California Press, 1974).

15. Howard Erdman, *The Swatantra Party and Indian Conservatism* (Cambridge: Cambridge University Press, 1967).

16. The Monopolies Inquiry Commission of 1965 found that the top seventy-five business houses (comprising 1,536 companies) accounted for 44% of the total paid-up capital of the private sector. (Government of India, Ministry of Law, Justice and Company Affairs, *Report of the High-powered Expert Committee on Companies and MRTP Acts* [New Delhi, 1978], p. 246). For an account of the sales of the top twenty industrial houses, see the estimate of the Centre to Monitor the Indian Economy reported in Pranab Bardhan, *The Political Economy of Development in India* (Oxford: Basil Blackwell, 1984), p. 105.

17. Although, as Steven R. Weisman's portrait of the younger business people in Rajiv Gandhi's generation showed, "young businessmen are less defensive than were their fathers. They believe that business can help India by doing well for itself." "Businessmen always used to be put down. People used to say 'What's so great about selling soap?' Now there's great respect for managerial and marketing skills, especially because the public sector is in such low repute" (Dilip Thakore, the young editor of Bombay's *Business World,* quoted by Weisman in "The Rajiv Generation," *New York Times Magazine,* April 20, 1986). Myron Weiner, in his 1962 discussion of organized business in India, noted that Indian businessmen refrain from public relations campaigns on behalf of free enterprise because they share public attitudes that value public over private goals. (*The Politics of Scarcity* [Chicago: University of Chicago Press, 1962], (p. 139).

18. We have been unable to confirm the report that such a proposal was offered.

19. See Nasir Tyabji, "Capitalism in India and the Small Industries Policy," *Economic and Political Weekly,* October 1980 (special no.).

20. G. K. Shirokov, *Industrialization of India* (Moscow: People's Publishing House, 1973; New Delhi, 1980), p. 74. Prem Shanker Jha in *India: A Political Economy of Stagnation,* (New Delhi: Oxford University Press, 1980) writes that licensing had "the not altogether unintended effect of creating a formidable bias against large and medium scale investment, and in favor of small scale investment" (p. 83). Shirokov implicitly and Jha explicitly suggest that this bias weights the scales in favor of low-priority over high-priority investment.

21. Isher Judge Ahluwalia, *Industrial Growth in India: Stagnation since the Mid-Sixties* (New Delhi, Oxford University Press, 1985), p. 160. George Rosen offers a similar evaluation of this phenomenon in his forthcoming book *Industrial Change in India, 1970–2000: Present State of Indian Manufactures and Outlook of the Same.*

22. The formations are briefly chronicled in Government of India, Ministry of Information and Broadcasting, *India, 1983* (Delhi, 1983), pp. 213, 214, 325.

23. Government of India, Ministry of Industrial Development, *Report of*

the *Industrial Licensing Policy Inquiry Committee* (New Delhi, 1969, *Main Report*, vol. 1, p. 148.

24. Ibid.

25. Ibid.

26. For an argument in favor of corporate takeovers as a vehicle of healthy competition, and opposition to placing government and its financial institutions in a decisive role in such takeovers, see S. Kumarasundaram, "Corporate Takeovers: The Indian Situation," *Economic and Political Weekly,* June 4, 1983.

27. Swraj Paul eventually won a court judgment that would have forced Escorts to register his shares. However, by that time Mr. Paul's Caparo group was said to have lost its enthusiasm for controlling Escorts or Delhi Cloth Mills, as *The Hindu* reported, "because of the prevailing prejudices against investment by non-resident Indians in this country (January 18, 1986).

28. "The term joint sector is customarily applied to a subset of legally private sector companies in which . . . both state government and the private sector participate in financing and management" (Howard Erdman, "Mangalore Chemicals and Fertilizers: A Case Study in India's Political Economy" (1984, typescript), p. 10. See also Erdman's earlier *Politics and Economic Development in India: The Gujarat State Fertilizer Company as a Joint Sector Enterprise* (Delhi: D. K. Publisher, 1973 and 1978).

29. Erdman, "Mangalore Chemicals and Fertilizers," p. 13. For a thoughtful discussion of the political environment in which joint and private sector firms operate, see Erdman's *Political and Industrial Management: Some Introductory Thoughts, Hypotheses and Cases,* (Bangalore: Indian Institute of Management, 1985, mimeograph). Erdman emphasizes the extent to which government exercises its power over firm policy; his case studies illustrate public-private interaction in detail. A useful review of issues concerning public sector enterprises, including the bureaucratic ideologies that affect them, is T. N. Chaturvedi and S. K. Goyal, eds., *Public Enterprises* (New Delhi: Indian Institute of Public Administration, 1984). Goyal's introduction summarizes official critiques of the joint sector, as escaping public accountability while benefiting from public financing (pp. xivff). For a comparable study of the relationship between public and private power in Western Europe, see Andrew Shonfield, *Modern Capitalism* (New York: Oxford University Press, 1969).

30. See Kochanek, *Business and Politics in India,* especially chap. 7.

31. *Asian Recorder, 1985,* p. 18248.

32. See *Keesing's Contemporary Archives,* April 9, 1982, p. 31414. Mr. Antulay went on trial for corruption charges in March 1984 (*Keesing's Contemporary Archives,* 1984, p. 33227). He was acquitted. See also "The Antulay Affair," in Arun Shourie, *Mrs. Gandhi's Second Reign* (New Delhi: Vikas, 1983).

33. For a summary and bibliography of studies of black money, see National Institute of Public Finance and Policy, "Aspects of Black Money in India" (1985, mimeograph), chap. 3. The Institute study, sponsored by the Ministry of Finance, advances what it considers a conservative estimate; tax-evaded income accounts for 15 percent of the gross domestic product at factor cost (p. 167). See also "The Parallel Economy: A Symposium on the Ramifications of the Black Money Phenomenon" *Seminar,* no. 283 (March 1983).

34. *Hindustan Times,* February 6, 1984.

35. Kochanek, *Business and Politics in India*, p. 329.

36. George Rosen has emphasized in his study of industrialization that approximately 60 percent of the total pre-tax profit earned by the 110 profit-making public-sector companies is produced by the three public-sector petroleum companies. The profits made by the 107 remaining public-sector companies "barely balance" the losses made by the 81 losing enterprises (*Industrial Change,* manuscript p. 32). Isher Ahluwalia, in her discussion of infrastructural constraints on industrial growth, demonstrates in detail inefficiencies ranging from the formulation of plans in the railway, coal, and electricity sectors to the final operational stages. See table 5.1(C) "Inefficiency and Mismanagement of Infrastructural Sectors," in *Industrial Growth in India,* pp. 83ff. The Government of India's Rajadhyaksha Committee on Power illustrated the extent of inefficiency from the realm of power generating, where the minimum of time over for hydropower projects was two years and the maximum nine, and cost overruns were typically over 100 percent and exceeded 400 percent in two cases (ibid., p. 87). A painstaking study of routinized corruption in irrigation, which attempts to specify both the scale of "rents" and the networks by which they are accumulated, is R. Wade, "The System of Administration and Political Corruption: Canal Irrigation in South India," *Journal of Development Studies*, 18, no. 3 (April 1982). For a discussion of other and similar evidence see study by National Institute of Public Finance and Policy, "Aspects of Black Money," pp. 257ff.

37. Bardhan cites World Bank, *World Development Report, 1982* to the effect that India has one of the highest ratios among developing countries (*Political Economy of Development,* p. 27). K. N. Raj cites data showing a general tendency toward rising ratios ("Some Observations on Economic Growth in India over the Period 1952–3 to 1982–3," *Economic and Political Weekly,* October 13, 1984). Bardhan agrees (p. 28). Both agree that the pattern of investment within the large-scale industrial sector in India "has shifted in favour of industries with relatively high capital-output ratios, such as chemical fertilizers, petrochemicals and electricity generation, transmission and distribution" (Bardhan, p. 27).

The debate between Bardhan and Raj in *Economic and Political Weekly* obscures the wide areas of agreement. For the full debate, see Ashutosh Varshney, "Political Economy of Slow Industrial Growth in India," *Economic and Political Weekly,* September 1, 1984; Raj, "Economic Growth in India"; and Pranab Bardhan, "Some Observations on Economic Growth in India," *Economic and Political Weekly,* December 22–29, 1984. The Varshney paper summarizes the work of the Social Science Research Council–sponsored project on slow industrialization. See also Barnett Rubin, "Comment on Slow Industrialization in India" (1984, mimeograph), which summarizes and criticizes aspects of the conference, suggesting the problem of political sacrifices on behalf of investment growth.

38. Bardhan's argument has significant overlap with Mancur Olson, *The Rise and Decline of Nations* (New Haven: Yale University Press, 1982). Olson argues that over time, in peaceful and stable democracies, distributional coalitions become more powerful and are unwilling to sacrifice current consumption for future benefit. See Bardhan, *Political Economy,* chap. 7, 8. See also Jha, *India: A Political Economy of Stagnation.*

39. For a systematic account of these differences among parties in Western

Europe, see Kenneth Janda, *Political Parties: A Cross National Survey* (New York: Free Press, 1980), item 5.05, "Secularization of Society," for each of the European parties analyzed in the Janda volume.

40. For a discussion of the self-identification of untouchables, see Mark Juergensmeyer, *Religion as Social Vision: The Movement Against Untouchability in 20th Century Punjab* (Berkeley and Los Angeles: University of California Press, 1982).

41. According to the 1981 census, there were 52 million tribals among India's 685 million people. Many tribals are Christians. We estimate that 7 of the 16 million persons classified as Christian in 1971 are tribals. The almost 3 million persons who are classified as belonging to other religious persuasions can be assumed to be mainly tribals. As very few tribals belong to other non-Hindu religious communities (Muslim, Sikh, Buddhist, or Jaina), we conclude that of India's 52 million tribals, 42 million (52 million minus 7 million Christians and 3 million other) have been counted as Hindus. For the data on which these estimates are based, see Government of India, Census Commission, Census of India, 1981, "Household Population by Religion of Head of Household," paper 3 of 1984 (Delhi, 1985), p. vii, and Government of India, Ministry of Information and Broadcasting, *India, 1984: A Reference Annual* (New Delhi, 1984), p. 14.

42. See three recent books on Jinnah and the formation of Pakistan: Ayesha Jalal, *The Sole Spokesman: Jinnah, the Muslim League and the Demand for Pakistan* (Cambridge: Cambridge University Press, 1985); Allen Hayes Merriam, *Gandhi vs. Jinnah: The Debate over the Partition of India* (Calcutta: Minerva, 1980); and Stanley A. Wolpert, *Jinnah of Pakistan* (New York: Oxford University Press, 1984).

43. See Reginald Coupland, *The Indian Problem: Report on the Constitutional Problem in India* (Oxford: Oxford University Press, 1944), 1:47, 128, 134, 151, for the evolution of statutory communalism.

44. For the Khilafat movement, see Gail Minault, *The Khilafat Movement: Religious Symbolism and Political Mobilization in India* (New York: Columbia University Press, 1982). For gurdwara reform and self-government, see M. J. Akbar, *India: The Siege Within: Challenges to a Nation's Unity* (Harmondsworth, England: Penguin, 1985), chap. 6, pp. 134–43.

45. In 1932, Gandhi launched a fast unto death against a novel provision of the "communal award" that extended to untouchables the separate electorates and reserved seats that already applied to religious and other minorities. Nehru initially was dismayed and annoyed; "I felt angry with him at his religious and sentimental approach to a political question." Reform of Hinduism would prove a costly diversion from the drive for independence, and his action was "a recognition, and in part an acceptance, of the communal award" that recognized separate electorates for Muslims and Sikhs. "Then came news," according to Nehru's own account, "of the tremendous upheaval all over the country, a magic wave of enthusiasm running through Hindu society, and untouchability appeared to be doomed" (quoted in Dorothy Norman, ed., *Nehru: The First Sixty Years* (New York: John Day, 1965), 1:272.

46. Coupland, *Indian Problem* 1:48.

47. Granville Austin, *The Indian Constitution* (New York: Oxford University Press, 1966), p. 151.

48. Nearly everyone present said they agreed. The Sikhs reluctantly dropped

their claims for reservation and weightage after being assured that Sikh scheduled castes would benefit if reservations were extended to other (Sikh) scheduled castes (Proceedings of the Advisory Committee meeting, May 11, 1949, in *Law Ministry Archives,* file CA/19(11)/Cons/49, as cited in Austin, *Indian Constitution,* pp. 154–55).

49. For balkanization or authoritarian rule, see Selig Harrison, *India: The Most Dangerous Decade* (Princeton: Princeton University Press, 1960). Paul Brass is cited from "Separatism in India (with Special Reference to Punjab)" (Paper presented at the Conference on India's Democracy., March 14–16, 1985).

50. The Vishwa Hindu Parishad is the "intellectual" branch of the RSS, which was founded in 1925. From 1980, RSS branches, membership, and public visibility grew by leaps and bounds. For a detailed account of its rise and success in the mid-1980s, see "Hindus: Militant Revivalism," *India Today,* May 31, 1986.

51. Even in 1905, aspects of Tilak's Poona Hindu symbolism traveled to Bengal, but without creating the wide popular base characteristic of the 1980s.

52. *Economic and Political Weekly,* January 7, 1986.

53. The Hindi Heartland and other regions are defined in chapter 6. For accounts of the support base for Hindu confessional politics, see Walter K. Andersen and Shridar D. Damle, *The Fraternity in Saffron: The Rashtriya Swayamsevak Sangh and its Affiliates: Organization and Ideology in Institution Building,* forthcoming; Craig Baxter, *The Jan Sangh: A Biography of an Indian Political Party* (Philadelphia: University of Pennsylvania Press, 1969); and our *Modernity of Tradition,* pt. 1.

54. Popular Hinduism as a form of social mobility departs from M. N. Srinivas's brahmanically oriented concept of "sanskritization." See M. N. Srinivas, *Caste in Modern India and Other Essays* (Bombay: Asia Publishing House, 1962). Lawrence A. Babb, "The Puzzle of Religious Modernity," in James R. Roach, ed., *India 2000: The Next Fifteen Years* (Riverdale, Md.: Riverdale, 1986), pp. 56–79, deals with three versions of contemporary popular Hinduism, the Radhasoami movement, and the cult of Sathya Sai Baba.

55. Anncharlott Eschmann, Hermann Kulke, and Gaya Charan Tripathi, eds., *The Cult of Jaganath and the Regional Tradition of Orissa* (New Delhi: Manohar, 1978), particularly the five essays by Kulke; and Burton Stein, *Peasant, State and Society in Medieval South India* (New Delhi: Oxford University Press, 1980).

56. See Philip Lutgendorf, "Sri Ramacaritamanasa: The Life of a Text" (Ph.D. diss., South Asia Language and Civilization Department, University of Chicago, 1986), for an account of the variety of forms that Ramayana recitation has taken.

57. Abdul Malik, "Conversions to Islam: Untouchables' Strategy for Protest in India, 1980–81" (M.A. paper, Department of Political Science, University of Chicago, 1985); George Mathew, "Politicization of Religion: Conversion to Islam in Tamil Nadu," pts. 1, 2, *Economic and Political Weekly,* June 19 and 26, 1982.

58. See, for example, Upendra Baxi, "Reflections on Reservation Crisis in Gujarat," *Mainstream,* June 8, 1985, pp. 15–22, and Mario Rodrigues, "Mahararashtra: Bhiwandi: Will the Peace Hold?" *Economic and Political Weekly,*

June 14, 1986, pp. 1049–50. See also Asghar Ali Engineer, ed., *Communal Riots in Post-independent India* (Hyderabad: Sangam, 1984).

59. In Stainislaus's case (*Stainislaus v. State of Madhya Pradesh* 1977 A.I.R. [S.C.] 908), the supreme court upheld laws of the Madhya Pradesh and Orissa state governments prohibiting conversion and penalizing those involved if force, fraud, inducement, or allurement was used by the person advocating conversion. Christians held that the freedom to propagate religion provided by article 25(1) of the constitution could result in conversion and that the limitations imposed by the two states' acts unconstitutionally restricted their religious freedom. Morarji Desai's Janata government, reflecting and responding to Hindu revivalist pressure, was on the verge of supporting a private member bill designed to extend the ruling of Stainislaus's case to all of India when it fell.

60. See our article "Rethinking Secularism: Genesis and Implications of the Text Book Controversy, 1977–79," in Lloyd I. Rudolph, ed., *Cultural Policy in India* (Delhi: Chanakya, 1984).

61. Akbar, *India*, pp. 197–98.

62. *Asian Recorder*, March 12–18, 1983, pp. 17074, and July 23–29, 1983, 17286.

63. See Lloyd I. Rudolph, "India and the Punjab," in Asia Society, *Asia Agenda Report 2* (Lanham, N.Y.: University Press of America, for the Asia Society, 1986). Mark Juergensmeyer, "The Logic of Religious Violence" Washington, D.C.: Woodrow Wilson International Center for Scholars, Smithsonian Institution, 1986, typescript, analyzes Sant Jarnail Singh Bhindranwale's speeches.

64. The massacre of "Bengali" Muslims at Nellie during the February 1983 election campaign was in fact perpetrated by Lalung tribals, not Hindus. For particulars, including the effects of the massacre on national and Muslim opinion, see *India Today*, February 28 and March 15, 1983. For an assessment of the Assam movement against "foreigners" that began in 1979 and was punctuated in August 1985 when Prime Minister Rajiv Gandhi signed an accord with leaders of the movement, see Sanjib Baruah, "Lessons of Assam," *Economic and Political Weekly*, February 15, 1986.

The 1985 court ruling declaring that an historic structure in Ayodhya (Faizabad district, Uttar Pradesh) was a temple, not a mosque, rocked the country. Hindus jubilantly proclaimed that many other mosques could now be reclaimed, and Muslims in Kashmir descrated Hindu temples there. Muslims held that the building in Ayodhya was the Babari mosque, established 350 years ago by Babar, the first Mughal ruler in India, and Hindus held that it was the Ramjanmabhoomi temple, birthplace of Rama, hero of the epic and sacred Hindu text, the *Ramayana*. For accounts of the dispute and the court judgment see Des Raj Goyal, "Ayodhya and After," *Mainstream*, March 15, 1986; a letter to *Mainstream* from Syed Shahabuddin, MP, in the May 10, 1986 issue; and S. Sahay, "A Close Look; Restoring Communal Harmoney, *The Statesman Weekly*, June 21, 1986.

65. *India Today*, January 31, 1986, p. 55.

66. A year earlier, in Rajiv Gandhi's December 1984 sweep of the eighth parliamentary election, a Muslim Congress-I candidate had carried the constituency by 1.3 million votes. Shahabuddin carried it in December 1985 by

700,000 even though the Congress-I candidate was the general secretary of the Jamiat-ul-Ulema-e-Hind, a national organization of orthodox Muslims, and two hundred *ulemas* from all over the country attempted to campaign on his behalf. See "Muslims: A Community in Turmoil," *India Today*, January 31, 1986, pp. 50–60, for details about by-elections and particulars of Muslim alienation from Congress-I.

67. Forty-eight Congress-I MPs defied a three-line party whip by absenting themselves at the time of the vote, and thirty more "mistakenly" pressed the "no" button. Pranab Mukherjee, Indira Gandhi's finance minister and senior member of her cabinet at the time of her assassination, was expelled from the party for organizing a movement within the party to make the vote on the Muslim Women's Bill a conscience vote, an action that would have challenged Rajiv Gandhi's leadership. By mid-July 1986, it was apparent that the Rajiv Gandhi government planned to enact a "voluntary uniform civil code" that would enable members of various communities to choose to be governed by a "secular" version of personal law rather than by the separate codes of their respective communities. "It is not every day," the *Times of India* editorialized, "that the country gives itself a new civil code nor, once enacted, can such fundamental parts of the law be altered without bitter controversy." Clearly, the prime minister hoped to not renew the war between "secularism" and "communalism" (*Times of India*, July 18, 1986).

68. According to orthodox Muslim opinion, the *shariat* (Muslim sacred law) holds that marriage is a contract, not a sacrament. When the contract is terminated by divorce, the husband's financial responsibilities are at an end except for repayment of the *mehr*, the payment with which a woman enters the marriage contract. These interpretations are disputed by liberal scholars of Muslim law, such as Professor Asaf A. A. Fyzee, and progressive Muslim politicians, such as Araif Mohammad Khan, who resigned from Rajiv Gandhi's cabinet over the Muslim Women Bill. For particulars of each position see "The Quaran: The Last Word," and "'My Faith Is Progressive,'" *India Today*, January 31, 1986, pp. 52–53 and p. 54. For the lack of cohesiveness among India's Muslims, see Myron Weiner, "India's Minorities: Who Are They? What Do They Want?" in James R. Roach, ed., *India 2000*, pp. 109–10.

69. Rajiv Gandhi's and his ministers' responses to the Shah Bano case are detailed in T. N. Ninan's interview with the prime minister in *India Today*, May 31, 1986, and Seema Mustafa, "Muslim Women Bill: Government's Dangerous Line in Lok Sabha," *Mainstream*, May 17, 1986. When law minister Asoke Sen admonished the house to attend to "the Muslim voice speaking on the floor of this House," the speaker intervened to censure him, pointing out that there were no Muslim or Hindu representatives in the house and that every member spoke for his constituency and himself. Steel minister K. C. Pant, who gave the principal speech in defense of the government's bill spoke of Hindu and Muslim "psyches." After arguing that "Hindu society had been able to regenerate itself," Pant expresesed the hope that Muslims would be able to do the same. Araif Mohammad Khan, the "progressive" Muslim minister in Rajiv Gandhi's government, resigned when the government decided to introduce a bill that would restore to the *ulema* or *mullahs* (Muslim priests) control over the interpretation of *shariat* (Quaranic law) with respect to Muslim personal law. For Khan's views see "My Faith Is Progressive,'" *India Today*, January 31, 1986.

70. *India Today*, May 31, 1986, p. 48.

71. For the effect of group consciousness on blacks' and scheduled castes' levels of political participation and on the tendency of these groups to vote together, see Sidney Verba, Bashiruddin Ahmed, and Anil Bhatt, *Caste, Race and Politics: A Comparative Study of India and the United States* (Beverly Hills, Calif.: Sage Publications, 1971). For a careful examination of Muslim voting in Bihar, which shows, inter alia, increasing Muslim electoral cohesiveness, see Harry W. Blair, *Voting, Caste, Community, Society: Explorations in Aggregate Data Analysis in India and Bangladesh* (New Delhi: Young Asia Publications, 1979). See chapter 6 for our discussion of a correlation between cohesiveness and proportion of Muslim voters in a constituency.

72. Myron Weiner and John Osgood Field note, on the basis of a study of tribal electoral behavior in the period 1952–72, that voting in tribal constituencies tends to reflect the rise and fall of the Congress vote in the rural areas of the same state. However, in 1967, "the national anti-Congress mood of 1967 had only limited impact on tribal constituencies," a finding in line with the 1972–84 electoral behavior we discuss in chapter 6 (Weiner and Field, "How Tribal Constituencies in India Vote," in Weiner and Field, eds., *Studies in Electoral Politics in the Indian States,* vol. 2, *Three Disadvantaged Sectors,* (New Delhi: Manohar, 1975), p. 108.

73. See chapter 6 below, where this point is developed in greater detail.

74. Of a total population in 1971 of 548 million, 80.09 percent were classified as rural, compared with 76.69 percent of a total population of 685 million in 1981. The proportion working in the agricultural sector declined between 1971 and 1981 from 69.77 (Government of India, Census Commission, Census of India, 1981, *Primary Census Abstract, General Population,* pt. IIB(i), "Figures at a Glance," pp. iii–iv). For sectoral income figures, see Government of India, Ministry of Planning, Central Statistical Organization, *Basic Statistics Relating to the Indian Economy, 1950–51—1979–80,* table 8, p. 16. We have used the data for the primary, secondary, and tertiary sectors to calculate shares for agriculture, industry, and services. These are rough approximations, but we are interested primarily in magnitudes and proportional relationships here.

75. According to Ronald J. Herring, "production in contemporary rural South Asia exhibits extensive evidence of interpenetration of social and technical organizations of production characteristic of modern capitalism with pre-capitalist relations of production" ("Economic Consequences of Local Power Configurations in Rural South Asia," in Meghnad Desai, Susanne Hoeber Rudolph, and Ashok Rudra, *Agrarian Power and Agricultural Productivity in South Asia* (Berkeley and Los Angeles: University of California Press and New Delhi: Oxford University Press, 1984). Herring's "interpenetration" thesis follows the evidence and interpretation in Pranab Bardhan and Ashok Rudra, "Interlinkages of Land, Labour, and Credit Relations," *Economic and Political Weekly,* February 1978 (annual no.). For agrarian-based conservative politics in Pakistan see Ronald J. Herring and Charles Kennedy, "The Political Economy of Farm Mechanization Policy: Tractors in Pakistan," in Raymond Hopkins, ed., *Food, Politics, and Agricultural Development* (Boulder, Colo.: Westview, 1979); Herring and M. Ghaffar Chaudry, "The 1972 Land Reforms in Pakistan and Their Economic Implications: A Preliminary Analysis" *Pakistan Development Review,* 11, no. 3 (Autumn 1972); and Herring "Zulfikar Ali

Bhutto and 'Eradication of Feudalism' in Pakistan," *Economic and Political Weekly,* March 22, 1980, where Herring concludes that Bhutto "sought selective accommodation [with "feudal" landlords] and transformation to facilitate concentration of political power and rationalization of the agricultural economy" (p. 599).

76. See Erdman, *Swatantra Party.*

77. We use the phrase "independent agrarian producers" for the bullock capitalists only. Small and marginal farmers (with under 2.5 acres) are disadvantaged with respect to market forces, access to state benefits, and return to family labor in ways that compromise their independence. The productivity of large holders (approximately over 15 acres) in turn is dependent on the availability of wage or dependent labor, and they are more oriented toward profit for capital accumulation than for independence.

78. V. Subramaniam estimates that 9 percent of India's "working population" (a term that refers to census-based occupational categories, some of which are counted as middle class) is middle class. See his "Representative Bureaucracy: A Reassessment," *American Political Science Review* 61, no. 4 (December 1967); p. 1015. Subramaniam's mode of estimation probably overstates the proportion, particularly with reference to the English-educated administrators, managers, and professionals referred to here. They and their families may constitute about 3 percent of the population, which makes this group small in proportional terms but large absolutely (about sixteen million in 1971).

79. Charan Singh's March 1979 proagrarian budget and his 1980 campaign themes, attacking Nehru's urban industrial bias and organized labor as privileged, created a backlash whose strength was a measure of their success. Charan Singh articulated these themes while campaigning in Andhra Pradesh in October 1979. See the *Deccan Herald, Hindu,* and *Indian Express* (Bangalore) for October 23 and 24, 1979. (We are grateful to V. K. Narasimhan, editor of the *Deccan Herald,* for providing these cuttings.)

80. The Congress-I minister for agriculture, Rao Birendra Singh, pushed vigorously for more favorable prices for agricultural products and inputs ("Appeasing the Rich Farm Lobby," *Economic and Political Weekly,* March 1, 1980). Finance Minister R. Venkataraman's temporary budget of March 1980, which provided virtually no relief for any category of taxpayer, did provide relief for the tax-paying farmers, who are by definition rich, allowing them to take into account the previous year's losses in the current year's declaration (*Times of India,* March 12, 1980). The two moves suggested appeals to both bullock capitalists and rich farmers.

81. Marc Galanter, "Who are the Other Backward Classes? An Introduction to a Constitutional Puzzle," *Economic and Political Weekly,* October 28, 1978. The most comprehensive account of the legal condition of the backward classes is Galanter's monumental *Competing Equalities: Law and the Backward Classes in India* (New Delhi: Oxford University Press, 1984). See our *Modernity of Tradition,* pt. 1; Robert L. Hardgrave, Jr., *The Nadars of Tamilnadu* (Berkeley and Los Angeles: University of California Press, 1969); Eugene Irshick, *Politics and Social Conflict in South India: The Non-Brahman Movement and Tamil Separatism* (New Delhi: University Press, Oxford, 1969).

82. The Janata government appointed a commission to look into the condi-

tion of backward classes (Mandal Commission), which reported after Mrs. Gandhi returned to power in 1980. Congress-I favored a policy of reservations based on economic backwardness, arguing that caste criteria were inappropriate, and delayed implementation of the Mandal Commission's report. For its findings, see *Times of India*, December 13, 1981, and note 92 below.

83. For a definition and examples, see our *Modernity of Tradition*, p. 24.

84. Bullocks capitalists are marginally affected by labor markets too, in that they sometimes employ even though they do not depend on casual or attached wage labor.

85. They benefit or suffer from the surplus value of their own labor, depending on efficiency, the ratio of producers to consumers in the household, and the size of the holding.

86. Charan Singh, *India's Economic Policy: The Gandhian Blueprint* (New Delhi: Vikas, 1978), p. 16.

87. For an account of the complex ideological and legal aspects of the backward classes movement, see Galanter, "Who Are the Other Backward Classes?" and Lelah Dushkin, "Backward Class Benefits and Social Class in India, 1920–1970," *Economic and Political Weekly*, April 7, 1980. See also Galanter, *Competing Inequalities*. Today the term "backward classes" loosely refers to lower *shudras*, castes located below the upper *shudras*, and below traditionally literate upper "twice-born" castes (e.g., Brahmans, Kshatriyas, Vaishyas), but above the ex-untouchables.

88. Ram Naresh Yadav, Karpoori Thakur, and Devraj Urs, the chief ministers of Uttar Pradesh, Bihar and Karnataka were from "backward classes." Studies that deal with specific backward classes include Chandrasekhar Bhatt, "The Reform Movement among the Waddors of Karnataka," in M. S. A. Rao, ed., *Social Movements in India*, vol. 1 (New Delhi: Manohar, 1978); Marcus F. Franda, *Small is Politics* (New Delhi: Wiley Eastern, 1979), which deals with backward classes in Bihar; M. S. A. Rao, "Political Elite and Caste Association," *Economic and Political Weekly*, May 18, 1968, an account of the Yadavas; and K. K. Verma, *Changing Role of Caste Associations* (New Delhi: National Publishing House, 1979), a study of the Kurmis.

89. These efforts reflected the commitment in the Janata manifesto of 1977 and the Lok Dal manifesto of 1979, which provided that "at least 25 percent of Groups A and B . . . jobs in the Central Government services will . . . be reserved for young men and women coming from [the socially and educationally backward classes . . . both Hindu and Muslim] as recommended by the Backward Classes Commission appointed in the fifties by the Union Government itself, under Article 340 of the Constitution" (Shyamal Basu, *Lok Dal Election Manifesto, 1979* [New Delhi, 1979], p. 29).

90. See Government of India, *Report of the Backward Classes Commission* (B. P. Mandal, Chair) (Delhi, 1982), as well as a resolution declaring the report unacceptable and a discussion of its reasoning in Government of India, Home Ministry, *Fourth Annual Report of the Minorities' Commission, 1981–82* (New Delhi, 1983), pp. 166–97. On the struggle over reservations, see Achyut Yagnik and Anil Bhatt, "The Anti-Dalit Agitation of Gujarat," *South Asia Bulletin* 4, no. 1 (Spring 1984).

91. See chapter 13 for our discussion of the new agrarianism.

92. We count as other status groups scheduled castes (15 percent), sched-

uled tribes (7 percent), and Muslims (11 percent). For various estimates of the "backward classes" proportion of the population, see Galanter, "Who are the Other Backward Classes?" Twenty-five percent is a conservative estimate but one in line with recent policy initiativeso to reserve places in government employment. The Mandal Commission identified a much higher proportion (37 percent) as backward but, in keeping with the supreme court's strictures in *Balaji v. Mysore* (1963) that reservations totaling more than 50 percent destroyed the meaning of backwardness, recommended that reservations for backward castes be only 27 percent in order to keep total reservations below 50 percent.

93. Parties representing the scheduled castes (e.g., the factionalized Republican party of India), the scheduled tribes (a large variety of local parties) and the Muslims (various Muslim leagues and several Uttar Pradesh parties of short duration) have proved notably unsuccessful in mobilizing and holding the support of the minority status groups they hoped to lead and represent. We have already adverted to the ultimate failure of the Swatantra party to lead and represent feudal landlords and capitalist farmers (the large landholders discussed in chapter 13). No party represents agricultural laborers as such. The Naxalite movement of the late 1960s used direct methods and violence to represent the interests of agricultural laborers. Repression and changed historical circumstances led to the movement's demise.

94. Biplab Dasgupta and W. H. Morris-Jones, *Patterns and Trends in Indian Politics: An Ecological Analysis of Aggregate Data on Society and Elections* (Bombay: Allied, 1976).

95. See William H. Riker, "The Number of Political Parties; A Reexamination of Duverger's Law," *Comparative Politics* (October 1976), for a reformulation and defense against Harry Eckstein's conclusion that Maurice Duverger's "law" ("the simple majority, single ballot system favors the two party system") "often lacks empirical fit, no matter how complicated the logic has been made" (Eckstein, "Political Parties," in *International Encyclopedia of the Social Sciences* [New York: MacMillan, 1968]; Duverger, *Political Parties*, trans. Barbara North and Robert North, rev. ed. [New York: Wiley, 1963], p. 217). Riker examines the Indian case "to investigate the theory that explains the variation in the number of candidates for office in single-member constituencies with plurality voting" (p. 93). He distinguishes three types of voting: "naive or sincere, under which the citizen always votes for the candidate of the party that stands first in his preference order"; "sophisticated voting, under which supporters of a third party vote for the party that stands second in their preference order"; and "disillusioned voting, under which some of the supporters of a large party [proportion larger than .6] "vote with a probability, p, for the party that stands first in their preference orders and, with a probability, 1-p for the party that stands second" (pp. 98–99). Riker concludes that "plurality voting can, through the motives of voters, guide the system to create and to destroy third parties" (p. 105). We do not accept Riker's implication that voters' preferences as rational actors in relationship to the electoral and party systems explain all the variance in the distribution of party vote shares in Indian elections. The motives that lead voters to support third parties representing communities, castes, classes, and regions or lead them to support independent candidates are not necessarily a function of preferences and strategic calculations that arise from within the electoral and

party systems. Even so, because the preferences, motives, and strategic calculations that Riker adduces do explain a large but indeterminant amount of the
variance that characterizes party voting in India, we believe they support our
argument that first-past-the-post voting contributes to centrism, as does Riker's
defense of Duverger's law.

96. Both figures are for 1980. See G. G. Mirchandani, *People's Verdict*
(New Delhi: Vikas, 1980), p. 127, for plurality victories in 1980 and p. 103
for number of multicornered contests in 1980 and 1977. In 1977, 438 of 540
contests were multicornered but 473 were won by a majority, a result reflecting
Janata's sweep in the northern states. For the 1977 majority and plurality win
figures see Government of India, Election Commission, *Report on the Sixth
General Election to the House of the People in India, 1977* (Delhi, 1978), 2 : 16.

97. This is markedly true for the AIADMK in Tamil Nadu; Telugu Desam
and Janata in Andhra and Karnataka too have cooperated with the center except during the time when Mrs. Gandhi was seen as attempting unfairly to
topple those governments.

Chapter 2

1. For recent, comparative discussions of state formation in Western Europe, see Charles Tilley, *The Formation of National States in Western Europe*
(Princeton: Princeton University Press, 1975). For a theory of the viceregal versus the parliamentary traditions, see Keith Callard, *Pakistan: A Political
Study.* (London: Allen and Unwin, 1958). For an account of European views
of Asian state formation, see Perry Anderson, *Lineages of the Absolutist State,*
(London: NLB, 1977), especially the appendix.

2. We take the term "stateness" from J. P. Nettl's seminal article, "The State
as Conceptual Variable," *World Politics* 20 (July 1968) : 566.

3. For a historical and analytic account of state formation in India, see our
"The Regional Kingdom and the Subcontinental Empire in Indian State Formation," in Paul Wallace, ed., *Region and Nation in India* (New Delhi: Oxford and IBH, 1985).

4. See, for example, A. L. Basham, *The Wonder that Was India: A Survey of
the History and Culture of the Indian Sub-Continent before the Coming of the
Muslims* (New York: Grove, 1959), chap. 4; Romila Thapar, *Asoka and the
Decline of the Mauryas* (Oxford: Oxford University Press, 1961); R. C. Ma-
jumdar and Amant Sadashiv Altekar, eds., *The Vakataka-Gupta Age (circa
200–500 A.D.)* (Banaras, India: Motilal Banarsi Dass for Bharatiya Itihas
Parishad, 1946). For a perspective that challenges the notion that ancient and
medieval empires wielded centralized power, see Burton Stein's account of the
Chola kingdoms, "The State and the Agrarian Order in Medieval South India:
A Historiographic Critique," in Burton Stein, ed., *Essays on South Asia* (Ho-
nolulu: University of Hawaii Press, 1975).

5. The Mughal period began with Babar in 1526 and is often considered to
have "ended" with the battles of Plassey and Panipat in 1757 and 1761, when
the ascendancy of British power begins. The literature on the Mughal empire
is well developed and varied. For a guide, see Satish Chandra's bibliographic
essay, "Writings on Social History of Medieval India: Trends and Prospects,"

in his *Medieval India: Society, the Jagirdari Crisis and the Village* (New Delhi: Macmillan India, 1982); M. Athar Ali, "The Mughal Empire in History" (Presidential Address, Thirty-third Session of the Indian History Congress, Section 2, Medieval India, Muzaffarpur, 1972); M. Athar Ali, "Towards an Interpretation of the Mughal Empire," *Journal of the Royal Asiatic Society,* 1978, no. 1; and Irfan Habib, *Agrarian System of Mughal India* (Bombay: Asia Publishing House, 1963).

6. Centralized fiscal mechanisms are described in detail in R. P. Kangle, ed. and trans., *The Kautiliya Arthasastra,* 2d ed., 3 vols., (Bombay: University of Bombay, 1960–65), a translation of a work that is generally dated at approximately 300 B.C. Habib, *Agrarian System of Mughal India,* chap. 7, deals with the ways in which the Mughals prevented *mansabdars* from inheriting estates and wealth and with the system's economic consequences.

7. See M. Athar Ali, *The Mughal Nobility under Aurangzeb* (Bombay Asia Publishing House, 1970).

8. There was one great struggle in protest from the nobility and the theocracy—the revolt of 1518—but once it had been quelled, the empire never really faced a serious revolt from within the ranks of its own bureaucracy. However, in the latter half of the eighteenth century, rebellions by subordinate chiefs multiplied. (Habib, *Agrarian System of Mughal India,* pp. 317–18.) See also Abdul Aziz, *The Mansabdari System and the Mughal Army* (Delhi: Idarah-I Adabiyut-I Delli, 1952).

9. V. S. Bhatnagar, *Life and Times of Sawai Jai Singh, 1688–1743* (Delhi: Impex, 1974).

10. Heinrich Zimmer, *Myths and Symbols in Indian Art and Architecture,* ed. Joseph Campbell (New York: Pantheon, 1946). For an account that gives strong attention to the symbolic realm, see John F. Richards, "The Formulation of Imperial Authority under Akbar and Jahangir," in John F. Richards, ed., *Kingship and Authority in South Asia* (Madison: University of Wisconsin Press, 1978).

11. For a summary of the imperial idea as revived by the Mughals, see Percival Spear, "The Mughals and the British," in A. L. Basham, ed., *A Cultural History of India,* (Oxford: Clarendon, 1975).

12. David Lelyveld, *Aligarh's First Generation* (Princeton: Princeton University Press, 1977).

13. Ali, "Towards an Interpretation," p. 47.

14. John F. Richards, "The Imperial Crisis in the Deccan," *Journal of Asian Studies,* 25, no. 2 (February 1976).

15. See, for example, M. I. Borah, trans., *Baharisthan-I-Ghaybi* (Mughal wars in Assam, Cooch Behar, Bengal, Bihar and Orissa during the reigns of Jahangir and Shah Jahan by Mirza Nathan) (Gauhati, India: Assam Department of Historical and Antiquarian Studies, 1936); Henry Beveridge, ed., and Alexander Rogers, trans., *The Tuzuk-i-Jahangiri, or Memoirs of Jahangir,* 2d ed. (Delhi: Munshiram Manoharlal, 1968).

16. Bernard S. Cohn, "The British and the Mughal Court in the Seventeenth Century" (University of Chicago, 1977, typescript); W. H. Moreland, *India at the Death of Akbar: An Economic Study* (Delhi: Atma Ram, 1961).

17. Kangle, *Kautiliya Arthasastra.*

18. See for example, J. Duncan Derrett, "Social and Political Thought and Institutions," in Basham, *Cultural History,* quoting Narada "with the rod of

chastisement (*danda*) he is to control all his subjects" (p. 132). On Hindu state theory, see also Charles Drekmeier, *Kingship and Community in Early India* (Stanford: Stanford University Press, 1962); Louis Dumont, "The Conception of Kingship in Ancient India," *Contributions to Indian Sociology* 56 (1961); U. N. Ghoshal, *A History of Indian Political Ideas* (New York: Oxford University Press, 1959).

19. The motives and objectives of Englishmen at the beginning of the century were mixed, as often controversial or contradictory as consensual, with high Tory imperialists and liberal reformers disagreeing over the meaning of the empire and the capacity of Indians for self-government. Reginald Coupland's *India: A Re-statement* (Oxford: Oxford University Press, 1945), provides a succinct statement of the issues and outcomes.

20. For a careful, detailed discussion of the failure of the Gandhian option, see Austin, *Indian Constitution*. As Austin observes, "Great As Gandhi's influence had been . . . he had not succeeded in converting either the country or his own party to his view of how Indians should . . . govern themselves" (p. 39).

21. The key figures were Prime Minister Jawaharlal Nehru; Deputy Prime Minister Vallabhbhai Patel; Rajendra Prasad, the Constituent Assembly's presiding officer and India's first president; and Maulana Abul Kalam Azad, education minister, Congress's most prominent Muslim leader and a Nehru confidant (Austin, *Indian Constitution*, p. 19).

22. Announced by the viceroy, Lord Mountbatten, on June 3, 1947, after obtaining the reluctant consent of Nehru. Gandhi, who was strongly opposed, was observing a day of silence when Mountbatten "discussed" the decision with him. For a narrative account of the historical background of partition and the events surrounding it, see H. V. Hodson, *The Great Divide: Britain, India, Pakistan* (London: Hutchinson, 1969). Nicholas Mansergh, ed., *The Transfer of Power, 1942–1947*, 12 vols. (London: Her Majesty's Stationery Office, 1970–83), provides in published form the official records bearing inter alia on partition. See also C. H. Philips and Mary Doreen Wainwright, eds., *The Partition of India: Policies and Perspectives, 1935–1946* (Cambridge: MIT Press, 1970).

23. For the most authoritative account, see V. P. Menon, *The Story of the Integration of the Indian States* (London: 1946). Menon was secretary to the States Ministry under Vallabhbhai Patel.

24. Partition, Mountbatten's authority and persuasion, and Patel's accomplishments at the States and Home Ministries made what had seemed a most unlikely prospect, integration of the princely states, become a reality. As late as December 1945, integration was not anticipated even by so committed a nationalist as Nehru. See S. Gopal, *Jawaharlal Nehru: A Biography*, vol. 1889–1947 (Cambridge: Harvard University Press, 1967), p. 321.

25. The best biographies of these two departed leaders are Hugh Toye, *The Springing Tiger: A Study of a Revolutionary* (London: Cassell, 1959), and N. D. Parikh, *Sardar Vallabhai Patel*, 2 vols. (Ahmadabad: Navajivan Press, 1953–56). Howard Spodek's "Sardar Vallabhai Patel at 100," *Economic and Political Weekly*, December 13, 1975, provides a new assessment of Patel's early career and explains some of the reasons for the Patel revival that accompanied the disillusionment with Mrs. Gandhi that began in 1973.

26. See Mansergh, *Transfer of Power*, vol. 4, *The Bengal Famine and the New Viceroyalty, 15 June 1943–31 August 1944*. Document 37, note by M. I. 2(a) gives the formation of the INA as July 8, 1943. It reports that Rash Behari

Bose, the interim president of the Indian Independence League, presented Subhas Chandra Bose to the League as its new president "who has adopted the title of "Mehtarji [*Netaji*] or Leader." Bose immediately announced the formation of a provisional government, declared his sincere belief in Japan's good intentions, and stated that India's hope for freedom lay in an Axis victory (p. 75). For a superb account of the military and political fortunes of the INA in its abortive effort to free India in the wake of Japanese forces, see Philip Mason, *A Matter of Honour: An Account of the Indian Army, Its Officers and Men* (Harmondsworth, England: Penguin, 1967).

27. Subhas Chandra Bose, *The Indian Struggle, 1920–1942* (Bombay: Asia Publishing House, 1964), p. 460.

28. Ibid., p. 454. Bose, like the early Hitler, proposed to protect labor and promote its welfare rather than create a state that represented its class interests and ideology: "The Azad [Free] India State will look after the welfare of the labourer . . . [and] the peasant will have to be given relief. . . . In this connection, institutions for the welfare of labour, like 'Arbeitsdienst' (services for labor), 'Winterhilfe' (winter welfare), 'Kraft durch Freude' (strength through joy) will be of great interest to India" (Bose, "Free India and Her Problems," in ibid., p. 457).

29. The young Bose's patron was C. R. Das, the Bengali trade unionist and democratic socialist who died in 1925. In time, his spiritual forefathers came to be Balwantrao Tilak and Bipin Chandra Pal, who allied in 1905 when the abortive partition of Bengal provided an issue around which extremists could rally at the national level. Their call for immediate independence and willingness to use violence and terrorism distinguished them from the moderates who believed that representative government and independence could be won with British help and cooperation. Mahadev Govind Ranade, the father of social reform, and his intellectual heir Gopal Krishna Gokhale, the greatest of the Indian liberals, represent a different strand from Tilak and B. C. Pal. Gokhale in turn became the young Gandhi's political guru and sponsor and Gandhi played the same role for Nehru. See Stanley A. Wolpert, *Tilak and Gokhale; Revolution and Reform in the Making of Modern India* (Berkeley and Los Angeles: University of California Press, 1962); John R. McLane, *Indian Nationalism and the Early Congress* (Princeton: Princeton University Press, 1977); B. R. Nanda, *Gokhale: The Indian Moderates and the British Raj* (Princeton: Princeton University Press, 1977); and Michael Brecher, *Nehru: A Political Biography* (Oxford: Oxford University Press, 1959). For the larger Bengali context of Bose's ideas, see Leonard Gordon, *Bengal: The Nationalist Movement, 1876–1940* (New York: Columbia University Press, 1974).

30. B. N. Pandey, a Nehru biographer, concludes that "their trial by court martial aroused the country [then in the midst of the 1946 election campaign] as nothing else could." They represented, for Nehru, India's fight for freedom (*Nehru*, [New York: Stein and Day, 1976], p. 254).

31. Pandey, *Nehru*, p. 254, citing Rajendra Prasad Papers, Report by Nehru on his visit to Malaya, 28 March 1946. See Gopal, *Nehru* 1:309–11, for an account of Nehru's visit to Malaya and the immediate rapport that was established between Nehru and Lord and Lady Mountbatten.

32. See Mason, *Matter of Honour*, pp. 513–22, where he describes Auchinleck's essential role. Paul Scott's *Raj Quartet*, particularly *A Division of the*

Spoils (London: Heinemann, 1975), provides a subtle account of raj and nationalist attitudes toward the (British) Indian Army and the INA.

33. For a full account, see Parikh, *Patel*.

34. Nehru wrote as "Chanakya," sometimes known as Kautiliya, the famous Mauryan (c. 320–185 B.C.) statesman to whom is ascribed the authorship of the *Arthasastra*, a text often characterized as Machiavellian in its depiction of statecraft. He entitled the essay, "The Rashtrapati" (father of the nation). The text, reproduced in Norman, *Nehru*, 1:498–501, appeared in *Modern Review* (Calcutta).

35. See Jayaprakash Narayan, *A Plea for the Reconstruction of Indian Polity* (Kashi, India: Sarva Seva Sangh, 1969), and W. H. Morris-Jones's trenchant critique in "The Unhappy Utopia: JP in Wonderland," *Economic Weekly*, June 25, 1960.

36. Nettl, "The State as Conceptual Variable," p. 566.

37. Barrington Moore, Jr., *Social Origins of Dictatorship and Democracy: Lord and Peasant in the Making of the Modern World* (Boston: Beacon, 1966). The quotation is from Jonathan M. Wiener, "Review of Reviews," *History and Theory 5* (1976):169 n. 124.

38. For autobiographical accounts that provide insights into the problematics of this transition, see that of an ICS officer whose experience spanned the British and Indian period, E. N. Mangat Rai (*Commitment My Style* [New Delhi: Vikas, 1973]) and of a civil servant who joined in the special recruitment just after independence, Mohan Mukerji (*Ham in the Sandwich* [New Delhi: Vikas, 1979]).

39. See, for example, Ernest Barker, *The Development of the Public Services in Europe* (New York: Oxford University Press, 1944).

40. For the shift from the ICS to the IAS, see B. B. Misra, *The Bureaucracy in India: An Historical Analysis of Development up to 1947* (New Delhi: Oxford University Press, 1977), pp. 299–308. Misra, citing Home Department file no. 30/28/47-ESB(S), reports that there were 980 ICS officers on January 1, 1947. Of these, 468 were Europeans, 352 were Hindus other than "depressed classes," and 101 were Muslims. The balance were from other religious and social communities (p. 306 n. 163).

41. As quoted in W. H. Morris-Jones, *The Government and Politics of India*, 3d. rev. ed. (London: Hutchinson, 1971), p. 26. Patel insisted, on pain of his own and the entire ICS's resignation, that the Drafting Committee of the Constituent Assembly include constitutional guarantees protecting conditions of service for the ICS comparable to those enjoyed under the raj. Patel told Constituent Assembly members opposed to guarantees for the ICS, "If you decide that we should not have the service at all, in spite of my pledged word, I will take the service with me and I will go. I will tell the servicemen, 'Let us go. The nation has changed.' They are capable of earning their living" (T. V. Kunhi Krishna, *Chavan and the Troubled Decade*, [Bombay: Somaiya Publications, 1971], p. 273, as quoted in Francine R. Frankel, *India's Political Economy, 1947–1977* [New Delhi: Oxford University Press, 1978], pp. 80–81 n. 24).

42. Jawaharlal Nehru, *Independence and After* (New York: John Day, 1950), p. 9, as quoted in Robert L. Hardgrave, Jr., *India: Government and Politics in a Developing Nation*, 3d ed. (New York: Harcourt Brace Jovanovich, 1980), p. 71.

43. Stanley Heginbotham has disaggregated four organizational ideologies of civil servants, among which the "colonial" is one. See his *Cultures in Conflict; The Four Faces of Indian Bureaucracy* (New York: Columbia University Press, 1975).

44. Philip Woodruff, *The Men Who Ruled India,* 2 vols. (New York: Schocken, 1967). Mason used Woodruff as a pseudonym when he published his remarkable if apologetic biographical and historical study of raj administrators. Also useful are B. B. Misra, *The Administrative History of India, 1834–1947* (Oxford: Oxford University Press, 1970); and David C. Potter, "Bureaucratic Change in India," and Bernard S. Cohn, "Recruitment and Training of British Civil Servants in India, 1600–1860," in Ralph Braibanti, ed., *Asian Bureaucratic Systems Emergent from the Imperial Tradition* (Durham, N.C.: Duke University Press, 1966). W. H. Morris-Jones's chapter on governance in *Government and Politics of India* (chap. 4) still provides the best short account of the services. Henry Hart has provided a thoughtful recent assessment of governance: "Political Leadership in India: Dimensions and Limits" (Paper presented at the Conference on India's Democracy, Princeton University, March 14–16, 1985).

45. V. Subramaniam reports that 89, 81, 77, 80, and 79 percent, respectively, of entrants to the Indian Foreign Service, IAS, Indian Police Service, Audit and Accounts Service, and Customs and Postal Services between 1957 and 1963 were from families whose father's occupation was "professional middle class," (e.g., higher or lower civil servant, employee of a private firm, schoolteacher, professor, doctor, and lawyer). See his *Social Background of India's Administrators* (New Delhi: Government of India, Publications Division, 1971), table 6. See also David C. Potter, "The Indian Civil Service Tradition within the Bureaucratic Structures of State Power in South Asia: 1919–1978" (Paper presented at the Sixth European Conference on Modern South Asian Studies, 1978; published as a pamphlet by the Centre National de la Recherche Scientifique [Paris], 1978).

46. For an insightful discussion of the strains between state servants and their political masters in India, see Richard P. Taub, *Bureaucrats under Stress* (Berkeley and Los Angeles: University of California Press, 1969).

47. For the original use of the term "representative bureaucracy," see J. Donald Kingsley, *Representative Bureaucracy,* (Yellow Springs, Ohio: Antioch Press, 1944); for an able critique see V. Subramaniam, "Representative Bureaucracy." For a more recent restatement, see Samuel Krislov, *Representative Bureaucracy* (Englewood Cliffs, N.J.: Prentice-Hall, 1974). Subramaniam presents data for six countries for 1957–63, showing the middle-class origins of their higher services (p. 1016). He also notes that such origins make a civil service more representative in a society where the middle classes compose 60 percent of the work force (e.g., the United States) than in one where they constitute 9 percent (e.g., India) (p. 1015).

48. At the state level, see, for example, Mangat Rai's discussion of the administrative-political collaboration in constructing the Punjab's contributions to economic development, including the Bhakra Dam and the Punjab Agricultural University at Ludhiana. He also provides microdata, of which much more is needed, to support or discredit the unproven proposition that the IAS is not development minded. His instances tend to fall fairly evenly on the pro and con sides of the argument. See, for example, *Commitment My Style,* p. 133.

For a detailed account of development work at the local level by senior officers, see Stanley Heginbotham, *Cultures in Conflict.*

49. Rai, *Commitment My Style,* pp. viii, ix.

50. For an account and explanation of bureaucratic responsiveness in the 1970s, see Dennis J. Encarnation, "The Indian Central Bureaucracy: Responsive to Whom?" *Asian Survey* 19, no. 11 (November 1979): 1126–45.

51. Cited in C. P. Bhambhri, *Administrators in a Changing Society* (New Delhi: National Publishing House, 1972), p. 24. For a series of case studies that illuminate the relationships between senior bureaucrats and politicians, see also his *Bureaucracy and Politics in India* (New Delhi: Vikas, 1971).

52. In September 1972, in a renewed effort, this time successful, to eliminate the guarantees Sardar Patel had insisted on putting in the 1950 constitution, Parliament passed the Former Secretary of State Service Officer (Conditions of Service) Bill. It became the Twentieth Amendment Act, 1972, revoking article 314 of the constitution, which had committed the Indian state to maintain the same conditions of service and rights as those enjoyed by ICS officers under the British raj. As a result, ICS officers served under the less favorable terms applicable to IAS officers.

53. D. P. Dhar, planning minister and a Gandhi loyalist "pleaded for a civil service which is committed not only to the policies and ideas enshrined in the Constitution but also the policies and programs of the ruling party which was backed by a majority of the people in the country" (quoted in Vishnu Sahay, "What Does it Mean," *Seminar,* cited by K. K. Tummala, *The Ambiguity of Ideology and Administrative Reform* [Bombay: Allied, 1977], p. 177).

54. The roster of national-level reassignments in 1975, 1977, and 1980 is long and complex, and they were by no means all mala fide. Illustrations of some widely considered to be so are the following: the abrupt removal of N. K. Mukherjee, ICS, as Home Secretary when the emergency was declared; Muhkerjee was posted to the Department of Tourism. T. C. A. Srinivasavardhan, due to retire, was replaced as home secretary by M. H. Burney when Congress returned to power in 1980. Burney had been secretary, Ministry of Information and Broadcasting, a critical emergency department and was considered an emergency stalwart. Burney was sent back to Orissa, to whose cadre he belonged, when Janata came to power. His next in line at the Ministry of Information and Broadcasting, M. K. N. Prasad, who handled press censorship under the emergency, was transferred by Janata to the relatively harmless Police Research Bureau. The director of the Central Bureau of Investigation under Janata was transferred by Congress in 1980 to his home state of Tamil Nadu. The 1980 Congress appointments most widely criticized were the promotion, over the seniority claims of many others, of P. S. Bhinder to police commissioner of Delhi and the promotion of Jag Mohan, Delhi development commissioner under the emergency, to lieutenant governor of Delhi (a union territory). Both were close to Sanjay Gandhi and figured centrally in the Shah Commission's examination of emergency excesses. They were associated with Sanjay's beautification programs that led inter alia to the highly controversial clearance of Muslim quarters around the Jama Masjid and Turkman Gate. Bhinder, in particular, was responsible for police arrangements when many poor Muslims who rioted at Turkman Gate against slum clearance and vasectomy camps died as a result of police firing (*Statesman,* April 13, 1980 and Government of India, Ministry of Home Affairs, *Shah Commission of Inquiry:*

Interim Report II [Delhi, 1978], chaps. 8, 9, particularly pp. 96–101, 120–46). For an up-close account by a craftsmanly administrator in the emergency, see Mohan Mukerji, *Non-story of a Chief Secretary During Emergency, Etcetera* (New Delhi: Associated Publishing House, 1982).

55. Rajni Kothari believed that the cure for a rule-bound and routinized bureaucracy characterized by lack of trust, confidence, and spontaneity was a radical restructuring of the relationship between bureaucracy and party: "The point of all this is to politicize the administration" (*Democratic Polity and Social Change in India* [Bombay: Allied, 1976], pp. 67–69). In the perspective of the 1980s, such a critique and cure need to address the balance between the legal obligations and programmatic obligations of civil servants on the one hand and demands for purely partisan resource and patronage allocation on the other. In "Where Are We Heading," *Express Magazine,* November 29, 1981, Kothari wrote a powerful polemic along lines similar to those advanced here. He argued for "an institutional framework that protects the country from both the cult of personality and the politics of survival."

56. See Ezra N. Suleiman, *Politics, Power and Bureaucracy in France: The Administrative Elite* (Princeton: Princeton University Press, 1974), chaps. 8, 9, pp. 181–238.

57. For an extended discussion of loyalty and team spirit in bureaucracies, see our "Authority and Power in Bureaucratic and Patrimonial Administration: A Revisionist Interpretation of Weber on Bureaucracy," *World Politics* 31 (January 1979).

58. The Administrative Reforms Commission found that the principal weakness of India's higher civil service (IAS) was the supremacy of the generalist and "generalism." Its solution was to recommend that specialists and experts be given more senior posts and to call for more professionalism in the outlook and training of the senior bureaucracy (Government of India, Ministry of Home Affairs, Administrative Reforms Commission, *Report of the Study Team on the Machinery of the Government of India and Its Procedures at Work* [New Delhi, 1968]), pt. 2, vol. 1, pp. 106–7. See also Shriman Maheshwari, *The Administrative Reforms Commission* (Agra, India: Lakshmi Narain Agarwal, 1972). For an account that argues that professionalization leads to rigidity, and that criticizes insulation of bureaucracies, see Encarnation, "Indian Central Bureaucracy."

59. Government of India, Ministry of Finance, *Study Group on Wages, Incomes and Prices: Report* (Delhi, 1978), tables 14, 15. (This is generally referred to as the Boothalingam Report.

60. For an early intimation of this problem, see Taub, *Bureaucrats under Stress.*

61. *Hindu,* June 23, 1984.

62. Ibid.

63. P. R. Brahmananda, *Productivity in the Indian Economy* (Bombay: Himalaya Publishing House, 1982), table 19.02.

64. R. N. Chopra, *Public Sector in India* (New Delhi, Intellectual Publishing House, [c. 1983]), p. 85. For an account of conflict between the IAS and technical officers in the public sector, see Howard Erdman, "Politics and Industrial Management: The IAS in Joint Sector Fertilizer Companies," *Journal of the Institute of Public Enterprises,* January–March 1986.

65. "An Indian Personality for Television: Report of the Working Group on

Software for Doordarshan," pt. 2, published unofficially in *Mainstream*, April 14, 21, and 28, 1984 and May 1984 (Nehru no.).

66. K. S. Bhat, "Tenure of the Chief Executives and Composition of the Board: Two Issues in SLPE Corporate Management" (Hyderabad, 1984, mimeograph). The author is on the faculty of the Institute of Public Enterprise, Osmania University Campus.

67. In January of 1986, the Ministry of Personnel and Administrative Reforms proposed a scheme by which newly appointed IAS officers would have no more than three appointments in their first eleven years, including the two probationary years; new entrants would be encouraged to specialize; senior officers in their seventeenth year would be subject to "data based performance assessment" before further promotion; officers would be selected into an "integrated management pool" from the three all-India services (Indian Police Service, IAS, Indian Forest Service) and other central services on the basis of proven administrative ability to fill senior positions in the administration; and entrants to the all-India services would be assigned to one of five zonal cadres instead of the present practice of assignment to a state, to break up the locality-based cliques and factions into which officers are now frequently drawn (*Times of India*, January 29, 1986; *Statesman*, January 18 and January 29, 1986).

68. *Statesman*, May 28, 1984.

69. Ibid.

70. See note 34 above.

71. Antulay resigned from his post as chief minister of Maharashtra after the Bombay high court held him culpable in exchanging cement allocations for party funds. He was later tried for extorting funds from businesses for the Pratibha Pratisthan Maharashtra, a trust said to support deserving artists and performers. After one dismissal by the supreme court, the case was still in the courts in April 1985 (*Asian Recorder*, July 2–8, 1985, p. 18391). Deputy Chief Minister Adik resigned after allegations of drunken and lascivious behavior to, from, and at an international trade fair in Germany. See *India Today*, May 15, 1984, pp. 20–24, for accounts of Antulay's and Adik's conduct.

72. See, for example, "Uttar Pradesh, Milking the State," *India Today*, May 31, 1984, pp. 76–79.

73. "Indira Gandhi and the Culture of Indian Politics," in Ashis Nandy, *At the Edge of Psychology: Essays in Politics and Culture* (New Delhi: Oxford University Press, 1980), p. 114.

74. See Philip Mason, *Matter of Honour.*

75. Defense Minister V. K. Krishna Menon, who presumably saw to Kaul's appointment as corps commander, was forced to resign over the deplorable state of readiness of the forces and poor military leadership and performance. There was sentiment inside and outside the army that the appointment of Kaul to command the forces facing China at the moment of imminent crisis was based on his connection with Menon and with his fellow Kashmiri, Prime Minister Jawaharlal Nehru, rather than on professional considerations. Some thought Kaul was being groomed for becoming chief of army staff. Kaul was relieved from command of IV Corps on November 20, 1962, by Lieutenant General Chaudhuri, who had just been appointed chief of army staff to replace General P. N. Thapar, who resigned on November 19. Kaul resigned from the army rather than accept the training command Chaudhuri offered to him. See

Rudolph and Rudolph, "Generals and Politicians in India," *Pacific Affairs* 37, no. 1 (Spring 1964); Lt. General B. N. Kaul, *The Untold Story* (Bombing: Allied, 1967); Neville Maxwell, *India's China War* (New York: Anchor, 1972); and J. P. Dalvi, *Himalyan Blunder* (Calcutta: Thacker, 1969).

76. See Stephen P. Cohen, *The Indian Army: Its Contribution to the Development of a Nation* (Berkeley and Los Angeles: University of California Press, 1971), and the same author's more recent assessment, "The Military," in Henry C. Hart, ed., *Indira Gandhi's India: A Political System Appraisal* (Boulder, Colo.: Westview, 1976). See also "Using the Army," *Seminar*, no. 308 (April 1985).

77. There was, for example, some controversy over the retirement of General Krishna Rao as chief of the army staff in 1983, when the succession was decided in favor of the less-senior General A. S. Vaidya and against the more-senior General S. K. Sinha, vice-chief of the army staff and generally considered in line for the chief of staff position, who resigned. The appointment was said to have been affected by personal and political considerations, regarded as unfortunate by members of the service. (See *Indian Express*, July 18 (editorial) and July 29 (letter), 1984; and see General Sinha's article in *Statesman*, May 2, 1984. The appointment of General T. N. Raina over more-senior officers in 1975 was controversial for the same reason.

78. Stephen P. Cohen, "The Military and Indian Democracy" (Paper presented at the Conference on India's Democracy, Princeton University, March 14–16, 1985). The next paragraph draws on this account.

79. See reports of Commissioner R. K. Triveldi's conference in December 1983, of seven national, seventeen regional, and eight registered parties (*Statesman*, December 4, 1983).

80. *Times of India*, December 13, 1983; *Indian Express*, December 15, 1983; *Hindustan Times*, December 15, 1983.

81. Following the revelation of taped conversations of Veerappa Moily, leader of the Congress party in Karnataka, offering a Rs. 200,000 bribe to C. Byre Gowda to defect from the Janata party and join Congress, the late Congress-I party secretary, C. M. Stephen, an articulate defender of the doctrine that all means are justified in politics, asserted the right of his party to encourage defection (*Times of India*, November 20, 1985).

82. For a critique of central control of the electronic media, see "An Indian Personality for Television."

83. Government of India, Ministry of Home Affairs, *Seventh Report of the National Police Commission* (Delhi, 1982), 7 (supplement note). For a careful overall view, see David H. Bayley, *The Police and Political Development in India* (Princeton: Princeton University Press, 1969).

84. *Third Report of the National Police Commission* (Delhi, 1980), p. 25.

85. The total number of Indian Police Service officers in 1978 was 2,344 (*Sixth Report of the National Police Commission* [Delhi, 1982], appendix, p. 59.

86. *Third Report of the National Police Commission*, p. 26.

87. *Second Report of the National Police Commission* (Delhi, 1979), p. 24.

88. Ibid., p. 25.

89. Reserve Bank of India, *Report on Currency and Finance, 1983–84* (Bombay, 1985), vol. 7, statement 80, p. 107.

90. Myron Weiner, "India's New Political Institutions," *Asian Survey* 16 (September 1976).

91. For a complete account of police and constabulary strikes see Cohen, "Military and Indian Democracy," p. 40.

92. *Leader,* February 1, 1980, cited in Paul Brass, "National Power and Local Politics in India: A Twenty-Year Perspective" (Paper presented at the Institute of Commonwealth Studies, University of London, 1982), p. 13.

93. *Hindu,* February 9, 1980.

94. Thus, a random example of Bihar administration of the sort one used to hear from indifferently administered princely states such as Udaipur in the 1920s, is that of Rudal Shah who suffered fourteen years of unlawful incarceration after being acquitted in 1968. Shah had the unique luck of having his case brought to the attention of the supreme court in 1982 by a law student (*Times of India,* August 4, 1983).

95. Kuldip Nayar, *Sunday* (Calcutta), July 24–30, 1983.

96. *Indian Express,* May 20, 1984.

97. *Indian Express,* May 20, 1984.

98. Hardgrave, *India,* p. 64.

99. Subhash Kashyap, "The Eighth Lok Sabha: A Profile of Its Members" *Indian and Foreign Review,* May 31, 1985.

100. For example, in a speech before the Rajasthan Political Sciences Association Meeting of fall 1975, Chief Minister Harideo Joshi condemned the wasting of time in Parliament, which detracted from the vital business to which ministers should attend (authors' notes of meeting).

101. *Illustrated Weekly,* January 1, 1984.

102. See ibid. and D. C. Wadhwa, *Promulgation of Ordinances: A Fraud in the Constitution of India* (Bombay: Orient Longman, 1983).

103. The atrophy that besets state assemblies is also evident in the fate of legislative committees. For a critical account of the inattentiveness of Uttar Pradesh cabinets to the reports of legislative committees, notably the committee on government assurances, see P. K. Srivastava "Legislature in Uttar Pradesh" (Ph.D. diss. Lucknow University, 1983), chap. 7.

104. The Harish Chandra Mathur Institute at Jaipur provides such training.

105. For an early critique, see Ivor Jennings, *Some Characteristics of the Indian Constitution* (Oxford: Oxford University Press, 1953). For a discussion of bargaining federalism, see Morris-Jones, *Government and Politics of India,* pp. 150–56.

106. Government of Tamil Nadu, *Report of the Centre-State Relations Inquiry Committee, 1971* (Madras, 1971).

107. "The party organization of the prime minister's Congress, instead of serving as an institution of recruitment and linkage between different levels of India's federal system, as it had before, became more unitary with control maintained by the Prime Minister. Presidents circulated almost annually, tickets for elections were allocated centrally" (Richard Sisson, "Prime Ministerial Power and the Selection of Ministers in India: Three Decades of Change," *International Political Science Review* 2, no. 2 [1981]: 150.

108. *State of Rajasthan v. Union of India,* 1977 A.I.R. 1361.

109. *Constituent Assembly Debates; Official Report,* 12 vols. (Delhi, 1946–50), 7:455, as quoted in Durga Das Basu, *Introduction to the Constitution of India,* 10th ed. (New Delhi: Prentice-Hall of India, 1983), p. 213.

110. Basu, *Introduction to Constitution,* 10th ed., p. 212.

111. *Surya v. Union of India,* 1982 A. 1982 Rajasthan 1, with respect to Tilak, confirmed that the president's pleasure under article 154(1) can be used

by the prime minister to dismiss any governor for political reasons without assigning any charge. Prabhudas Patwari was similarly dismissed in Tamil Nadu in October 1980. See Durga Das Basu, *Constitutional Law of India* (New Delhi: Prentice-Hall of India, 1983), p. 164 n. 12; see also Basu, *Introduction to Constitution*, 10th ed., p. 219 n. 8a. See Bhagwan Dua's critical remarks in "India: Congress Dominance Revisited" (Paper presented at the Thirty-seventh Annual Meeting of the Association for Asian Studies, Philadelphia, March 1985). See also his *Presidential Rule in India* (New Delhi: Chand, 1979), a severe indictment of the partisan use of this power, and "India: A Study in the Pathology of a Federal System," *Journal of Commonwealth and Comparative Politics* 19 (November 1981).

112. Basu, *Introduction to Constitution*, 10th ed., p. 311.

113. *Constituent Assembly Debates* 9 : 177, cited in ibid.

114. Ibid., pp. 308–11, where Basu lists each case. Janata used the device nineteen times.

115. Ibid., p. 312.

Chapter 3

1. Nettl's "measure" of "stateness" is evoked by the question "Is there a historical tradition . . . for the existence, primacy, autonomy and sovereignty of a state? Do the political ideas and theories of the society, past or present, incorporate a notion of a state, and what role do they assign to it?" ("The state as Conceptual Variable," p. 566.)

2. One index of the intensified struggle is the fact that fourteen of thirty-seven amendments (the twenty-fourth through the thirty-seventh) prior to the emergency (June 25, 1975) occurred after the 1971 parliamentary election. The twenty-fourth amendment was an attempt to reverse *Golak Nath*, discussed below.

3. Articles 19, 20, 21, 22, 31, 31a, 31b, and 368.

4. *Golak Nath v. State of Punjab* 1967 A.I.R. (S.C.) 1643. It reversed *Shankari Prasad v. Union of India* 1951 A.I.R. (S.C.) 458, which held that no part of the constitution was unamendable, and *Sajjan Singh v. State of Rajasthan* 1964 A.I.R. (S.C.) 845.

5. For a discussion of the forty-second amendment and other constitutional developments under the emergency, see Michael Henderson, "Setting India's Democratic House in Order: Constitutional Amendments," *Asian Survey* 19, no. 10 (October 1979).

6. Part 4, articles 36–51.

7. *Keshavananda Bharati v. State of Kerala* [1973] 4 S.C.C. 225; 1973 A.I.R. (S.C.) 1461. The eleven opinions of the case run to over seven hundred pages. They have been abridged in M. C. J. Kagzi, *The Keshavananda's Case* (Delhi: Metropolitan, 1973). Surendra Malik, ed., *The Fundamental Rights Case: The Critics Speak!* (Lucknow: Eastern Book Co., 1975), provides a summary of the arguments (pp. 1–52); six articles interpreting the decision and its eleven opinions, by N. S. Bindra, N. A. Palkhivala, K. Subba Rao, P. K. Tripathi, Upendra Baxi, and Joseph Minattur (pp. 53–158); and an "Analytical Summary of the Case" in seven parts prepared by Malik (pp. 225–304), who

also supplies an "editorial" introduction. The book is self-confessedly mis-named: "Though the case primarily involved the validity of Constitution Amendments and should have been so popularly named, the name 'Funda-mental Rights Case' was popularized by the daily newspapers apparently be-cause *Keshavananda Bharati* was a sequel to *Golak Nath* which had held the Fundamental Rights unamendable" (p. 5). Upendra Baxi observes that "al-though [*Keshavananda*] is in the ultimate analysis a judicial decision, it is not just a reported case on some Articles of the Indian Constitution. Indeed, I be-lieve that it is, in some sense, the Indian Constitution of the future" (p. 130). See also George H. Gadbois, Jr., "Judicial Review in India" (Paper presented at the American Political Science Association, New York, September 3–6, 1981).

8. *Constituent Assembly Debates* 9:1195.

9. *Constituent Assembly Debates* 9:1662–63, cited in Austin, *Indian Constitution,* p. 263.

10. Austin, *Indian Constitution,* p. 264.

11. See articles by Kuldip Nayar and Nani A. Palkhivala in *Indian Express,* May 14 and May 16, 1980. A. K. Ayyar and K. M. Munshi were the strongest advocates in the Constituent Assembly's rights subcommittee of limitations on fundamental rights. They were supported by a galaxy of members of the as-sembly's senior advisory committee, including K. M. Panikkar, G. B. Pant, C. Rajagopalachari, and Sardar Patel. The rank and file of the assembly re-sisted and blocked substantial limitations favored by the leadership. Rau's pro-posal that directive principles should override fundamental rights was sup-ported by K. T. Shah, K. M. Munshi, and Dr. Ambedkar. See Austin, *Indian Constitution,* pp. 68–78, for the debate on fundamental rights and the discus-sion of directive principles. See also Rajeev Dhavan, *The Supreme Court of India and Parliamentary Sovereignty* (New Delhi: Sterling, 1976).

12. According to Austin, "The desire to restrict the purview of the courts in certain matters was not restricted to 'liberals' like Ayyar and Rau. Patel led the way in giving the Executive authority, largely unsupervised by the courts, to impose preventive detention. He had also opposed the inclusion in the Con-stitution of rights to secrecy of correspondence and to inviolability of an indi-vidual's person and home." In the Advisory Committee's discussion of "due process" limitations on abolition of the zamindari system of agrarian in-termediaries, Patel's strong-state views converged with Nehru's view of the state as an agent of social transformation: "'There is a danger,' Patel said, 'that a certain old type of judges may misinterpret this new process of law'" (*Indian Constitution,* p. 175).

13. The fears of the socialists were realized when early state acts abolishing intermediaries ("feudal" landlords) were subject to long delays from frequent appeals to the courts. Nehru forced through the first constitutional amend-ment in 1951, which removed such acts from court review by placing them in a ninth schedule of the constitution under newly inserted clauses, 31A and 31B of article 31, dealing with the acquisition of property by the state and with the amount of compensation. Further amendments to article 31 followed in 1955 (fourth amendment), 1964 (seventh amendment), and 1971 (twenty-sixth amendment). On four more occasions after the first amendment and prior to the emergency (June 1975), additional state acts were placed in the ninth schedule as a result of the fourth, seventeenth, twenty-ninth (1972), and

thirty-fourth (1974) amendments. Wholesale use of the ninth schedule was resorted to under the emergency. These uses by Parliament of its amending
power provided a less direct but effective procedure for limiting judicial
review.

14. Nani A. Palkhivala, *Our Constitution Profaned and Defiled*, (New
Delhi: Macmillan India, 1974), p. 135.

15. Ibid., p. 137.

16. The Gandhi government's brief in the habeas corpus case of 1976 argued that under an emergency there were no constitutional, statutory, common law, or natural law restraints on the state in depriving citizens of liberty or
even life. See Kuldip Nayar, *The Judgment: Inside Story of the Emergency
in India* (New Delhi: Vikas, 1977), p. 123 for Attorney General Niren De's
brief on behalf of the government. A more detailed account of doctrines at
issue in the habeas corpus case is given in David Selbourne, *An Eye to India:
The Unmasking of Tyranny* (Harmondsworth, England: Penguin, 1977), pp.
145–50.

17. For an excellent discussion of the political significance of Kumaramangalam, see Frankel, *India's Political Economy*, chap. 10, 11.

18. For Mohan Kumaramangalam's legal theory see his *Constitutional
Amendments: The Reason Why* (New Delhi: All India Congress Committee,
November 1971). In it, he argued that the twenty-fourth, twenty-fifth, and
twenty-sixth amendments (reasserting the amending power of Parliament,
asserting the primacy of directive principles over fundamental rights, and
abolishing the privy purses of the princes) and the substitution of the word
"amount" for the word "compensation" in article 31C to ease acquisition of
property, gave Parliament "the power to determine where the line is to be
drawn between the preservation of private property rights on the one hand and
the assertion of the rights of the community on the other" (p. 29).

19. Justive V. R. Krishna Iyer in *Statesman*, April 7, 1980.

20. Justice P. N. Bhagwati in *Statesman*, April 3, 1980.

21. Narayan's letter of May 16, 1973, is reproduced in Kuldip Nayar, ed.,
The Supercession of Judges (New Delhi: Indian Book Co., 1973), pp. 69–72.

22. Articles 19(f) and article 31.

23. Article 31 governs state acquisition of property, providing that it is acquired by law and for public purposes. After three amendments, the first,
fourth, and seventeenth, failed to preclude judicial review that enforced the
payment of adequate compensation (market value), the twenty-fifth amendment (1971) substituted the word "amount" for "compensation." Even so, the
majority in *Keshavananda* (1973) held that the amount fixed by the legislature
cannot be arbitrary or illusory. Articles 14 and 19 guarantee equal protection
under the law and of fundamental rights.

24. The amendment added article 31A, which holds that no law providing
for the acquisition by the state of any "estate" shall be deemed void on the
ground that it is inconsistent with the rights conferred by articles 14, 19,
or 31; it also added 31B which established the ninth schedule. See G. G.
Mirchandani, *Subverting the Constitution* (Columbia, Mo.: South Asia Books,
1977), chap. 7, for an analysis of the history of its use and abuse. Of the 188
laws protected from judicial review by the Ninth Schedule, 102 were placed
there by the thirty-ninth and fortieth amendments passed under the emer-

gency. See pp. 162–73 for the titles of all acts placed in the ninth schedule, including the objectionable matter bill which enabled the censuring of parliamentary debates.

25. The fourth amendment added article 31(2) making the adequacy of compensation nonjusticiable. When the courts responded, in *Cooper v. Union of India* 1970 A.I.R. (S.C.) 564, that the very word "compensation" implied full monetary value (i.e., market value), the twenty-fifth amendment substituted the word "amount" for the word "compensation" in article 31C and provided that laws implementing certain directive principles of state policy (part 4) calling for redistribution of resources could not be voided for inconsistency with articles 14, 19, or 31.

26. Article 368.

27. *Keshavananda* upheld the validity of the twenty-fifth amendment, article 31C, which provided that no act of Parliament that includes a declaration designed to give effect to directive principles 39B and 39C would be declared void "on the ground that it is inconsistent with, or takes away or abridges any of the rights conferred by article 14, 9, or 31." The state is enjoined to direct its policy toward securing, under 39B, that the "ownership and control of the material resources of the community are so distributed to subserve the common good" and, under 39C, that "the operation of the economic system does not result in the concentration of wealth and means of production to the common detriment." Both tests seem to provide substantial policy space for a "socialist" Parliament. See report on the *Minerva Mills* case in *Times of India*, May 10, 1980. For the view that *Keshavananda* did not preclude court review of the constitutionality of legislation passed under the provisions laid down by article 31C, see Durga Das Basu, *Introduction to the Constitution of India*, 6th ed. (New Delhi: Prentice-Hall of India, 1976), p. 103.

28. See Uma Vasudeva's interview with Sanjay Gandhi of August 6, 1975, published as an appendix to her *Two Faces of Indira Gandhi*, (New Delhi: Vikas, 1977), especially pp. 201–7. For Sanjay Gandhi's tactical retreat from his anti-Russian and anticommunist views in that interview, see his interview in *Surya*, July 1979, p. 32.

29. It explicitly excluded the courts from entertaining questions relating to the ground or reasons for the president's "satisfaction" in issuing an emergency proclamation on the advice of the council of ministers and allowed the president to make multiple (concurrent) declarations.

30. For a discussion of the seniority convention, see articles by Nayar, Justice J. M. Shelat, K. S. Hegde, A. N. Grover, M. C. Chagla, and N. A. Palkhivala in Nayar's *Supersession of Judges*. Kumaramangalam's defense in Parliament of the supersession of the three senior supreme court judges, when A. N. Ray was appointed chief justice to replace the retiring S. M. Sikri, is reproduced by Nayar, pp. 78–92. Kumaramangalam argued that it was the government's "duty . . . to come to the conclusion whether a particular person is fit to be appointed the Chief Justice of the Court because of his outlook, because of his philosophies expressed in his . . . opinions." See also his *Judicial Appointments* (New Delhi: Oxford and IBH, 1973). See also Rajeev Dhavan and Alice Jacob, *Selection and Appointment of Supreme Court Judges: A Case Study* (Bombay: Tripathi, 1978).

31. The invalidating was supported by all five judges: Ray, Beg, Khanna,

Chandrachud, and Mathew. The basic structure argument was that of the last three (*Keesing's Contemporary Archives*, January 16, 1976, p. 27525). See also Basu, *Introduction to Constitution*, 6th ed., pp. 325–26, particularly n. 3.

32. Upendra Baxi, *The Indian Supreme Court and Politics* (Lucknow: Eastern Book Co., 1980), p. 193.

33. *Keshavananda* was a confusing decision because it failed to define or provide an agreed list of its components. The government did not want merely a clarification for the sake of some three hundred writs that challenged laws for violating basic structure and were pending in various courts; it also wanted reversal of the doctrine and of its positive consequences for judicial review. But the Andhra Pradesh case that might have tested the doctrine and that was being heard by a partial ("constitution") bench, was not pursued by the full bench (all thirteen justices) convened by Justice Ray and was later dismissed by a constitution bench of the court. See Baxi, *Indian Supreme Court*, pp. 70–76; *Keesing's Contemporary Archives*, January 16, 1976, p. 27526; and Kuldip Nayar, *Judgment*, p. 94. Nayar claims that Chief Justice A. N. Ray "came to know that the majority of judges were not in favour of reviewing the case" (i.e., *Keshavananda*).

34. "A Fresh Look at Our Constitution: Some Suggestions" (1975, mimeograph). See also Kuldip Nayar, *Judgment*, p. 115. Nayar attributes authorship to B. K. Nehru and Rajni Patel.

35. Article 83 of the constitution of the Fifth Republic, cited as source, does not deal with the judiciary but with the community of French ex-colonial countries. Article 64, chapter 8, "The Judicial Authority" deals with the Supreme Council of Justice. That article coincides roughly with the description attached to "A Fresh Look": "Composed of fourteen members, its president is the president of the republic and its vice-president is the justice minister. It also includes twelve persons chosen for six year terms, six from outside the national assembly but elected by two-thirds majorities within it, four elected judges representing each category of the judiciary, and two members of the legal profession appointed by the president from outside the membership of the national assembly and the judiciary," p. 12.

36. By deleting those sections of article 13 of India's present constitution that make fundamental rights justiciable.

37. The rights specified are freedom of speech and expression; freedom of peaceable assembly; freedom of association; freedom of movement; freedom to have, hold, and use property; and freedom to carry on an occupation.

38. Baxi, *Indian Supreme Court*, pp. 34–35.

39. Justices Chandrachud, Beg, Ray, and Bhagwati constituted the majority (*Keesing's Contemporary Archives*, June 18, 1976, p. 27781). According to Kuldip Nayar, the decision "came as a surprise and disappointed many people because it was believed that Chandrachud and Bhagwati would support habeas corpus" (*Judgment*, p. 124).

40. Quoted in Norman D. Palmer, "India in 1975: Democracy in Eclipse" *Asian Survey* 16, no. 2 (February 1976): 104.

41. For a significant challenge on these and other grounds by Indian intellectuals, see M. C. Chagla et al., *Nationwide Demand for Postponement of Constitution Amendment Bill* (New Delhi, National Book Centre, 1976),

which contains a "Statement by Intellectuals," signed by 375 of India's leading academics, journalists, writers, and professionals (pp. 51–52).

42. It did so by stipulating that legislation stated to give effect to the directive principles could not be impugned as violations of articles 13 and 19 (fundamental rights). The twenty-fifth amendment had attempted to do this (see note 26 above). For useful contemporary accounts, see S. P. Sathe, "Forty-Fourth Constitutional Amendment," *Economic and Political Weekly,* October 23, 1976; S. V. Kogekar, "Constitutional Amendment Bill, *Economic and Political Weekly,* October 16, 1976. See also Rajeev Dhavan, *The Amendment: Conspiracy or Revolution?* (Allahabad: Wheeler, 1978).

43. Another provision of the forty-second amendment that weakened judicial review and the court's capacity to "balance" Parliament was one that raised from five to seven the number of judges for a constitution bench and required a majority of five to validate decisions. For further analysis of the forty-second (initially forty-fourth) amendment, see references in note 41 above. See also Mirchandani, *Subverting the Constitution,* which deals with the thirty-eighth amendment (denying the courts the power to review a presidential proclamation of emergency), the thirty-ninth (retroactively barring the courts from examining electoral disputes involving inter alia the prime minister), and the forty-second; and our "To the Brink and Back: Representation and the State in India," *Asian Survey* 18, no. 4 (April 1978):397–99.

44. *Times of India,* February 12, 1978. The prime minister made his decision in the face of strong pressure by "a veritable Who's Who of the legal profession." A *Statesman* editorial called for a "supersession . . . to end all supersessions" or "a third 'ultimate' supersession." See Henry J. Abraham, "'Merit' or 'Seniority'? Reflections on the Politics of Recent Appointment to the Chief Justiceship of India," *Journal of Commonwealth and Comparative Politics* 16, no. 3 (November, 1978):305.

45. For details, see *Times of India,* January 1, 1978; *Hindu,* April 21, 1978; *Indian Express,* August 8, 1978; *Overseas Hindustan Times,* September 14, 1978; and *Asian Recorder,* January 8–14, 1979, pp. 14685–86, and June 4–10, 1979, pp. 14919–20.

46. Mrs. Gandhi's formal case for the proclamation of emergency's being "a Constitutional step" is given in Government of India, Ministry of Home Affairs, *Shah Commission on Inquiry: Interim Report I* (Delhi, 1978), paragraphs 5.61, 5.62, pp. 26–29. Mrs. Gandhi explicitly denies that "the Emergency was declared for personal reasons, namely to stultify the judgment [of the Allahabad High Court] by extra-legal means and to maintain my position as Prime Minister by extra-constitutional methods" (p. 29). She charges that there was an "internal disturbance" that threatened India's security: "the Judgment of the Allahabad High Court was . . . seized upon by the opposition," she stated in a written reply to the Shah Commission, "to whip up political frenzy against me."

Critical evaluations of the declaration of emergency and its use can be found in Nayar, *Judgment;* Vasudeva, *Two Faces of Indira Gandhi;* Nayantara Sahgal, *Indira Gandhi's Emergence and Style* (New Delhi: Vikas, 1978); and Selbourne, *Eye to India.* The most scathing and historically and philosophically informed interpretations of the emergency can be found in Arun Shourie's *Symptoms of Fascism* (New Delhi: Vikas, 1978). For a generally positive interpretation, see Marie C. Carras, *Indira Gandhi in the Crucible of Leadership* (Boston: Beacon, 1979).

47. For an authoritative detailed account of the abuses of power or "excesses" see Shah *Commission of Inquiry: Interim Report I*, pp. 17–32. The Shah Commission report was withdrawn from the market in March 1980, after Mrs. Gandhi returned to power, and government booksellers were ordered to return their copies to government.

The second paragraph of Prime Minister Gandhi's midnight letter to the president of India recommending that he declare an emergency states: "I would have like to have taken this to Cabinet but unfortunately this is not possible tonight. I am, therefore, condoning or permitting a departure from the Government of India (Transaction of Business Rules, 1961), as amended up-to-date by virtue of my powers under Rule 12 thereof. I shall mention the matter to the Cabinet first thing tomorrow morning" (p. 25). Paragraph 5.66, p. 29, of the Shah Commission's report deals with the validity of Mrs. Gandhi's use of rule 12 to justify her failure to submit the emergency decision to her cabinet colleagues (Council of Ministers). For a defense of this use, see Carras, *Indira Gandhi*, pp. 218–23. According to Carras, Mrs. Gandhi told her that she did not "consult the ministers" prior to the decision because "she was fearful of leaks and felt that secrecy had to be maintained at all costs" (p. 221). See Shourie, "Spineless Stalwarts," in *Symptoms of Fascism* (pp. 212–215), for an account of Mrs. Gandhi's premeditation in declaring the emergency.

48. The provision sought to remedy and prevent one of the most significant restrictions of civil and political rights during the emergency, the censorship of press reports of parliamentary debates and proceedings under the Prevention of Publication of Objectionable Matters Act. The fortieth amendment, also passed during the emergency, placed the act in the ninth schedule, where it became immune from judicial review.

49. See clauses 42, 40, 3, and 37 of the Forty-fourth Amendment Bill (later the forty-fourth amendment) and *Overseas Hindustan Times,* May 10, 1979. See also Henderson, "Setting India's Democratic House in Order," p. 953. *The Shah Commission: Interim Report I,* paragraphs 5.80, 5.81, pp. 31–33, refers to the "gross irregularities by which the provisions of the Maintenance of Internal Security Act and provisions of the Defence of India Rules were misused to the detriment of political opponents." Their provisions "were not complied with, either at the behest of Smt. Indira Gandhi or her aides and orders were made without any grounds, without any satisfaction or maintenance of any record regarding the satisfaction of competent authorities; and personal liberty of many citizens was taken away and they continued to remain deprived of liberty for substantial periods even in the face of safeguards which were incorporated against misuse of section 16A of MISA."

On September 23, 1980, the Gandhi Congress-I government reinstated preventive detention via presidential ordinance (the National Security Ordinance). It authorized detention of persons to prevent them from acting in a manner prejudicial to the defense or security of India and on the grounds of the security of a state and the maintenance of services essential to the life of the community. Since 1950 there have been only two brief periods—January to May 1970 and March 1977 to September 22, 1980—when India has been without central authority to use preventive detention. The September ordinance, unlike the notorious MISA used during the emergency, is subject to provisions of the forty-fifth amendment, such as the requirement that a detained person be informed of the reason for his arrest, that an advisory board composed of sitting or former high court judges review the circumstances of arrest within two months, and that individual acts as well as the ordinance (or subsequent legislation) can be challenged in a court of law.

Another ordinance issued in September amended the criminal procedure code by making executive rather than judicial magistrates responsible for enforcing provisions of section 108, which barred attempts to bring into hatred and contempt the government established by law, by the following means: the preaching of disaffection, including disloyalty and feelings of enmity toward the government (but not comments disapproving of the government's action), imputations of lack of patriotism on the part of religious or linguistic groups, the preaching of communal or religious disharmony, and deliberate and malicious acts intended to outrage religious feelings. The danger is that overzealous executives intent on pleasing higher authorities may treat allegations about expression as proof. For an analysis of both ordinances see S. Sahay, "A Close Look: That Law Again," *The Statesman Weekly*, October 4, 1980, p. 12, and "MISA in Another Garb," *Economic and Political Weekly*, September 27, 1980, which argues that loopholes in the National Security Ordinance appear to have restored "all the hateful provisions" of the emergency period of MISA (p. 1602).

50. The forty-fourth amendment reduced from two months to one month the period, if Parliament is not sitting, for which an emergency proclamation is valid before being approved by a (now) two-thirds parliamentary vote. The 1950 constitution already provided that approval of a proclamation of emergency can be given by Parliament for six months only, with six-month extensions thereafter, and for special measures to guard against emergency proclamations if Parliament is dissolved.

51. *Statesman, Times of India, Indian Express, and Hindustan Times* of May 10 and 11, 1980.

52. The court's opinion specifically mentions that article 31(C) as it stood prior to the forty-second amendment, that is, when it provided that directive principles of state policy—articles 39B and 39C—could override fundamental rights, is compatible with the basic structure argument. It is the much wider 1976 effort to extend the precedence to any law "containing a declaration that it is for giving effect to" directive principles, that was struck down (*Times of India*, May 10, 1980).

53. Basu, *Introduction to Constitution*, ed. 6, pp. 249–50, lays out the nature of the advisory process and describes its use up to 1975.

54. See ibid., pp. 294–99, for an account of the provisions and use of article 356(1), which provides that the president by proclamation may impose president's rule when satisfied that a state's government cannot be carried on in accordance with the provisions of the constitution. "It has been strongly urged," Basu writes, "that the power under Article 356 cannot be used to dismiss a Ministry so long as it commands the confidence of the majority in the State Legislature. But since the use of the power rests on the subjective satisfaction of the President, its propriety cannot be questioned by the Courts" (p. 298).

55. For an account of the parliamentary debate, including Home Minis-

ter Zail Singh's statements that "his Government was merely following the precedent set by the Janata Government in 1977," see *Hindustan Times,* March 28, 1980.

56. The special courts bill, contrary to Janata's original intent, was amended in Parliament to give such courts jurisdiction over all abuses of power, not merely those committed under the emergency (*Overseas Hindustan Times,* May 17, 1979).

57. See *The Indian Express,* February 20, 1980, for a critical editorial, "End of Special Courts," that decried their demise on "an obscure technicality."

58. *Hindustan Times,* September 23, 1979; *Indian Express,* September 25, 1979. Arun Shourie's "Haryana Cases: What Next?" in *Institutions in the Janata Phase* (Bombay: Popular Prakashan, 1980), pp. 52–57, discusses the purely political nature of the Harayan government and public prosecutor's decision. Soon after the dismissal of the case, Bhajan Lal's government defected en masse to Congress-I to save itself from dissolution.

59. After repeated and protracted delays to accommodate Maneka Gandhi or her counsel, a single nonattendance by plaintiff, the noted journalist Romesh Thapar, was used to dismiss the case.

60. *Stateman,* February 24, 1980.

61. *Times of India,* March 15, 1980.

62. *Hindustan Times,* September 13, 1979.

63. The justices presiding over the special courts, appointed six months earlier under the Janata government, discovered on January 15 and February 14, shortly after Mrs. Gandhi was elected, that the rules of business of the Home and Law ministries were not specifically allocated the function of setting up such courts at the time of setting up the special courts (May 20, 1979), but only in September (*Times of India,* February 19, 1980; *Indian Express,* February 20, 1980).

64. *Indian Express,* April 27, 1980. Abdul Ghani, the victim, declared in September of 1979 that the Matador by which he was hit and injured was driven by Sanjay Gandhi. On cross-examination in April, 1980, he reported that the accident was his own fault and the Matador was driven by one Chattar Singh.

65. Kuldip Nayar in *Indian Express,* April 30, 1980.

66. *Times of India,* May 7, 1980. For accounts and citations from the two cases see *Indian Express,* September 25, 1979, and May 3, 1980; *Times of India,* January 19, May 3, and May 7, 1980; and Arun Shourie's extended critical analyses, "Preaching High, Practicing Low," *Indian Express,* May 22 and 23, 1980. Citations that follow from the May decision are from *Times of India,* May 3, 1980; from the Delhi magistrate, *Times of India,* May 7, 1980. For a thoughtful consideration of the issues in the *Minerva Mills* case, see A. G. Noorani, "The Supreme Court on Constitutional Amendments," in A. G. Noorani, ed. *Public Law in India* (New Delhi: Vikas, [1981?]), pp. 293–300.

67. Girilal Jain, "Authoritarian or Indecisive?" in *Times of India,* April 23, 1980.

68. Upendra Baxi, "Judicial Terrorism: Some Thoughts on Justice Tulzapurkar's Pune Speech" *Mainstream,* January 1, 1983, p. 17 n. 1.

69. For a sharply critical and detailed account of the political dimension of the transfer of judges in Mrs. Gandhi's post-1980 government, see Shourie,

Mrs. Gandhi's Second Reign, pp. 264–307. The Law Commission proposed the one-third rule in its report of 1979 and recommended that "this would normally be done by initial appointment and not by transfer," presumably to avoid the punitive implications of transfer (Government of India, Ministry of Law, Justice and Company Affairs, Law Commission of India, *Eightieth Report on the Methods of Appointment of Judges* [Delhi: 1980], p. 33). For the Indira Gandhi government's proposals, see *Hindu*, July 16, 1983. For the supreme court strictures on the Uttar Pradesh High Court, see *Asian Recorder*, July 16–22, 1985, p. 18417. For a discussion of the supreme court's views, see "Judge Transfer Case," *India Today*, January 31, 1982.

70. For the blinding of 31 victims by the police in Bhagalpur, Bihar, see Shourie, *Mrs. Gandhi's Second Reign*, pp. 322–35. For a discussion of legal aspects of police brutality, see A. G. Noorani, "Deaths in Police Custody," *Economic and Political Weekly*, July 13, 1985.

71. See Government of India, Ministry of Law, Social Justice and Company Affairs, *Processual Justice to the People: Report of the Expert Committee on Legal Aid* (New Delhi, 1973) (V. R. Krishna Iyer, chairman), and *Report on Judicare: Equal Justice—Social Justice* (New Delhi, 1978), (P. N. Bhagwati, chairman).

72. See Upendra Baxi, "Taking Suffering Seriously: Social Action Litigation Before the Supreme Court of India," *Social Justice Reporter*, 1983 [n.d.]; Rajeev Dhavan, "Managing Legal Activism: Reflecting on India's Legal Aid Programme" (1984, typescript); Marc Galanter, "Patterns of Legal Services in India," (1982, mimeograph).

73. The phrase is Upendra Baxi's; see his "Judicial Terrorism," p. 14.

74. Imtiaz Ahmad, "Some Results of the Traffic in Law," response to Upendra Baxi, "Understanding the Traffic of 'Ideas' in Law between America and India," in Robert M. Crunden, ed., *Traffic of Ideas between India and America* (Delhi: Chanakya, 1985).

75. For a discussion of the "docket explosion," leading to a backlog of possibly six hundred thousand cases pending in 1978 before the state high courts and the supreme court, see Upendra Baxi, "The Courts in Crisis," in his *The Crisis of the Indian Legal System* (New Delhi: Vikas, 1982), p. 61; see also Rajeev Dhavan, *The Supreme Court under Strain: The Challenge of Arrears* (Bombay: Tripathi, 1978).

76. Anjali Deshpande, in discussing the "humiliation" of the Government of India in the case, cites Federal Judge John F. Keenan's judgment in refusing United States jurisdiction over the case: "The Union of India is a world power in 1985, and its courts have the proven capacity to mete out fair and equal justice. To deprive the Indian judiciary of this opportunity . . . would be to revive a history of subservience and subjugation from which India has emerged" ("A Day of Shame," *Mainstream*, June 14, 1986).

77. For an account of Justice Tulzapurkar's attack on the two justices, see Baxi, "Judicial Terrorism."

78. Ibid., p. 12.

79. In "Socialism, Constitution and Country," Justice Reddy wished to see directive principles incorporated into fundamental rights. However, he also criticized the court for striking down habeas corpus under the emergency (*Mainstream*, January 26, 1983).

80. *India Today*, May 31, 1986.
81. Alexander Hamilton, James Madison, and John Jay, *The Federalist; or, The New Constitution* (Everyman's Library, 1911), p. 264.
82. See *Statesman Weekly*, September 27, 1980, for the names and dates of retiring justices.

Chapter 4

1. For a recent review of the Congress's historical dimension, see Richard Sisson and Stanley Wolpert, eds., *The Indian National Congress: The Preindependence Phase* (Berkeley and Los Angeles: University of California Press, forthcoming). For a recent account of Congress and the party system in the postindependence period, see James Manor, "Parties and the Party System" (Paper presented at the Conference on India's Democracy, Princeton, March 14–16, 1984).
2. See our *Modernity of Tradition*, pp. 237–40. John Broomfield argues that Gandhi's symbolic politics, organizational reforms, and economic program were relevant to the twentieth century because he "recognized the need to deal with the problems of the peasantry—still a majority of the world's population." He wrestled with a crucial problem of that world: "the construction of an economic and political order in which the peasantry could have a full role" ("Gandhi: A Twentiety-Century Anomaly?" in *Mostly About Bengal* [New Delhi: Manohar, 1982], p. 196). For Congress's educated elite dimension, see Anil Seal, *The Emergence of Indian Nationalism: Competition and Collaboration in the Later Nineteenth Century* (Cambridge: Cambridge University Press, 1968). For the growth of early populist cultural movements see John R. McLane, *Indian Nationalism and Early Congress*, and Rajat K. Ray, "The Moderates, Extremists and Revolutionaries: Bengal 1900–1908," in Sisson and Wolpert, *Indian National Congress*.
3. Myron Weiner's *Party Building in a New Nation*, (Chicago: University of Chicago Press, 1967), and Paul Brass's *Factional Politics in an Indian State* (Berkeley and Los Angeles: University of California Press, 1966), provide accounts of how Congress party organizations articulated at the district level with local social formations, notabilities, and entrepreneurs. Stanley A. Kochanek's, *The Congress Party of India: The Dynamics of One-Party Democracy*, (Princeton: Princeton University Press, 1968), provides an account of the structure and dynamics of the Congress party in its heyday. See also Rajni Kothari, *Party Systems and Election Studies*, Occasional Papers of the Center for Developing Societies (Bombay: Allied, 1967).
4. See W. H. Morris-Jones, "Bargaining Federalism," in *The Government and Politics of India*, 3d. rev. ed. (London: Hutchinson, 1971), p. 150–56.
5. "Pressure at the margin" was Rajni Kothari's characterization ("The Congress System in India," in *Party Systems and Election Studies*). See also W. H. Morris-Jones, "Parliament and Dominant Party: Indian Experience," in *Parliamentary Affairs* 17 (Summer 1964).
6. N. G. Goray, *Report* (Presented at the First Conference of the Praja Socialist Party, Allahabad, December 1953). Shriman Narayan, speaking as a general secretary of the Congress party in 1957, echoed Mehta's view: "Economically underdeveloped countries like ours can hardly afford the luxury of

opposition only for the sake of opposition" (*A Plea for Ideological Clarity* [New Delhi: Indian National Congress, 1957], p. 25). These and like issues are more fully discussed in Susanne Hoeber Rudolph, "Consensus and Conflict in Indian Politics," *World Politics* 13 (April 1961), 385–99.

7. "Governability" became a worldwide issue in the seventies. See, for example, Michel Crozier, Samuel P. Huntington, and Joy L. Watanuki *The Crisis of Democracy: Report on the Governability of Democracy to the Tri-Lateral Commission* (New York: New York University Press, 1975).

8. Kochanek, *Congress Party*, p. 423.

9. See, for example, Francine Frankel, *India's Green Revolution* (Princeton, Princeton University Press, 1971), pp. 213–14; Pravin Seth, "Indian Electoral Behaviour: Pattern of Continuity and Change," *Indian Journal of Political Science* 34, no. 2 (April–June 1973); and Rajni Kothari, "The Political Change of 1967," *Economic and Political Weekly*, January 1971 (annual no.).

10. See Kochanek's complex and interesting discussion of changes in party structure and mechanics in "Mrs. Gandhi's Pyramid: The New Congress," in Hart, *Indira Gandhi's India*. Myron Weiner noted the weakness of Mrs. Gandhi's constituency organization in the 1971 election compared with the organization of the undivided Congress ("The 1971 Elections and the Indian Party System," *Asian Survey* 11, no. 12 [December 1971]: 1154). A more critical judgment is that of Arun Shourie in *Indian Express,* May 10, 1980: "There is really no Congress at all. It is just a collection of time-servers who have gathered around two individuals as they regard these two as the dispensers of spoils." See also James Manor, "Party Decay and Political Crisis in India," *The Washington Quarterly* 4, no. 3 (Summer 1981), and "The Decay of Party Organization in India," *Round Table* 272 (October 1978).

11. See S. Gopal, *Nehru*, 2: 149–55.

12. Paul Wallace discusses the plebiscitary nature of the 1980 election: "In this plebiscitary version of a parliamentary election, the choice was clearly between former Prime Minister Indira Gandhi, caretaker Prime Minister Charan Singh and Jagjivan Ram. These three prominent individuals were seen as the only major, realistic aspirants for the prime ministership. Other party candidates or parties themselves receded to secondary importance in the electioneering" ("Plebiscitary Politics in India's 1980 Parliamentary Elections: Punjab and Haryana," *Asian Survey* 20, no. 6 [June 1980]). We observed the election in 1980. Party posters throughout northern India featured the faces and personalities of the three principal candidates rather than, as in the past, the party symbols and slogans.

13. Carras, *Indira Gandhi*, p. 24ff; Carras speaks of "a problem" which mars her ability to function well as a political leader under certain conditions: she is severely limited in her ability to reach people at an intermediate level, though she functions extremely well in large crowds and at intimate gatherings. This inability might not create very serious problems under ordinary circumstances, but for a leader, it is a very serious handicap; and in Indian politics, where personal relationships count for so much, this flaw can be disastrous . . . one of her major shortcomings as a leader (thought one newspaper editor) was her inability to evoke trust and loyalty, along with her reluctance to formulate decisions jointly with others (p. 52) See also Zareer Masani, *Indira Gandhi: A Biography* (New York: Crowell, 1975).

14. Kothari interpreted the deinstitutionalization of party in parallel with the rise of the centralizing administrative state. Noting that Nehru and Patel valued the pluralistic nature of Congress, he contrasted their commitment with subsequent tendencies to substitute state control for party support (*Democratic Polity and Social Change*, pp. 24–27).

15. Myron Weiner, *India at the Polls: The Parliamentary Elections of 1977* (Washington, D.C.: American Enterprise Institute, 1978), pp. 24–27.

16. For accounts of deinstitutionalization under the emergency and the election of 1977, see James Manor, "Where Congress Survived: Five States in the Indian General Election of 1977," *Asian Survey* 18, no. 8 (August 1978); Ram Joshi and Kirtidev Desai, "Towards a More Competitive Party System in India," *Asian Survey* 18, no. 11 (November 1978); and "Sanjay Spreads His Wings," *India Today* (June 16–30, 1980).

17. Brass, "National Power and Local Politics."

18. Samuel Eldersveld and Bashiruddin Ahmed, *Citizens and Politics: Mass Political Behavior in India* (Chicago: University of Chicago Press, 1978), p. 274. At the same time they observe that "the level of loyalty to parties is still considerable and probably close to the level of many western societies."

19. Paul Brass, "Political Participation, Institutionalization and Stability in India," *Government and Opposition* (Winter 1969); Hardgrave, *India*, p. 231; Richard Sisson and William Vanderbok, "Mapping the Indian Electorate: Trends in Party Support in Seven National Elections" *Asian Survey* 23, no. 10 (October 1983); Albert Johnson in a study of voting behavior in Madurai, Tamil Nadu's second largest city, found that "identification with a political party is a must for candidates to be recognized by electors." Voters cast their ballots more for parties and their leaders than they did for particular candidates ("Voting Behaviour and Political Participation with Reference to Madurai City," [Ph.D. diss., Madurai Kamaraj University, 1985], p. 153).

20. *Overseas Hindustan Times*, December 2, 1976.

21. *India Today*, January 16–31, 1980.

22. After Ram's resignation and the creation of the Congress for Democracy, Mrs. Gandhi tried to save the situation by cutting Sanjay's share of tickets to about twenty and allocating the rest to incumbents and party regulars, but to no avail. See Weiner, *India at the Polls*, pp. 15–16, and see also *Seminar*, no. 211 (March 1977) for the names of those involved and the text of their statement.

23. Rameshray Roy, "Election Studies: Selection of Congress Candidates," pt. 1, "The Formal Criteria," *Economic and Political Weekly*, December 31, 1966. This is the first of a five-part article; parts 2 ("Pressures and Counter Pressures"), 3 ("Claims and Counter Claims"), and 4 and 5 ("Structure of Authority in the Congress") were published on January 7, January 14, and February 11, 1967.

24. See also W. H. Morris-Jones, "Candidate Selection: The Ordeal of the Indian National Congress, 1966–67," in M. S. Rajan, ed., *Studies in Politics: National and International*, (New Delhi: Vikas, 1971).

25. *Keesing's Contemporary Archives* summed up informed press opinion when it observed: "The majority of the Congress (I) candidates (for the nine state assembly elections in May, 1980) were reported to have been selected by Mr. Sanjay Gandhi, the younger son of the Prime Minister. Mr. H. N. Bahuguna, who had resigned as general secretary of the Congress (I) on May 1 . . . said that he had been completely ignored in the selection of candidates,

and alleged that Mr. Gandhi controlled 'not only the party but even the government machinery.'" (November 21, 1980, p. 30573).

26. Senior state leaders were accommodated by the allocation of a few tickets to their family members, but their factional followings and policy preferences were overwhelmed by the number of tickets given to Sanjay loyalists by his lieutenants ("Sanjay Spreads His Wings," pp. 34–38).

27. Congress-I won over two-thirds of the seats in Gujarat, Madhya Pradesh, Orissa, Rajasthan, and Uttar Pradesh and won majorities in Bihar, Maharashtra, and Punjab. In Tamil Nadu, the ninth state to go to the polls in May 1980, the AIADMK (All India Dravida Munnetra Kazhagam) in alliance with the two Communist parties (CPI-M [Marxist] and CPI) defeated the DMK–Congress-I alliance. We count as Sanjay loyalists Arjun Singh (Madhya Pradesh), Janaki Ballav Patnaik (Orissa), Jaganath Pahadia (Rajasthan), and Viswanath Pratab Singh (Uttar Pradesh). The Uttar Pradesh case was rather special. The Congress-I parliamentary party on June 6 unanimously elected Sanjay Gandhi its leader in the face of a statement by Mrs. Gandhi that her son would not be given any post in the union or state governments. The party provided for the contingency that Mrs. Gandhi might not relent by asking her to nominate any other suitable person. Her choice was V. P. Singh. Two additional Sanjay loyalists had assumed office in January and February 1980 when defections in Karnataka, Haryana, and Himachal Pradesh enabled the Congress-I to form governments in those states. We count Gundu Rao (Karnataka) and Ram Lal (Himachal Pradesh) as Sanjay loyalists (*Keesing's Contemporary Archives* July 4, 1980, pp. 30328–29, and November 21, 1980, pp. 30573-74.

28. Samuel J. Eldersveld, *Political Parties in American Society* (New York: Basic Books, 1982), p. 145. For accounts of the decline or transformation of party in America, see, for example, Jeane Kirkpatrick, *Dismantling the Parties* (Washington, American Enterprise Institute, 1978); Thomas E. Patterson, *The Mass Media Election: How Americans Choose their President* (New York: Praeger, 1980); Robert Agranoff, "The New Style of Campaigning: The Decline of Party and the Rise of Candidate-Centered Technology," in Jeff Fishel, ed., *Parties and Elections in an Anti-party Age* (Bloomington, Ind.: Indiana University Press, 1978); David S. Broder, *The Party's Over: The Failure of Politics in America* (New York: Harper and Row, 1972); and Norman Nie, Sidney Verba, and John R. Petrocik, *The Changing American Voter* (Cambridge: Harvard University Press, 1976).

29. *Sunday* (Calcutta), March 13–19, 1983, p. 27.

30. For the "France in India," see Fritz Stern, "The Giant from Afar: Visions of Europe from Algiers to Tokyo," *Foreign Affairs 56*, no. 1 (October 1977): 111–35.

31. For a lengthy, sympathetic but not uncritical account of Rajiv's attempt to create cadre organizations, see "Readying the Ranks," *India Today*, September 15, 1983. The two parliamentary secretaries were Ahmed Mohammed Patel and Oscar Fernandes. Patel was president of the Gujarat State Youth Congress. The coordinators were paid nominal sums to supply political information about constituencies (*India Today*, January 31, 1985).

32. Rajiv Gandhi appears to have been serious about intraparty elections, which he attempted to have held by October 1982. They did not come about except in five states, for the same reasons as before: a high degree of state-level factionalism that led to forged party memberships and fake enrollments, rendering elections meaningless (*India Today*, September 15, 1983). For a de-

tailed discussion of the history of these issues see Kochanek, *Congress Party*, pp. 214–32.

33. For a report of the Bombay centenary meeting and Rajiv Gandhi's speech, see *India Today*, January 15, 1986, p. 53. For his comment on intra-party elections, see the interview in *India Today*, May 31, 1986, p. 46, and the article entitled "Dissident Dangers," pp. 16–17.

34. The dissidents included, in addition to Mukherjee, Congress working president Kamalapathi Tripathi; Gundu Rao, former chief minister of Karnataka; Madhav Singh Solanki, former chief minister of Gujarat; V. C. Shukla, former minister in Mrs. Gandhi's cabinet; Jaganath Mishra, former chief minister of Bihar; S. S. Mohapatra, former Congress general secretary; and others. For accounts, see *Indian Express* and *Times of India*, June 1–3, 1986.

35. In 1984, Congress contested 508 seats, 339 held by incumbent Congressmen and 169 held by opposition parties. For the figures on federal funding, see Nagindas Sanghavi, "Patterns of Political Control," *Economic and Political Weekly*, December 15, 1984.

36. *India Today*, February 28, 1985.

37. The guidelines recommended, for example, that approximately 60 percent of the party's nominees be under forty-five years old, that 20 percent be women, and that serious consideration be given to professionals, such as engineers, doctors, scientists, educationists, and management experts (*Overseas Hindustan Times*, February 16, 1985). While no comprehensive statistical account of the results are available, the press at the time found evidence of compliance. It was reported, for example, that in Orissa, 95 Congress-I candidates were under age forty-five, that in Rajasthan more than half of the Congress-I candidates had never contested before and 30 were lawyers, doctors and engineers, and that in Uttar Pradesh, of 254 new candidates, 38 were women and 50 were active members of Congress-sponsored organizations. Although the press gave credence to the "clean" look of most Congress-I nominees, it also reported that liquor racketeers, smugglers, and persons associated with rigging elections and other forms of political fraud, the kind of bad characters associated with nominations in the Indira-Sanjay era, also received tickets. In Karnataka, for example, the former chief minister Gundu Rao was dropped, but the unprincipled S. Bangarappa and Veerappa Moily, former leader of the Congress opposition in the assembly who allegedly offered an MLA Rs. 200,000 to defect, were given tickets ("Assembly Elections," *India Today*, February 28, 1985).

38. See chapter 6, p. 206. See also *The Statesman Weekly*, March 16, 1985; *India Today*, March 31, 1985; and United News of India, *Backgrounders*, March 14, 1985.

39. An *India Today* study of selected states concluded that "the electorate did not welcome the new entrants with any exuberance." In Madhya Pradesh, where new entrants did worse than in any other state, of 150 renominees, 120 (80 percent) were elected, but of 93 new nominees, only 40 (43 percent) were elected. In Uttar Pradesh, the respective proportions were 66 and 60 percent. In the 100 constituencies in Uttar Pradesh where new nominees replaced incumbents, only 30 won ("Congress(I): Unexpected Setbacks," *India Today*, March 31, 1985), pp. 17–21.

40. The chief ministers and the dates of their nominations are as follows: J. Vengal Rao, February 28, 1978; Dr. M. Chenna Reddy, March 6, 1978;

T. Anjaiah, October 11, 1980; Bhavanam Venkataram Reddy, February 24, 1982; and V. B. Reddy, September 16, 1982. In January 1983, the Telugu Desam led by N. T. Rama Rao decisively defeated the Congress-I in a state assembly election. In March 1985, when Har Deo Joshi again became chief minister of Rajasthan, he became the state's twelfth in eight years. Andhra Pradesh and Rajasthan are not exceptional cases.

41. *India Today,* January 31, 1983.

42. Ibid. The Karnataka governor asked Hegde to be caretaker chief minister until the assembly elections in March 1985.

43. The five chief ministers who continued in office were: N. D. Tiwari (Uttar Pradesh), Virbhadra Singh (Himachal Pradesh), Madhav Singh Solanki (Gujarat), J. B. Patnaik (Orissa), and Vasantrao Patil (Maharashtra). Mammanapillai O. H. K. Farook remained as the chief minister of the union territory of Pondicherry. New chief ministers took office in Rajasthan (Har Deo Joshi, an eight-term MLA who had been an All India Congress Committee member since 1949, general secretary and president of the Rajasthan Congress committee and chief minister), in Bihar (Bindeshwari Dubey, a ranking trade unionist in a state with the nation's largest public-sector investment, ally of factional leader Jaganath Mishra and president of the Bihar Congress committee when he became chief minister), and in Madhya Pradesh (Motilal Vohra, identified with the P. C. Sethi faction rather than with the faction of outgoing chief minister Arjun Singh but, like Dubey, president of the state Congress committee when he became chief minister).

44. K. K. Katyal's comments on this turn of events capture much of the interpretative response:

The sternness with which Mr. Patil was dealt with made sense only in the context of the Centre's anxiety to prevent the re-emergence of state bossism, although Mr. Patil's derisive references to "computer boys" too could not have been liked in Delhi. Otherwise, it was no breach of discipline on the part of the outgoing Chief Minister to have drawn attention to the locked doors of the Congress (I) offices in the *talukas,* or even to suggest that the Prime Minister give up direct responsibility of running the party. (*Hindu,* June 15, 1985, international edition)

45. In retrospect, G. K. Reddy found Rajiv Gandhi "relatively free" of responsibility for previous toppling operations in which both Congress-I and opposition chief ministers had been arbitrarily replaced by those more acceptable to Indira Gandhi–led Congress-I governments at the center. Reddy cited as evidence in support of this historical reconstruction Rajiv Gandhi's advice to the governors of Andhra Pradesh and Karnataka that they allow N. T. Rama Rao and Ramakrishna Hegde to continue in office as heads of caretaker governments when, in the light of the 1984 parliamentary election results, they sought to dissolve their assemblies and opt for fresh elections. The prime minister, Reddy wrote, "has been particularly keen on maintaining a good working relationship with all non-Congress (I) Chief Ministers to avoid the impression of discrimination. The harsh attacks he made on some of them during the heat of the electoral campaigns have been forgotten" and most are supporting his policies on "matters relating to larger national interests" ("Governors Will Ask CMs to Face Assembly," *Hindu,* August 19, 1985, international edition).

46. "Bid for Consensus on More Issues," *Hindu,* August 10, 1985, international edition.

Chapter 5

1. Kochanek, *Congress Party*, p. 427, and Eric da Costa, *Times of India*, January 30, 1967, as quoted in Dua, *Presidential Rule in India*, pp. 232–33.

2. We count as the "Janata vote" the vote shares won in 1971, the election immediately preceding the 1977 election, by those parties who came together in 1977 to form the Janata. The parties included are the Jan Sangh (7.4 percent), the Congress-O (10.4 percent), the Swatantra (3 percent), which merged with the BKD in 1974 to form the Bharatiya Lok Dal (BLD), the Samyukia Socialist party (2.4 percent), the Praja Socialist party (1 percent), and the BKD (3.3 percent), for a total vote share of 27.5 percent.

In 1977, the "Janata vote" is that cast for the party formed just prior to the 1977 parliamentary election (i.e., 43 percent). In 1980, we count as the Janata vote the vote shares of Janata's then erstwhile components, the Lok Dal (9.4 percent) and Janata (18.9 percent), and of the Lok Dal's coalition government (July–December 1979) and 1980 electoral alliance partner, the Congress-U (U for Devraj Urs, who became president of the anti-Indira Congress faction in September 1978) (5.3 percent), for a total of 33.6 percent.

3. The late V. O. Key, Jr., introduced the concept of critical elections in *Southern Politics in State and Nation* (New York: Knopf, 1949) and used it in various editions of his *Politics, Parties and Pressure Groups* (New York: Crowell) (various editions, the last being the fifth, published in 1964). The concept was formally elaborated in Key's "A Theory of Critical Elections," *Journal of Politics* 18 (1955). Walter Dean Burnham extended and empirically elaborated the term in his "The Changing Shape of the American Political Universe," *American Political Science Review* (1965), and *Critical Elections and the Mainsprings of American Politics*, (New York: Norton, 1970). Duncan McCrae, James Meldrum, Walter Dean Burnham, John D. Sprague, David Butler, Donald Stokes and others have further elaborated or applied the concept in analyses of political change in the United States and Britain.

4. See, for a discussion of the importance of participation, Lloyd I. Rudolph, "Continuity and Change in Electoral Behavior: The 1971 Parliamentary Elections in India," *Asian Survey* 11, no. 2 (December 1971):1123. See also Daniel Graves, "Political Mobilization in India: The First Party System," *Asian Survey* 16, no. 9 (September 1976).

5. An important part of this translation was accomplished by the late Raj Krishna, professor of economics at Delhi University and a senior member of the Janata's planning commission, whose death in 1985 was a great loss to rationalized Gandhianism and to Indian policy.

6. Ashis Nandy, "Indira Gandhi and the Culture of Indian Politics," in his *At the Edge of Psychology*.

7. See, for his autobiography, Narayan's *Toward Struggle,* ed. Yusuf Meherally (Bombay: Padma, 1946), and a selection of his writings in *Socialism to Sarvodaya* (Madras: Socialist Book Centre, 1956). For an account of his recent politics, see Minoo Masani, *Is J. P. the Answer?* (New Delhi: Macmillan India (1975). See also Gordon Fellman's "Indian Socialists and Jayaprakash Narayan: A Study in Political Sociology and Biography" (Ph.D. diss., Harvard University, 1963), which has not been published because of objections raised by Herbert Passin, who holds some of the material that Fellman used.

8. The initial clash between Morarji Desai and Charan Singh occurred soon

after Mrs. Gandhi dissolved Parliament and announced an election on January 18, 1977. Charan Singh, as the leading proponent, since 1974, of "one party" expected to be made its chairman and to lead it in the forthcoming election. Desai was more senior and commanded, it seemed, wider support. The initial struggle between them was patched up by Vajpayee's formula, which provided that Desai be chairman and Charan Singh vice-chairman, with the understanding that Charan Singh enjoy final authority for the allocation of tickets in all of northern India (where Vajpayee's former party had the largest stakes). The issue of leadership of the parliamentary party and thus of the government should Janata form one was to be decided after the election. See L. K. Advani, *The People Betrayed* (New Delhi: Vision Books, 1979), pp. 16–17. For documents of interactions in this period, see Arun Gandhi, *The Morarji Papers* (New Delhi: Vision Books, 1983).

9. Atal Behari Vajpayee, leader of the largest fraction but not himself in contention, has provided a revealing firsthand account of the leadership selection:

It is no secret that when the PM was to be elected in March 1977, members of the erstwhile Jan Sangh and the Socialists were in favour of Mr. Jagjivan Ram. They felt that the elevation of a Harijan to the Prime Ministership of our country would have a positive impact, and that his proven administrative acumen as well as his ability to get along with people of diverse backgrounds would be an asset to the new administration. However, when this proposal was put before Chaudhry Charan Singh, he rejected it outright and indicated that he would support Mr. Morarji Desai who had suffered during the Emergency rather than accept a person who had moved the motion in Parliament for approval of the Emergency. Once two of the three senior leaders had come together, the claim of the third was not further pressed ("All Responsible for Janata Crisis," *Indian Express*, August 2, 1979).

10. According to Vajpayee's account:

The manner in which this crisis [over national leadership] erupted and was 'resolved' contained an important portent of how crises would be handled in the Janata party in the coming years: the sad fact is that in this, as in later crises, the members of Parliament and the national executive of the party were not taken into confidence about the negotiations that were going on behind the scenes. When the Janata MPs assembled in the Gandhi Peace Foundation hall they were taken by surprise at the announcement that the leader of the parliamentary party would be chosen by consensus. . . . The wrangle was not confined to the Prime Ministership. Having conceded the Prime Ministership to Congress-O, the BLD group sought the Party Presidentship for themselves. However, the others could not be persuaded and with great reluctance, Chaudhry Charan Singh agreed to Mr. Chandra Shekhar's nomination" ("All Responsible for Janata Crisis").

See also Janardan Thakur, "The Janata Debacle," chap. 7 in *Indira Gandhi and Her Power Game*, (New Delhi: Vikas, 1979), pp. 110–15.

11. We say "resulted from a tacit bargain" in part because L. K. Advani, president of the former Jan Sangh party and minister for information and broadcasting in the Janata government, says that the division was a natural consequence of Morarji Desai's decision not to foist persons chosen by the Central Parliamentary Board on the states. "It was only in Bihar where though the Jan Sangh was the largest single group, its decision to support Karpoori

Thakur for Chief Ministership *gave the impression as if* [our emphasis] the Jan Sangh and the BLD between themselves had divided eight states half-and-half . . . the impression that it had been the result of a deal was extremely unfortunate" (*People Betrayed*, p. 20). Subsequent developments in 1978, when the efforts to unseat BLD chief ministers failed, and in 1979, when they succeeded, made it clear that what may have been a tacit "deal" initially quickly became an explicit understanding whose "violation" was treated as a casus belli by the Charan Singh–led BLD (Advani, ibid., chap. 12). Nana Deshmukh, general secretary of the Janata, and a leading RSS and Jan Sangh spokesman, also denies that there was a deal between the BLD and the Jan Sangh to divide the states. See his *R.S.S.: Victim of Slander* (New Delhi: Vision Books, 1979), pp. 125–28.

12. L. K. Advani denies what most observers credit, that the undissolved Akhil Bharatiya Vidyarthi Parishad and Bharatiya Mazdoor Sangh were the student and labor wings of the former Jan Sangh. As proof of their "scrupulously non-political" nature he says that the Jan Sangh in 1973 launched "its own" Bharatiya Yuva Sangh (Youth Organization) and by 1975 was "seriously thinking of floating an all India trade union body" (*People Betrayed*, p. 78).

13. By far the best study of the Rashtriya Swayamsevak Sangh (Volunteers in the Service of the Nation, commonly denoted as RSS or RSSS) and its relationship with the Jan Sangh is Walter Andersen, "The Jan Sangh: Ideology and Organization in Party Behavior" (Ph.D. diss., University of Chicago, 1975). Other recent studies include the polemically critical book by Des Raj Goyal, *Rashtriya Swayamsevak Sangh* (New Delhi: Radha Krishna, 1979), and the apologia by Nana Deshmukh, *R.S.S.* Goyal is the editor of *Secular Democracy*, a journal devoted to the exposure of "communism," and Deshmukh is chairman of the Deen Dayal Research Institute, an organization that attempts to bridge the divide between the "cultural" concerns of the RSS and the political concerns of the Jan Sangh. Craig Baxter's earlier study, *Jan Sangh*, like Andersen's work, provides a useful antidote to more "committed" studies.

14. The practice of "entrepreneurial" fundraising became a matter of party dissension when Madhu Limaye, then a party secretary, used it to attack Prime Minister Desai via his son, Kanti. Limaye asked Desai on August 15, 1978, whether Kanti had his permission to collect Rs. 8,000,000 (about $1,000,000). C. B. Gupta, Janata party treasurer, stated a day later that he had authorized Kanti Desai to collect funds for the assembly election because leaders of all constituents of the party collected funds separately and spent them on their own groups (*Keesing's Contemporary Archives*, December 8, 1978, p. 29345).

15. Organizational elections scheduled for October 31, 1978, were "postponed" by party president Chandra Shekhar on September 4 and never seriously considered thereafter. Baru Sengupta reports that the postponement, proposed by Madhu Limaye and supported by the party president, was thought by the "Jan Sangh" group to be "mainly the work of the Congress-O" whose leaders were then disproportionately influential. "In their bid to capture the party committees," Sengupta writes, "all the former constituents had resorted to bogus membership. About . . . 5.18 million membership forms were deposited with the Party offices . . . no one knew the ratio of genuine to bogus membership. . . . All the constituents of the Janata Party were afraid that the Jan Sangh group would capture almost all the committees in the Hindi-speaking states . . . (and thought) there might be bloodshed in some

. . . specially in U.P. and Bihar" (*Last Days of the Morarji Raj* [Calcutta: Ananda, 1979], p. 19). According to H. N. Bahuguna, then a member of Desai's government, "Any independent observer will tell you that RSS volunteers took charge of enrollment of members. . . . In every [Uttar Pradesh] village this happened. Everywhere the Jan Sangh kept running parallel offices" (Interview in *Sunday* [Calcutta], as cited by Des Raj Goyal in *Rashtriya Swayamsewak Sangh*, p. 193).

16. According to Nana Deshmukh's after-the-fact interpretation, "those who had come from the Jan Sangh felt that to sustain the politics of change which had emerged out of the JP movement and to keep away from the deleterious politics of power, they must make sacrifices. This is why in spite of the fact that they constituted almost one-third of the 302 members of the Lok Sabha they never aspired to prime minister or deputy prime ministership. . . . The idea at the back of their mind was that recriminations about the allotment of portfolios or the number of seats in the cabinet could hamper the party from becoming a harmonious organization (*R.S.S.*, pp. 51–52).

17. See Lloyd I. Rudolph and Susanne Hoeber Rudolph, "The Text Book Controversy," in Lloyd I. Rudolph, ed., *Cultural Policy in India*.

18. The drop in percentage vote shares for Janata between March and June 1977 was as follows: Haryana, −23 percent; Bihar −22; Uttar Pradesh, −20; Jammu and Kashmir, −16; Rajasthan, −16; Madhya Pradesh, −11; Himachal Pradesh, −8; Orissa, −3; Tamil Nadu, −1; and West Bengal, −1. In Punjab, there was a slight increase (+2 percent).

19. For a summary of the background controversy over corruption charges against Kanti Desai and against relatives of Charan Singh, see *Keesing's Contemporary Archives*, December 8, 1978, pp. 29344–45.

20. Charan Singh asked Desai to prove his statement at Bhavnagar on January 15, 1978, that the charges were "unfounded and mischievous" and to go ahead with the inquiry that Desai had suggested at that time. A public inquiry would help maintain the good name of the government, which was "going down steeply with every passing day." The letter was the opening round of charges and countercharges about each other's relatives that eventuated in a 1980 report finding prima facie evidence incriminating members of both men's families (Thakur, *Indira Gandhi and Her Power Game*, p. 116).

21. Shekhar, a former Congressman, was alleged to have insured the selection of defectors from Congress as candidates (*Keesing's Contemporary Archives*, December 8, 1978, p. 29343). It should be noted that, except for its very small dissident Congress fraction, none of the components of the Janata prior to 1977 had organizational or electoral bases in Andhra Pradesh or Karnataka.

22. Ibid.

23. The effects of Desai's alleged efforts was to reopen the June 1977 settlement allocating control of state governments to the BLD and Jan Sangh fractions. Two days later, thirty-eight of seventy-six Janata members of the Haryana state assembly party met at Desai's house and voted unanimously that they lacked confidence in (BLD) Chief Minister Devi Lal's leadership. Both Uttar Pradesh and Haryana BLD chief ministers ultimately survived formal tests of their leadership in May and June, but the Haryana chief minister contributed to the evolving schism by reorganizing his cabinet to exclude all former Congress-O, Congress for Democracy, and Socialist party members.

24. Desai was sympathetic to the "freedom of religion" bill that, by creating

penalties for conversion, alarmed Christians; he supported a constitutional amendment bill that opened up the way to ban cow slaughter throughout the country; he was committed to nationwide prohibition; and he encouraged official moves by the Ministry of Education and other funding and certifying bodies to purge textbooks and research that interpreted Mughal rule in political rather than communal terms.

A private member bill introduced in the Lok Sabha (lower house) in December 1978 by O. P. Tyagi, a leading member of the Jan Sangh fraction of the Janata party, made it a criminal offense to use "force, fraud and inducement" to bring about religious conversions. Christians felt alarmed and threatened because their philanthropic activities, such as hospitals and schools, could be regarded as "inducements." Des Raj Goyal accused the RSS of holding that "change of religions subverts the loyalty to nation" and that "followers of religions born outside India (e.g., Islam, Christianity) . . . are excluded . . . from the concept of national rights of citizenship" (*Rashtriya Swayamsewak Sangh,* p. 20). Government also introduced the Constitution (Fiftieth Amendment) Bill, making cow protection a concurrent subject. When it passed, the center planned to introduce legislation banning cow slaughter. Such an act would particularly affect West Bengal and Kerala, the two states explicitly and unequivocally opposed to such a ban, in part because of their strong Communist parties and in part because of their large and influential Muslim and Christian populations. This effort aroused criticism in the Janata itself and ultimately aborted.

Desai's efforts to impose prohibition on the country were more successful than his moves to stop conversions or end cow slaughter, although he was far from his objective of total prohibition within four years when his government fell after twenty-eight months in office. Public drinking in bars, clubs, and restaurants was banned in most states and the number of dry days (no liquor sold in stores) per month substantially increased.

Desai's first moves in support of Hindu literary and historical interests occurred in mid-1977 when he (1) supported the withdrawal of government purchases and distribution of history books that, according to the minister of education, did not sufficiently celebrate certain Hindu kings or the perfidy of Muslim rulers and (2) reorganized the Indian Council of Historical Research and encouraged the formation of the Indian History and Cultural Society to rival the Indian History Congress, which had endorsed the textbooks withdrawn by government.

25. Created on May 28, 1977 under the Commissions of Inquiry Act, the Shah Commission produced its *Interim Report I* on March 11, 1978; subsequently two further volumes were published. Booksellers were officially instructed to withdraw the volumes when Mrs. Gandhi's government returned to power in January 1980.

26. The Indian constitution has no provision for impeaching a prime minister; it provides only for impeaching a president. The Commissions of Inquiry Act (1952) provides for a procedure not unlike that of American grand juries to ascertain whether sufficient evidence exists for the government to prosecute.

27. Besides advocating the use of the emergency's notorious preventive detention law, MISA, to arrest Mrs. Gandhi, Charan Singh made clear in his June 28, 1978, statement that she should be punished and suffer as her victims did. Mrs. Gandhi should be arrested immediately and kept in Chandigarh in

the same circumstances in which Lok Nayak (People's Leader) Jayaprakash Narayan was kept. JP developed a kidney condition that required dialysis after his release and ultimately led to his death. (See his *Prison Diary* [Bombay Popular Prakashan, 1977].) Mrs. Gandhi should also be kept in Delhi's notorious Tihar Jail, as had Gayatri Devi and Vijaya Raje Scindia, the former maharanis of Jaipur and Gwalior who were active political opponents of Mrs. Gandhi. Those two women had not been accorded the treatment commonly provided educated political prisoners but instead had shared cells with "common criminals." Charan Singh's sense of proportion (and history) is reflected in his final remarks: "Of course, in any other country, she would have by now been facing trial on the lines of the historic Nuremberg trial." See Advani, *The People Betrayed*, p. 31, for Singh's statements. Archarya J. P. Kripalani reports of Desai that "the Prime Minister is said to have given assurances to Mrs. Gandhi when he met her for the first time after assuming high office that he would save her but he could not save her son." When asked by a correspondent "why his government was not expediting the cases against Mrs. Gandhi," he replied, "has she not suffered enough?" (*The Nightmare and After* [Bombay: Popular Prakashan, 1980], p. 207.)

28. On June 17, Prime Minister Desai told a press conference that the government would decide in two or three months whether Mrs. Gandhi *could be* prosecuted on the basis of the Shah Commission reports but that, in any case, no special procedure or laws with retroactive effect would be used.

29. The government could have acted immediately by using its power under MISA, the notorious preventive detention act used by Mrs. Gandhi under the emergency, which Charan Singh had previously condemned and which the Janata government was pledged to repeal. The government's failure to arrest Mrs. Gandhi, said Charan Singh, has led the "people [to] think that we in the Government are a pack of impotent people who cannot govern the country" (*Keesing's Contemporary Archives*, December 8, 1978, p. 29344).

30. The report left it to the "collective wisdom" of the House what the punishment should be. The committee found that Mrs. Gandhi had instituted false charges against four officials who gathered information on Sanjay Gandhi's automobile firm, Maruti, Ltd., in response to questions tabled in the House. It also held that Mrs. Gandhi had misused the office of prime minister to protect the firm's interests.

31. On December 1, while Parliament was considering Mrs. Gandhi's fate, the supreme court held that Parliament had the legislative competence to create special courts. They were to try high public or political officers for offences such as those detailed in the Shah Commission reports investigating the conduct of Mrs. Gandhi and others under the emergency. Contrary to the Desai's assurance in June that the government would not enact any special procedure not already provided for by the country's legal system or enact any new law with retroactive effect, the Desai government supported the bill. See Upendra Baxi, "The Saga of Special Courts," in *Indian Supreme Court*, pp. 209–13. See also *Times of India*, February 10, 1980, and *Indian Express*, February 20, 1980, for the narrow and controversial ground on which a lower court declared the special court unconstitutional. See *Keesing's Contemporary Archives*, December 8, 1978, p. 29349, for the prime minister's press conference of June 17, at which he made his initial assurances.

32. The three-member cabinet group that helped to negotiate this compromise in December, 1978, consisted of George Fernandes, Madhu Dandavate, and Ravinder Varma. L. K. Advani was also associated with the group. In De-

cember 1978, the two antagonists, by referring the charges to a retired justice, also found a way to live with mutual charges of corruption against their respective family members. On April 28, 1979, the Desai government referred to Justice C. A. Vaidialingam the Rajya Sabha debate on its motion, adopted on August 10, 1978, that inter alia called for the chief justice of India to inquire whether any prima facie case was established against the family members of Desai and Charan Singh in respect of any of the charges made in the debate so as to justify a formal inquiry under the Commissions of Inquiry Act, 1952. The chief justice, despite his earlier (August 24, 1978) concurrence, eventually refused because critics had made him and the prime minister, whose pet scheme this was, realize that his involvement as a "designated person" would not be a proper role for a chief justice. A. G. Noorani's excellent column, "The Vaidialingam Inquiry" provides a historical and legal critique of the inquiry's procedure and findings (*Indian Express*, February 18, 1980).

33. The positive effects of A. B. Vajpayee and L. K. Advani's role in negotiating Charan Singh's return to the Janata government in January 1979, were off-set by the fortuitously simultaneous part the Jan Sangh fraction played in bringing down Uttar Pradesh's BLD chief minister, Ram Naresh Yadav. See *Keesing's Contemporary Archives*, December 7, 1979, p. 29970.

34. Dual membership had troubled the secularists in the party, primarily socialists such as Madhu Limaye, from the outset. They considered membership in the Janata and the RSS, the militant Hindu cultural wing of the former Jan Sangh, incompatible.

35. Dismissed from the cabinet in June 1978, Raj Narain was removed from the party's national executive on June 12, 1979, on the grounds that he had criticized the party's leaders and called for a change in the government. On the twenty-third, he resigned from the party in order to build "a real Janata party." When the monsoon session opened on July 9, thirteen former BLD members of the Janata parliamentary party resigned to join Raj Narain on the opposition benches. Fourteen more resigned on the tenth, and twenty-two on the eleventh. Forty-seven joined Raj Narain's group that, on the tenth, had adopted the name Janata party (Secular). On July 11, the Janata government lost its majority. By July 14, seventy-two MPs had defected from the Janata parliamentary party, and on the sixteenth Charan Singh, who had remained silent from the beginning of the session, resigned from the government and party and was elected leader of the Janata party (Secular). See *Keesing's Contemporary Archives*, December 7, 1979, pp. 29971–72.

36. Janata split for a third time in April when the Congress-O and the socialist remnant again invoked the communalism issue to drive the Jan Sangh fraction out of the party. More sinned against than sinning with respect to party loyalty and discipline, it formed the BJP. By invoking the Janata name it hoped to continue to be associated with JP's legacy of Gandhian ideology and antiauthoritarianism and thus prevent the BJP from becoming the minor party of upper-caste Hindus from Hindi Heartland states that the Jan Sangh had been.

37. The parliamentary election of January 1980 did reveal that Jagjivan Ram was a paper tiger. The Janata vote under his leadership dropped from 43 to 9 percent, a decline, to be sure, for which there were a variety of causes. His equanimity, which had contrasted favorably with that of his colleagues, de-

serted him. He had some cause. The more orthodox section of the Jan Sangh constituency in Janata who, in the event, could not stomach an untouchable as their leader, apparently sat on their hands where they did not sabotage the Janata campaign. Nor did he make a showing in the constituency that was expected to support him, the Harijans, who rejected him too by voting as much or more for Congress-I or Lok Dal as for Janata. Janata won only one scheduled caste constituency, Ram's own. Like Charan Singh, Ram abruptly discovered the Jan Sangh's communal potential. Abandoning his long-standing Jan Sangh alliance, he left Janata in March 1980, and soon found a minor berth in Congress-U.

38. On July 18, when President Sanjiva Reddy asked Chavan to try to form a government, the distribution of seats in the Lok Sabha was as follows: Janata, 206; Janata (Secular) 76; Congress, 75; Congress-I, 71; smaller parties, 77; and unattached, 33. Minus the speaker and five vacant seats, the House totaled 538, which meant a majority required support from 270 members. On July 22, Chavan informed the president that he could not form a government but that an alliance under Charan Singh's leadership could. On the twenty-sixth, President Reddy, in the first of two controversial actions, asked Charan Singh rather than Desai to form a government but to seek a vote of confidence by the third week of August. See *Keesing's Contemporary Archives*, December 7, 1979, p. 29972.

39. Indira Gandhi made her support of his government contingent on the withdrawal of court cases pending against herself and Sanjay and on exclusion from Charan Singh's cabinet of former cabinet colleagues, such as T. A. Pai and Karan Singh, who had testified against her before the Shah Commission. These demands were unacceptable to Charan Singh's coalition partner, the Chavan-led Congress-U.

40. See note 38 above.

Chapter 6

1. Richard Sisson and William Vanderbok have noted the increasing weakness of Congress in the Hindi-speaking states ("Mapping the Indian Electorate, II," *Asian Survey* 24, no. 10 [October 1984]). Harold Gould, in an analysis of the 1980 election, noted that Congress's political fate "had been determined by party performance in the Hindi Belt primarily" ("Second Coming: The 1980 Elections in the Hindi Belt," *Asian Survey* 20, no. 6 [June 1980]).

2. For an earlier effort to characterize India regionally, displaying socioeconomic indicators by region, see Susanne Hoeber Rudolph and Lloyd I. Rudolph, eds., *Education and Politics in India: Studies in Organization, Society and Policy* (Cambridge: Harvard University Press, 1972; New Delhi: Oxford University Press, 1973), pp. 51–67. The effects of regional profiles on social organization are discussed in our *Modernity of Tradition*, pt. 4, pp. 76–79.

3. *India Today*, January 16–31, 1980.

4. Gopal Krishna, "Electoral Participation and Political Integration," in

Center for the Study of Developing Societies, *Context of Electoral Change in India* (Delhi: Academic Books, 1969), p. 37.

5. It should not be assumed that there is a valid or reliable way to determine whether candidates "represent" tribal, community, economic class, or national identities and interests. The CPI-M thinks of itself as a class party, and Jharkand thinks of itself as a tribal party. Yet, to varying degrees, CPI-M candidates in northeastern India represent tribal identities and interests as well as those of class, and the Jharkand party in Bihar represents class as well as tribe, as does the Congress party in Madhya Pradesh. All three regions are centers of large but culturally and economically quite different tribal populations.

6. We are grateful to DCM Data Products of New Delhi and Messrs. S. U. Ullal, S. K. Maggu, and P. R. Shankar Kumar of that organization for providing us with data on party voting in Muslim constituencies for 1977 and 1980. We did not have, unfortunately, comparable data for 1971. The data for 1984 were compiled by us on the basis of the constituencies identified by the DCM group for 1977 and 1980.

7. The interpretation of all three sets of electoral data on minorities is subject to global (or ecological) fallacies because we infer minority party preferences and changes in party preferences from constituency-wide aggregate data and not from direct evidence of how minority voters cast their ballots. Nevertheless, such an interpretation of the party preferences of minority voters is better grounded than impressionistic accounts or nonanalytic inferences based on undifferentiated aggregate data.

8. Our calculations, on the basis of 1980 electoral data (Government of India, Election Commission, *Report on the Seventh General Elections to the House of the People in India, 1980,* vol. 2 [New Delhi, 1982]).

9. Our calculations, on the basis of preliminary results, provided by the Election Commission in unpublished form.

10. See People's Union for Democratic Rights and People's Union for Civil Liberties, *Who Are the Guilty* (Delhi, 1984), p. 3, for accounts of the role of Bhangis in the Delhi violence.

11. See, for example, Imtiaz Ahmad, "Indian Muslims and Electoral Politics," *Economic and Political Weekly*, March 11, 1967; H. A. Gani, *Muslim Political Issues and National Integration* (New Delhi: Sterling, 1978); R. A. Schermerhorn, *Ethnic Plurality in India;* Bashiruddin Ahmed, "Process of Integration," *Seminar*, no. 240 (August 1979); and Harry W. Blair, "Religion and Voting Behavior: The Muslim Community in Bihar, 1958–72, in *Voting, Caste, Community, Society.*

12. Kenneth Janda cites the poll of a 3,537-person sample in *Political Parties.*

13. Our finding that Muslim voters in Muslim-majority constituencies have found their interests and identity better represented by confessional than by national centrist parties is compatible with that of Harry Blair for Muslim electoral behavior in Bihar's state assembly elections through the 1972 poll. He concludes that "Muslim candidates . . . have been getting their votes more and more from areas of substantial Muslim population." See his "Religion and Voting Behavior," p. 41.

Of the ten Muslim-majority constituencies, three each are in Kashmir and Kerala, where Muslim parties (the National Conference and the Muslim League) articulate and represent Muslim interests and identity. Three more are in CPI-M—ruled West Bengal, where an additional twenty-two of that state's forty-two parliamentary seats have Muslim populations of 20 to 50 percent. The tenth is in the union territory of Lakshadweep.

14. For the use of the concept of political universes, see Walter Dean Burnham, *Critical Elections*.

15. For a sophisticated, skeptical assessment of Congress's future that places the assessment in the context of the Kothari and Morris-Jones characterizations of the early party, see James Manor, "Parties and the Party System."

16. International comparisons suggest that India's vote swings are more like those in Britain's parliamentary than those in America's presidential system with its national plebiscitary orientation. In Great Britain in eight parliamentary elections prior to 1984, vote swings were in the range of 1 to 4 percent in six elections and 4.1 to 8 percent in five, in the United States in eight presidential elections prior to 1984, vote swings were in the range of 5 to 9 percent in four elections and 11 to 20 percent in three. For a comparative discussion of volatility, see Ivor Crewe and David Denver, eds., *Electoral Change in Western Democracies: Patterns and Sources of Electoral Volatility* (New York: St. Martin's, 1985), p. 34, 106.

17. The very wide swings in Mrs. Gandhi's popularity reported by the Indian Institute of Public Opinion in 1980 are compatible with this analysis. The institute's cumulative measure on the question, "On the whole what is your opinion of the performance of Prime Minister Indira Gandhi—very good, fair, bad, very bad?" ranged between a high of 260 in 1972, just after the victory in the Bangladesh war, and a low of 63 in 1974, just before the emergency (Bashiruddin Ahmed, "Trends and Options," *Seminar*, no. 248 [April 1980]). See also Ahmed's "The Crisis of Change," *Seminar*, no. 242 October, 1979), for an analysis that reinforces our interpretation in much of this chapter and chapter 4.

18. See, for a similar argument, Manor's "Parties and the Party System."

19. Hindi Heartland, South, West, East, and North. These are the regions used in our analysis of the transformation of the Congress party earlier in this chapter (table 9), where the states and union territories that compose them are detailed. Historical, economic, and cultural determinants that justify our use of these regions for policy and political analysis are presented in our *Education and Politics in India*.

20. Anand Kumar locates the bifurcation that expressed itself in the 1967 election partly in the rise of a demand for regional languages that invigorated agitational politics in both North and South in the 1966–69 period. After the elections of 1967, support for regional languages became first a legitimate and then a dominant political stand across the parties. See Anand Kumar, "Political Philosophy of Peripheral Capitalism: Making the State's Agenda in Colonial and Post-Colonial India" (Ph.D. diss., Department of Sociology, University of Chicago, 1985).

21. The phenomenon of steady electoral adherence to Congress in the West and South, and the insulation of those regions from the votes swings of 1967 and 1977, was noted by Sisson and Vanderbok in their "Mapping the Indian Electorate [I]" (October 1983). Gould, in his analysis of the 1980 parliamentary election, noted "the political volatility and unpredictability which has characterized the Hindi Belt throughout the Indira Gandhi era" ("The Second Coming").

22. The Indian government responded to these common programs by appointing the Sakaria Commission. A sample of the kind of policy recommendations entailed in the demand for stronger state powers is contained in the various published and mimeographed materials of the Seminar on Centre-State Relations held in Bangalore on August 5–7, 1983. The seminar was organized by the Economic and Planning Council of the Government of Karnataka in association with the Institute for Social and Economic Change, Bangalore, and the Centre for Policy Research, New Delhi. The proposals of the seminar were summarized in "Seminar on Centre-State Relations, Bangalore, August 5–7, 1983 (mimeographed press release, July 8, 1983). The tendencies of the seminar, which was attended by academic and policy intellectuals, not politicians, are presented in a volume of stimulating and well-researched background papers: Government of Karnataka, *Seminar on Centre-State Relations* (Bangalore, [c. 1983]). See also "Keynote Address by President of the Seminar, VKRV Rao" (c. 1983, mimeograph). The political note in the seminar, and it was a low-key one, was *Inaugural Speech by Shri Ramakrishna Hegde, Chief Minister, Karnataka* (Bangalore: Economic and Planning Council, 1983). See also John R. Wood, ed., *State Politics in Contemporary India: Crisis or Continuity?* (Boulder, Colo.: Westview, 1985).

23. In December 1984, the party captured 1,959 assembly segments in the states that went to the polls in March 1985, but they captured only 1,438 in the March poll, a decline of 27 percent. Between the January 1980 parliamentary election and the June 1980 state assembly election, the difference had been between 1,888 segments and 1,513 seats, or a loss of 20 percent (*India Today,* March 31, 1985). The Congress-I had held 1,475 seats in the assemblies of the ten major states that went to the polls in March 1985, but it won only 1,438 of the seats whose results were announced immediately after the election, for a net loss at the time of 37 seats or 2.5 percent.

24. *Statesman Weekly,* March 16, 1985; *India Today,* March 31, 1985; and United News of India, *Backgrounders* March 14, 1985.

Chapter 7

1. For theoretical treatments of related issues see Anthony Downs, *An Economic Theory of Democracy* (New York: Harper and Row, 1965), and Donald Wittman's critique showing how producer rather than consumer or voter sovereignty can govern market and electoral outcomes, "Parties as Utility Maximizers," *American Political Science Review* 67, no. 2 (June 1973). We distinguish our models from Charles E. Lindblom's by integrating his two domains of "politics" (i.e., public authority and markets) into state and popular sovereignty, with the latter expressed in the collective and individual action of citizens as voters, producers, or consumers. See Lindblom's *Politics and Markets: The World's Political Economic Systems Compared* (New York: Basic Books, 1977). We do not treat market relationships in demand and command politics as a necessarily autonomous domain because we take the existence, viability, and quality of markets to be dependent on state decisions and policies that, in a circular fashion, depend on the "balance" of command and demand politics in particular contexts.

2. Lindblom, "The Science of Muddling Through," *Public Administration Review* 19 (Spring 1959): 79–88.

3. See Lindblom's *Politics and Markets,* where he contrasts incremental and synoptic rationality.

4. "It may be necessary," Jon Elster writes of the dichotomous view of investment and consumption, "at some point to take one step backwards in order to be able later on to take two steps forwards. An instance of this pattern is investment—consuming less now in order to be able to consume more later on." An "intentional agent" must be able to say "yes to unfavorable options now in order to say yes to very, very favorable ones in the future . . . the suboptimal action only makes sense in view of future gains that it makes possible" (*Making Sense of Marx* [Cambridge: Cambridge University Press, 1985], pp. 108–9).

5. See Hollis Chenery et al., *Redistribution with Growth* (Oxford: Oxford University Press, 1977).

6. See Morris David Morris, *Measuring the Condition of the World's Poor: The Physical Quality of Life Index* (New York: Pergamon, 1979).

7. Amartya Sen, "Public Action and the Quality of Life in Developing Countries," *Oxford Bulletin of Economics and Statistics,* no. 43 (1981): 310–16. In another article, Sen notes that Sri Lanka also does not incur heavy military expenditures ("Conflicts in Access to Food," *Mainstream,* January 8, 1983). The implication is that Sri Lanka therefore can afford the food subsidies. Presumably India, which aspires to be a regional and world power, cannot be a free rider on other actors' defense expenditures.

8. John Toye, *Public Expenditures and Indian Development Policy, 1960–70* (Cambridge: Cambridge University Press, 1981), p. 68.

9. Theodore Schultz, *Investing in People: The Economics of Population Quality* (Berkeley and Los Angeles: University of California Press, 1981); Gunnar Myrdal, *Asian Drama: An Inquiry into the Poverty of Nations* (New York: Twentieth Century Fund, 1968).

10. Myrdal, *Asian Drama,* p. 1916. For a critique of this view, see John Toye, *Public Expenditures,* pp. 67–70.

11. We do not accept Mancur Olson's charge that such a partial explanation must be rejected because it is "ad hoc." His search for the universal independent variable that will explain economic growth and decline ignores their multiple and contextual determination. See his *Rise and Decline of Nations.*

12. This argument is more strongly developed in Schultz's *Investing in People.*

13. For Sen's argument, see "How is India Doing," *New York Review of Books,* December 16, 1982. This article and a similar one in *Mainstream* spawned a lively debate. See Sen, "Conflicts in Access to Food"; K. N. Raj, "Chinese Data and Amartya Sen," *Mainstream,* January 15, 1983; Sen and Raj, "Amartya Sen vs. K. N. Raj on Chinese Data," *Mainstream,* February 12, 1983; and Sen, "Reply to K. N. Raj," *Mainstream,* February 19, 1983. See also Ranjit Sau, "Growth, Stagnation and Fluctuation in Indian Economy," and Sen, "India: The Doing and the Undoing," *Economic and Political Weekly,* February 12, 1983. We have profited from Barnett Rubin's argument for a connection beween the alleviation of poverty and participatory democracy in his "Private Power and Public Investment in India: A Study in the Political Economy of Development" (Ph.D. diss., University of Chicago, 1982).

Chapter 8

1. Alexis de Tocqueville may have been the first modern social theorist to address the generic problem of the relationship between improving economic and status conditions of the many and collective action directed at regime change. In his *Old Regime and the French Revolution*, (Garden City, N.Y.: Doubleday Anchor, 1955), he pointed out that France's peasants under improving economic circumstances became increasingly discontent with residual "feudal" exactions (e.g., corvee, market controls and costs, hunting privileges) while Prussia's oppressed and exploited serfs remained docile and obedient. A century later in his study of Prussian landworkers, Max Weber argued that most preferred insecurity with freedom to security with domination (*Schriften des Vereins für Sozialpolitik*, vol. 60, *Die Verhältnisse der Landarbeiter im Oestelbischen Deutschland* (Berlin: Duncker and Humbolt, 1892). Charles Tilley's recent study, *From Mobilization to Revolution* (Reading, Mass.: Addison-Wesley, 1978), provides a "partial synthesis" between causal and purposive explanation of collective action that leads to revolution and rebellion. Our "Determinants and Varieties of Agrarian Mobilization," in Desai, Susanne Hoeber Rudolph, and Rudra, *Agrarian Power and Agricultural Productivity in South Asia*, gives equal attention to why radical collective action does not and does occur.

2. Donald S. Zagoria, "China by Daylight," *Dissent* 2 (April 1975). Criticisms of Mancur Olson's bold attempt in *Rise and Decline of Nations* to explain economic growth in Western industrial democracies by a single variable—the degree to which vested interest groups pursuing redistributive goals retard or block collective action to promote allocative efficiency and collective goods—suggest the perils of relying on one variable. For critiques of Olson's approach to collective action problems generally, see Russell Hardin, *Collective Action* (Baltimore: Johns Hopkins University Press, 1982), chaps. 2, 3, 7; and Albert O. Hirschman, *Shifting Involvements* (Princeton: Princeton University Press, 1982), chap. 5. Essays in Dennis Mueller, ed., *The Political Economy of Growth* (New Haven: Yale University Press, 1983), challenge Olson's single-variable approach to economic growth and decline. An important attempt to explain growth using economic variables only can be found in E. F. Dennis, *Why Growth Rates Differ* (Washington, D.C.: Brookings Institution, 1967).

3. Rubin, "Private Power and Public Investment," fig. 6, pp. 174–75. Rubin finds inflation the crucial determinant of gross capital formation. Compare Paul Peretz, *The Political Economy of Inflation in the United States* (Chicago: University of Chicago Press, 1983).

4. See also Pranab Bardhan, *Political Economy of Development*. Bardhan argues that the nature of the "dominant coalition" determines the rate and prospects of economic growth.

5. Mueller, *Political Economy of Growth*, p. 3. (The following quotations are from the same page.)

6. Myrdal, *Asian Drama*.

7. See Albert O. Hirschman, *Shifting Involvements*, Princeton, Princeton University Press, 1982, chapter 5, where he criticizes Mancur Olson's theories of collective action as reflecting concern about the effects of 1960s-like mobilizations.

8. For a summary and critique of "overloaded government," see Colin Crouch, "The State Capital and Liberal Democracy."

9. See Claus Offe, *Contradictions of the Welfare State*, particularly chap. 2, "Ungovernability: The Renaissance of Conservative Theories of Crisis," pp. 65–87.

10. See Crozier, Huntington, and Watanuki, *Crisis of Democracy*, and Samuel P. Huntington and Joan M. Nelson, *No Easy Choice: Political Participation in Developing Countries* (Cambridge: Harvard University Press, 1976).

11. "In the years since independence, Indian economic growth has been much faster than in the colonial period. From 1948 to 1969, real national income rose by 3.3 percent per year . . . acceptable estimates for 1900–1946 . . . show a compound growth rate of real national income amounting to 0.7 percent a year in the last half century of colonial rule. Population growth was 0.8 percent a year from 1900 to 1946 and rose to 2.4 percent a year in 1948–1969. Therefore, *per capita* income has grown by 0.9 percent per year since independence, compared with a more or less stagnant level from 1900 to 1946" (Angus Maddison, *Class Structure and Economic Growth: India and Pakistan since the Moghuls* [New York: Norton, 1971], p. 76). Calculations based on table A-2 (p. 165) and B-1 (p. 167) show that per capita income between 1900 and 1936 increased from Rs. 71 to Rs. 78.

12. World Bank, *World Development Report, 1984* (New York: Oxford University Press, 1984), table 1, pp. 218–19.

13. The calibration and synchronization of political periods (regime types and type of politics) with our measures of demand politics and of economic performance are complicated by the facts that demand politics and economic performance data are sometimes given on the basis of calendar year (January 1–December 31) and sometimes on the basis of financial year (April 1–March 31), that political events occur stochastically, and that five-year plan periods (starting in 1951) have been modified by a plan "holiday" (or annual plans) (1966–67 through 1968–69) and by a one-year reduction in the fifth plan (from 1974–79 to 1974–78).

14. See, for example, Weiner, *India at the Polls*, p. 68, and Hardgrave, *India*.

15. John Mellor, *Developing Rural India* (Ithaca, N.Y.: Cornell University Press, 1968), p. 87.

16. See James Warner Bjorkman, "Public Law 480 and the Policies of Self-Help and Short-Tether: Indo-American Relations, 1965–68," in Lloyd I. Rudolph and Susanne Hoeber Rudolph, eds., *The Regional Imperative: The Administration of U.S. Foreign Policy Towards South Asian States Under Presidents Johnson and Nixon* (New Delhi: Concept, 1980; Atlantic Highlands, N.J.: Humanities Press, 1981).

17. For an interpretation of the election, see our "New Era for India," in S. P. Varma and Iqbal Narain, eds., *Fourth General Election in India* (Hyderabad: Orient Longman, 1970), pp. 1–17.

18. Baldev Raj Nayar, *Violence and Crime in India: A Quantitative Study* (New Delhi: Macmillan India, 1975), p. 24. For a study covering earlier years, see David H. Bayley, "Violent Public Protest in India: 1900–1960," *Indian Journal of Political Science* 24 (1963). The treatment of political riots and deaths in G. Bingham Powell, Jr.'s more recent *Contemporary Democracies: Participation, Stability, and Violence* (Cambridge: Harvard University Press, 1982) is unsatisfactory for our purposes, because Powell "simply" adds up

events and divides by a number of years to arrive at measures of political riots and deaths, does not control for population (i.e., uses absolute rather than per capita figures in making comparisons among states), and makes no attempt to deal with contextual time-bound relationships between political and economic conditions and levels of political riots and deaths. (See his tables 2.3 [p. 22], [p. 232]).

19. *Keesing's Contemporary Archives,* November 19–26, 1966, pp. 217–24.

20. Lloyd I. Rudolph, Susanne Hoeber Rudolph, and Karuna Ahmed, "Student Politics and National Politics in India," *Economic and Political Weekly,* July 1971 (special no.). We have put quotation marks around "indiscipline" to mitigate a necessarily negative implication. The various causes, reasons, forms, and levels of student "indiscipline" can both promote and undermine representational processes and policy dialogue.

21. There is an extensive literature on the Naxalbari rebellion, the Naxalite movement and violence, and Naxalism. Naxalbari village has in fact supplied Indian English with terms for agrarian radicalism and rebellion. Among the leading works on Naxalite politics are Marcus F. Franda, *Radical Politics in West Bengal* (Cambridge: MIT Press, 1971); Mohan Ram, *Maoism in India* (New Delhi: Vikas, 1971); Bhabani Sen Gupta, *Communism in Indian Politics* (New York: Columbia University Press, 1972); Biplab Dasgupta, *The Naxalite Movement* (Bombay: Allied, 1974); J. C. Johri, *Naxalite Politics in India* (Delhi: Institute of Constitutional and Parliamentary Studies, 1972); and Sohail Jawaid, *The Naxalite Movement in India* (New Delhi: Associated Publishing House, 1979).

22. *Keesing's Contemporary Archives,* November 28–December 5, 1970, p. 24319.

23. Ibid., pp. 24319–20. See also sources for table 23.

24. Government of India, Ministry of Home Affairs, *Report, 1971–72* (Delhi, 1972).

25. Kochanek, "Mrs. Gandhi's Pyramid."

26. "Demonstrations, strikes, bandhs, etc. imposed unusual strains on the law and order machinery. . . . Student unrest . . . has been a cause for serious concern" (Government of India, Ministry of Home Affairs, *Report, 1973–74* [Delhi, 1974], p. 1).

27. See Ghanshyam Shah, *Protest Movements in Two Indian States* (New Delhi: Ajanta, 1977); John R. Wood, "Extra-Parliamentary Opposition in India: An Analysis of Populist Agitators in Gujarat and Bihar" *Pacific Affairs* 48 (Fall 1975):313–34; and Dawn E. Jones and Rodney W. Jones, "Urban Upheaval in India: The Nav Nirman Riots in Gujarat," *Asian Survey* 16, no. 11 (November 1976):1012–23.

28. See our "Determinants and Varieties of Agrarian Mobilization."

29. Isher Judge Ahluwalia, *Industrial Growth in India.*

Chapter 9

1. For a review of relevant theory, see J. David Greenstone, "Group Theories," in Fred Greenstein and Nelson Polsby, eds., *The Handbook of Political Science,* vol. 4 (Reading, Mass.: Addison-Wesley, 1975). Samuel Beer's *British Politics in the Collectivist Age* (New York: Knopf, 1966) reviews the effect of

the socialist state on British pluralism. Robert A. Dahl, *Who Governs?* (New Haven: Yale University Press, 1961), offers a classical recent defense of the pluralist position; Arthur F. Bentley, *The Process of Government* (Chicago: University of Chicago Press, 1908), and David B. Truman, *The Governmental Process* (New York: Knopf, 1953), offer earlier justifications. Mancur Olson's *The Logic of Collective Action: Public Goods and the Theory of Groups* (Cambridge: Harvard University Press, 1980) deals with the problem in the language of public goods theory.

2. See, for example, Stephen S. Cohen, *Modern Capitalist Planning; The French Model* (Cambridge: Harvard University Press, 1979); Leo Panitch, "The Development of Corporatism in Liberal Democracies," *Comparative Political Studies* 10, no. 1 (April 1977); Richard Willey, "Trade Unionism and Political Parties in the Federal Republic of Germany," *Industrial Labor Relations Review* 28 (1974); Shonfield, *Modern Capitalism*; Philippe C. Schmitter, "Modes of Interest Intermediation and Models of Societal Change in Western Europe," in *Comparative Political Studies* 10, no. 1 (April 1977); and Gerhard Lehmbruch, "Liberal Corporatism and Party Government," *Comparative Political Studies* 10, no. 1 (April 1977).

3. "The interest group structure can be characterized as pluralist . . . even increasingly so in its multiplicity, autonomy and fragmentation" (Philippe C. Schmitter and Donald Brand, "Organizing Capitalists in the United States: The Advantages and Disadvantages of Exceptionalism" [Paper presented at a meeting of the American Political Science Association, September 1979], p. 68. Schmitter and Brand lay much of the causal burden for American pluralism on the antitrust tradition (p. 69ff). Grant McConnell, *Private Power and American Democracy* (New York: Alfred A. Knopf, 1966), provided an important critique. See also Theodore Lowi, "American Business, Public Policy, Case Studies and Political Theory," *World Politics* 16 (1964).

4. Mobilizations that overflow formal political processes have a family resemblance to what Samuel P. Huntington calls political decay. Our point is that such mobilizations are problematic but not necessarily degenerative. We stress here that new forms, such as demand groups, can arise in response to crises of mobilization. See Huntington's *Political Order in Changing Societies* (New Haven: Yale University Press, 1968).

5. For a view that assumes that interests already exist, as against the emphasis here on the demand group as a form that is continuously emergent, see Suzanne Berger, ed., *Organizing Interests in Western Europe: Pluralism, Corporatism and the Transformation of Politics* (Cambridge: Cambridge University Press, 1981). Berger's formulation begs the question of representation of the unorganized and unmobilized. The demand group creates consciousness and organization as part of the process of representation and bargaining.

6. Kochanek, *Business and Politics in India*, p. xii.

7. Clifford Geertz, *Agricultural Involution: The Process of Ecological Change in Indonesia* (Berkeley and Los Angeles: University of California Press, 1970), pp. 81–82.

Chapter 10

1. For the disparity in growth of employment between public and private organized sectors, see Government of India, Ministry of Labour, Labour Bu-

reau, *The Indian Labour Yearbook, 1982* (Chandigarh and Simla, 1983). In the American context, Richard A. Cloward and Francis Fox Piven have shown the propensity of public bureaucracies to consume resources intended for wider and poorer publics (*The Politics of Turmoil: Essays in Poverty, Race, and the Urban Crisis* [New York: Vintage, 1972]). Of the 3.5 million increase in Indian public employment between 1966 and 1975, 1.5 million was in community and social services.

2. See, for example, Michael J. Piore and Charles F. Sabel, *The Second Industrial Divide: Possibilities for Prosperity* (New York: Basic Books, 1984), and Charles F. Sabel, *Work and Politics: The Divisim of Labor in Industry* (New York: Cambridge University Press, 1982).

3. Rakhahari Chatterji, *Unions, Politics and the State: A Study of Labour Politics* (New Delhi: South Asian Publishers, 1980).

4. Economic Intelligence Service, *Basic Statistics Relating to the Indian Economy* (Bombay, 1980), table 9.14.

5. For an account of the destructiveness and violence that prevailed in 1969, see *Keesing's Contemporary Archives,* January 31—February 7, 1970, p. 23800. The CPI-M home minister of 1969, who was accused of deploying the police in ways that favored labor and left agitators, in 1977 became chief minister of a more orderly and peaceable Bengal. Bakul H. Dholakia and Ravindra H. Dholakia, "State Income Inequalities and Inter-state Variations in the Growth of Real Capital Stock," *Economic and Political Weekly,* September 20, 1980, reports that between 1961 and 1971 West Bengal dropped from first to fourth in rank by per capita income (table 1, p. 158).

6. *Statesman,* March 8, 1980.

7. Government of India, Ministry of Labour, Labour Bureau, *The Indian Labour Yearbook, 1975 and 1976* (Delhi, 1979). See table 2.02 for the range of wages.

8. See, for example, table 4, in Ministry of Finance, Study Group on Wages, Incomes and Prices, *Report* (hereafter *Boothalingam Report* (Delhi, 1978) which shows the minimum emoluments of two public-sector enterprises in Bangalore at Rs. 723 and 684 per month, compared with Rs. 473 and 463 for two private engineering firms at Calcutta and Faridabad. One would want far more complete figures to affirm the point in the text with full confidence.

9. This survey covers all "factories" that average fifty workers or more with the aid of power or one hundred or more without the aid of power (Government of India, Ministry of Labour, Labour Bureau, *Labour Statistics under the Annual Survey of Industries, 1975—76* [Delhi, 1978]).

10. Ibid., pp. 73—84.

11. Labour Bureau, *Indian Labour Yearbook, 1975 and 1976,* table 2.17, p. 49, shows that 99 percent of all central government employees in 1975 earned less than Rs. 1,000 per month.

12. "Neutralization" in dearness allowance was calculated thus: up to 100 percent of the inflation index for pay levels below Rs. 301 and 75 percent for pay levels between Rs. 301 and Rs. 900, for every increase of eight points in the price index average over twelve months, under recommendations of the pay commission given effect after January 1973 (Labour Bureau, *Indian Labour Yearbook, 1975 and 1976,* p. 49).

13. *Boothalingam Report,* tables 14, 15, pp. 118—19. Table 15 compares erosion for peons and secretaries to government, and table 14 shows similar erosion for senior management in the public-sector firms.

14. Ibid., table 17, which shows the maximum for central government peons at Rs. 398, Life Insurance Corporation peons at 799, and banking peons at 675.

15. Ibid., table 19, p. 123.

16. Ibid., table 15, p. 119.

17. The Boothalingam Commission reported top real-value emoluments of Rs. 3,188 after taxes in 1973 and top real-value emoluments of Rs. 1,871 after taxes in 1978 (ibid.).

18. Dharma Kumar, "Changes in Income Distribution and Poverty in India: A Review of the Literature," *World Development* 2, no. 1 (January 1, 1974): 39. Kumar adds that accepting the change in the ratio "involves many implicit assumptions about the absence of intersectoral transfers, etc." For example, she reports that a microstudy by Sheldon R. Simon on Senapur, Uttar Pradesh, between 1954 and 1964 found that "while average per capita income from non-agricultural sources increased by 133 percent, largely because of transfers from migrants to cities, the agriculturist class as a group benefitted most in contrast to traders and landowners, and within this group the untouchable chamars gained" (p. 39).

19. For a discussion of the validity of this figure, and its meaning, see chapter 12 below.

20. The balance in agriculture were in "livestock, forestry, fishing, plantations, etc." (2.4 percent); the balance in industry, in "mining, quarrying" (0.6 percent); and the balance in services, in "trade and commerce" (5.6 percent) and "transportation, storage and communications" (2.4 percent). (Figures from Economic Intelligence Service, *Basic Statistics,* table 15.1.)

21. *Boothalingam Report,* table 6, pp. 108–10.

22. Government of India, Ministry of Labour, Labour Bureau, *Rural Labour Enquiry, 1974–5: Summary Report* (Delhi, 1978), p. 15.

23. Kumar reports from the Herdt and Baker study that only in Punjab, Madras, and Kerala were real wages higher in 1967–68 and 1968–69 than in the preceding thirteen years; "in all other states studied, with one exception, real wages were lower" ("Income Distribution and Poverty"). See R. W. Herdt and E. A. Baker, "Agricultural Wages, Production, and High Yielding Varieties," *Economic and Political Weekly,* March 25, 1972. If we treat the terms of trade between the agricultural and other sectors (measured primarily by the price of food grains relative to the price of manufactured goods) as an indirect indicator of the relationship of workers' earnings in the agricultural and other sectors, we find, according to data assembled by Isher Ahluwalia, that "there has been a declining trend since the mid-sixties in the terms of trade of agricultural vis-a-vis non-agriculture" (*Industrial Growth in India,* p. 44). Ahluwalia relies primarily on data from A. S. Kahlon and D. S. Tyagi, *Agricultural Price Policy in India* (Bombay: Allied, 1983), in constructing table 3.4, p. 45.

24. Montek Ahluwalia, "Rural Poverty and Agricultural Performance in India," *Journal of Development Studies* 14 (April 1978).

25. Reply to "Starred Question No. 901" in Lok Sabha on April 27, 1978 as reported in Economic Intelligence Service, *Basic Statistics,* table 15.4. The figure for 1975 of 5.772 million has been adjusted to 5.5 million to take account of the growth in the labor force over fifteen months.

26. Labour Bureau, *Indian Labour Yearbook, 1975 and 1976,* table 2.01. Of the 51,609 factories covered under the act in 1974, only 31,404 furnished returns, a factor that somewhat biases the figures.

27. See Labour Bureau, *Rural Labour Enquiry, 1974–75*, p. 47 for the average daily earnings of male rural laborers.

28. We apply the 33 percent of operational holders holding units of a .01–2.5 acres (see our table 40, chapter 13) to the number of persons in the rural labor force in 1971–72 (126 million).

29. *Boothalingam Report*, table 7, p. 111. Sixteen industries are compared as to employment and average per capita daily earnings (1971–72). The largest discrepancies were in rubber and rubber products and chemicals, the smallest in leather and leather products and wood and wood products.

30. See D. A. S. Jackson, "Wage Policy and Industrial Relations in India," *Economic Journal* 82 (March 1972).

31. As the citations that follow suggest, research on Indian trade unions is mostly quite dated, having been conducted in the fifties and sixties. However, the earlier work provides a valuable introduction and significant evidence about the continuity of the tradition of state domination. See V. B. Karnik, *Indian Trade Unions: A Survey* (Bombay: Manaktalas, 1966), and *Strikes in India* (Bombay: Manaktalas, 1967); Harold Crouch, *Trade Unions and Politics in India* (Bombay: Manaktalas, 1966); Van Dusen Kennedy, *Unions, Employers and Government* (Bombay: Manaktalas, 1966); Charles A. Myers and Subbiah Kannapan, *Industrial Relations in India*, rev. ed. (Bombay: Asia Publishing House, 1970); and Oscar Ornati, *Jobs and Workers in India* (Ithaca, N.Y.: Cornell University Press, 1955).

E. A. Ramaswamy's *The Worker and His Union* (Bombay: Allied, 1977), an analysis of textile trade unions in Coimbatore, was, according to his teacher, M. N. Srinivas, the first social scientific study of trade unions by an Indian national (p. ix). Ramaswamy's student, Kuriakose Mamkoottam, produced another, *Trade Unionism: Myth and Reality, Unionism in the Tata Iron and Steel Company* (New Delhi: Oxford University Press, 1982). Finally E. A. Ramaswamy and Uma Ramaswamy's *Industry and Labour* (New Delhi: Oxford University Press, 1981) provided an excellent overview of industrial relations, while Sukomal Sen's *Working Class of India: History of Emergence and Movement 1830–1970* (Columbia, Mo.: South Asia Books, 1977) provided an excellent historical account of workers and trade unions. Chatterji's *Unions* also represents a significant example of this recent literature. For new work, see Manju Baruah Parikh, "Labor-Capital Relations in the Indian Textile Industry" (Ph.D. diss. in progress, University of Chicago), comparing the Ahmedabad and Coimbatore models of trade union action. See also Santosh Sood, *Trade Union Leadership in India: A Case Study* (New Delhi: Deep and Deep, 1984).

32. See, for example, Stephen P. Cohen, *Modern Capitalist Planning*, and Shonfield, *Modern Capitalism*.

33. A significant example was the reversal by government in April 1981 of the agreement between the Life Insurance Corporation and the Life Insurance Corporation union on levels of dearness allowance and bonus (including retroactive payments). The government acted in the face of a supreme court stay order upholding the settlement. It alleged that the formula adopted bore no relation to those prevailing with respect to other public-sector undertakings. In other years, according to government, Life Insurance Corporation emoluments exceeded increases in the consumer price index. The conflict highlights state efforts to rationalize and control wages and union efforts to maintain or

increase the real income of their members in the vast administered-price sector of the organized economy. See *Hindu,* February 7, 1981, February 14, 1981, and April 11, 1981, international edition.

34. Geertz, *Agricultural Involution,* pp. 81–82. Geertz in turn draws on A. Goldenwieser, "Loose Ends of a Theory on the Individual Pattern and Involution in Primitive Society," in R. Lowie, ed., *Essays in Anthropology Presented to A. L. Kroeber* (Berkeley and Los Angeles: University of California Press, 1936).

35. Adolph Sturmthal, "Industrial Relations Strategies," in Adolph Sturmthal and James G. Scoville, *The International Labor Movement in Transition* (Urbana: University of Illinois Press, 1973), pp. 30–31.

36. Skocpol, *States and Social Revolutions.*

37. Sturmthal and Scoville have related trade union movements to economic development. See Sturmthal, "Economic Development and Labour Movement," in Arthur A. Ross, ed., *Industrial Relations and Economic Development,* (London: Macmillan, 1966), pp. 165–84 and "Industrial Relations Strategies" and Scoville, "Some Determinants of the Structure of Labor Movements," in Sturmthal and Scoville, *International Labor Movement.*

38. For additional comparative views, see Ernest Barker, *The Development of the Public Services in Europe* (New York: Oxford University Press, 1944; Hamden, Conn.: Archon, 1977); Alexander Gershenkron, *Economic Backwardness in Historical Perspective* (Cambridge: Harvard University Press, 1962); J. David Greenstone, *Labor in American Politics* (New York: Vintage, 1969); David L. Horowitz, *Italian Labor Movement* (Cambridge: Harvard University Press, 1963); Joseph La Polambara, *The Italian Labor Movement* (Ithaca, N.Y.: Cornell University Press, 1957); Val R. Lorwin, *The French Labor Movement* (Cambridge: Harvard University Press, 1954); Peter Losche, "Stages in the Evolution of the German Labor Movements," in Sturmthal and Scoville, *International Labor Movement,* pp. 101–22; François Sellier, "The French Workers' Movement and Political Unionism," in ibid., pp. 79–100; and Richard J. Willey, "Trade Unionism and Political Parties in the Federal Republic of Germany," *Industrial and Labor Relations Review* 28 (October 1974):38–59. A useful recent account of German Trade Unions and of the Deutsche Gewerkschaftsbund is contained in Federal Government of Germany, *Bulletin* 3 (January 30, 1980).

39. The measure used is "value added in manufacturing (millions of 1970 dollars)." The figure for India is $8,973 million. Figures for "centrally planned economies" are not given.

40. For accounts of organization among agricultural workers in South India, see Marshall M. Bouton, *Agrarian Radicalism in South India* (Princeton: Princeton University Press, 1985); and Ronald J. Herring, *Land to the Tiller: The Political Ecconomy of Agrarian Reform in South Asia* (New Haven: Yale University Press, 1983).

41. The Essential Services Maintenance Ordinance of July 27, 1981, empowered the government to declare any service essential if it is connected with matters about which Parliament has the constitutional authority to pass legislation, and to issue an order prohibiting strikes in it for six months. The prohibition can be extended for a maximum of an additional six months. Persons commencing, taking part in, inciting, or instigating strikes can be arrested by any police officer without warrant and tried summarily by specially empow-

ered magistrates who can impose jail sentences and fines. Except for the provision of summary trials and stiffer penalties, powers to ban strikes are already available, not only to the center but also to state governments under existing laws, including the Industrial Disputes Act (1947). See *Hindu,* August 8, 1981, international edition; BM in *Economic and Political Weekly,* August 1 and 8, 1981, pp. 1254–55 and 1299.

42. BM in his *Economic and Political Weekly* column of August 8, 1981, argues that the ordinance and subsequent legislation was "widely held to be prelude to the clamping of some kind of wage and DA [dearness allowance] freeze." When the labor minister "was pushed to the sidelines" and the Home Ministry took charge, "the management of industrial relations . . . began to be looked upon as a problem of administration and law and order. Inevitably, the Ordinance was sponsored by the Home Ministry. It is the policemen, and not labour and conciliation officers, who will now handle labour and labour disputes" (p. 1299).

N. Ram in a dispatch from Washington entitled "The Pound of Flesh" suggests that, "contrary to the version put out by Indian officialdom for home consumption," the antistrike ordinance was related to the "stiff degree of conditionality" associated with the largest loan ($6 billion) negotiated in the history of the International Monetary Fund (*Hindu,* August 7, 1981, international edition).

43. We are indebted to Sandip Pendse "Labour, The Datta Samant Phenomenon," pts. 1, 2, *Economic and Political Weekly,* April 18 and 25, 1981, for these terms. Other standard accounts also deal with the history of trade unionism in terms of phases. The best recent account of both national and state developments can be found in Chatterji's *Unions.* In the Bombay area, Pendse distinguishes the "red flag wave" led by the AITUC of the early years of independence; the period of legalism, about a decade after independence when recourse to state conciliation machinery and productivity deals under the slogans of patriotism and "free and responsible" were the order of the day; the period of militancy (1963–67), when George Fernandes was the preeminent leader of service-sector workers, Congress popularity was at a low ebb, newer sections of workers were becoming organized, and CITU, after its formation in 1970, began to provide a channel for new militancy; the period of the Shiv Sena wave (1966–70), when local chauvinism and anticommunism gave the Maharashtrian nationalist Shiv Sena control of more than four hundred factories in Bombay; and the Datta Samant era, which Pendse dates from the Godrej incident of 1972, characterized by "militancy, direct action, disregard for legal proprieties," challenge to established unions, and "above all worker support" as workers "looking for a leader capable of challenging an established union began to flock to him" (pp. 695–96).

44. Chatterji, *Unions,* p. 222.

45. John Echeverri-Gent, "An Analysis of Causes behind the Authoritarianism of the Gandhi Regime in India" (Seminar paper, University of Chicago, Department of Political Science, 1976, typescript).

46. Chatterji, *Unions,* p. 223.

47. For the establishment of apex bodies, see Labour Bureau, *Indian Labour Yearbook, 1975 and 1976,* p. 108; see also Chatterji, *Unions,* p. 232.

48. *Times of India,* November 25, 1975. For an account of the Indian Labour Conference and the Standing Committee on Labour, see Labour Bureau,

Indian Labour Yearbook, 1975 and 1976, p. 105 and references. For Joint Management Councils, see pp. 110–12. Joint councils of management were inspired in part by the Yugoslav experience, and encouraged by the Industrial Policy Resolution of 1956. The second, third, and fourth five-year plans contained programs to extend the councils, but by the end of the fifth plan they covered no more than 1,290 of the establishments employing five hundred or more workers (Alak Ghosh, *Indian Economy,* p. 437).

49. For an extended discussion of the Indian Labour Conference and the Standing Labour Committee, see Kamala Mathur and N. R. Sheth, *Tripartism in Labour Policy: The Indian Experience* (New Delhi: Shri Ram Centre for Industrial Relations, 1969). For the agenda decision, see p. 6. For an early criticism of the passive role of the Indian Labour Conference, see Bhagaram Tulpule, "ILC Evades Main Issues," *Economic and Political Weekly,* May 4, 1968.

50. The bonus had been 4 percent until 1972, when, in response to exigent demands, Mrs. Gandhi raised it to 8.33 percent. Under the emergency, legislation was enacted specifying that the bonus need only be paid by enterprises that had a "surplus." The law provoked more skillful company accounting. The history of the bonus is discussed in *Boothalingam Report,* p. 78. For the bonus settlement of 1980, which for the first time in the public sector linked the bonus to productivity by the settlement affecting railways and post and telegraphs, see *Financial Express,* February 13, 1980.

51. Government of India, Ministry of Information and Broadcasting, *India, 1976: A Reference Annual* (Delhi, 1976), pp. iii, vii.

52. Ibid.

53. *Statesman,* October 27, 1975.

54. For general accounts of state influence, see Subbiah Kannapan, "Many Facets of Government Influence on Industrial Relations in India," and S. D. Punekar, "Aspects of State Intervention in Industrial Relations in India: An Evaluation," both in Ross, *Industrial Relations.*

55. See Bhagaram Tulpule, "The Industrial Relations Bill, 1978," pts. 1, 2, *Economic and Political Weekly,* October 14 and November 11, 1978.

56. See *Hindustan Times,* April 4, 1980, and Radha Iyer in *New Delhi,* December 10, 1979. For a more general discussion, see S. B. Kale, "Verification of Membership of Trade Unions: Procedures and Practice," *Indian Journal of Industrial Relations* (July 1966): 50–69.

57. The central government advised the president not to consent to the Indian Trade Unions (West Bengal Amendment) Bill of 1969 which provided for compulsory recognition of representative unions selected by means of secret ballot (Chatterji, *Unions,* p. 193).

58. The Bharatiya Mazdoor Sangh, a smaller apex federation, then affiliated with the Jan Sangh, wanted proportionate representation in the negotiating process, and the Hind Mazdoor Sabha, a socialist apex federation, wanted an independent body to decide the representative nature of rival claimants. All these procedures seek to escape a secret ballot (*Hindustan Times,* February 9, 1980).

59. See, for example, Centre of Indian Trade Unions, *Constitution* (CITU, Calcutta: 1970).

60. The National Commission on Labour (1969) recommended that a single bargaining agent be determined by procedures selected by an indepen-

dent Industrial Relations Commission (Government of India, Ministry of Labour, *Report of the National Commission on Labour,* [Delhi: 1969]). The Industrial Relations Bill of 1978 would have required a union to be supported by 65 percent for it to become sole negotiating agent, a very stringent condition. Union support would have made possible either a secret ballot or check-off authorization as the basis of determining union support (Tulpule, "Industrial Relations Bill," p. 1719). But the bill was never passed.

61. Ministry of Labour, Report of the National Commission on Labour, p. 322.

62. See, for example, an early account, A. J. Fonseca, *Wage Determination and Organized Labour in India* (New Delhi: Oxford University Press, 1964); and V. K. R. V. Rao, "Incomes Policy and Industrial Relations," *Indian Journal of Industrial Relations* (July 1973): 1–13, and *Inflation and India's Economic Crisis* (New Delhi: Vikas, 1973).

63. Government of India, Ministry of Labour, Labour Bureau, *Wage Fixation in Industry and Agriculture in India* (Delhi, 1974), pp. 63–64.

64. Labour Minister Narain Dutt Tiwari announced government's decision to reinstitute wage boards at the annual conference of the All-India Organization of Employers on April 24, 1981. The government, he said, could not allow wages to be determined by market forces. But wage boards are unlikely to work in the eighties when they failed in the seventies. Employers are skeptical about them; many trade unions, following the recommendations of the National Commission on Labour (1969), believe them to be a retrograde measure compared with collective bargaining and bipartite negotiations; and government has no control over profits, dividends, and prices. See Narendra Sharma, "Wage Boards: Shot in the Dark?" *Mainstream,* May 23, 1981, pp. 4–5.

65. Ministry of Labour, *Report of the National Commission on Labour,* pp. 43–44.

66. Sturmthal, "Industrial Relations Strategies," p. 18. See also H. J. Habakkuk, *American and British Technology in the Nineteenth Century* (Cambridge: Cambridge University Press, 1962).

67. Chatterji, *Unions,* p. 214. The official count of "federations" by the Government of India's Labour Bureau reports a much higher number of federations, eighty-five in 1975. We use Chatterji's figure because it bears some relationship to power and influence, while the Labour Bureau adheres to a formal legal definition (Labour Bureau, *Indian Labour Yearbook, 1982,* table 4.05, p. 80).

68. The *Report of the National Commission on Labour* recommended a minimum for recognition of 10 percent or one hundred per firm, whichever is lower (p. 296).

69. The state of Bombay collected data on unregistered unions in the forties and reported that it had 350 unions in 1947, of which 250 were registered, and 468,078 members, of whom 370,449 were in the registered unions (Government of India, Ministry of Labour, Labour Bureau, *The Indian Labour Yearbook, 1947–48* [Delhi, 1949], p. 106).

70. Chatterji, *Unions,* compares the three states.

71. In 1976, public-sector disputes accounted for 153 disputes as against 1,306 in the private sector (Government of India, Ministry of Labour, Labour Bureau, *Pocket Book of Labour Statistics, 1978* [Chandigosh and Simla, 1978], table 7.8, p. 161. Public-sector employment rose by 69 percent between 1966 and 1981, private-sector by 8.9 percent.

72. "Partnership of the kind Gandhi had in mind was not based on class-conflict, but on class cooperation. In a healthy partnership, there is no conflict of interests between partners, only there is concurrence of unity of interests" (S. R. Vasavada, G. Ramanujam, R. K. Malviya, and Ramanandandas, in Ministry of Labour, *Report of the National Commission on Labour*, p. 495). For the original, see Mohandas K. Gandhi, *Towards Non-Violent Socialism* ed. Bharatan Kumarappa (Ahmadabad: Navajivan Publishing House, 1951).

73. Kamal Nayan Kabra, Anil C. Itteyerali, and Vijay P. Ojha, in "Manday Losses, Wages, Profits and Prices," *Mainstream*, August 25, 1981, pp. 13–15, convincingly discredit the economic assumptions justifying the antistrike ban ordinance by showing that lost workdays are not associated with losses in industrial production. Paradoxically, they show a positive association, one that is "not very weak," of 0.58.

74. Ministry of Labour, *Report of the National Commission on Labour*, p. A3.

75. Evidence before the commission February 1, 1969, at Bombay (ibid., p. 492). Jha's characterization omits the fact that British laissez-faire at its peak was mortally opposed to industrial "combinations."

76. S. R. Vasavada et al., Minute of Dissent, p. 492. The dissenters relied heavily upon Gandhian premises and philosophy.

77. Ibid., p. 493.

78. Raj Krishna, "Economic Development of India," p. 140.

79. Ramaswamy and Ramaswamy, *Industry and Labour*, pp. 197–98. In 1947 and again in 1950, efforts were made to amend or replace the Indian Trade Unions Act of 1926. They envisaged "statutory union recognition, compulsory collective bargaining, exclusive bargaining rights to trade unions fulfilling certain requirements, and the conferment on recognized unions of the right to collect subscriptions and hold meetings within company premises." These bills lapsed along with Parliament on the eve of the first general elections in 1952.

After the election, V. V. Giri as labor minister, sought to resuscitate these bills but was blocked, despite efforts to gain Nehru's support, by state and party opposition. Government ministries with many employees—such as railways, defense, and post and telegraphs—did not want to be statutorily compelled to bargain with a trade union. The fledgling Indian National Trade Union Congress (INTUC), the recently created Congress party labor wing, was in no position to compete with Communist and socialist unions if the law required recognition of the largest union as the exclusive bargaining agent for workers in particular factories. See also Myers and Kannappan, *Industrial Relations*, p. 320, 343 n. 34, and V. V. Giri, *Labour Problems in Indian Industry* (Bombay: Asia Publishing House, 1955).

Bhagaram Tulpule has provided a consistently informed and articulate viewpoint in favor of regulated conflict for more than ten years through journals of opinion, notably *Economic and Political Weekly*. See also E. A. Ramaswamy's reasoned defense of bargaining within a union in the context of union democracy, "The Indian Management Dilemma," *Asian Survey* 23, no. 8 (August 1983).

80. For an excellent review of the Janata government's aborted Industrial Relations Bill of 1978 in the context of the history of trade union relations in India, see Bhagaram Tulpule's "The Industrial Relations Bill, 1978."

81. The first pay commission reported in 1946–47. The second pay commission issued its recommendations concerning central government employees during the second plan period: (The Commission of Enquiry on Emoluments and Conditions of Service of Central Government Employees, 1957–59, cited in Labour Bureau, *Wage Fixation,* p. 8).

82. The Committee on Wage Policy (Chakravarti Committee) of 1973 precipitated a substantial national debate on wage policy. While its deliberations did not result in a policy, they did produce a wage cell in the Ministry of Labour (Chatterji, *Unions,* p. 192). The Labour Bureau's *Wage Fixation* "codified" prior practice in its technical report.

83. See, for example, the promulgation of guidelines with respect to dearness allowance and wages by the Bureau of Public Enterprise in 1979 and the union response demanding that these be arrived at by negotiations between unions and management, not unilaterally by government (*Times of India,* September 15, 1979). The same sequence was repeated in 1983 ("Doing Away with Collective Bargaining," *Economic and Political Weekly,* November 26, 1983).

84. For a theoretical statement of the role of trade unions in development in India, see Asoka Mehta, "The Mediating Role of the Trade Union in Underdeveloped Countries," *Economic Development and Cultural Change* (October 1957):16–23.

85. A. K. Dasgupta, *A Theory of Wage Policy* (New Delhi: Oxford University Press, 1976), p. 36 (Agarwal, 563).

86. Ornati, *Jobs and Workers in India* (Ithaca, N.Y.: Cornell University Press, 1955), p. 157.

87. S. A. Dange, one of the founders of the CPI and its principal strategist since the 1964 split, said of the results of the January 1980 parliamentary elections that the Indian people had chosen "well and wisely" by electing the Indira Gandhi–led Congress-I. The party's national council accepted his resignation as chairman in February and passed, by a vote of one hundred to five, a resolution rejecting Dange's policy of support for the Congress-I and calling instead for "unity of the left and democratic forces." On April 13, it met again to expel him. Some of Dange's followers formed a new party, the All-India Communist party, in April. Roza Desphande, the new party's leader and Dange's daughter, said the party would support the Congress-I, which represented the "national bourgeoisie" and supported "democratic socialism." The AITUC, which Dange also headed as its president, survived the split with little damage, as did the CPI. It may be that the era of CPI–Congress-I collaboration, which foundered during the emergency and Sanjay Gandhi's rise to power, has finally come to an end.

Chapter 11

1. Morris David Morris has argued persuasively that if the English experience of urban work in the early stage of industrialization was indeed horrendous—and he questions whether the rural-to-urban transition was as sharp as it has been made out—the Indian experience as he observed it in Bombay and Jamshedpur was different, leading to a less alienated work force ("The Labour Market in India," in Wilbert F. Moore and Arnold S. Feldman, eds., *Labour*

Commitment and Social Change in Developing Areas [New York: Social Science Research Council, 1960]). "Historical evidence indicates that the transformation of a rural, traditionally organized population into a committed industrial labour force has not been socially difficult in India" (p. 199). Richard D. Lambert speaks of a "village based set of interpersonal relational norms which are inferred throughout the traditional society and are carried over into the factory"; he speaks also of the margin of safety provided to a worker by "property rights" in a factory job. The two together, he suggests, operate to increase the worker's sense of security (*Workers, Factories and Social Change in India* [Princeton: Princeton University Press, 1963], pp. 92–93).

2. The reference is, of course, to Peter Laslett, *The World We Have Lost*, 3d ed. (New York: Scribner, 1973).

3. See, for example, Warren Ilchman and T. N. Dhar, "Student Unrest and Educational Unemployment," *Economic and Political Weekly,* July 1970 (special no.).

4. See Rudolph, Rudolph, and Ahmed, "Student Politics and National Politics in India"; Rudolph and Rudolph, *Education and Politics in India,* especially preface, introductions to parts 2 and 3, chaps. 1, 2, and 11, chap. 7 by Harold Gould, "Educational Structures and Political Processes in Faizabad District, Uttar Pradesh," and chap. 12 by Carolyn Elliott, "The Problem of Autonomy: The Osmania University Case"; Phillip Altbach, *Turmoil and Transition: Higher Education and Student Politics in India,* (Bombay: Lalvani, 1968); and Joseph DiBona, *Change and Conflict in the Indian University* (Durham, N.C.: Duke University Press, Program in Comparative Studies, 1969).

5. For a theoretical and empirical location of this problem, see Ronald Dore, *The Diploma Disease: Education, Qualification and Development* (Berkeley and Los Angeles: University of California Press, 1976).

6. Tata Services, *Statistical Outline of India, 1978* (Bombay, 1977), p. 121.

7. The Forty-second Amendment Act, passed under the emergency, provided for education to become the joint responsibility of center and states. It had previously been a state responsibility only.

8. See Gould, "Educational Structures," for a detailed account of the way Uttar Pradesh political entrepreneurs use educational institutions as part of their machines. The exceptionally strong vested interest of Uttar Pradesh politicians in intermediate and preuniversity institutions helps account for Uttar Pradesh's delay in shifting to the ten-plus-two system of secondary education.

9. The term "primary" is used for grades 1–5 in Indian educational statistics and "middle" for grades 6–8, but "elementary" is used comprehensively for both and has come into official use only recently to mark a new emphasis on grades 1–8. Together these grades are receiving larger funds under the sixth plan, to increase enrollment in grades 6–8—which was only 35 percent of the age cadre in 1973—while continuing to increase primary school enrollment, which was 84 percent. Our table 32 uses the category primary, not elementary.

10. The allocations are from Government of India, Ministry of Information and Broadcasting, *India, 1977–78: A Reference Annual* (Delhi, 1977), p. 51; the figures for enrollments add up those for primary and middle schools to get those for "elementary," and are from Government of India, Ministry of Education, *Education in India, 1971/72* (New Delhi, 1977), p. 13.

11. For an argument that the dilution of Indian higher education was also accompanied by substantial upgrading and differentiation, see our *Education and Politics in India,* chap. 4.

12. Ibid., chap. 1.

13. Rudolph, Rudolph, and Ahmed, "Student Politics."

14. Their percentages in the indiscipline group and in the all-India sample were about the same.

15. Other factors positively associated with student indiscipline included the presence of postgraduate (master's degree level) students (Rudolph, Rudolph, and Ahmed, "Student Politics," table 8, coeducational colleges (ibid., table 3), and older institutions (21–75 years old) (ibid., table 12).

16. A leading example was the defeat of the Congress chief, Kamaraj Nadar, by a student leader in the 1967 general election.

17. D. E. Jones and R. W. Jones, "Urban Upheaval in India."

18. For the key role of students in the JP movement, see Minoo Masani, *Is J. P. the Answer?* See also John R. Wood, "Extra-parliamentary Opposition."

19. Jones and Jones, "Urban Upheaval in India."

20. Rudolph and Rudolph, "Cultural Policy, Textbook Controversy and Indian Identity," in A. J. Wilson and Dennis Dalton, eds., *The States of South Asia* (London: Christopher Hurst, 1983).

21. Schultz, *Investing in People.*

22. Government of India, Planning Commission, *Draft Five Year Plan, 1978–83* (Delhi, 1978), p. 229.

23. For further remarks on ten-plus-two, see note 34.

24. Government of India, University Grants Commission, *Report for the Year 1979–80* (New Delhi, 1980), p. 10.

25. See Louise Fernandes, "Karnataka's Moneyspinning Colleges," *Sunday* (Calcutta), April 19, 1981. The entrepreneurial, Sanjay Gandhi–backed chief minister, Gundu Rau, was the chief figure in the medical college founding spree, which yielded many political, and possibly financial, advantages for him and his faction.

26. Planning Commission, *Sixth Five Year Plan, 1980–85,* annexure 13.9, p. 220.

27. Planning Commission, Committee of Experts on Unemployment, *Report* (New Delhi, 1973), cited by Alak Ghosh, *Indian Economy,* pp. 81–82.

28. Government of India, Ministry of Planning, Department of Statistics, National Sample Survey, Thirty-second Round (1977–78), *Some Key Results of the Survey on Employment-Unemployment* (Delhi, 1979). Estimates for usual-status (i.e., chronic) unemployment are always lower than for weekly status, and estimates for daily status are always higher.

29. The rate was 4.56 percent in urban areas and 2.62 percent in rural. Another calculation based on thirty-second round data but organized by states and union territories yielded 4.8 percent as the all-India level of unemployment, with the rates in Kerala (13.6 percent) and Delhi (10.7 percent) among the highest (ibid.).

30. Planning Commission, *Draft Five Year Plan, 1978–83* (Janata), p. 94; *Sixth Five Year Plan, 1980–85* (Congress-I), p. 217.

31. Planning Commission, *Sixth Five Year Plan, 1980–85,* p. 206.

32. Ibid., annexure 13.2, p. 214.

33. The precise figures were 1,009,000 in the NSS data extrapolated for

1980 from NSS sources (ibid., annexure 13.9, p. 220), and 1,355,500 for educated job seekers on the live register, June 1979 (Economic Intelligence Service, *Basic Statistics*, table 15.10).

34. Congress-I, in its plan calculations, conceived of the educated unemployed as including matriculates, students with ten years of high school, which
would raise the figure of all educated unemployed to between 3,472,000 (NSS
figures, 1980) and 6,936,000 (live registers of unemployed, 1979).

35. The first figure is from *Sixth Five Year Plan*, annexure 13.7, p. 220. The
figure is 3,152,000 in Economic Intelligence Service, *Basic Statistics*, table
15.10. This table aggregate "higher secondary passed" and intermediates/
undergraduates. These are students who, under the old system when high
school ended at the tenth year, were considered collegiate level. With the shift
to the ten-plus-two system, which brings high school up to the twelfth year,
the intermediate level comes to be attached to the secondary. The live register
figures cited in the previous note do not break out intermediate.

36. A. N. Agarwal, *Indian Economy*, 5th rev. ed. (New Delhi: Vikas, 1979),
pp. 528–29.

Chapter 12

1. Myron Weiner and John Osgood Field show that voter turnouts in state
elections were generally higher in urban than in rural constituencies in the
1957 and 1962 elections, but that the gap narrowed in 1967 and 1972 ("India's Urban Constituencies" *Comparative Politics* 8, no. 2 [January 1976]).
Samuel Eldersveld and Bashiruddin Ahmed show that urban and rural voters
do not hold significantly different political attitudes, for example, with respect
to forms of political involvement (*Citizens and Politics*, pp. 45–47).

2. Weiner, *The Politics of Scarcity*, p. 160.

3. Between October 1984 and April 1985, the BLD changed its name to
the Dalit Mazdoor Kisan party (DMKP). See Robert L. Hardgrave, Jr., and
Stanley A. Kochanek, *India: Government and Politics in a Developing Nation*
(New York: Harcourt Brace Jovanovich, 1986), p. 249. Assessments of the
BLD/DMKP's performance in the December 1984 parliamentary election can
be found in Harold Gould," A Sociological Perspective on the Eighth Parliamentary Election in India," and Paul R. Brass, "The 1984 Parliamentary Election in Uttar Pradesh," *Asian Survey*, 26, no. 6 (June 1986), pp. 630–52 and
653–69.

4. Raj Krishna, "Small Farmer Development," *Economic and Political
Weekly*, May 26, 1979, p. 913.

5. See A. M. Khusro, *An Analysis of Agricultural Land in India by Size of
Holding and Tenure* (Delhi: Institute of Economic Growth, 1964); see also
Dharm Narain and P. C. Joshi, "Magnitude of Agricultural Tenancy," *Eco-
nomic and Political Weekly*, September 27, 1969.

6. Government of India, Ministry of Information and Broadcasting, *India,
1973: A Reference Annual* (New Delhi, 1973), p. 213.

7. Under most state acts, intermediaries were given the right to keep lands
up to ceiling maximums for "self-cultivation." By dividing their estates among
family members and engaging in other forms of *benami* (spurious) transfers,

many intermediaries managed, at least in the short run, to keep large holdings under their de facto control (Kusum Nair, *Blossoms in the Dust: The Human Element in Indian Development* [London: Duckworth, 1961]). Nair provided one of the earliest accounts of poor tenants' acquiescence in claims by landlords to prior rights that legitimated tenant removals.

8. For an account sympathetic to the Dazhai Production Brigade, the model commune for the Chinese approach, and its ideological and technical innovations, see Mitch Meisner, "In Agriculture Learn from Dazhai: Theory and Practice in Chinese Rural Development" (Ph.D. diss., University of Chicago, 1977). For an account of the post-Mao reversals, see Tsou Tang, Michael Brecher, and Mitch Meisner, "Organization, Growth, and Equality in Xiyand County," pts. 1, 2 *Modern China*, 5, nos. 1–2 (January, April 1979).

9. Government of India, Planning Commission, *Report of the Indian Delegation to China on Agrarian Cooperatives* (New Delhi, 1956). See also Government of India, Ministry of Food and Agriculture, *Report of the Indian Delegation to China on Agricultural Planning and Techniques* (New Delhi, 1956).

10. Sarwar Lateef, *Economic Growth in China and India, 1950–1980* (London: Economic Intelligence Unit, 1976), p. 72. For more recent estimates, see D. Gale Johnson, "The World Food Situation: Developments during the 1970's and Prospects for the 1980's," in William Fellner, ed., *Contemporary Economic Problems* (Washington, D.C.: American Enterprise Institute, 1980), p. 325. For the "responsibility system," see Nicholas R. Lardy, *Agriculture in China's Modern Economic Development* (New York: Cambridge University Press, 1983), pp. 217ff. James R. Townsend and Brantly Womack, *Politics in China* (Boston: Little, Brown, 1986) appendix B, table 1, p. 433, reports the average annual increase in grain production between 1978 and 1982 as 3.8 percent. Between 1978–79 and 1983–84 in India it was 3.3 percent.

11. Cited in Frankel, *India's Political Economy*, p. 137.

12. Ibid.

13. *Congress Bulletin*, January–February 1959, cited in ibid., p. 162.

14. For the formation and course of the Swatantra party, see Erdman, *Swatantra Party*.

15. Herring, *Land to the Tiller*, chap. 9.

16. For a recent government account, see Government of West Bengal, *Economic Review, 1979–80* (Alipore, 1980), pp. 13–14. Franda's *Small is Politics* provides a positive account.

17. Frankel, *India's Political Economy*, p. 258.

18. Ibid., p. 276.

19. B. S. Minhas, "Perspective for Development—1961 to 1976: Implications of Planning for a Minimum Level of Living" (New Delhi: Planning Commission, 1962), reprinted in T. N. Srinivasan and P. K. Bardhan, eds., *Poverty and Income Distribution in India* (Calcutta: Statistical Publishing Society, 1974).

20. K. N. Raj, "Economic Perspective of Self-reliance" and V. K. R. V. Rao, "Agricultural Production," in Government of India, Ministry of Information and Broadcasting, *The Meaning of Self-reliance* (Delhi, 1965).

21. According to one high-ranking World Bank official who was active at that time and since in shaping policy toward India, the Bell Report created a

receptive climate in India "for measures of agricultural improvement which greatly facilitated the subsequent profound changes in agricultural technology." On the other hand, he questioned "whether any important redirections of policy brought about through the influence or advice of the World Bank or the Consortium would not have been brought about anyway by the government of India" (I. P. M. Cargill, "Efforts to Influence Recipient Performance, Case Study of India," in John P. Lewis and Ishan Kapur, *The World Bank Group: Multilateral Aid and the 1970's* [Lexington, Mass.: Lexington, 1973], pp. 92–93). L. K. Jha, a senior advisor to Prime Minister Lal Bahadur Shastri during the period of 1964–66, observed with respect to Cargill's arguments, "It should be emphasized that the basic principles of the new agricultural policy had been accepted and approved within the Government of India before the Crawford Report" ("Comment: Leaning Against Open Doors?" in Lewis and Kapur, *World Bank*, pp. 98–99).

22. For accounts of American opinion and role, see James Bjorkman, "Public Law 480," and Arthur Goldsmith, "Foreign Aid and Agricultural Development in India: A Study of the Interaction between Donor and Recipient" (Washington, D.C.: Development Strategy Division, World Bank, 1985, mimeograph).

23. Chester Bowles, *Promises to Keep* (New York: Harper and Row, 1971), chap. 43; John P. Lewis, *Quiet Crisis in India* (Washington, D.C.: Brookings Institution, 1962).

24. Average annual wheat production in West Bengal, Orissa, and Assam grew by 26 percent between 1967–70 and 1972–75, and by another 12 percent in the period of 1975–78 (World Bank, *Economic Situation and Prospects of India* [New Delhi, 1979], pp. 40–41).

25. Among the early statistical studies supporting this point of view is Pranab Bardhan, "Green Revolution and Agricultural Labour," *Economic and Political Weekly*, July 1970 (special no.). Bardhan modified his conclusion in the light of trends after 1968 in "Variations in Agricultural Wages: A Note," *Economic and Political Weekly*, May 26, 1973. Important early pessimistic American accounts were Frankel's *India's Green Revolution;* Wolf Ladejinsky's "How Green is the Green Revolution," *Economic and Political Weekly*, December 29, 1973; and Daniel Thorner's "Capitalist Farming in India," *Economic and Political Weekly*, December 27, 1969.

26. Francine Frankel and Karl von Vorys, "The Political Challenge of the Green Revolution: Shifting Patterns of Peasant Participation in India and Pakistan," policy memorandum no. 38 (Princeton: Center for International Affairs, Princeton University, 1972), p. 13.

27. "Indian planners and politicians." T. N. Srinivasan argues, "had poverty amelioration and reduction in inequalities as major objectives of planning long before the World Bank, the International Labor Organization, and assorted do-gooders discovered the bottom 40 percent, basic needs, and so on." Srinivasan cites Nehru, while introducing the third five-year plan to Parliament in 1960, as asking where the 42 percent growth in national income and the 20 percent growth in per capita income has gone; he also cites Pitamber Pant's "pioneering paper" in 1962 for the Perspective Planning Division of the Planning Commission, "Perspectives of Development—India 1960–61 to 1975–76: Implications of Planning for a Minimum Level of Living," a paper

which, according to Srinivasan, "contains all the essentials of the so-called basic needs approach to development" ("Comment," in John Mellor, ed., *India: A Rising Middle Power* Boulder, Colo.: Westview, 1979, pp. 112–13).

28. See Kochanek, "Mrs. Gandhi's Pyramid"; Weiner, "The 1971 Elections and the Indian Party System"; Frankel, *India's Political Economy*, pp. 444–45.

29. Minhas, "The Current Development Debate" (Paper presented at the University of Chicago Conference on Indian Development, December 9, 1977), p. 20.

30. Minhas, "The Planning Process: Objectives and Policy Frame," in *Commerce* pamphlet series, (Bombay: Vora, 1969), republished in B. S. Minhas, *Planning and the Poor* (New Delhi: Chand, 1974); M. L. Dantwala, *Poverty in India: Now and Then* (Bombay: Macmillan, 1973); V. M. Dandekar and N. Rath, *Poverty in India: Dimensions and Trends* (Poona: Gokhale Institute, 1971); Pranab Bardhan, "On the Minimum Level of Living and the Rural Poor," *Indian Economic Review 5*, no. 1 (April 1970); V. S. Vyas, "Institutional Change, Agricultural Production, and Rural Poverty," *Commerce*, August 19, 1972. For a summary of the work through the early seventies and its varying methodologies and assumptions, see Dharma Kumar, "Income Distribution and Poverty in India."

31. B. S. Minhas, who resigned from the Planning Commission on December 5, 1973, because he regarded the plan estimates as out of line with realistic revenue and cost estimates, discusses the National Development Council decision in the text of a note laid on the table of the Lok Sabha on February 27, 1974 (*Planning and the Poor*, p. 128). For a "left" attack on Minhas as a propagator of anti-national facts and a defense of D. P. Dhar, see *Link*, December 16, 1973.

32. International Labor Organization, *Employment Growth and Basic Needs: A One-World Problem* (Geneva: ILO, 1976); Dag Hammarskjold Foundation, *What Now: Another Development* (Upsala, 1975).

33. Chenery et al., *Redistribution with Growth*, p. xiii.

34. Mahbub al Huq, "Employment in the 1970's: A New Perspective," *International Development Review* 13 (December 1971).

35. Morris, *Measuring Conditions of World's Poor*.

36. The Small Farmer Development Agency was proposed in the fourth five-year plan to guarantee bank credit to small farmers and to stimulate other services to such farmers (Government of India, Planning Commission, *Fourth Five Year Plan, Draft, 1969–74* [Delhi, 1974], p. 116). The Drought Prone Areas Program was launched in 1971. The Food for Work, Antyodhya, and Employment Guarantee Scheme began under Janata governments.

37. S. L. Shetty, *Structural Retrogression in the Indian Economy Since the Mid-Sixties* (Bombay: Saneeksha Trust, 1978), p. 59.

38. Under the Small Farmer Development Agency program, small farmers are allowed up to 25 percent and marginal farmers and laborers up to 33 percent of the investment costs of minor irrigation, land development, soil conservation, etc., as well as very low interest loans (Government of India, Ministry of Information and Broadcasting, *India, 1980: A Reference Annual* [Delhi, 1980], p. 247). Frankel's early pessimistic assessment of the Small Farmer Development Agency and Marginal Farmers and Agricultural Labourers Scheme, based on interviews in 1973, is to be found in her *India's Political Economy*, p. 498. Raj Krishna's 1979 assessment is based on a variety of government and

private studies that cover a longer period. The specifics in our paragraph are from his "Small Farmer Development."

39. Ministry of Information and Broadcasting, *India, 1977–1978*, p. 240.

40. *Keesing's Contemporary Archives*, July 8, 1977, p. 28434.

41. Ibid.

42. See, for example, Rajni Kothari, *Footsteps into the Future: Diagnosis of the Present with a Design for an Alternative* (Hyderabad: Orient Longman, 1974), and Ernst Friedrich Schumacher, *Small is Beautiful: Economics as if People Mattered* (New York: Harper and Row, 1975).

43. For a systematic development of the argument for an agriculture-led growth policy, see John Mellor, *The New Economics of Growth: A Strategy for India and the Developing World* (Ithaca, N.Y.: Cornell University Press, 1976). John P. Lewis is associated with similar views. See, for example, his "Reviving American Aid to India: Motivation, Scale, Uses, Constraints" and "Revived Aid: A Possible Scenario," in Mellor, *India*, pp. 301–49.

44. The hope of linking investment in agriculture to an employment-consumption-investment cycle was embodied in the section on employment of the Janata government's version of the sixth five-year plan (Planning Commission, *Draft Five Year Plan, 1978–83*), p. 9ff. Janata also reduced plan investment in social services from 15.8 to 13.5 percent and in transport and communication from 17.6 to 15.3 percent (pp. 17–18).

45. Ronald J. Herring and Rea M. Edwards, "Guaranteeing Employment to the Rural Poor: Social Functions and Class Interests in the EGS in Western India" (Paper presented at the meeting of the Association for Indian Studies, April 2–4, 1982, Chicago); John Echeverri-Gent, "Making Employment an Entitlement: Maharashtra's Employment Guarantee Scheme," in "Pro-poor Policy Implementation: A Comparative Study of the Implementation of Policies to Help the Rural Poor" (Ph.D. diss., Department of Political Science, University of Chicago, 1986), chap. 2.

46. Ministry of Information and Broadcasting, *India, 1980*, p. 254.

Chapter 13

1. See table 40. Sown area was about 308 million acres in 1976–77 (calculated from table 1.1–2 in Economic Intelligence Service, *Basic Statistics.*

2. We attend below to the controversy concerning the changing proportions of cultivators and agricultural laborers between 1961–71. The figures for 1971 are taken from table 3 in Census of India, 1981, *Provisional Population Totals: Workers and Non-workers*, p. 43. This table shows 95.5 million cultivators in 1961, 75 million in 1971, and 91.4 million in 1981. The comparable figures for agricultural laborers are 31.3, 47, and 55.4 million.

3. See table 40.

4. See our discussion of Weber's methodology in "Authority and Power."

5. The question of whether the new technology of the green revolution is scale neutral or to what size it is scale neutral was preceded by discussion among economists of the proposition that there is an inverse relationship between farm size and yield. The larger farms were thought to produce less per unit of land than smaller farms. The statistical evidence mounted at the time—

before the green revolution inputs became available and before the oil price rises of 1973 and 1979 reduced the cost advantages of larger-scale mechanized agriculture—already tended to support the negative relationship between size and productivity per unit of land. Herring has provided an excellent summary of the course of the debate, concluding that the yields are typically, if often weakly, inversely proportional to size of holding (*Land to the Tiller*). Two articles by Sen "An Aspect of Indian Agriculture," *Economic and Political Weekly*, February 1962 (annual no.), and "Size of Holding and Productivity," *Economic and Political Weekly*, February 1964 (annual no.), set off the debate. Ashok Rudra, in "Farm Size and Yield Per Acre," *Economic and Political Weekly*, July 1968 (special no.), concluded that there was no statistically significant relationship between size and yield, and in "More on Returns to Scale in Indian Agriculture," *Economic and Political Weekly*, October 26, 1968, found the correlations primarily negative as predicted but statistically significant in only a few cases. N. Bhattacharya and G. Saini in "Farm Size and Productivity: A Fresh Look," *Economic and Political Weekly*, June 24, 1974, and Krishna Bharadwaj in *Production Conditions in Indian Agriculture* (Cambridge: Cambridge University Press, 1974), have also made important contributions to the issue of size and productivity.

Biplab Dasgupta, *The New Agrarian Technology and India* (New Delhi: Macmillan India, 1977), reviewed the evidence before the oil price rises in 1973 and 1979. His arguments favoring the relative efficiency of mechanized agriculture have been seriously undercut by the rise in operating costs subsequent to 1973. Nor does he attend to the effects of the quality and commitment of labor, a consideration that favors the efficiency of operating units whose scale is commensurate with higher-quality family labor. Finally, he does not consider the long-run benefits from relying on the renewal resources associated with bullock power, or the depletable and high-cost resources associated with mechanized farming.

6. For a discussion of the condition of these classes see Kalpana Bardhan, "Rural Employment, Wages and Labor Markets in India: A survey of Research," pts. 1–3, *Economic and Political Weekly*, June 26, July 2, and July 9, 1977.

7. An example that documents the problem is Vyas's microstudy in Gujarat, which showed that between 1967–68 and 1970–71, the average per-acre use of fertilizer on small farms was between one-fourth and one-fifth that on all farms and the use of other modern inputs was even lower (V. S. Vyas, "Structural Change in Agriculture and the Small Farm Sector," *Economic and Political Weekly*, January 10, 1976). See also Dasgupta, *New Agrarian Technology*.

8. Raj Krishna, "Small Farm Development." Krishna's figure for land controlled by small farmers is higher than ours because he defines small farmers differently.

9. James O. Harrison, "Agricultural Modernization and Income Distribution: An Economic Analysis of the Impact of New Seed Varieties on the Crop Production of Large and Small Farms in India" (Ph.D. diss., Princeton University, 1972), pp. 2–3.

10. C. Mutiah, "The Green Revolution: Participation by Small and Large Farmers," *Indian Journal of Agricultural Economy* (January–March 1971): 57–58. G. S. Bhalla and G. K. Chadha, "Green Revolution and Small Peas-

ant," *Economic and Political Weekly,* May 15, 1982, documents similar crop-ping patterns for large and small farmers in Punjab, except in cotton.

11. Kalpana Bardhan, "Rural Employment," pt. 1, A-37.

12. Pravin Visaria and S. K. Sanyal, "Trends in Rural Unemployment in In-dia: Two Comments," *Economic and Political Weekly,* January 29, 1977. Ac-cording to the 1981 census, the proportions of "cultivators" and "agricultural laborers" varied as follows between 1961 and 1981: 1961, 52.34 and 17.17 percent, respectively; 1971, 42.91 and 26.88 percent; and 1981: 41.53 and 25.16 percent. (Census of India, 1981, *Provisional Population Totals: Workers and Non-workers,* table 4.)

13. For example the NSS found in 1970 that in small cultivator households (2.5 acres and below), 30 percent were engaged in agriculture, 64 percent were not gainfully employed, and 6 percent were working outside the agricultural sector. Of those employed in agriculture, 39 percent worked on family farms and 61 percent worked for wages on others' farms (Government of India, Min-istry of Planning, Department of Statistics, National Sample Survey, Twenty-fifth Round [July–September 1970], *Time Disposition, Wage Rate and Atti-tude Towards Employment Opportunities outside Village for the Weaker Sections of the Rural Population of India,* no. 223 [Delhi, 1976], table 1A, p. 18).

14. See chapter 1 for a more detailed discussion of the contribution of bullock capitalists to centrism. We have drawn on our "Agrarian Mobiliza-tion," pp. 318–22, for this discussion. We first considered the problem of bullock capitalism in "The Centrist Future of Indian Politics," *Asian Survey* 20, no. 6 (June 1980). An excellent empirical account that pursues a similar argument while stressing a different interpretation of the bullock capitalist category is Harry W. Blair, "Rising Kulaks and Backward Classes in Bihar, *Economic and Political Weekly,* January 12, 1980.

15. Prem Vashishtha, in a comparison in Ferozepur district of Punjab, showed that none of the 29 tractor-using farms but 106 of the 121 non–tractor-using farms met the top two standards of a six-category measure of economic efficiency (ratio of optimal output and the actual output subject to the farmer's budget constraint) ("Measurement of Private Efficiency Under Di-verse Technologies in Indian Agriculture," *Sankhya,* ser. C, vol. 39, pt. 4 [1978]).

16. Merle Fainsod's excellent study of collectivization, *Smolensk under So-viet Rule* (Cambridge: Harvard University Press, 1958), not only provides vivid detail for the process but also makes it clear how difficult it was to distin-guish kulaks from other peasants, discussing the remarkable lineage, affinal, and economic interdependence among rich, middle, and poor peasants.

17. Walter Neale, personal communication.

18. Rudra more or less excludes bullock capitalists from his analysis of rele-vant categories in the rural landscape, precisely because their relations with other classes are nonantagonistic. See his "Class Relations in Indian Agricul-ture," *Economic and Political Weekly,* pts. 1–3, June 8, 10, and 17, 1978, where he treats them and smallholders as "not constituting any class."

19. See note 13 above for data indicating that 39 percent of smallholders were working entirely on their own farms.

20. Pranab Bardhan, in a Bengal study, avoids the problem of deducing

"self-employed" from size categories by using data that build categories specifically on self-employment and the employment of others. He shows that even West Bengal, an area that is thought to have fewer self-employed and more employers and employed than other parts of India, has 29 percent self-employed ("Agrarian Class Formation in India," *Journal of Peasant Studies,* 10, no. 1 [October 1982]). Bardhan is adapting the categories of J. Roemer, *A General Theory of Exploitation and Class* (Cambridge: Harvard University Press, 1982).

21. Charan Singh, an important voice of bullock capitalism, made it clear in his speech as prime minister to the Andhra Pradesh Kisan Advocates Forum, October 22, 1979, that he hoped to forge such relations (*Hindustan Times,* October 23, 1979).

22. Government of India, Ministry of Agriculture and Irrigation, Directorate of Economics and Statistics, *Indian Agriculture in Brief* (Delhi, 1975), table 2–1(a).

23. The number of eight-hour days worked on the farm in a year per adult family worker was 78 in Thanjavur, 87 in Cuddapah, 42 in Alleppey and Quilon, 79 in Hooghly, and 24 in Parganas, as against 263 in Meerut and Muzzafarnagar, 267 in Amritsar and Ferozepur, and 239 in Nasik (ibid., table 2.1[a]).

24. Census of India, 1981, "Provisional Population Totals: Workers and Non-workers," table 1, pp. 31–34.

25. The figures for West Godavari, Andhra Pradesh, and Coimbatore/Salem in Tamil Nadu show higher levels of adult family labor per year (160 and 202 days, respectively) than the southern districts cited in note 23 above. Marshall Bouton identifies two of five zones in Thanjavur District dominated by cultivation based on family labor on middle-sized holdings, and Joan Mencher finds that many holdings in Chingleput rely on family labor. See Bouton, *Agrarian Radicalism in South India;* Mencher, *Agriculture and Social Structure in Tamil Nadu* (Bombay: Allied, 1978), p. 197.

26. In 1970–71, the average size of a "large-sized" operational holding of 10 acres or above was 23.8 acres (S. K. Sanyal, "Trends in Rural Unemployment in India: Comment," *Economic and Political Weekly,* January 19, 1977).

27. Rudra, "Class Relations," and Herring, *Land to the Tiller.*

28. Barrington Moore, Jr., *Dictatorship and Democracy.*

29. For a more extended argument that the bullock capitalist gains were reflected in voting patterns, see our "Agrarian Mobilization."

30. For example, Frankel, in *India's Green Revolution,* and K. N. Raj, "Trends in Rural Unemployment in India," *Economic and Political Weekly,* August 1976 (special no.), saw polarization in the transformation being wrought by the coming of commercial agriculture and the green revolution.

31. The two do not always reach the same conclusions. Economists rely more on the NSS's data because its field staffs are more permanent and professional than those of the census and its questions, concepts, and methods more sophisticated.

32. E. P. Thompson, *The Making of the English Working Class* (New York: Pantheon, 1964).

33. K. N. Raj, "Trends in Rural Unemployment."

34. Ibid., p. 1289. We do not refer to Raj's figure of 11.83 percent in appendix B, table B-1, row 3, column 3, because he does not accept the 30.66 per-

cent of row 1, column 7. In any case, no combination of Raj's figures in rows 1 and 3 exceeds the total of column 2 (38.71 percent) for "own account workers" and "unpaid family labor." Inter alia, Raj's argument involved showing that, after a brief increase following the land reforms of the mid-1950s, there had been a decline in the proportion of small holdings from 22.7 percent "own account workers" in 1960–61 to 18.1 percent in 1964–65 (row 1, columns 3 and 5), a corresponding increase in the proportion of "employers" from 5.8 percent in 1960–61 to 13.8 percent in 1964–65 (row 5, columns 3 and 5), and an increase in the proportion of "employees" (wage workers) from 16.6 percent in 1960–61 to 21.9 percent in 1972–73 (row 7, columns 3 and 7).

35. Ibid., pp. 1287–88.

36. Visaria and Sanyal, "Trends in Rural Unemployment."

37. See footnotes in appendix B, table B-1 for Visaria's grounds for differing with Raj. Visaria held that while there had been an increase in the number of "employers," it had been much smaller (2 vs. 8 percent) than Raj had calculated (table B-1, rows 5 and 6, column 5). Visaria agreed that there had been a large increase in "employees" (rows 7 and 8, columns 3 and 7) but took issue with Raj on the question of family farms. Visaria's reconstruction of the figures on which Raj had based his conclusions showed that the number of "own account workers" had increased rather than decreased between 1960–61 and 1972–73, from 22.7 to 25.9 percent.

38. Ashok Rudra, "Hiring of Labour by Poor Peasants," *Economic and Political Weekly,* January 10, 1976.

39. Thomas Rosin, "Adaptive Strategy and Tradition in Rajputana" (Paper presented at the meeting of the Association of Asian Studies, San Francisco, March 26, 1983). It was in fact the better-off farmers who provided the labor when they rented out their capital equipment and/or tools.

40. Raj, "Trends in Rural Unemployment," p. 1286.

41. Sanyal's reading of the proportion of households not operating land entertains the possibilities of a large decrease (from 23 to 9.6 percent) and a small decrease (from 28.2 to 27.4 percent) before opting for a small increase of 3 percent. The principal difference between Raj and Sanyal related to the allocation of "nonagricultural holdings" in the NSS eighth round of 1953–54. Although "nonagricultural holders" were not counted in the subsequent rounds used in appendix B, table B-2 as an element in the smallholder category, Raj included them in his calculations for 1953–54 but did not include them in calculating numbers and percentages for 1960–61 and 1970–71. The result, according to Sanyal's revisions, was to "inflate" the proportion of smallholders in 1953–54 by 17.3 percent and to understate the proportion of households without land by the same amount. Most of the differences between Raj's and Sanyal's interpretation of changes in landholding between 1953–54 and 1970–71 are accounted for by their contrasting treatment of "nonagricultural holders." Sanyal also took issue with Raj over his treatment of those households that leased out land and were counted as not operating land. Heads of such households were owners or petty rentiers. According to Sanyal, there are as many households leasing out as leasing in among those counted as "not operating land." By excluding the leasing-out households, Sanyal calculated that there could have been a sharp decline, from 23 to 9.6 percent, in those not operating land.

42. By family farms, we refer not only to "own account workers" but also

to "unpaid family labor," which increased between 1960–61 and 1972–73 by about 3 percent (appendix B, table B-1). We do not enter here into the Chayanovian questions of which agricultural producers working on family farms were better and which worse off under specified conditions over time. Politically, it seems unlikely that "unpaid family labor" would engage in polarizing political participation even if, as we are inclined to doubt, a substantial proportion of them were and felt more miserable due to decreased consumption and incomes.

We agree with Ronald J. Herring's thesis in "Chayanovism vs. Neoclassical Perspectives on Land Tenure and Productivity Interaction," in E. Paul Durrenberger, ed., *Chayanov, Peasants and Economic Anthropology* (New York: Academic Press, 1984) that tiny plots are more productive per acre than large traditional farms. With substantially more consumers than producers and a limited amount of land, the only way to feed the family is to work harder, better, and longer. The policy implications for Herring are to "correct the terms of trade with agriculture" through subsidizing prices and inputs, providing credit and infrastructure, raising labor productivity on small farms, reducing taxes, and so forth. For the book that brought Chayanov to the attention of Western scholars and applied his concepts to India see A. V. Chayanov, *The Theory of Peasant Economy*, ed. Daniel Thorner et al. (Homewood, Ill.: Irwin, 1966).

43. Vyas, "Structural Change."

44. Ibid., p. 30.

45. M. L. Dantwala and C. H. Shah, *Evaluation of Land Reform* (Bombay: University of Bombay Press), 1:35–60.

46. Vyas, "Structural Change," p. 30. The tenancy reforms in Kerala in which 40 percent of the operational holdings were turned over to tenants also shifted land from a smaller number of owners to a larger number of tenants, accelerating deconcentration but leaving the problem of agricultural labor to be dealt with by other means (Centre for Development Studies, "Poverty, Unemployment, and Development Policy: A Case Study of Selected Issues with Reference to Kerala" (New York: United Nations, 1975), pp. 69–71, cited in Herring, "Abolition of Landlordism in Kerala: A Redistribution of Privilege," *Economic and Political Weekly*, June 28, 1980.

47. Ashok Rudra, A. Majid, B. D. Talib, "Big Farmers of Punjab: Some Preliminary Findings of a Sample Survey," *Economic and Political Weekly*, September 27, 1969.

48. Montek Ahluwalia, "Rural Poverty and Agricultural Performance," p. 319; Bhalla and Chadha, "Green Revolution."

49. Montek Ahluwalia, "Rural Poverty and Agricultural Performance," p. 315.

50. Other factors include conditions of tenancy, population pressure on land reducing the size of holdings, and technological change that, by displacing labor, weakens the economic position of both landless labor and small farmers who rely in part on wage employment.

51. Montek Ahluwalia, "Rural Poverty and Agricultural Performance," p. 316.

52. Ibid., p. 319.

53. The authors divide cultivators into size classes. The marginal and small size classes, below 5 acres (classes I and II) spent Rs. 92.82 and 97.96 on fertil-

izer per annum as against Rs. 112.46 and 112.26 among the two size classes above 12.5 acres. Small farmers spent more on draft cattle, Rs. 175.93 and Rs. 168.20 for classes I and II, while class VI spent only Rs. 36.76. The figures were reversed for diesel and electricity; classes I and II spent Rs. 14.3 and 29.48, while classes V and VI spent Rs. 38.29 and 49.67 (Bhalla and Chadha, "Green Revolution," p. 831).

54. They continue to produce higher output per acre even though they "have lost their traditional edge of higher yield rates" (ibid.).

55. Bharadwaj, in *Production Conditions in Indian Agriculture,* had noted disparities in cropping patterns and explored the "distress cropping" of the poor.

56. Alexander E. George, "Land Reforms: Study in Jhorgram," *Economic and Political Weekly,* January 23, 1982. If Dasgupta's study of seven Intensive Agricultural District Projects tends to support the concentration thesis of Rudra, Majid, and Talib, C. H. Hanumantha Rao's examination of the distribution of gains from new agricultural technology tends to support Bhalla and Chadha's thesis that large farmers benefited proportionately (but not absolutely) more from the new inputs. See Dasgupta, "India's Green Revolution," *Economic and Political Weekly,* February 1977 (annual no.) and C. H. Hanumantha Rao, *Technological Change and the Distribution of Gains in Indian Agriculture* (New Delhi: Macmillan India, 1977).

57. Herring, "'A Paddy Field Is Not a Factory': Production Relations and Redistributive Policy in South India" (Paper presented at the Wisconsin Conference on South Asia, Madison, November 7–8, 1980).

58. For the problems that arise if one tries to translate size of holdings into categories characterizing relationship to cultivation (e.g., self-cultivation vs. cultivation by hired labor, see note 20 above, and adjacent discussion in text. The 33 percent of households operating 0.01–2.49 acres are overwhelmingly self-cultivating, except perhaps in rice regions. Most of those cultivating holdings from 2.5 to 15 acres would rely primarily on household and family labor.

59. See Erdman, *Swatantra Party,* and Frankel, *India's Green Revolution,* for the formation of the Swatantra by cultivator groups at several national meetings, notably by N. G. Ranga of the Andhra Kisan Sabha. These groups were soon joined by industrial and "feudal" interests. We have drawn for this discussion on our "Agrarian Mobilization," pp. 331–34.

60. Harekrishna Singh Surjeet, "Upsurge," *Seminar,* no. 267 (November 1981), p. 16.

61. Quoted in Gail Omvedt, "Rasta Roko [Block Roads!], Kulaks and the Left," *Economic and Political Weekly,* November 18, 1981, p. 1937. Omvedt uses a recent publication in Marathi, *Yodh Shetkari,* edited by Vijay Paralkar and containing articles, conversations, and speeches originally published in *Manus* magazine, to depict Joshi's ideology, socioeconomic analysis, and policy prescriptions. For a comparative view of these issues, see our "Agrarianism in India and America," *Emerging Sociology* (Meerut, Uttar Pradesh) 2, no. 1 (1980).

62. Quoted in Omvedt, "Rasta Roko," p. 1937.

63. For example, Herring concludes his essay on Chayanovian vs. neoclassical perspectives by arguing that tiny plots are more productive per acre than large traditional farms. See note 42 above.

64. Surjeet, "Upsurge," p. 16.

65. Omvedt, who is a critic of the new agrarianism, believes that the mainstream left "nurtured the soil in which the movement grows" ("Rasta Roko," p. 1937).

66. For example, the National Security Act and the Essential Services Act, barring strikes. See chapter 10 above.

67. Singh, *India's Economic Policy.*

68. For example, the twenty-three-day "long march" from Jalgaon to Nagpur in December 1980 in support of price and wage increases was supported by a shaky six-party front composed of the Congress-U, the Janata party, the Peasants and Workers party, the Lok Dal, the CPI-M, and the CPI.

69. Farmers' agitations took place in Maharashtra, Gujarat, Tamil Nadu, Uttar Pradesh, Andhra Pradesh, Karnataka, and other states. See "Farmers' Agitation," *Times of India,* December 4, 1980; *Statesman,* December 13, 1980, overseas edition; *Hindu,* January 3, 13, 14, and 17, 1981; and "Precarious Peace," *India Today,* November 30, 1981.

70. "Farmers' Agitation," *Times of India,* December 20, 1980. Except for 1951–52 (when the series began), the index was adverse to agriculture for twelve years (until 1963–64), ranging from 89.10 in 1955–56 to 100 in 1960–61. Starting in 1964–65, the index became favorable to agriculture, reaching a high of 134.13 in 1973–74 but declining thereafter. See *Boothalingam Report,* table 27, p. 131.

71. See, for example, Jack Hayward, *The One and Indivisible French Republic* (New York: Norton, 1973).

72. Joshi's agitations in 1980 led the Government of Maharashtra to raise the support price of onions and to give cash concessions to cultivators of cotton, sugar cane, paddy, *jawar,* and *bajra* ("Farmers' Agitation," *Times of India,* December 20, 1980).

73. The Tamil Nadu Land Development Bank reported in early 1981 that 90 percent of its loans were in arrears (*Hindu,* February 3, 1981). Like other government-sponsored credit agencies in Tamil Nadu, it found it expedient, in the face of Naidu-led mobilizations, to ignore its arrears. The M. G. Ramachandran AIADMK government subsequently risked the wrath of Tamil Nadu farmers when it cracked down on nonpayment of electricity bills. The power of organized farmers in Tamil Nadu was already apparent in 1972 when the Karunanidhi DMK government enacted the Cultivating Tenants Arrears of Rents (Relief) Act cancelling past arrears on condition that current rents (July 1, 1971, to June 30, 1972) be paid. This moratorium has been sporadically renewed in recent years. Already in the 1970s, secure tenants and owner cultivators, not rent-collecting landlords, were the dominant voice in Tamil Nadu agricultural policy. For an account of recent trends in Tamil Nadu's agricultural economy and politics, including evidence of the reemergence of Naxalite protest, see "Myths and Facts behind Agrarian Unrest," *Economic and Political Weekly,* December 12, 1981.

74. Although we recognize the political mystification that Rama Rao's celluloid god image represented, other determinants also played a role in his and his party's victory. Congress misrule, including a disregard for the requirements of Andhra Pradesh's self-esteem and autonomy, played an important role, but so did agrarian interests. According to Bhabani Sen Gupta, "He [N. T. Rama Rao] seems to have worked out . . . a line that divides the social elements he wants to carry with himself from those he may have to fight down

or isolate as political opponents. In the former category are clustered all peasants. . . . In this massive mixed constituency, he has a distinct bias towards the rural people. . . . NTR has no intention of taxing the income of rich farmers. . . . His targets are the 'mean Mughals of Delhi,'" politicians, corrupt contractors, businessmen, bureaucrats, and "high brow intellectuals—elements that have cut off big slices of the nation's resource cake" (N. T. Rama Rao, "The Saffron Caesar," *India Today,* May 31, 1984). The stands taken by Janata in Karnataka and by the Telugu Desam once they were in power also show the strength of agrarian interests: "Soon after taking the oath of office . . . Chief minister Hegde said at a news conference that the Government would give top priority to farmers problems . . . the Government would order judicial inquiries into the recent police firings and withdrawal of cases connected with farmers' agitation." (*Overseas Hindustan Times,* January 20, 1983); "The Telugu Desam's economic resolution called for a reorganization of the existing mechanism to fix prices of agricultural commodities to provide a fair deal to farmers. . . ." (*Overseas Hindustan Times,* June 9, 1983.)

75. For an insider's view of the CPI-M predicament, see Hare Krishna Konar, *Agrarian Problems of India,* (Calcutta, Jour Saha, 1977). There is a considerable literature on Naxalism. See, for example, Asish Kumar Ray, *The Spring Thunder and After* (Calcutta: Minerva, 1975); Sankar Ghosh, *The Disinherited State: A Study of West Bengal, 1967–70* (Hyderabad: Orient Longman, 1971); Franda, *Radical Politics in West Bengal;* Mohan Ram, *Maoism in India;* Dasgupta, *Naxalite Movement;* and Sen Gupta, *Communism in Indian Politics.*

76. The following two paragraphs have profited from Sanjib Baruah, "Getting a Fair Share: Politics and the Poor in Rural India" (Ph.D. diss., University of Chicago, 1983), pt. 2, "West Bengal: The Marxist Idiom of Rural Poor Politics."

77. George, "Land Reforms."

78. Dasgupta, "Gram Banglar Sreni Binyas," *Desh-Hitaishi* 18 (Autumn 1980): 91–92 (Calcutta CPI-M West Bengal State Committee), cited in Baruah, "Getting a Fair Share," p. 206. Baruah demonstrates a similar class overlap in Meerut, Uttar Pradesh, which he contrasts with West Bengal.

79. Herring, *Land to the Tiller.*

80. Pranab Bardhan showed that Rs. 15 per person for thirty days at *rural* pricees was equivalent to Rs. 20 per person at all-India 1960–61 prices, adopted as minimum by the Planning Commission in 1962. This is the expenditure thought by Dandekar and Rath's pioneering study to correspond with a consumption of 2,250 calories per day ("The Incidence of Rural Poverty in the States," *Economic and Political Weekly,* February 1973 [annual no.]; see also Dandekar and Rath, *Poverty in India*).

81. Michelle S. McAlpin and Morris David Morris, "Nutrition, Malnutrition and Disease: Some Economists' Questions about Definitions and Methodology" (Paper presented to the South Asia Political Economy Group, Project II, sponsored by the Social Science Research Council, New York, and the Indian Council of Social Science Research, New Delhi, 1982, mimeograph).

82. P. V. Sukhatme, "Nutrition Policy: Need for Reorientation," *Economic and Political Weekly,* June 28, 1980. T. N. Srinivasan in "Malnutrition: Some Measurement and Policy Issues" (1979, mimeograph), concludes on statistical grounds that malnutrition levels are substantially overestimated (cited in McAlpin and Morris, "Nutrition, Malnutrition and Disease," p. 114).

83. Morris David Morris argues that if the World Bank per capita income data for India are corrected to take account of purchasing-power parity, at least 50 percent of the population of 359 million placed under the poverty line by Chenery et al. (in *Redistribution with Growth*) would move above it, reducing the poverty figure to 180 million (*Measuring Condition of World's Poor,* p. 12).

84. Prior to Ahluwalia's effort, the most widely used studies were Dharma Kumar's "Income Distribution and Poverty" and Minhas's, *Planning and the Poor.*

85. Ahluwalia, "Rural Poverty and Agricultural Performance," pp. 303−4.

86. Ibid., p. 304.

87. Planning Commission, *Seventh Five Year Plan, 1985−90,* 2 : 4.

88. Ahluwalia notes that the findings are for nominal, not real, consumption expenditure ("Rural Poverty and Agricultural Performance, p. 319).

89. Table 13 in Morris, *Measuring Condition of World's Poor,* exhibits the PQLI changes in selected countries.

90. The literacy index was based on percentages. For life expectancy and infant mortality, the worst performance in 1950 was set equal to zero and the best performance expected by the year 2000 set equal to 100. The range for life expectancy was from thirty-eight to seventy-seven years; for infant mortality, from 229 to 7 deaths per thousand live births.

91. Government of India, Ministry of Planning, Central Statistical Organization, Department of Statistics, *Statistical Pocket Book, India 1980* (Delhi 1981), table 12, p. 17.

92. Morris, *Measuring Condition of World's Poor,* table 13.

93. Economic Intelligence Service, *Basic Statistics,* table 12.5. The table is based on a private communication to the service by Professor M. Mukherjee, who has worked out the table for each state. Professor Mukherjee's per capita state domestic product ranking in table 12.5 is for 1975−76. We have used 1970−71 data from table 18 in Central Statistical Organization, *Statistical Pocket Book, India 1980,* pp. 24−25, to rank Kerala eleventh in 1970−71. Table 18 has also been used below for Punjab's and Uttar Pradesh's state domestic products.

94. Even though the categories used in the 1971 and 1981 censuses ("workers" and "nonworkers with secondary employment" vs. "main workers" and "marginal workers" are not strictly comparable, the 1981 census commissioner, P. Padmanabha, compares "work participation rates" between the two. As he puts it: "At the 1981 census it was considered desirable to obtain as detailed a profile of the working characteristics of the population as possible without losing the possibility of some comparability with the 1961 and the 1971 results. . . . The questions have been formulated so as to first attempt to divide the population into those who have worked any time at all during the last year and those who have not worked at all. Having classified the population into these broad groups, the next attempt has been to divide those who have worked any time into two groups, namely those who have worked in some economic activity over a period of six months or more or in both the agricultural seasons and those whose work can be considered marginal or secondary" (Census of India, 1981, *Provisional Population Totals: Workers and Non-workers,* statement 1, p. 3). For an extended discussion of various methods for estimating unemployment, see chapter 11 above. See also M. L. Dantwala, "Rural Employment."

95. Raj Krishna, "Rural Unemployment: A survey of Concepts and Estimates for India" (mimeograph), cited in Kalpana Bardhan, "Rural Employment," pt. 2, p. 1067. The likelihood that rural employment has been improving may be contradicted by the Labour Bureau's rural labor survey, which found that unemployment had increased between 1964–65 and 1974–75. However, its time series is vulnerable to the criticism that 1964–65 was an unusually good agricultural year and 1974–75 an unusually bad one. See Labour Bureau, *Rural Labour Enquiry, 1974–75,* chap. 2, table 4, p. 15.

96. The first report was contained in Pranab Bardhan's "Green Revolution and Agricultural Labour," the second in his "Variations in Agricultural Wages."

97. Deepak Lal, "Agricultural Growth, Real Wage, and the Rural Poor in India," *Economic and Political Weekly,* June 26, 1974. See also A. V. Jose, "Trends in Real Wage Rates of Agricultural Labourers," *Economic and Political Weekly,* Review of Agriculture, March 30, 1974.

98. Kalpana Bardhan, "Factors Affecting Wage Rates for Agricultural Labour," *Economic and Political Weekly,* June 30, 1973.

99. Ahluwalia, "Rural Poverty," pp. 310–18.

100. Pranab Bardhan, "Green Revolution and Agricultural Labour" and "Variations in Agricultural Wages."

101. Herring, "Paddy Field," p. 27.

102. Kalpana Bardhan, "Rural Employment," pt. 2, p. 168.

103. Ahluwalia, "Rural Poverty," p. 316.

104. Census of India, 1981, *Provisional Population Totals: Workers and Non-workers,* table 3, pp. 43–47. We have calculated the percentages from the figures provided. Punjab's increase of 38 percent in the number of employed agricultural laborers was 17 percent above the national average, while Bihar (where many of the Punjab's migrant workers originate) and Kerala (which experienced a decrease) were 2 and 22 percentage points below it, respectively.

105. C. H. Hanumantha Rao, *Technological Change.* Rao's study focused on Ferozepur in Punjab. For a review of the literature on tractorization and its consequences see Kalpana Bardhan, "Rural Employment," pt. 2, p. 1064.

106. According to the 1981 census, the proportion of employed agricultural laborers and of cultivators in Kerala declined between 1971 and 1981 by 0.004 and 20 percent, respectively, despite 18 and 22 percent increases at the all-India level (calculated from table 3 in *Provisional Population Totals: Workers and Non-workers,* pp. 43–44.

107. T. Scarlett Epstein, *Economic Development and Social Change in South India* (New Delhi: Oxford University Press, 1962); Jan Breman, *Patronage and Exploitation: Changing Agrarian Relations in South Gujarat, India* (Berkeley and Los Angeles: University of California Press, 1974).

108. Herring, "Paddy Field"; Sheila Bhalla, "New Relations of Production in Haryana Agriculture," *Economic and Political Weekly,* March 27, 1976.

109. Bouton, *Agrarian Radicalism in South India.*

110. Raj Krishna, "Small Farmer Development." See also Bhalla and Chadha, "Green Revolution."

111. The 1951–52 data are from Reserve Bank of India, *All India Rural Credit Survey 1* (Bombay, n.d.), pt. 2, table 18.1; 1961–62 and 1970–71 data are from *Monthly Commentary on Indian Economic Conditions* 18, no. 73 (1976) (annual no.).

112. Reserve Bank of India, *Report on Currency and Finance, 1981–82* (Bombay, 1983), vol. 1, table II-17, p. 149.

113. Planning Commission, *Sixth Five Year Plan, 1980–85*, p. 109.

114. The small farmers' share in outstanding commercial bank short-term loans is about the same (37 percent) as in the current loans reported in table 42, suggesting that their capacity to gain a share of short-term loans equivalent to their proportion of households is not recent. See statement 41 cited in table 42.

115. Sixty-eight percent of cooperative loans were short-term loans in 1980–81 (Reserve Bank of India, *Report on Currency and Finance 1981–82*, 1:175.

116. Planning Commission, *Sixth Five Year Plan, 1980–85*, p. 109.

117. Central Statistical Organization, *Statistical Pocket Book, India 1980*, table 18, p. 24. The range between the top- and bottom-ranked states in 1970–71 was from Rs. 1,030 to Rs. 402; and in 1977–78, from Rs. 1,962 to Rs. 735.

118. Krishna Bharadwaj, "Economic Development: Reflections on Regional Differentiation in India," *Religion and Society* 28, no. 2 (June 1981): 26.

119. Ahluwalia, "Rural Poverty," table 3a, p. 305.

120. Bharadwaj, "Economic Development," table 9, p. 21.

121. Thompson, *English Working Class.*

122. Weber, *Die Verhältnisse der Landarbeiter.*

123. Raj Krishna, "Economic Development of India." According to Krishna, the agricultural work force was 72 percent in 1911. The census report of 1981 shows 70 percent for 1961 and 1971 and 67 percent for 1981 (*Provisional Population Totals: Workers and Non-workers*, Table 4, p. 48. The 1981 census suggests a slight decrease (about 3 percent) in the agricultural work force; recent critiques attribute that change to underenumeration in backward areas that have high agricultural workforces. See J. N. Sinha, "1981 Census Economic Date: A Note," *Economic and Political Weekly*, February 6, 1982. Sinha believes that if the figures are adjusted for underenumeration, there is no change.

124. Ibid. The 1971 and 1981 figures appear to be comparable, while many observers attribute much of the increase from 17 to 26 percent between 1961 and 1971 to changes in the census categorization.

125. Cultivators increased between 1971 and 1981 from seventy-five to ninety-one million and agricultural laborers from forty-seven to fifty-five million (Census of India, 1981, *Provisional Population Totals: Workers and Non-workers*, table 3, p. 43).

126. For similarly pessimistic accounts with respect to Bangladesh, see Peter Bertocci, "Structural Fragmentation and Peasant Classes in Bangladesh" (Paper presented at the Sixth Annual Wisconsin Conference on South Asia, Madison, November 4–6, 1977), and Geoffrey D. Wood, "Class Differentiation and Power in Bandakgram: The Minifundist Case," in M. Ameerul Huq, *Exploitation and the Rural Poor: A Working Paper on the Rural Power Structure in Bangladesh* (Comilla: Bangladesh Academy for Rural Development, 1976).

127. See table 40 above.

128. See Baruah, "Getting a Fair Share." Baruah's microanalysis reveals that poor cultivators and workers in Meerut district, Uttar Pradesh, use caste

and jati idiom for political discourse and find class terms alien or incomprehensible, while those in West Bengal have assimilated class terms, that is, they understand themselves and their political universe in such terms. We count the Meerut context as more representative of the rural poor than the West Bengal context, where the CPI-M has come to prevail.

129. For the basis of this discussion, see our "Agrarian Mobilization," pp. 298–301. For an account that confronts many of the issues in this and previous sections, see Myron Weiner, "Capitalist Agriculture, Peasant Farming and Well Being in Rural India" (1983, mimeograph).

130. Bouton, *Agrarian Radicalism in South India*; Mencher, *Agriculture and Social Structure*; K. C. Alexander, *Agrarian Tension in Thanjavur* (Hyderabad: National Institute of Community Development, 1975), "Genesis of Agrarian Tension in Thanjavur: Findings of a Research Study,' *Economic and Political Weekly*, December 6, 1975, and *Peasant Organizations in South India* (New Delhi: Indian Social Institute, 1981); and André Beteille, "Agrarian Relations in Tanjore District, South India," *Sociological Bulletin* 21, no. 2 (1972). Another work that canvasses the objective conditions of the rural poor is V. K. Ramchandran, *Inequality in the Distribution of Land Holdings and Assets Among Households in Gokilapuram Village: A Report from a Field Survey*, working paper no. 31 (Madras: Madras Institute of Development Studies, 1983).

131. For a discussion of such ecological variations see David Ludden, "Productive Power in Agriculture: A survey of Work on the Local History of British India," in Desai, S. H. Rudolph, and Rudra, *Agrarian Power and Agricultural Productivity*. The social structure of these "old wet" areas stands in contrast to newly irrigated areas, such as Indian Punjab, where irrigation was superimposed on an agrarian structure characterized by family farmers and relatively more egalitarian status orders.

132. Beteille, "Agrarian Relations," pp. 144–45.

133. Mencher, *Agriculture and Social Structure*, p. 197.

134. For an important discussion of the correlations between objective determinants and agrarian radicalism, see Donald S. Zagoria, "The Ecology of Peasant Communism in India," *American Political Science Review* 15, no. 1 (March 1971), p. 152.

135. Bouton measures agrarian radicalism by vote shares of the Communist parties in the general elections and their control of Panchayats, the level and intensity of economic disputes, support for and membership in the Communist parties and their Agricultural Workers' Union, and "radical" attitudes on agrarian issues (*Agrarian Radicalism in South India*, chap. 6).

136. For details, see ibid., chap. 7, table 43, p. 163.

137. Ibid., p. 162.

138. Ibid., p. 165.

139. James O. Harrison, "Agricultural Modernization and Income Distribution," pp. 2–3; Mutiah, "Green Revolution," pp. 57–58. Mutiah found that holders under 5 acres accounted for 39 percent of the cultivated area but 42 percent of the high-yielding variety area. Harrison shows that operators under 3.8 acres used as much new technology and inputs per unit operated as medium and large operators did.

140. Alexander, *Peasant Organizations*, p. 102.

141. Ibid., pp. 100–2.

142. Mahavir Mahtu and Dhanak Mandal, the men found guilty in the killings, were hanged at Bhagalpur Central Jail on November 9, 1983 (*Hindustan Times*, November 10, 1983).

143. For an account of Communist leadership in the 1940s see B. S. Baliga, *Tanjore District Handbook* (Madras: Madras Government Press, 1957). See also Hari P. Sharma, "The Green Revolution in India: A Prelude to a Red One," in Kathleen Gough and Hari P. Sharma, *Imperialism and Revolution in South Asia* (New York: Monthly Review, 1973). For the more recent context of national left party lines, see Sen Gupta, *Communism in Indian Politics*.

144. Alexander, *Peasant Organizations*, p. 97. Alexander describes how the Madras government appointed the district judge of Thanjavur to arbitrate a wage dispute in 1940. When he offered equal seating to Harijan labor leaders, the symbolic gesture "gave a tremendous boost to the morale of the labourers." Alexander also points out that the CPI's initial organizing efforts were made easier by Congress's reluctance prior to independence to encourage class interests and by the Self-Respect Movement's and Justice party's preoccupation with Brahman social and economic dominance in urban professional life (p. 95).

145. For details, see ibid., pp. 95–99.

146. Gene D. Overstreet and Marshall Windmiller, *Communism in India* (Berkeley and Los Angeles: University of California Press, 1959), p. 273.

147. Protenant legislation included the Tanjore Tenants and Penniyal Protection Act (1952); the Madras Cultivating Tenants Protection Act (1955), and the Madras Cultivating Tenants Act (Payment of Fair Rent Act) (1956). By these acts, Congress governments met the demands of the CPI-M's Tamil Nadu Tillers Association with respect to tenant cultivators and converted a dissatisfied into a satisfied class.

148. See Lloyd I. Rudolph, "Urban Life and Populist Radicalism: Dravidian Politics in Madras," *Journal of Asian Studies* 20, no. 3 (May 1961); Robert L. Hardgrave, Jr., *The Dravidian Movement* (Bombay: Popular Prakashan, 1965); and Marguerite Ross Barnett, *The Politics of Cultural Nationalism in South India* (Princeton: Princeton University Press, 1976).

149. See Susanne Hoeber Rudolph, "From Madras: A View of the Southern Film," *Yale Review* 60, no. 3 (March, 1971), and Robert L. Hardgrave, Jr., "Politics and the Film in Tamil Nadu: The Stars and the DMK," *Asian Survey* 13, no. 3 (March 1973).

150. A survey by Gift Siromoney showed that M. G. Ramachandran, chief minister of Tamil Nadu in the late seventies and early eighties, had more support from agricultural laborers than from any other of seven occupational categories ("Parliamentary Elections in Tamil Nadu: Report of a Pre-Election Survey Conducted in December, 1979," *Religion and Society*, 29, no. 3 [September 1982], table 4). Forty-six to forty-eight percent of Ramachandran's supporters were landless laborers. By contrast, both Indira Gandhi and M. Karunanidhi drew their strongest support from office workers and professionals, and Morarji Desai drew his from traders.

151. Brindavan C. Moses, "An Analysis of the Electoral Politics in Tamil Nadu Since 1967," *Religion and Society* 29, no. 3 (September 1982), p. 46ff.

152. Breman, *Patronage and Exploitation*; John Echeverri-Gent, "Cooperation, Conflict and Ideology" (Seminar paper, Department of Political Science,

University of Chicago, 1979, typescript); Juergensmeyer, *Religion as Social Vision.*

153. See Beteille, "Agrarian Relations."

154. Ministry of Agriculture and Irrigation, *Indian Agriculture in Brief,* table 2.1a.

155. Henry Orenstein, *Gaon: Conflict and Cohesion in an Indian Village* (Princeton: Princeton University Press, 1965), p. 28.

156. Breman, *Patronage and Exploitation,* pp. 95, 155.

157. Adrian C. Mayer, *Caste and Kinship in Central India: A Village and Its Region* (Berkeley and Los Angeles: University of California Press, 1960), p. 80.

158. M. C. Pradhan, *The Political System of the Jats of Northern India* (Oxford: Oxford University Press, 1966), p. 26.

159. Sinha, "1981 Census Economic Data."

160. Epstein, *Economic Development and Social Change.*

161. James C. Scott, *The Moral Economy of the Peasant* (New Haven: Yale University Press, 1976).

162. Moore, *Dictatorship and Democracy;* Frankel, *India's Political Economy.*

163. Orenstein, *Gaon,* p. 257.

164. Breman, *Patronage and Exploitation,* p. 227.

165. Ibid., pp. 219, 256.

166. Charles Valentine offers a critique in *Culture and Poverty* (Chicago: University of Chicago Press, 1968).

167. Mark Juergensmeyer, "Culture of Deprivation: Three Case Studies in Punjab," *Economic and Political Weekly,* February 1979 (annual no.).

168. The Sadhupur, Deoli, and Kestara atrocities in Uttar Pradesh are discussed by Abdul Malik, "Monthly Massacres of Untouchables" (Course paper, Department of Political Science, University of Chicago, 1982, typescript). They are also reported in *Hindu, Indian Express,* and *Statesman* for November 20–28, 1981, January 1–27, 1982, and April 18, 1982. See also *Keesing's Contemporary Archives,* September 17, 1980, p. 31703. For the murder of fourteen Harijans in Pipar, Bihar, by Kurmi landlords, see *Economic and Political Weekly,* November 28, 1981. A number of accounts of the police show the state's weakness and lack of autonomy. See also Arun Sinha, "Class War, Not Atrocities Against Harijans," *Journal of Peasant Studies 9,* no. 3 (April 19, 1982).

169. Alexander, *Peasant Organizations,* p. 102. For a discussion of the symbolic politics of atrocities see Paul Brass, "National Power and Local Politics."

170. *Hindu,* February 9, 1980, quoted in Brass, "National Power and Local Politics," p. 19.

171. The organized sector would include the Communist-led mobilizations in Thanjavur district in the sixties, which eventuated in trade unions that negotiated a number of three-year contracts between agricultural workers and employers in the late sixties and early seventies; the Maharashtra sugar industry's INTUC, MMS, and Lal Nishan unions, which organize harvest workers as well as sugar mill workers; the Kerala State Karshaka Tozhilai Union, linked to the CPI-M, which represents the interest of workers under the Kerala Agri-

cultural Workers Act and in related job actions. For Thanjavur trade union organization, see Bouton, "Sources of Agranian Radicalism." For Maharashtra, see Amrita Abraham, "Maharashtra Sugar Workers' Cautious Response," *Economic and Political Weekly,* December 5, 1981. For Kerala, see Herring, "Paddy Field," p. 33.

172. For the literature on Naxalism, see chapter 8, note 21, and note 75 above.

Conclusion

1. See Charles Taylor, "Interpretation and The Sciences of Man" and "Understanding and Ethnocentricity," in *Philosophy and the Human Sciences: Philosophical Papers II* (Cambridge: Cambridge University Press, 1985).

2. See Fred Hirsch, *The Social Limits to Growth* (Cambridge: Harvard University Press, 1976).

3. See Arend Lijphart, "The Comparable-Cases Strategy in Comparative Research," *Comparative Political Studies* 8, no. 2 (June 1975).

4. We follow Weber in creating a model or ideal type of political economy and in recognizing that it is one way, our way, of identifying a subject worthy of explanation. See our critical discussion of Weber on models of versus models for particular subjects of study in "Authority and Power." In formulating our theory of demand and command polities, we have built on a wide variety of theoretical and empirical works, only some of which can be mentioned here: Joseph Schumpeter, *Capitalism, Socialism and Democracy* (New York: Harper and Brothers, 1950); Shonfield, *Modern Capitalism;* Lindblom, *Politics and Markets;* Alec Nove, *The Soviet Economic System* (London: Allen and Unwin, 1980); and Alec Nove, *The Economics of Feasible Socialism* (London: Allen and Unwin, 1983).

5. Our critique of rational choice theory has benefited greatly from the recent work of Amartya Sen, Thomas Schelling, and Albert O. Hirschman. See particularly Sen's "Rational Fools: A Critique of the Behavioural Foundations of Economic Theory," in *Choice, Welfare and Measurement* (New Delhi: Oxford University Press, 1982); Schelling's *Choice and Consequence* (Cambridge: Harvard University Press, 1984); and Hirschman's "Against Parsimony: Three Easy Ways of Complicating Some Categories of Economic Discourse," *Economics and Philosophy* 1 (1985), as well as his earlier *Shifting Involvements.*

6. See Albert O. Hirschman, *Exit, Voice, and Loyalty* (Cambridge: Harvard University Press, 1970).

7. See Robert Axelrod, "The Emergence of Cooperation Among Egoists," *American Political Science Review* 75, no. 2 (June 1981).

8. This line of argument is elaborated in our "Agrarian Mobilization."

9. For a recent, systematic, critical challenge to Marx's thought from a rational choice perspective, see Elster, *Making Sense of Marx.*

10. See Lisa Anderson, "State in the Middle East and North America," regarding oil-producing Middle Eastern states that do not have to extract resources from society and, as a result, can act independently, including in ways that shape or trigger social formations and ideas.

11. See Ralf Dahrendorf, *Class and Class Conflicts in Industrial Society* (Stanford: Stanford University Press, 1959), for a view of class based on the division between those with and without public authority, a notion that has a family resemblance to the interpretation being advanced here.

Author Index

501

Subject Index

The pursuit of Lakshmi, the fickle goddess of prosperity and good fortune, is a metaphor for the aspirations of the state and people of independent India. In the latest of their distinguished contributions to South Asian studies, scholars Lloyd I. Rudolph and Susanne Hoeber Rudolph focus on this modern-day pursuit by offering a comprehensive analysis of India's political economy.

India occupies a paradoxical place among nation states: it is both developed and underdeveloped, rich and poor, strong and weak. These contrasts locate India in the international order. The Rudolphs' theory of demand and command polities provides a general framework for explaining the special circumstances of the Indian experience.

Contrary to what one might expect in a country with great disparities of wealth, no national party, right or left, pursues the politics of class. Instead, the Rudolphs argue, private capital and organized labor in India face a "third actor"—the state. Because the dominance of the state makes class politics marginal, the state is itself an element in the creation of the centrist-oriented social pluralism that has characterized Indian politics since independence.

In analyzing the relationship between India's politics and its economy, the Rudolphs maintain that India's economic performance has been only marginally affected by the type of regime in power—authoritarian or democratic. More important, they show that rising levels of social mobilization and personalistic rule have contributed to declining state capacity and autonomy. At the same time, social mobilization has led to a more equitable distribution of economic benefits and political power, which has enhanced the state's legitimacy among its citizens.

The scope and explanatory power of *In Pursuit of Lakshmi* will make it essential for all those interested in political economy, comparative politics, Asian studies and India.

LLOYD I. RUDOLPH and SUSANNE HOEBER RUDOLPH are both professors of political science at the University of Chicago. Susanne Hoeber Rudolph is president of the Association of Asian Studies; Lloyd I. Rudolph is chair of the Committee on International Relations at the University of Chicago. The Rudolphs are the authors of numerous books on India, including *The Modernity of Tradition* and *Gandhi*, both published by the University of Chicago Press.

A Chicago Original Paperback

The University of Chicago Press

Cover photograph: *Lakshmi*, Halebid, Karnataka, by Lloyd I. Rudolph.

ISBN 0-226-73139-